ELSEVIER'S DICTIONARY OF NUTRITION AND FOOD PROCESSING

ELSEVIER'S DICTIONARY OF NUTRITION AND FOOD PROCESSING

in

English, German, French and Portuguese

compiled by

H.E. PHILIPPSBORN

2002
ELSEVIER
Amsterdam – Boston – London – New York – Oxford – Paris
San Diego – San Francisco – Singapore – Sydney – Tokyo

ELSEVIER SCIENCE B.V.
Sara Burgerhartstraat 25
P.O. Box 211, 1000 AE Amsterdam, The Netherlands

First edition 2002

Library of Congress Cataloging in Publication Data
A catalog record from the Library of Congress has been applied for.

British Library Cataloguing in Publication Data
Elsevier's dictionary of nutrition and food processing in
English, German, French and Portuguese
1.Nutrition - Dictionaries 2.Food industry and trade -
Dictionaries 3.English language - Dictionaries - French
4.English language - Dictionaries - German 5.English
language - Dictionaries - Portuguese
I.Philippsborn, H. E., 1936- II.Dictionary of nutrition and
Food processing
613.2'03

ISBN 0444510176

ISBN: 0-444-51017-6

∞ The paper used in this publication meets the requirements of ANSI/NISO Z39.48-1992 (Permanence of Paper).
Printed in The Netherlands.

PREFACE

Nutrition has obviously always been one of the main preoccupations of mankind, since its very beginning. In Egypt as well as in Mesopotamia between the Tigris and the Euphrates, from the mountains of East Asia Minor to the Persian Gulf, we find a variety of developed cultures. More than 5,000 years ago, not far away from Cairo, the Egyptians already understood the production of beer. Recipes of this most ancient alcoholic beverage were found written on the walls of the pyramides. The prime material in these times already was malt, and also orge and the juice of dates, ginger and honey. The production of beer demands a certain type of agricultural know-how, for maintaining the cultivation of cereals, not only orge, but also emmer, an ancient wheat type, cereals which were also used as food. In Genesis 41, we read about the seven years of plenty in the "land of Egypt" and the beginning of seven years of sore famine (about 1700 B.C.). "And when all the land of Egypt was famished, the people cried to Pharaoh for bread, and Pharaoh said unto all the Egyptians, Go unto Joseph, what he saith to you, do. And the famine was over all the face of the earth: and Joseph opened all the store-houses, and sold unto the Egyptians, and the famine was sore in the land of Egypt. And all countries came into Egypt to Joseph to buy grain, because the famine was sore in all the earth." (American Standard Version 1901); and even Joseph's brothers came "from the land of Canaan to buy food".

About 2000 B.C. we find in the Mesopotamian region extensive plantations of cereals, fruits and vegetables, with artificial irrigation systems (canals invented for this purpose), transporting water from the rivers, such as the Euphrates. We find in Genesis 13:2 "And Abram (from the town of Ur) was very rich in cattle". Cattle raising and sheep breeding was already an important activity, and people worried about the climate as says Deuteronomy 11:14 "That I (GOD) will give you rain of your land in his due season, the first rain and the latter rain, that thou mayest gather in the corn, and thy wine, and thine oil". People already knew how to store the corn, wheat and emmer harvested from their wide fields. Continues Deuteronomy : 7,8,9 "thy GOD bringeth thee into a … land of wheat and barley, and vines and fig-trees and pomegranates, a land of olive-trees and honey; a land wherin thou shalt eat bread without scarceness". People already knew what to do with the corn, how to make bread.

Winegrowing is also one of the most ancient agricultural activities, started when men passed fom the nomade state of life to settling in colonies. Winegrowing required plant cultivation, steady work and attention. Noah, after the Deluge had passed (2300 B.C.) as to Genesis 9:20,21 "…began to be a husbandman (farmer), and planted a vineyard: And he drank of the wine, and was drunken, and he was uncovered within his tent". Wine was easily produced by fermentation of the grape juice. In Egypt, the Pharaohs used wine with their funerals, preocupied with their "life-after-life" without this great beverage; and, much later, as literature is telling us, Cleopatra (69-30 B.C.), queen of Egypt (51-30 B.C.) offered wine to Marcus Antonius, Roman statesman (82-30 B.C.), as wine had the reputation of "helping to turn love to be more lovely"; and whereas Caesar (100-44 B.C.) distributed beer to his soldiers, celebrating his crossing of the Italian boundary river Rubicon, thus initiating in 49 B.C. the civil war against Pompey (106-48 B.C.) (as Plutarch, his biographer, 46-119 A.D., is telling us), calling the drink "cerevisia". Zeus, the king of gods in Greek mythology, preferred to cultivate vine, and offered the grapes to his son Dionysus, who created the wine as a beverage, turning himself into Bacchus, the Greek god of wine, of springtime flowering and ecstasy. From Greece the wine passed to the Roman Empire, and the emperors took care of their "special reserves", cultivated in special regions where an outstanding quality could be obtained. The Romans, going northwards, spreaded the art of viticulture until Europe, and until the end of their empire they had established winegrowing areas at, e.g., Champagne, Bordeaux etc., areas which still produce excellent wines. The viticulture followed the Moselle river of 515 km of extension, going from France to Germany, from the Vosges Mountains into the Rhine at the town of Koblenz, and the wine continued on the hilly riversides of the Rhine, producing the wonderful qualities of the Rheinland-Pfalz region (Rhineland-Palatinate).

Caesar introduced beer into Britannia, when the Germanic tribes still used the famous Met, the Germanic precursor of beer fermented from honey. During the Middle Ages both beverages - beer and wine - were cultivated, further developed and refined, and we have to be grateful to the monks living in the monasteries all over Europe, who dedicated themselves to these tasks.

We have seen two great products accompanying the evolution of agriculture since the beginning of mankind. Other beverages accompanied the produce of the fields: Russia makes its vodka from rye and wheat, Scotland produces its famous whisky from malted barley and from the rice cultures of the Japanese Island came the saki to us.

In 1532 the first sugar distillery (engenhoca) was founded in Brazil, in Vila de São Vicente. Colonization continued with the foundation of the town of Santos by Brás Cubas, under Martim Afonso in 1545, who had been sent by Portugal to exploit the coastal region of Brazil. The Portuguese already had some knowledge of sugarcane planting because sugar, of Asian origin, was planted on the Madeira Islands, on the Azores and on Cabo Verde (Cap Vert Islands). There was a great market for this very valuable product in Europe since the Middle Ages, commercialized at high price levels, even being part of testaments and estates, assets left by a person at his death. The Portuguese Crown could thus be sure of consumers for this new product to be planted at the coastal regions of the new colony, Brazil. Portugal, however, had no money for this huge enterprise and turned to the rich Jewish merchants, already responsible for Portuguese navigation and proprietors of the fleets of ships, for ships to transport the sugarcane from the colony to the Metropolis and for financing the sugar enterprise as a whole. The Jewish merchants, persecuted by the Portuguese Crown a couple of years earlier, had emigrated from Portugal to the Netherlands. This way, the Brazilian sugarcane reached the Netherlands via Portugal and the final product, the refined sugar, was traded by the Jewish merchants in Flanders, because only they had the know-how of sugar refining. Already at that time, they were a great trading people who owned many trading spots all over Europe and had already established the base of Europe's trade and commerce. The monoculture of sugarcane was one of the great economic cycles of Brazil's history. At the first cane sugar plantations, people discovered how to make use of the liquid residue of raw sugar (açúcar mascavo). The slaves tasted this still not fermented liquid and started distillation. Sugar cane cutting; cane milling; fermentation; distillation and aging: at that moment one of the greatest spirits was developed, called "cachaça", or "pinga". Cachaça proved to be money, and slaves were bought in Africa and payed for with this beverage. Today cachaça is a Brazilian export article; in Europe it is a speciality. One can take it pure, or in the form of a "caipirinha", that is, putting small slices of the local small green lemon and adding plenty of cane sugar (European beet sugar does not give the same delicious taste - this, however, is a subjective fact of experience, not of science!).

What is nutrition? Nutrition is the intake and assimilation of nutrients with the purpose of energy gain, for maintaining the body, for "body building", and for replacement of active substances. Nutrition is the basis for all metabolic processes. The human body needs ready nutrients (in contrast to plants). The main constituents of nutrition are carbohydrates and fats, proteins, starch, mineral salts, resulting from the structural activity of green plants. Human nutrition is derived from the vegetable kingdom, from the flora, or, via plants, from the animal kingdom, from the fauna.

Carbohydrates belong to the group of organic compounds. The simple ones are sugars, glucose and sucrose. More complex ones are polysaccharides, as glycogen, starch etc. Glucose is an essential intermediate in the food conversion process for the obtention of energy. Fats are a mixture of lipids, mainly triglycerides and are a mean of storing energy from nutrition. It can be obtained directly from food, however carbohydrates can be transformed into fats in the body and stored in tissues. Animal fats and vegetable oils contain fatty acids as a component, on which the melting point of the product depends and thus the transformation possibilities as additives in other final products, e.g., as a fat hardening additive in margarines etc. Fats have twice the calorific value of carbohydrates. Proteins are also a group of organic compounds, consisting of amino acids, being essential for the body, e.g., for the muscular system and tissues. Like enzymes and hormones, they are important for promoting certain functions. Proteins are built up in the body from amino acids and these are obtained from the digestion of proteins in the food. Mineral salts, inorganic food components, do not produce energy like, e.g., fats, but they are essential for structural purposes, like, e.g., calcium for the bones, and for regulation of processes. The distribution of these salts is responsible for the exchange of liquids between cells, by osmosis. We find calcium in dairy products, and all the minerals in milk and in vegetables and fruits, and iron especially in green plants like spinach.

Specific functions have vitamins, organic compounds found in food, often as provitamins, i.e. vitamin precursors, enzymes, which are proteins acting in catalyzing processes of biochemical reactions within the body, essential elements, for normal growth and maintenance such as phosphorus, potassium, magnesium etc. and trace elements, being present in very small quantities, like iron, iodine, selenium etc. These elements may be cofactors, components responsible for the catalytic activity of the enzyme, or they may be part of other molecules, like cobalt, contained in the structure of vitamin B12. The body consumes energy for mechanical activity, as the functioning of the muscular system, for chemical activity maintaining biosynthetic processes and for osmotic activity, comprising the transport of substances, e.g., through the intestinal wall for resorption of nutrients. Fats, together with carbohydrates, constitute for the body the basis for energy, which is obtained by oxidation of these nutrients and transformed into chemical energy, carried by ATP, adenosine triphosphate, a nucleotide.

Nutritional therapy is the treatment of diseases by regimens, i.e. by systematic dietary plans, increasing or diminishing the nutrition as a whole, or only certain components of the diet. It comprises also the selection of certain nutrients in conformity with the disease to be treated, the preventive nutrition (e.g. against cholesterol accumulation in the blood), curative nutrition and nutritional supplementation e.g. with vitamins and mineral salts.

Plants use inorganic material as nutrients, i. e. forming organic substances of their own from carbon dioxide of the air and the salt solutions in the soil. Plants produce carbohydrates by photosynthesis, the process by which inorganic substances are composed into organic compounds. Energy for this process is absorbed by the chlorophyll pigment. Photosynthesis occurs in the presence of sunlight.

Photosynthesis can be considered to be the basis for human (and animal) nutrition, and thus for life as a whole, as life depends on plants for food. Thus all agricultural growth and work depends on this synthesis process - resulting from this fact that:

Earth bears the basis of life, its produce, the diversity of plants - and thus the agricultural research and farming activities are the ultimate, food-supplying source for men, his nutrition-providing guarantee of maintenance, of growth and health.

Henry Erwin Philippsborn, June 2002

SUBJECT AREAS AND SUBFIELDS

Raw Materials / Consumer Goods / Chemical Starting Material / Industrialized Products

Nutritional Science

Agr.: Agriculture
Farming: Agricultural Produce; Biological Agriculture; Botany; Horticulture: fruits, vegetables, viticulture; Climatology; Soil; Soil Treatment
Livestock: Cattle Breeding; Poultry Farming; Fish; Game; Apiculture

Prod.: Products and Production Terminology
Prime Material: Natural Prime Material; Industrial Prime Material; Chemical Starting Material
Industrialized Products: Food Processing Technology; Auxiliary Products: additives, ingredients, antioxidants, preservatives; Aromas: flavour notes, flavour chemicals; Foodstuff Colorants; Vitamins in Nutrition; Water Supply: drinking water, mineral water; Baby Nutrition; Bakery; Beverages; Butchery; Confectionary; Dairy Products; Gastronomy; Spices

Biochem.: Biochemistry
Nutritional Science; Food Biochemistry; Microbiology; Enology; Fermentation

Med.: Medical Terms
a) Anatomy; Regimens; Diets; Nutritional Diseases; b) Veterinary Science

THEMENKREISE UND UNTERTEILUNGEN

Rohmaterial / Verbrauchsgüter / Konsumgüter

Chemisches Ausgangsmaterial / Industrialisierte Produkte

Ernährungswissenschaft

Agr.: Landwirtschaft
Nutztierzucht: Landwirtschaftliche Produkte; Biologische Landwirtschaft; Botanik; Anbau von Früchten, Gemüse; Weinbau; Klimakunde; Boden; Bodenbearbeitung
Viehhaltung: Großviehzucht; Geflügelzucht; Fisch; Wild; Bienenzucht

Prod.: Produkte und Produktionsterminologie
Rohmaterial: Natürliches Rohmaterial; Industrielles Rohmaterial; Chemische Ausgangsprodukte
Industrialisierte Produkte: Technologie der Nahrungsmittelverarbeitung; Hilfsprodukte: Additive; Zutaten, Antioxidantien, Konservierungsmittel; Aromas: Geschmacksnoten, Geschmacksstoffe; Lebensmittelfarbstoffe; Vitamine in Lebensmitteln; Wasserversorgung: Trinkwasser, Mineralwasser; Bäckerei; Gastronomie; Getränke; Gewürze; Molkereiprodukte; Kleinkindernährung; Konditorei / Süßwaren; Schlachterei

Biochem.: Biochemie
Ernährungswissenschaft; Lebensmittelbiochemie; Mikrobiologie; Önologie; Gärung

Med.: Medizinische Fachausdrücke
a) Anatomie; Diätpläne; Diät; Ernährungsstörungen; b) Tiermedizin

SUJETS ET SOUS-CHAMPS

Matières Premières / Biens de Consommation /

Produits de Départ Chimiques / Produits Industrialisés

Bromatologie – Sciences de la Nutrition

Agr.: Agriculture
Exploitation Agricole: Produits Agricoles; Agriculture Biologique; Botanique; Horticulture: les fruits, les légumes, la viticulture; Climatologie; le Sol; Traitement du Sol
Élevage: Élevage du Bétail; Aviculture; Poissons; Gibier; Apiculture

Prod.: Produits et Terminologie de la Production
Matières Premières: Matière Brute Naturelle; Matière Brute Industrielle; Produits Chimiques de Départ
Produits Industrialisés: Technologie du Traitement des Denrées; Produit Auxiliaire: additifs, ingrédients; antioxygènes, agents préservatifs; Arôme: notes aromatisantes, matière chimique pour arômes; Colorants pour Produits Alimentaires; Vitamines dans la Nutrition; Provision d'Eau: eau potable, eau minérale; Nutrition du Bébé; Boissons; Boulangerie; Boucherie; Confiserie; Épices; Gastronomie; Produits Laitiers

Biochim.: Biochimie
Bromatologie; Biochimie des Denrées Alimentaires; Microbiologie; Œnologie; Fermentation

Méd.: Termes Médicaux
a) Anatomie; Régimes; Diètes; b) Art Vétérinaire

TEMÁTICA E SUBDIVISÕES

Matérias Primas / Produtos de Consumo / Material Básico Químico / Produtos Industrializados

Bromatologia

Agr.: Agricultura Superior
Lavoura: Produção Agrícola; Agricultura Biológica; Botânica; Horticultura: frutas, legumes, vinicultura; Climatologia; Solo; Tratamento do Solo
Pecuária: Bovinocultura; Avicultura; Peixes; Caça; Apicultura

Prod.: Produtos e Terminologia de Produção
Matérias Primas: Matérias Primas Naturais; Matérias Primas Industrializadas; Matérias Primas Químicas
Produtos Industrializados: Tecnologia de Transformação de Alimentos; Produtos Auxiliares: aditivos, ingredientes, antioxidantes, conservantes; Aromas: notas de sabor, produtos químicos para sabores sintéticos; Corantes Alimentícios; Vitaminas na Nutrição; Fornecimento de Água: água potável, água mineral; Açougue; Nutrição Infantil; Bebidas; Condimentos; Confeitaria; Gastronomia; Laticínios; Panificação

Biochem.: Bioquímica
Ciência da Nutrição; Bioquímica dos Alimentos; Microbiologia; Enologia; Fermentação

Med.: Termos Médicos
a) Anatomia; Regimes; Dietas; Doenças Nutricionais; b) Veterinária

Basic Table

A

1 **abdomen**
(Med.)
(Anatomy.)
d Abdomen *n*; Bauch *m*; Unterleib *m*
f abdomen *m*; ventre *m*
p abdômen *m*; abdome *m*; ventre *m*; barriga *f*

2 **abortion; miscarriage**
(Med.)
(Veterinary: abortive processes in animals caused by accidents, fights etc.)
d Fehlgeburt *f*
f avortement *m*; fausse couche *f*
p aborto *m*

3 **abruptly pinnate leaf**
(Agr.)
(Botany: leaf form.)
d paarig gefiedertes Blatt *n*
f feuille *f* paripennée
p folha *f* paripenada

4 **absence of cholesterol in milk grades**
(Med.)
(Baby nutrition.)
d Abwesenheit *f* von Cholesterin in den Milchsorten
f absence *f* de cholestérol dans les laits
p ausência *f* de colesterol nos leites

5 **absolute alcohol; pure alcohol**
(Prod.)
(C_2H_5OH; ethanol; ethyl alcohol.)
d absoluter Alkohol *m*; reiner Alkohol *m*
f alcool *m* absolu
p álcool *m* absoluto

6 **absorbable substance**
(Prod.)
(Food processing technology and flavour research and production.)
d aufsaugbare Substanz *f*; absorbierbare Substanz *f*
f substance *f* absorbable
p substância *f* absorvível; substância *f* suscetível de ser absorvida

7 **absorbed energy**
(Med.)
(Body processes which consume, i.e. absorb, energy are: mechanic, osmotic and chemical work.)
d Energieverbrauch *m*
f énergie *f* absorbée
p energia *f* absorvida

8 **absorbent power of bentonite**
(Prod.)
(Food processing technology; used in the production of beer, wine and juices in clarification processes.)
d absorbierende Kraft *f* des Bentonites
f pouvoir *m* absorbant de la bentonite
p poder *m* absorvedor da bentonita

9 **absorption capacity**
(Agr.)
(Ref. e.g. to the soil structure.)
d Absorptionsfähigkeit *f*
f capacité *f* d'absorption
p capacidade *f* de absorção

10 **absorption of orally administered vitamins**
(Med.)
(Vitamins in medicine and veterinary science.)
d Absorption *f* von mündlich verabfolgten Vitaminen; Absorbieren *n* von mündlich verabfolgten Vitaminen; Aufnahme *f* von mündlich verabfolgten Vitaminen
f absorption *f* des vitamines administrées oralement
p absorção *f* de vitaminas administradas oralmente

11 **absorption of vitamins by tissues**
(Med.)
(Veterinary; ref. to animals under veterinary vitamin treatment.)
d Aufnahme *f* von Vitaminen durch das Gewebe
f absorption *f* des vitamines par le tissu
p absorção *f* de vitaminas pelos tecidos

12 **absorption velocity of sugar**
(Med.)
(Most rapidly absorbed is glucose, followed by saccharose.)
d Absorptionsgeschwindigkeit *f* von Zucker; Aufnahmegeschwindigkeit *f* des Zuckers
f vitesse *f* de l'absorption du sucre
p velocidade *f* de absorção do açúcar

* **acajou** → **961**

* **acajou nut** → **961**

13 **acaracide**
(Agr.)
(Pesticide type.)
d Akarazid *n*; Milbenmittel *n*
f acaracide *m*
p acaracida *m*

14 **accelerated filtration; rapid filtration**
(Prod.)
(Filtration process by means of rapid filters, steel containers through which the water is pumped. Filters can be regenerated after loading by flushing.)
d beschleunigtes Filtrieren *n*; Schnellfiltration *f*
f filtration *f* accélérée
p filtração *f* acelerada; filtração *f* rápida

15 **accelerate** *v* **maturity; speed** *v* **up maturity**
(Agr.)
(Horticulture; viticulture etc.)
d Reife beschleunigen
f accélérer la maturité
p acelerar a maturidade

16 **accelerate** *v* **the decomposition**
(Biochem.)
(Ref. to oxidant or reductant (reducing agent) activity.)
d Zerfall beschleunigen; Zersetzung beschleunigen
f accélérer la décomposition
p acelerar a decomposição

17 **acceleration of aging**
(Biochem.)
(Enology: wine treatment and production.)
d Erhöhung *f* der Alterungsschnelligkeit
f accélération *f* du vieillissement
p aceleração *f* de envelhecimento

18 **acceleration of dissolution**
(Prod.)
(Food processing technology.)
d Erhöhung *f* der Löslichkeitsrate
f accélération *f* de la dissolution
p aceleração *f* da dissolução

19 **accident in development**
(Biochem.)
(Ref. to negative (bacterial etc.) unforeseen influence.)
d Entwicklungsstörung *f*
f accident *m* de développement
p acidente *m* de desenvolvimento

20 **accompanied continuation of the fermentation process; controlled continuation of the fermentation process**
(Biochem.)
(Fermentation in nutritional science.)
d begleitete Fortsetzung *f* des Gärungsprozesses
f suivi *m* du processus de la fermentation
p acompanhamento *m* do processo da fermentação

21 **acescence; acescency**
(Biochem.)
(Wine disease: transformation of alcohol into acetic acid by the microorganism "Mycoderma aceti".)
d Versauerung *f*
f acescence *f*
p azedamento *m*; acescência *f*

* **acescency → 21**

22 **acetaldehyde; ethanal; acetic aldehyde**
(Biochem.)
(C_2H_4O; ref. to food biochemistry: used as fermentation activator in enology (wine production).)
d Acetaldehyd *n*
f acétaldéhyde *m*
p acetaldeído *m*

23 **acetates**
(Prod.)
(Salts or esters of acetic acid; prime material in aroma synthesis; in aroma/fragrance production.)
d Acetate *npl*
f acétates *mpl*
p acetatos *mpl*

24 **acetic** *adj*
(Prod.)
(Food processing technology.)
d essigsauer
f acétique
p acético

25 **acetic acid; vinegar acid; ethanoic acid**
(Prod.)
($C_2H_4O_2$; Food preservative No. CEE: E 260.)
d Essigsäure *f*
f acide *m* acétique
p ácido *m* acético

26 **acetic acid fermentation**
(Biochem.)
($C_2H_4O_2$; acetic acid = ethanoïc acid; food preservation additive.)
d Essigsäuregärung *f*; Essigsäurefermentation *f*
f fermentation *f* d'acide acétique
p fermentação *f* de ácido acético

* **acetic aldehyde → 22**

27 **acetic ester**
(Biochem.)
(Fermentation in nutritional science.)
d Essigester *m*
f ester *m* acétique
p éster *m* acético

28 **acetify** *v*
(Prod.)
(Food processing technology)

d mit Essig säuern; mit Essig ansäuern
f acétifier
p acetificar

29 **acetobacter**
(Biochem.)
(Microbiology; bacteria, genus "Acetobacteriaceae", which oxidizes alcohol, forming acetic acid. "Acetobacter pasteurianum" is used in the production of vinegar; also found in beer wort.)
d Acetobacter *m*
f acétobacter *m*
p acetobacter *m*

30 **acetoin**
(Prod.)
($C_4H_8O_2$; fermentation product; flavour ingredient in cheese, margarine, sweets; in creams ripened for churning processes.)
d Acetoin *n*
f acétoïne *f*
p acetoína *f*

31 **acetone; dimethyl ketone; 2-propanone**
(Prod.)
(C_3H_6O; prime material in aroma synthesis; aroma/fragrance production.)
d Aceton *n*; Dimethylketon *n*; 2-Propanon *n*
f acétone *f*; diméthylcétone *f*; 2-propanone *f*
p acetona *f*; dimetilcetona *f*; 2-propanona *f*

32 **acetophenone**
(Prod.)
(C_8H_8O; benzene derivative; prime material in aroma synthesis.)
d Acetophenon *n*
f acétophénone *f*
p acetofenona *f*

33 **acetylation**
(Biochem.)
(Reaction of introduction of an acetyl group into an organic compound.)
d Acetylierung *f*
f acétylation *f*
p acetilação *f*

34 **acetylcholine**
(Biochem.)
($C_7H_{17}NO_3$; neurotransmitter; formed in body tissues from choline.)
d Acetylcholin *n*
f acétylcholine *f*
p acetilcolina *f*

35 **acetylcholinesterase**
(Biochem.)
(Acetylcholine hydrolyzing enzyme.)
d Acetylcholinesterase *f*
f acétylcholinestérase *f*
p esterase *f* de acetilcolina

36 **acetyl-CoA**
(Biochem.)
(Acetyl coenzyme A; ref. to carbohydrate metabolism.)
d Acetyl-CoA *n*
f acétyl-CoA *f*
p acetil-CoA *f*

37 **acetylene**
(Prod.)
(C_2H_2; prime material in aroma synthesis.)
d Acetylen *n*
f acétylène *m*
p acetileno *m*

* **acetylene dichloride → 1633**

38 **acetylsalicylic acid**
(Prod.)
($C_9H_8O_4$; antioxidant.)
d Acetylsalicylsäure *f*
f acide *m* acétylsalicylique
p ácido *m* acetilsalicílico

39 **achlorhydria**
(Med.)
(Absence of hydrochloric acid (muriatic acid) in the stomach.)
d Achlorhydrie *f*
f achlorhydrie *f*
p acloridria *f*

40 **acid-base balance**
(Med.)
(Phosphorus interacts in the control of the hydrogen ion concentration of the body, promoting the acid-base balance of the organism.)
d Säure-Base-Gleichgewicht *n*
f balance *f* acide-basique; équilibre *m* acide-basique
p equilíbrio *m* ácido-básico

41 **acid diet**
(Med.)
(Alimentary regimen: sour, acid-containing, diet; nutrition.)
d saure Diät *f*
f diète *f* acide
p dieta *f* ácida

42 **acid-forming food**
(Med.)
(Alimentary regimen; diet.)
d säurebildende Lebensmittel *npl*
f denrées *fpl* alimentaires acidifiantes
p produtos *mpl* alimentícios formadores de ácidos; alimentos *mpl* acidíferos

43 acid-free diet
(Med.)
(Alimentary regimen.)
d säurefreie Diät *f*
f diète *f* sans acides; diète *f* exempte d'acides
p dieta *f* isenta de ácidos

44 acidic *adj*
(Prod.)
(Food processing technology; turning acid, producing acid.)
d säuernd
f acidifère
p acidífero

45 acidification
(Prod.)
(Dairy plant technology: Cheese production process, transformation of curd lactose into lactic acid by hydrolysis.)
d Säuerung *f*
f acidification *f*
p acidificação *f*

* **acidification of the medium → 3538**

46 acidified milk
(Prod.)
(Dairy product, e.g. in curd production.)
d gesäuerte Milch *f*
f lait *m* acidifié
p leite *m* acidificado

47 acidifier
(Prod.)
(Food processing technology: food preservation; also taste improvement.)
d Säuerungsmittel *n*
f acidificateur *m*
p acidulante *m*

48 acidify *v*; **acidulate** *v*; **turn** *v* **acid**
(Prod.)
(Food processing technology; to add leaven (sourdough) to a bread dough.)
d ansäuern
f acidifier; aciduler
p acidificar; acidular; acidar

49 acidity
(Prod.)
(Food processing technology; aroma/fragrance research and production.)
d Säuregehalt *m*; Säuregrad *m*
f acidité *f*
p acidez *f*

50 acidity of the grape
(Agr.)
(Viticulture.)
d Säuregehalt *m* der Weinbeere
f acidité *f* du grain de raisin
p acidez *f* da uva

51 acidity regulation
(Biochem.)
(Enology.)
d Einstellung *f* des Säuregehaltes; Regulierung *f* des Säuregehaltes
f réglage *m* de l'acidité
p regulação *f* da acidez

52 acid medium
(Biochem.)
(Food processing technology: action conditions of food preservatives.)
d saures Medium *n*; saures Milieu *n*
f milieu *m* acide
p meio *m* ácido

53 acidosis
(Med.)
(Impaired acid/alkali balance of the blood; the pH value should be 7.4.)
d Acidose *f*; Gewebsübersäuerung *f*; krankhafte Säuregehaltserhöhung *f* des Blutes
f acidose *f*
p acidose *f*

54 acid radical; acyl
(Biochem.)
(Nutritional science: atoms or molecules having unpaired electrons. Originated from heat or UV-light; radicals are very reactive.)
d Säureradikal *n*
f radical *m* acide; acyle *m*
p radical *m* ácido; acila *f*

55 acid soil
(Agr.)
(Soil with a high acid content, with pH between 0 and 6.5)
d saurer Boden *m*
f sol *m* acide
p solo *m* ácido

* **acid solution → 5116**

* **acidulate** *v* **→ 48**

56 acidulation
(Prod.)
(Food processing technology.)
d Säuerung *f*; Ansäuerung *f*
f acidulation *f*
p acidulação *f*

57 acidulous *adj*
(Prod.)
(Food processing technology; e.g. food characteristic.)

d säuerlich
f acidulé
p acídulo; acidulado

58 **acidulous taste**
(Prod.)
(Food processing technology, research and production: product characteristic.)
d säuerlicher Geschmack *m*
f goût *m* acidulé
p gosto *m* acídulo; paladar *m* acidulado

59 **acid value**
(Prod.)
(Food processing technology. Value that determines the contents of free organic acids in fats, solvents etc.)
d Säurezahl *f*
f indice *m* d'acide
p valor *m* de acidez

60 **acid whey**
(Prod.)
(Dairy plant subproduct, e.g. from cheese production.)
d saures Laktoserum *m*; Sauermolke *f*; saure Molke *f*
f lactosérum *m* acide
p lacto-soro *m* ácido; soro *m* ácido de leite

61 **acorn**
(Agr.)
(Nut of the oak tree (genus "Quercus").)
d Eichel *f*
f gland *m*
p bolota *f*; glande *f*

62 **acrid** *adj*
(Prod.)
(Aroma/flavour note.)
d herb; herbe
f âpre
p acre

63 **acrolein; 2-propenal**
(Prod.)
(C_3H_4O; appears during glycerol heating, e.g. excessive heating of fats, having a typical unpleasant odour.)
d Acrolein *n*
f acroléine *f*
p acroleína *f*

64 **actin**
(Biochem.)
(Anatomy; contractile muscle protein; ref. to enzymatic body processes of adenosine triphosphate utilization.)
d Actin *n*
f actine *f*
p actina *f*

65 **actinization; treatment by actinism**
(Prod.)
(Actinism is the property of light to produce chemical changes; in food processing technology: conservation method for milk by calorific treatment.)
d Aktinisierung *f*; Behandlung *f* durch Aktinität
f actinisitation *f*; traitement *m* par actinisme
p actinisação *f*; tratamento *m* por actinismo

66 **actinomycosis; lumpy jaw**
(Med.)
(Veterinary; infection of cattle, swine and humans; disease of the mouth and jaw.)
d Aktinomykose *f*
f actinomycose *f*
p actinomicose *f*

67 **activated charcoal**
(Prod.)
(In food processing technology: auxiliary in treatment processes because of its adsorption properties.)
d aktivierte Holzkohle *f*
f charbon *m* actif
p carvão *m* vegetal ativo

68 **activation of fermentation**
(Biochem.)
(Fermentation in nutritional science.)
d Aktivierung *f* der Gärung
f activation *f* de la fermentation
p ativação *f* da fermentação

69 **activator**
(Biochem.)
(Enzymatic activity activation: calcium (Ca), potassium (Ka), magnesium (Mg) etc.)
d Aktivator *m*; Beschleuniger *m*
f activateur *m*
p ativador *m*

70 **active carotenoid**
(Biochem.)
(Ref. to provitamin A.)
d aktives Carotenoid *n*
f caroténoïde *m* actif
p carotenóide *m* ativo

71 **active dry yeast**
(Biochem.)
(Microbiology; yeast characteristic, yeast production.)
d aktive Trockenhefe *f*
f levure *f* sèche active
p fermento *m* seco ativo

72 **active proteins**
(Biochem.)
(Participating in cellular life: e.g. enzymes, immunoglobulins.)
d aktive Proteine *npl*
f protéines *fpl* actives
p proteínas *fpl* ativas

73 **actomyosin**
(Biochem.)
(Anatomy; contractile muscle protein complex; adenosine triphosphate conversion for energy production.)
d Actomyosin *n*
f actomyosine *f*
p actomiosina *f*

74 **acute** *adj*
(Med.)
(Vitamin deficiency.)
d akut
f aigu
p agudo

75 **acute enteritis**
(Med.)
(Inflammation of the small intestine, e.g. caused by salmonella-infected foodstuffs.)
d akute Dünndarmentzündung *f*
f entérite *f* aiguë
p enterite *f* aguda

76 **acute toxicity**
(Med.)
(Food processing technology.)
d akute Toxizität *f*; akute Giftigkeit *f*
f toxicité *f* aiguë
p toxicidade *f* aguda

77 **acyclic monoterpenes**
(Prod.)
($C_{10}H_{16}$; e.g. myrcene; source of aroma/fragrance prime material.)
d azyklische Monoterpene *npl*
f monoterpènes *mpl* acycliques
p monoterpenos *mpl* acíclicos

* **acyl → 54**

78 **Adam's apple**
(Med.)
(Anatomy; laryngeal prominence; male body part.)
d Adamsapfel *m*
f pomme *f* d'Adam
p pomo-de-adão *m*; gogó *m*

79 **adaptation easiness**
(Biochem.)
(Microbiology; e.g. of microorganisms; ref. to biochemical research in nutritional science.)
d Anpassungsleichtigkeit *f*
f souplesse *f* d'adaptation
p facilidade *f* de adaptação

80 **adaptation of a vine sort to the climate**
(Agr.)
(Climatology; viticulture.)
d Anpassung *f* einer Rebsorte an das Klima; Klimaanpassung *f* einer Rebsorte
f adaptation *f* d'un cépage au climat
p adaptação *f* de uma espécie de cepa ao clima

81 **adaptation of a vine sort to the soil**
(Agr.)
(Viticulture.)
d Anpassung *f* einer Rebsorte an den Boden; Bodenanpassung *f* einer Rebsorte
f adaptation *f* d'un cépage au sol
p adaptação *f* de uma espécie de cepa ao solo

82 **adapted milk**
(Prod.)
(Dairy product; i.e. babymilk.)
d Säuglingsmilch *f*
f lait *m* pour nourrissons
p leite *m* para bebê; leite *m* adaptado

83 **adapted vine sort**
(Agr.)
(Viticulture.)
d adaptierte Rebsorte *f*; angepasste Rebsorte *f*
f cépage *m* adapté
p espécie *f* de cepa adaptada

84 **add** *v* **a superdosage of chlorine**
(Prod.)
(Water supply; drinking water and tap water treatment.)
d hochchlorieren
f additionner un superdosage en chlore
p adicionar uma superdosagem de cloro

* **added in the form of droplets → 2865**

85 **Addison's disease**
(Med.)
(Named after T. Addison (1793-1860), British physician; insufficiency of the adrenal glands; metabolic disease.)
d Addison-Krankheit *f*
f maladie *f* d'Addison
p doença *f* de Addison

* **additive → 480**

86 **add** *v* **tannin to the must**
(Prod.)
(Food processing technology.)
d dem Most Gerbstoff beigeben; dem Most

Gerbstoff hinzugeben
f ajouter du tannin au moût; ajouter du tanin au moût; tanniser le moût; taniser le moût
p adicionar tanino ao mosto

87 adenine
(Biochem.)
($C_5H_5N_5$; important in the formation of coenzyme-active principles; base of DNA and RNA.)
d Adenin *n*
f adénine *f*
p adenina *f*

88 adenosine
(Biochem.)
($C_{10}H_{13}N_5O_4$. Adenine riboside. Biochemically important regarding the liberation of energy in the muscles; see ATP.)
d Adenosin *n*
f adénosine *f*
p adenosina *f*

89 adenosine diphosphate; ADP
(Biochem.)
($C_{10}H_{15}N_5O_{10}P_2$; ref. e.g. to energetic metabolism.)
d Adinosindiphosphat *n*
f biphosphate *m* d'adénosine
p difosfato *m* de adenosina; adenosina *f* difosfato

90 adenosine monophosphate; AMP
(Biochem.)
(5-adenylic acid. $C_{10}H_{14}N_5O_7P$; e.g. ref. to muscle metabolism.)
d Adenosinmonophosphat *n*
f monophosphate *m* d'adénosine
p monofosfato *m* de adenosina; adenosina *f* monofosfato

91 adenosine triphosphate; ATP
(Biochem.)
($C_{10}H_{16}N_5O_{13}P_3$. Compound cont. ribose, adenine and three phosphate groups. Energy storage for metabolic and transport processes in cells; inhibit enzymatic browning of e.g. sliced apples, potatoes etc.)
d Adenosintriphosphat *n*; ATP *n*
f adénosine-triphosphate *f*; A.T.P. *f*
p trifosfato *m* de adenosina

92 adequate stability of suspensions
(Prod.)
(Food processing.)
d ausreichende Stabilität *f* der Suspensionen
f stabilité *f* suffisante des suspensions
p estabilidade *f* suficiente das suspensões

93 adipic acid
(Prod.)
($C_6H_{10}O_4$; used e.g. as baking powder additive.)
d Adipinsäure *f*
f acide *m* adipique
p ácido *m* adípico

94 adipoma; lipoma
(Med.)
(Benign tumor of fat cells.)
d Fettgewebegeschwulst *f*; Fettgeschwulst *f*; gutartige Fettgeschwulst *f*; Lipom *n*
f adipome *m*; lipome *m*; tumeur *m* de prolifération du tissu adipeux
p adipoma *m*; lipoma *m*

95 adiposalgia
(Med.)
(Adiposis type.)
d schmerzhafte Adipositas *f*
f adiposalgie *f*
p adipose *f* dolorosa

96 adipose *adj*
(Med.)
(Ref. to adiposis.)
d adipös; fetthaltig
f adipeux
p adiposo

97 adipose tissue
(Med.)
(E.g. due to supernutrition.)
d Fettgewebe *n*; adipöses Gewebe *n*
f tissu *m* adipeux
p tecido *m* adiposo

98 adiposis
(Med.)
(Accumulations of fat in the body, e.g. due to excessive food consumption; obesity.)
d Fettsucht *f*
f adiposité *f*
p adipose *f*

99 adiposuria; lipuria
(Med.)
(Presence of fat in the urine.)
d Lipurie *f*, Fettharnen *n*
f adiposurie *f*
p lipuria *f*, adiposuria *f*

* **ADP → 89**

* **adsorbent → 100**

100 adsorbing agent; adsorbent
(Biochem.)
(Ref. to an adsorbing substance (on its surface fixing molecules), without alteration of the

chemical compound; in nutritional science.)
d Adsorptionsmittel *n*
f adsorbant *m*
p adsorvente *m*

101 adsorption chromatography
(Prod.)
(In aroma/flavour research and production: separation process type for analysis.)
d Adsorptionschromatographie *f*
f chromatographie *f* par adsorption
p cromatografia *f* por adsorção

102 adsorption power
(Prod.)
(Aroma/fragrance research and production.)
d Adsorptionskraft *f*
f pouvoir *m* adsorbant; pouvoir *m* d'adsorption
p poder *m* de adsorção

103 adsorption power of solid carriers
(Prod.)
(Aroma/fragrance research and production.)
d Adsorptionskraft *f* fester Trägersubstanzen
f pouvoir *m* adsorbant de supports solides; pouvoir *m* d'adsorption de supports solides
p poder *m* de adsorção de suportes sólidos

104 adulteration
(Prod.)
(Foodstuff adulteration.)
d Verfälschung *f*
f adultération *f*
p adulteração *f*

105 adventitious plants
(Agr.)
(Botany; biologic agriculture: plants occurring sporadically in other than their usual places: weeds.)
d wildwachsende Pflanzen *fpl*
f plantes *fpl* adventices
p plantas *fpl* adventícias

106 adventitious roots
(Agr.)
(Botany: root form.)
d Stützwurzeln *fpl*; Stelzwurzeln *fpl*
f racines *fpl* adventives
p raízes *fpl* adventícias

*** aeolian erosion → 1537**

107 aeration
(Prod.)
(Product processing in food processing technology.)
d Auflockerung *f*
f aération *f*
p aeração *f*

108 aerial root
(Agr.)
(Botany: root form.)
d Luftwurzel *f*
f racine *f* aérienne
p raiz *f* aérea

109 aerobe
(Biochem.)
(Microbiology; microorganism that lives only in the presence of oxygen.)
d Aerobier *m*; Aerobiont *m*
f aérobe *m*
p aeróbio *m*

110 aerobic bacteria
(Biochem.)
(Microbiology; free oxygen requiring bacteria.)
d aerobe Bakterien *fpl*
f bactéries *fpl* aérobies
p bactérias *fpl* aeróbias

111 aerobic fermentation
(Biochem.)
(Nutritional science; fermentation process used for the aerobic decomposition of organic material by means of microorganisms or by enzymes.)
d aerobe Gärung *f*; aerobes Gärungsverfahren *n*
f fermentation *f* aérobie
p fermentação *f* aeróbia

112 aerobic respiration
(Biochem.)
(Decomposition of foodstuffs, carbohydrates, into carbon dioxide and water; it is a reaction requiring oxygen.)
d aerobe Atmung *f*
f respiration *f* aérobie
p respiração *f* aeróbia

113 aerobiosis
(Biochem.)
(Microbiology; development of microorganisms in the presence of air; e.g. brewing process: growing phase of yeast; in nutritional science.)
d Aerobiose *f*
f aérobiose *f*
p aerobiose *f*

114 aerosol
(Prod.)
(Food processing technology; colloidal system containing gas and a dispersion medium; in nutrition for distribution of foamy products, e.g. whipped cream.)
d Aerosol *n*
f aérosol *m*
p aerossol *m*

115 affection of allergic origin; disease of allergic origin
(Med.)
(Baby nutrition.)
d Beschwerde *f* allergischen Ursprunges; Krankheit *f* allergischen Ursprunges
f affection *f* d'origine allergique; maladie *f* d'origine allergique
p afecção *f* de origem alérgica; doença *f* de origem alérgica

116 aflatoxin
(Biochem.)
(Microbiology; food poison, originated by "Aspergillus flavus" and "Aspergillus parasiticus". Occurs mainly in cereals, nuts and oily seeds.)
d Aflatoxin *n*
f aflatoxine *f*
p aflatoxina *f*

117 afterbirth
(Med.)
(Veterinary: Placenta and membranes expelled after birth of a mammalian fetus: of young animals, cubs etc.)
d Nachgeburt *f*
f arrière-faix *m*; délivre *m*
p secundinas *f*

118 after-fertilizing
(Agr.)
(Soil treatment.)
d Nachdüngung *f*
f refumaison *f*
p readubação *f*

119 afterhardening
(Biochem.)
(Food processing technology: product characteristic: e.g. after treatment, storage.)
d Nachhärtung *f*
f post-durcissement *m*; durcissement *m* postérieur; durcissement *m* retardé
p pós-endurecimento *m*

* **afters → 1592**

120 aftertaste
(Prod.)
(Flavour persistence, flavour modification in the mouth over a longer period; food processing technology; e.g. ref. to organoleptic food evaluation.)
d Nachgeschmack *m*
f arrière-goût *m*; postsaveur *f*
p gosto *m* secundário; sabor *m* residual

121 agalactia
(Med.)
(Low milk production in a woman; absence of milk production; ref. to baby nutrition.)
d Agalaktose *f*
f agalactose *f*
p agalactia *f*

122 agar-agar; gelose
(Prod.)
(Gelatinous colloidal additive in food production e.g. in soups, ice creams, gelatines and meat and fish pastes, gelling additive or stabilizer. A non-digestible galactose-related complex.)
d Agar-Agar *n/m*
f agar-agar *m*; gélose *f*
p agar-agar *m*

123 agastric anaemia
(Med.)
(Anaemia due to iron-resorption troubles.)
d agastrische Anämie *f*; agastrische Blutarmut *f*
f anémie *f* agastrique
p anemia *f* agástrica

124 age as quality factor
(Agr.)
(Viticulture; e.g. ref. to wine and to vine.)
d Alter *n* als Qualitätsfaktor
f âge *m* comme facteur de qualité
p idade *f* como fator de qualidade

125 aged wine
(Biochem.)
(Enology; wine characteristic and wine quality factor.)
d gealterter Wein *m*
f vin *m* âgé
p vinho *m* envelhecido

126 ageusia
(Med.)
(Loss of the sense of taste.)
d Geschmacksverlust *m*; Ageusie *f*
f agueusie *f*
p ageusia *f*, ageustia *f*

127 agglomeration
(Prod.)
(Food processing technology; e.g. instant full-cream milk production: powder particle production, then agglomeration of these particles, followed by the drying process of the agglomerate.)
d Agglomeration *f*, Zusammenballung *f*, Anhäufung *f*
f agglomération *f*
p aglomeração *f*

128 agglutination
(Prod.)
(Food processing technology, e.g. of materials like pastes, doughs etc.)

d Agglutination *f*; Verklebung *f*; Verklumpung *f*
f agglutination *f*
p aglutinação *f*

* **agglutination of blood platelets → 130**

129 **aggregate fruit**
(Agr.)
(Botany: fruit type.)
d Sammelfrucht *f*
f pseudocarpe *m* composé
p pseudofruto *m* composto

130 **aggregation of blood platelets; agglutination of blood platelets**
(Med.)
(Ref. to thrombocytes.)
d Aggregation *f* von Blutplättchen; Zusammenballung *f* von Blutplättchen
f agrégation *f* des plaquettes sanguines
p agregação *f* das plaquetas do sangue

131 **aging of wine**
(Biochem.)
(Enology.)
d Alterung *f* des Weines
f vieillissement *m* du vin
p envelhecimento *m* do vinho

132 **aging of wine in bottles**
(Biochem.)
(Enology.)
d Alterung *f* des Weines in Flaschen
f vieillissement *m* du vin en bouteilles
p envelhecimento *m* do vinho em garrafas

133 **aglycone**
(Biochem.)
(Non-sugar group of the glycosides.)
d Aglykon *n*
f aglycone *m*
p aglicônio *m*

134 **agricultural area; arable land; soil; ploughable land; plowable land**
(Agr.)
(Soil type. Loose, fertile surface on which plants grow; farmland.)
d Ackerland *n*; Ackerboden *m*; landwirtschaftliches Anbaugebiet *n*; Ackerkrume *f*; Oberboden *m*
f terre *f* de culture; terre *f* arable; sol *m*; terre *f* fertile agricole
p terra *f* de planta; terra *f* arável; solo *m* fértil-agrícola

* **agricultural crop → 1406**

135 **agricultural foodstuffs of high nutritional value**
(Agr.)
(Aim of biologic agriculture, biologic farming system.)
d landwirtschaftliche Lebensmittel *npl* hohen Nährwertes
f denrées *fpl* agricoles de haute qualité nutritive
p gêneros *mpl* alimentícios agrícolas de alto valor nutritivo

136 **agricultural industry**
(Agr.)
(Agricultural produce marketing.)
d landwirtschaftliche Industrie *f*
f industrie *f* agricole; agro-industrie *f*
p indústria *f* agrícola

137 **agricultural practice**
(Agr.)
(Agricultural habits of working etc.)
d landwirtschaftliche Praktiken *fpl*
f pratiques *mpl* agricoles
p práticas *fpl* agrícolas

138 **agricultural prime material**
(Prod.)
(Prime material.)
d landwirtschaftliches Rohprodukt *n*; Agrarrohprodukt *n*
f matière *f* première agricole
p matéria *f* prima agrícola

139 **agricultural produce**
(Agr.)
(Agricultural produce; farm produce.)
d Landwirtschaftsprodukte *npl*
f produits *mpl* agricoles
p produtos *mpl* agrícolas

140 **agricultural sales period; harvest time**
(Agr.)
(Agricultural produce: Period of the year destined for sale of agricultural products: beef cattle etc. Climatology. Agricultural period.)
d Ernte *f*; Erntezeit *f*
f saison *f* des récoltes; saison *f* de la récolte; temps *m* de la moisson
p safra *f*; período *m* da safra; período *m* de colheita

141 **agricultural supply gap**
(Agr.)
(Agricultural produce: Period before harvest time.)
d Versorgungslücke *f* von Agrarprodukten; landwirtschaftliche Versorgungslücke *f*; Zwischenerntezeit *f*
f période *f* agricole de soudure
p entressafra *f*

142 agricultural techniques
(Agr.)
(Promoting agricultural produce.)
d landwirtschaftliche Technik *f*; landwirtschaftliche Verfahren *npl*; Agrotechnik *f*
f techniques *fpl* agricoles
p técnicas *fpl* agrícolas

143 agricultural zones
(Agr.)
(Climatology and soils.)
d landwirtschaftliche Zoneneinteilung *f*
f zones *fpl* d'implantation agricole
p zoneamento *m* agrícola

144 agriculture; husbandry
(Agr.)
(Agricultural produce: soil cultivation, livestock raising and crop production and sales.)
d Agrikultur *f*; Ackerbau *m*; Landwirtschaft *f*
f agriculture *f*
p agricultura *f*

145 agrobiologic system
(Agr.)
(Biological agriculture.)
d agrobiologisches System *n*
f système *m* agrobiologique
p sistema *m* agrobiológico

146 agronomic potential of the soil
(Agr.)
(Biological agriculture.)
d agronomisches Potential *n* des Bodens
f potentiel *m* agronomique des sols
p potencial *m* agronômico dos solos

147 agronomy
(Agr.)
(Agricultural produce: Agricultural science.)
d Landwirtschaftswissenschaft *f*; Agronomie *f*
f agronomie *f*
p agronomia *f*

148 agrumen flavonoids
(Biochem.)
(Nutritional science. Ref. to citrus fruits.)
d Agrumenflavonoide *npl*; Flavonoide *npl* der Zitrusfrüchte
f flavonoïdes *mpl* d'agrumes
p flavonoídes *fpl* cítricos

149 agrumen oils
(Prod.)
(Food processing technology: citrus oils (from citrus fruits).)
d Agrumenöle *npl*; Öle *npl* der Zitrusfrüchte
f huiles *fpl* des agrumes
p óleos *mpl* cítricos

* **air chamber → 152**

150 air classification; pneumatic separation
(Prod.)
(Food processing technology and processes; pneumatic classifying process for particles of small grain size; e.g. cleaning of grainy fruits.)
d Windsichtung *f*; pneumatische Klassierung *f*
f classification *f* par air; classement *m* par le courant d'air
p classificação *f* por corrente de ar; separação *f* pneumática

151 air-dry wood; seasoned timber
(Agr.)
(Agricultural produce: Agricultural byproduct.)
d lufttrockenes Holz *n*
f bois *m* séché à l'air
p madeira *f* seca ao ar

152 air space; air chamber
(Agr.)
(Poultry farming: Lining the eggshell internally, two membranes form the air space or air chamber, situated on the larger end of the egg.)
d Luftkammer *f*
f chambre *f* à air
p câmara *f* de ar

153 alanine
(Biochem.)
($C_3H_7NO_2$; non-essential amino acid. Part of the pantothenic acid molecule, which is part of the vitamin B complex; ingredient in human milk and in cow's milk.)
d Alanin *n*
f alanine *f*
p alanina *f*

154 albumen
(Prod.)
(Nutritional science; white of an egg. Dried egg white, containing ovalbumin, an protein. Plant nutrient in certain reserve plant tissues.)
d Albumen *n*; Eiweiß *n*
f albumen *m*
p albume *m*; albúmen *m*

155 albumin
(Biochem.)
(Nutritional science; water-soluble protein: From the dried white of eggs, used for sugar refining and clarifying of certain liquids. Nutrient in foods.)

d Albumin *n*
f albumine *f*
p albumina *f*

* **albumin of white of egg → 3939**

156 albuminoid *adj*
(Prod.)
(Food processing technology.)
d albuminoid; eiweißähnlich
f albuminoïde
p albuminóide

157 albuminoids; scleroprotein
(Med.)
(Anatomy; fibrous protein: Elastin; keratin; collagen.)
d Albuminoide *npl*; Skleroprotein *n*
f albuminoïdes *mpl*; scléroprotéine *f*
p albuminoídes *mpl*; escleroproteína *f*

158 albuminous *adj*
(Prod.)
(Food processing technology; having the characteristics of, or containing albumins.)
d albuminös; eiweißhaltig
f albumineux
p albuminoso

159 albuminuria
(Med.)
(E.g. serum proteins in the urine; can be due to kidney disease, or to exercise.)
d Albuminausscheidung *f*
f albuminurie *f*
p albuminuria *f*

160 alcohol addition to the wine
(Prod.)
(Enology; addition operation.)
d Alkoholzusatz *m* zum Wein
f vinage *m*
p adição *f* de álcool ao vinho

161 alcoholemia
(Med.)
(Alcohol concentration in one litre of blood in the body; maximum level after one hour of absorption.)
d Alkoholämie *f*
f alcoolémie *f*
p alcoolemia *f*

* **alcoholic beverage → 163**

162 alcoholic degree
(Prod.)
(Food processing technology, research and production; chemistry.)
d Alkoholgrad *m*
f degré *m* alcoolique
p grau *m* alcoólico; graduação *f* alcoólica

163 alcoholic drink; alcoholic beverage; potable
(Prod.)
(Food processing technology.)
d alkoholisches Getränk *n*
f boisson *f* alcoolique; boisson *f* alcoolisée
p bebida *f* alcoólica

164 alcoholic fermentation
(Biochem.)
(Beer brewery process of ethanol, grain-alcohol production. Wine production. Fermentation in nutritional science.)
d alkoholische Fermentation *f*; alkoholische Gärung *f*; Alkoholgärung *f*
f fermentation *f* alcoolique
p fermentação *f* alcoólica

165 alcoholic tincture
(Prod.)
(Flavour research and production: extraction process.)
d alkoholische Tinktur *f*
f teinture *f* alcoolique
p tintura *f* alcoólica

166 alcoholic tinctures
(Prod.)
(Aroma/flavour research and production: extraction process: (flavour) product obtained by alcoholic maceration of fresh plants and alcohol in equal parts.)
d alkoholische Auszüge *mpl*
f alcoolatures *fpl*
p alcoolatos *mpl*

167 alcohol 95 per cent
(Prod.)
(C_2H_5OH; mixture of 95% of ethanol and water.)
d Weingeist *m*
f alcool *m* officinal; esprit-de-vin *m*
p álcool *m* etílico

* **alcohol-soluble** *adj* **→ 5096**

168 alcohol-water mixtures
(Prod.)
(Food processing technology.)
d Alkohol-Wasser-Mischungen *fpl*
f mélanges *mpl* d'alcool et d'eau
p misturas *fpl* alcool/água

169 aldehyde C_{11}; methyl octyl acetaldehyde
(Prod.)
(Aroma prime material; e.g. orange-peel flavour.)
d Aldehyd C_{11} *n*; Methyloctylacetaldehyd *n*

f aldéhyde C_{11} *m*; acétaldéhyde *m* de méthyloctyle
p aldeído C_{11} *m*; acetaldeído *m* de metiloctila; metiloctilacetaldeído *m*

170 **aldehyde C_{12}; methyl nonyl acetaldehyde; 2-methyl-undecanal**
(Prod.)
(Aroma prime material; e.g. fruity note.)
d Aldehyd C_{12} *n*; Methylnonylacetaldehyd *n*
f aldéhyde C_{12} *m*; acétaldéhyde *m* de méthylnonyle
p aldeído C_{12} *m*; acetaldeído *m* de metilnonila; metilnonilacetaldeído *m*

171 **aldehyde C_5; n-valeraldehyde; valeric aldehyde**
(Prod.)
($C_5H_{10}O$; aroma prime material; fruit-like to nutty flavour notes.)
d Aldehyd C_5 *n*; n-Valeraldehyd *n*
f aldéhyde C_5 *m*; aldéhyde *m* n-valérique
p aldeído C_5 *m*; aldeído n-valérico *m*

172 **aldehyde C_6; n-hexanal; caproic aldehyde**
(Prod.)
($C_6H_{12}O$; aroma prime material; e.g. apple-like flavour note; odour-masking additive.)
d Aldehyd C_6 *n*; n-Hexanal *n*
f aldéhyde C_6 *m*; n-hexanal *m*
p aldeído C_6 *m*; n-hexanal *m*

173 **aldehydic note**
(Prod.)
(Aroma research and production.)
d aldehydische Note *f*
f note *f* aldéhydique
p nota *f* aldeídica

174 **aldosterone**
(Med.)
($C_{21}H_{28}O_5$; hormone which controls the kidney's excretion of salt and water; regulation of the salt/water balance of the body.)
d Aldosteron *n*
f aldostérone *f*
p aldosterona *f*

175 **ale**
(Prod.)
(Food processing technology; English, slightly bitter, top fermenting beer type.)
d Ale *n*; englisches helles, obergäriges Bier *n*
f ale *f*; bière *f* anglaise blonde (*de fermentation haute*)
p cerveja *f* clara inglesa de alta fermentação

176 **aleurone**
(Biochem.)
(Protein present e.g. in seeds.)
d Aleuron *n*; Pflanzenreserveeiweiß *n*
f aleurone *f*
p aleurona *f*

* **alfa,delta-diaminovaleric acid → 3930**

* **alfalfa → 3293**

177 **alga**
(Biochem.)
(Plants of simple structure containing chlorophyll: photosynthesis ability.)
d Alge *f*
f algue *f*
p alga *f*

178 **alginate**
(Prod.)
(Alginic acid salt; complex polysaccharide; used e.g. in food industrialization as stabilizer, thickening agent, emulsifier; texture improving ingredient etc.)
d Alginat *n*
f alginate *m*
p alginato *m*

179 **alginic acid**
(Prod.)
($(C_6H_8O_6)n$; auxiliary product; complex polysaccharide extracted from algae, seaweeds. Binding agent in ice-cream, sweets, meat products. No. CEE: E 400; texture improving ingredient.)
d Alginsäure *f*
f acide *m* alginique
p ácido *m* algínico

180 **alimentary**
(Med.)
(Nutrition.)
d lebensmittelbezüglich; nahrungsmittelbezogen
f alimentaire
p alimentar

181 **alimentary anaemia**
(Med.)
(Vitamin deficiency in nutrition.)
d alimentäre Anämie *f*; ernährungsbedingte Blutarmut *f*
f anémie *f* alimentaire
p anemia *f* alimentar

* **alimentary antioxidant → 2299**

182 **alimentary aroma**
(Prod.)
(Flavour chemicals.)
d Nahrungsmittelaroma *n*

f arôme *m* alimentaire
p aroma *m* alimentício; aroma *m* alimentar; aroma *m* para fins alimentícios

183 alimentary bolus
(Med.)
(Soft food mass used in feeding by tube.)
d Nahrungsbolus *m*
f bol *m* alimentaire
p bolo *m* alimentar

184 alimentary comportment
(Med.)
(Nutrition.)
d Ernährungsverhalten *n*; Verhalten *n* in Bezug auf die Ernährung
f comportement *m* alimentaire
p comportamento *m* alimentar

185 alimentary compulsion
(Med.)
(Psychologic condition.)
d psychologischer Ernährungszwang *m*
f compulsion *f* alimentaire
p compulsão *f* alimentar

186 alimentary contamination
(Biochem.)
(Microbiology; nutritional science.)
d Lebensmittelverseuchung *f*; Lebensmittelkontamination *f*
f contamination *f* alimentaire
p contaminação *f* alimentar

* **alimentary diabetes → 1617**

187 alimentary dystrophy
(Med.)
(Nutritional disorder.)
d ernährungsbedingte Dystrophie *f*
f dystrophie *f* alimentaire
p distrofia *f* alimentar

188 alimentary fats
(Prod.)
(Food processing technology; the fats have their origin in some fatty acids (saturated and unsaturated fatty acids).)
d Nahrungsfette *npl*
f graisses *fpl* alimentaires
p gorduras *fpl* alimentícios; gorduras *fpl* alimentares

189 alimentary intolerance
(Med.)
(Nutrition and its disorders.)
d nahrungsbezügliche Intoleranz *f*; Intoleranz *f* gegen Nahrungsmittel
f intolérance *f* alimentaire
p intolerância *f* alimentar

190 alimentary intoxication of sucklings
(Med.)
(Baby nutrition.)
d nahrungsbedingte Säuglingsvergiftung *f*
f intoxication *f* alimentaire des nourrissons
p intoxicação *f* alimentar dos lactentes

191 alimentary liquid
(Med.)
(Artificial nutrition methods.)
d Nährflüssigkeit *f*
f liquide *m* alimentaire
p líquido *m* alimentar

192 alimentary peptide
(Biochem.)
(Nutritional science.)
d Nahrungsmittelpeptid *n*; nahrungsmittelbezügliches Peptid *n*
f peptide *m* alimentaire
p peptídeo *m* alimentar

193 alimentary proteins
(Biochem.)
(Nutritional science.)
d Nährproteine *npl*; Ernährungseiweiß *n*
f protéines *fpl* alimentaires
p proteínas *fpl* alimentares

194 alimentary supply
(Med.)
(Take-in of foodstuffs with addition of certain vitamins not synthesized by the human body.)
d Nahrungsmittelzufuhr *f*
f apport *m* alimentaire
p aporte *m* alimentar

195 alimentary supply-deficiency of essential fatty acids
(Biochem.)
(Nutritional science, food research and production.)
d Nahrungsmittelzufuhrmangel *m* an essentiellen Fettsäuren; Mangel *m* an essentiellen Fettsäuren bedingt durch fehlerhafte Nahrungsmittelzufuhr
f carence *f* d'apport alimentaire en acides gras essentiels
p carência *f* de aporte alimentar de ácidos graxos essenciais

196 alimentary therapy
(Med.)
(Treatment by nutrition.)
d Ernährungstherapie *f*
f thérapeutique *f* alimentaire
p terapêutica *f* alimentar

197 alimentary toxicosis
(Med.)
(Food processing technology.)

d Nahrungstoxikose *f*
f toxicose *f* alimentaire
p toxicose *f* alimentar

198 alimentary usage
(Prod.)
(Food processing technology, food research and production.)
d Gebrauch *m* zu Ernährungszwcken
f usage *m* alimentaire
p uso *m* alimentício

199 alimentation
(Med.)
(Feeding; intake of nutriments.)
d Ernährung *f*
f alimentation *f*
p alimentação *f*

* **alimentation by duodenal tube → 3827**

200 alimentation for disease prevention
(Biochem.)
(Nutrition in medicine; nutritional therapy.)
d Ernährung *f* zur Krankheitsvorbeugung
f alimentation *f* pour la prévention de maladies
p alimentação *f* para a prevenção de doenças

201 alimentation for treatment of diseases
(Biochem.)
(Nutrition in medicine; nutritional therapy.)
d Ernährung *f* zur Krankheitsbehandlung
f alimentation *f* pour le traitement de maladies
p alimentação *f* para o tratamento de doenças

202 aliphatic *adj*
(Biochem.)
(Nutritional science. Ref. to organic compounds with open-chain structure.)
d aliphatisch
f aliphatique
p alifático

203 alkali
(Biochem.)
(Base dissolving in water, yielding ions of hydroxide.)
d Alkali *n*
f alcali *m*
p álcali *m*

204 alkaligenous diet
(Med.)
(Alimentary regimen; ovolactovegetable nutrition.)
d alkalisierende Diät *f*
f diète *f* alcalisante
p dieta *f* alcalizante

205 alkaline medium
(Biochem.)
(Food processing technology: action condition of food preservatives.)
d alkalisches Medium *n*
f milieu *m* alcalin
p meio *m* alcalino

206 alkaline soil
(Agr.)
(Soil with a high alkali content, above pH 7.3.)
d alkalischer Boden *m*
f sol *m* alcalin
p solo *m* alcalino

207 alkalinization of urine
(Med.)
(Lactovovegetable diet may be the origin, increasing the uric acid solubility and its excretion.)
d Alkalisierung *f* des Harns
f alcalisation *f* de l'urine
p alcalização *f* da urina; alcalinização *f* da urina

208 alkali spring
(Med.)
(Ref. to fountain water types.)
d alkalische Quelle *f*
f source *f* alcaline
p fonte *f* alcalina

209 alkaloid
(Biochem.)
(Basic nitrogenous organic plant compound, with physiologic, i.e. therapeutic or toxic, effect.)
d Alkaloid *n*
f alcaloïde *m*
p alcalóide *m*

210 alkaloids extraction
(Med.)
(Therapy.)
d Auszug *m* von Alkaloiden
f extraction *f* des alcaloïdes
p extração *f* de alcalóides

211 alkaloids isolation
(Biochem.)
(Biochemical process.)
d Isolierung *f* von Alkaloiden
f isolement *m* des alcaloïdes
p isolação *f* de alcalóides

212 alkanes; paraffins
(Prod.)
(C_nH_{2n+2}; saturated (open-chain) hydrocarbons; e.g. butyric acid ($C_4H_8O_2$); source of prime material for esters as bases for synthetic flavouring ingredients and fragrance bases.)

d Alkane *npl*; Grenzkohlenwasserstoffe *mpl*; Paraffine *npl*
f alcanes *mpl*; paraffines *fpl*
p alcanos *mpl*; parafinas *fpl*

213 alkenes; olefins; olefines
(Prod.)
(C_nH_{2n}; unsaturated hydrocarbons; source of prime material for fragrance/aroma production.)
d Alkene *npl*; Olefine *npl*
f alcènes *mpl*; oléfines *fpl*
p alcenos *mpl*; olefinas *fpl*

214 allergen
(Med.)
(Allergy causing substance, e.g. a specific foodstuff or foodstuff ingredient.)
d Allergen *n*
f allergène *m*
p alérgeno *m*; alergênio *m*

215 allergen in child nutrition
(Med.)
(Baby nutrition. Antigen that causes allergy.)
d Allergen *n* in Kinderernährung
f allergène *m* dans la nutrition infantile
p alergênio *m* na nutrição infantil; alergênico *m* na nutrição infantil; alérgeno *m* na nutrição infantil

216 allergic eczema
(Med.)
(Baby nutrition. Condition of allergic origin e.g. of not correctly nursed babies.)
d allergisches Ekzem *n*; allergische Juckflechte *f*; allergischer Hautausschlag *m*
f eczéma *m* allergique
p eczema *m* alérgico

217 allergic process
(Med.)
(Nutrition.)
d allergischer Prozess *m*
f processus *m* allergique
p processo *m* alérgico

218 allergic shock
(Med.)
(E.g. due to intolerance to proteins of cow's milk, esp. regarding baby nutrition.)
d allergischer Schock *m*
f choc *m* allergique
p choque *m* alérgico

219 allergy
(Med.)
(Body hypersensitivity, e.g. related in some cases to certain foods.)
d Allergie *f*
f allergie *f*
p alergia *f*

220 allergy diseases of alimentary origin
(Med.)
(Nutrition.)
d allergische Krankheiten *fpl* mit auf Nahrungsmitteln bezüglichen Ursprunges; nahrungsmittelbezogene allergische Krankheiten *fpl*
f maladies *fpl* allergiques d'origine alimentaire
p doenças *fpl* alérgicas de origem alimentar

*** allheal → 5650**

221 allolactose
(Biochem.)
(Sugar form, lactose modification, lactose isomer.)
d Allolactose *f*
f allolactose *f*
p alolactose *f*

222 allotment
(Agr.)
(Biological agriculture: small plot of land for domestic cultivation.)
d Schrebergarten *m*
f jardin *m* ouvrier
p horta *f* doméstica

223 alloxan
(Med.)
($C_4H_2N_2O_4$; uric acid oxidation product.)
d Alloxan *n*
f alloxane *f*
p aloxano *m*

224 alloxazine
(Biochem.)
(Structural part of lactoflavin ($C_{17}H_{20}N_4O_6$), i.e. of riboflavin (vitamin B_2).)
d Alloxazin *n*
f alloxazine *f*
p aloxazina *f*

225 alluvial plain; alluvial soil
(Agr.)
(Soil composed of alluvium, e.g. deposited by running water.)
d Schwemmland *n*; Schwemmboden *m*; aufgeschwemmter Boden *m*
f terrain *m* alluvial; sol *m* alluvial
p terra *f* de aluvião; solo *m* aluvial

*** alluvial soil → 225**

226 allyl caproate
(Prod.)
($C_9H_{16}O_2$; Caproic acid allyl ester; aroma

prime material; flavouring agent: e.g. rum-like to fruity, mango, passion fruit notes.)
d Allylcapronat *n*
f caproate *m* d'allyle
p capronato *m* de alila

227 **allyl isothiocyanate**
(Prod.)
(C_4H_5NS; In nature: seeds of "Brassica nigra L."; volatile mustard oil; flavour prime material.)
d Allylisothiocyanat *n*
f isothiocynate *m* d'allyle
p isotiocianato *m* de alila

228 **almond**
(Agr.)
(Agricultural produce. "Prunus dulcis syn. Prunus amygdalus"; drupaceous fruit.)
d Mandel *f*
f amande *f*
p amêndoa *f*

229 **almond cookie; almond cooky**
(Prod.)
(Confectionary.)
d Mandelgebäck *n*
f pâtisserie *f* aux amandes
p biscoito *m* de amêndoas

* **almond cooky → 229**

230 **almond oil**
(Prod.)
(Agricultural produce. Oil of "Prunus dulcis".)
d Mandelöl *n*
f huile *f* d'amandes
p óleo *m* de amêndoas

231 **aloe**
(Agr.)
(Botany: "Aloe vera L."; medicinal herb.)
d Aloe *f*
f aloès *m*
p aloés *m*; babosa *f*

232 **alpha-aminobutyric acid; 2-aminobutanoic acid**
(Biochem.)
($C_4H_9NO_2$; Occurs during cheese maturation.)
d Alpha-Aminobuttersäure *f*
f acide *m* alpha-aminobutyrique
p ácido *m* alfa-aminobutírico

* **alpha tocopherol → 5764**

233 **alpha-tocopherol concentration**
(Biochem.)
(Nutritional science; ref. to vitamin as an antioxidant.)
d Alpha-Tocopherol-Konzentration *f*
f concentration *f* d'alpha-tocophérol
p concentração *f* de alfa-tocoferol

* **alpkase → 1038**

234 **alteration agents of wine**
(Biochem.)
(Enology: Microbiology; e.g. ref. to bacteria acting in the wine.)
d Veränderung hervorrufende Stoffe *mpl* des Weines
f agents *mpl* d'altération du vin
p agentes *mpl* de alteração do vinho

235 **alteration of immunologic function**
(Med.)
(Modification of immunologic function e.g. by nutritional factors.)
d Veränderung *f* der Immunfunktion
f altération *f* de la fonction immunitaire
p alteração *f* da função imunológica

* **alteration of nutriments → 3602**

236 **alteration suffered by the aroma note**
(Prod.)
(Taste; aroma research and production, e.g. alteration by aging; oxidation of the flavour note.)
d Veränderung *f*, welche die Geschmacksnote erlitt
f altération *f* subie par la note d'arôme
p alteração *f* sofrida pelo aroma

* **alternation of cultures → 1448**

237 **alternative agricultural production**
(Agr.)
(Biological agriculture, biologic farming system.)
d alternative Landwirtschaftsproduktion *f*; alternative Agrarproduktion *f*
f production *f* agricole alternative
p produção *f* agrícola alternativa

238 **alternative agriculture**
(Agr.)
(See organic agriculture; organic farming; biological agriculture.)
d alternative Agrikultur *f*; Alternativlandwirtschaft *f*
f agriculture *f* alternative
p agricultura *f* alternativa

239 **alternative ways of production**
(Agr.)
(Biological agriculture.)
d alternative Produktionswege *mpl*

f voies *fpl* alternatives de production
p caminhos *mpl* alternativos de produção

240 altocumulos
(Agr.)
(Climatology: Fleecy clouds approx. 2,500-6,000 m high, forming a lamellar or flocculent layer.)
d Schäfchenwolken *fpl*
f altocumulus *m*
p alto-cúmulo *m*

241 aluminium; aluminum
(Prod.)
(Al; Foodstuff colorant; prime material for food (surface) dye production.)
d Aluminium *n*
f aluminium *m*
p alumínio *m*

242 aluminium oxide
(Prod.)
(Water supply: Al_2O_3; element eventually contained in form of traces in mineral water.)
d Aluminiumoxid *n*
f oxyde *m* d'aluminium
p óxido *m* de alumínio

* **aluminium silicate → 587**

* **aluminum → 241**

243 amandine tart
(Prod.)
(Cake shop product.)
d Mandeltörtchen *n*
f amandine *f*
p torta *f* de amêndoas

244 amaranth
(Prod.)
(Foodstuff colorant; $C_{20}H_{11}N_2Na_3O_{10}S_3$. Food dye (E 123) in some countries.)
d Amaranthrot *n*
f amarante *f*; rouge *m* de l'amarante
p amaranto *m*; vermelho-amaranto *m*

245 amine
(Biochem.)
(Nutritional science; amino group ($-NH_2$); organic compound which is derived from ammonia.)
d Amin *n*
f amine *f*
p amina *f*

246 amino acid
(Biochem.)
(Organic, water-soluble compounds, with an amino ($-H_2$) and carboxyl (-COOH) group linked to the alfa-carbon atom. Proteins consist of ca. 20 amino acids. Essential a. must be present in the diet.)
d Aminosäure *f*
f amino-acide *m*; acide *m* aminé
p aminoácido *m*

247 amino acid composition
(Prod.)
(Food processing technology: e.g. eggs.)
d Aminosäurenzusammensetzung *f*; Zusammensetzung *f* an Aminosäuren
f composition *f* en acides aminés
p composição *f* de aminoácidos

248 amino acid metabolism
(Med.)
d Aminosäurestoffwechsel *m*
f métabolisme *m* des amino-acides
p metabolismo *m* dos aminoácidos

249 amino acid mixtures
(Med.)
(E.g. in parenteral (intravenous) nutrition: protein supply.)
d Aminosäurengemische *npl*
f mélanges *mpl* d'amino-acides
p misturas *fpl* de aminoácidos

* **2-aminobutanoic acid → 232**

250 aminopeptidase
(Biochem.)
(Proteolytic (peptides hydrolyzing) enzyme.)
d Aminopeptidase *f*
f aminopeptidase *f*
p aminopeptidase *f*

* **aminosuccinic acid → 458**

251 ammonia
(Agr.)
(NH_3; soil treatment; active principle of ammoniacal fertilizers; raw material.)
d Ammoniak *n*
f ammoniaque *m*
p amoníaco *m*

* **ammoniacal fertilizer → 252**

252 ammoniac fertilizer; ammoniacal fertilizer
(Agr.)
(Soil treatment. Nitrogen source for plants; raw material.)
d Ammoniakdünger *m*
f engrais *m* ammoniacal
p adubo *m* amoniacal

253 ammonium alginate
(Prod.)
(Food processing technology: e.g. texture improving ingredient.)

d Ammoniumalginat *n*
f alginate *m* d'ammonium
p alginato *m* de amônio

* **ammonium bicarbonate → 254**

* **ammonium carbonate → 522**

254 **ammonium hydrogen carbonate; ammonium bicarbonate**
(Prod.)
(NH_4HCO_3; e.g. component of the leavening agent: Hartshorn (Hirschhornsalz).)
d Ammoniumhydrogencarbonat *n*; Ammoniumbicarbonat *n*; Hirschhornsalz *n*
f hydrogénocarbonate *m* d'ammonium; bicarbonate *m* d'ammonium
p bicarbonato *m* de amônio

255 **ammonium nitrate**
(Prod.)
(NH_4NO_3; Fertilizing active principle: Nitrogen source for plants; raw material.)
d Ammoniumnitrat *n*; salpetersaures Ammoniak *n*; Ammonsalpeter *m*
f nitrate *m* d'ammonium
p nitrato *m* de amônio

256 **ammonium phosphate**
(Prod.)
($(NH_4)H_2PO_4$; monobasic; food processing technology: e.g. used in baking powder, in fermentation and caramel production.)
d Ammoniumphosphat *n*
f phosphate *m* d'ammonium
p fosfato *m* de amônio

257 **amoebae** *pl*
(Med.)
(Genus "Amoeba", "Entamoeba histolytica Schaudimm"; e.g. dysentery causing parasite.)
d Amöben *fpl*; Wechseltierchen *npl*
f amibes *fpl*
p amebas *fpl*

258 **amoebiasis; amoebic dysentery**
(Med.)
(Diarrhoea caused by amoeba "Entamoeba histolytica".)
d Amöbenruhr *f*
f amibiase *f*; diarrhée *f* amibienne
p amebíase *f*

* **amoebic dysentery → 258**

* **AMP → 90**

259 **amphibian**
(Agr.)
(Class "Amphibia"; cold-blooded vertebrates, e.g. frogs.)
d Lurche *f*
f amphibien *m*
p anfíbio *m*

260 **amygdalin**
(Prod.)
(Aromas; $C_{20}H_{27}NO_{11}$; Prussic acid containing glucoside; occurs in seeds, almonds, cherry stones; gives characteristic odour after hydrolysis. Bitter almonds can have a severe toxic effect.)
d Amygdalin *n*
f amygdaline *f*
p amigdalina *f*

261 **amyl acetate**
(Prod.)
($C_7H_{14}O_2$; isoamyl acetate; banana oil; aroma prime material; pear to banana-like flavour note.)
d Amylacetat *n*
f acétate *m* d'amyle
p acetato *m* de amilo

262 **amylase**
(Biochem.)
(Beer brewing process: Ensyme group. Diastase. Degradation of starch and other polysaccharides. Production of maltose and glucose.)
d Amylase *f*
f amylase *f*
p amilase *f*; amilíase *f*

263 **amylic fermentation**
(Biochem.)
(Nutritional science; amyl alcohol production from cane sugar.)
d Amylgärung *f*
f fermentation *f* amylique
p fermentação *f* amílica

264 **amylic odour**
(Biochem.)
(Nutritional science; ref. to fermentation processes: undesirable effect.)
d Amylgeruch *m*
f odeur *f* amylique
p odor *m* amílico

265 **amylopectin**
(Prod.)
(Food processing technology; polysaccharide, 80% starch, used in mash types; e.g. in baby food.)
d Amylopectin *n*
f amylopectine *f*
p amilopectina *f*

266 amylose
(Biochem.)
(Linear chain polysaccharide and constituent of starch.)
d Amylose *f*
f amylose *f*
p amilose *f*

267 anabolism
(Med.)
(Growth, synthesis and formation of new tissues.)
d Anabolismus *m*
f anabolisme *m*
p anabolismo *m*

268 anaemic *adj*
(Med.)
(State of health due to vitamin deficiency in nutrition.)
d anämisch; blutarm
f anémique
p anêmico

269 anaerobe
(Biochem.)
(Microbiology; organism capable to live without oxygen.)
d Anaerobier *m*; Anaerobiont *m*
f anaérobie *m*
p anaeróbio *m*

270 anaerobic germ
(Biochem.)
(Microbiology; food biochemistry; ref. to a contaminating agent.)
d anaerober Keim *m*
f germe *m* anaérobie
p germe *m* anaeróbio; gérmen *m* anaeróbio

271 anaerobic respiration
(Biochem.)
(Respiration without the presence of molecular oxygen: Cellular respiration.)
d anaerobe Atmung *f*
f respiration *f* anaérobie
p respiração *f* anaeróbia

272 anaerobiosis
(Biochem.)
(Microbiology; life of the organism capable to live without oxygen.)
d Anaerobiose *f*; sauerstoffloses Leben *n*
f anaérobiose *f*
p anaerobiose *f*

273 anaerobiotic fermentation
(Biochem.)
(Nutritional science; fermentation process; e.g. alcoholic fermentation: ethylalcohol production by hexoses through enzyme activity of yeast.)
d anaerobe Gärung *f*
f fermentation *f* anaérobie
p fermentação *f* anaeróbia

274 analgesic
(Med.)
(Pain-relieving drug.)
d Analgetikum *n*
f analgésique *m*
p analgésico *m*

275 anallergic *adj*
(Med.)
(Characteristic of a substance which does not provoke allergy.)
d anallergisch; nicht allergisch
f anallergique
p não alérgico

276 analytical techniques
(Prod.)
(Food processing technology.)
d Analyseverfahren *npl*
f techniques *fpl* de l'analyse
p técnicas *fpl* analíticas

277 analytic control
(Biochem.)
(Fermentation in nutritional science: Food processing technology.)
d analytische Kontrolle *f*
f contrôle *m* analytique
p controle *m* analítico

278 analytic criterions; analytic standards
(Biochem.)
(Nutritional science.)
d analytische Kriterien *npl*
f critères *mpl* analytiques
p critérios *mpl* analíticos

* **analytic standards → 278**

279 anaphylaxis
(Med.)
(Caused by repeating parenteral (intravenous) protein supply: parenteral nutrition problem.)
d Anaphylaxie *f*, Überempfindlichkeit *f*
f anaphylaxie *f*
p anafilaxia *f*

280 anasarca
(Med.)
(Generalized oedema; can be due to vitamin B_1 deficiency. Veterinary: cattle disease.)
d Anasarka *n*; Wassersucht *f* des Unterhautgewebes

f anasarque *f*; hydropisie *f* du tissu cellulaire
p anasarca *f*; edema *m* do tecido celular

281 anchoiade; anchovy sauce
(Prod.)
(Gastronomy; sauce made of oil and crushed anchovies.)
d Anschovistunke *f*
f anchoïade *f*
p molho *m* de anchovas

282 anchovy
(Agr.)
(Edible fish "Engraulis encrasicholus".)
d Anschovis *f*; Sardelle *f*; gesalzene Sardelle *f*
f anchois *m*
p anchova *f*

283 anchovy butter
(Prod.)
(Gastronomy; prepared with anchovies, condiments and egg yolk.)
d Anschovisbutter *m*
f beurre *m* d'anchois
p manteiga *f* de anchovas

* **anchovy sauce → 281**

284 angelica
(Agr.)
(Botany: "Angelica archangelica"; aromatic herb; used in confectionary.)
d Engelwurz *f*; Brustwurz *f*; Angelika *f*
f angélique *f*
p angélica *f*

285 animal albumin
(Prod.)
(Food processing technology; nutrient.)
d tierisches Albumin *n*
f albumine *f* animale
p albumina *f* animal

286 animal cell
(Med.)
(Anatomy; unit of animal structure.)
d tierische Zelle *f*
f cellule *f* animale
p célula *f* animal

287 animal fat
(Prod.)
(Food processing technology.)
d tierisches Fett *n*
f graisse *f* animale
p gordura *f* animal

* **animal fattening → 2085**

288 animal for slaughter; beef cattle
(Agr.)
(Cattle breeding. Animals raised for alimentation purpose.)
d Schlachtvieh *n*
f bétail *m* de boucherie
p gado *m* para abate; rês *f* de corte

289 animal lipids
(Biochem.)
(Nutrition; dietary constituents: e.g. milk.)
d tierische Lipide *npl*; Lipide *npl* tierischen Ursprungs
f lipides *mpl* animaux
p lipídios *mpl* animais; lipides *mpl* de origem animal

290 animal note
(Prod.)
(Taste; aroma research and production; e.g. in dairy products.)
d tierursprüngliche Note *f*
f note *f* animale
p nota *f* de origem animal

291 animal nutrition
(Med.)
(Veterinary science.)
d Tierernährung *f*
f alimentation *f* animale
p nutrição *f* animal

292 animal pelage
(Med.)
(Veterinary science; veterinary anatomy.)
d Haarkleid *n* des Tieres
f pelage *m* de l'animal
p pelagem *f* do animal; pelame *m*

293 animal protection
(Agr.)
(Aim of biologic agriculture, biologic farming system.)
d Tierschutz *m*
f protection *f* des animaux
p proteção *f* dos animais

294 animal protein
(Biochem.)
(Nutritional science.)
d Protein *n* tierischer Herkunft
f protéine *f* animale
p proteína *f* animal

295 animals destined for alimentation
(Agr.)
(Livestock: farm animals.)
d zu Nahrungszwecken vorgesehene Tiere *npl*
f animaux *mpl* destinés à l'alimentation
p animais *mpl* destinados para a alimentação

296 animal's hock
(Med.)
(Animal's anatomy, e.g. horse.)
d Sprunggelenk *n*
f jarret *m*
p jarrete *m*

297 animal toxin
(Med.)
(Food processing technology.)
d tierisches Toxin *n*; tierischer Giftstoff *m*
f toxine *f* animale
p toxina *f* animal

298 anisaldehyde; anisic aldehyde
(Prod.)
($C_8H_8O_2$. Flavour (aroma) prime material: e.g. anise, apricot, peach notes; condiment.)
d Anisaldehyd *n*
f aldéhyde *m* anisique
p aldeído *m* anísico

299 anise
(Agr.)
(Botany: "Pimpinella anisum"; medicinal herb, flavouring agent in cooking.)
d Anis *m*
f anis *m*
p anis *m*

300 anise alcohol; 4-methoxybenzyl alcohol
(Prod.)
(Flavour chemicals: $C_8H_{10}O_2$; ref. to elaboration of aromas: organic chemistry.)
d Anisalkohol *m*; 4-Methoxybenzylalkohol *m*
f alcool *m* anisique; alcool *m* méthoxy-4 benzylique
p álcool *m* anísico; álcool *m* methoxi-4 benzílico

301 aniseed
(Agr.)
(Botany. Seed of anise e.g. for flavouring.)
d Anissamen *m*
f graine *f* de l'anis
p semente *m* do anis

302 anise note
(Prod.)
(Taste; aroma research and production.)
d Anisnote *f*
f note *f* d'anis
p nota *f* de anis; nota *f* de erva-doce

303 anise oil
(Prod.)
("Pimpinella anisum L."; Volatile oil of this fruit; aromas; flavouring agent e.g. in the production of candies.)
d Anisöl *n*
f essence *f* d'anis; huile *f* d'anis
p essência *f* de anis; óleo *m* de anis

304 anise oil tincture
(Prod.)
(Aroma/flavour research and production: extraction process.)
d Anisöltinktur *f*; Anisölauszug *m*
f teinture *f* d'essence d'anis
p tintura *f* de essência de anis

305 anisette
(Prod.)
(Beverages.)
d Anisette *m*; Anislikör *m*
f anisette *f*
p licor *m* de anisete

* **anisic aldehyde → 298**

306 anisylpropanal
(Prod.)
(Aroma prime material; e.g. anise to fennel-like flavour.)
d Anisylpropanal *n*
f anisylpropanal *m*
p anispropanal *m*

307 ankle
(Med.)
(Anatomy.)
d Knöchel *m*
f malléole *f*; cheville *f*
p tornozelo *m*

308 anorexia
(Med.)
(Loss of appetite.)
d Anorexie *f*
f anorexie *f*
p anorexia *f*

309 anorexia nervosa
(Med.)
(Psychological illness, generally of female adolescents, during late puberty; foodstuff intake aversion.)
d nervöse Anorexie *f*; Pubertätsmagersucht *f*
f anorexie *f* mentale
p anorexia *f* nervosa

310 anosmia
(Med.)
(Loss (partial or complete) of the sense of smell.)
d Geruchssinnmangel *m*; Geruchssinnverlust *m*
f anosmie *f*
p anosmia *f*

311 ant
(Agr.)
(Plant-destructive insect; family "Formicidae".)
d Ameise *f*
f fourmi *f*
p formiga *f*

312 antacid *adj*
(Med.)
(Ref. to an antacid: drug which neutralizes hydrochloric acid of the stomach in e.g. digestive disorders.)
d säureneutralisierend; säurebindend
f antiacide
p antiácido

313 anther
(Agr.)
(Botany: Pollen bearing stamen part, on the top of the filament.)
d Staubbeutel *m*
f anthère *f*
p antera *f*

* **anthocyan → 314**

314 anthocyanin; anthocyan
(Prod.)
(Natural foodstuff colorant of fruits and some vegetables, used for colouring butter, cheese, butcher shop's products and bakery products; cancer antagonist e.g. in beetroot.)
d Anthocyan *n*
f anthocyane *f*
p antocianina *f*; antociana *f*

315 anthranilic acid
(Prod.)
($C_7H_7NO_2$; o-aminobenzoic acid; base for aroma/fragrance production.)
d Anthranilsäure *f*
f acide *m* anthranilique
p ácido *m* antranílico

316 anthraquinone blue
(Prod.)
(Anthraquinone: $C_{14}H_8O_2$; prime material for food colorants, e.g. used in baker's products, in patisserie, fancy cakes, ice creams, cheese etc. See Government regulations.)
d Anthraquinonblau *n*
f bleu *m* anthraquinonique
p azul *m* de antraquinona

317 antiallergic protection
(Med.)
(Baby nutrition: characteristic of human milk.)
d Allergieschutz *m*; Schutz *m* gegen Allergie
f protection *f* antiallergique
p proteção *f* antialérgica

318 antibacterial activity
(Biochem.)
(In nutritional science, in food biochemistry; microbiology.)
d antibakterielle Aktivität *f*
f activité *f* antibactérienne
p atividade *f* antibacteriana

319 antibiotic
(Med.)
(Substance derived from microorganism that is used to destroy other sensitive microorganisms.)
d Antibiotikum *n*
f antibiotique *m*
p antibiótico *m*

320 antibody
(Med.)
(Antibody formation is stimulated by bacterial toxins. Antibodies are e.g. the basis of allergy.)
d Antikörper *m*
f anticorps *m*
p anticorpo *m*

321 anticaking agent
(Prod.)
(Auxiliary used for inhibiting the caking effect, glueing effect in food, e.g. calcium silicate.)
d Antiklebmittel *m*
f antimottant *m*
p agente *m* antiaderente

322 anticline; saddle
(Agr.)
(Soil; ref. to a geological formation.)
d Antiklinale *f*; Sattel *m*
f anticlinal *m*
p anticlinal *m*; aresta *f* de anticlinal

323 anticoagulant
(Prod.)
(Auxiliary used in slaughterhouse processes to inhibit blood coagulation; used also in food products.)
d Antikoagulans *n*; Antikoagulierungsmittel *n*
f anticoagulant *m*
p anticoagulante *m*; agente *m* anticoagulante

324 antidiarrheal regimen for the baby
(Med.)
(Regimens in nutritional diseases related to infant/baby nutrition.)
d Diätplan *m* gegen Durchfall des Säuglings
f régime *m* antidiarrhéique du nourrisson
p regime *m* antidiarréico do lactente; regime *m* antidiarréico do récem-nascido *m*

325 **antidote**
(Med.)
(Remedy against poisonous effects; also used in veterinary.)
d Antidot *n*; Antidoton *n*; Gegengift *n*; Gegenmittel *n*
f antidote *m*; contrepoison *m*
p antídoto *m*; contraveneno *m*

326 **antienzyme**
(Biochem.)
(Specific enzyme inhibiting agent.)
d Antienzym *n*
f antienzyme *f*
p antienzima *f*

327 **antifermentative** *adj*
(Biochem.)
(Microbiology; food biochemistry; microbiology.)
d antifermentativ; gärungswidrig
f antifermentatif
p antifermentativo

328 **antifungal essay**
(Biochem.)
(Microbiology; nutritional science; food biochemistry.)
d Antischimmeltest *m*
f essai *m* antifongique
p ensaio *m* antifungo

329 **antigen**
(Med.)
(Strange substance to the body which causes production of antibodies; substance of bacterial or viral origin.)
d Antigen *n*
f antigène *m*
p antígeno *m*

330 **antigen-antibody reaction**
(Med.)
(Alimentary allergy: the immunological response against antigens (strange dangous substances against which the body produces antibodies).)
d Antigen-Antikörperreaktion *f*
f réaction *f* d'antigène-anticorps
p reação *f* antígeno-anticorpo

331 **antiinfective** *adj*
(Med.)
d antiinfektiös; der Ansteckung entgegenwirkend; die Ansteckung verhindernd
f anti-infectieux
p antiinfeccioso

332 **antiinfective property of the milk**
(Med.)
(Baby nutrition. Human milk.)
d antiinfektiöse Eigenschaft *f* der Milch
f propriété *f* anti-infectieuse du lait
p propriedade *f* antiinfecciosa

333 **antiinfective protection**
(Med.)
(Baby nutrition: characteristic of human milk.)
d antiinfektiöser Schutz *m*; Schutz *m* gegen Ansteckung
f protection *f* anti-infectieuse
p proteção *f* antiinfecciosa

334 **antimould agent**
(Biochem.)
(Fungicides, fungistatic agents in nutritional science are e.g. propionic acid ($C_3H_6O_2$) and sorbic acid ($C_6H_8O_2$); mold/yeast inhibitor.)
d Mittel *n* gegen Pilzbefall
f antifongique *m*
p agente *m* antifungo

335 **antioxidant**
(Biochem.)
(Food processing technology: e.g. Vitamin C and derivatives (E No.: E 300, 301).)
d Antioxidant *n* (*pl Antioxidanzien, Antioxidantia*)
f antioxydant *m*
p antioxidante *m*

336 **antioxidant active principles in mother's milk**
(Med.)
(Baby nutrition: e.g. vitamin E as milk ingredient.)
d Antioxidationswirkstoff *m* in der Muttermilch
f agent *m* antioxydant dans le lait maternel
p princípio *m* ativo antioxidante no leite maternal

337 **antioxidant activity**
(Biochem.)
(Nutritional science; food biochemistry.)
d antioxidierende Aktivität *f*; antioxidierende Wirksamkeit *f*
f activité *f* antioxydante
p atividade *f* antioxidante

338 **antioxidant activity of ascorbic acid**
(Biochem.)
(Nutritional science; ref. to antioxidant activity of vitamin C.)
d antioxidierende Aktivität *f* der Ascorbinsäure; antioxidierende Wirksamkeit *f* der Ascorbinsäure
f activité *f* antioxydante de l'acide ascorbique
p atividade *f* antioxidante do ácido ascórbico

339 antioxidant activity of spices
(Biochem.)
(Nutritional science; ref. to meat products/processing: e.g. rosemary extracts.)
d antioxidierende Aktivität *f* von Gewürzen; antioxidierende Wirksamkeit *f* von Gewürzen
f activité *f* antioxydante des condiments
p atividade *f* antioxidante dos condimentos

340 antioxidant activity of tocopherols
(Biochem.)
(Nutritional science; e.g. ref. to vitamin E activity in restructured meat, in meat processing.)
d antioxidierende Aktivität *f* von Tocopherolen; antioxidierende Wirksamkeit *f* von Tocopherolen
f activité *f* antioxydante des tocophérols
p atividade *f* antioxidante dos tocoferois

341 antioxidant defence
(Med.)
(Inhibition of oxidation processes.)
d antioxidierende Abwehr *f*
f défense *f* antioxydante
p defesa *f* antioxidante

342 antioxidant factor
(Biochem.)
(Nutritional science: e.g. vitamin E.)
d Faktor *m* antioxidierender Wirkung; Antioxidationsfaktor *m*
f facteur *m* antioxydant
p fator *m* antioxidante

343 antioxidant function
(Biochem.)
(Nutritional science; e.g. of alpha-tocopherol (vitamin E).)
d Antioxidantfunktion *f*
f fonction *f* antioxydante
p função *f* antioxidante

344 antioxidant nutrients
(Biochem.)
(Nutritional science.)
d antioxidierende Nährstoffe *mpl*
f nutriments *mpl* antioxydants
p nutrientes *mpl* antioxidantes

345 antioxidant potential
(Biochem.)
(Nutritional science; ref. to restructured meat in meat processing.)
d Antioxidantpotential *n*
f potentiel *m* antioxydant
p potencial *m* antioxidante

346 antioxidant potential of food ingredients
(Biochem.)
(Nutritional science; ref. to restructured meat in meat processing.)
d Antioxidantpotential *n* von Nahrungsmittelzutaten
f potentiel *m* antioxydant des ingrédients alimentaires
p potencial *m* antioxidante dos ingredientes alimentícios

347 antioxidant properties
(Biochem.)
(Nutritional science; food biochemistry.)
d antioxidierende Eigenschaften *fpl*
f propriétés *fpl* antioxydantes
p propriedades *fpl* antioxidantes

348 antioxidative action
(Biochem.)
(Food biochemistry.)
d antioxidative Wirkung *f*
f action *f* antioxydante
p ação *f* antioxidante

349 antioxidative protection
(Biochem.)
(Nutritional science.)
d antioxidierender Schutz *m*
f protection *f* antioxydante
p proteção *f* antioxidante

350 antiparasitic *adj*
(Agr.)
(Biological agriculture: substance which acts against parasites.)
d antiparasitär; antiparasitisch
f antiparasitaire
p antiparasítário

351 antiparasitic battle
(Agr.)
(Pest control activity.)
d Schädlingsbekämpfung *f*
f lutte *f* antiparasitaire; lutte *f* contre les parasites
p luta *f* antiparasitária; luta contra os parasitas

352 antipellagra factor
(Med.)
(Ref. e.g. to vitamin B complex.)
d Antipellagrafaktor *m*
f facteur *m* antipellagreux
p fator *m* antipelagroso

353 antipellagrous vitamin
(Med.)
(Ref. to vitamin B_2.)
d Antipellagravitamin *n*
f vitamine *f* antipellagreuse
p vitamina *f* antipelagra

354 antirachitic vitamin
(Med.)
(Ref. to vitamin D.)
d antirachitisches Vitamin *n*
f vitamine *f* antirachitique
p vitamina *f* anti-raquítica

355 antiscorbutic factor
(Med.)
(E.g. L-ascorbic acid (vitamin C).)
d Antiskorbutfaktor *m*
f facteur *m* antiscorbutique
p fator *m* antiescorbuto

356 antiscorbutic vitamin
(Med.)
(Ref. to vitamin C.)
d Antiskorbutvitamin *n*
f vitamine *f* antiscorbutique
p vitamina *f* antiescorbútica

357 antisialogogue
(Med.)
(Salivation inhibiting substance.)
d Speichelfluss *m* hemmendes Mittel
f antisialogogue *m*
p antissiálico *m*; agente *m* antissiálico

358 antispattering agent
(Prod.)
(Used in frying-processes, e.g. lecithin ($C_{43}H_{88}NO_9P$).)
d Antispritzmittel *n*
f anti-éclaboussant *m*
p agente *m* antiestalante

359 antistaling agent
(Prod.)
(Auxiliary in food processing technology; see stale.)
d Additiv *n* gegen Altbackenwerden
f agent *m* antirassissement
p aditivo *m* contra envelhecimento de produtos de panificação

360 antiviral *adj*
(Med.)
(Medical microbiology.)
d antiviral; dem Virus entgegenwirkend; den Virus verhindernd
f antiviral
p antiviral

361 antivitamin
(Biochem.)
(Compounds of vitamin-similar structure, which are capable of displacing a vitamin from its site.)
d Antivitamin *n*
f antivitamine *f*
p antivitamina *f*

362 antivitaminic *adj*
(Biochem.)
(Ref. to antivitamins.)
d vitaminfeindlich; vitaminzerstörend
f antivitaminique
p antivitamínico

363 antixerophthalmic vitamin
(Med.)
(Ref. to vitamin A.)
d antixerophthalmisches Vitamin *n*
f vitamine *f* antixérophtalmique
p vitamina *f* antixeroftálmica

364 anus
(Med.)
(Anatomy; faeces discharging end of the alimentary canal.)
d After *m*
f anus *m*
p ânus *m*

365 apastia
(Med.)
(Neurological condition.)
d Nahrungsaufnahmeverweigerung *f*
f apastie *f*
p apastia *f*; abstinência *f* de alimentos

366 aperitif
(Prod.)
(Beverages. Appetizing alcoholic drink.)
d Aperitif *m*
f apéritif *m*
p aperitivo *m*

367 aphagia
(Med.)
(Inability to swallow.)
d Schluckunvermögen *n*
f aphagie *f*
p afagia *f*

368 aphid; greenfly
(Agr.)
(Biological agriculture; ref. to destruction of cultures by this insect.)
d Blattlaus *f*
f aphidé *m*; puceron *m*; puceron *m* du chou
p pulgão *m*; afídio *m*; piolho-de-planta *m*; piolho-dos-vegetais *m*

369 apiarist; beekeeper
(Agr.)
(Apiculture.)
d Imker *m*; Bienenzüchter *m*
f apiculteur *m*
p apicultor *m*; criador *m* de abelhas

370 **apiary**
(Agr.)
(Apiculture: Bee house.)
d Apiarium *n*; Bienenhaus *n*; Bienenstand *m*
f rucher *m*
p apiário *m*

371 **apiculture**
(Agr.)
(Apiculture.)
d Bienenzucht *f*
f apiculture *f*; élevage *m* d'abeilles
p apicultura *f*

372 **apoenzyme**
(Biochem.)
(Unchangeable protein part of enzyme structure which, in combination with a coenzyme, determines the enzyme specificity.)
d Apoenzym *f*; Apoferment *n*
f apoenzyme *f*
p apoenzima *f*

373 **apoferritin**
(Biochem.)
(Protein ferritin part, iron storage of the intestinal mucosa.)
d Apoferritin *n*
f apoferritine *f*
p apoferritina *f*

* **appearance → 459**

374 **appendix**
(Med.)
(Anatomy; vermiform appendix.)
d Wurmfortsatz *m*
f appendice *m*
p apêndice *m*

* **appetence → 375**

375 **appetency; appetence**
(Med.)
(Strong desire. In this specific case related to food-tasting, food intake.)
d Appetenz *f*
f appétence *f*
p apetência *f*

376 **appetite**
(Med.)
d Appetit *n*
f appétit *m*
p apetite *m*

377 **appetite of the baby; appetite of the infant**
(Med.)
(Baby nutrition.)
d Appetit *m* des Säuglings
f appétit *m* du nourrisson
p apetite *m* do bebê; apetite *m* do lactente

* **appetite of the infant → 377**

378 **appetizer**
(Prod.)
(Gastronomy.)
d Appetitbissen *m*; Appetithappen *m*
f hors-d'œuvre *m*
p petisco *m*

379 **appetizing; palatable** *adj*
(Prod.)
(Gastronomy; characteristics of food which stimulate the desire of eating.)
d appetitanregend; appetitlich
f appétissant
p apetitoso; apetitivo

380 **apple**
(Agr.)
(Agricultural produce. Genus "Malus"; pome fruit.)
d Apfel *m*
f pomme *f*
p maçã *f*

* **apple acid → 3346**

381 **apple butter**
(Prod.)
(Sweet seasoned apple spread prepared with cider.)
d Apfelaufstrich *m*
f beurre *m* de pomme
p manteiga *f* de maçã; creme *m* de maçã; conduto *m* à base de maçã

382 **apple jack; cider brandy**
(Prod.)
(Apple brandy; alcoholic beverage made from fermented apple juice (cider).)
d Apfelbranntwein *m*; Apfelschnaps *m*
f calvados *m*; calva *m*; eau-de-vie *f* de cidre
p aguardente *m* de maçã

383 **apple juice**
(Prod.)
(Food processing technology, non-alcoholic beverage made from apples.)
d Apfelsaft *m*
f jus *m* de pommes
p suco *m* de maçã

384 **apple-like aroma note**
(Prod.)
(Flavour note, flavour chemicals; elaboration of aromas: organic chemistry.)

d apfelartige Geschmacksnote *f*
f note *f* de saveur pomme
p nota *f* sabor de maçã

385 **apple-pancake**
(Prod.)
(Gastronomy.)
d Apfelpfannkuchen *m*; Apfeleierkuchen *m*
f beignet *m* aux pommes
p panqueca *f* de maçã

386 **apple turnover**
(Prod.)
(Bakery. Little flaky pastry cake with apple stuffing.)
d Apfelblätterteigkuchen *m*
f chausson *m* aux pommes
p folhado *m* de maçã

387 **application of vitamins in feed**
(Med.)
(Veterinary science. Livestock nutrition.)
d Einsatz *m* von Vitaminen in Futtermitteln
f application *f* des vitamines dans des fourrages
p emprego *m* de vitaminas em rações

388 **applied biotechnological science**
(Biochem.)
(Nutritional science.)
d angewandte Wissenschaft *f* der Biotechnologie
f science *f* appliquée de biotechnologie
p ciência *f* aplicada de biotecnologia

389 **appreciation of a flavouring agent**
(Prod.)
(Aroma/fragrance research and production.)
d Beurteilung *f* eines Geschmacksstoffes
f appréciation *f* d'un aromatisant
p apreciação *f* de un aromatizante

390 **appreciation of the wine quality**
(Biochem.)
(Enology.)
d Einschätzung *f* der Weinqualität; Würdigung *f* der Weinqualität
f appréciation *f* de la qualité du vin
p apreciação *f* da qualidade do vinho

391 **apricot**
(Agr.)
("Prunus armeniaca". Edible stone fruit, containing vitamins (A, B_1, B_2, C, nicotinic acid, iron etc.).)
d Aprikose *f*
f abricot *m*
p abricó *m*; damasco *m*

392 **apricot flavour note**
(Prod.)
(Flavour prime material e.g. isoamyl butyrate $C_9H_{18}O_2$; butyric acid isoamyl ester; aroma/flavour note of fruit essences; elaboration of aromas: organic chemistry.)
d Aprikosengeschmacksnote *f*
f note *f* saveur abricot
p nota *f* de sabor de damasco

393 **apricot nectar**
(Prod.)
(Nectar: beverage made from fruit juice and fruit pulp.)
d Aprikosennektar *m*
f nectar *m* d'abricots
p néctar *m* de damascos

394 **aqueous distillation residue**
(Prod.)
(Food processing technology; flavour production: separation process.)
d wässriger Destillationsrückstand *m*
f résidu *m* aqueux de la distillation
p resíduo *m* aquoso da destilação

395 **aqueous phase**
(Prod.)
(Food processing technology; emulsions, dispersions etc.)
d wässrige Phase *f*
f phase *f* aqueuse
p fase *f* aquosa

396 **aqueous phase within the fatty phase**
(Prod.)
(Food processing technology; e.g. emulsion elaboration.)
d wässrige Phase *f* in der Fettphase
f phase *f* aqueuse dans la phase grasse
p fase *f* aquosa dentro da fase gordurosa

397 **aqueous solution**
(Prod.)
(Food processing technology.)
d wässrige Lösung *f*
f solution *f* aqueuse
p solução *f* aquosa

398 **aquifer**
(Prod.)
(Water-bearing layer, e.g. drinking water source.)
d Aquifer *m*
f nappe *f* aquifère
p camada *f* aqüífera

* **arable land → 134**

399 **arachidic acid**
(Prod.)
($C_{20}H_{40}O_2$; arachic acid; prime material; fatty

acid present in some types of vegetable oil, esp. peanut oil.)
d Arachinsäure *f*
f acide *m* arachidique
p ácido *m* araquídico; ácido *m* eicosânico

400 **arachidonic acid**
(Biochem.)
(Nutritional science; $C_{20}H_{32}O_2$; this essential fatty unsaturated acid is important as a structural element for phospholipids, constituents of all cells. Production intermediate for prostaglandin.)
d Arachidonsäure *f*
f acide *m* arachidonique
p ácido *m* araquidônico

* **arachis oil → 4056**

401 **araucaria; Norfolk Island pine**
(Agr.)
(Botany: "Araucaria angustifolia".)
d Araukarie *f*; Norfolk-Chile-Tanne *f*; Andentanne *f*
f araucaria *m*
p araucária *f*; pinheiro-do-paraná *m*; pinheiro-brasileiro *m*

402 **arboricultural technique; method of fruit tree culture**
(Agr.)
(Biological agriculture.)
d Technik *f* der Fruchtbaumkultur; Verfahren *n* der Fruchtbaumkultur
f technique *f* arboricole; méthode *f* de l'arboriculture fruitière
p técnica *f* da arboricultura; método *m* da cultura de árvores frutíferas

403 **areola**
(Med.)
(Anatomy; body part: tissue ring around the breast nipple.)
d Warzenhof *m*; Brustwarzenhof *m*
f aréole *f*
p auréola *f*; aréola *f*

404 **arginine**
(Biochem.)
($C_6H_{14}N_4O_2$; amino acid, originated from the decomposition of nitrogenated foodstuff. Important in protein synthesis and urea formation by the liver; ingredient in human milk and in cow's milk.)
d Arginin *n*
f arginine *f*
p arginina *f*

405 **arginine-rich vegetable protein**
(Biochem.)
(Nutritional science; e.g. soya derivative.)
d argininreiches Pflanzenprotein *n*; Pflanzeneiweiß *n* reich an Arginin
f protéine *f* végétale riche en arginine
p proteína *f* vegetal rica em arginina

406 **ariboflavinosis**
(Med.)
(Ref. to riboflavin (vitamin B_2) deficiency.)
d Ariboflavinose *f*
f ariboflavinose *f*
p arriboflavinose *f*

407 **aridity of the soil**
(Agr.)
(Soil; also Climatology; ref. to insufficient rainfall for agricultural purposes.)
d Dürre *f* des Bodens
f aridité *f* du sol
p aridez *f* do solo

408 **arid soil**
(Agr.)
(Soil: Excessively dry soil of sparse vegetation.)
d dürrer Boden *m*
f sol *m* aride
p solo *m* árido

409 **arnica**
(Agr.)
(Botany: "Arnica montana L."; medicinal herb.)
d Arnika *f*; Wohlverleih *m*
f arnica *m*
p arnica *f*

410 **arnica tincture**
(Prod.)
(Aroma/flavour research and production: extraction process.)
d Arnikatinktur *f*; Arnikaauszug *m*
f teinture *f* d'arnica
p tintura *f* de arnica

411 **aroma**
(Prod.)
(Flavour; savoury odour; food additive, artificial flavouring agent.)
d Aroma *n*
f arôme *m*
p aroma *m*

412 **aroma dispersion**
(Prod.)
(Aroma/fragrance research and production.)
d Aromadispersion *f*
f dispersion *f* d'arôme
p dispersão *f* de aroma

413 aroma exhalation
(Prod.)
(Flavour notes, flavour chemicals and their properties, elaboration of aromas.)
d Aromaabgabe *f*; Aromafreisetzung *f*
f émission *f* d'arôme
p emissão *f* de aroma; exalação *f* de aroma

414 aroma extracts; flavour extracts
(Prod.)
(Aroma/flavour research and production.)
d Aromaextrakte *mpl*; Geschmacksstoffauszüge *mpl*
f extraits *mpl* aromatiques
p extratos *mpl* aromáticos

415 aroma fragility
(Prod.)
(Aromas/flavours and their chemical characteristics.)
d Aromaschwäche *f*; Aromavergänglichkeit *f*
f fragilité *f* des arômes
p fragilidade *f* dos aromas

416 aroma of the vine sort
(Biochem.)
(Enology; viticulture; wine production.)
d Aroma *n* der Rebsorte
f arôme *m* de cépage
p aroma *m* da espécie de cepa

417 aroma potentiation; flavour potentiating
(Prod.)
(Food processing technology; e.g. by means of table salt or sodium glutamate.)
d Geschmacksanhebung *f*; Geschmacksverstärkung *f*
f renforcement *m* de la saveur
p realçamento *m* do sabor

418 aroma refinement
(Prod.)
(Aroma/flavour quality.)
d Aromaverfeinerung *f*
f affinement *m* de l'arôme
p refinamento *m* do aroma

419 aroma reincorporation into the concentrate
(Prod.)
(Aroma/flavour research and production, distillation/extraction processes.)
d Wiedereinführung *f* der Aromen in das Konzentrat
f réincorporation *f* des arômes au concentré
p reincorporação *f* dos aromas nos concentrados

420 aromas of culinary preparations
(Prod.)
(Gastronomy; e.g. to flavour research and production.)
d Aromen *npl* kulinarischer Zubereitungen
f arômes *mpl* des préparations culinaires
p aromas *mpl* das preparações culinários

421 aromatic balance
(Prod.)
(Food processing technology; flavours/aromas.)
d Aromagleichgewicht *n*
f équilibre *m* aromatique
p equilíbrio *m* aromático

422 aromatic benzene derivatives
(Prod.)
(Basis for aroma/fragrance production.)
d aromatische Benzolderivate *npl*
f dérivés *mpl* aromatiques du benzène
p derivados *mpl* aromáticos do benzeno; derivados *mpl* aromáticos do benzol

423 aromatic compounds
(Prod.)
(E.g. source of fragrance/aroma prime material.)
d aromatische Verbindungen *fpl*
f composés *mpl* aromatiques
p compostos *mpl* aromáticos

424 aromatic note
(Prod.)
(Taste; aroma research and production.)
d aromatische Note *f*
f note *f* aromatique
p nota *f* aromática

425 aromatic products for use in foodstuff
(Prod.)
(Aroma/flavour chemicals; additives.)
d aromatische Produkte *npl* zum Gebrauch in Nahrungsmitteln
f produits *mpl* aromatiques à usage alimentaire
p produtos *mpl* aromáticos de uso alimentício

426 aromatic substance
(Prod.)
(Aroma/flavour research and production; auxiliary product; ingredient.)
d aromatische Substanz *f*; aromatischer Stoff *m*
f substance *f* aromatique
p substância *f* aromática

427 aromatic synthetic prime material
(Prod.)
(Chemical starting material for aroma/fragrance production.)
d aromatischer Syntheserohstoff *m*
f matière *f* première aromatique de synthèse
p matéria *f* prima aromática de síntese

* **aromatic toluene derivatives → 428**

428 **aromatic toluol derivatives; aromatic toluene derivatives**
(Prod.)
(Chemical starting material for aroma/fragrance production.)
d aromatische Toluolderivate *npl*
f dérivés *mpl* aromatiques du toluène
p derivados *mpl* aromáticos do tolueno

429 **aromatic vinegar**
(Prod.)
(Gastronomy; vinegar preparation containing herbs like dill etc.)
d Kräuteressig *m*
f vinaigre *m* aux fines herbes
p vinagre *m* de ervas finas

430 **aromatization of foodstuffs**
(Prod.)
(Food processing technology; introduction of aromas, flavouring agents, in food products.)
d Lebensmittelaromatisierung *f*
f aromatisation *f* de denrées
p aromatização *f* de produtos alimentícios

431 **aromatize** *v*
(Prod.)
(Aroma/flavour addition: food processing technology.)
d würzen
f aromatiser
p aromatizar

432 **aromatized yoghurt; flavoured yoghurt**
(Prod.)
(Food processing technology; dairy products; aroma/flavour notes.)
d aromatisierter Joghurt *m*
f yaourt *m* aromatisé; yogourt *m* aromatisé
p iogurte *m* com aroma

433 **aromatizing characteristics**
(Prod.)
(Aroma/flavour addition to foodstuffs.)
d aromatisierende Eigenschaften *fpl*
f caractéristiques *fpl* aromatisantes
p caraterísticas *fpl* aromatizantes

434 **aromatizing force**
(Biochem.)
(Characteristic of aroma chemicals; biochemistry of aroma elaboration.)
d aromatisierende Kraft *f*
f puissance *f* aromatique; puissance *f* de l'arôme
p poder *m* aromatizador; força *f* aromatizante; força *f* do aroma

435 **arrowroot**
(Agr.)
(Botany: "Maranta arundinacea" (after an Italian botanist of the XVI century); starch-yielding plant. Edible starch.)
d Pfeilwurz *f*
f maranta *m*
p maranta *f*; araruta *f*

436 **arsenic**
(Biochem.)
(As. Toxic element, sometimes present in foodstuffs in faint traces. Arsenic trioxide is used as insecticide and weed killer.)
d Arsen *n*
f arsenic *m*
p arsênio *m*

437 **artemisia; wormwood**
(Agr.)
(Botany: "Artimisia vulgaris L.".)
d Beifuß *m*
f armoise *f*
p artemísia *f*

438 **arteriosclerosis**
(Med.)
(Due to calcium deposits in the arteries.)
d Arteriosklerose *f*; Arterienverkalkung *f*
f artériosclérose *f*
p arteriosclerose *f*

439 **artery**
(Med.)
(Anatomy; blood transport vessel away from the heart.)
d Schlagader *f*; Arterie *f*
f artère *f*
p artéria *f*

440 **artesian ground-water surface**
(Prod.)
(Water supply. Geological site where the ground water is under natural pressure and thus flows (gushing forth) to the surface naturally.)
d artesische Grundwasserschicht *f*
f nappe *f* artésienne
p lençol *m* de água artesiano

441 **artesian well**
(Agr.)
(Deep well with natural, to the surface directed water flow.)
d artesischer Brunnen *m*
f puits *m* artésien
p poço *m* artesiano

442 **artichoke**
(Agr.)
(Agricultural produce. "Cynara Scolymus L."; edible vegetable.)
d Artischocke *f*

f artichaut *m*
p alcachofra *f*

443 articulations; joints
(Med.)
(Animal's anatomy: contacting part between two bones.)
d Gelenke *npl*
f jointures *fpl*; articulations *fpl*
p articulações *fpl*

444 artificial aroma; synthetic flavour
(Prod.)
(Flavour chemicals; e.g. based on organic chemistry.)
d künstliches Aroma *n*; synthetischer Geschmacksstoff *m*
f arôme *m* artificiel; arôme *m* synthétique
p aroma *m* artificial; aroma *m* sintético

445 artificial deficiencies
(Med.)
(E.g. of vitamins.)
d künstliche Mangelzustände *mpl*
f états *mpl* de carence artificielle
p estados *mpl* de carência artificial; condições *fpl* de carência artificial

446 artificial feeding
(Med.)
(E.g. gavage)
d künstliche Ernährung *f*
f alimentation *f* artificielle
p alimentação *f* artificial

* **artificial fertilizer → 1057**

447 artificial honeycomb
(Agr.)
(Apiculture.)
d künstliche Honigwabe *f*
f rayon *m* de miel artificiel
p favo *m* artificial de mel

448 artificial insemination
(Med.)
(Veterinary: animal raising treatment.)
d künstliche Befruchtung *f*
f insémination *f* artificielle
p inseminação *f* artificial

449 artificial nursing
(Med.)
(Baby nutrition.)
d künstliches Stillen *n*
f allaitement *m* artificiel
p amamentação *f* artificial

450 ascarid; ascaris
(Med.)
("Ascaris lumbricoides": a parasitic nematode worm.)
d Askaris *m*; Spulwurm *m*
f ascaride *m*; ascaris *m*
p ascárida *m*; ascarídeo *m*; lombriga *f*

* **ascaris → 450**

451 ascending colon
(Med.)
(Anatomy; part of the large intestine.)
d aufsteigender Grimmdarm *m*
f côlon *m* ascendant
p cólon *m* ascendente

452 ascomycetes
(Biochem.)
(Microbiology: important microorganisms for the production of cheese: e.g. penicillum: "Penicillum roqueforti" (Roquefort cheese), "Penicillum candidum" = "Penicillum caseicolum" (Camembert cheese).)
d Askomyceten *npl*; Schlauchpilze *mpl*
f ascomycètes *mpl*
p ascomicetos *mpl*

* **ascorbic acid → 5755**

453 ascorbic acid powder
(Prod.)
(Vitamin C form. $C_6H_8O_6$; antioxidant.)
d Ascorbinsäurepulver *n*
f acide *m* ascorbique poudre
p ácido *m* ascórbico em pó

454 asparagine
(Biochem.)
($C_4H_8N_2O_3$; non-essential amino acid.)
d Asparagin *n*
f asparagine *f*
p asparagina *f*

* **asparaginic acid → 458**

455 asparagus
(Agr.)
(Agricultural produce. Genus "Asparagus". "Asparagus officinalis".)
d Spargel *m*
f asperge *f*
p aspargo *m*; espargo *m*

456 asparagus bed
(Agr.)
(Truck farming; Genus "Asparagus"; common vegetable having edible tender shoots.)
d Spargelbeet *n*
f planche *f* d'asperges
p canteiro *m* de espargos

457 **aspartame**
(Prod.)
($C_{14}H_{18}N_2O_5$; additive; aspartic acid and phenylalanine derivative: synthetic sweetener.)
d Aspartam *n*
f aspartame *m*; aspartam *m*
p aspartame *m*

458 **aspartic acid; asparaginic acid; aminosuccinic acid**
(Prod.)
($C_4H_7NO_4$; amino acid; its beta-amide is $C_4H_8N_2O_3$; ingredient in human milk and cow's milk.)
d Asparaginsäure *f*
f acide *m* aspartique
p ácido *m* aspártico

459 **aspect; appearance**
(Prod.)
(Final products, e.g. in gastronomy.)
d Aussehen *n*; Aspekt *m*
f aspect *m*
p aspecto *m*; aspeto *m*; aparência *f*

460 **aspergillus**
(Biochem.)
("Aspergillus fumigatus"; food poison; causes aspergillosis; skin and lung inflammations. "Aspergillus flavus" produces an antibiotic.)
d Kolbenschimmelpilz *m*
f aspergillus *m*
p aspergilo *m*

461 **aspic jelly**
(Prod.)
(Gastronomy; jelly (e.g. of meat) flavourized with pepper grains, lemon etc., used as garnish.)
d Aspik *m*
f aspics *mpl*
p geléia *f* de "aspic"

462 **aspiration**
(Med.)
(Flavour perception.)
d Einatmung *f*
f aspiration *f*
p aspiração *f*

463 **ass; donkey; jackass**
(Agr.)
(Livestock. "Equus asinus"; e.g. beast of burden.)
d Esel *m*
f âne *m*; baudet *m*
p burro *m*; jumento *m*; asno *m*; jegue *m*

464 **asthma**
(Med.)
(Baby nutrition. Condition of allergic origin e.g. of not correctly nursed babies.)
d Asthma *n*
f asthme *m*
p asma *f*

465 **asthmatic child**
(Med.)
(Baby nutrition. Child with a condition of allergic origin e.g. if not correctly nursed.)
d asthmatisches Kind *n*
f enfant *m* asthmatique
p criança *f* asmática

466 **ataxia**
(Med.)
(Veterinary: Incoordination of muscular movements.)
d Ataxie *f*
f ataxie *f*
p ataxia *f*; incoordenação *f* muscular

467 **atherosclerosis**
(Med.)
(Nutritional diseases: fatty plaque development in the arteries; nutritional factors can influence condition.)
d Atherosklerose *f*
f athérosclérose *f*
p aterosclerose *f*

468 **atmospheric nitrogen fixation**
(Agr.)
(Botany; soil microorganisms and plants.)
d Luftstickstoff-Fixierung *f*; Festsetzung *f* atmosphärischen Stickstoffes
f fixation *f* de l'azote atmosphérique
p fixação *f* do nitrogênio atmosférico

469 **atmospheric precipitation**
(Agr.)
(Climatology: deposit on the earth surface of rain, snow etc.)
d atmosphärischer Niederschlag *m*; atmosphärische Ausfällung *f*
f précipitation *f* atmosphérique
p precipitação *f* atmosférica

* **ATP → 91**

470 **atrophy**
(Med.)
(Veterinary: Tissue degeneration.)
d Atrophie *f*
f atrophie *f*
p atrofia *f*

471 **attenuation of the bitter taste**
(Prod.)
(Food processing technology; organoleptic

food evaluation.)
d Verbesserung *f* des bitteren Geschmackes; Milderung *f* des bitteren Geschmackes
f atténuation *f* du goût amer; atténuation *f* de la saveur amère
p atenuação *f* do gosto amargo; atenuação *f* do sabor amargo

472 attenuation of violent notes
(Prod.)
(In aroma/fragrance research and production; ref. to aroma note characteristics.)
d Abschwächung *f* der zu heftigen Noten; Milderung *f* der zu heftigen Noten
f atténuation *f* des notes violentes
p atenuação *f* das notas violentas

473 aubergine; eggplant
(Agr.)
(Agricultural produce. "Solanum melongena". Edible ovoid fruit.)
d Aubergine *f*; Eierpflanze *f*; Eierfrucht *f*
f aubergine *f*
p berinjela *f*

474 aurantiamarin
(Prod.)
($C_{22}H_{31}O_{15}$; aroma prime material, flavour chemical obtained from the rind of "Citrus auranthium L."; e.g. used for liqueurs, cakes etc.)
d Aurantiamarin *n*
f aurantiomarine *f*
p aurantiamarina *f*

475 autolysis
(Biochem.)
(E.g. of cell parts; enzymatic autodigestion.)
d Autolyse *f*; Selbstauflösung *f*
f autolyse *f*
p autólise *f*

476 autolytic fermentation
(Biochem.)
(Autolysis: Tissue breakdown by self-produced enzymes.)
d autolytische Gärung *f*
f fermentation *f* autolytique
p fermentação *f* autolítica

477 automatic addition
(Prod.)
(Foodstuff processing equipment.)
d automatische Zugabe *f*; automatische Hinzufügung *f*
f adjonction *f* automatique
p adição *f* automática; adicionamento *m* automático; acrescimento *m* automático

478 autoxidation
(Biochem.)
(Nutritional science; flameless reaction of a substance with air-oxygen by room temperature: Food autoxidation leads to quality decrease.)
d Autoxidation *f*
f autoxydation *f*
p auto-oxidação *f*

479 autoxidation of unsaturated fatty acids
(Biochem.)
(Phenomenon in nutritional science.)
d Autoxidation *f* ungesättigter Fettsäuren
f autoxydation *f* des acides gras insaturés
p auto-oxidação *f* de ácidos graxos insaturados

480 auxiliary; additive; auxiliary product
(Prod.)
(Food processing technology; preservation agents, antioxidants, emulsifiers, thickeners.)
d Hilfsmittel *n*; Hilfsprodukt *n*; Zusatzstoff *m*
f adjuvant *m*; produit *m* auxiliaire
p produto *m* auxiliar; aditivo *m*

* **auxiliary product → 480**

481 auxin
(Agr.)
(Botany. Plant hormone; phytohormone; substance which promotes cell elongation in the plant.)
d Auxin *n*
f auxine *f*
p auxina *f*

* **aversion to a foodstuff → 2301**

* **aviary → 2555**

482 avicultural production
(Agr.)
(Poultry farming: raising and treatment of poultry for commercial (sales) purposes.)
d Geflügelproduktion *f*
f production *f* avicole
p produção *f* avícola

483 avitaminosis
(Med.)
(Vitamin deficiency disease.)
d Avitaminose *f*; Vitaminmangel *m*
f avitaminose *f*
p avitaminose *f*

484 avocado; avocado pear
(Agr.)
(Agricultural produce; "Persea; Persea americana"; edible, pulpy South-American fruit; very common in e.g. Brazil.)
d Avocado *f*; Avocato *f*

f avocat *m*
p abacate *m*

* **avocado pear → 484**

485 **avoidance of nutriments**
(Med.)
(Nutrition in medicine.)
d Vermeidung *f* von Nahrungsmitteln
f suppression *f* d'aliments
p evitação *f* de alimentos

486 **azelaic acid**
(Prod.)
($C_9H_{16}O_4$; 1,7-heptanedicarboxylic acid; e.g. prime material in aroma production.)
d Azelainsäure *f*
f acide *m* azélaïque
p ácido *m* azeláico

487 **azoic dyes**
(Prod.)
(Food colorants: See Government regulations.)
d Azofarbstoffe *mpl*
f colorants *mpl* azoïques
p corantes *mpl* azóicos

488 **Azores cheese**
(Prod.)
(Dairy product. Cheese produced on the Azores Islands from cow's milk; seasoned cheese type.)
d Azorenkäse *m*
f fromage *m* des Açores
p queijo *m* dos Açores

489 **azo rubi lake**
(Prod.)
(Foodstuff colorant; E number: E 122.)
d Azorubinfarblack *m*
f laque *m* d'azorubine
p laca *f* de azo-rubina

490 **azotobacter**
(Biochem.)
(Microbiology: atmospheric nitrogen-fixing soil bacteria.)
d Azotobacter *m*
f azotobactérie *f*
p azotobacter *m*

491 **azoturia**
(Med.)
(Abnormal high presence of nitrogen compounds in urine, tissue-destruction symptom, e.g. in diabetes mellitus.)
d Azoturie *f*
f azoturie *f*
p azoturia *f*

B

492 **babassu oil**
(Prod.)
(Brazilian palm (Tupi Indian: wawa'su): "Orbygnia martiana". Also "Orbygnia barbosiana". Oil for food preparations. Prime material.)
d Babassuöl *n*
f huile *f* de babassu
p óleo *m* de babaçu

493 **Babcock test process**
(Prod.)
(Food processing technology: Volumetric control procedure determining the fat contents of milk.)
d Babcock-Testverfahren *n*
f processus *m* d'essai Babcock; acido-butyrométrie *f*
p processo *m* de teste Babcock

* **baby → 3725**

* **baby nutrition → 2913**

* **baby's bottle → 727**

* **bacilli → 4737**

494 **bacitracin**
(Biochem.)
(Microbiology: nutritional science: antibiotic produced by the bacteria "Bacillus subtilis"; polypeptide.)
d Bacitracin *n*
f bacitracine *f*
p bacitracina *f*

* **backbone → 5151**

495 **back fat of pork**
(Prod.)
(Butchery.)
d Rückenspeck *m*
f lard *m* dorsal de porc
p toucinho *m* dorsal

* **background note → 553**

496 **bacon**
(Prod.)
(Food processing technology: salted, smoked side of a pig.)
d Speck *m*
f lard *m*
p toucinho *m* defumado

497 **bacteria**
(Biochem.)
(Microbiology: microorganisms e.g. in food poisoning, causing alimentary infections; generally salmonella.)
d Bakterien *fpl*
f bactéries *fpl*
p bactérias *fpl*

498 **bacterial accidents**
(Biochem.)
(Microbiology: negative bacterial influence in cultivation.)
d bakterielle Störungen *fpl*; bakterielle Unfälle *mpl*
f accidents *mpl* bactériens
p acidentes *mpl* bacterianos

499 **bacterial action**
(Biochem.)
(Microbiology: food biochemistry, fermentation in nutritional science.)
d bakterielle Wirkung *f*
f action *f* bactérienne
p ação *f* bacteriana

500 **bacterial alterations**
(Biochem.)
(Fermentation in nutritional science: Food processing technology.)
d bakterielle Veränderungen *fpl*
f altérations *fpl* bactériennes
p alterações *fpl* bacterianas

501 **bacterial degradation; degradation due to bacteria**
(Biochem.)
(Fermentation in nutritional science.)
d bakterienbedingter Abbau *m*
f dégradation *f* d'origine bactérienne
p degradação *f* de origem bacteriana

502 **bacterial deviations**
(Biochem.)
(Fermentation in nutritional science, food processing technology: enology.)
d bakterielle Abweichungen *fpl*
f déviations *fpl* bactériennes
p desvios *mpl* bacterianos

503 **bacterial growth**
(Biochem.)
(Food biochemistry, e.g. in fermentation processes.)
d Bakterienwachstum *n*
f croissance *f* bactérienne
p crescimento *m* das bactérias; crescimento *m* bacteriano

504 **bacterial inoculum**
(Biochem.)
(Material for inoculation purposes: food biochemistry, e.g. in fermentation processes.)
d bakterielles Inokulationsmaterial *n*
f inoculum *m* bactérien
p inóculo *m* bacteriano

505 **bacterial product**
(Biochem.)
(Microbiology; food biochemistry.)
d Bakterienprodukt *n*
f produit *m* bactérien
p produto *m* bacteriano

506 **bacterial strains**
(Biochem.)
(Microbiology.)
d bakterielle Stränge *mpl*
f espèces *fpl* de bactéries; souches *fpl* de bactéries
p espécies *fpl* bacterianas

507 **bacteria of malolactic fermentation**
(Biochem.)
(Enology: wine fermentation in nutritional science: e.g. ref. to "Lactobacillus".)
d Bakterien *fpl* der malolaktischen Gärung
f bactéries *fpl* de la fermentation malolactique
p bactérias *fpl* da fermentação malolática

508 **bactericide**
(Biochem.)
(Chemical and/or physical agent which destroys bacteria. Used to eliminate pathogenic agents; also used in conservation processes.)
d Bakterizid *n*
f bactéricide *m*
p agente *m* bactericida

509 **bacteriologic characteristics**
(Agr.)
(Biological agriculture.)
d bakteriologische Eigenschaften *fpl*
f caractéristiques *fpl* bactériologiques
p caraterísticas *fpl* bacteriológicas

510 **bacteriologic criteria**
(Biochem.)
(Microbiology; bacteriologic standards; nutritional science.)
d bakteriologische Kriterien *npl*
f critères *mpl* bactériologiques
p critérios *mpl* bacteriológicos

511 **bacteriology**
(Biochem.)
(Microbiology; science of bacteria.)
d Bakteriologie *f*
f bactériologie *f*
p bacteriolologia *f*

512 **bacteriostat**
(Biochem.)
(Microbiology; nutritional science; e.g. food additive that inhibits bacterial multiplication (proliferation).)
d Bakteriostat *m*
f agent *m* bactériostatique
p agente *m* bacteriostático

513 **bacteriostatic effect**
(Biochem.)
(Microbiology, also medical aspects.)
d bakteriostatische Wirkung *f*
f effet *m* bactériostatique
p efeito *m* bacteriostático

514 **bacteriostatic force**
(Biochem.)
(Biochemistry of essences; microbiology.)
d bakteriostatische Kraft *f*
f pouvoir *m* bactériostatique
p poder *m* bacteriostático

515 **bacteriostatics**
(Biochem.)
(Microbiology; food additives which inhibit the growth and multiplication of bacteria, without killing them.)
d Bakteriostatika *npl*
f bactériostatiques *mpl*
p agentes *mpl* bacteriostáticos

516 **bacterium cell**
(Biochem.)
(Microbiology; unit of bacterial structure.)
d Bakterienzelle *f*
f cellule *f* bactérienne
p célula *f* de bactéria

517 **bactofugation**
(Prod.)
(Food processing technology. Belgian milk-treatment process for elimination of the bacteria by centrifugation at pasteurizing temperatures.)
d Baktofugation *f*
f bactofugation *f*
p bactofugação *f*

* **bag → 5608**

518 **baker's yeast**
(Prod.)
(Bakery and brewery prime material: living single-cell organism, "Saccharomyces cervisiae".)
d Backhefe *f*

f levure *f* de boulanger; levure *f* de boulangerie
p fermento *m* de panificação

519 bakery
(Prod.)
(Establishment for the production and sale of baked products.)
d Bäckerei *f*
f boulangerie *f*
p padaria *f*

520 bakery goods
(Prod.)
(Bakery product.)
d Backwaren *fpl*
f pâtisseries *fpl*
p produtos *mpl* de padaria; produtos *mpl* de panificação; produtos *mpl* de pastelaria

521 baking additives; bakings ingredients
(Prod.)
(Auxiliary product in baking processes; e.g. substances which promote fermentation. Also water-retention additives, e.g.: sorbitol, milk.)
d Backzutaten *fpl*
f ingrédients *m* pour la pâtisserie
p aditivos *mpl* de panificação

522 baking powder; ammonium carbonate
(Prod.)
(Auxiliary; leavening agent.)
d Backpulver *n*
f levure *f* chimique; carbonate *m* d'ammonium
p fermento *m* em pó; carbonato *m* de amônio

* **baking sheet cake → 838**

* **bakings ingredients → 521**

523 balance between sugar and acidity
(Biochem.)
(Enology; nutritional science of wine production.)
d Ausgeglichenheit *f* zwischen Zucker- und Säuregehalt
f équilibre *m* sucre-acidité
p equilíbrio *m* entre o teor de açúcar e de ácido

524 balance between sugar and alcohol
(Biochem.)
(Enology, wine production.)
d Zucker-Alkohol-Gleichgewicht *n*
f équilibre *m* sucre/alcool
p equilíbrio *m* açúcar/álcool

525 balanced diet
(Med.)
(Alimentary regimen.)
d ausgeglichene Diät *f*
f diète *f* équilibrée
p dieta *f* equilibrada; dieta *f* balanceada

* **balance of alimentary ration → 2328**

526 balance of physiologic functions
(Med.)
(Nutritional therapy: vitamins, trace elements electrolytes in diets.)
d Gleichgewicht *n* der physiologischen Funktionen
f équilibre *m* des fonctions physiologiques
p equilíbrio *m* das funções fisiológicas

527 balance of volatile particles
(Prod.)
(Aroma/flavour chemicals.)
d Gleichgewicht *n* flüchtiger Körper
f équilibre *m* de corps volatils
p equilíbrio *m* de corpos voláteis

528 bamboo shoots
(Agr.)
(Agricultural produce. Genus "Bambusa"; edible sprouts.)
d Bambussprösse *mpl*
f pousses *fpl* de bambou
p brotos *mpl* de bambu

529 banana
(Agr.)
(Agricultural produce. Genus "Musa" of the family "Musaceae", the banana family. Edible fruit, with important content of vitamin B and carotene convertible into vitamin A.)
d Banane *f*
f banane *f*
p banana *f*

530 banana-like aroma note
(Prod.)
(Prime material e.g. isoamyl acetate: banana oil ($C_7H_{14}O_2$). Flavour note, ref. to flavour chemicals; elaboration of aromas: organic chemistry.)
d bananenartige Geschmacksnote *f*
f note *f* saveur de banane
p nota *f* sabor de banana

* **Bang's disease → 793**

531 Banting diet; bantingism
(Med.)
(Diet poor in carbohydrates and fats. After Frederick Grant Banting, Canadian physician (1891-1941), insulin discoverer (1921); Nobel prize 1923.)
d Banting-Diät *f*
f diète *f* à Banting; bantingisme *m*
p dieta *f* de Banting

* **bantingism → 531**

532 **bap; small round loaf**
(Prod.)
(Bakery; ref. to bread type.)
d kleines Rundbrot *n*
f petite boule *f*
p broa *f*; broinha *f*

533 **barb**
(Agr.)
(Apiculture. Bee anatomy: part of the bee sting.)
d Widerhaken *m* des Bienenstachels
f barbe *f* de l'aiguillon d'abeille; barbe *f* du dard
p farpa *f* do ferrão da abelha

534 **barbecue**
(Prod.)
(Gastronomy.)
d Spießbraten *m*
f brochette *f* de viande
p brochete *f* de carne

535 **barbel**
(Agr.)
("Barbus barbus", freshwater fish.)
d Barbe *f*
f barbeau *m*
p barbo *m*

536 **barium sulphate**
(Prod.)
($BaSO_4$; element contained in traces in mineral water.)
d Bariumsulfat *n*
f sulfate *m* de baryum
p sulfato *m* de bário

537 **bark of the black alder; winterberry**
(Agr.)
(Botany: "Alnus glutinosa"; "Ilex verticillata"; medicinal herb.)
d Schwarzerlenrinde *f*; Faulbaumrinde *f*
f écorce *f* de la bourdaine; écorce *f* de l'aulne noir
p casca *f* do amieiro negro

538 **barley**
(Agr.)
(Agricultural produce. Genus "Hordeum"; cereal.)
d Gerste *f*
f orge *f/m*
p cevada *f*

539 **barley bread**
(Prod.)
(Bakery product.)
d Gerstenbrot *n*
f pain *m* d'orge
p pão *m* de cevada

540 **barley field**
(Agr.)
(Agricultural produce: Barley cultivation.)
d Gerstenfeld *n*
f champ *m* d'orge
p cevadal *m*

541 **barley sugar**
(Prod.)
(Food processing technology.)
d Gerstenzucker *m*
f sucre *m* d'orge
p açúcar *m* de cevada

542 **barm**
(Biochem.)
(Microbiology: nutritional science: brewing processes: organisms which transform, by fermentation, malt sugars in alcohol and thus the must in beer.)
d Bierhefe *f*
f levure *f* de bière
p lêvedo *m* de cerveja

543 **bar of chocolate**
(Prod.)
(Confectionary.)
d Tafel *m* Schokolade
f tablette *f* de chocolat
p barra *f* de chocolate

544 **barrow; castrated male pig**
(Agr.)
(Livestock.)
d kastrierter Eber *m*; kastriertes männliches Schwein *n*
f porc *m* châtré
p porco *m* castrado

* **barysphere → 1839**

545 **basal diet**
(Med.)
(Alimentary regimen; e.g. diet which contains all essential nutrients in balanced condition; a light integral diet; e.g. in case of gastrointestinal disease.)
d Basisdiät *f*, leichte Vollkost *f*
f diète *f* basale
p dieta *f* básica; dieta *f* basal

546 **basal fertilizer**
(Agr.)
(Soil treatment.)
d Grunddünger *m*
f fertilisant *m* basal
p fertilizante *m* básico

547 **basal leaf**
(Agr.)
(Botany; scaly bulb (e.g. onion) leaf.)
d Zwiebelschuppe *f*
f écaille *f* du bulbe
p catáfilo *m*

548 **basal metabolic rate**
(Med.)
(Related to the muscular mass and the body surface area: approx. 1,500 kcal/day.)
d Rate *f* des Grundstoffwechsels; Grundumsatzrate *f*
f taux *m* du métabolisme basal
p taxa *f* metabólica basal

549 **basal metabolism**
(Med.)
(Approx. 1,600 kcal daily, resting and on empty stomach.)
d Grundumsatz *m* des Stoffwechsels
f métabolisme *m* basal
p metabolismo *m* basal

550 **based on lactose** *adv*
(Biochem.)
(Nutritional science; ref. to foodstuffs.)
d auf Basis von Laktose; auf Milchzuckerbasis
f à base de lactose
p à base de lactose

551 **basic diet**
(Med.)
(Alimentary regimen; e.g. diet having the property of neutralizing acids.)
d basische Diät *f*
f diète *f* basique
p dieta *f* de caráter alcalino

* **basic food → 5202**

552 **basic food industry**
(Prod.)
(Food processing technology and production.)
d Grundnahrungsmittelindustrie *f*
f industries *fpl* de produits alimentaires de base
p indústrias *fpl* de produtos alimentícios de base

* **basic foodstuffs → 5202**

553 **basic note; bottom note; background note**
(Prod.)
(In aroma/fragrance research and production; ref. to aroma note characteristics.)
d Basisnote *f*; Grundnote *f*
f note *f* de fond; note *f* de base; note *f* de queue
p nota *f* de fundo

554 **basic whey; sweet whey**
(Prod.)
(Subproduct of dairy food processing technology: originated from cheese production.)
d Süßmolke *f*
f lactosérum *m* doux
p lacto-soro *m* doce; soro *m* doce de leite

555 **basil; sweet basil**
(Agr.)
(Botany. Genus "Ocimum". Aromatic herb used as seasoning.)
d Basilienkraut *n*; Basilikum *n*
f basilic *m*
p manjericão *m*; manjericão-cheiroso *m*; alfavaca *f*

* **basil seasoned soup → 556**

556 **basil soup; basil seasoned soup**
(Prod.)
(French gastronomic specialty.)
d Basilienkrautsuppe *f*; Basilikumsuppe *f*
f soupe *f* au basilic; soupe *f* au pistou; soupe *f* de légumes au basilic
p sopa *f* de manjeiricão; sopa *f* temperada com manjeiricão

557 **basis of alimentation**
(Prod.)
(Food processing technology, research and production.)
d Ernährungsgrundlage *f*
f base *f* de l'alimentation
p base *f* da alimentação

558 **basis of feedstuff ration**
(Agr.)
(Products from biological agriculture.)
d Base *f* der Futtermittelration
f base *f* de la ration animale
p base *f* da ração animal

559 **basis of poultry alimentation**
(Agr.)
(Poultry farming; aviculture.)
d Ernährungsbasis *f* des Geflügels
f alimentation *f* de base des volailles
p base *f* de alimentação das aves

560 **bass**
(Agr.)
(Freshwater or marine edible fish; family "Centrarchidae".)
d Wolfsbarsch *m*
f bar *m*; loup *m*
p perca *f*

561 **batter**
(Prod.)
(Food processing technology; flour/egg mixture for food coating before frying.)

d geschlagener Mehl/Eier-Teig *m*
f pâte *f* à frire à base de farine et d'œufs
p massa *f* de empada; massa *f* de empadão

562 **batter for pancake**
(Prod.)
(Food processing technology.)
d Pfannkuchenteig *m*
f pâte *f* à beignets
p massa *f* para crepes; massa *f* para panquecas

* **bay → 3142**

563 **beak**
(Med.)
(Veterinary science; anatomy; the bill.)
d Schnabel *m*
f bec *m*
p bico *m*

564 **bean**
(Agr.)
(Agricultural produce; e.g. "Phaseolus". Leguminous climbing plant having pods and seeds.)
d Bohne *f*
f haricot *m*
p feijão *m*

* **bean curd → 5511**

* **bean runner → 565**

565 **bean sprout; bean runner**
(Prod.)
(Gastronomy: edible young shoots)
d Bohnenkeimling *m*
f pousse *f* de haricot
p broto *m* de fejão

* **bear *v* fruit → 2394**

* **beast of burden → 3992**

* **bed → 4216**

566 **bee; honeybee; hive bee**
(Agr.)
(Apiculture. "Apoidea"; "Apis mellifera L.".)
d Biene *f*; Honigbiene *f*; Imme *f*
f abeille *f*; abeille *f* mellifique
p abelha *f*; abelha *f* de mel; abelha *f* domêstica

567 **beef**
(Prod.)
(Butchery.)
d Rindfleisch *n*
f viande *f* bovine
p carne *f* bovina

568 **beef; beefsteak**
(Prod.)
(Butchery; Cattle meat type.)
d Steak *n*
f bifteck *m*
p bife *m*; bisteca *f*

* **beef broth → 1311**

* **beef cattle → 288**

* **beef extract → 3430**

* **beefsteak → 568**

569 **beef stew**
(Prod.)
(Gastronomy; type of meat meal.)
d Schmorbraten *m*
f bœuf *m* en daube
p carne *f* refogada

570 **beef tallow**
(Prod.)
(Edible fat of animal origin; prime material in food processing technology.)
d Rindertalg *m*
f suif *m* de bœuf
p sebo *m* de boi

571 **beehive**
(Agr.)
(Apiculture. Place for bee housing.)
d Bienenkorb *m*; Bienenstock *m*; Bienenkasten *m*
f ruche *f*; ruche *f* en paille; ruche *f* en bois
p colméia *f*

* **beekeeper → 369**

572 **beer clarification; clarification of beer**
(Prod.)
(Food processing technology: Beer brewing techniques: Beer brewery process of impurity elimination by filtering e.g. with addition of PVP (polyvinylpyrrolidone) type.)
d Bierklärung *f*; Klärung *f* des Bieres
f clarification *f* de la bière
p clarificação *f* da cerveja

* **beer on draught → 1774**

573 **beer without alcohol; non-alcoholic beer**
(Prod.)
(Beverages: Alcohol-free beer type.)
d alkoholfreies Bier *n*
f bière *f* sans alcool; bière *f* non-alcoolique
p cerveja *f* sem álcool; cerveja *f* isenta de álcool

574 **bee smoker**
(Agr.)
(Apiculture. Beekeeper protection.)
d Imkerpfeife *f*
f pipe *f* d'apiculteur; enfumier *m* d'apiculteur
p cachimbo-fumigador *m* de apicultor

575 **bee sting ointment**
(Agr.)
(Apiculture. Beekeeper protection.)
d Bienengiftsalbe *f*
f pommade *f* contre les piqûres d'abeilles
p pomada *f* contra picadas de abelhas

576 **beeswax**
(Agr.)
(Apiculture. Product secreted by bees for honeycomb construction.)
d Bienenwachs *m*
f cire *f* d'abeille
p cera *f* de abelha

577 **beet**
(Agr.)
(Beet as "Runkelrübe" is used as feedstuff; in the USA this term identifies also the (edible) "beetroot".)
d Runkelrübe *f*
f betterave *f* fourragère
p beterraba *f* de forragem

578 **beetroot**
(Agr.)
("Beta vulgaris". Common red beet; edible beet.)
d Rotebeete *f*
f betterave *f* rouge
p beterraba *f*

579 **beet sugar**
(Agr.)
(Agricultural produce, obtained from the beetroot.)
d Rübenzucker *m*
f sucre *m* de betteraves
p açúcar *m* de beterraba

580 **bee veil**
(Agr.)
(Apiculture. Beekeeper protection.)
d Bienenschleier *m*
f voile *m* d'apiculteur
p véu *m* protetor do apicultor

581 **beginning of the vintage; start of grape harvest**
(Agr.)
(Viticulture, winegrowing.)
d Anfang *m* der Weinernte; Anfang *m* der Weinlese
f début *m* de la vendange
p começo *m* da vindima

582 **begin of fermentation; fermentation start**
(Biochem.)
(Fermentation.)
d Gärungsbeginn *m*
f début *m* de fermentation
p início *m* de fermentação

583 **behaviour correction by nutrition; nutritional behaviour correction**
(Med.)
(Behaviour deviations: e.g. addiction types.)
d Betragenskorrektur *f* durch Ernährung; ernährungsbedingte Betragensverbesserung *f*
f correction *f* nutritionnelle du comportement
p correção *f* nutricional do compartamento

584 **behaviour of the chicks**
(Agr.)
(Poultry farming. The behaviour of the chicks gives information about the comfort (temperature etc.) of the aviary, brooder.)
d Verhalten *n* der Küken
f comportement *m* des poussins
p comportamento *m* dos pintos

585 **behenic acid; docosanoic acid**
(Prod.)
($C_{22}H_{44}O_2$; saturated fatty acid; constituent of fats (milk, seeds) and marine animal oils. Food prime material.)
d Behensäure *f*
f acide *m* béhénique
p ácido *m* beênico

* **bell pepper → 5385**

586 **belly**
(Prod.)
(Butchery. Meat, ventral part of the pork.)
d Wanne *f*
f ventre *m*
p barrigueira *f*; aba *f*

587 **bentonite; aluminium silicate**
(Prod.)
(Auxiliary. Protein adsorption agent, used in wine and beer production.)
d Bentonit *n*
f bentonite *f*
p bentonita *f*

588 **benzaldehyde; benzoic aldehyde**
(Prod.)
(C_7H_6O; toluene derivative; ref. to aroma synthesis; prime material.)
d Benzaldehyd *n*

f benzaldéhyde *m*; aldéhyde *m* benzoïque
p aldeído *m* benzóico

589 **benzene; benzol**
(Prod.)
(C_6H_6; prime material in aroma synthesis.)
d Benzol *n*
f benzène *m*
p benzeno *m*

* **benzenecarboxylic acid → 590**

* **benzine → 4118**

590 **benzoic acid; benzenecarboxylic acid**
(Prod.)
($C_7H_6O_2$; food preservative.)
d Benzoesäure *f*; Benzolcarbonsäure *f*
f acide *m* benzoïque
p ácido *m* benzóico

* **benzoic aldehyde → 588**

* **benzol → 589**

* **2,3-benzopyrrole → 2882**

591 **benzyl alcohol**
(Prod.)
(C_7H_8O; prime material (esp. its aliphatic esters) for aroma/fragrance production.)
d Benzylalkohol *m*
f alcool *m* benzylique
p álcool *m* benzílico

592 **benzyl cinnamate; cinnamein**
(Prod.)
($C_{16}H_{14}O_2$; aroma; flavouring agent: apricot-rum-peach-like note; for honey-cherry-plum-notes.)
d Benzylcinnamat *n*
f cinnamate *m* de benzyle
p benzilcinamato *m*

593 **bergamot taste**
(Prod.)
(Aroma/flavouring agent: Linalyl acetate: $C_{12}H_{20}O_2$.)
d Bergamottgeschmack *m*
f saveur *f* bergamote
p sabor *m* de bergamota

594 **beriberi**
(Med.)
(Disease due to vitamin B_1 (thiamin) deficiency.)
d Beriberi *f*
f béribéri *m*
p beribéri *m*

595 **beriberic** *adj*
(Med.)
(Disease due to vitamin B_1 (thiamin) deficiency.)
d beriberisch
f béribérique
p beribérico

596 **beriberic diet**
(Med.)
(Alimentary regimen; vitamin B_1 (thiamin) deficient regimen.)
d Beriberi verursachende Diät *f*
f diète *f* béribérique
p dieta *f* beribérica; dieta *f* causadora de beribéri

597 **beriberi heart**
(Med.)
(Due to vitamin B_1 (thiamin) deficiency.)
d Beriberiherz *n*
f cœur *m* béribérique
p coração *m* beribérico

598 **berry**
(Agr.)
(Botany. Small fruit with a fleshy pericarp.)
d Beere *f*
f baie *f*
p bago *m*

599 **berry selection**
(Agr.)
(Viticulture. "Beerenauslese" is a German wine type, indicating that the berries were selected one by one.)
d Beerenauslese *f*
f sélection *f* de baies
p seleção *f* de uvas

600 **beta-carotene; provitamin A**
(Prod.)
($C_{40}H_{56}$; vitamins in nutrition; retinol precursor.)
d Beta-Carotin *n*; Provitamin A *n*
f bêta-carotène *m*; provitamine A *f*
p beta-caroteno *m*; provitamina A *f*

601 **beta-carotene as pure substance**
(Prod.)
(Beta-carotene ($C_{40}H_{56}$) as provitamin A.)
d Beta-Carotin *n* als Reinsubstanz
f bêta-carotène *m* comme substance pure
p beta-caroteno *m* como substância pura

602 **beta-carotene dispersed in vegetable oil**
(Prod.)
(Food processing technology, product characteristic: e.g. for food dying; food colorant.)
d Beta-Carotin *n* in Pflanzenöl dispergiert

f bêta-carotène *m* dispersé dans une huile végétale
p beta-caroteno *m* disperso em óleo vegetal

603 beta-carotene dispersible in cold water
(Biochem.)
($C_{40}H_{56}$; carotenoids; provitamin A; yellow food dye.)
d Beta-Carotin *n* dispergierbar in kaltem Wasser; kaltwasserdispergierbares Beta-Carotin *n*
f bêta-carotène *m* dispersible dans l'eau froide
p beta-caroteno *m* dispersível em água fria

604 betaine; trimethylglycocol
(Prod.)
($C_5H_{11}NO_2$. Product found in the beetroot, "Beta vulgaris". Prime material e.g. for medicinal application.)
d Betain *n*
f bétaïne *f*
p betaína *f*

* **beta-lupulic acid → 3300**

605 beta-oxidation; ß-oxidation
(Biochem.)
(Oxidative fatty-acid decomposition, phase of the fatty acid metabolism.)
d Beta-Oxidation *f*; ß-Oxidation *f*
f bêta-oxydation *f*; ß-oxydation *f*
p oxidação beta *f*; beta-oxidação *f*; oxidação-ß *f*

606 better solubility
(Biochem.)
(Production techniques in nutritional science.)
d bessere Löslichkeit *f*
f solubilité *f* meilleure
p solubilidade *f* melhor

* **beverage → 1788**

607 beverage powders; drink powders
(Prod.)
(Beverages.)
d Trinkpulver *npl*
f poudres *fpl* pour boissons
p pós *mpl* de refresco

* **BHA → 822**

* **BHT → 823**

608 bicyclic monoterpenes
(Prod.)
($C_{10}H_{16}$; e.g. pinene; aroma/fragrance prime material: Constituent of many volatile oils.)
d bizyklische Monoterpene *npl*
f monoterpènes *mpl* bicycliques
p monoterpenos *mpl* bicíclicos

609 bifid factor
(Med.)
(Baby nutrition. Ref. to the "Lactobacillus bifidus" of the intestinal flora of the newborn, promoted by his mother's milk.)
d Bifidusfaktor *m*
f facteur *m* bifide
p fator *m* bífido

610 bifidus fermented milk
(Prod.)
(Dairy product; ref. to the anaerobic bacteria "Bifidobacterium bifidus" used as lactic ferment.)
d bifidfermentierte Milch *f*; mit Bifidusbakterien gegärte Milch *f*
f lait *m* fermenté au bifidus
p leite *m* fermentado com bífidos

611 bilberry; blueberry
(Agr.)
(Genus "Vaccinium"; sweet edible fruit; berry.)
d Heidelbeere *f*; Blaubeere *f*
f airelle *f*; myrtille *f*
p arando *m*; mirtilo *m*

612 bile
(Med.)
(In the gall bladder stored liver fluid, helps fat digestion in the duodenum.)
d Galle *f*
f bile *f*
p bile *f*

613 bile acid
(Med.)
(E.g. cholic acid.)
d Gallensäure *f*
f acide *m* biliaire
p ácido *m* biliar

614 biliary calculus; gallstone
(Med.)
(Formed, e.g. of cholesterol, in the gall bladder; formation can be inhibited by alimentary regimen.)
d Gallenstein *m*
f calcul *m* biliaire
p cálculo *m* biliar

615 binder
(Prod.)
(Auxiliary products.)
d Bindemittel *n*
f liant *m*
p aglutinante *m*

616 binding power
(Biochem.)
(Biochemical reaction in food biochemistry.)

d Bindungskraft *f*
f pouvoir *m* liant
p poder *m* ligante; poder *m* de ligação

617 **binding protein**
(Med.)
(Veterinary; e.g. ref. to subcellular vitamin transfer in the animal body.)
d Bindungsprotein *n*
f protéine *f* liante
p proteína *f* de ligação

618 **bindweed**
(Agr.)
(Botany. "Convolvulus"; twining plant, weed.)
d Winde *f*
f liseron *m*
p convólvulo *m*; convolvulácea *f*

619 **bioavailability**
(Biochem.)
(Active principles e.g. trace elements, vitamins.)
d Bioverfügbarkeit *f*
f biodisponibilité *f*
p biodisponibilidade *f*

620 **biochemical adsorption**
(Biochem.)
(Enzymatic activation; in nutritional science.)
d biochemische Adsorption *f*
f adsorption *f* biochimique
p adsorção *f* bioquímica

* **biochemical breakdown → 621**

621 **biochemical decomposition; biochemical breakdown**
(Biochem.)
(Food biochemistry.)
d biochemischer Abbau *m*
f décomposition *f* biochimique
p decomposição *f* bioquímica

622 **biochemical effect of micronutrients**
(Biochem.)
(Nutritional science; food biochemistry.)
d biochemische Wirkung *f* der Mikronährstoffe; biochemischer Effekt *m* der Mikronährstoffe
f effet *m* biochimique des micronutriments
p efeito *m* bioquímico dos micronutrientes

623 **biochemical systems**
(Biochem.)
(Biochemical research in nutritional science.)
d biochemische Systeme *npl*
f systèmes *mpl* biochimiques
p sistemas *mpl* bioquímicos

624 **biochemistry of lipids**
(Biochem.)
(Branch of food biochemistry important for food processing technology.)
d Biochemie *f* der Fettstoffe
f biochimie *f* des lipides
p bioquímica *f* dos lipídios

625 **biodegradation**
(Biochem.)
(Microbiology; natural destruction of organic substances by microorganisms.)
d biologischer Abbau *m*
f biodégradation *f*
p biodegradação *f*

626 **biodynamic agriculture; biodynamic farming**
(Agr.)
(Biological agriculture; organic agriculture; organic farming.)
d biodynamische Agrikultur *f*; biodynamische Landwirtschaft *f*
f agriculture *f* biodynamique
p agricultura *f* biodinâmica

* **biodynamic farming → 626**

627 **biodynamic method**
(Agr.)
(Biological agriculture and foodstuff production only with fertilizers of plant and animal origin.)
d biodynamische Methode *f*
f méthode *f* biodynamique
p método *m* biodinâmico

628 **bioenergetic** *adj*
(Biochem.)
(Bioenergetics, exchanges and transformations of energy.)
d bioenergetisch
f bioénergétique
p bioenergético

629 **bioenergetic oxidoreduction**
(Biochem.)
(Vitamin biochemistry.)
d bioenergetischer Oxidationsreduktions-Prozess *m*; bioenergetische Oxidationsreduktion *f*
f oxydoréduction *f* bioénergétique
p óxido-redução *f* bioenergética

630 **bioequivalency**
(Biochem.)
(Vitamin biochemistry.)
d Bioäquivalenz *f*
f bioéquivalence *f*
p bioequivalência *f*

631 biologic acidification
(Biochem.)
(Food processing technology; nutritional science.)
d biologische Säuerung *f*
f acidification *f* biologique
p acidificação *f* biológica

632 biological activity
(Biochem.)
(Vitamins.)
d biologische Aktivität *f*; biologische Wirksamkeit *f*
f activité *f* biologique
p atividade *f* biológica

633 biological agriculture; biologic farming
(Agr.)
(Biological agriculture: without using chemical fertilizers, pesticides etc.)
d biologische Agrikultur *f*; biologischer Ackerbau *m*
f agriculture *f* biologique
p agricultura *f* biológica

634 biological-dynamical agricultural management
(Med.)
(As to Rudolf Steiner (1861-1925), German philosopher, founder of the anthroposophy.)
d biologisch-dynamische Wirtschaftsweise *f*
f administration *f* agricole biologique-dynamique
p gerenciamento *m* biológico-dinâmico da agricultura

* **biological fruit tree culture → 641**

635 biological harmlessness
(Biochem.)
(Nutritional science.)
d biologische Unbedenklichkeit *f*
f innocuité *f* biologique
p inocuidade *f* biológica

636 biologically active compounds
(Biochem.)
(Nutritional science.)
d biologisch aktive Verbindungen *fpl*; biologisch wirkende Verbindungen *fpl*
f composés *mpl* biologiquement actifs
p compostos *mpl* biologicamente ativos

637 biologically active compounds of medical interest
(Med.)
(Vitamins.)
d biologisch aktive Verbindungen *fpl* medizinischen Interesses
f composés *mpl* biologiquement actifs d'intérêt médical
p compostos *mpl* biologicamente ativos de interesse medicinal

638 biological oxygen demand
(Biochem.)
(Oxygen volume required for the biochemical degradation of organic material contained in 1 l of water, during 5 days/20°C. In nutritional science: measure of microbial activity.)
d biologischer Sauerstoffbedarf *m*
f demande *f* biologique en oxygène
p demanda *f* biológica de oxigênio

639 biological techniques in the nutritional field
(Biochem.)
(Nutritional science.)
d biologische Verfahrenstechnik *f* auf dem Ernährungsgebiet
f techniques *fpl* biologiques dans le domaine de l'alimentation
p técnicas *fpl* biológicas no campo da alimentação

640 biologic antioxidant effect
(Biochem.)
(Vitamin biochemistry.)
d biologischer antioxidierender Effekt *m*; biologische antioxidierende Auswirkung *f*
f effet *m* biologique antioxydant
p efeito *m* biológico antioxidante

641 biologic arboriculture; biological fruit tree culture
(Agr.)
(Biological agriculture.)
d biologische Baumkultur *f*; biologische Obstbaumkultur *f*
f arboriculture *f* biologique; arboriculture *f* fruitière biologique
p arboricultura *f* biológica; cultura *f* biológica de árvores frutíferas

642 biologic balance of the cells; biologic cellular balance
(Biochem.)
(Nutritional science.)
d biologische Ausgeglichenheit *f* der Zellen
f équilibre *m* biologique des cellules
p equilíbrio *m* biológico das células

643 biologic battle
(Agr.)
(Biological agricultural pest control method.)
d biologischer Kampf *m*
f lutte *f* biologique
p luta *f* biológica

* **biologic cellular balance → 642**

644 biologic culture of cereals
(Agr.)
(Biological agriculture.)
d biologische Getreidekultur *f*
f culture *f* biologique de céréales
p cultura *f* biológica de cereais

645 biologic equilibrium
(Agr.)
(Concern of biological agriculture; organic agriculture; organic farming.)
d biologisches Gleichgewicht *n*
f équilibre *m* biologique
p equilíbrio *m* biológico

* **biologic farming → 633**

646 biologic fruit cultures
(Agr.)
(Biological agriculture.)
d biologische Obstkulturen *fpl*
f cultures *fpl* biologiques de fruits
p culturas *fpl* biológicas de frutas

647 biologic importants of nutrients
(Biochem.)
(Nutritional science; food biochemistry.)
d biologische Wichtigkeit *f* der Nährstoffe
f importance *f* biologique des nutriments
p importância *f* biológica dos nutrientes

648 biologic life
(Agr.)
(In soils; soil treatment.)
d biologisches Leben *n*
f vie *f* biologique
p vida *f* biológica

649 biologic processes
(Agr.)
(Biological agriculture and foodstuff production.)
d biologische Prozesse *mpl*
f processus *mpl* biologiques
p processos *mpl* biológicos

650 biologic production of fruits
(Agr.)
(Biological agriculture.)
d biologischer Obstanbau *m*
f production *f* biologique de fruits
p produção *f* biológica de frutas

651 biologic reactions
(Agr.)
(Biological agriculture.)
d biologische Reaktionen *fpl*
f réactions *fpl* biologiques
p reações *fpl* biológicas

652 biologic stability
(Biochem.)
(Nutritional science; food biochemistry.)
d biologische Stabilität *f*
f stabilité *f* biologique
p estabilidade *f* biológica

653 biologic stabilization
(Biochem.)
(Nutritional science; food biochemistry.)
d biologische Stabilisierung *f*
f stabilisation *f* biologique
p estabilização *f* biológica

654 biopotency
(Med.)
(Medical and veterinary; e.g. ref. to vitamin transport in the human (or animal) body.)
d Biopotenz *f*; biologische Leistungsfähigkeit *f*
f biopotentiel *m*; biopuissance *f*
p biopotência *f*

655 bios
(Biochem.)
(Yeast growth factor, especially for barm (brewery's yeast): BIOS I: inositol (vitamin B_2); BIOS II: biotin.)
d Bios *n*
f bios *m*
p bios *m*

656 biosynthesis
(Biochem.)
(Synthesis of a chemical substance (e.g. a protein) within the living body.)
d Biosynthese *f*
f biosynthèse *f*
p biossíntese *f*

657 biosynthesis of the terpenes
(Biochem.)
(Hydrocarbons $(C_{10}H_{16})_n$ in essential oils; ref. to synthesis of flavour chemicals.)
d Biosynthese *f* der Terpene
f biosynthèse *f* des terpènes
p biossíntese *f* dos terpenos

658 biosynthetic differences
(Biochem.)
(Nutritional science; food biochemistry.)
d biosynthetische Unterschiede *fpl*
f différences *fpl* biosynthétiques
p diferenças *fpl* biossintéticas

659 biotin
(Prod.)
($C_{10}H_{16}N_2O_3S$. Vitamin H, present in vegetables, levures, grains, egg white etc.; medicinal application.)
d Biotin *n*

f biotine *f*
p biotina *f*

660 **birch tree**
(Agr.)
(Botany: "Betula Alba". The white wood is used e.g. as firewood. Its sap is used e.g. for sugar production, alcoholic beverages and in cosmetics.)
d Birke *f*
f bouleau *m*
p bétula *f*

661 **bird**
(Agr.)
(Port.: ave: big bird. Pássaro: small bird.)
d Vogel *m*
f oiseau *m*
p ave *f*; pássaro *m*

* **birds → 4292**

662 **biscuit; cookie**
(Prod.)
(Bakery. Dry baked product. Cake shop product, of light flour, rich in fats and sugars with high energetic content.)
d Biskuit *n*; leichtes Gebäck *n*
f biscuit *m*
p biscoito *m*

663 **biscuit industry**
(Prod.)
(Bakery. Biscuit production: hard, crisp and dry products.)
d Keksfabrik *f*
f biscuiterie *f*
p fábrica *f* de biscoitos

664 **bison; wisent; buffalo**
(Agr.)
(Cattle breeding: "Bison bicon", "Bison bison" (American); "Bison bonasus", also called "Bison auroque" (European). Bovine mammals.)
d Bison *m*; Wisent *m*; Büffel *m*
f bison *m*; buffle *m*
p bisão *m*; búfalo *m*

665 **bisque**
(Prod.)
(Gastronomy, vegetable cream soup.)
d Gemüsecremesuppe *f*; sämige Gemüsesuppe *f*
f potage *m* crémeux aux légumes
p sopa *f* de creme de legumes

666 **bite**
(Med.)
(Veterinary science; injury caused by an animal.)
d Biss *m*
f morsure *f*
p mordida *f*

667 **bite** *v*
(Med.)
(Biting process: to seize a portion of food with teeth.)
d beißen
f mordre
p morder

668 **bitter almond**
(Agr.)
(Agricultural produce. "Prunus dulcis amara".)
d bittere Mandel *f*; Bittermandel *f*
f amande *f* amère
p amêndoa *f* amarga

669 **bitter chocolate**
(Prod.)
(Confectionary.)
d Bitterschokolade *f*
f chocolat *m* amer
p chocolate *m* amargo

670 **bitter drink**
(Prod.)
(Alcoholic drink of plant and fruit extracts and bitter additives like e.g. gentian. Appetite stimulating alcoholic carbonated beverage.)
d Bitter *m*
f bitter *m*
p tônico *m* amargo

671 **bittering agent**
(Prod.)
(Additive; flavouring agent like hop.)
d Bitterstoff *m*
f matière *f* amère; principe *m* amer; amérisant *m*
p princípio *m* amargo

672 **bitterness; bitter taste**
(Prod.)
(Gastronomy; e.g. ref. to the taste, palatability.)
d Bitterkeit *f*; bitterer Geschmack *m*
f amertume *f*; goût *m* amer; saveur *f* amère
p amargor *m*; amargura *f*; gosto *m* amargo; sabor *m* amargo

673 **bitter orange**
(Agr.)
(Agricultural produce. "Citrus aurantium".)
d Bitterorange *f*
f orange *f* amère
p laranja-da-terra *f*; laranja-amarga *f*; laranja-azeda *f*

* **bitter taste → 672**

674 **bixin**
(Prod.)
($C_{25}H_{30}O_4$; carotenoidcarboxylic acid from the seeds of "Bixa orellana L.". Foodstuff colorant.)
d Bixin *n*
f bixine *f*
p bixina *f*

675 **blackberry**
(Agr.)
(Agricultural produce; berry; genus "Rubus"; soft fruit.)
d Brombeere *f*
f mûre *f* sauvage
p amora *f* silvestre; amora *f* negra

676 **black currant**
(Agr.)
(Agricultural produce. "Phyllanthus distichus". Soft fruit; berry.)
d schwarze Johannisbeere *f*
f cassis *m*
p groselha *f* preta

677 **black earth; chernozem**
(Agr.)
(Dark soil with profound humus horizon. Chernozemic soil: found in subhumid and temperate zones.)
d Schwarzerden *fpl*
f terre *f* noire; tchernozem *m*
p terras *fpl* pretas

678 **black elder**
(Agr.)
(Botany: "Sambucus nigra L."; medicinal plant.)
d schwarzer Holunder *m*
f sureau *m* noir
p sabugueiro *m*

679 **black forest tart**
(Prod.)
(Bakery; cake shop product: cream cake with cherries.)
d Schwarzwälder-Kirschtorte *f*
f clafoutis *m* de la Forêt-Noire; clafoutis *m* aux cerises
p torta *f* de cerejas tipo floresta negra

680 **blackhead**
(Med.)
(Veterinary: intestinal and liver disease of poultry.)
d ansteckende Darm- und Leberentzündung *f* des Geflügels
f entéro-hépatite *f* infectieuse des volailles
p entero-hepatite *f* infecciosa das aves

681 **black pepper**
(Agr.)
(Agricultural produce. Genus "Piper nigrum" of the family "Piperaceae". Intensively cultivated e.g. in Brazil. A condiment.)
d schwarzer Pfeffer *m*
f poivre *m* noir
p pimenta-negra *f*; pimenta-do-reino *f*

682 **black pudding; blood pudding**
(Prod.)
(Gastronomy; butcher's shop product; blood sausage.)
d Blutwurst *f*
f boudin *m*
p chouriço *m*; morcela *f*

683 **black tea**
(Agr.)
(Agricultural produce. "Camellia sinensis"; black: made of fermented and dried leaves.)
d schwarzer Tee *m*
f thé *m* noir
p chá *m* preto

684 **black tongue disease**
(Med.)
(Veterinary science; e.g. poultry disease: Tissue ulcerations and inflammations due to nicotinic acid deficiency.)
d Schwarze-Zungen-Krankheit *f*
f maladie *f* de la langue noire
p doença *f* da língua preta

685 **bladebone**
(Prod.)
(Butchery. Meat part.)
d Bug *m*
f épaule *f*
p paleta *f*; pá *f*

686 **blanch** *v*
(Prod.)
(Food processing technology; thermal (scalding) pre-treatment of e.g. vegetables and fruits, to interrupt enzymatic action.)
d blanchieren; abbrühen; überbrühen
f blanchir
p branquear por escaldadura

687 **blanching**
(Prod.)
(Food processing technology; thermal (scalding) pre-treatment of e.g. vegetables and fruits, to interrupt enzymatic action.)
d Blanchieren *n*; Abbrühen *n*; Überbrühen *n*
f blanchiment *m*
p branqueamanto *m* por escaldadura

* **bleeding → 2616**

688 **blend of condiment; seasoning mix**
(Prod.)
(Additive; e.g. ketchup.)
d Würzemischung *f*
f condiment *m* composé
p mistura *f* de condimentos

689 **blend of condiments ready for use; seasoning mix ready for use**
(Prod.)
(Gastronomy; e.g. mayonnaise.)
d gebrauchsfertige Würzemischung *f*
f condiments *mpl* composés prêts à l'emploi
p condimento *m* composto pronto para uso

690 **block**
(Prod.)
(Bakery; e.g. presentation form of baker's yeast.)
d Blöckchen *n*
f bloc *m*
p bloquinho *m*

691 **blood clot**
(Med.)
(Thrombogenic processes, e.g. due to incorrect nutritional habits.)
d Blutgerinnsel *n*
f caillot *m*
p coágulo *m*

692 **blood coagulation**
(Med.)
(Nutrition in medicine.)
d Blutgerinnung *f*
f coagulation *f* sanguine
p coagulação *f* do sangue

693 **blood disease**
(Med.)
d Blutkrankheit *f*
f maladie *f* du sang
p enfermidade *f* do sangue

* **blood glucose concentration → 697**

694 **blood platelet**
(Med.)
(Thrombocyte.)
d Blutplättchen *n*
f plaquette *f* sanguine
p plaqueta *f* do sangue

* **blood pudding → 682**

695 **blood sugar**
(Med.)
(Glucose concentration in blood. Normal value on empty stomach: 80-120 mg/%.)
d Blutzucker *m*
f glycémie *f*
p glicemia *f*

696 **blood sugar increase; elevation of blood sugar**
(Med.)
(Glucose concentration in blood. Normal value on empty stomach: 80-120 mg/%.)
d Blutzuckerspiegelerhöhung *f*
f élévation *f* de sucre sanguin; augmentation *f* du taux de sucre sanguin
p aumento *m* do açúcar no sangue; elevação *f* da taxa do açúcar no sangue

697 **blood sugar level; blood glucose concentration**
(Med.)
(Glucose concentration in blood: measured in mg per 100 ml.)
d Blutzuckerspiegel *m*
f taux *m* de la glycémie; taux *m* de glucose
p taxa *f* de glicemia; taxa *f* de glicose no sangue

698 **blood sugar reduction; decrease in the blood sugar level; reduction of blood glucose concentration**
(Med.)
(Glucose concentration in blood. Normal value on empty stomach: 80-120 mg/%.)
d Blutzuckerspiegelsenkung *f*
f abaissement *m* de la glycémie; abaissement *m* du taux de glucose
p redução *f* da glicemia; redução *f* da taxa glicêmica; redução *f* da taxa de glicose no sangue

699 **blood sugar value**
(Med.)
(Glucose concentration in blood. Normal value on empty stomach: 80-120 mg/%.)
d Blutzuckerwert *m*
f valeur *f* de sucre sanguin; taux *m* de sucre sanguin
p valor *m* do açúcar no sangue; taxa *f* de açúcar no sangue

700 **bloom**
(Prod.)
(Food processing technology; e.g. white discoloration in form of a film on chocolate.)
d Fettreif *m*
f givre *m* gras; blanchiment *m* gras
p embranquecimento *m* gorduroso

* **bloom → 701, 702**

701 **blossom; bloom**
(Agr.)
(Botany; flower(s) of a seed plant.)
d Blüte *f*

f fleur *f*
p flor *f*

702 blossom; bloom
(Agr.)
(Botany; state of bearing flowers.)
d Erblühen *n*; Aufgehen *n*
f floraison *f*; épanouissement *m* (*de la fleur*)
p florescência *f*

703 blossoming period
(Agr.)
(Botany.)
d Blütezeit *f*
f période *f* de fleuraison; temps *m* de floraison
p tempo *m* de floração

*** blueberry → 611**

704 blue cheese
(Prod.)
(Dairy product; cheese type containing the mold "Penicillium roqueforti".)
d Blaukäse *m*; blauer Käse *m*
f bleu *m*
p queijo *m* azul

705 blue mold culture
(Prod.)
(Dairy plant technology: cheese mold.)
d Kultur *f* blauer Schimmelpilze; Kultur *f* blauen Schimmelpilzes
f culture *f* en moisissures bleues
p cultura *f* de bolor azul

706 boar
(Agr.)
(Livestock; male hog, reproducer.)
d Eber *m*
f verrat *m*
p porco *m* macho

*** body note → 2657**

707 body weight
(Med.)
(Anatomy.)
d Körpergewicht *n*
f poids *m* du corps
p peso *m* do corpo; peso *m* corporal

708 body weight gain in chicks
(Med.)
(Veterinary; ref. to chicken farming, feed supplementation with vitamins etc.)
d Körpergewichtsgewinn *n* der Küken
f augmentation *f* de poids du corps des poussins
p aumento *m* do peso dos pintos; aumento *m* ponderal dos pintos

709 boil *v*
(Prod.)
(Food processing technology.)
d sieden
f bouillir
p ferver

710 boil *v* **down**
(Prod.)
((Domestic) food processing technology; to turn more compact; to reduce in bulk by boiling.)
d einkochen; konzentrieren durch Verdampfen
f réduire par ébullition; concentrer
p reduzir por ebulição; fazer conserva

711 boiled meat
(Prod.)
(Gastronomy; meat prepared in boiled water.)
d Suppenfleisch *n*
f viande *f* bouillie; bœuf *m* pour le pot-au-feu
p carne *f* cozida; carne *f* para ensopado

*** boiler scale → 4854**

712 boiling point
(Prod.)
(Food processing technology; product specification: temperature at which a liquid boils.)
d Siedepunkt *m*
f point *m* d'ébullition
p ponto *m* de ebulição

713 boil *v* **over** (the milk boils over)
(Prod.)
(Food processing technology; ref. to a liquid, milk etc.)
d überkochen (*die Milch kocht über*)
f se sauver (*le lait se sauve*)
p subir fervendo; entornar fervendo (*o leite sobe, entorna fervendo; o leite sobe, entornando fervendo*)

714 boil *v* **the milk; bring** *v* **milk to the boil; scald** *v* **the milk**
(Prod.)
(Dairy product; food processing technology: Temperature slightly below the boiling point.)
d Milch aufkochen; Milch zum Kochen bringen
f bouillir le lait
p esquentar o leite; ferver o leite; deixar o leite; levantar fervura

715 bone *v* **a fish**
(Prod.)
(Food processing technology; e.g. in gastronomy.)
d Fisch entgräten

f désosser un poisson
p tirar as espinhas do peixe

716 boneless *adj*
(Prod.)
(Food processing technology; ref. to meat characteristics.)
d ausgebeint; knochenfrei
f désossé
p desossado

717 bone marrow
(Med.)
(Marrow contained within the bones cavities.)
d Knochenmark *n*
f moelle *f* des os
p medula *f* óssea

718 bone meal fertilizer
(Agr.)
(Soil treatment. Bone meal supplies phosphorus; soil conditioner.)
d Knochenmehldüngemittel *n*
f engrais *m* d'os
p fertilizante *m* de farinha de osso

719 bone powder
(Agr.)
(Soil treatment; element for soil enrichment.)
d Knochenpulver *n*
f poudre *f* d'os
p pó *m* de osso

720 boost *v* **fermentation; step** *v* **up fermentation**
(Biochem.)
(Fermentation in nutritional science.)
d Gärung ankurbeln
f intensifier la fermentation
p estimular a fermentação; intensificar a fermentação

721 borage
(Prod.)
(Gastronomy. "Borago officinalis"; used for aromatizing dishes.)
d Borretsch *m*
f bourrache *m*
p borragem *f*

722 boric acid
(Prod.)
(H_3BO_3; preservative for foodstuff, e.g. margarine.)
d Borsäure *f*
f acide *m* borique
p ácido *m* bórico

723 borneol; 2-camphanol
(Prod.)
($C_{10}H_{18}O$; prime material for aroma/fragrance production.)
d Borneol *m*
f bornéol *m*
p borneol *m*

724 boron deficiency
(Agr.)
(Botany; trace element (Bo); necessary for plant germ development; present in larger quantities in legumes.)
d Bormangel *m*
f carence *f* en bore
p carência *f* de boro

* **borsch → 725**

725 borscht; borsch
(Prod.)
(Russian gastronomy (Yiddish: borsht). Soup prepared from meat, beets and Kwass (Russian alcoholic beverage).)
d Borschtsch *m*; Rotebeetesuppe *f*
f bortsch *m*; bortch *m*; soupe *f* à la betterave
p sopa *f* de beterraba

726 bottle *v*
(Prod.)
((Domestic) food processing technology: e.g. to preserve fruits in bottles. As to J. Weck (1841-1914) who introduced this process in Germany.)
d einwecken
f confire
p fazer conserva por cozimento em vidros

727 bottle; baby's bottle
(Med.)
(Baby nutrition. For baby bottle-feeding e.g. on milk.)
d Flasche *f*; Säuglingsflasche *f*
f biberon *m*
p mamadeira *f*; biberão *m*

728 bottled beer
(Prod.)
(Beverages. Beer type.)
d Flaschenbier *n*
f bière *f* en canettes; bière *f* en bouteilles
p cerveja *f* em garrafas; cerveja *f* engarrafada

729 bottled milk
(Med.)
(Dairy product.)
d Flaschenmilch *f*
f lait *m* en bouteilles
p leite *m* engarrafado; leite *m* em garrafa

730 bottled wine
(Prod.)
(Enology; preservation method.)

d auf Flaschen abgezogener Wein *m*
f vin *m* embouteillé
p vinho *m* engarrafado

731 **bottle-feed** *v*
(Med.)
(Baby nutrition. Baby bottle-feeding, e.g. on milk.)
d mit der Flasche aufziehen
f nourrir au biberon
p dar mamadeira

732 **bottom fermentation**
(Prod.)
(Food processing technology; ref. to beer brewing process and beer characteristic.)
d Untergärung *f*
f fermentation *f* basse
p baixa fermentação *f*

* **bottom note → 553**

733 **bottom yeast**
(Prod.)
(Food processing, e.g. beer brewing technology.)
d untergärige Hefe *f*
f levure *f* basse
p levedura *f* de baixa fermentação

734 **botulinic clostridium**
(Biochem.)
(Microbiology; food poisoning bacteria, esp. in canned meat and tinned sausages.)
d Clostridium *n* des Botulismus
f clostridium *m* botulinique
p clostridium *m* botulínico

735 **botulism**
(Med.)
(Food poisoning by toxin produced by the bacterium clostridium botulinum.)
d Botulismus *m*
f botulisme *m*
p botulismo *m*

736 **bouillon; broth**
(Prod.)
(Gastronomy; clear soup; beef tea.)
d Brühe *f*; Bouillon *f*
f bouillon *m*; consommé *m*
p caldo *m* de carne

* **bouillon cube → 5241**

737 **bouquet of the aroma**
(Prod.)
(In aroma/fragrance research and production; metaphor ref. to aroma note.)
d Aromabukett *n*
f bouquet *m* d'arôme
p buquê *m* do aroma

738 **bovine coccidosis**
(Med.)
(Veterinary; disease of the cattle caused by coccidia.)
d Rinderkokzidiose *f*
f coccidiose *f* du bétail
p coccidiose *f* do gado

* **ß-oxidation → 605**

739 **braise** *v*
(Prod.)
(Food processing technology: cooking slowly in a closed pot.)
d schmoren
f braiser; dauber
p refogar

740 **braise**
(Prod.)
(Gastronomy; e.g. a piece of meat cooked slowly in a closed pot.)
d Geschmorte *n*
f bœuf *m* en daube
p refogado *m*

741 **braising**
(Prod.)
(Food processing technology: cooking slowly in a closed pot.)
d Schmoren *n*
f étouffée *f*; estouffade *f*
p estufagem *f*; processo *m* de refogar

742 **bran; ground fodder cereal**
(Agr.)
(Livestock nutrition: Coarse residue of cereal seed coats.)
d Schrot *m/n*; Getreideschrot *m/n*
f blé *m* égrugé
p farelo *m*; farelo *m* de trigo

743 **bran cake**
(Agr.)
(Livestock nutrition: See bran.)
d Kleie *f*
f son *m*
p farelo *m* em forma de bolo

744 **branch; twig**
(Agr.)
(Botany. Subdivision of a stem.)
d Ast *m*; Zweig *m*
f branche *f*; rameau *m*
p galho *m*; ramo *m*

745 branched-chained alcohol
(Biochem.)
(Ref. to e.g. aroma synthesis.)
d Alkohol *m* verzweigter Kette
f alcool *m* à chaîne ramifiée
p álcool *m* de cadeia ramificada

746 branded butter
(Prod.)
(Dairy product.)
d Markenbutter *f*
f beurre *m* de marque
p manteiga *f* com marca de fábrica; manteiga *f* de marca registrada

747 brandy
(Prod.)
(Alcoholic beverage made by distillation of wine.)
d Weinbrand *m*; Branntwein *m*
f eau-de-vie *f* de vin
p aguardente *m* de vinho

748 brawn
(Prod.)
(Gastronomy; jellied meat.)
d Sülze *f*
f viande *f* en gelée; gelée *f* de viande
p geléia *f* de carne

749 brawn of pork; head cheese
(Prod.)
(Gastronomy; jellied pork meat; Butcher's product.)
d Schweinesülze *f*; gesülzter Schweinskopf *m*
f fromage *m* de tête; hure *f* de porc; marbrade *f*
p geleia *f* de carne de porco; cabeça *f* de porco em geléia

750 Brazil nut
(Agr.)
(Agricultural produce; "Bertholletia excelsa"; drupe; stone fruit (fruit called after the Brazilian Federal State of Pará: Brazil nut-plantation region).)
d Paranuss *f*
f noix *f* du Brésil
p castanha-do-pará *f*

751 bread
(Prod.)
(Bakery.)
d Brot *n*
f pain *m*
p pão *m*

752 bread crumb
(Prod.)
(Bakery subproduct.)
d Brotkrümel *m*; Brotkrume *f*
f mie *f* de pain
p migalha *f* de pão; farelo *m* de pão

753 bread crust
(Prod.)
(Bakery product; part of the bread.)
d Brotkruste *f*, Brotrinde *f*
f croûte *f* de pain
p crosta *f* de pão

754 bread flour
(Prod.)
(Bakery product; prime material for bread making processes.)
d Brotmehl *n*
f farine *f* panifiable
p farinha *f* panificável

755 breadfruit tree
(Agr.)
(Brazilian tree "Artocarpus incisa", bearing the breadfruit.)
d Brotfruchtbaum *m*
f arbre *m* à pain
p fruta-pão *f* (*pl frutas-pães, frutas-pão*); rima *f*

* **break → 5579**

756 breakfast
(Prod.)
(Gastronomy.)
d Frühstück *n*
f petit déjeuner *m*
p café *m* da manhã

* **breast-feed** *v* **→ 3776**

757 breast of veal
(Prod.)
(Gastronomy.)
d Kalbsbrust *f*
f tendron *m* de veau
p peito *m* de vitela

758 breed adapted to local conditions
(Agr.)
(Biological agriculture.)
d den lokalen Bedingungen angepasste Rasse *f*
f race *f* adaptée aux conditions locales
p raça *f* adaptada às condições locais

* **breeder → 763**

* **breeding animal → 763**

759 breeding comb
(Agr.)
(Apiculture; movable frame hive construction.)
d Brutwabe *f*

f rayon *m* à couvain
p favo *m* de cria

760 breeding hen
(Agr.)
(Poultry farming, chicken farming.)
d Zuchthenne *f*
f poule *f* couveuse
p matriz *f*; galinha *f* reprodutora

761 breeding of slaughterhouse animals
(Agr.)
(Livestock for butchery.)
d Zucht *f* von Schlachttieren
f élevage *m* des animaux de boucherie
p criação *f* de animais de abate

762 breeding sow
(Agr.)
(Livestock: Gestation period is four months. The sow can farrow (giving birth to) two litters a year.)
d Zuchtschwein *n*
f truie *f*
p porca *f* de criação

763 breeding stock; breeding animal; breeder
(Agr.)
(Cattle breeding: reproducers.)
d Zuchttier *n*
f animal *m* reproducteur; animal *m* d'élevage
p animal *m* de reprodução; animal *m* reprodutor

764 breed of hog
(Agr.)
(Livestock: classification of a type of hog.)
d Schweinerasse *f*
f race *f* de porc
p raça *f* de suínos

765 Bresse hen
(Agr.)
(Poultry farming: Fowl of French origin with high-quality meat.)
d Bresse-Huhn *n*
f poularde *f* de Bresse
p galinha *f* Bresse

766 brewery
(Prod.)
(Food processing technology and production, beer production facilities.)
d Brauerei *f*; Bierbrauerei *f*
f brasserie *f*
p cervejaria *f*; indústria *f* de cerveja

767 brewing
(Prod.)
(Beer production; brewery process.)
d Brauen *n*
f brassage *f*
p brassagem *f*; mosturação *f*

768 brewing process
(Prod.)
(Beer production.)
d Brauereiprozess *m*
f processus *m* de production de bière
p processo *m* de produção de cerveja

769 brie cheese
(Prod.)
(Dairy product; soft white-surface cheese made of cow's milk.)
d Briekäse *m*
f brie *m*
p queijo *m* tipo brie

770 brilliancy
(Prod.)
(Food processing technology: ref. to certain product aspects, e.g. beer, wine.)
d Klarheit *f*
f limpidité *f*; brillance *f*
p limpidez *f*

771 brilliant black
(Prod.)
(Foodstuff colorant; E number: E 151)
d Brillantschwarz *n*
f noir *m* brillant
p negro *m* brilhante

772 brim *v*; **overflow** *v*
(Prod.)
(Food processing technology. See also "boil over".)
d überlaufen
f déborder
p transbordar

773 brine
(Prod.)
(Food processing technology: with common salt saturated water or solution.)
d Sole *f*; Lake *f*; Salzlake *f*; Salzwasser *n*
f saumure *f*; eau *f* saline; eau *f* salée
p salmoura *f*; água *f* salina

* **bring** *v* **milk to the boil → 714**

774 bring *v* **to the boil**
(Prod.)
(Food processing technology.)
d aufkochen lassen
f faire bouillir
p deixar levantar fervura; fazer ferver

* **brisling → 5167**

775 **brittle**
(Prod.)
(Confectionary; caramelized candy of nuts.)
d Krokant *m*
f nougatine *f*
p caramelado *m* crocante de nozes

776 **brittle granules**
(Prod.)
(Food processing technology: physical product presentation form.)
d sprödes Granulat *n*
f granulé *m* friable
p granulado *m* friável

777 **broad bean**
(Agr.)
(Agricultural produce; "Vicia faba"; e.g. German dish, elaborated with yet unripe green seeds: Saubohnen mit Speck (broad beans with bacon).)
d Saubohne *f*; Puffbohne *f*; große Bohnen *fpl*
f fève *f* de marais; grosse fève *f*
p fava *f*; fava-do-brejo *f*; feijão *m* fava

778 **broad-spectrum antiseptic**
(Med.)
(Antibiotics showing effect against a wide spectrum of bacteria.)
d Breitbandantiseptikum *n*
f antiseptique *m* à large spectre
p antisséptico *m* de amplo espectro

779 **broccoli**
(Agr.)
("Brassica oleracea"; leafy vegetable.)
d Brokkoli *pl*; Spargelkohl *m*
f brocoli *m*
p brócolis *m*; brócolos *m*

* **broil** *v* → **2589**

780 **broiled chicken**
(Prod.)
(Gastronomy.)
d gegrilltes Hähnchen *n*; gegrilltes Hühnchen *n*
f poulet *m* grillé
p frango *m* grelhado

* **broiler** → **4727**

781 **broiler fattening**
(Agr.)
(Poultry farming.)
d Masthuhnmästung *f*
f engrais *m* de poularde
p engorda *f* de frangos

782 **broiler rearing**
(Agr.)
(Poultry farming.)
d Mastgeflügelzucht *f*
f élevage *m* de poulardes
p criação *f* de frangos de engorda; criação *f* de galinhas jovens de engorda

* **bromelain** → **783**

783 **bromelin; bromelain**
(Biochem.)
(Food biochemistry; plant (pineapple) protease, protein hydrolyzing; e.g. used in meat tenderizing.)
d Bromelin *n*
f bromelaïne *f*
p bromelina *f*

784 **bromine**
(Prod.)
(Br. Additive as tablet salt (sodium chloride) contains trace elements, such as bromine, iodine.)
d Brom *n*
f brome *m*
p bromo *m*

* **bronchial tube** → **785**

785 **bronchus; bronchial tube**
(Med.)
(Anatomy; air passage beyond the trachea.)
d Bronchien *fpl*; Luftröhrenast *m*
f bronches *fpl*; arbre *m* bronchique
p brônquios *mpl*

786 **brood**
(Agr.)
(Poultry farming; ref. the young of a bird.)
d Brut *f*
f couvée *f*; nichée *f*
p ninhada *f*

* **broth** → **736**

787 **brown** *v*
(Prod.)
(Food processing technology; e.g. meat browned in fat.)
d bräunen
f rissoler; revenir
p dourar

* **brown ale** → **1507**

788 **brown bread**
(Prod.)
(Bakery product; made of whole wheat flower.)
d Schwarzbrot *n*

f pain *m* noir; pain *m* bis
p pão *m* preto

* **Brownian movement → 1227**

789 **browning; browning reaction**
(Biochem.)
(Change in food coloration due to enzymatic (oxidation of phenols: apple cut) or non-enzymatic (long conservation time, heat: protein-amino acid-sugar: Maillard reaction) phenomena.)
d Bräunung *f*; Bräunungsreaktion *f*
f brunissement *m*; réaction *f* de brunissement
p escurecimento *m*; reação *m* de escurecimento marrom

* **browning reaction → 789**

790 **brown lake**
(Prod.)
(Foodstuff colorant; E numbers: E 110 + 122 + 151.)
d brauner Farblack *m*; Braunlack *m*
f laque *m* brun
p laca *f* castanha; laca *f* marrom

791 **brown rice**
(Agr.)
(Agricultural produce. Whole unpolished rice without its husk.)
d Integralreis *m*; brauner Reis *m*
f riz *m* entier; riz *m* cargo
p arroz *m* integral

792 **brown sugar**
(Agr.)
(Agricultural produce. Unrefined sugar.)
d brauner Rohzucker *m*
f cassonade *f*
p açúcar *m* mascavo

793 **brucellosis; Malta fever; Mediterranean fever; Bang's disease**
(Med.)
(Veterinary: zoonosis: disease which can be transmitted from animals to humans.)
d Brucellose *f*; Bangsche Krankheit *f*
f brucellose *f*; fièvre *f* de Malte
p brucelose *f*; febre *f* de Malta

794 **Brussels sprouts**
(Agr.)
(Agricultural produce. "Brassica oleracea gemmifera"; mustard family; cabbage with edible green heads.)
d Rosenkohl *m*
f chou *m* de Bruxelles
p couve-de-bruxelas *f*

795 **bubble gum**
(Prod.)
(Food processing technology; product like chewing gum which can be blown.)
d Ballonkaugummi *n*; Knallkaugummi *n*
f bubble *m*
p chiclete *m* de bola

* **bubbly → 1022**

796 **buccal microflora**
(Med.)
(Microflora of the mouth, influenced by saccharose (cane sugar) intake.)
d Mikroflora *f* des Mundes; Mikroflora *f* der Mundhöhle
f microflore *f* buccale
p microflora *f* bucal

797 **buck**
(Agr.)
(Male hare. Family "Leporidae", esp. genus "Lepus".)
d Rammler *m*
f bouquin *m*
p macho *m* de lebre

* **buck → 2676**

798 **buckwheat**
(Agr.)
(Agricultural produce. "Polygonum fagopyram L."; cereal grain.)
d Buchweizen *m*
f sarrasin *m*
p trigo *m* sarraceno; trigo-mouro *m*; fagópiro *m*

799 **buckwheat bread**
(Prod.)
(Food processing technology, research: ancient bread type. "Fagopyrum", family "Polygonaceae".)
d Buchweizenbrot *n*
f pain *m* de sarrasin
p pão *m* de trigo sarraceno; pão *m* de trigo-mouro; pão *m* de fagópiro

800 **bud**
(Agr.)
(Botany: initial state of a flower.)
d Knospe *f*
f bourgeon *m*; bouton *m* de fleur
p botão *m* de flor

801 **budding**
(Agr.)
(Botany; plants: formation of buds.)
d Knospen *fpl* treiben
f bourgeonnement *m*
p germinação *f* de botões

* **buffalo → 664**

802 **buffer phenomenon**
(Biochem.)
(Nutritional science, food biochemistry.)
d Puffererscheinung *f*
f phénomène *m* tampon
p fenômeno *m* tampão

803 **buffer solution**
(Biochem.)
(Nutritional science: The buffer is a substance which does not change the pH-value of a solution, e.g. acid salts and weak bases.)
d Pufferlösung *f*
f solution-tampon *f*; tampon *m*
p solução *f* tampão

804 **bulb**
(Agr.)
(Botany; underground plant bud.)
d Zwiebel *f*
f bulbe *m*
p bulbo *m*

805 **Bulgarian lactobacillus**
(Biochem.)
(Food biochemistry: e.g. ingredient of yoghurt. Production process.)
d bulgarische Milchsäurebakterie *f*; bulgarischer Laktobazillus *m*
f lactobacille *m* bulgare
p lactobacilo *m* búlgaro

806 **bulk density**
(Prod.)
(Food processing technology.)
d Schüttgewicht *n*
f densité *m* apparente
p densidade *f* aparente; peso *m* aparente

807 **bull**
(Agr.)
(Cattle breeding. Male of the cattle family.)
d Bulle *m*; Stier *m*
f taureau *m*
p touro *m*

* **bunch → 1169**

* **bunch of grapes → 1170**

808 **burgundy wine**
(Agr.)
(Viticulture. French wine, winegrowing area around Dijon; white and red wine.)
d Burgunder *m*; Burgunderwein *m*
f bourgogne *f*
p vinho *m* de Borgonha

809 **burn** *v*; **overburn** *v*
(Prod.)
(Food processing technology.)
d anbrennen
f brûler; cramer
p queimar

810 **butane**
(Prod.)
(C_4H_{10}; aroma/flavour research and production: in extraction processes.)
d Butan *n*
f butane *m*
p butano *m*

* **2,3-butanedione → 1623**

811 **butter biscuit**
(Prod.)
(Dry butter biscuit with a rectangular form; cake shop product.)
d Butterkeks *m*
f petit-beurre *m*
p biscoito *m* amanteigado

812 **butterfat**
(Prod.)
(Dairy product; prime material (fat of milk) for ice cream production.)
d Rahm *m*; Sahne *f*; Creme *f*; Krem *m*
f crème *f*
p nata *f* de leite; creme *m*

813 **butterfly**
(Agr.)
(Biological agriculture. Insect; the chrysalis, pupa is the intermediate stage between the caterpillar and the adult butterfly. The caterpillar is destructive to plants and trees.)
d Schmetterling *m*
f papillon *m*
p borboleta *f*; mariposa *f*

814 **butter-like taste**
(Prod.)
(Flavouring agent: Diacetyl; 2,3-Butanedione: $C_4H_6O_2$.)
d butterartiger Geschmack *m*
f saveur *f* beurre
p sabor *m* manteiga

815 **butter lipids**
(Biochem.)
(Food biochemistry.)
d Butterfettstoffe *mpl*
f lipides *mpl* du beurre
p lipídios *mpl* da manteiga

816 **buttermilk**
(Prod.)
(Dairy product: acid milk of butter production residue.)

d Buttermilch *f*
f babeurre *m*; lait *m* de beurre
p soro *m* de manteiga; leite *m* de manteiga

817 buttermilk cure
(Med.)
(Slimming treatment.)
d Buttermilchkur *f*
f cure *f* de lait de beurre; cure *f* de babeurre
p regime *m* à base de soro de manteiga

818 butter production
(Prod.)
(Dairy plant activity.)
d Butterherstellung *f*; Butterproduktion *f*
f production *f* de beurre
p produção *f* de manteiga

819 buttery *adj*
(Prod.)
(Aroma/flavour note.)
d butterig; buttrig
f au beurre
p amanteigado

820 buttock
(Prod.)
(Butcher's product; meat joint; rump.)
d Schwanzstück *n*
f culotte *f*
p rabada *f*

821 butyl acetate
(Prod.)
($C_6H_{12}O_2$; acetic acid ester; synthetic prime material for fruity aroma/flavour notes.)
d Butylacetat *n*
f acétate *m* de butyle
p acetato *m* de butila

822 butylated hydroxyanisole; BHA
(Prod.)
($C_{11}H_{16}O_2$; food antioxidant: preservation additive.)
d Butylhydroxyanisol *n*; BHA *n*
f butylhydroxyanisol *m*; BHA *m*
p butil-hidroxianisol *m*; BHA *m*

823 butylated hydroxytoluene; BHT
(Prod.)
($C_{15}H_{24}O$; food antioxidant: preservation additive.)
d Butylhydroxytoluol *n*; BHT *n*
f butylhydroxytoluène *m*; BHT *m*
p butil-hidroxitolueno *m*; BHT *m*

824 butyric acid
(Prod.)
($C_4H_8O_2$; aroma prime material, e.g. butter-like flavour.)
d Buttersäure *f*
f acide *m* butyrique
p ácido *m* butírico

825 butyric fermentation
(Biochem.)
(Butyric acid: $C_4H_8O_2$; obtained by carbohydrate fermentation; prime material for artificial flavours.)
d Buttersäuregärung *f*
f fermentation *f* butyrique
p fermentação *f* butírica

826 butyrification
(Prod.)
(Food processing technology: transformation of fats into butter.)
d Verbutterung *f*
f butyrification *f*
p butirificação *f*

827 by enzymatic means
(Biochem.)
(Enzymatic processes in biochemistry.)
d auf enzymatischem Wege
f par voie enzymatique
p por via enzimática

C

828 **cabbage**
(Agr.)
(Agricultural produce. "Brassica oleracea capitata".)
d Kohl *m*
f chou *m*
p couve *f*

829 **cabbage lettuce; lettuce**
(Agr.)
(Agricultural produce. "Lactuca sativa".)
d Kopfsalat *m*; Lattich *m*
f laitue *f*; laitue *f* pommée
p alface *f*

830 **cacao**
(Agr.)
(Agricultural produce. Seeds (cocoa beans; cacao beans) of the tree "Theobroma cacao", from which cocoa is made as well as chocolate etc.)
d Kakao *m*
f cacao *m*
p cacau *m*

831 **cacao beans**
(Prod.)
(Chocolate production. "Theobroma cacao", fatty seed, prime material.)
d Kakaobohne *f*
f amande *f* de cacao; fève *f* de cacao
p semente *f* do cacau

832 **cacao butter; cocoa butter**
(Prod.)
("Theobroma cacao"; theobroma oil.)
d Kakaobutter *f*
f beurre *m* de cacao
p manteiga *f* de cacau

833 **cadaverine**
(Biochem.)
($C_5H_{14}N_2$; pentamethylenediamine. Occurs e.g. in meat and fish putrefaction: An amine formed by lysine decarboxylation decomposition; meat, fish decomposition.)
d Cadaverin *n*
f cadavérine *f*
p cadaverina *f*

834 **caecum; cecum**
(Med.)
(Anatomy; blind pouch at the beginning of the large intestine.)
d Blinddarm *m*
f cæcum *m*
p ceco *m*; cecum *m*

* **café → 840**

835 **caffeic acid**
(Prod.)
($C_9H_8O_4$; 3,4-dihydroxycinnamic acid; e.g. constituent of plants, e.g. coffee beans, potatoes, tobacco.)
d Kaffeesäure *f*
f acide *m* caféique
p ácido *m* caféico

836 **caffeine**
(Biochem.)
($C_8H_{10}N_4O_2$; occurs in coffee, tea, guaraná and mate.)
d Koffein *n*
f caféine *f*
p cafeína *f*

837 **caffeinism; chronic caffeine intoxication**
(Med.)
(Caffeine occurs in coffee, tea, guaraná and mate.)
d Koffeinvergiftung *f*; chronische Vergiftung *f* durch den Kaffee
f caféisme *m*; intoxication *f* chronique par le café
p cafeinismo *m*; intoxicação *f* crônica pelo café

838 **cake on baking tin; baking sheet cake**
(Prod.)
(Bakery. Baker's shop product; flat cake made on the griddle.)
d Blechkuchen *m*
f galette *f*
p bolo *m* de tabuleiro

839 **cakes**
(Prod.)
(Bakery. Baker's product. Cake shop product.)
d Kuchen *mpl*
f gâteaux *mpl*
p bolos *mpl*

840 **cake shop; café**
(Prod.)
(Cake and coffee serving establishment.)
d Konditorei *f*
f pâtisserie *f* confiserie
p confeitaria *f*; café *m*

841 **calcareous soil**
(Agr.)
(Soil type.)
d Kalkboden *m*; kalkhaltiger Boden *m*

f sol *m* calcaire
p solo *m* calcário

842 calcium
(Biochem.)
(Ca. Trace element with hepatic activity, promoting glycogenesis.)
d Calcium *n*
f calcium *m*
p cálcio *m*

843 calcium acetate
(Prod.)
($C_4H_6CaO_4.H_2O$; additive in food processing technology; e.g. food preservative.)
d Calciumacetat *n*
f acétate *m* de calcium
p acetato *m* de cálcio

844 calcium alginate
(Prod.)
(Food processing technology: e.g. texture improving ingredient.)
d Calciumalginat *n*
f alginate *m* de calcium
p alginato *m* de cálcio

845 calcium ascorbate
(Prod.)
($(C_6H_7O_6)_2Ca.2H_2O$; vitamin C derivative; antioxidant.)
d Calciumascorbat *n*
f ascorbate *m* de calcium
p ascorbato *m* de cálcio

846 calcium benzoate
(Prod.)
($C_{14}H_{10}CaO_4.3H_2O$; food preservative.)
d Calciumbenzoat *n*
f benzoate *m* de calcium
p benzoato *m* de cálcio

847 calcium bicarbonate
(Prod.)
($Ca(HCO_3)_2$; element contained in traces in mineral water.)
d Calciumbicarbonat *n*
f bicarbonate *m* de calcium
p bicarbonato *m* de cálcio

848 calcium carbonate
(Prod.)
($CaCO_3$. Constituent of the bones; foodstuff colorant: (surface) dye.)
d Calciumcarbonat *n*
f carbonate *m* de calcium
p carbonato *m* de cálcio

849 calcium citrate
(Prod.)
($Ca_3(C_6H_5O_7)_2.4H_2O$; additive in food processing technology; prime material in the production of citric acid.)
d Calciumcitrat *n*
f citrate *m* de calcium
p citrato *m* de cálcio

850 calcium deficiency
(Agr.)
(Livestock breeding: Animal nutrition; foodstuff ration deficiency.)
d Kalkmangel *m*
f carence *f* en calcium
p deficiência *f* de cálcio; carência *f* de cálcio

851 calcium deposit
(Prod.)
(Water supply: tap water production.)
d Kalkablagerung *f*
f dépôt *m* en calcium
p depósito *m* de cálcio

852 calcium deposit within the limits of hot water
(Prod.)
(Water supply: water treatment; water quality.)
d Kalkablagerung *f* im Heißwasserbereich
f dépôt *m* en calcium dans les limites d'eau chaude
p depósito *m* de cálcio dentro dos limites da água quente

853 calcium D-pantothenate
(Prod.)
($(C_9H_{16}NO_5)_2Ca$. Vitamin B_5; Calcium salt of D pantothenoic acid.)
d Calcium-D-Pantothenat *n*
f D-pantothénate *m* de calcium
p d-pantotenato *m* de cálcio

854 calcium lactate
(Prod.)
($C_6H_{10}CaO_6.5H_2O$; additive in food processing (E 327).)
d Calciumlaktat *n*
f lactate *m* de calcium
p lactato *m* de cálcio

855 calcium-nitrogen fertilizer
(Agr.)
(Soil treatment. Fertilizer type.)
d Kalkstickstoffdünger *m*
f engrais *m* de chaux et azote
p fertilizante *m* de nitrocálcio

856 calcium oxalate
(Med.)
(CaC_2O_4; produced by oxalic acid, found in some vegetable types. Abnormal high

presence of oxalates in the urine is called oxaluria.)
d Calciumoxalat *n*
f oxalate *m* de calcium
p oxalato *m* de cálcio

857 **calcium oxide**
(Prod.)
(CaO; e.g. water supply: water treatment: water hardening agent.)
d Calciumoxid *n*
f oxyde *m* de calcium
p óxido *m* de cálcio

858 **calcium phosphate**
(Prod.)
(Present in fishbones: very small fishbones, swallowed with the tiny fishes, are considered to be a calcium source.)
d Calciumphosphat *n*
f phosphate *m* de calcium
p fosfato *m* de cálcio

859 **calcium propionate**
(Prod.)
($C_6H_{10}CaO_4$; additive in food processing; e.g. food preservative.)
d Calciumpropionat *n*
f propionate *m* de calcium
p propionato *m* de cálcio

860 **calcium separation**
(Prod.)
(Water supply: water treatment; water quality.)
d Kalkabscheidung *f*
f séparation *f* de calcium
p separação *f* de cálcio

861 **calcium sulphate**
(Prod.)
($CaSO_4.2H_2O$; substance contained in traces in mineral water.)
d Calciumsulfat *n*
f sulfate *m* de calcium
p sulfato *m* de cálcio

862 **calcium sulphite**
(Prod.)
($CaSO_3.2H_2O$; additive in food processing; preservative for fruit juices; antioxidant.)
d Calciumsulfit *n*
f sulfite *m* de calcium
p sulfito *m* de cálcio

863 **calcium supply**
(Prod.)
(Food processing technology: e.g. by consumption of whole small fishes.)
d Calciumzufuhr *f*
f apport *m* en calcium
p aporte *m* de cálcio

* **calculus → 5438**

864 **calf** (*pl* calves)**; yearling calf; heifer**
(Agr.)
(Livestock; ref. to the young of cattle. A heifer has not yet produced a calf and is less than three years of age.)
d Kalb *n*; Färse *f*
f veau *m*
p bezerra *f*; novilha *f*; vitela *f* (= *novilha: less than one year old*)

865 **calf diphtheria**
(Med.)
(Veterinary; cattle disease.)
d Kälberdiphterie *f*
f diphtérie *f* des veaux
p difteria *f* das novilhas

866 **caloric restriction**
(Med.)
(Dietetics, nutrition.)
d Kalorieneinschränkung *f*
f restriction *f* calorique
p restrição *f* calórica

867 **caloric supply**
(Biochem.)
(Nutritional science; food biochemistry.)
d Kalorienzufuhr *f*
f apport *m* calorique
p aporte *m* calórico

868 **caloric value**
(Biochem.)
(Nutritional science; food biochemistry, ref. to a nutrient.)
d Kalorienwert *m*
f valeur *f* calorique
p valor *m* calórico

869 **calorie**
(Prod.)
(Thermal unit in food processing technology; represents the thermal quantity necessary to make pass 1 liter of water from 14.5° C to 15.5° C at normal atmospheric pressure.)
d Kalorie *f*
f calorie *f*
p caloria *f*

* **calorie ration → 872**

870 **calorie-reduced foods**
(Med.)
(Alimentary regimen.)
d kalorienreduzierte Nahrungsmittel *npl*

f produits *mpl* alimentaires à valeur calorique réduite
p produtos *mpl* alimentícos com teor reduzido de calorias

871 calorimetry
(Prod.)
(Measure of produced heat; regarding foodstuff it refers to its combustion in the presence of oxygen. Direct calorimetry: by means of a calorimeter. Indirect calorimetry: by calculation.)
d Kalorimetrie *f*, Wärmemessung *f*
f calorimétrie *f*
p calorimetria *f*

872 calory ration; calorie ration
(Med.)
d Kalorienration *f*
f ration *f* calorique
p cota *f* de calorias

873 calve *v*
(Med.)
(Veterinary: to give birth to a calf.)
d abkalben
f vêler
p parir

874 calving
(Med.)
(Veterinary: giving birth to a calf.)
d Abkalben *n*
f vêlage *m*; vêlement *m*
p parição *f* da vaca

875 calyx; cup
(Agr.)
(Botany; part of the flower structure, formed by the sepals.)
d Kelch *m*
f calice *m*
p cálice *m*

876 camembert cheese
(Prod.)
(Dairy product; surface-ripened soft French cheese.)
d Camembert-Käse *m*
f camembert *m*
p queijo *m* camembert

877 camomile; chamomile
(Prod.)
("Anthemis nobilis". Medical herb. The essential oil is used as flavouring agent.)
d Kamille *f*
f camomille *f*
p camomila *f*

878 camomile tea; chamomile tea
(Prod.)
(Tea, infusion, made of herbs like "Matricaria chamomilla L.", "Anthemis nobilis"; e.g. an aromatic digestive tonic.)
d Kamillentee *m*
f infusion *f* de camomille
p chá *m* de camomila

* **2-camphanol → 723**

879 canapé
(Prod.)
(Gastronomy; white bread/toast appetizer with delicatessen.)
d Kanapee *n*
f canapé *m*
p canapê *m*

880 candida
(Biochem.)
(Microbiology; "Candida utilis" ("Torula utilis"): yeast type, of interest in food processing technology.)
d Candida *f*
f candida *m*
p cândida *f*

881 candied fruits
(Prod.)
(Food processing technology; candied: coated or baked with sugar.)
d kandierte Früchte *fpl*
f fruits *mpl* candis
p frutas *fpl* cristalizadas

882 candied lemon peel
(Prod.)
(Baking ingredient in food processing technology.)
d Zitronat *n*; Sukkade *f*
f zeste *m* de citron confit
p doce *m* cristalizado da casca de cidra; doce *m* cristalizado da casca de cidrão

883 candy *v*
(Prod.)
(Food processing technology: e.g. to cover a fruit with crystallized sugar.)
d kandieren; mit Zuckerguss überziehen
f candir
p cobrir com açúcar cristalizado

884 candy *v* **fruits**
(Prod.)
(Food processing technology: prepare fruits in sugar, e.g. for conservation.)
d Konfitüre machen
f confire des fruits
p preparar doce de frutas

885 cane juice; sugarcane juice
(Agr.)
(Agricultural produce: Agricultural subproduct; juice obtained from sugar cane by crushing.)
d Zuckerrohrsaft *m*
f vesou *m*
p caldo-de-cana *m*

886 cane molasses
(Prod.)
(Yeast production plant material: Yeast propagation substrate.)
d Rohrzuckermelasse *f*
f mélasse *f* de canne à sucre
p melaço *m* de cana-de-açucar

887 cane sugar
(Agr.)
(Agricultural produce. "Saccharum officinarum".)
d Rohrzucker *m*
f sucre *m* de canne
p cana-de-açúcar *f*

888 canine tooth; eyetooth
(Med.)
(Anatomy.)
d Eckzahn *m*
f dent *f* canine
p dente *m* canino

889 canned fish
(Prod.)
(Food processing technology.)
d Fischkonserve *f*
f conserve *f* de poisson
p conserva *f* de peixe; peixe *m* enlatado

890 canned food; tinned food
(Prod.)
(Food processing technology.)
d Dosenkonserven *fpl*
f conserves *fpl* en boîtes
p conservas *fpl* em latas

891 canned food production; tinned food production
(Prod.)
(Food processing technology and production.)
d Konservenproduktion *f*
f fabrication *f* de conserves
p produção *f* de conservas

892 canned fruits; tinned fruits
(Prod.)
(Food processing technology.)
d eingemachte Früchte *fpl*; Obstkonserve *f*; Fruchtkonserve *f*
f fruits *mpl* en conserve; conserve *f* de fruits
p frutas *fpl* em conserva; conserva *f* de frutas

893 canned meat; tinned meat
(Prod.)
(Food processing technology. Industrialized packaging type of foodstuff product.)
d Fleischkonserve *f*
f conserve *f* à viande; conserve *f* de viande
p carne *f* enlatada

894 canned milk; tinned milk
(Prod.)
(Dairy product.)
d Dosenmilch *f*; Büchsenmilch *f*
f lait *m* en boîte
p leite *m* em lata; leite *m* enlatado

895 canned minced meat in lard
(Prod.)
(Gastronomy; French specialty.)
d Schmalzfleisch *n* in Dosen
f rillettes *fpl*
p carne *f* picada em banha enlatada

896 canned vegetables
(Prod.)
(Food processing technology. Industrialized packaging type of foodstuff product.)
d Gemüsekonserve *f*
f conserve *f* de légumes
p legumes *mpl* em conservas

897 cannery; canning industry
(Prod.)
(Food processing technology and its industrial branch of foodstuff preservation.)
d Konservenindustrie *f*
f conserverie *f*; industrie *f* des conserves
p indústria *f* de conservas

* **canning industry → 897**

* **canola → 4565**

* **canola oil → 4566**

898 canthaxanthin
(Agr.)
($C_{40}H_{52}O_2$. Poultry farming; carotenoid used e.g. as poultry-ration additive for poultry meat and egg colouring.)
d Canthaxanthin *n*
f cantaxantine *f*
p cantaxantina *f*

899 capacity of egg laying
(Agr.)
(Poultry farming.)
d Legeleistung *f*

f capacité *f* pondeuse
p capacidade *f* de postura

900 capacity of water retention
(Agr.)
(Soils and plants.)
d Kapazität *f* der Wasserzurückhaltung
f capacité *f* de rétention en eau
p capacidade *f* de retenção de água

901 caper
(Prod.)
(Genus "Capparis". Ingredient used for seasoning.)
d Kaper *f*
f câpre *f*
p alcaparra *f*

902 capon
(Agr.)
(Poultry farming. Male chicken castrated to improve quality of the meat.)
d Kapaun *m*
f chapon *m*
p capão *m*

903 caponization
(Agr.)
(Poultry farming. Castration of male chicken to improve quality of the meat.)
d Kapaunisierung *f*
f chaponnage *f*
p capação *f* do frango; capadura *f* do frango

904 capric acid; decanoic acid
(Prod.)
($C_{10}H_{20}O_2$; fruit aroma/flavour prime material; occurs as ester in milk fat, coconut oil and fish oil.)
d Caprinsäure *f*
f acide *m* caprique
p ácido *m* cáprico

905 caproic acid; hexanoic acid
(Prod.)
($C_6H_{12}O_2$; ingredient in coconut, some types of cheese; triglyceride in cow's milk and goat's milk.)
d Capronsäure *f*
f acide *m* caproïque
p ácido *m* capróico

906 caproic acid allyl ester
(Prod.)
(See allyl caproate; flavour chemical.)
d Capronsäure-Allylester *m*
f ester *m* allylique de l'acide caproïque
p éster *m* alílico do ácido capróico

* **caproic aldehyde → 172**

907 caprylic acid; octanoic acid
(Prod.)
($C_8H_{16}O_2$; fatty acid; triglyceride; ingredient in cow's milk, goat's milk, in coconut etc.)
d Caprylsäure *f*
f acide *m* caprylique
p ácido *m* caprílico

908 capsanthin
(Prod.)
($C_{40}H_{58}O_3$; carotenoid red pigment, e.g. of paprika; food dye.)
d Capsanthin *n*
f capsantéine *f*
p capsanteína *f*

909 capsid
(Biochem.)
(Microbiology, outer protein virus structure, virus capsule.)
d Virushülle *f*
f capside *f* de virus
p capsídeo *m* do vírus

910 captive groundwater levels
(Prod.)
(Water supply: possible situation of groundwater between the geological layers.)
d eingefangene Grundwasserschichten *fpl*
f nappes *fpl* d'eau souterraines captives
p lençois *mpl* de água subterrânea represados; lençois *mpl* de água subterrânea alçaponados

* **carabao → 5824**

911 caramel
(Prod.)
(Food processing technology: brown burnt sugar; candy type; food dye.)
d Karamel *m*
f caramel *m*
p caramelo *m*

912 caramelization
(Prod.)
(Sugar transformation into caramel by means of heat and acids. This reaction provides a brown colour. Food additive.)
d Karamelisierung *f*
f caramélisation *f*
p caramelização *f*

913 caramelize *v*
(Prod.)
(Food processing technology; processing of sugar into caramel; to cover with caramel.)
d karamelisieren
f caraméliser
p caramelizar

914 caraway
(Agr.)
(Botany. "Carum carvi L."; aromatic herb.)
d Kümmel *m*
f cumin *m*
p alcarávia *f*; cominho-armênio *m*; cariz *m*

915 caraway oil
(Prod.)
(Aroma/flavour agent, e.g. for cookies.)
d Kümmelöl *n*
f huile *f* de cumin
p óleo *m* de cominho

916 carbohydrase
(Biochem.)
(Enzyme, as amylase; used e.g. in the production of beer, wines, alcohols etc., also in dairy products.)
d Carbohydrase *f*
f carbohydrase *f*
p carboidrase *f*

917 carbohydrate
(Biochem.)
(Carbon, oxygen and hydrogen compound, basic formula $C_n(H_2O)_n$.)
d Kohlenhydrat *n*
f glucide *m*; hydrate *m* de carbone
p carboidrato *m*; hidrato *m* de carbono; glucídio *m*

918 carbohydrate fermentation
(Med.)
(Enzymatic decomposition of carbohydrates in the body for energy provision.)
d Kohlenhydratgärung *f*
f fermentation *f* des glucides
p fermentação *f* dos carboidratos

919 carbohydrate-free *adj*
(Prod.)
(Food processing technology. Properties of certain nutrients.)
d kohlenhydratfrei
f exempt de glucides
p isento de carboidratos

920 carbohydrate metabolism
(Med.)
(Biochemical changes undergone by carbohydrates within the body.)
d Kohlenhydratstoffwechsel *m*
f métabolisme *m* des glucides
p metabolismo *m* dos carboidratos

921 carbohydrate-reduced
(Prod.)
(Food processing technology; ref. to properties of certain nutrients.)
d kohlenhydratreduziert
f réduit en glucides
p reduzido em carboidratos

922 carbohydrate-rich *adj*
(Prod.)
(Food processing technology; ref. to properties of certain nutrients.)
d kohlenhydratreich
f riche en glucides
p rico em carboidratos

923 carbohydrates of agricultural origin
(Biochem.)
(E.g. sucrose (saccharose; sugar); ref. to biochemical research, e.g. in genetic engineering; nutritional science.)
d Kohlenhydrate *npl* landwirtschaftlicher Herkunft
f hydrates *mpl* de carbone d'origine agricole
p hidratos *mpl* de carbono de origem agrícola

924 carbohydrates of the milk
(Biochem.)
(Food biochemistry: lactose compounds.)
d Kohlenhydrate *npl* der Milch
f glucides *mpl* du lait
p carboidratos *mpl* do leite

925 carbohydrate surcharge
(Biochem.)
(Nutritional science.)
d Kohlenhydratüberbelastung *f*
f surcharge *f* glucidique
p sobrecarga *f* de carboidratos

926 carbon
(Prod.)
(Aromas; E.g. constitutional part of odoriferous foodstuff molecules.)
d Kohlenstoff *m*
f carbone *m*
p carbono *m*

927 carbon atom chain
(Biochem.)
(Nutritional science.)
d Kohlenstoffatomkette *f*
f chaîne *f* d'atomes de carbone
p cadeia *f* de átomos de carbono

928 carbon cycle in nature
(Biochem.)
(Nutritional science.)
d Kohlenstoffkreislauf *m* in der Natur
f cycle *m* de carbone dans la nature
p ciclo *m* do carbono na natureza

929 **carbon dioxide**
(Biochem.)
(CO_2; carbonic anhydride; e.g. in brewery and wine production. Transformation of sugar molecules by brewery fermentation process into alcohol and CO_2. This is e.g. the moment of the origin of beer.)
d Kohlendioxid *n*
f gaz *m* carbonique; dioxyde *m* de carbone
p gás *m* carbônico; dióxido *m* de carbono

930 **carbon dioxide pressure**
(Biochem.)
(Enology; wine production techniques.)
d Kohlendioxiddruck *m*; Druck *m* des Kohlendioxides
f pression *f* de dioxyde de carbone
p pressão *f* do dióxido de carbono

* **carbon dioxide produced by fermentation**
→ **2133**

931 **carbonic maceration**
(Biochem.)
(Enology: technology of wine production.)
d Kohlendioxidmazeration *f*; Ziehenlassen *n* unter Kohlendioxid
f macération *f* carbonique
p maceração *f* carbônica

932 **carbonyl derivatives**
(Prod.)
(Food processing technology; aroma/fragrance research and production.)
d Carbonylderivate *npl*
f dérivés *mpl* carbonylés
p derivados *mpl* de carbonila

933 **carboxymethylcellulose**
(Prod.)
(Additive; as emulsifier used in the production of sweets, candies etc.; outstanding water absorption properties.)
d Carboxymethylcellulose *f*
f carboxyméthylcellulose *f*
p carboximetilcelulose *f*

934 **carboxypeptidase**
(Biochem.)
(Proteolytic pancreatic enzyme: Breakdown of polypeptides into dipeptides.)
d Carboxypeptidase *f*
f carboxypeptidase *f*
p carboxipeptidase *f*

935 **carcinogenic effect**
(Med.)
(Ref. to certain dietary considerations.)
d krebsfördernde Wirkung *f*
f effet *m* cancérigène
p efeito *m* cancerígeno

936 **carcinoprophylaxis**
(Med.)
(Ref. to certain dietary considerations.)
d Krebsprophylaxe *f*, Krebsvorbeugung *f*
f cancérophylaxie *f*
p profilaxia *f* ao câncer

937 **cardamom**
(Prod.)
("Elettaria cardamomum"; ginger family; ingredient: its seeds are used as a condiment.)
d Kardamom *n*
f cardamome *f*
p cardamomo *m*

938 **cardia**
(Med.)
(Anatomy; opening of the upper part of the stomach: oesophagus (gullet) connection.)
d Magenmund *m*
f cardia *m*
p cárdia *f*

939 **cardiac diet**
(Med.)
(Alimentary regimen.)
d Herzdiät *f*, Herzschonkost *f*
f diète *f* cardiaque
p dieta *f* cardíaca; regime *m* nutricional para o coração

940 **cardiopathy**
(Med.)
(Heart disease e.g. due to incorrect nutritional habits.)
d Herzleiden *n*
f cardiopathie *f*
p cardiopatia *f*

941 **cardiovascular complication**
(Med.)
(Caused by erroneous nutrition.)
d herzgefäßebezügliche Verschlimmerung *f*; kardiovaskuläre Komplikation *f*
f complication *f* cardiovasculaire
p complicação *f* cardiovascular

942 **cardiovascular diseases**
(Med.)
(Caused by erroneous nutrition.)
d herzgefäßebezügliche Krankheiten *fpl*; kardiovaskuläre Krankheiten *fpl*
f maladies *fpl* cardiovasculaires
p doenças *fpl* cardiovasculares

943 **cariogenic** *adj*
(Med.)
(Tooth related effect caused by sweets, candies.)

d kariesverursachend; Zahnfäule verursachend
f cariogénique
p cariogênico

944 carious *adj*
(Med.)
(Tooth related effect caused by sweets, candies.)
d kariös; von Zahnfäule befallen
f carié; carieux
p cariado

945 carious tooth
(Med.)
(Anatomy. Tooth related effect caused by sweets, candies.)
d kariöser Zahn *m*
f dent *f* carieuse
p dente *m* cariado

946 carmine
(Prod.)
(Red pigment obtained from dried female "Coccus cacti L." = cochineal; foodstuff colorant (see cochineal).)
d Carminrot *n*
f carmin *m*
p vermelho *m* carmim

947 carminic acid
(Prod.)
($C_{22}H_{20}O_{13}$; red glucosidal dyestuff obtained from "Coccus cacti L." = cochineal; see "cochineal" and "carmine"; food dye, food colorants.)
d Carminsäure *f*
f acide *m* carminique
p ácido *m* carmínico

948 carnitine
(Med.)
($C_7H_{15}NO_3$; nutritional science: substance especially present in the muscle cells; takes part in the oxidation of fatty acids.)
d Carnitin *n*
f carnitine *f*
p carnitina *f*

949 carob; locust bean; St.John's bread
(Agr.)
(Botany; "Ceratonia siliqua", leguminous tree; pulp and pod of this tree (also locust bean), having a sweet taste, as to the legend, served as a nutrient to St. John in the dessert.)
d Johannisbrot *n*; Karube *f*
f caroube *f*
p alfarroba *f*

950 carotenaemia; xanthaemia
(Med.)
(Presence of carotene in blood, causing pseudojaundice: yellow skin.)
d Carotinämie *f*; Karotinämie *f*
f caroténémie *f*
p carotenemia *f*

951 carotene
(Prod.)
($C_{40}H_{56}$; orange pigment, foodstuff colorant. Also ß-carotene = provitamin A.)
d Carotin *n*
f carotène *m*
p caroteno *m*

952 carotenoid
(Prod.)
(Natural and synthetic food dyestuff of orange colour.)
d Carotenoid *n*
f caroténoïde *m*
p carotenóide *m*

953 carp
(Agr.)
("Cyprinus carpio L.". A freshwater fish, raised for food.)
d Karpfen *m*
f carpe *f*
p carpa *f*

* **carpel → 4195**

954 carrageen
(Prod.)
(Food processing technology; algue "Chondrus crispus"; emulsifier, stabilizer; texture improving ingredient (E 407).)
d irländisches Moos *n*; Carrageen *n*
f carragheen *m*
p carragena *f*

955 carrier
(Prod.)
(Aroma/fragrance research and production.)
d Trägersubstanz *f*
f support *m*
p suporte *m*

956 carrot
(Agr.)
(Agricultural produce. "Daucus carota", edible root.)
d Wurzel *f*; Mohrrübe *f*; gelbe Rübe *f*
f carotte *f* longue
p cenoura *f*

* **carrying out of the fermentation process → 2136**

957 **cartilage**
(Med.)
(Anatomy. Elastic skeleton tissue.)
d Knorpel *m*
f cartilage *m*
p cartilagem *f*

* **carve** *v* → **1468**

958 **casein**
(Prod.)
(Dairy product; prime material; 80% of milk protein is casein; constituent of cheese and occurs when milk curdles by the action of rennet.)
d Casein *n*
f caséine *f*
p caseína *f*

959 **casein hydrolysate**
(Biochem.)
(Nutritional science.)
d Caseinhydrolysat *n*
f hydrolysat *m* de caséine
p produto *m* de hidrólise da caseína

960 **caseiniform albumin**
(Prod.)
(Food processing technology.)
d kaseinförmiges Albumin *n*; kaseinförmiges Eiweiß *n*
f albumine *f* caséiniforme
p albumina *f* caseiforme

961 **cashew; cashew nut; acajou; acajou nut**
(Agr.)
("Anacardium occidentalis" (Tupi: aka'yu); very common e.g. in Brazil. The kernel is used for preparing compote and the edible nut is roasted.)
d Kajunuss *f*; Cashewnuss *f*
f cajou *m*; noix *f* d'anacarde; noix *f* de cajou; anarcade *f*; amande *f* de cajou
p caju *m*; castanha *f* de caju; noz *f* de cajú

* **cashew nut → 961**

* **cassava → 3373**

962 **cassia; senna leaves**
(Agr.)
(Botany; genus "Cassia". Medicinal herb.)
d Kassie *f*; Sennesblätter *npl*
f casse *f*; séné *m*; feuilles *fpl* de séné
p cássia *f*; folhas *fpl* de sena

* **cassia bark → 963**

963 **cassia cinnamon; cassia bark; Chinese cinnamon**
(Prod.)
(Additive; "Cinnamonum cassia"; aromatic spice.)
d chinesischer Zimt *m*
f cannelle *f* de Chine
p canela-da-China *f*

964 **caster sugar; castor sugar**
(Prod.)
(Food processing technology: refined sugar type.)
d Streuzucker *m*
f sucre *m* semoule
p açúcar *m* em pó

965 **castor oil**
(Agr.)
(Agricultural produce. Pressed from the seeds of "Ricinus communis L.". Used in medicine as cathartic (laxative); also used for industrial purposes.)
d Rizinusöl *n*
f huile *f* de ricin
p óleo *m* de rícino

966 **castor-oil plant**
(Agr.)
(Botany: "Ricinus communis Palma Christi"; Medicinal plant: Cold-pressed seed oil.)
d Rizinus *m*
f ricin *m*
p rícino *m*; mamona *f*

* **castor sugar → 964**

967 **castrate** *v*
(Agr.)
(Livestock: to turn the animal unable to reproduce.)
d kastrieren
f châtrer
p castrar

* **castrated male pig → 544**

968 **castration**
(Agr.)
(Livestock: Turning the animal unable to reproduce.)
d Kastration *f*
f castration *f*
p castração *f*

969 **catabolism**
(Med.)
(Decomposing metabolism under energy release.)
d Katabolismus *m*
f catabolisme *m*
p catabolismo *m*

970 **catalase**
(Biochem.)
(Microbiology; microorganism-produced enzyme which exists e.g. in milk. Catalase test for determination of the bacteriologic quality of the milk.)
d Katalase *f*
f catalase *f*
p catalase *f*

971 **catalysis**
(Biochem.)
(Nutritional science; increase in the rate of chemical reaction induced by a catalyst.)
d Katalyse *f*
f catalyse *f*
p catálise *f*

972 **catalyzer**
(Biochem.)
(In biochemistry: enzymes, proteins which catalyze biochemical reactions; ref. to nutritional science.)
d Katalysator *m*
f catalyseur *m*
p catalisador *m*

973 **caterpillar**
(Agr.)
(Larva; stage between the egg and e.g. an adult butterfly; problem causing larva in biologic agriculture.)
d Raupe *f*
f chenille *f*
p lagarta *f*

* **catsup → 3063**

974 **cattle**
(Agr.)
(Cattle breeding. Bovine animals raised for use.)
d Rindvieh *n*; Rind *n*; Rinder *npl*
f espèce *f* bovine; bovins *mpl*; bœuf *m*
p gado *m* bovino

* **cattle breeding → 975**

975 **cattle raising; cattle breeding**
(Agr.)
(Livestock (farm animals; here: the cow family) raising for profit.)
d Rinderzucht *f*
f élevage *m* bovin; élevage *m* du bétail
p bovinocultura *f*

976 **cattle-raising zoning**
(Agr.)
(Soil; ref. to the formation of livestock, cattle breeding zones.)
d viehwirtschaftliche Zoneneinteilung *f*; Zoneneinteilung *f* für die Viehwirtschaft
f zonage *m* de l'élevage du bétail; zones *fpl* d'implantation pour l'élevage du bétail
p zoneamento *m* pecuário

977 **cattle slaughter; cattle slaughtering**
(Prod.)
(Slaughthouse (abattoir) activity; meat production.)
d Viehschlachtung *f*
f abattage *m* du bétail
p abate *m* de gado

* **cattle slaughtering → 977**

978 **cauliflower**
(Agr.)
(Agricultural produce. "Brassica oleracea botrytis".)
d Blumenkohl *m*
f chou-fleur *m*
p couve-flor *m*

979 **cause of the interruptions of fermentation; reason for the interruptions of fermentation**
(Biochem.)
(Fermentation in nutritional science.)
d Ursache *f* der Gärungsstockungen
f cause *f* des arrêts de la fermentation
p causa *f* das paralizações da fermentação

980 **caviar**
(Prod.)
(Gastronomy; food: roe (e.g. of sturgeon).)
d Kaviar *m*
f caviar *m*
p caviar *m*

981 **cayenne pepper**
(Agr.)
("Capsicum fructescens" (Tupi: kyinha). A hot pepper type of long red fruits.)
d spanischer Pfeffer *m*
f piment *m* de Cayenne; piment *m* rouge
p pimenta-malagueta *f*; malagueta *f*

* **cecum → 834**

982 **cedar**
(Agr.)
(Botany; genus "Cedrus"; coniferous evergreen tree.)
d Zeder *f*
f cèdre *m*
p cedro *m*

983 **celeriac**
(Agr.)
(Agricultural produce. "Apium graveolens

rapaceum", having edible roots.)
d Sellerie *m*
f céleri-rave *m*
p aipo-rábano *m*; salsão *m*

984 **celery**
(Agr.)
(Agricultural produce; "Apium graveolens dulce"; having edible leafstalks.)
d Stangensellerie *m*
f céleri *f*
p aipo *m*

985 **cell culture**
(Biochem.)
(Biochemical research in nutritional science.)
d Zellenkultur *f*
f culture *f* cellulaire; culture *f* des cellules
p cultura *f* celular

* **cell gearing → 986**

986 **cell machinism; cell gearing**
(Biochem.)
(Cell-functioning system; e.g. ref. to biochemical research in nutritional science.)
d Zellengetriebe *n*
f machinerie *f* cellulaire
p engrenagem *f* celular

* **cell membrane → 4213**

987 **cell nucleus**
(Biochem.)
(Cell constituents, cell structure: controlling part of the cell, containing the genetic (DNA) material; e. g. in genetic engineering; nutritional science.)
d Zellkern *m*
f noyau *m* cellulaire
p núcleo *m* da célula; núcleo *m* celular

988 **cell proliferation**
(Biochem.)
(Nutritional science; Processes in aroma production from plant prime material.)
d Zellwucherung *f*; starke Zellvermehrung *f*
f prolifération *f* de cellules
p proliferação *f* de células

989 **cell protease; proteolytic cellular enzyme**
(Med.)
(Biochemical reactions within the cells.)
d Zellprotease *f*; proteolytisches Zellenenzym *n*
f protéase *f* cellulaire; enzyme *f* protéolytique cellulaire
p protease *f* celular; enzima *f* proteolítica celular

990 **cell surface receptors**
(Med.)
(Veterinary; e.g. ref. to vitamin transport in the animal body.)
d Zelloberflächenrezeptoren *mpl*
f récepteur *m* de la surface cellulaire
p receptores *mpl* da superfície celular

991 **cellular genetics**
(Biochem.)
(Genetic engineering, e.g. nutritional science.)
d Zellengenetik *f*, Zellulargenetik *f*
f génétique *f* cellulaire
p genética *f* celular

992 **cellular nutrition**
(Med.)
(Nutrition in medicine; e.g. ref. to metabolism.)
d Zellenernährung *f*
f nutrition *f* cellulaire
p nutrição *f* celular

993 **cellular poison**
(Med.)
(E.g. of some mushrooms: the "death cap", also "death cup" (Amanita phalloides). German: Knollenblätterpilz.)
d Zellgift *n*
f poison *m* cellulaire
p veneno *m* celular

994 **cellulase**
(Med.)
(Veterinary; cellulose downbreaking enzyme in the intestine of ruminants.)
d Cellulase *f*
f cellulase *f*
p celulase *f*

995 **cellulose**
(Med.)
(Polysaccharide, forming the plant structure; indigestible dietary fibre component, acting as roughage in the intestine.)
d Zellulose *f*
f cellulose *f*
p celulose *f*

996 **cellulose cell wall**
(Agr.)
(Botany; plant cell constituents, cell structure; e.g. in genetic engineering; nutritional science.)
d cellulosehaltige Zellwand *f*
f membrane *f* squelettique cellulosique
p membrana *f* de celulose

997 **cellulose fibre**
(Agr.)
(Botany. Plant constituent.)
d Zellulosefaser *f*

f fibre *f* cellulosique
p fibra *f* de celulose

998 **cell wall**
(Agr.)
(Botany; cell structure.)
d Zellwand *f*
f paroi *f* cellulaire; paroi *f* des cellules
p parede *f* celular

999 **central nervous system**
(Med.)
(CNS; brain and spinal cord; ref. olfactory stimulation, nervous cells system: aroma/flavour research: ref. to odoriferous molecules perceptivity and perceptibility.)
d zentrales Nervensystem *n*
f système *m* nerveux central
p sistema *m* nervoso central

* **centrifugal clarification → 1148**

* **centrifugal scumming → 4863**

1000 **centrifugal sedimentation**
(Prod.)
(Food processing technology; production process: separation procedure.)
d Zentrifugalablagerung *f*
f sédimentation *f* centrifuge
p sedimentação *f* centrifugal

1001 **centrifugated milk**
(Prod.)
(Dairy product.)
d zentrifugierte Milch *f*
f lait *m* centrifugé
p leite *m* centrifugado

1002 **centrifugation**
(Prod.)
(Centrifuging process in sugar production: sugar syrup treatment by rotation; separation of the crystals.)
d Abschleuderung *f*
f turbinage *m*
p centrifugação *f*

1003 **cepe; edible boletus**
(Agr.)
(Botany. Genus "Boletus edulis"; edible boletus: mushroom.)
d Steinpilz *m*
f cèpe *m*
p boleto *m* comestível

1004 **cereal diet**
(Med.)
(Highest stage of macrobiotic method of nutrition on whole grains, containing 79% of carbohydrates; as to Christoph Wilhelm Hufeland (1762-1836), German physician.)
d Getreidenahrung *f*; Getreidekost *f*
f régime *m* de céréales
p regime *m* à base de cereais; dieta *f* à base de cereais

1005 **cereal feedstuff**
(Agr.)
(Livestock nutrition.)
d Getreidefutter *n*
f fourrage *m* de céréales; céréales *fpl* fourragères
p cereal *m* forrageiro; cereal *m* forraginoso

1006 **cereal grains**
(Agr.)
(Agricultural produce.)
d Getreidekörner *npl*
f grains *mpl* de céréales
p grãos *mpl* de cereais

1007 **cereal plains; plains of cereal cultivation**
(Agr.)
(Soil; area under cultivation.)
d Getreideanbauebenen *fpl*
f plaines *fpl* céréalières; plaines *fpl* de culture des céréales
p planícies *fpl* de cultivo de cereais

1008 **cereal protein**
(Biochem.)
(Nutritional science.)
d Getreideprotein *n*
f protéine *f* céréale
p proteína *f* cereal

1009 **cereals**
(Agr.)
(Agricultural produce.)
d Getreide *n*
f céréales *fpl*
p cereais *mpl*

1010 **cereal selection**
(Prod.)
(Food processing technology, research.)
d Getreideauswahl *f*
f sélection *f* des céréales
p seleção *f* dos cereais

1011 **cereals for panification**
(Agr.)
(Agricultural produce; ref. to bread-baking prime material: e.g. rye, wheat.)
d Brotgetreide *n*
f céréales *fpl* panifiables
p cereais *mpl* para panificação

1012 cerebral-cortical necrosis
(Med.)
(Veterinary.)
d zerebral-kortikaler Brand *m*
f nécrose *f* cérébrale-corticale
p necrose *f* córtico-cerebral

1013 cerebral nutrition; nutrition of the brain
(Med.)
(Nutrition of cerebral tissue.)
d Ernährung *f* des Gehirns
f nutrition *f* du cerveau
p nutrição *f* do cérebro

1014 cerebral tissues
(Med.)
(Anatomy.)
d Gehirngewebe *npl*
f tissus *mpl* cérébraux
p tecidos *mpl* cerebrais

1015 cerebrosides
(Med.)
(Galactose containing lipids, found in nerve tissue, necessary for myelin synthesis; galactose is an ingredient of human milk.)
d Sphingogalaktoside *npl*
f cérébrosides *mpl*
p cerebrósidos *mpl*

1016 cervix
(Med.)
(Veterinary; animal anatomy; cervix uteri; uterus passage.)
d Gebärmutterhals *m*
f col *m* de l'utérus
p cérvix *m*; colo *m* uterino

1017 cestoda
(Med.)
(Veterinary; tapeworm; class of the phylum of platyhelminthes: parasite.)
d Bandwurm *m*
f cestode *m*
p cestóide *m*

1018 cetonic rancidity; cetonic rancidness
(Biochem.)
(Nutritional science; can occur in butter and other kinds of fatty foodstuff, caused by penicillium or aspergillus fungi.)
d ketonische Ranzigkeit *f*
f rance *m* cétonique
p ranço *m* cetônico

* **cetonic rancidness → 1018**

1019 Ceylon cinnamon
(Agr.)
(Botany. "Cinnamomum zeylanicum" (Sri Lanka). Aromatic spice from the dried bark.)
d Ceylon-Zimt *m*
f cannelle *f* de Ceylan
p canela *f* de Ceilão

* **chaff → 2769**

1020 chaff of oats
(Agr.)
(Agricultural produce, subproduct.)
d Spreu *f* des Hafers
f balle *f* d'avoine
p debulho *m* da aveia

1021 chalybeate spring
(Med.)
(Iron salt fountain water types.)
d Eisenquelle *f*
f source *f* ferrugineuse
p fonte *f* ferruginosa

* **chamomile → 877**

* **chamomile tea → 878**

1022 champagne; bubbly
(Biochem.)
(Enology: effervescent wine; in this case not the French champagne of the province of Champagne, but a similar wine type made elsewhere.)
d Schaumwein *m*; Sekt *m*
f vin *m* mousseux; mousseux *m*
p vinho *m* espumante

1023 champagne wine
(Prod.)
(Beverages. German "Sekt" is used but not correct; the real champagne is a French red or white sparkling wine of controlled origin. "Sekt" is a similar wine made e.g. in Germany.)
d Champagner *m*; Sekt *m*
f champagne *m*
p champanhe *m*

1024 chanterelle
(Agr.)
(Botany; "Cantharellus cibarius"; edible mushroom.)
d Pfifferling *m*
f chanterelle *f*, girolle *f*
p cantarelo *m*

1025 characteristic aromatic note
(Prod.)
(Aroma/flavour note.)
d charakteristische aromatische Note *f*
f note *f* aromatique caractéristique
p nota *f* aromática caraterística

1026 **characteristic odour**
(Prod.)
(Aroma/fragrance research and production.)
d charakteristischer Geruch *m*
f odeur *f* caractéristique
p odor *m* caraterístico; cheiro *m* caraterístico

1027 **characteristics of essential oils; characteristics of ethereal oils**
(Prod.)
(Aroma/flavour research and production.)
d charakteristische Eigenschaften *fpl* ätherischer Öle
f caractéristiques *fpl* des huiles essentielles
p caraterísticas *fpl* dos óleos essenciais

* **characteristics of ethereal oils → 1027**

1028 **charcoal**
(Agr.)
(Agricultural produce: subproduct; carbon produced from wood by partial burning, "charring".)
d Holzkohle *f*
f charbon *m* de bois
p carvão *m* vegetal

1029 **chard; Swiss chard**
(Agr.)
(Botany. "Beta vulgaris var. cicla L.". Vegetable.)
d Mangold *m*
f poirée *f*; bette *f*; blette *f*
p acelga *f*

1030 **charqui; jerked beef**
(Prod.)
(Butchery; dried up beef and some other meat types, known in Brazil and other South American countries. In Brazil: salted cow meat in large pieces.)
d Trockenfleisch *n*
f charqui *f*; viande *f* séchée au soleil
p charque *m*; carne-seca *f*; carne-de-sol *f*; jabá *m/f*

1031 **chartreuse liqueur**
(Prod.)
(Beverages. French liqueur made by maceration of herbs.)
d Chartreuse *m*; Chartreuse-Kräuterlikör *m*
f chartreuse *f*
p licor *m* Chartreuse

1032 **cheap cuts**
(Prod.)
(Gastronomy; less noble meat part e.g. for boiling, cooking.)
d Kochfleisch *n* minderer Güte
f basse *f*
p carne *f* de segunda

1033 **cheek**
(Med.)
(Anatomy.)
d Backe *f*; Wange *f*
f joue *f*
p face *f*

1034 **cheekbone; zygomatic bone**
(Med.)
(Anatomy; bones; "Arcus zygmaticus".)
d Jochbein *n*; Backenknochen *m*
f os *m* malaire
p osso *m* zigomático; arcada *f* zigomática

* **cheese cake → 1037**

1035 **cheese drying**
(Prod.)
(Food processing technology: cheese production process: a slow dehydration process.)
d Käsetrocknung *f*
f hâlage *m*
p secagem *f* do queijo; desidratação *f* do queijo

1036 **cheese enzyme**
(Biochem.)
(Nutritional science: enzyme which coagulates the raw milk.)
d Käseenzym *n*
f fromase *f*; enzyme *f* du fromage
p enzima *f* do queijo

1037 **cheese flan; cheese cake**
(Prod.)
(Cake shop product.)
d Käsekuchen *m*
f tarte *f* au fromage
p torta *f* de ricota; bolo *m* de queijo

1038 **cheese from the Alps; alpkase**
(Prod.)
(Dairy product; Swiss cheese type, similar to Emmenthaler.)
d Alpenkäse *m*; Bergkäse *f*
f fromage *m* de montagne
p queijo *m* suiço

1039 **cheese lipids**
(Biochem.)
(Nutritional science; food biochemistry.)
d Käsefettstoffe *mpl*
f lipides *mpl* du fromage
p lipídios *mpl* de queijo

1040 **cheese packaged in wedges**
(Prod.)
(Dairy product; dairy plant packing process.)

d in Keilform abgepackter Käse *f*
f fromage *m* empaqueté en coins
p queijo *m* empacotado em forma de cunha

1041 **cheese plant**
(Prod.)
(Dairy subplant for cheese production.)
d Käsefabrikationsanlage *f*
f installation *f* de production de fromages; fromagerie *f*
p instalação *f* produtora de queijos

1042 **cheese products**
(Prod.)
(Dairy product; eventually flavoured with acetoin.)
d Käseprodukte *fpl*
f fromages *mpl*
p queijos *mpl*

1043 **cheese refinement**
(Prod.)
(Food processing technology; food industrialization.)
d Käseveredelung *f*
f affinage *m* du fromage
p refinação *f* do queijo; refinamento *m* do queijo

1044 **cheese rind**
(Prod.)
(Dairy technology, dairy product: rind of hard cheese.)
d Käserinde *f*
f croûte *f* du fromage
p casca *f* do queijo

1045 **cheese spread**
(Prod.)
(Food processing technology: cheese type.)
d Streichkäse *m*
f fromage *m* à tartiner
p queijo *m* cremoso; queijo-creme *m*

1046 **cheese wheel rapped in foil**
(Prod.)
(Dairy product, ready for transport.)
d Käserad *n* in Folie gewickelt
f meule *f* de fromage empaquetée dans des feuilles
p rodela *f* de queijo embrulhada em folha

1047 **cheese with internal mould**
(Prod.)
(Dairy plant technology: e.g. Gorgonzola-type: Italian-type soft cheese.)
d Käse *m* mit innerem Schimmelbefall
f fromage *m* avec moisissures internes
p queijo *m* com bolor interno

1048 **cheese with washed out rind**
(Prod.)
(Dairy plant technology: e.g. Münster-type, of fine aromatic taste.)
d Käse *m* mit ausgewaschener Rinde
f fromage *m* à croûte lavée
p queijo *m* de casca lavada

1049 **cheilosis**
(Med.)
(Inflammation of the lips. Nutritional disorder, vitamin B_2 deficiency.)
d Lippenentzündung *f*
f chéilose *f*
p quilose *f*; queilose *f*

* **chelate formation → 1053**

1050 **chelating ability**
(Biochem.)
(Nutritional science; ref. to restructured meat in meat processing: ref. to phosphates.)
d Chelatisierungsvermögen *n*
f capacité *f* de la formation d'un chélate
p capacidade *f* de formação de um quelato

1051 **chelating agent**
(Biochem.)
(Nutritional science: complexing agent; inhibits enzymatic reactions.)
d Komplexbildner *m*; Sequestrierungsmittel *n*
f chélateur *m*; agent *m* chélateur; séquestrant *m*; agent *m* séquestrant
p seqüestrante *m*

1052 **chelating power**
(Biochem.)
(Nutritional science; ref. to restructured meat in meat processing.)
d Chelatbildungskraft *f*
f pouvoir *m* de chélation
p poder *m* de quelatização

1053 **chelation; chelate formation**
(Biochem.)
(Food biochemistry.)
d Chelatisierung *f*; Chelatbildung *f*
f chélation *f*; formation *f* d'un chélat
p quelatização *f*; formação *f* de um quelato

1054 **chemical acidification**
(Prod.)
(Dairy plant technology: Curd preparation.)
d chemische Säuerung *f*
f acidification *f* chimique
p acidificação *f* química

* **chemical analysis of feed → 1055**

1055 **chemical assay of feed; chemical analysis of feed**
(Biochem.)
(Test to confirm the presence of certain substances, such as vitamins.)
d chemische Untersuchung *f* der Futtermittel; chemische Analyse *f* der Futtermittel
f essai *m* chimique des fourrages; analyse *f* chimique des fourrages
p exame *m* químico das rações; análise *f* química das rações

1056 **chemical composition of the soil**
(Agr.)
(Soils; soil treatment.)
d chemische Beschaffenheit *f* des Bodens; chemische Zusammensetzung *f* des Bodens
f composition *f* chimique du sol
p composição *f* química do solo

1057 **chemical fertilizer; artificial fertilizer**
(Agr.)
(Soil treatment; e.g. potash fertilizer; nitrogen fertilizer.)
d Kunstdünger *m*
f engrais *m* chimique; engrais *m* artificiel
p fertilizante *m* químico

1058 **chemical improver for panification**
(Prod.)
(Food processing technology: active ingredient.)
d chemischer Brotteigverbesserer *m*
f améliorant *m* chimique pour la panification
p melhorador *m* químico para panificação

1059 **chemical inertia**
(Prod.)
(Aroma/flavour research and production, ref. to solvent characteristics, solvent qualities.)
d chemisch inerter Charakter *m*
f inertie *f* chimique
p inércia *f* química

1060 **chemical interaction**
(Prod.)
(Food processing technology and aroma/flavour research and production.)
d chemische Wechselwirkung *f*
f interaction *f* chimique
p interação *f* química

1061 **chemical interaction between foodstuff and aroma**
(Prod.)
(Food processing technology and aroma/flavour research and production.)
d chemische Wechselwirkung *f* zwischen Nahrungsmittel und Aroma
f interaction *f* chimique entre l'aliment et l'arôme
p interação *f* química entre o produto alimentício e o aroma

1062 **chemical nature of micronutrients**
(Biochem.)
(Nutritional science.)
d chemische Natur *f* der Mikronährstoffe
f nature *f* chimique des micronutriments
p natureza *f* química dos micronutrientes

1063 **chemical oxidation**
(Biochem.)
(Nutritional science; food biochemistry.)
d chemische Oxidation *f*
f oxydation *f* chimique
p oxidação *f* química

1064 **chemical preservation processes**
(Prod.)
(Food processing technology: acidifying, pickling, salting, smoking.)
d chemische Konservierungsverfahren *npl*
f traitements *mpl* préservatifs chimiques
p processos *mpl* químicos de conservação

1065 **chemical reactions**
(Biochem.)
(Food biochemistry; chemical change; interaction between chemicals.)
d chemische Reaktionen *fpl*
f réactions *fpl* chimiques
p reações *fpl* químicas

1066 **chemoreceptors**
(Med.)
(Aroma/flavour perception.)
d Chemorezeptoren *mpl*
f chimiorécepteurs *mpl*
p químiorreceptores *mpl*

* **chernozem → 677**

1067 **cherry**
(Agr.)
(Agricultural produce; genus "Prunus", drupe.)
d Kirsche *f*
f cerise *f*
p cereja *f*

1068 **cherry brandy**
(Prod.)
(Beverages. Brandy made from cherries.)
d Kirschwasser *n*; Kirschgeist *m*
f eau *f* de cerise; kirsch *m*
p aguardente *m* de cereja

1069 **cherry flan**
(Prod.)
(Cake shop product: fruit flan.)

d Kirschtorte *f*
f tarte *f* aux cerises
p torta *f* de cerejas

1070 **cherry juice**
(Prod.)
(Beverages; cherry drink.)
d Kirschensaft *m*
f jus *m* de cerises; cerisette *f* (*fermented*)
p suco *m* de cereja

1071 **cherry liqueur**
(Prod.)
(Beverages; aperitif liqueur, made by maceration of cherries and sugar addition.)
d Kirschlikör *m*
f guignolet *m*; guignolet kirsch *m*
p licor *m* de cereja

1072 **chervil**
(Agr.)
(Botany; "Anthriscus cerefolium". Edible aromatic herb; leaves used as condiment, e.g. in soups; seeds used for extraction of essential oil.)
d Kerbel *m*; Kerbelkraut *n*
f cerfeuil *m*
p cerefólio *m*; cerefolho *m*

1073 **chestnut; marron**
(Agr.)
(Agricultural produce. Edible fruit; genus "Castanea"; Spanish chestnut: marron: "Castanea sativa".)
d echte Kastanie *f*; Esskastanie *f*; Marone *f*
f châtaigne *f*; marron *m*
p castanha *f*

1074 **chew** *v*
(Med.)
(Initiation of the chemical digestion process. The enzyme ptyalin, contained in the saliva, breaks down the starch.)
d kauen
f mâcher
p mastigar

1075 **chewing gum**
(Prod.)
(On basis of synthetic and vegetable resins; with addition of sugar or sweeteners, acids and flavouring agents.)
d Kaugummi *n*
f gomme *f* à mâcher
p goma *f* de mascar

1076 **chick**
(Agr.)
(Poultry farming. "Gallus gallus"; newly hatched chicken; starter.)
d Küken *n*
f poussin *m*
p pinto *m*

1077 **chicken breed**
(Agr.)
(Poultry farming; classification of animal type.)
d Hühnerrasse *f*
f race *f* de poule
p raça *f* de galinha; linhagem *f* de galinha

1078 **chicken broth**
(Prod.)
(Gastronomy.)
d Hühnerbrühe *f*
f bouillon *m* de poule
p caldo *m* de galinha

1079 **chicken cholera**
(Med.)
(Veterinary; ref. to poultry; microbe "Pasteurella multocida".)
d Hühnercholera *f*; Geflügelcholera *f*
f choléra *m* des poules; choléra *m* aviaire
p cólera *f* das galinhas; cólera *f* avícula

1080 **chicken farming**
(Agr.)
(Poultry farming.)
d Hühnerzucht *f*
f élevage *f* de volleiles
p criação *f* de galinhas

1081 **chicken meat**
(Agr.)
(Poultry farming.)
d Hühnerfleisch *n*
f viande *f* de poulet
p carne *f* de frango

1082 **chickpea**
(Agr.)
(Agricultural produce; "Cicer arietinum"; leguminous herb: edible seeds (like peas).)
d Kichererbse *f*
f pois *m* chiche
p grão-de-bico *m*

1083 **chickpea mash; chickpea purée**
(Prod.)
(Gastronomy.)
d Kichererbsenpüree *n*
f purée *f* de pois chiches
p purê *m* de grãos-de-bico

* **chickpea purée → 1083**

1084 **chick starter ration**
(Agr.)
(Poultry farming: poultry nutrition.)

d Kükenration *f*
f ration *f* pour poussins
p ração *f* para pintos

1085 **chicory**
(Agr.)
(Agricultural produce; "Cichorium intybus"; edible plant, e.g. for salads.)
d Zichorie *f*; Wegwarte *f*
f chicorée *f*
p chicória *f*

1086 **child resistant to infections**
(Med.)
(Baby nutrition.)
d gegen Ansteckungen widerstandsfähiges Kind *n*
f enfant *m* résistant aux infections
p criança *f* resistente às infecções

* **Chile salpetre → 5042**

1087 **chill** *v*
(Prod.)
(Food processing technology; cooling of foodstuff without obtaining the freezing point.)
d kühlen
f réfrigérer
p refrigerar

1088 **chilling process**
(Prod.)
(Food processing technology; ref. to temperature decrease for foodstuff conservation without freezing.)
d Kühlprozess *m*
f processus *m* de réfrigération
p processo *m* de refrigeração

1089 **chin**
(Med.)
(Anatomy.)
d Kinn *n*
f menton *m*
p queixo *m*

* **Chinese cinnamon → 963**

* **chinoleine → 4543**

* **chitlins → 1090**

1090 **chitterlings; chitlins**
(Prod.)
(Meat product: intestines of hogs, cattles, ready as food.)
d Kuttel *f*; Kaldaune *f*
f tripe *f*
p tripas *fpl*

1091 **chive**
(Agr.)
(Agricultural produce. "Allium schoenoprasum".)
d Schnittlauch *m*
f ciboulette *f*
p cebolinha *f*

1092 **chlorella**
(Biochem.)
(Microbiology; green alga; protein-producing microorganisms; protein source.)
d Chlorella *f*
f chlorelle *f*
p clorela *f*

1093 **chlorides**
(Prod.)
(Component of table salt, together with sodium. Essential for maintaining the body's fluid balance.)
d Chloride *npl*
f chlorures *mpl*
p cloretos *mpl*

1094 **chlorinated solvents**
(Prod.)
(E.g. methylene chloride (dichloromethane): CH_2Cl_2; used in extraction processes in aroma/flavour research and production.)
d chlorierte Lösungsmittel *npl*
f solvants *mpl* chlorés
p solventes *mpl* clorados

1095 **chlorination**
(Prod.)
(Water supply; water treatment by means of chlorine for disinfection.)
d Chlorierung *f*
f chloration *f*
p cloração *f*

1096 **chlorination of the water**
(Prod.)
(Water supply; water treatment by means of chlorine for disinfection.)
d Chloren *n* des Wassers
f chloration *f* d'eau
p cloração *f* da água

1097 **chlorine**
(Prod.)
(Cl. Bleaching agent for flour, fats etc. Disinfectant. Used in water treatment. Macromineral ingredient in some type of animal foodstuff.)
d Chlor *n*
f chlore *m*
p cloro *m*

1098 **chlorine deficiency**
(Med.)
(Veterinary: E.g. mineral deficiency in some foodstuff type.)
d Chlormangel *m*
f carence *f* en chlore
p deficiência *f* de cloro

1099 **chlorine dioxide; chlorine peroxide**
(Prod.)
(ClO_2; water supply treatment: chlorine liberating substance.)
d Chlordioxid *n*
f dioxyde *m* de chlore
p dióxido *m* de cloro

* **chlorine peroxide → 1099**

1100 **chlorine-sensitive** *adj*
(Agr.)
(Biological agriculture; ref. to certain plants.)
d chlorempfindlich
f sensible au chlore
p sensível ao cloro

1101 **chlorogenic acid**
(Prod.)
($C_{16}H_{18}O_9$; found in coffee beans and in many vegetable products; can be the cause of blackening of cut potatoes.)
d Chlorogensäure *f*
f acide *m* chlorogénique
p ácido *m* clorogênico

1102 **chlorophyll**
(Prod.)
(Plant pigment; foodstuff colour; essential in the photosynthesis process.)
d Chlorophyll *n*; Blattgrün *n*
f chlorophylle *f*
p clorofila *f*

1103 **chlorophyllase**
(Biochem.)
(Nutritional science; chlorophyll hydrolyzing plant enzyme, causing browning of green vegetables (greenstuff).)
d Chlorophyllase *f*
f chlorophyllase *f*
p clorofilase *f*

1104 **chloroplast**
(Biochem.)
(Photosynthesis site located in the cytoplasm; ref. to biochemical research in nutritional science.)
d Chloroplast *n*
f chloroplaste *m*
p cloroplasto *m*

1105 **chlortetracycline**
(Biochem.)
($C_{22}H_{23}ClN_2O_8$; Nutritional science: antibiotic; origin: "Streptomyces aureofaciens"; used in foodstuff conservation.)
d Chlortetracyclin *n*
f chlortétracycline *f*
p clorotetraciclina *f*

1106 **chocolate**
(Prod.)
(Candy with a soft centre and chocolate coating; as to the legend originally named after the French Count Plessis-Praslin (1598-1675), whose cook is said to be the inventor.)
d Praline *f*
f praliné *m*; bonbon *m* au chocolat; crotte *f* en chocolat
p bombom *m* de chocolate

1107 **chocolate coating of ice cream**
(Prod.)
(Food processing technology.)
d Schokoladenüberzug *m* des Speiseeises
f couverture *f* au chocolat de la glace
p cobertura *f* de chocolate do sorvete

1108 **chocolate powder**
(Prod.)
(Food processing technology; e.g. ice cream additive.)
d Schokoladenpulver *n*
f chocolat *m* en poudre
p chocolate *m* em pó

* **chocolate truffle → 5582**

1109 **choice of vine sorts; selection of vine sorts**
(Agr.)
(Viticulture; wine production; ref. to quality characteristics.)
d Wahl *f* der Rebsorte; Auswahl *f* der Rebsorte
f choix *m* des cépages; sélection *f* des cépages
p escolha *f* da espécia da cepa; seleção *f* da espécie da cepa

1110 **cholesterol**
(Med.)
(Fat-like substance in blood. Elevated blood levels of cholesterol should be avoided as health impairing (e.g. atheroma). Also: A vitamin D precursor.)
d Cholesterin *n*
f cholestérol *m*
p colesterol *m*

1111 **cholesterolemia**
(Med.)
(Excess of cholesterol in blood.)

d Cholesterinämie *f*
f cholestérolémie *f*
p colesterinemia *f*

1112 **cholesterol in blood circulation**
(Med.)
(Nutrition in medicine.)
d Cholesterin *n* im Blutkreislauf
f cholestérol *m* dans la circulation du sang
p colesterol *m* na circulação do sangue

1113 **cholesterol level**
(Med.)
(Cholesterol concentration in blood.)
d Cholesterinspiegel *m*
f taux *m* de cholestérol
p taxa *f* de colesterol

1114 **cholesterol-rich foodstuffs**
(Prod.)
(Food processing technology; food composition.)
d cholesterinreiche Nahrungsmittel *npl*
f aliments *mpl* riches en cholestérol
p alimentos *mpl* ricos em colesterol

1115 **choline**
(Biochem.)
($C_5H_{15}NO_2$. Inhibits fatty deposits in the body. Hypotensive active agent. Synthesis of phospholipids. Also : Poultry dietary supplementation.)
d Cholin *n*
f choline *f*
p colina *f*

1116 **choline chloride**
(Med.)
($C_5H_{14}ClNO$. Lipotropic factor which promotes the utilization of fats: E.g. liver treatment. In veterinary: Nutritional factor, e.g. supplementary dietary source for poultry.)
d Cholinchlorid *n*
f chlorure *m* de choline
p cloreto *m* de colina

1117 **chondrichthyes**
(Agr.)
(Cartilaginous fish type.)
d Knorpelfische *mpl*
f chondrichtyens *mpl*
p condrictios *mpl*

* **chop → 1470**

* **chop** *v* **→ 1468**

* **chorizo sausage → 1819**

1118 **chowder**
(Prod.)
(Gastronomy; seafood soup; seafood stew.)
d Suppe *f* aus Meeresfrüchten
f potage *m* des fruits de mer
p caldeirada *f* de frutos do mar

1119 **chromatography**
(Prod.)
(Food processing technology; chromatographic analysis: Analytical method in biochemistry (e.g. in nutritional science) for identifying the composition of substances.)
d Chromatographie *f*; chromatografische Adsorptionsanalyse *f*
f chromatographie *f*
p cromatografia *f*

1120 **chromium**
(Med.)
(Cr. Trace element, in the metabolism of carbohydrates: cofactor; glucose tolerance factor.)
d Chrom *n*
f chrome *m*
p cromo *m*

1121 **chromosome**
(Med.)
(Genes-bearing threadlike structure contained in the nucleus of a cell.)
d Chromosom *n*
f chromosome *m*
p cromossomo *m*

1122 **chronic** *adj*
(Med.)
(Vitamin deficiency.)
d chronisch
f chronique
p crônico

* **chronic caffeine intoxication → 837**

1123 **chronicle respiratory disease; C.R.D.**
(Med.)
(Veterinary: Poultry; microorganism "Mycoplasma gallisapticum"; pleuropneumonia-like organisms together with "Escheria Coli".)
d chronische Atmungsbeschwerden *fpl*
f maladie *f* respiratoire chronique
p doença *f* crônica respiratória

* **chrysalis → 4505**

* **chrysophrys → 4866**

1124 **churn** *v*
(Prod.)
(Dairy process of butter production; milk and

cream churning.)
d buttern; kirnen (*Margarine*)
f baratter
p fazer manteiga

1125 **churning**
(Prod.)
(Dairy process: agitation of cream in the churn in butter production, eliminating the buttermilk.)
d Buttern *n*
f barattage *m*
p processo *m* de agitação para produção de manteiga

1126 **chyme**
(Med.)
(Also in veterinary. Partly digested food mass in the stomach.)
d Chymus *m*
f chyme *m*
p quimo *m*

1127 **chymotrypsin**
(Med.)
(Pancreas enzyme; acts in the protein digestion; splitting of proteins and polypeptides.)
d Chymotrypsin *n*
f chymotrypsine *f*
p quimotripsina *f*

1128 **cider**
(Prod.)
(Beverages. Cider: slightly alcoholic apple juice beverage; German Apfelmost: generally non-alcoholic, but in South Germany slightly alcoholic made from fermented apple juice.)
d Apfelmost *m*
f cidre *m*
p sidra *f*; cidra *f*

* **cider brandy → 382**

1129 **cider vinegar**
(Prod.)
(Food processing technology.)
d Obstessig *m*; Apfelweinessig *m*
f vinaigre *m* de cidre
p vinagre *m* de cidra

1130 **cilantro leaves; coriander leaves**
(Agr.)
(Botany. "Coriandrum sativum", used in flavouring.)
d Korianderblätter *npl*
f feuilles *fpl* de coriandre
p folhas *fpl* de coentro

1131 **ciliary protozoa**
(Med.)
(Unicellular parasitic organisms, having cilia or flagella for locomotion.)
d Wimpertierchen *npl*
f ciliés *mpl*
p ciliados *mpl*

1132 **cinchona bark infusion**
(Prod.)
(Tea of the dried bark of "Cinchona officinalis L." (C. ledgeriana).)
d Chinarinden-Aufguss *m*
f tisane *f* de l'écorce du quinquina
p infusão *f* da casca da quina

* **cineol → 1986**

* **cinnamein → 592**

* **cinnamic alcohol → 1137**

1133 **cinnamon**
(Agr.)
(Bark of various species of "Cinnamonum" used in flavouring.)
d Zimt *m*; Kaneel *m*
f cannelle *f*
p canela *f*

1134 **cinnamon bark**
(Prod.)
(Cinnamon tree "Cinnamomum zeylanicum": natural source of aroma/fragrance prime material.)
d Zimtbaumrinde *f*; Borke *f* des Zimtbaumes
f écorce *f* du cannelier
p casca *f* da canela

1135 **cinnamon oil**
(Prod.)
(Cassia oil or Chinese cinnamon oil. Aroma; flavouring agent.)
d Zimtöl *n*
f essence *f* de cannelle
p essência *f* de canela

1136 **cinnamon tincture**
(Prod.)
(Aroma/flavour research and production: extraction process.)
d Zimttinktur *f*; Zimtauszug *m*
f teinture *f* de cannelle
p tintura *f* de canela

1137 **cinnamyl alcohol; cinnamic alcohol**
(Prod.)
($C_9H_{10}O$; aroma prime material, e.g. sweet flavour; strawberry note, raspberry note.)
d Zimtalkohol *m*

f alcool *m* cinnamique
p álcool *m* cinâmico

1138 cirrostratus
(Agr.)
(Climatology. Uniform-layer type of cloud, 6,000 to 12,000 m high.)
d Schleierwolken *fpl*
f cirrostratus *m/mpl*
p cirros-estratos *mpl*; cirros-estrato *mpl*

1139 cirrus
(Agr.)
(Climatology. White clouds in form of small filaments, bearing ice crystals, 6,000 to 12,000 m high.)
d Federwolke *f*
f cirrus *m*
p cirro *m*

1140 citral
(Prod.)
($C_{10}H_{16}O$; aroma prime material, flavour chemical; e.g. in non-alcoholic drinks; lemon-peel like; flavour improver.)
d Citral *n*
f citral *m*
p citral *m*

1141 citric acid
(Prod.)
($C_6H_8O_7.H_2O$. Additive; acidulant used in confectionary, beverages etc. No. CEE: E 150.)
d Zitronensäure *f*
f acide *m* citrique
p ácido *m* cítrico

* **citric acid cycle → 3079**

1142 citronellal
(Prod.)
($C_{10}H_{18}O$; aroma prime material, e.g. citrus-like, fresh flavour note.)
d Citronellal *n*
f citronnellal *m*
p citronelal *m*

1143 citronellol
(Prod.)
($C_{10}H_{20}O$; aroma prime material.)
d Citronellol *n*
f citronnellol *m*
p citronelol *m*

1144 citronellyl nitrile
(Prod.)
(Aroma prime material, e.g. fresh herbaceous flavour note.)
d Citronellylnitril *n*
f citronnellylnitrile *m*
p citronelilnitrila *n*

1145 citrus fruits
(Agr.)
(Agricultural produce: Oranges, lemons etc.)
d Zitrusfrüchte *fpl*
f agrumes *mpl*
p frutas *fpl* cítricas

1146 citrus fruits essences
(Prod.)
(Aroma/flavour research and production; essence note.)
d Zitrusfruchtessenzen *fpl*
f essences *fpl* d'agrumes
p essências *fpl* de frutas cítricas

1147 citrus-like flavour note
(Prod.)
(Flavour note, flavour chemicals; elaboration of aromas: organic chemistry.)
d zitrusartige Geschmacksnote *f*
f note *f* de saveur citronnée
p nota *f* de sabor cítrica

* **citrus note → 2692**

1148 clarification by centrifugation; centrifugal clarification
(Prod.)
(Food processing technology: ref. to enology; also fruit juices etc.)
d Klärung *f* durch Schleudern; Klärung *f* durch Zentrifugierung
f clarification *f* par centrifugation
p clarificação *f* por centrifugação

1149 clarification by filtration
(Prod.)
(Food processing technology: ref. to enology; also fruit juices etc.)
d Klärung *f* durch Filtrierung
f clarification *f* par filtration
p clarificação *f* por filtração

* **clarification of beer → 572**

1150 clarification of the must
(Prod.)
(Enology; also fruit juices etc.)
d Klärung *f* des Mostes
f clarification *f* du moût
p clarificação *f* do mosto

1151 class
(Agr.)
(Botany; flora/fauna: Classification of living organisms; taxonomy.)
d Klasse *f*

f classe *f*
p classe *f*

1152 **classical vinification**
(Agr.)
(Viticulture.)
d klassische Weinbereitung *f*
f vinification *f* classique
p vinificação *f* clássica

1153 **claudication**
(Med.)
(Veterinary; animal raising and treatment: limping.)
d Hinken *n*
f claudication *f*
p claudicação *f*; capengar *m*

1154 **clay soil**
(Agr.)
(Soil; argillaceous soil type of very small particles, containing more than 40% of argil.)
d Tonboden *m*
f sol *m* argileux
p solo *m* argiloso

1155 **clear must; pure must**
(Prod.)
(Must from fruits, grapes etc.: product aspect.)
d klarer Most *m*
f moût *m* limpide
p mosto *m* límpido

1156 **cleft graft**
(Agr.)
(Botany; grafting method: Insertion of the scion into the cleft stock.)
d Pfropfungseinsatz *m* in den gespaltenen Wildling
f insertion *f* de greffe dans l'entaille du porte-greffe
p encaixamento *m* de ramo na fenda do porta-enxerto; garfagem *f*

1157 **clementine**
(Agr.)
(Agricultural produce. "Citrus reticulata". Type-selection by the French Trappist monk Père Clément.)
d Klementine *f*; Clementine *f*
f clémentine *f*
p tangerina *f* tipo clementina

1158 **climate-adapted varieties; varieties adapted to the climate**
(Agr.)
(Biological agriculture.)
d klimaangepasste Arten *fpl*; dem Klima angepasste Arten *fpl*
f variétés *fpl* adaptées au climat
p variedades *fpl* adaptadas ao clima

1159 **climatic conditions**
(Agr.)
(Climatology.)
d klimatische Bedingungen *fpl*
f conditions *fpl* climatiques
p condições *fpl* climáticas

1160 **climatic conditions for viticulture**
(Agr.)
(Climatology in winegrowing.)
d klimatische Bedingungen *fpl* für den Weinbau
f conditions *fpl* climatiques pour la viniculture
p condições *fpl* climáticas para a vinicultura

1161 **climatic uncertainty**
(Agr.)
(Climatology.)
d klimabezogene Ungewissheit *f*; klimatische Unsicherheit *f*
f aléa *m* climatique
p imprevisibilidade *f* climática

1162 **climatology**
(Agr.)
(Science of climates, branch of meteorology.)
d Klimakunde *f*
f climatologie *f*
p climatologia *f*

* **climber → 5713**

1163 **clinical nutrition**
(Med.)
(Nutrition in medicine.)
d klinische Ernährung *f*; Ernährung *f* in der Klinik
f nutrition *f* clinique
p nutrição *f* clínica

* **clip** *v* **→ 4947**

* **close of fermentation → 1287**

1164 **clotting salt**
(Prod.)
(Food processing technology; product characteristics.)
d verklumpendes Salz *n*
f sel *m* formant des grumeaux
p sal *m* formando torrões

* **cloudiness → 5595**

* **clouding → 5595**

1165 **clove**
(Agr.)
("Syzygium aromaticum syn. Eugenia aromatica". Used as a spice.)

d Gewürznelke *f*
f clou *m* de girofle
p cravo-da-índia *m*

1166 clove of garlic; garlic clove
(Agr.)
("Allium sativum". Bulb part, used in cookery.)
d Knoblauchzehe *f*
f gousse *f* d'ail
p dente *m* de alho

1167 clove oil
(Prod.)
(Auxiliary in confectionery; contains e.g. eugenol and vanillin.)
d Nelkenöl *n*
f essence *f* de girofle
p essência *f* de cravos-da-índia

1168 clover
(Agr.)
(Botany: "Trifolium"; e.g. leguminous forage herbs; also used as green manure (in biological agriculture).)
d Klee *m*
f trèfle *m*
p trevo *m*

1169 cluster; bunch
(Agr.)
(Botany; cluster of grapes; bunch of grapes.)
d Traube *f*
f grappe *f*
p cacho *m*

1170 cluster of grapes; bunch of grapes
(Agr.)
(Viticulture.)
d Weintraube *f*
f grappe *f* de raisin; raisin *m*
p cacho *m* de uvas

1171 coagulable *adj*
(Prod.)
(Dairy process; e.g. proteins becoming insoluble. Rennin is an enzyme that coagulates milk.)
d gerinnbar; koagulierbar
f coagulable
p coagulável

1172 coagulate *v*
(Prod.)
(Food processing technology.)
d koagulieren; gerinnen
f coaguler; cailler (*milk*)
p coagular

1173 coagulation
(Prod.)
(Dairy process. Proteins become insoluble. Rennin is an enzyme that coagulates milk.)
d Koagulation *f*; Koagulieren *n*; Gerinnen *n*
f coagulation *f*; coagulage *m* (*du lait*)
p coagulação *f*

1174 coagulation process
(Biochem.)
(Nutritional science: e.g. referring to the passage of a colloidal substance from a sol (a fluid colloidal system) to a gel (a more solid colloid).)
d Koagulationsprozess *m*; Gerinnungsprozess *m*
f processus *m* de coagulation
p processo *m* de coagulação

1175 coarse brown bread; peasant bread
(Prod.)
(Bakery product.)
d Landbrot *n*; Bauernbrot *n*
f pain *m* de campagne
p pão *m* preto grosso; pão *m* da roça

1176 coarse-grained salt
(Prod.)
(Food processing technology; salt type, having a coarse grain of small crystals.)
d grobgekörntes Salz *n*
f sel *m* grenu
p sal *m* grosso

1177 coarsely grained
(Prod.)
(Food processing technology: powder aspect definition.)
d grobkörnig
f granulé grossièrement; grenu
p granulado de forma grossa

1178 coating for food stuff protection
(Prod.)
(Food processing technology: This kind of protection coating is in some cases made of an edible substance.)
d Schutzüberzug *m* eines Lebensmittels
f enrobage *m* protecteur d'un produit alimentaire
p revestimento *m* protetor de um produto alimentício; cobertura *f* protetora de um produto alimentício

1179 cobalamin reduction
(Biochem.)
(Vitamin B_{12} activity.)
d Cobalaminreduktion *f*
f réduction *f* de la cobalamine
p redução *f* da cobalamina

1180 **cobalt**
(Biochem.)
(Co. Micromineral; contained in the structure of vitamin B_{12}.)
d Kobalt *n*
f cobalt *m*
p cobalto *m*

1181 **cobalt deficiency**
(Agr.)
(Livestock breeding; animal nutrition: mineral deficiency causing various diseases in farm animals.)
d Kobaltmangel *m*
f carence *f* en cobalt
p deficiência *f* de cobalto

1182 **cocarboxylase**
(Biochem.)
($C_{12}H_{19}ClN_4O_7P_2S.H_2O$. Nutritional science: coenzyme; important for decarboxylation processes, e.g. decomposition of "glucides" and their transformation in lipids.)
d Cocarboxylase *f*
f cocarboxylase *f*
p cocarboxilase *f*

1183 **coccus; spherical bacteria**
(Med.)
(Veterinary; microorganism; parasites.)
d Kokken *fpl*; Kugelbakterien *fpl*
f cocci *mpl*; bactéries *fpl* sphériques
p cocos *mpl*; bactérias *fpl* de forma arredondada

1184 **cochineal**
(Prod.)
(Red foodstuff colorant (e.g. used in yoghurts) made from the cochineal "Dactylopius coccus" insect; contains carminic acid, $C_{22}H_{20}O_{13}$; carmine.)
d Koschenille *f*
f cochenille *f*
p cochonila *f*; cochinilha
f

1185 **cochineal tincture**
(Prod.)
(Aroma//flavour research and production: extraction process; cochineal is used as food dye, e.g. in yoghurts.)
d Cochenilletinktur *f*; Koschenilleauszug *m*; Auszug *m* der roten Schildlaus
f teinture *f* de cochenille
p tintura *f* de cochonilha

1186 **cock**
(Agr.)
(Poultry breeding. "Gallus gallus". Male domestic fowl.)
d Hahn *m*
f coq *m*
p galo *m*

1187 **cockerel**
(Agr.)
(Poultry farming: "Gallus gallus". Young male fowl.)
d Hähnchen *n*
f petit coq *m*; poulet *m*
p galeto *m*; frango *m* novo

* **cockscomb → 1242**

1188 **cocktail snack**
(Prod.)
(Confectionary; small cereal products, e.g. salty biscuit, cookies.)
d Cocktailhappen *m*; zum Cocktail gereichter Appetithappen *m*
f amuse-gueule *m* servi avec le cocktail
p salgadinho *m* para coquetel

1189 **cocoa**
(Prod.)
(Powdered cacao beans; ingredient; prime material.)
d Kakaopulver *n*
f cacao *m* en poudre
p cacau *m* em pó

* **cocoa butter → 832**

1190 **coconut**
(Agr.)
(Agricultural produce; coconut-palm fruit.)
d Kokosnuss *f*
f coco *m*; noix *f* de coco
p coco *m*

1191 **coconut milk**
(Prod.)
(Gastronomy.)
d Kokosmilch *f*
f lait *m* de coco
p leite *m* de coco

1192 **coconut oil; copra oil**
(Prod.)
(Fatty oil extracted from the fleshy part of the coconut.)
d Kokosöl *n*; Kopra-Öl *n*
f huile *f* de coco; huile *f* de copra(h)
p óleo *m* de coco; copraol *m*

1193 **cocoon**
(Agr.)
(Biological agriculture: pest: covering of a larva while it passes through the pupa stage.)
d Kokon *m*
f cocon *m*
p casulo *m*

1194 cod; small cod
(Agr.)
(Young codfish, e.g. small cod of the Baltic sea.)
d Dorsch *f*
f petite morue *f*
p badejo *m*

1195 codfish
(Prod.)
(Cod family "Gadidae"; fresh codfish; seafood. German Dorsch is a small cod, esp. from the Baltic Sea.)
d Kabeljau *m*
f morue *f*; cabillaud *m*
p bacalhau *m*

1196 cod-liver oil
(Prod.)
(Natural vitamin source (A and D). Prime material. From cod (family "Gadidae").)
d Kabeljaulebertran *m*
f huile *f* de foi de morue
p óleo *m* de fígado de bacalhau

1197 coenzyme
(Biochem.)
(Nutritional science: Certain vitamins are coenzyme precursors.)
d Coenzym *n*
f coenzyme *m/f*
p coenzima *f*

1198 coffee; real coffee
(Agr.)
(Agricultural produce. Genus "Coffea"; prepared from the seeds by roasting and grinding etc.)
d Kaffee *m*; Bohnenkaffee *m*
f café *m*; café *m* en grains
p café *m*; café *m* em grãos

1199 coffee bean
(Agr.)
(Agricultural produce. Genus "Coffea"; seeds of the coffee plant.)
d Kaffeebohne *f*
f grain *m* de café
p grão *m* de café

1200 coffee extract
(Prod.)
(Food processing technology.)
d Kaffee-Extrakt *m*
f extrait *m* de café
p extrato *m* de café

1201 coffee grounds
(Prod.)
(Coffee residue e.g. in the cup.)
d Kaffeesatz *m*
f marc *m* de café
p borra *f* do café

1202 coffee of low caffeine contents
(Prod.)
(Food processing technology: caffeine extraction from coffee by means of organic solvents.)
d koffeinarmer Kaffee *m*
f café *m* pauvre en caféine
p café *m* com baixo teor de cafeína

1203 coffee powder
(Prod.)
(Food processing technology.)
d Kaffeepulver *n*
f café *m* en poudre
p café *m* em pó

1204 coffee roasting
(Prod.)
(Food processing technology.)
d Kaffeerösten *n*; Kaffeeröstung *f*
f torréfaction *f* du café
p torrefação *f* do café

1205 cognac
(Prod.)
(Beverages. Brandy, distilled from white wine, produced in a region of France.)
d Cognac *m*
f cognac *m*
p conhaque *m*

1206 cohesion of meat particles
(Biochem.)
(Nutritional science; ref. to restructured meat in meat processing.)
d Kohäsion *f* von Fleischteilchen; innerer Zusammenhalt *m* von Fleischteilchen
f cohésion *f* des particules de la viande
p coesão *f* das partículas da carne

*** coitus → 1354**

1207 cola drink
(Prod.)
(Carbonated beverage on the basis e.g. of fruit and kola nut extracts)
d Kolagetränk *n*
f cola *m*
p bebida *f* à base de cola

1208 cold conservation
(Prod.)
(Food processing technology.)
d Kältekonservierung *f*
f conservation *f* par le froid
p conservação *f* pelo frio

1209 **cold cuts**
(Prod.)
(Butchery.)
d Aufschnitt *m*
f viande *f* froide en tranches
p frios *mpl*

1210 **cold dispersible dry powder**
(Prod.)
(Food processing technology, product characteristic.)
d kaltdispergierbares Trockenpulver *n*
f poudre *f* sèche dispersible à froid
p pó *m* seco dispersível a frio

1211 **cold expression**
(Prod.)
(Aroma/flavour research and production: separation process.)
d Kaltauspressen *n*
f expression *f* à froid
p expressão *f* a frio

1212 **cold extraction of essential oils**
(Prod.)
(Food processing technology; prime material processing; also: ref. to aroma/flavour research and production.)
d kalte Essenzextraktion *f*, Auszug *m* ätherischer Öle auf kaltem Wege
f extraction *f* d'essence à froid
p extração *f* de óleos essenciais a frio

1213 **cold meat assortment**
(Prod.)
(Gastronomy; cold assortment of beef, ham etc.)
d kalte Platte *f*
f assiette *f* anglaise
p prato *m* de frios sortidos

1214 **cold storage**
(Prod.)
(Foodstuff storage method.)
d Aufbewahrung *f* unter Kühlung; Einlagerung *f* unter Kühlung; Kühllagerung *f*
f emmagasinage *m* sous réfrigération; entreposage *m* sous réfrigération; entreposage *m* frigorifique
p armazenamento *m* sob refrigeração

1215 **cold water dispersible**
(Prod.)
(Product property. Product characteristic in processing.)
d dispergierbar in kaltem Wasser
f dispersible à l'eau froide
p dispersível em água fria

1216 **cold water dispersible dry vitamin powder**
(Prod.)
(Vitamin presentation form.)
d Vitamintrockenpulver *n* dispergierbar in kaltem Wasser
f poudre *f* sèche vitaminique dispersible dans l'eau froide
p pó *m* vitamínico seco dispersível em água fria

* **coleslaw → 4994**

1217 **coliform bacteria**
(Med.)
(Enterobacter; Escherichia; Klebsielle.)
d Kolibakterien *fpl*
f colibacilles *mpl*
p bactérias *fpl* coliformes

1218 **colitis**
(Med.)
(Inflammation of the colon.)
d Kolitis *f*
f colite *f*
p colite *f*

1219 **collagenous tissue**
(Med.)
(Anatomy: Fibrous protein within the connective skin tissue, bones etc. Approx. 1/3 of the body protein of mammals.)
d Kollagen *n*
f collagène *m*
p colágeno *m*; colagênio *m*

* **collagen proportion → 1220**

1220 **collagen rate; collagen proportion**
(Prod.)
(Food processing evaluation methods: Fibrous protein; rate of collagen is used in analytical evaluation of meat products.)
d Kollagenanteil *m*
f taux *m* de collagène
p taxa *f* de colágeno; cota *f* de colagênio

1221 **collagen structure**
(Med.)
(Anatomy.)
d Kollagenstruktur *f*
f structure *f* collagénique
p estrutura *f* do colágeno; estrutura *f* do colagênio

1222 **collect *v* the liquids**
(Prod.)
(Aroma/flavour production: ref. to distillation processes.)
d Flüssigkeiten auffangen
f recueillir les liquides
p recolher os líquidos

1223 **colloid**
(Biochem.)
(Nutritional science: Particles dispersed within another substance: e.g. milk, gelatin and resins.)
d Kolloid *n*
f colloïde *m*
p colóide *m*

1224 **colloidal clay**
(Prod.)
(Food processing technology; used in the production of beer, wine and juices in clarification processes.)
d kolloidaler Ton *m*
f argile *f* colloïdale
p argila *f* coloidal

1225 **colloidal colorant**
(Biochem.)
(Food biochemistry.)
d kolloidaler Farbstoff *m*
f colorant *m* colloïdal
p corante *m* coloidal

1226 **colloidal material**
(Biochem.)
(Nutritional science: colloidal chemistry.)
d kolloidales Material *n*
f matière *f* colloïdale
p material *m* coloidal

1227 **colloidal movement; Brownian movement**
(Biochem.)
(Nutritional science: colloidal chemistry; random movement of microscopic solid particles, as to British Botanist Robert Brown (1773-1858).)
d kolloidale Bewegung *f*; Brownsche Bewegung *f*
f mouvement *m* colloïdal; mouvement *m* brownien
p movimento *m* coloidal; movimento *m* de Brown

1228 **colloidal-osmotic pressure**
(Biochem.)
(Nutritional science: colloidal chemistry.)
d kolloidal-osmotischer Druck *m*
f pression *f* colloïde-osmotique
p pressão *f* coloidal-osmótica

1229 **colloidal solution**
(Biochem.)
(Nutritional science: colloidal chemistry.)
d kolloidale Lösung *f*
f solution *f* colloïdale
p solução *f* coloidal

1230 **colloidal state**
(Biochem.)
(Nutritional science: colloidal chemistry.)
d kolloidaler Zustand *m*
f état *m* colloïdal
p estado *m* coloidal

1231 **colloidal system**
(Biochem.)
(Nutritional science: colloidal chemistry; ref. to colloid behaviour.)
d kolloidales System *n*
f système *m* colloïdal
p sistema *m* coloidal

1232 **Colorado potato beetle**
(Agr.)
(Biological agriculture. "Leptinotarsa decemlineata"; pest problem: potato beetle that feeds on potato leaves.)
d Kartoffelkäfer *m*; Koloradokäfer *m*
f doryphore *m*
p caruncho *m*; broca *f*; escaravelho *m* da batateira

1233 **colorant**
(Prod.)
(Foodstuff colorant.)
d Farbstoff *m*
f matière *f* colorante
p corante *m*

1234 **colostrum**
(Med.)
(Veterinary science, e.g. ref. to bovines: transmission of antibodies and immunoglobulin to the young cattle.)
d Vormilch *f*; Kolostrum *n*
f colostrum *m*
p colostro *m*

1235 **colour**
(Prod.)
(Food processing and gastronomy; ref. to product aspect.)
d Farbe *f*
f couleur *f*
p cor *f*

1236 **colour improvement**
(Prod.)
(Food processing technology; production of beer, wine and juices.)
d Farbverbesserung *f*
f amélioration *f* de la couleur
p melhora *f* na coloração

1237 **colour intensification**
(Biochem.)
(Nutritional science: Enology.)
d Farbintensivierung *f*; Farbverstärkung *f*

f intensification *f* de la couleur
p intensificação *f* da cor

1238 **colour lakes**
(Prod.)
(Foodstuff colorant.)
d Farblacke *mpl*
f laques *mpl* colorants
p corantes *mpl* em forma de laca

1239 **colour modification**
(Biochem.)
(Enology, e.g. certain chemical process in red wines during aging.)
d Farbveränderung *f*
f modification *f* de la couleur
p modificação *f* da cor

1240 **coltsfoot**
(Agr.)
(Botany: "Tussilago farfara", "Tussilago integerrima". Coughwort. Medicinal plant.)
d Huflattich *m*
f tussilage *m*; pas-d'âne *m*
p tussilagem *f*; unha-de-cavalo *f*

1241 **column chromatography**
(Prod.)
(Chromatographic analysis: Analytical method in food processing technology.)
d Säulenchromatographie *f*
f chromatographie *f* sur colonnes
p cromatografia *f* em colunas

1242 **comb; cockscomb**
(Agr.)
(Poultry farming. Soft red crest on the top of the head of domestic fowl.)
d Kamm *m*; Hahnenkamm *m*
f crête *f*; crête *f* de coq
p crista *f*; crista *f* de galo

* **combined diet → 3596**

1243 **comfrey**
(Agr.)
(Botany: "Symphytum officinalis L."; medicinal herb.)
d Beinwell *m*; Schwarzwurz *f*
f grande consoude *f*
p consólida *f*; consolda *f*

1244 **coming up; sprouting; germination**
(Agr.)
(Botany; springing up of a plant.)
d Keimen *n*; Treiben *n*
f pousse *f*
p brotamento *m*; brotadura *f*; germinação *f*; brotação *f*

1245 **common bile duct**
(Med.)
(Anatomy; resulting from the junction of the common hepatic duct and the cystic duct.)
d gemeinsamer Gallengang *m*
f canal *m* cholédoque
p canal *m* colédoco

1246 **common hepatic duct**
(Med.)
(Anatomy; hepatic duct; bile duct, transporting bile from the liver.)
d Lebergang *m*
f canal *m* hépatique
p canal *m* hepático comum

1247 **common rice**
(Agr.)
(Agricultural produce. Rice which has not yet undergone any treatment.)
d gemeiner Reis *m*
f riz *m* ordinaire
p arroz *m* comum

* **communicable disease → 5553**

1248 **comparison between biologic agriculture and conventional agriculture**
(Agr.)
(Biological agriculture: evaluation of activity, results etc.)
d Vergleich *m* zwischen der biologischen Landwirtschaft und der herkömmlichen Landwirtschaft
f comparaison *f* entre l'agriculture biologique et l'agriculture conventionnelle
p comparação *f* entre a agriculture biológica e a agricultura convencional

1249 **complementary characteristics of the bases**
(Biochem.)
(Ref. to DNA double helix.)
d Basenkomplementarität *f*
f caractéristiques *fpl* complémentaires des bases; complémentarité *f* des bases
p caraterísticas *fpl* complementares das bases entre si

1250 **complementary feed supply**
(Agr.)
(Livestock nutrition.)
d zusätzliche Futermittelzufuhr *f*
f apport *m* complémentaire de fourrage
p aporte *m* complementar de forragens; fornecimento *m* complementar de forragens

1251 **complementation**
(Prod.)
(Food processing technology; addition to foodstuffs of nutritional auxiliary products.)

d Komplementierung *f*; Zugabe *f*
f complémentation *f*
p complementação *f*

* **complete clear** *adj* → **1254**

1252 complete fermentation
(Biochem.)
(Fermentation; e.g. in beer production, wine production etc.)
d Ausgärung *f*
f fermentation *f* totale
p fermentação *f* total

1253 complete fertilizer
(Agr.)
(Soil treatment. Fertilizer type, containing nitrogen (N), potassium (K), and phosphorus (P).)
d Volldünger *m*
f engrais *m* intégral
p adubo *m* integral

1254 complete limpid *adj*; **complete clear** *adj*
(Biochem.)
(Food biochemistry, products etc.)
d vollkommen klar; vollständig rein
f parfaitement limpide
p completamente límpido

1255 complex
(Biochem.)
(Nutritional science; ref. to chemical associations.)
d Komplex *m*
f complexe *m*
p complexo *m*

1256 complex aroma
(Prod.)
(Aroma/flavour association.)
d komplexes Aroma *n*
f arôme *m* complexe
p aroma *m* complexo

1257 complex compounds
(Prod.)
(Aroma/flavour research of synthetic material.)
d komplexe Zusammensetzungen *fpl*; komplexe Verbindungen *fpl*
f composés *mpl* complexes
p compostos *mpl* complexos

1258 complex-forming ability
(Biochem.)
(Nutritional science.)
d Komplexbildungsfähigkeit *f*
f aptitude *f* à former des complexes
p abilidade *f* de formar complexos

1259 components of odoriferous material; fragrance components
(Prod.)
(In research of synthetic aroma/flavour chemicals and flavour notes.)
d Riechstoffbestandteile *npl*
f constituants *mpl* odorants
p componentes *mpl* de matérias odoríferas; componentes *mpl* de fragrâncias

1260 composition of agricultural products
(Agr.)
(Agricultural produce; ref. e.g. to further treatment, processing, for standardizing purposes.)
d Zusammensetzung *f* der Landwirtschaftsprodukte
f composition *f* des produits agricoles
p composição *f* dos produtos agrícolas

1261 composition of biologic agricultural products
(Agr.)
(Biological agriculture and its production.)
d Zusammensetzung *f* der Produkte der biologischen Landwirtschaft; Zusammensetzung *f* der Produkte biologischer Agrikultur
f composition *f* des produits de l'agriculture biologique
p composição *f* dos produtos da agricultura biológica

1262 composition of bread
(Prod.)
(Bakery; ref. to ingredients e.g. milk, fatty bodies, sugar.)
d Brotzusammensetzung *f*
f composition *f* du pain
p composição *f* do pão

1263 composition of cereal grain
(Biochem.)
(Nutritional science: share in carbohydrate e.g. as starch, fatty bodies, proteins, water.)
d Getreidekornzusammensetzung *f*
f composition *f* du grain de céréale
p composição *f* do grão de cereal

1264 composition of cow's milk
(Biochem.)
(Food biochemistry: e.g. containing: proteins; calcium; phosphorus; lipids; water; lactose.)
d Zusammensetzung *f* der Kuhmilch
f composition *f* du lait de vache
p composição *f* do leite de vaca

1265 composition of margarines
(Prod.)
(Food processing technology; e.g. dairy

product made from vegetable oil, skim milk etc.)
d Zusammensetzung *f* der Margarinen
f composition *f* des margarines
p composição *f* das margarinas

1266 **composition of mineral elements**
(Prod.)
(Water supply; ref. to mineral water quality.)
d Mineralstoffzusammensetzung *f*
f composition *f* en corps minéraux
p composição *f* referente dos minerais; composição *f* do teor mineral

1267 **composition of odoriferous components**
(Prod.)
(Aroma/flavour research.)
d Komposition *f* von Riechstoffkomponenten
f composition *f* en composés odorants
p composição *f* de componentes odoríficos

1268 **composition of the buccal microflora**
(Med.)
(Microflora of the mouth, influenced by saccharose (cane sugar) intake.)
d Zusammensetzung *f* der Mikroflora des Mundes; Zusammensetzung *f* der Mikroflora der Mundhöhle
f composition *f* de la microflore buccale
p composição *f* da microflora bucal

1269 **composition of the foodstuff ration**
(Prod.)
(Food processing technology.)
d Zusammenstellung *f* der Nahrungsmittelration
f composition *f* de la ration alimentaire
p composição *f* da ração alimentícia; composição *f* da ração de alimentos

1270 **compost**
(Agr.)
(Mixture of organic matter for fertilizing; ref. to organic agriculture; organic farming; concern of biological agriculture.)
d Kompost *m*
f compost *m*
p adubo *m* orgânico

1271 **compote**
(Prod.)
(Sweet cooked fruit dessert; e.g. confectionery's product.)
d Kompott *n*
f compote *f*
p compota *f*

1272 **compound eye**
(Agr.)
(Apiculture: Bee anatomy: bee eye.)
d Insektenauge *n*; Facettenauge *n*; Netzauge *n*
f œil *m* composé; œil *m* à facettes
p olho *m* composto

1273 **compound fertilizer**
(Agr.)
(Soil treatment. Fertilizer compound, containing various active agents.)
d Mehrnährstoffdünger *m*
f engrais *m* complet
p fertilizante *m* composto

1274 **compounds having antioxidant activity**
(Biochem.)
(Nutritional science; ref. to restructured meat in meat processing.)
d Verbindungen *fpl* mit Antioxidantwirkung
f composés *mpl* ayant de l'activité antioxydante
p compostos *mpl* tendo atividade antioxidante

1275 **compounds of the family of terpenoids**
(Prod.)
(Basis of fragrance/aroma prime material.)
d Verbindungen *fpl* der Familie der Terpenoide
f composés *mpl* de la famille des terpénoïdes
p compostos *mpl* da família dos terpenóides

1276 **compression**
(Agr.)
(Ref. to soil treatment, biological agriculture:soil compression (by passing with heavy machines) harms its structure.)
d Zusammendrücken *n*
f tassement *m*
p compressão *f*

1277 **concentrate**
(Prod.)
(Food processing technology; fruit juices, vegetable products are produced from concentrates obtained by thermal treatment of originally hydrated raw material: Reconstituted food.)
d Konzentrat *n*
f concentré *m*
p concentrado *m*

1278 **concentrated fruit juices**
(Prod.)
(Aroma/flavour research and production.)
d konzentrierte Fruchtsäfte *mpl*
f jus *mpl* concentrés de fruits
p sucos *mpl* de frutas concentrados

1279 **concentrated poultry ration**
(Agr.)
(Poultry farming; ref. to poultry nutrition.)
d Geflügelfutterkonzentrat *n*
f ration *f* avicole concentrée
p ração *f* concentrada para aves

1280 concentrated sugared milk types
(Med.)
(Baby nutrition.)
d gezuckerte konzentrierte Milchsorten *fpl*
f laits *mpl* concentrés sucrés
p qualidades *fpl* de leite concentrados açucarados

1281 concentration
(Prod.)
(Food processing technology, the process of concentrating.)
d Konzentration *f*
f concentration *f*
p concentração *f*

1282 concentration appreciation
(Med.)
(Olfactory stimulation, nervous cells system: aroma/flavour research: ref. to odoriferous molecules.)
d Konzentrationsbeurteilung *f*; Abschätzung *f* der Konzentration
f appréciation *f* de la concentration
p apreciação *f* de concentração

1283 concentration by evaporation
(Prod.)
(Food processing technology, e.g. of milk.)
d Konzentration *f* durch Verdampfung
f concentration *f* par évaporation
p concentração *f* por evaporação

1284 concentration of juices
(Prod.)
(Aroma/flavour research and production.)
d Saftkonzentrierung *f*
f concentration *f* des jus
p concentração *f* de sucos

1285 concentration of tannins
(Biochem.)
(Enology.)
d Gerbstoffkonzentration *f*
f concentration *f* des tanins; concentration *f* des tannins
p concentração *f* dos taninos

1286 concentration process
(Prod.)
(Food processing technology: e.g. evaporation.)
d Konzentrationsverfahren *n*
f procédé *m* de concentration
p processo *m* de concentração

1287 conclusion of fermentation; close of fermentation
(Biochem.)
(Nutritional science.)
d Beendigung *f* der Gärung
f achèvement *m* de la fermentation
p conclusão *f* da fermentação

1288 concrete
(Prod.)
(Flavour/fragrance research and production: Essence prepared by extraction and evaporation.)
d Konkret *n*
f concrète *f*
p concreto *m*

1289 condensation
(Prod.)
(Conversion from the vapor state to the liquid or solid state.)
d Kondensation *f*
f condensation *f*
p condensação *f*

1290 condensation liquid
(Prod.)
(Aroma/flavour production: ref. to distillation processes.)
d Kondensationsflüssigkeit *f*
f liquide *m* de condensation
p líquido *m* de condensação

1291 condensation product of amino acid
(Prod.)
(Aspartame: aspartic acid and phenylalanine.)
d Kondensationsprodukt *n* der Aminosäuren
f produit *m* de condensation des amino-acides
p produto *m* de condensação dos aminoácidos

* **condensed milk → 1991**

1292 condensed phase
(Prod.)
(Aroma/flavour production: ref. to distillation processes.)
d kondensierte Phase *f*
f phase *f* condensée
p fase *f* condensada

1293 condensed whey
(Prod.)
(Subproduct of dairy food processing technology: originated from serum evaporation, fat content approx. 50%; used in animal feeding.)
d kondensierte Molke *f*; Kondensmolke *f*
f lactosérum *m* concentré
p lacto-soro *m* condensado; soro *m* concentrado de leite

1294 condiment; seasoning
(Prod.)
(Natural products for flavour intensification:

e.g. mustard, vinegar; ingredients.)
d Würze *f*
f condiment *m*
p condimento *m*

1295 **conductibility**
(Med.)
(Olfactory stimulation, nervous cells system: aroma/flavour research: ref. to odoriferous molecules.)
d Leitfähigkeit *f*
f conductibilité *f*
p condutibilidade *f*

1296 **confectionary**
(Prod.)
(Sweets, chocolates, all types of cakes and flans, layer cakes and fruit tarts.)
d Konditoreiware *fpl*; Süßwaren *fpl*
f confiseries *fpl*
p produtos *mpl* de confeitaria

* **confectioner's sugar → 2831**

1297 **conformation of polypeptide chains**
(Biochem.)
(Nutritional science: protein biochemistry: ref. to protein structure.)
d Aufbau *m* der Polypeptidketten
f conformation *f* des chaînes polypeptidiques
p conformação *f* das cadeias polipeptídicas

1298 **congeal** *v*
(Prod.)
(Food processing technology.)
d gefrieren
f congeler
p congelar

1299 **conger eel**
(Agr.)
("Conger oceanicus"; marine eel; edible fish.)
d Meeraal *m*
f congre *m*; anguille *f* de mer
p congro *m*

1300 **conic papilla**
(Med.)
(Anatomy; one kind of tongue protuberance related to the taste buds.)
d konische Zungenpapille *f*; konische Geschmacksknospe *f*
f papille *f* conique
p papila *f* cônica

* **coniferous trees → 1301**

1301 **conifers; coniferous trees**
(Agr.)
(Botany. Evergreen trees, gymnosperms, with needle leaves; their softwood is used for timber or in industrialization processes, as pulp prime material.)
d Nadelhölzer *npl*; Koniferen *fpl*
f conifères *fpl*
p árvores *fpl* coníferas

1302 **conjugated proteins**
(Biochem.)
(Nutritional science; single proteins: constituted only of amino acids. Conjugated proteins: constituted of amino acid and other substances.)
d zusammengesetzte Proteine *npl*
f protéines *fpl* conjuguées
p proteínas *fpl* conjugadas

1303 **conjunctivitis**
(Med.)
(Can be the consequence of vitamin B_2 deficiency.)
d Bindehautentzündung *f*
f conjonctivite *f*
p conjuntivite *f*

1304 **consanguinity**
(Med.)
(Veterinary: Importance in breed classification and determination and in productivity.)
d Blutsverwandtschaft *f*
f consanguinité *f*
p consangüinidade *f*

1305 **consecutive flowering time**
(Agr.)
(Biological agriculture.)
d aufeinanderfolgende Blütezeiten *fpl*
f floraisons *fpl* échelonnées
p florescências *fpl* consecutivas

1306 **consequences of the interruption of fermentation**
(Biochem.)
(Fermentation in nutritional science.)
d Folgen *fpl* der Gärungsstockung; Folgen *fpl* des Gärungsabbruches
f conséquences *fpl* de l'arrêt de la fermentation
p conseqüências *fpl* da paralização da fermentação

1307 **conservation**
(Prod.)
(Food conservation processes; preservation.)
d Haltbarmachung *f*
f conservation *f*
p conservação *f*

1308 **conservation temperatures**
(Prod.)
(Food processing technology.)

d Konservierungstemperaturen *fpl*
f températures *fpl* de conservation
p temperaturas *fpl* de conservação

1309 **consistency**
(Biochem.)
(Nutritional science: product characteristic: ref. e.g. to adherence properties of a product.)
d Konsistenz *f*
f consistance *f*
p consistência *f*

1310 **consistent dough; firm dough**
(Prod.)
(Bakery.)
d fester Teig *m*
f pâte *f* consistante
p massa *f* consistente

1311 **consommé; beef broth**
(Prod.)
(Gastronomy. Clear soup; beef stock.)
d Fleischbrühe *f*
f bouillon *m* de viande
p caldo *m* de carne

1312 **constipation; obstipation**
(Med.)
(Roughage-rich diet can be prescribed.)
d Stuhlverstopfung *f*; Obstipation *f*
f constipation *f*
p constipação *f*; prisão *f* de ventre

1313 **constitution of the cluster of grapes**
(Agr.)
(Viticulture; bunch of grapes; ref. to the biologic constitution of the fruit.)
d Verfassung *f* der Weintraube; Konstitution *f* der Weintraube
f constitution *f* de la grappe de raisin
p constituição *f* do cacho de uvas

1314 **consumer goods**
(Prod.)
(Food processing technology; foodstuff production; goods which directly satisfy human needs and wishes.)
d Konsumgüter *npl*
f biens *mpl* de consommation
p bens *mpl* de consumo

1315 **consumer goods industry**
(Prod.)
(Food processing technology; foodstuff production and marketing; goods which directly satisfy human needs and wishes.)
d Konsumgüterindustrie *f*
f industrie *f* de biens de consommation
p indústria *f* de bens de consumo

1316 **consumption of animal fat**
(Prod.)
(Food processing technology.)
d Tierfettkonsum *m*; Konsum *m* tierischer Fette
f consommation *f* de graisse animale
p consumo *m* de gordura animal

1317 **consumption of cereals**
(Agr.)
(Agricultural produce and marketing.)
d Getreidekonsum *m*
f consommation *f* des céréales
p consumo *m* de cereais

1318 **consumption of veal**
(Prod.)
(Gastronomy; calf meat.)
d Kalbfleischkonsum *m*
f consommation *f* de veau
p consumo *m* de carne de vitela

1319 **consumption of vegetable fat**
(Prod.)
(Food processing technology.)
d Pflanzenfettkonsum *m*; Konsum *m* pflanzlicher Fette
f consommation *f* de graisse végétale
p consumo *m* de gordura vegetal

1320 **contact poison**
(Agr.)
(Ref. to insecticides.)
d Kontaktgift *n*
f poison *m* de contact
p toxina *f* de contato

1321 **contain *v* erosion; dam *v* erosion**
(Agr.)
(Soil treatment.)
d Erosion eindämmen
f endiguer l'érosion
p conter a erosão

1322 **contaminated food**
(Biochem.)
(Food biochemistry.)
d infizierte Lebensmittel *npl*; verseuchte Lebensmittel *npl*
f denrées *fpl* contaminées
p alimentos *mpl* contaminados

1323 **content**
(Prod.)
(Food processing technology.)
d Gehalt *m*
f teneur *f*; richesse *f*
p conteúdo *m*; teor *m*

1324 **content of dry matter; rate of dry matter**
(Prod.)
(Aroma/flavour research and production,

distillation/extraction processes.)
d Trockenstoffgehalt *m*
f taux *m* de matière sèche
p taxa *f* de matéria seca

1325 content of esters
(Biochem.)
(Aroma/fragrance research and production in food biochemistry.)
d Gehalt *m* an Estern
f teneur *f* en esters
p teor *m* de ésteres

* **contents of residual sugar in the grape marc → 4680**

* **continuity of taste perception → 4114**

1326 continuous cheese-making process
(Prod.)
(Dairy plant technology.)
d kontinuierliches Käseherstellungsverfahren *n*
f procédé *m* de fabrication continuée de fromage
p processo *m* contínuo de produção de queijo

1327 continuous countercurrent extraction
(Prod.)
(Aroma/flavour research and production, ref. to extraction processes.)
d kontinuierliche Gegenstromextraktion *f*
f extraction *f* à contre-courant continu
p extração *f* a contracorrente contínua

1328 continuous current
(Prod.)
(Aroma/flavour production technology: solvents in extraction processes.)
d kontinuierlicher Strom *m*; stetiger Strom *m*
f courant *m* continu
p corrente *f* contínua

1329 continuous cutting of frozen meat blocks
(Prod.)
(Food processing technology; ref. to meat industrialization.)
d kontinuierliche Zerkleinerung *f* von Gefrierfleischblöcken
f découpe *f* continue de blocs de viande congelée
p trituração *f* contínua de blocos de carne congelada

1330 continuous extraction
(Prod.)
(Aroma/flavour research and production.)
d kontinuierliche Extraktion *f*
f extraction *f* continue
p extração *f* contínua

1331 continuous intestinal irrigation
(Med.)
(Irrigation process of washing a hollow organ, e.g. with water.)
d Dauereinlauf *m*; fortdauernde Darmspülung *f*; Dauerklistier *n*
f irrigation *f* intestinale continue
p lavagem *f* intestinal contínua; clister *m* contínuo

1332 continuous liquid agitation
(Prod.)
(Food processing technology.)
d kontinuierliche intensive Flüssigkeitsbewegung *f*
f agitation *f* continue du liquide
p agitação *f* contínua do líquido

1333 continuous rectification
(Prod.)
(Food processing technology.)
d kontinuierliche Rektifikation *f*; stetige Rektifikation *f*
f rectification *f* continue
p retificação *f* contínua

1334 contractions; labour
(Med.)
(Veterinary; ref. to cattle breeding, cattle reproduction and treatment.)
d Zusammenziehungen *fpl*; Wehen *fpl*
f contractions *fpl*
p contrações *fpl*

* **controlled continuation of the fermentation process → 20**

1335 convalescent diet; diet of convalescence
(Med.)
(Diet for gradually recovering health after sickness.)
d Rekonvaleszenzdiät *f*; Genesungsdiät *f*; Diät *f* der Gesundung
f diète *f* de convalescence; diète *f* reconstituante
p dieta *f* de convalescença; dieta *f* reconstituinte

1336 convenience food
(Prod.)
(Food processing technology. Foodstuff which is prepared for easy and immediate consumption.)
d Lebensmittelfertigprodukt *n*
f aliment *m* prêt à l'emploi
p produtos *mpl* alimentícios de conveniência; alimentos *mpl* prontos para consumo

1337 conventional agriculture
(Agr.)
(Opposed to biological agriculture.)
d konventionelle Landwirtschaft *f*; herkömmlicher Ackerbau *m*

f agriculture *f* conventionnelle
p agricultura *f* convencional

1338 convert
(Med.)
(Ref. to metabolic processes.)
d umwandeln
f convertir
p converter; transformar

1339 cook *v*
(Prod.)
(Food processing technology.)
d kochen
f cuire
p cozinhar; cozer

1340 cook *v* **au gratin**
(Prod.)
(Food processing technology: cooking procedure that forms a brown superficial crust on the food during baking.)
d überbacken
f gratiner
p gratinar

1341 cooked cheese
(Prod.)
(Dairy plant technology: e.g. Swiss cheese, of elastic texture, having a nutlike aroma.)
d gekochter Käse *m*
f fromage *m* à pâte cuite
p queijo *m* cozido

1342 cooked sugar
(Prod.)
(Food processing technology.)
d gekochter Zucker *m*
f sucre *m* cuit
p açúcar *m* cozido

1343 cooked vegetables
(Prod.)
(Gastronomy.)
d gekochtes Gemüse *n*
f légumes *mpl* cuits
p legumes *mpl* cozidos

* **cookie → 662**

1344 cooking process
(Prod.)
(Food processing technology.)
d Kochprozess *m*
f processus *m* de la cuisson
p processo *m* de cozimento

1345 cooking refinement
(Prod.)
(Gastronomy.)
d Verfeinerung *f* der Küche
f raffinement *m* de la cuisine
p refinamento *m* da cozinha

1346 cooking resistant *adj*
(Prod.)
(Food processing technology: product property.)
d kochfest
f résistant à la cuisson
p resistente ao cozimento

1347 cooking time
(Prod.)
(Food processing technology.)
d Kochzeit *f*
f temps *m* de cuisson
p tempo *m* de cozimento

1348 cool *v* **down**
(Prod.)
(Dairy plant technology of cheese production.)
d abkühlen
f refroidir
p esfriar

1349 cooling
(Prod.)
(Food processing technology.)
d Abkühlung *f*
f refroidissement *m*
p resfriamento *m*

1350 cooling brine
(Prod.)
(Food processing technology: cooling process: as a cold-carrying medium (German: Kälteträger).)
d Kühlsole *f*
f saumure *f* pour refroidissement; saumure *f* de réfrigération
p salmoura *f* de refrigeração

* **cooling of the must → 4647**

1351 copper
(Med.)
(Cu. Trace element. Enzyme (transaminase) activator in the liver.)
d Kupfer *n*
f cuivre *m*
p cobre *m*

1352 copper deficiency
(Med.)
(Veterinary: ref. to cattle breeding; Cu-deficiency; mineral deficiency; catalyzing factor for iron, iron-fixation.)
d Kupfermangel *m*

f carence *f* en cuivre
p deficiência *f* de cobre

* **copra oil → 1192**

1353 **coprecipitates**
(Biochem.)
(Nutritional science; precipitate type.)
d Copräzipitate *npl*
f coprécipités *mpl*
p co-precipitados *mpl*

1354 **copulation; coitus**
(Agr.)
(Cattle breeding; reproduction purpose.)
d Kopulation *f*; Koitus *m*
f copulation *f*; coït *m*
p copulação *f*; coito *m*

* **coriander leaves → 1130**

1355 **coriander seed**
(Agr.)
(Botany. "Coriandrum sativum". Used in flavouring.)
d Koriandersamen *m*
f grains *mpl* de coriandre; coriandre *f* en grain
p sementes *mpl* de coentro

* **corn → 2551**

1356 **corn bread; hoecake**
(Prod.)
(Bakery product. Indian corn bread.)
d Maisbrot *n*
f pain *m* de maïs
p pão *m* de milho

1357 **corncob; corn on the cob**
(Agr.)
(Botany; Indian corn.)
d Maiskolben *m*
f épi *m* de maïs
p espiga *f* de milho

1358 **corned beef**
(Prod.)
(Gastronomy.)
d Cornedbeef *n*; Rindfleisch *n* in Dosen
f corned-beef *m*; viande *f* de bœuf en conserve
p presuntada *f*

1359 **cornflakes**
(Prod.)
(Food processing technology: crisp breakfast cereal to be served in milk.)
d Cornflakes pl; geröstete Maisflocken *fpl*
f corn-flakes *mpl*
p flocos *mpl* de milho

1360 **cornmeal**
(Prod.)
(Agricultural subproduct: meal ground from maize (corn), "Zea mays".)
d Maismehl *n*
f farine *f* de maïs
p fubá *m*; farinha *f* de milho

* **corn on the cob → 1357**

1361 **corn starch**
(Prod.)
(Maize, corn, polysaccharide $(C_6H_{10}O_5)_n$; prime material for aroma/fragrance production.)
d Maisstärke *f*
f amidon *m* de maïs
p amido *m* de milho

1362 **corn syrup**
(Prod.)
(Food processing technology; e.g. as succedaneum for malt.)
d Maissirup *m*
f sirop *m* de maïs
p xarope *m* de milho

1363 **coronaropathies**
(Med.)
(Heart disease e.g. promoted by excess of cholesterol concentration in blood.)
d Koronarerkrankungen *fpl*; koronare Herzkrankheiten *fpl*
f coronaropathies *fpl*
p doenças *fpl* coronárias

1364 **coronary thrombosis**
(Med.)
(Blood clot (thrombus) formation in the coronary area.)
d Koronarthrombose *f*; Thrombose *f* der Herzkranzgefäße
f thrombose *f* coronaire
p trombose *f* coronária

1365 **corpulence; corpulency**
(Med.)
(Obesity: excess of fat accumulation due to higher fat consumption than necessary for energy production.)
d Korpulenz *f*; Beleibtheit *f*; Wohlgenährtheit *f*
f corpulence *f*
p corpulência *f*

* **corpulency → 1365**

1366 **corral**
(Agr.)
(Livestock raising; cattle confining place.)
d Vieheinzäunung *f*

f clôture *f* pour le bétail; étable *f* pour les bovides
p curral *m*; cercado *m*

1367 **correct *v* a flavour note**
(Prod.)
(Aroma/flavour research and application.)
d eine Geschmacksnote korrigieren
f corriger une flaveur
p corrigir um sabor

1368 **correct alimentary supply of essential fatty acids**
(Prod.)
(Food processing technology: research and production.)
d angemessene Nahrungsmittelzufuhr *f* an essentiellen Fettsäuren; ausgewogene Zufuhr *f* von essentiellen Fettsäuren durch Nahrungsmitteleinnahme
f apport *m* alimentaire correct en acides gras essentiels
p aporte *m* alimentar correto de ácidos graxos essenciais

1369 **correction of deficiencies**
(Med.)
(Nutrition in medicine.)
d Mangelerscheinungskorrektion *f*; Ausgleich *m* von Mangelerscheinungen
f correction *f* de carences
p correção *f* de carências

1370 **correction of sugar contents**
(Prod.)
(Beverages; ref. to the production of wine and juices.)
d Korrektion *f* des Zuckergehaltes
f correction *f* de la teneur en sucre
p correção *f* do teor de açúcar

1371 **correct nutrition**
(Med.)
(Dietary problems.)
d korrekte Ernährung *f*; richtige Ernährung *f*
f alimentation *f* correcte
p alimentação *f* correta; nutrição *f* correta

1372 **correct *v* soil deficiencies; repair *v* soil deficiencies**
(Agr.)
(Biological agriculture: soil treatment.)
d Bodenmangelzustände korrigieren; Mangelzustände des Bodens beheben
f corriger les carences du sol
p corrigir as carências do solo

* **cortisol → 2779**

1373 **corysa**
(Med.)
(Veterinary; ref. to fowl disease of the respiratory tract, caused by the bacterium "Hemophilus gallinarum".)
d Nasenschleimhautentzündung *f*
f inflammation *f* de la muqueuse des fosses nasales
p doença *f* da coriza; coriza *f*

1374 **cottage cheese**
(Prod.)
(Dairy product: fresh, soft, white cheese.)
d Hüttenkäse *m*
f cottage *m*
p requeijão *m* caseiro; requeijão *m* tipo "cottage"

* **cottage loaf → 2724**

1375 **cotton candy**
(Prod.)
(Candy made of sugar spun around a stick; confectionary.)
d Zuckerwolle *f*
f barbe-à-papa *f*
p algodão *m* doce

1376 **cottonseed oil**
(Prod.)
(Prime material; Important vegetable oil for human nutrition; obtained by extraction or squeezing of the seeds of "gossypium".)
d Baumwollsaatöl *n*
f huile *f* de coton; huile *f* de graines de coton
p óleo *m* da semente de algodão

1377 **cottonseed protein**
(Biochem.)
(Highly nutritious vegetable protein.)
d Baumwollsaatprotein *n*
f protéine *f* de graine de coton
p proteína *f* da semente do algodão

1378 **cotyledon; seed leaf; seed lobe**
(Agr.)
(Botany: Seed plant: embryo part.)
d Samenblatt *n*; Keimblatt *n*
f cotylédon *m*
p cotilédone *m/f*

1379 **coumarin**
(Prod.)
($C_9H_6O_2$; aroma/flavour prime material; extracted from the tonka bean, or synthetic.)
d Kumarin *n*
f coumarine *f*
p cumarina *f*

1380 **countercurrent; counterflow**
(Prod.)
(Aroma/flavour production: ref. to distillation processes.)
d Gegenstrom *m*
f contre-courant *m*; courant *m* opposé
p contra-corrente *f*; corrente *f* oposta

1381 **countercurrent exhaustion**
(Prod.)
(Food processing and flavour production technology: solvents in extraction processes, extraction-process type.)
d Gegenstromerschöpfungsprozess *m*; Erschöpfung *f* durch das Gegenstromprinzip
f épuisement *m* par contre-courant
p esgotamento *m* por contracorrente

* **countercurrent principle → 1382**

* **counterflow → 1380**

1382 **counterflow principle; countercurrent principle**
(Prod.)
(Food processing technology; ref. to distillation process.)
d Gegenstromprinzip *n*
f principe *m* de contre-courant
p princípio *m* de contracorrente

1383 **courgette; zucchini; summer squash**
(Agr.)
("Cucurbita pepo", used cooked as a vegetable.)
d Zucchetto *m*; Zucchini *f*
f courgette *f*
p abobrinha *f*

1384 **course of fermentation; run of fermentation**
(Biochem.)
(Fermentation in nutritional science.)
d Ablauf *m* der Gärung; Gärungsablauf *m*; Verlauf *m* der Gärung; Gärungsverlauf *m*
f déroulement *m* de la fermentation; marche *f* de la fermentation; cours *m* de la fermentation
p decurso *m* da fermentação; curso *m* da fermentação; evolução *f* da fermentação

1385 **cow**
(Agr.)
(Cattle breeding; genus "Bos", adult female of cattle.)
d Kuh *f*
f vache *f*
p vaca *f*

1386 **cowpat**
(Agr.)
(Biological agriculture: cow dung dropping.)
d Kuhfladen *m*
f bouse *f* de vache
p bosta *f*

1387 **cow's milk**
(Prod.)
(Dairy product.)
d Kuhmilch *f*
f lait *m* de vache
p leite *m* de vaca

1388 **crab**
(Agr.)
(Edible marine crustacean. Freshwater crab: in German: Flusskrebs; in Portuguese: caranguejo-do-rio, caranguejo-de-água-doce.)
d Krabbe *f*; Taschenkrebs *m*
f crabe *m*; tourteau *m*
p caranguejo *m*

1389 **crabmeat**
(Prod.)
(Gastronomy.)
d Krabbenfleisch *n*
f chair *f* de crabe; chair *f* de tourteau
p carne *f* de caranguejo

1390 **cracker**
(Prod.)
(Bakery product; crispy, dry, thin bakery product.)
d Teegebäck *n*; Keks *m*
f cracker *m*; gâteau *m* sec
p cracker *m*; biscoito *m*; bolacha *f*

1391 **cranberry**
(Agr.)
(Agricultural produce; "Vaccinium"; small red berry.)
d Preiselbeere *f*; Kronsbeere *f*
f airelle *f* rouge
p murtinho *m*

* **crayfish → 3129**

* **C.R.D. → 1123**

1392 **cream cake slice**
(Prod.)
(Cake shop product.)
d Cremeschnitte *f*
f tranche *f* de gâteau à la crème
p pedaço *m* de torta de creme

1393 **cream cheese**
(Prod.)
(Dairy product.)
d Rahmkäse *m*
f fromage *m* à la crème
p queijo *m* amanteigado

1394 **cream cheese, Swiss type**
(Prod.)
(Dairy product; fresh cheese type, not salted.)
d Schweizer Frischkäse *m*
f fromage *m* frais de type suisse; suisse *m*
p queijo *m* fresco tipo suiço

1395 **creamed**
(Prod.)
(Food processing technology; product characteristic.)
d gecremt; gekremt
f crémé
p ao creme

1396 **cream puff**
(Prod.)
(Cake shop product; chou pastry.)
d Windbeutel *m*
f chou *f* à la crème
p bomba *f* de creme

1397 **creamy** *adj*
(Prod.)
(Aroma/flavour note; food processing technology.)
d sahnig
f crémeux
p cremoso

1398 **creamy taste**
(Prod.)
(Gastronomy.)
d sahniger Geschmack *m*
f saveur *f* crémeuse
p sabor *m* cremoso

1399 **creatinine**
(Med.)
(Ref. to creatine excretion through the kidney in the urine; kidney functioning.)
d Kreatinin *n*
f créatinine *f*
p creatinina *f*

* **creeper → 5713**

1400 **crepe**
(Prod.)
(Gastronomy; thin pancake.)
d Krepp *f*
f crêpe *f*
p crepe *m*

1401 **crescent rolls; crescents**
(Prod.)
(Bakery product.)
d Hörnchen *n*
f croissant *m*
p meia-lua *f*

* **crescents → 1401**

1402 **cress**
(Agr.)
(Botany: "Nasturtium officinale"; used in salads.)
d Brunnenkresse *f*
f cresson *m* de fontaine
p agrião *m*

1403 **crisp** *adj*
(Prod.)
(Characteristic of bakery products, like rolls, crackers.)
d knusperig; knusprig; resch; rösch
f croustillant; croquant; craquant
p crocante

1404 **crispbread**
(Prod.)
(Bakery product.)
d Knäckebrot *n*
f pain *m* croustillant
p pão *m* sueco

1405 **crisp quality**
(Prod.)
(E.g. of bread crust.)
d knusperige Beschaffenheit *f*
f caractère *m* croustillant
p qualidade *f* crocante

* **crocus → 4784**

1406 **crop; agricultural crop**
(Agr.)
(Agricultural produce.)
d Ernte *f*
f récolte *f*
p colheita *f* agrícola

1407 **crop of a bird**
(Med.)
(Veterinary; fowl anatomy: gullet enlargement for food intake and preliminary digestion processes.)
d Kropf *m* des Vogels
f jabot *m*
p papo *m*

1408 **crop rotation**
(Agr.)
(Crop alternation on arable land.)
d Fruchtfolge *f*
f culture *f* alternante; rotation *f* culturale; assolement *m* des cultures
p folhamento *m*; rotação *f* de cultura; alternação *f* de cultura

1409 croquette
(Prod.)
(Gastronomy; e.g. round minced meat mass fried with egg and bread crumbs.)
d Krokette *f*
f croquette *f*
p croquete *m*

1410 croquettes ready for frying
(Prod.)
(Food processing technology.)
d bratfertige Kroketten *fpl*
f croquettes *fpl* prêtes à cuire
p croquetes *mpl* prontos para fritura

1411 cross; hybridism
(Agr.)
(Cattle breeding; e.g. selective crossing for cattle-race improvement.)
d Kreuzung *f*; Hybridenzüchtung *f*
f croisement *m*; hybridation *f*
p cruzamento *m*; hibridação *f*

1412 crosslinked vitamin A
(Biochem.)
(Nutritional science: Reticulation for e.g. higher antioxidant stability.)
d vernetztes Vitamin A *n*
f vitamine A *f* réticulée
p vitamina A *f* reticulada

1413 crosslinking agent
(Biochem.)
(Nutritional science: ref. to the crosswise connecting process of parallel atom chains, forming a complex molecule: polymer formation.)
d Vernetzer *m*
f réticulant *m*; agent *m* de réticulation
p agente *m* de reticul ação

1414 crown of tapeworm hooks
(Med.)
(Crown of the hooks of the taenia, parasitic platyhelminthic worm. Fixing structures.)
d Hakenkranz *m* des Bandwurms
f crochets *mpl* de fixation du ténia
p espícula *f* da tênia

1415 crucifers
(Agr.)
(Botany; "Cruciferae"; e.g. cabbage, mustard, rape; used as green manure in biologic agriculture.)
d Kreuzblütler *mpl*
f crucifères *fpl*
p crucíferas *fpl*

1416 crude egg
(Prod.)
(Gastronomy.)
d rohes Ei *n*
f œuf *m* cru
p ovo *m* cru

1417 crude protein contents
(Biochem.)
(Nutritional science: Total protein quantity of a chemical environment, e.g. milk.)
d Rohproteingehalt *m*
f teneur *f* en matières protéiques brutes
p teor *m* em proteínas brutas

1418 crude vegetables
(Agr.)
(Biological agriculture produce.)
d rohes Gemüse *n*
f végétaux *mpl* crus
p vegetais *mpl* crus

1419 crumble *v*
(Prod.)
(Food processing technology.)
d zerbröckeln; zerkrümeln
f émietter
p esmigalhar

1420 crumbly *adj*
(Prod.)
(Product characteristic, e.g. of biscuits, cookies.)
d bröcklig; bröckelig
f cassant; friable
p esfarelável

1421 crumblyness
(Prod.)
(Food processing technology, e.g. characteristic of bakery products.)
d Bröckligkeit *f*; Bröckeligkeit *f*
f friabilité *f*
p esfarelamento *m*

1422 crumbly solid
(Prod.)
(Food processing technology: product characteristic.)
d bröcklige Festsubstanz *f*
f solide *m* friable
p sólido *m* esfarelável

1423 crush *v*; **mash** *v*
(Prod.)
(Food processing technology: e.g. flour obtention.)
d zerdrücken; zermalmen; zerquetschen
f écraser; broyer
p esmagar; triturar

* **crushed sugarcane husks → 5307**

1424 **crushing**
(Prod.)
(Treatment of malt in brewery.)
d Zerkleinerung *f*; Zerstoßung *f*; Zermahlung *f*
f concassage *m*; broyage *m*
p trituração *f*

1425 **crushing process**
(Prod.)
(Food processing technology, separation technique.)
d Zermalmungsprozess *m*; Zerquetschungsprozess *m*
f processus *m* d'écrasement
p processo *m* de esmagamento

1426 **crush** *v* **the grape**
(Agr.)
(Viticulture.)
d die Beere zerdrücken
f écraser le raisin
p esmagar a uva; triturar a uva

1427 **crush** *v* **to flour; mash** *v* **until the obtention of flour**
(Prod.)
(Food processing technology: manioc and cassava preparation.)
d zu Mehl zermalmen
f écraser en farine; broyer en farine
p triturar até formar farinha

1428 **crustaceans**
(Agr.)
(Class "Crustacea". Lobsters, crabs, shrimps.)
d Krebstiere *npl*; Schalentiere *npl*
f crustacés *mpl*
p crustáceos *mpl*

1429 **crust of bread; heel of bread**
(Prod.)
(Term for the final crusty end pieces of a bread loaf.)
d Knust *m*
f croûton *m* de pain; quignon *m*
p bico *m* do pão

1430 **crust of brown bread**
(Prod.)
(Hard exterior of dark brown bread made of whole wheat flower.)
d Schwarzbrotrinde *f*; Schwarzbrotkruste *f*
f croûte *f* de pain noir
p crosta *f* do pão preto

1431 **cryptogam**
(Agr.)
(Botany; plant that reproduces by spores, e.g. alga, fern, fungus.)
d Kryptogamme *fpl*; Sporenpflanze *f*
f cryptogame *m*
p criptógamo *m*

1432 **crystalline beta-carotene authorized as food dye**
(Prod.)
($C_{40}H_{56}$. Food stuff processing.)
d kristallines Beta-Carotin *n* als Nährmittelfarbstoff genehmigt
f bêta-carotène *m* cristallin autorisé comme colorant alimentaire
p beta-caroteno *m* cristalino autorizado como corante alimentício

1433 **crystalline powder**
(Prod.)
(Food processing technology: product characteristic.)
d kristallinisches Pulver *n*; kristallines Pulver *n*
f poudre *f* cristalline
p pó *m* cristalino

1434 **crystalline sodium ascorbate**
(Biochem.)
(Nutritional science: vitamin C, used as an antioxidant.)
d kristallines Natriumascorbat *n*
f ascorbate *m* de sodium cristallin
p ascorbato *m* de sódio cristalino

1435 **crystalline structure of amino acids**
(Biochem.)
(Protein biochemistry, protein structure.)
d Kristallstruktur *f* de Aminosäuren
f structure *f* cristalline des acides aminés
p estrutura *f* cristalina dos aminoácidos

1436 **crystallization fineness**
(Prod.)
(Food processing technology.)
d Kristallisationsfeinheit *f*
f finesse *f* de la cristallisation
p fineza *f* de cristalização; finura *f* de cristalização

1437 **crystallization pattern**
(Prod.)
(Food processing technology; ref. to solutions in freezing processes.)
d Kristallisierungsschema *n*
f schéma *m* de la cristallisation
p esquema *f* da cristalização

1438 **crystallization phenomenon**
(Prod.)
(Food processing technology.)
d Kristallisationsphänomen *n*; Kristallisationserscheinung *f*
f phénomène *m* de cristallisation
p fenômeno *m* de cristalização

1439 **crystallized oil**
(Prod.)
(Food processing technology.)
d kristallisiertes Öl *n*
f huile *f* cristallisée
p óleo *m* cristalizado

1440 **crystal sugar; granulated sugar**
(Prod.)
(Food processing technology; processed product of agricultural origin.)
d Kristallzucker *m*
f sucre *m* cristallisé
p açúcar *m* cristalizado; açúcar *m* cristal

1441 **cube sugar; lump sugar**
(Prod.)
(Food processing technology.)
d Würfelzucker *m*
f sucre *m* en morceaux
p açúcar *m* em cubinhos; açúcar *m* em quadradinhos

1442 **cucumber**
(Agr.)
(Agricultural produce; of the gourd family "Cucumis sativus"; cucurbit.)
d Gurke *f*
f concombre *m*
p pepino *m*

* **cucurbit → 4500**

1443 **culinary art**
(Prod.)
(Gastronomy.)
d Kochkunst *f*
f art *m* culinaire
p arte *f* culinária

1444 **culinary culture**
(Prod.)
(Gastronomy.)
d kulinarische Kultur *f*
f culture *f* culinaire
p cultura *f* culinária

* **culinary herbs → 2686**

1445 **culinary utilization**
(Prod.)
(Gastronomy.)
d kulinarische Verwertung *f*
f utilisation *f* culinaire
p utilização *f* culinária

1446 **cull** *v*; **select** *v*
(Prod.)
(To remove undesirable substances out of a lot. E.g. to cull the grains one by one; culled grains are used for animal ration.)
d auslesen; aussortieren
f trier
p selecionar; escolher por triagem

1447 **cultivated feedstuff**
(Agr.)
(Livestock nutrition.)
d kultivierte Futtermittel *npl*
f fourrages *mpl* cultivés
p forragens *fpl* cultivadas

1448 **culture rotation; alternation of cultures**
(Agr.)
(Soil treatment, avoiding soil wear.)
d Wechselwirtschaft *f*; Kulturenabwechslung *f*
f alternance *f* des cultures
p alternância *f* das culturas

1449 **culture treatment**
(Agr.)
(Biological agriculture; ref. to cultivation procedures.)
d Kulturenbehandlung *f*; Behandlung *f* der Kulturen
f traitement *m* des cultures
p tratamento *m* das culturas

1450 **cumene; cumol; isopropylbenzene**
(Prod.)
(C_9H_{12}; benzene derivative; ref. to aroma synthesis; prime material.)
d Cumol *m*
f cumène *m*
p cumeno *m*; cumol *m*

1451 **cumin**
(Agr.)
(Agricultural produce. "Cuminum cyminum"; used as spice.)
d echter Kümmel *n*
f cumin *m* officinal
p cominho *m*

* **cuminal → 1452**

1452 **cuminaldehyde; cuminal; p-isopropylbenzaldehyde**
(Prod.)
($C_{10}H_{12}O$; benzene derivative; ref. to aroma synthesis; prime material.)
d Cuminaldehyde *n*
f cuminaldéhyde *m*
p cuminaldeído *m*; cumaldeído *m*

1453 **cumin seed**
(Prod.)
("Cuminum cyminum"; aromatizing seeds are used as additives in bakery and in cheese production.)

d Samen *m* des echten Kümmels
f graines *fpl* du cumin
p semente *m* do cominho; grãos *mpl* do cominho

* **cumol → 1450**

1454 **cumulation toxin**
(Med.)
(Food processing technology.)
d Kumulationstoxin *n*; Speicherungsgift *n*
f toxine *f* de cumulation
p toxina *f* de cumulação; toxina *f* de acumulação

1455 **cumulonimbus**
(Agr.)
(Climatology; specific cloud form; approx. 1,000 to 6,000 m high; thunder storm-announcing cloud.)
d Kumulonimbus *m*; Gewitterwolke *f*
f cumulonimbus *m*
p cúmulo-nimbo *m*

1456 **cumulus**
(Agr.)
(Climatology; specific cloud form; approx. 600-2,000 m high.)
d Kumulus *m*; Haufenwölkchen *n*
f cumulus *m*
p cúmulo *m*

* **cup → 875**

1457 **cupric sulphate**
(Prod.)
($CuSO_4$; used for insecticide (Bordeaux) mixture, (e.g. against mildew) for treatment of useful plants and vine: e.g. treatment of the "white disease" of vines caused by "Oidium".)
d Kupfer(II)sulfat *n*
f sulfate *m* de cuivre
p sulfato *m* cúprico

1458 **curative nutrition**
(Med.)
(Nutritional science in therapy.)
d heilende Ernährung *f*
f nutrition *f* curative
p nutrição *f* curativa

1459 **curative treatment**
(Agr.)
(Biological agriculture. e.g. ref. to plant protection.)
d heilende Behandlung *f*; wiederherstellende Behandlung *f*
f traitement *m* curatif
p tratamento *m* curativo

1460 **curcumin; curcumin yellow**
(Prod.)
($C_{21}H_{20}O_6$; turmeric yellow from "Curcuma longa L."; foodstuff dye.)
d Kurkumin *n*; Kurkumingelb *n*
f curcumine *f*; jaune *m* de curcuma
p curcumina *f*; amarelo *m* curcumina

* **curcumin yellow → 1460**

1461 **curd cheese**
(Prod.)
(Dairy product: fresh, unsalted, cow-milk cheese.)
d Quark *m*
f caillebotte *f*
p ricota *f*

1462 **curdled milk; junket**
(Prod.)
(Dairy product; soured milk type.)
d Dickmilch *f*
f lait *m* caillé
p coalhada *f*

1463 **curd syneresis**
(Prod.)
(Dairy process, occurring in cheese vats: Separation of the liquid from the cheese in a settled state.)
d Quarksynärese *f*; Quarksynäresis *f*
f synérèse *f* de caillebotte
p sinérese *f* da ricota

* **curly kale → 3060**

1464 **currant**
(Prod.)
(Seedless crystallized raisin, used as baking ingredient.)
d Korinthe *f*
f raisin *m* de Corinthe
p corinto *m*

1465 **curry**
(Prod.)
(Indian pungent spice.)
d Curry *n*
f curry *m*; cari *m*
p caril *m*

1466 **curry rice**
(Prod.)
(Gastronomy.)
d Curryreis *m*
f riz *m* au curry
p arroz *m* ao caril; arroz *m* preparado com caril

1467 **custom-produced blends of vitamins**
(Prod.)
(For incorporation into foodstuffs.)
d kundenorientierte Vitaminmischungen *fpl*

f mélanges *mpl* sur mesure de vitamines
p misturas *fpl* vitamínicas sob encomenda

1468 **cut** *v*; **chop** *v*; **carve** *v*
(Prod.)
(Food processing technology, e.g. meat.)
d schneiden; durchhauen; zerlegen; tranchieren
f trancher
p cortar; partir; talhar

* **cut** *v* → **4947**

1469 **cuticle of the dents**
(Med.)
(Anatomy. Cuticula dentis.)
d Zahnschmelzoberhäutchen *n*
f cuticule *f* de la dent
p cutícula *f* dental

1470 **cutlet; chop**
(Prod.)
(Meat product; meat slice.)
d Kotelett *n*
f côtelette *f*
p costeleta *f*

1471 **cutting; slicing**
(Prod.)
(Food processing technology; aroma/essence production e.g. from fruits.)
d Zerschneiden *n*
f découpage *m*
p trincho *m*; retalhação *f*

1472 **cutting section**
(Prod.)
(Unit of dairy machine for cheese production.)
d Schneidevorrichtung *f*; Schneideeinheit *f*
f équipement *m* à couper
p seção *f* de corte

1473 **cutting to any shape**
(Prod.)
(Ref. to meat industrialization.)
d Zerkleinerung *f* in beliebiger Form
f découpe *f* de forme variable
p corte *m* em pedaços em todas as formas

1474 **cutting up**
(Prod.)
(Meat treatment.)
d Aufschneiden *n*
f découpe *f*
p corte *m*; talha *f*; talhamento *m*

1475 **cuttlefish; squid**
(Prod.)
(Marine mollusk; genus "Sepia"; seafood; calamary. Loligo brasiliensis Blainv.)
d Tintenfisch *m*
f seiche *f*; calmar *m*
p lula *f*; calamar *m*

1476 **cut** *v* **up**
(Prod.)
(Butcher's activity: cutting a carcass of an animal into pieces.)
d ausschlachten
f dépecer
p talhar; abrir

1477 **cyanocobalamin**
(Prod.)
($C_{63}H_{90}CoN_{14}O_{14}P$. Vitamin B_{12} derivative.)
d Cyanocobalamin *n*
f cyanocobalamine *f*
p cianocobalamina *f*

1478 **cyanosis**
(Med.)
(Veterinary; bluish coloration of the skin due to insufficient oxygen in the blood.)
d Zyanose *f*; Blausucht *f*
f cyanose *f*; maladie *f* bleue
p cianose *f*

1479 **cyclamate sodium**
(Prod.)
(Food processing technology: synthetic sweetener. A sodium salt.)
d Natriumcyclamat *n*
f cyclamate *m* sódique
p ciclamato *m* de sódio

1480 **cyclization**
(Prod.)
(In food processing chemistry, biochemistry etc.: formation of rings in a chemical compound.)
d Zyklisierung *f*
f cyclisation *f*
p ciclização *f*

1481 **cyclobutane; tetramethylene**
(Prod.)
(C_4H_8; source of fragrance/aroma prime material.)
d Cyclobutan *n*
f cyclobutane *m*
p ciclobutano *m*

1482 **cyclohexane; hexamethylene**
(Prod.)
(C_6H_{12}; used in the extraction of essential oils; source of fragrance/aroma prime material.)
d Cyclohexan *n*
f cyclohexane *m*
p ciclohexano *m*

1483 cyclohexanol; hexalin
(Prod.)
($C_6H_{12}O$; benzene derivative; ref. to aroma synthesis; prime material.)
d Cyclohexanol *n*; Hexcalin *n*
f cyclohexanol *m*; hexaline *f*
p cicloexanol *m*; hexalina *f*

1484 cyclohexylethanol
(Prod.)
(Aroma prime material, e.g. green, mint-like flavour.)
d Cyclohexylethanol *m*
f cyclohexyléthanol *m*
p ciclohexiletanol *m*

1485 cyclohexylethyl acetate
(Prod.)
($C_{10}H_{18}O_2$; aroma prime material, e.g. raspberry flavour.)
d Cyclohexylethylacetat *n*
f acétate *m* de cyclohexyléthyle
p acetato *m* de ciclohexiletila

1486 cyclopentane; pentamethylene
(Prod.)
(C_5H_{10}; source of fragrance/aroma prime material.)
d Cyclopentan *n*
f cyclopentane *m*
p ciclopentano *m*

1487 cyclopropane; trimethylene
(Prod.)
(C_3H_6; source of fragrance/aroma prime material.)
d Cyclopropan *n*
f cyclopropane *m*
p ciclopropano *m*

1488 cyst
(Med.)
(Veterinary; tumor in form of a sac filled with liquid or semi-solid matter.)
d Zyste *f*; Balggeschwulst *f*
f kyste *m*
p cisto *m*; quisto *m*

1489 cysteine
(Biochem.)
($C_3H_7NO_2S$; sulphur-containing amino acid, to be oxidized to cystine ($C_6H_{12}N_2O_4S_2$). This is present in proteins as a metabolic sulphur source.)
d Cystein *n*; Zystein *n*
f cystéine *f*
p cisteína *f*

1490 cystic duct
(Med.)
(Anatomy; joining with the common hepatic duct, forming the common bile duct: bile movement in and out of the gall bladder.)
d Gallenblasengang *m*
f canal *m* cystique
p canal *m* cístico

1491 cystine
(Biochem.)
($C_6H_{12}N_2O_4S_2$; non-essential amino acid; ingredient in human and in cow's milk.)
d Cystin *n*; Zystin *n*
f cystine *f*
p cistina *f*

1492 cytoplasm
(Biochem.)
(Cell constituents, cell structure: substance surrounding the cell nucleus; e.g. in genetic engineering; nutritional science.)
d Cytoplasma *n*; Zellplasma *n*
f cytoplasme *m*
p citoplasma *m*

1493 cytosine
(Med.)
($C_4H_5N_3O$; pyrimidine (nitrogen containing) base in the nucleic acid; related to genetic information.)
d Cytosin *n*
f cytosine *f*
p citosina *f*

D

1494 **dabble** *v*
(Prod.)
(Food processing technology and production.)
d bespritzen
f mouiller
p borrifar

1495 **daily iodine requirements**
(Med.)
(Adults approx. 200 mg; recommendation: use of iodized table salt.)
d täglicher Jodbedarf *m*
f besoins *mpl* quotidiens d'iode; besoins *mpl* journaliers d'iode
p necessidades *fpl* cotidianas de iodo

1496 **daily recommended vitamin requirements**
(Med.)
(Avoiding deficiencies.)
d empfohlene tägliche Vitaminbedarfsmenge *f*
f dose *f* vitaminique quotidienne recommandée
p dose *f* diária recomendada de vitaminas

1497 **daily requirement**
(Prod.)
(E.g. of vitamins.)
d Tagesbedarf *m*
f besoin *m* journalier
p necessidade *f* diária

1498 **daily water requirement**
(Med.)
(Daily water requirement of an adult of 70 kg: 2.5-3 l.)
d täglicher Wasserbedarf *n*
f besoin *m* journalier d'eau
p necessidade *f* diária de água

1499 **dairy**
(Prod.)
(Establishment for milk transformation.)
d Molkerei *f*
f laiterie *f*
p leiteria *f*; leitaria *f*

1500 **dairy cow; milk cow; milker**
(Agr.)
(Cattle breeding.)
d Milchkuh *f*
f vache *f* laitière
p vaca *f* leiteira

1501 **dairy produce; dairy products**
(Prod.)
(Food processing technology.)
d Molkereiprodukt *n*
f produit *m* de la laiterie; produits *mpl* laitiers
p produto *m* de leiteria; produto *m* de leitaria; laticínios *mpl*

* **dairy products → 1501**

1502 **dairy subproducts**
(Agr.)
(Dairy: food processing technology: food industrialization.)
d Molkereinebenprodukte *npl*
f sous-produits *mpl* de l'industrie du lait; sous-produits *mpl* de la laiterie
p subprodutos *mpl* da indústria leiteira

* **dam → 1681**

1503 **damaged cluster of grapes**
(Agr.)
(Viticulture: bunches of grapes: grape harvest.)
d beschädigte Weintraube *f*
f grappe *f* de raisin variée; raisin *m* varié
p cacho *m* de uvas danificados

* **dam** *v* **erosion → 1321**

1504 **dampen** *v*
(Prod.)
(Food processing technology and production.)
d anfeuchten; befeuchten
f humecter; mouiller légèrement
p umedecer

* **dandelion greens → 1505**

1505 **dandelion leaves; dandelion greens**
(Agr.)
(Botany. "Taraxacum officinale"; herb. Leaves can be used in salads.)
d Löwenzahnblätter *npl*
f feuilles *fpl* de pissenlit
p folhas *fpl* de dente de leão

1506 **Danish pastry**
(Prod.)
(Cake shop product.)
d Blätterteigschweinsohr *n*
f palmier *m*
p mil-folhas *fpl* tipo "orelha de porco"

1507 **dark beer; brown ale**
(Prod.)
(Food processing technology; beverage: beer type.)
d dunkles Bier *n*

f bière *f* brune
p cerveja *f* escura

1508 **dash; pinch**
(Prod.)
(Food processing technology and production.)
d Prise *f*; Messerspitze *f* voll
f prise *f*; pincée *f*
p pitada *f*

1509 **dates**
(Agr.)
(Agricultural produce. Edible fruit of the "Phoenix dactylifera" (palm).)
d Datteln *fpl*
f dattes *fpl*
p tâmaras *fpl*

1510 **deacidification**
(Prod.)
(Reduction/elimination of acids. Elimination of free fatty acids during refinement of fatty globules; cheese production: Milk undergoes a deacidification process by addition of neutralizing additives.)
d Entsäuerung *f*
f désacidification *f*
p desacidificação *f*

1511 **decaffeinated** *adj*
(Prod.)
(Food processing technology: ref. to coffee; coffee type.)
d koffeinfrei
f décaféiné
p descafeinado

1512 **decaffeinated coffee**
(Prod.)
(Food processing technology.)
d kaffeinfreier Kaffee *m*
f café *m* décaféiné
p café *m* descafeinado

1513 **decanal**
(Prod.)
(n-Decanal; aldehyde C_{10}; flavour prime material; e.g. citrus note.)
d Decanal *n*
f decanal *m*
p decanal *m*

* **decanoic acid → 904**

1514 **decantation** (drawing off a liquid)
(Prod.)
(Separation of liquid from its sediments into another container: e.g. beer brewery process; also: wine production; see also decantation (pouring a liquid from one vessel into another).)
d Dekantieren *n*; Dekantation *f*; Abklären *n*; Abgießen *n*
f décantage *m*; décantation *f*
p decantação *f*

1515 **decantation** (pouring a liquid from one vessel into another)
(Prod.)
(See decantation (drawing off a liquid).)
d Umgießen *n*; Umfüllung *f*
f transvasement *m*; soutirage *m*
p transvasamento *m*

1516 **decarboxylase**
(Biochem.)
(Nutritional science: enzymes which accelerate the decarboxylation process of amino acids.)
d Decarboxylase *f*
f décarboxylase *f*
p decarboxilase *f*

1517 **decarboxylation**
(Biochem.)
(Nutritional science: Enzymatic reaction.)
d Decarboxylierung *f*
f décarboxylation *f*
p decarboxilação *f*

1518 **deciduous tree**
(Agr.)
(Botany; tree which looses its leaves each year.)
d Laubbaum *m*
f arbre *m* de feuilles caduques
p árvore *f* de folha caduca

1519 **decoction method**
(Prod.)
(Food processing technology; brewery process; flavour extraction by boiling.)
d Dekoktionsverfahren *n*
f méthode *f* de décoction
p método *m* de decocção

1520 **decomposition of foodstuffs**
(Biochem.)
(Food biochemistry: Disintegration caused by bacteria and fungi.)
d Zersetzung *f* von Nahrungsmitteln
f décomposition *f* alimentaire
p decomposição *f* de produtos alimentícios; decomposição *f* de alimentos

1521 **decomposition of starch**
(Prod.)
(Food processing technology: e.g. industrial glucose production.)
d Stärkespaltung *f*

f décomposition *f* de l'amidon
p decomposição *f* do amido

* **decomposition risks → 1598**

* **decrease in the blood sugar level → 698**

1522 **decrease of mineral supply**
(Biochem.)
(Food biochemistry: ref. to mineral plant constituents important for the human body.)
d Verringerung *f* der Mineralienzufuhr
f diminution *f* d'apport en minéraux
p diminuição *f* do aporte de minerais; diminuição *f* do fornecimento de minerais

1523 **deep-freezing of fruits**
(Prod.)
(Food processing technology; food conservation.)
d Tiefkühlen *n* von Obst; Tiefgefrieren *n* von Obst
f congélation *f* des fruits; surgélation *f* des fruits
p congelamento *m* de frutas

1524 **deep-freezing of meat**
(Prod.)
(Food processing technology; food conservation.)
d Tiefkühlen *n* des Fleisches; Tiefgefrieren *n* von Fleisch
f congélation *f* de la viande; surgélation *f* de la viande
p congelamento *m* da carne

1525 **deep-freezing process**
(Prod.)
(Food processing technology; food preservation.)
d Tiefkühlverfahren *n*
f processus *m* de surgélation
p processo *m* de congelamento

1526 **deep-frozen** *adj*
(Prod.)
(Food processing technology; food conservation method.)
d tiefgefroren; tiefgekühlt
f surgelé
p congelado

1527 **deep-frozen fish filet**
(Prod.)
(Food processing technology; food preservation.)
d tiefgekühltes Fischfilet *n*
f filet *m* de poisson surgelé
p filete *m* de peixe congelado

1528 **deep-frozen food**
(Prod.)
(Food processing technology; food conservation method.)
d Tiefkühlkost *f*; Tiefkühlspeise *f*; tiefgefrorene Nahrungsmittel *npl*
f aliments *mpl* surgelés
p produtos *mpl* alimentícios congelados; alimentos *mpl* congelados

1529 **deep-frozen meat**
(Prod.)
(Butchery.)
d Tiefkühlfleisch *n*; tiefgekühltes Fleisch *n*
f viande *f* surgelée
p carne *f* congelada

1530 **deep-frozen minced meat**
(Prod.)
(Food processing technology, meat industrialization.)
d tiefgekühltes Hackfleisch *n*; tiefgekühltes Gehackte *n*
f viande *f* hachée surgelée
p carne *f* picada congelada

1531 **defective tooth**
(Med.)
(Anatomy.)
d kranker Zahn *m*
f dent *f* gâtée
p dente *m* estragado

1532 **deferrization**
(Prod.)
(Elimination of iron e.g. of water used for foodstuff treatment)
d Enteisenung *f*; Enteisenen *n*
f déferrisation *f*
p eliminação *f* de traços ferro

1533 **defibration**
(Prod.)
(Food processing technology: e.g. of sugar cane.)
d Entfaserung *f*
f défibrage *m*
p desfibramento *m*

1534 **deficiencies of the soil; soil deficiencies**
(Agr.)
(Biological agriculture: soil characteristics.)
d Mangelzustand *m* des Bodens
f carences *fpl* du sol
p carências *fpl* do solo

1535 **deficiency**
(Med.)
(Vitamin deficiency.)
d Mangel *m*

f carence *f*
p carência *f*

1536 **definitive host**
(Med.)
(Veterinary; in parasitology: organism susceptible to "lodging" a parasite definitively, where the parasite has its sexual reproduction.)
d Hauptwirt *m*
f hôte *m* définitif
p hospedeiro *m* definitivo

1537 **deflation; wind erosion; aeolian erosion**
(Agr.)
(Soil; soil erosion caused by the wind.)
d Deflation *f*; Winderosion *f*
f déflation *f*; érosion *f* éolienne
p deflação *f*; erosão *f* pelo vento

1538 **defrosting of deep-frozen food**
(Prod.)
(Food processing technology; thawing out of agricultural products from a deep-frozen state.)
d Auftauen *n* tiefgefrorener Nahrungsmittel
f décongélation *f* d'aliments surgelés
p descongelamento *m* de produtos alimentícios congelados

1539 **degasifying of the wine; degassing of the wine**
(Biochem.)
(Enology.)
d Entgasen *n* des Weines
f dégazage *m* du vin; dégagement *m* gazeux du vin
p desgasificação *f* do vinho

* **degassing of the wine → 1539**

1540 **deglutition**
(Med.)
(Baby nutrition. Act of swallowing.)
d Hinunterschlucken *n*
f déglutition *f*
p deglutição *f*

* **degradation due to bacteria → 501**

1541 **degraded soil**
(Agr.)
(Soil: worn out soils.)
d abgetragener Boden *m*
f sol *m* dégradé
p solo *m* desgastado

1542 **degreasing of leather**
(Agr.)
(Leather treatment; tanning process.)
d Lederentfettung *f*
f dégraissage *m* du cuir
p desengraxamento *m* de couro

1543 **degree of ripeness**
(Agr.)
(Botany; ref. e.g. to fruit/plant development.)
d Reifegrad *m*
f degré *m* de maturité
p grau *m* de madureza; grau *m* de maturação

1544 **degree of unsaturation of fatty acids**
(Biochem.)
(Nutritional science; related to product susceptibility to oxidative deterioration.)
d Grad *m* der Ungesättigtheit von Fettsäuren
f degré *m* d'insaturation d'acides gras
p grau *m* de insaturação de ácidos graxos

1545 **degust** *v*; **taste** *v*
(Prod.)
(Gastronomy.)
d kosten; abschmecken; probieren
f déguster; goûter; essayer; jouir de; savourer
p degustar; provar; saborear

1546 **dehisced fruit**
(Agr.)
(Botany; fruits spreading seeds at maturity, e.g. opening seed pods.)
d Streufrucht *f*
f fruit *m* déhiscent
p fruto *m* deiscente

1547 **dehydrated foodstuffs**
(Prod.)
(Food processing technology.)
d entwässerte Lebensmittel *npl*
f denrées *fpl* alimentaires déshydratées
p produtos *mpl* alimentícios desidratados

1548 **dehydrated powdered vegetables**
(Med.)
(Baby nutrition.)
d Trockengemüse *n* in Pulverform
f légumes *mpl* déshydratés en poudre
p verduras *fpl* desidratadas em forma de pó

1549 **dehydrated vegetables**
(Prod.)
(Food processing technology.)
d dehydratisiertes Gemüse *n*
f légumes *mpl* déshydratés
p verduras *fpl* desidratadas

1550 **dehydrated whey powder**
(Prod.)
(Subproduct of dairy food processing technology: originated from serum desiccation of the lactoserum.)

d dehydrierte Trockenmolke *f*; dehydrierte Molke *f* in Pulverform
f lactosérum *m* déshydraté en poudre
p lactó-soro *m* em pó desidratado; soro *m* de leite desidratado em pó

1551 **dehydration**
(Prod.)
(Food processing technology; elimination reaction, separating water from a compound.)
d Dehydratation *f*; Dehydratisierung *f*; Wasserentzug *m*
f déshydratation *f*
p desidratação *f*

1552 **dehydrofreezing**
(Prod.)
(Food processing technology; food conservation method.)
d Tiefkühlung *f* durch Dehydratation
f congélation *f* par déshydratation
p congelamento *m* por desidratação

1553 **dehydrogenases**
(Biochem.)
(Nutritional science: these enzymes promote cell oxidation removing hydrogen (H) from the substrate. Specific dehydrogenases: lactic dehydrogenase; alcohol dehydrogenase, etc.)
d Dehydrogenasen *fpl*
f déshydrogénases *fpl*
p dehidrogenases *fpl*

1554 **delayed aging of wine**
(Biochem.)
(Enology; e.g. depending on environmental storage temperatures.)
d verzögerte Alterung *f* des Weines
f vieillissement *m* retardé du vin
p envelhecimento *m* retardado do vinho

1555 **delay** *v* **lipid oxidation**
(Biochem.)
(Nutritional science; ref. to restructured meat in meat processing.)
d Lipidoxidation verzögern
f retarder l'oxydation lipidique
p retardar a oxidação lipídica

* **demand for foodstuff → 2319**

1556 **demineralization**
(Prod.)
(Water supply; water treatment; removal of mineral salts.)
d Entmineralisierung *f*
f déminéralisation *f*
p desmineralização *f*

1557 **demineralization of bones**
(Med.)
(Nutrition in medicine; e.g. loss of body minerals as calcium salts.)
d Entmineralisierung *f* der Knochen; Knochenentmineraliserung *f*
f déminéralisation *f* osseuse
p desmineralização *f* óssea

1558 **demineralization of lactoserum; demineralization of whey**
(Biochem.)
(Food biochemistry.)
d Entmineralisierung *f* des Laktoserums
f déminéralisation *f* du lactosérum
p desmineralização *f* do lacto-soro

* **demineralization of whey → 1558**

1559 **demographic explosion**
(Agr.)
(Ecology; excessive and rapid growth of population.)
d Bevölkerungsexplosion *f*
f explosion *f* démographique
p explosão *f* demográfica *f*

1560 **denaturated alcohol**
(Prod.)
(Ref. to methylated alcohol; can also be denaturated with other substances; unsuitable for human consumption.)
d vergällter Alkohol *m*
f alcool *m* dénaturé
p álcool *m* desnaturado

1561 **denaturated lipoprotein**
(Biochem.)
(Nutritional science.)
d denaturiertes Lipoprotein *n*
f lipoprotéine *f* dénaturée
p lipoproteína *f* desnaturada

1562 **denaturation**
(Biochem.)
(Thermal treatment can produce protein-denaturation promoting action of digestive enzymes. Ref. to alcohol: addition of substances to turn it undrinkable.)
d Denaturierung *f*
f dénaturation *f*
p desnaturação *f*

* **denatured component → 1563**

1563 **denatured constituent; denatured component**
(Biochem.)
(Nutritional science.)
d denaturierter Bestandteil *m*

f constituant *m* dénaturé
p constituinte *m* desnaturado

1564 **denitrification of the soil**
(Agr.)
(Soil; soil treatment: nitrate/nitrite reduction.)
d Denitrifikation *f* des Bodens
f dénitrification *f* du sol
p desnitrificação *f* do solo

1565 **density**
(Prod.)
(Quantity/mass of a substance related to unit volume: food production technology; flavour research and production.)
d Densität *f*
f densité *f*
p densidade *f*

1566 **density of plantation**
(Agr.)
(Agricultural methods.)
d Dichte *f* der Anpflanzung
f densité *f* de plantation
p densidade *f* da plantação

1567 **density of the grape must**
(Biochem.)
(Enology.)
d Traubenmostdensität *f*; Dichte *f* des Traubenmostes; Dichtigkeit *f* des Traubenmostes
f densité *f* du moût *m* de raisin
p densidade *f* do mosto de uvas

1568 **dental caries**
(Med.)
(Caries of the dentine, caused by sugar-decomposing bacteria.)
d Dentinerweichung *f*; Zahnschmelzkaries *f*; Zahnfäule *f*
f carie *f* dentaire
p cárie *f* dentária

1569 **dental crown**
(Med.)
(Anatomy; tooth-body part.)
d Zahnkrone *f*
f couronne *f* de dents
p coroa *f* de dentes

1570 **dental diseases**
(Med.)
(E.g. caries, sugar-related.)
d Zahnkrankheiten *fpl*
f maladies *fpl* des dents
p doenças *fpl* dos dentes

1571 **dental enamel**
(Med.)
(Anatomy.)
d Zahnschmelz *m*
f émail *m* des dents
p esmalte *m* dos dentes

1572 **dental plaque**
(Med.)
(Bacteria layer on the teeth, causing caries, a nutrition-related disease.)
d Zahnbelag *m*
f plaque *f* dentaire
p placa *f* dentária

1573 **dental pulp**
(Med.)
(Anatomy. Mass in the pulp cavity of the center of the tooth.)
d Zahnmark *n*
f pulpe *f* dentaire
p polpa *f* dental

* **dentin → 1574**

1574 **dentine; dentin**
(Med.)
(Anatomy. Calcified tooth-body part.)
d Dentin *n*; Zahnbein *m*
f dentine *f*
p dentina *f*

1575 **dentition**
(Med.)
(Anatomy)
d Zahnung *f*
f dentition *f*
p dentição *f*

1576 **deodorization**
(Prod.)
(Food processing technology; odour elimination treatment, generally of fats; in milk processing.)
d Deodorisierung *f*
f désodorisation *f*
p desodorização *f*

1577 **depectinization**
(Biochem.)
(Nutritional science: Fruit juice clarification; Fruit pulp clearing treatment; e.g. by enzymatic methods.)
d Entpektinisierung *f*; Pektinentzug *m*
f dépectination *f*
p depectinização *f*

1578 **deposit** *v*
(Prod.)
(Food processing technology; deposit forming, accumulating, to sediment.)
d ablagern

f déposer
p depositar

1579 **depot fat**
(Med.)
(Storage fat, ref. e.g. to supernutrition.)
d angelagertes Fett *n*; Fettanlagerung *f*
f dépôt *m* de graisses
p depósito *m* de gordura

1580 **depression of the freezing point**
(Prod.)
(Food processing technology.)
d Gefrierpunkterniedrigung *f*
f abaissement *m* du point de congélation
p abaixamento *m* do ponto de congelamento

* **depth erosion → 4402**

1581 **derivatives**
(Prod.)
(Food processing technology.)
d Derivate *npl*
f dérivés *mpl*
p derivados *mpl*

1582 **derivatives with an aromatic nucleus**
(Biochem.)
(Nutritional science; chemistry: ref. to an organic compound showing multiple double bonds.)
d Derivate *npl* mit aromatischen Kern
f dérivés *mpl* à noyau aromatique
p derivados *mpl* com núcleo aromático

1583 **dermatitis**
(Med.)
(Veterinary; skin inflammation.)
d Hautentzündung *f*
f dermatite *f*; dermite *f*
p dermatite *f*

1584 **dermatosis**
(Med.)
(Veterinary; generic designation for skin disease, especially those ones without inflammation.)
d Dermatose *f*
f dermatose *f*
p dermatose *f*

1585 **desalination**
(Prod.)
(Water supply; water treatment: salt reduction.)
d Entsalzung *f*
f dessalement *m*
p dessalinização *f*

1586 **desalinize** *v*; **desalt** *v*
(Prod.)
(Water supply: water treatment.)
d entsalzen
f dessaler
p dessalinizar

* **desalt** *v* **→ 1586**

1587 **descending colon**
(Med.)
(Anatomy; part of the large intestine.)
d absteigender Grimmdarm *m*
f côlon *m* descendant
p cólon *m* descendente

1588 **desertification of the soil**
(Agr.)
(Soil destruction, e.g. by mismanagement.)
d Versandung *f* des Bodens; Bodenzerstörung *f*
f désertification *f* des sols
p desertificação *f* do solo

1589 **desiccate** *v*; **dry** *v*
(Prod.)
(Food processing technology; food preservation by drying.)
d dörren; trocknen
f dessécher; déshydrater
p dessecar

1590 **desiccation**
(Prod.)
(Food processing technology: dehydration; food preservation by drying methods.)
d Austrocknung *f*
f dessiccation *f*
p dessecação *f*

1591 **desoxyribonucleic acid; DNA**
(Med.)
(Constituent of the chromosomes; determinates the hereditary characteristics, controlling the protein synthesis, parting from the amino acids. The structure is that of a double helix.)
d Desoxyribonucleinsäure *f*; DNS *f*
f acide *m* désoxyribonucléique; ADN *m*
p ácido *m* desoxirribonucléico *m*; DNA *m*

1592 **dessert; afters**
(Prod.)
(Gastronomy.)
d Nachtisch *m*; Nachspeise *f*; Dessert *n*
f dessert *m*
p sobremesa *f*

1593 **dessert; sweet**
(Prod.)
(Gastronomy.)
d Süßspeise *f*

f entremets *m*; entremets *m* sucré
p doce *m* de sobremesa

1594 **destruction of pathogenic germs**
(Biochem.)
(Microbiology: here, germ is a disease-causing microorganism.)
d Zerstörung *f* pathogener Keime
f destruction *f* des germes pathogènes
p destruição *f* de germes patogênicos

1595 **detection threshold**
(Med.)
(Aroma/flavour perception.)
d Ermittlungsschwelle *f*; Feststellungsschwelle *f*
f seuil *m* de détection
p limiar *m* de detecção

1596 **deterioration; spoilage**
(Prod.)
(Food processing technology, research and production: foodstuff decay.)
d Verderblichkeit *f*; Schlechtwerden *n*
f détérioration *f*
p deterioração *f*

1597 **deterioration by various microorganisms**
(Biochem.)
(Microbiology.)
d Zerfall *m* durch verschiedene Mikroorganismen
f dégradation *f* par divers microorganismes
p degradação *f* por diversos microorganismos

1598 **deterioration risks; decomposition risks**
(Biochem.)
(Microbiology.)
d Zerfallsrisiko *n*; Dekompositionsrisiko *n*
f risques *mpl* de détérioration; risques *mpl* de décomposition
p riscos *mpl* de deterioração; riscos *mpl* de decomposição

1599 **determination method by thin layer chromatography**
(Prod.)
(Flavour research and production.)
d Dünnschichtchromatographiebestimmungs-methode *f*; Bestimmungsmethode *f* der Dünnschichtchromatographie
f méthode *f* de dosage par chromatographie en couches minces; méthode *f* de dosage par chromatographie sur couche mince
p método *m* de determinação por cromatografia de camada fina

1600 **determination of acidity**
(Biochem.)
(Enology.)
d Bestimmung *f* des Säuregehaltes
f détermination *f* de l'acidité
p determinação *f* da acidez

1601 **determination of sugar richness**
(Biochem.)
(Enology.)
d Bestimmung *f* der Zuckerreichaltigkeit
f détermination *f* de la richesse en sucre
p determinação *f* da riqueza do teor de açúcar

* **detoxication → 1602**

1602 **detoxification; detoxication**
(Biochem.)
(Nutritional science: Elimination of toxic substances in foodstuff.)
d Entgiftung *f*; Detoxifikation *f*
f détoxication *f*
p desintoxicação *f*; eliminação *f* de substâncias tóxicas

1603 **devastation of the culture; ravage of the culture**
(Agr.)
(Destruction of cultures, e.g. by insects.)
d Verheerung *f* der Kulturen
f dégâts *mpl* des cultures
p devastação *f* das culturas

1604 **development of feathers**
(Agr.)
(Poultry raising and treatment.)
d Befiederung *f*
f développement *m* du plumage
p empenamento *m*

1605 **development of grape overmaturation sauternes type**
(Biochem.)
(Enology.)
d Entwicklung *f* der Edelfäule
f développement *m* de la pourriture noble
p desenvolvimento *m* da sobrematuração nobre; desenvolvimento *m* da supermaturação nobre

1606 **development of nutrition**
(Prod.)
(Food processing technology; foodstuff production.)
d Entwicklung *f* der Ernährung
f évolution *f* de l'alimentation
p evolução *f* da nutrição

1607 **development of processed foodstuffs**
(Prod.)
(Food processing, research, production and marketing.)
d Entwicklung *f* der weiterverarbeiteten Nahrungsmittel

f développement *m* des produits alimentaires transformés
p desenvolvimento *m* dos produtos alimentícios de transformação

1608 development of rancid flavour
(Biochem.)
(Nutritional science: quality-reducing factor in meat processing.)
d Entwicklung *f* ranzigen Geschmacks
f développement *m* de flaveur rance
p desenvolvimento *m* de sabor rançoso

1609 development of the leaves
(Agr.)
(Botany.)
d Blattentwicklung *f*
f développement *m* foliaire
p desenvolvimento *m* das folhas; desenvolvimento *m* foliar

1610 development of the wine bouquet
(Biochem.)
(Enology; e.g. depending on environmental storage temperatures.)
d Entwicklung *f* des Weinbuketts
f développement *m* du bouquet du vin
p desenvolvimento *m* do buquê du vinho

1611 deviation of heat
(Prod.)
(Food processing technology.)
d Wärmeabführung *f*; Wärmeableitung *f*
f déviation *f* de chaleur
p desvio *m* de calor

1612 dextran
(Med.)
(Polysaccharide. Medicinal application: Blood plasma expander.)
d Dextran *n*
f dextrane *m*
p dextrano *m*

1613 dextrin; starch gum
(Prod.)
($(C_6H_{10}O_5)_n$; carbohydrate; intermediate product of starch digestion; e.g. prime material for aroma/fragrance production.)
d Dextrin *n*; Stärkegummi *n*
f dextrine *f*
p dextrina *f*

1614 dextrin-maltose
(Prod.)
(Baby nutrition. Milk ingredient in industrial milk types.)
d Dextrin-Maltose-Anteil *m*
f dextrine-maltose *m*
p dextrina-maltose *f*

* **dextrose → 2571**

1615 d-gluconic acid delta-lactone; gluconolactone
(Prod.)
($C_6H_{12}O_6$; acidifying agent in foodstuff.)
d d-Gluconsäure-delta-lacton *n*
f delta-lactone *m* de l'acide gluconique
p delta-lactona *f* do ácido glucônico

1616 diabetes
(Med.)
(Metabolism disorder with thirst and urine quantity increase.)
d Diabetes *m*
f diabète *m*
p diabetes *m/f*

1617 diabetes mellitus; alimentary diabetes
(Med.)
(Hyperglycaemia due to insufficient carbohydrate utilization of the body.)
d Diabetes *m* mellitus; Zuckerharnruhr *f*; Zuckerkrankheit *f*
f diabète *m* sucré
p diabetes *m* melito

1618 diabetic acidosis
(Med.)
(Due to diabetic mellitus: Increased level of ketone bodies in the organism: fat metabolism deficiency.)
d diabetische Acidose *f*
f acidose *f* diabétique
p acidose *f* diabética

1619 diabetic bread
(Med.)
(Regimens, diets: Carbohydrate-reduced bread without sugar addition, in regimen for diabetics.)
d Diabetikerbrot *n*
f pain *m* diabétique
p pão *m* para diabéticos

1620 diabetic coma
(Med.)
(Diabetes mellitus, carbohydrate-metabolism disorder.)
d diabetisches Koma *n*
f coma *m* diabétique
p coma *m* diabético

1621 diabetic diet
(Med.)
(Alimentary regimen; e.g. ref. to distribution of permitted carbohydrate ration over various daily meals.)
d Diabetesdiät *f*

f diète *f* pour diabétiques
p dieta *f* para diabético

1622 **diabetic marmalade**
(Med.)
(Regimens, diets: Carbohydrate-reduced and without sugar addition, in regimen for diabetics.)
d Diabetikermarmelade *f*
f marmelade *f* diabétique
p geléia *f* para diabéticos

1623 **diacetyl; 2,3-butanedione**
(Prod.)
($C_4H_6O_2$. Aroma prime material, butter-like flavour; in ice-cream, desserts and confectioneries aroma notes.)
d Diacetyl *n*
f diacétyle *m*
p diacetila *f*

1624 **dialysis**
(Med.)
(In general: particle-separation in a liquid mixture through a membrane.)
d Dialyse *f*
f dialyse *f*
p diálise *f*

1625 **diaphragm**
(Med.)
(Anatomy; muscle, separating the thoracic and abdominal cavities.)
d Zwerchfell *n*; Diaphragma *n*
f diaphragme *m*
p diafragma *m*

1626 **diarrhea; diarrhoea**
(Med.)
(E.g. due to intolerance to proteins of cow's milk, esp. regarding baby nutrition.)
d Durchfall *m*; Diarrhö *f*; Diarrhöe *f*
f diarrhée *f*
p diarréia *f*

1627 **diarrheal; diarrhoeal** *adj*
(Med.)
(Ref. to intolerance to proteins of cow's milk, esp. regarding baby nutrition.)
d diarrhöisch; durchfallsbezüglich
f diarrhéique
p diarréico

1628 **diarrhea of ablactation**
(Med.)
(Baby care.)
d Entwöhnungsdurchfall *m*; Entwöhnungsdiarrhöe *f*
f diarrhée *f* d'ablactation
p diarréia *f* ablactação

* **diarrhoea → 1626**

* **diarrhoeal** *adj* **→ 1627**

1629 **diastase**
(Biochem.)
(Nutritional science: beer brewery process: Wort production through hydrolysis of starch by diastase in malted barley, occurring in the production of sucrose and maltose.)
d Diastase *f*
f diastase *f*
p diástase *f*

1630 **diastasic activity; diastatic activity**
(Biochem.)
(Nutritional science; e.g. measure for sugar production in meal by means of its own amides and diastase.)
d Diastaseaktivität *f*
f activité *f* diastasique
p atividade *f* diastásica; atividade *f* diastática

* **diastatic activity → 1630**

1631 **diatomaceous earth; infusorial earth; kieselguhr**
(Prod.)
(Food processing technology. Kieselguhr; diatomite: filtering additive esp. in brewery processes.)
d Diatomeenerde *f*; Kieselgur *f*; Infusorienerde *f*
f terre *f* à diatomées; tripoli *m*; kieselguhr *m*; kieselgur *m*
p diatomito *m*; terra *f* de infusórios; terra *f* diatomácea; tvipole *m*

1632 **dice** *v*
(Prod.)
(Gastronomy.)
d würfeln; in Würfel schneiden
f couper en petits carrés
p cortar em cubos

1633 **dichloroethylene; acetylene dichloride**
(Prod.)
($C_2H_2Cl_2$; chlorinated solvent, e.g. for fats; also aroma/flavour research and production. Raw material.)
d Dichloräthylen *n*
f dichloréthylène *m*
p dicloroetileno *m*

* **dichloromethane → 3493**

* **dicotyledon → 1634**

1634 **dicotyledonous angiosperm; dicotyledon**
(Agr.)
(Botany. Angiospermae having two seed leaves.)

d zweikeimblättriger Decksamen *m*
f angiosperme *f* dicotylédone; dicotylédone *f*
p angiosperma *f* dicotiledônea

1635 **diet**
(Med.)
(Eating as to dietary rules; consuming dietary products e.g. reduced in calories, sugar-free foods etc.)
d Diät *f*
f diète *f*
p dieta *f*

1636 **diet; regimen**
(Med.)
(Health-promoting nutrition plan.)
d Diät *f*; Schonkost *f*
f diète *f*; régime *m*
p dieta *f*; regime *m*

1637 **diet adjustment**
(Med.)
(Alimentary regimen.)
d Diätanpassung *f*
f ajustement *m* diététique
p adequação *f* dietética

1638 **dietary beer**
(Prod.)
(Food processing technology; beer type nearly without any carbohydrates which could be harmful in case of diabetes.)
d Diätbier *n*
f bière *f* diététique
p cerveja *f* para dieta; cerveja *f* dietética

1639 **dietary levels of selected vitamins**
(Med.)
(Veterinary; ref. to feed composition.)
d Diätniveaus *npl* ausgewählter Vitamine; Wertstufen *fpl* ausgesuchter Vitamine in der Diät
f niveaux *mpl* diététiques de vitamines sélectionnées
p níveis *mpl* dietéticos de vitaminas selecionadas

1640 **dietary products**
(Prod.)
(Food processing technology: products for use in diets.)
d diätetische Produkte *npl*
f produits *mpl* diététiques
p produtos *mpl* dietéticos

1641 **dietary treatment**
(Med.)
(Veterinary; ref. to animal treatment by diets and vitamin supplementations.)
d Diätbehandlung *f*
f traitement *m* diététique
p tratamento *m* por dieta

1642 **diet change**
(Med.)
(Alimentary regimen.)
d Diätwechsel *m*
f changement *m* de la diète
p mudança *f* de dieta

1643 **diet deficiency**
(Med.)
(Ref. to insufficient vitamin supply.)
d Mangeldiät *f*
f carence *f* diététique
p deficiência *f* dietética

1644 **dietetic** *adj*
(Med.)
(Regimens, diets: the use of products in special diets.)
d diätetisch
f diététique
p dietético

1645 **dietetic albuminuria**
(Med.)
(Proteinuria; presence of serum proteins in the urine.)
d diätetische Albuminurie *f*
f albuminurie *f* diététique
p albuminuria *f* dietética

1646 **dietetic correction**
(Med.)
(Diet alteration; nutrition.)
d dietätische Korrektion *f*; Ausgleich *m* der Diät
f correction *f* diététique
p correção *f* dietética

1647 **dietetic error**
(Med.)
(Often the cause of intestinal malfunction, due to lack of dietary fibres called "roughage" in diets.)
d Ernährungsfehler *m*
f erreur *f* diététique
p error *m* dietético

1648 **dietetic food**
(Med.)
(Regimens, diets.)
d Diätnahrungsmittel *npl*
f produits *mpl* alimentaires de régime
p produtos *mpl* alimentícios dietéticos; alimentos *mpl* dietéticos

1649 **dietetic improvement**
(Biochem.)
(Nutritional science: dietetics, nutrition.)

d diätetische Verbesserung *f*
f amélioration *f* diététique
p melhoramento *m* dietético

1650 **dietetic intervention; intervention through dietetics**
(Med.)
(Nutrition in therapy.)
d Diätintervention *f*; Eingriff *m* seitens diätischer Maßnahmen
f intervention *f* diététique
p intervenção *f* dietética

1651 **dietetic measures**
(Med.)
(Nutrition in medicine.)
d dietätische Maßnahmen *fpl*
f mesures *fpl* diététiques
p medidas *fpl* dietéticas

1652 **dietetic milk**
(Prod.)
(Food processing technology.)
d Diätmilch *f*
f lait *m* de régime
p leite *m* para regime

1653 **dietetic nutriment**
(Med.)
(Nutritional therapy.)
d dietätisches Nahrungsmittel *n*
f aliment *m* diététique
p alimento *m* dietético

1654 **dietetic properties**
(Med.)
(Food processing technology: dietetic food.)
d diätetische Eigenschaften *fpl*
f propriétés *mpl* diététiques
p propriedades *fpl* dietéticas

1655 **dietetic protection**
(Med.)
(Nutritional therapy.)
d Diätschutz *m*; Schutz *m* durch diätischer Maßnahmen
f protection *f* diététique
p proteção *f* dietética

1656 **dietetic science**
(Med.)
(Nutrition.)
d Ernährungswissenschaft *f*
f science *f* alimentaire
p ciência *f* da alimentação

1657 **dietetics for children; infantile dietetics**
(Med.)
(Science of diets in baby/child nutrition.)
d Kinderdiätetik *f*
f diététique *f* infantile
p dietética *f* infantil; dietética *f* para crianças

1658 **dietetic solution; solution via dietetics**
(Med.)
(Medical solutions through dietetic methods.)
d diätetische Lösung *f*; Lösung *f* durch diätetische Methoden
f solution *f* diététique; solution *f* par la diététique
p solução *f* dietética; solução *f* por métodos dietéticos

1659 **dietetic vitamin products**
(Prod.)
(Vitamins in nutrition.)
d diätetische Vitaminprodukte *npl*
f produits *mpl* diététiques vitaminiques
p produtos *mpl* dietéticos com vitaminas

1660 **diet for children**
(Med.)
(Baby nutrition.)
d Kinderdiät *f*
f diète *f* infantile
p dieta *f* infantil; dieta *f* para crianças

* **diet of convalescence → 1335**

1661 **diet variation**
(Med.)
(Alimentary regimen.)
d Diätabwechslung *f*
f variation *f* de la diète
p variação *f* de dieta

1662 **differential vaporization**
(Prod.)
(Aroma/flavour production: ref. to distillation processes.)
d differentielle Vaporisierung *f*; differentielle Vaporisation *f*
f vaporisation *f* différentielle
p vaporização *f* diferencial

1663 **differential volatilization**
(Prod.)
(Aroma/flavour production: separation procedure of liquid phases.)
d differentielle Flüchtigkeit *f*
f volatilisation *f* différentielle
p volatilização *f* diferencial

1664 **difficult sedimentation; difficult settling process**
(Biochem.)
(Nutritional science: ref. to sedimentation processes.)
d schwieriger Sedimentationsprozess *m*; schwer zu erwirkender Niederschlag *m*

f sédimentation *f* difficile; processus *m* de sédimentation difficile
p sedimentação *f* difícil; processo *m* de difícil sedimentação

* **difficult settling process → 1664**

1665 **digestibility**
(Med.)
(Assimilation of nutrients, amounts to about 95%.)
d Verdaulichkeit *f*
f digestibilité *f*
p digestibilidade *f*

1666 **digestibility of cereal products; digestibility of cereals**
(Med.)
(Assimilation of nutrients.)
d Verdaulichkeit *f* von Getreideprodukten
f digestibilité *f* des produits céréaliers
p digestibilidade *f* de produtos cereais

* **digestibility of cereals → 1666**

1667 **digestibility of cow's milk**
(Med.)
(Baby nutrition.)
d Verdaulichkeit *f* von Kuhmilch
f digestibilité *f* du lait de vache
p digestibilidade *f* de leite de vaca

1668 **digestible** *adj*
(Med.)
(Digestibility.)
d verdaulich
f digestible
p digestível; digerível

1669 **digestion**
(Med.)
(Food breakdown process for assimilation by the body.)
d Verdauung *f*
f digestion *f*
p digestão *f*

1670 **digestive enzymes**
(Med.)
(Anatomy: Secretion of digestive glands in the body.)
d Verdauungsenzyme *npl*
f enzymes *fpl* digestives
p enzimas *fpl* digestivas

1671 **digestive ferment**
(Med.)
(Anatomy: ref. to the digestion process.)
d Verdauungsferment *n*
f ferment *m* digestif
p fermento *m* digestivo

1672 **digestive immunity**
(Med.)
(Nutrition in medicine.)
d Verdauungsimmunität *f*
f immunité *f* digestive
p imunidade *f* digestiva

1673 **digestive intolerance**
(Med.)
(Nutritional disorders.)
d Verdauungsunverträglichkeit *f*
f intolérance *f* digestive
p intolerância *f* digestiva

1674 **digestive juice; gastric juice**
(Med.)
(Digestion process.)
d Verdauungssaft *m*; Magensaft *m*
f suc *m* digestif; suc *m* gastrique
p suco *m* digestivo; suco *m* gástrico

1675 **digestive malabsorption**
(Med.)
(Nutrition: nutrients in the alimentary canal.)
d digestive Absorptionsstörung *f*; den Verdauungsprozess betreffende Aufnahmestörung *f*
f malabsorption *f* digestive
p má absorção *f* digestiva

1676 **digestive pathology**
(Med.)
(Nutrition in medicine: digestive diseases.)
d Verdauungspathologie *f*
f pathologie *f* digestive
p patologia *f* digestiva

1677 **digestive system**
(Med.)
(Human anatomy.)
d Verdauungsapparat *m*
f système *m* digestif
p órgãos *mpl* de digestão

1678 **digestive tract**
(Med.)
(Anatomy.)
d Verdauungstrakt *m*
f tractus *m* gastro-intestinal
p trato *m* digestivo

* **digestive trouble due to overnutrition → 2876**

1679 **digestive utilization of proteins**
(Med.)
(Proteins of good utilization: e.g. dairy products.)

d Ausnutzung *f* der Proteine durch die Verdauung
f utilisation *f* digestive des protéines
p utilização *f* digestiva das proteínas

1680 **dihydro-beta-ionone**
(Prod.)
(Aroma/flavour prime material.)
d Dihydro-beta-Ionon *n*
f dihydro-bêta-ionone *f*
p dihidro-beta-ionona *f*

1681 **dike; dam**
(Agr.)
(Construction of earth for water-flow stopping and for confining water etc.)
d Deich *m*; Damm *m*
f digue *f*
p dique *m*

1682 **dillherb oil**
(Prod.)
(Aroma/flavour prime material. "Anethum graveolens L.".)
d Dillkrautöl *n*
f huile *f* d'aneth
p óleo *m* da erva do aneto

1683 **dillseed oil**
(Prod.)
(Aroma/flavour prime material. "Anethum graveolens L.".)
d Dillsamenöl *n*
f huile *f* de la semence d'aneth
p óleo *m* da semente do aneto

1684 **dilute** *v*; **thin** *v*
(Prod.)
(Aroma/flavour research and application.)
d verdünnen
f délayer; diluer
p diluir

1685 **diluted**
(Prod.)
(Aroma/flavour research and application.)
d verdünnt
f dilué
p diluído

1686 **diluted mixture**
(Prod.)
(Aroma/fragrance research and production.)
d verdünnte Mischung *f*
f mélange *m* dilué
p mistura *f* diluída

1687 **dilute** *v* **under cold; dilute** *v* **under cold application**
(Prod.)
(Food processing technology.)
d verdünnen bei Kälte; verdünnen unter Kälteanwendung
f délayer à froid
p diluir sob frio

* **dilute** *v* **under cold application → 1687**

1688 **dilute** *v* **under heat; dilute** *v* **under heat application**
(Prod.)
(Food processing technology.)
d verdünnen bei Wärme; verdünnen unter Wärmeanwendung
f délayer à chaud
p diluir sob calor

* **dilute** *v* **under heat application → 1688**

1689 **dilution**
(Prod.)
(Aroma/flavour research and application.)
d Verdünnung *f*
f dilution *f*
p diluição *f*

1690 **dimethylacetal**
(Prod.)
($C_4H_{10}O_2$; aroma/fragrance prime material.)
d Dimethylacetal *n*
f diméthylacétal *m*
p dimetilacetal *m*

* **dimethyl ketone → 31**

1691 **dimethylphenylethylcarbinol**
(Prod.)
(Aroma/fragrance prime material, e.g. herbal flavour note.)
d Dimethylphenylethylcarbinol *n*
f diméthylphényléthylcarbinol *m*
p dimetilfeniletilcarbinol *m*

* **dinner → 1998**

* **dip → 4839**

1692 **diphenyl**
(Agr.)
($C_{12}H_{10}$. Fungistat, e.g. for transportation of oranges and other types of fruit.)
d Diphenyl *n*
f diphényle *m*
p difenilo *m*

1693 **disaccharide**
(Biochem.)
(Nutritional science: sugars with two monosaccharides combined with elimination of one water molecule.)

d Disaccharid *n*
f disaccharide *m*
p dissacáride *m*; dissacarose *f*

1694 **disaccharide intolerance**
(Med.)
(Insufficient digestion capacity for saccharose, maltose or lactose. Hereditary disease.)
d Disaccharidunverträglichkeit *f*
f intolérance *f* aux disaccharides
p intolerância aos dissacaretos

1695 **discharge**
(Prod.)
(Food production technology.)
d Entleerung *f*
f vidage *f*
p escoamento *m*

1696 **discoloration**
(Prod.)
(Food colorants: Elimination of colorants and pigments, generally from cooking oils etc.)
d Entfärbung *f*
f décoloration *f*
p descoloração *f*

1697 **discoloration of edible oils**
(Biochem.)
(Food biochemistry: Colour elimination from a foodstuff; in refinement procedures.)
d Entfärbung *f* von Speiseölen
f décoloration *f* des huiles alimentaires
p descoloração *f* de óleos comestíveis

1698 **discontinuous extraction**
(Prod.)
(Aroma/flavour research and production; extraction process type.)
d diskontinuierliche Extraktion *f*
f extraction *f* discontinue
p extração *f* descontínua

1699 **discontinuous extraction by solvent circulation**
(Prod.)
(Aroma/flavour research and production, extraction process type.)
d diskontinuierliche Extraktion *f* unter Lösungsmittelumlauf
f extraction *f* discontinue avec circulation de solvant
p extração *f* descontínua sob circulação de solvente

1700 **discontinuous extraction with agitation**
(Prod.)
(Aroma/flavour research and production, extraction process type.)
d diskontinuierliche Extraktion *f* mit intensiven Umrührungsbewegungen
f extraction *f* discontinue avec agitation
p extração *f* descontínua sob agitação

1701 **discontinuous extraction with solvent agitation and circulation**
(Prod.)
(Aroma/flavour research and production, extraction process type.)
d diskontinuierliche Extraktion *f* unter intensiver Bewegung und mit Umlauf des Lösungsmittels
f extraction *f* discontinue avec agitation et circulation du solvant
p extração *f* descontínua sob agitação e circulação do solvente

1702 **discontinuous rectification**
(Prod.)
(Aroma/flavour research and production.)
d diskontinuierliche Rektifikation *f*
f rectification *f* discontinue
p retificação *f* descontínua

1703 **disease identification by organ checking**
(Med.)
(Veterinary; ref. to slaughterhouse technology: disease research by examination of the animal body.)
d Krankheitsbestimmung *f* durch Organbeschau
f identification *f* des maladies par les organes
p identificação *f* das doenças pelos órgãos

* **disease of allergic origin → 115**

1704 **disease of the blood-forming organs; disease of the hematopoietic organs**
(Med.)
(Anatomy.)
d Erkrankung *f* der blutbildenden Organe; Erkrankung *f* der hämatopoetischen Organe
f maladie *f* des organes hématopoïétiques
p enfermidade *f* dos órgãos hematopoéticos

* **disease of the hematopoietic organs → 1704**

1705 **disease outbrake**
(Med.)
(Veterinary; e.g. ref. to livestock and poultry diseases.)
d Krankheitsausbruch *m*
f apparition *f* soudaine des maladies
p surto *m* de doença

1706 **diseases nutritionally correctable; diseases remediable by nutrition**
(Med.)
(Nutritional therapy; diets etc.)
d ernährungskorregierbare Krankheiten *fpl*;

durch Ernährung besserungsfähige Krankheiten *fpl*
f maladies *fpl* corrigibles par l'alimentation
p doenças *fpl* corregíveis pela alimentação

1707 diseases of baby cattle; diseases of young stock
(Med.)
(Veterinary: ref. to farm animal raising and treatment.)
d Aufzuchtskrankheiten *fpl*
f maladies *fpl* d'élevage
p doenças *fpl* das crias

* **diseases of young stock → 1707**

* **diseases remediable by nutrition → 1706**

1708 dish; meal
(Prod.)
(Gastronomy.)
d Gericht *n*; Speise *f*
f mets *m*
p refeição *f*; prato *m*

1709 disinfect *v*
(Med.)
(Food processing technology; water treatment.)
d entkeimen; desinfizieren
f désinfecter
p desinfetar

1710 disinfected
(Prod.)
(Water supply treatment.)
d entkeimt; desinfiziert
f désinfecté
p desinfetado

1711 disinfection bath against arachnids
(Med.)
(Veterinary cattle treatment by immersion or by shower.)
d Desinfektionsbad *n* gegen Zecken
f bain *m* acaracide
p banho *m* carrapaticida

1712 disinfection process
(Prod.)
(Food processing technology; e.g. water treatment.)
d Entkeimungsverfahren *n*
f processus *m* de désinfection
p processo *m* de desinfecção

1713 disintegration
(Biochem.)
(E.g. separation into constituting elements.)
d Desintegration *f*
f désintégration *f*; désagrégation *f*
p desintegração *f*; desagregação *f*

1714 dismineralized water
(Prod.)
(Water supply.)
d entmineralisiertes Wasser *n*
f eau *f* déminéralisée
p água *f* desmineralizada

* **dispersant → 1718**

1715 disperse *v*
(Prod.)
(Aroma/flavour research and production: ref. to a system of various phases (dispersed system), having a continuous phase and another, finely divided, dispersed phase.)
d dispergieren
f disperser
p dispergar

1716 dispersed phase
(Biochem.)
(System of various phases (dispersed system), having a continuous phase (dispersing agent) and another, finely divided, dispersed phase.)
d disperse Phase *f*; dispergierte Phase *f*
f phase *f* dispersée
p fase *f* dispersa

1717 dispersibility
(Biochem.)
(Food processing technology: e.g. raw material characteristic.)
d Dispersionskraft *f*
f dispersibilité *f*; pouvoir *m* dispersant; force *f* dispersive
p poder *m* de dispersão; força *f* de dispersão

1718 dispersing agent; dispersant
(Prod.)
(Auxiliary which promotes the formation of dispersion.)
d Dispersionsmittel *n*
f agent *m* dispersant
p dispersante *m*; dispergente *m*

1719 dispersing effect
(Biochem.)
(Ref. to dispersibility, to the action of dispersing additives.)
d Dispergierungseffekt *m*
f effet *m* dispersant
p efeito *m* dispersante

1720 dispersing properties
(Biochem.)
(Ref. to dispersibility, to the action of dispersing additives.)

d dispergierende Eigenschaften *fpl*
f caractéristiques *fpl* dispersantes
p caraterísticas *fpl* dispersantes; propriedades *fpl* dispersantes

1721 **dispersion**
(Prod.)
(Aroma/flavour research and production: ref. to a system of various phases (dispersed system), having a continuous phase and another, finely divided, dispersed phase.)
d Dispersion *f*
f dispersion *f*
p dispersão *f*

1722 **dispersion in hardened peanut fat**
(Prod.)
(Food processing technology; product preparation, like beta-carotene dispersed in peanut oil.)
d Dispersion *f* in gefestigtem Erdnussfett
f dispersion *f* dans la graisse d'arachide durcie
p dispersão *f* em gordura sólida de amendoim

1723 **dispersion in soybean oil**
(Prod.)
(Food processing technology; product preparation, like beta-carotene dispersed in soybean oil.)
d Sojaöldispersion *f*
f dispersion *f* dans l'huile de soja
p dispersão *f* em óleo de soja

1724 **dispersion of the aqueous phase**
(Prod.)
(Food processing technology; e.g. emulsion elaboration.)
d Dispersion *f* der wässrigen Phase
f dispersion *f* de la phase aqueuse
p dispersão *f* da fase aquosa

1725 **dissociated diet**
(Med.)
(Alimentary regimen by H. Hay, U.S. physician; e.g. separate intake of protein-rich food and carbohydrate-rich food.)
d Trennkost *f*; Haysche Trennkost *f*
f diète *f* dissociée
p dieta *f* de dissociação

1726 **dissolution**
(Biochem.)
(E.g. liquefaction.)
d Auflösung *f*
f dissolution *f*
p dissolução *f*

1727 **dissolution in the saliva**
(Med.)
(Food constituents, before swallowing: Initiaton of action of salivary amylases.)
d Auflösung *f* im Speichel
f dissolution *f* dans la salive
p dissolução *f* na saliva

1728 **dissolving power**
(Prod.)
(Food processing technology: product characteristic.)
d Auflösungskraft *f*
f pouvoir *m* de dissolution
p poder *m* dissolvente; poder *m* de dissolução

1729 **dissolving velocity**
(Prod.)
(Food processing technology: product characteristic.)
d Auflösungsgeschwindigkeit *f*
f vitesse *f* de dissolution
p velocidade *f* de dissolução

1730 **distillate**
(Prod.)
(Aroma/flavour production: ref. to distillation processes: distillation product.)
d Destillat *n*
f distillat *m*
p destilado *m*; produto *m* de destilação

* **distillation front → 2198**

1731 **distillation of the fermented product**
(Prod.)
(Aroma/flavour research and production.)
d Destillation *f* des gegärten Produktes; Destillation *f* des Gärungsproduktes
f distillation *f* du produit fermenté
p destilação *f* do produto fermentado

1732 **distillation of the maceration product**
(Prod.)
(Aroma/flavour research and production.)
d Destillation *f* des Mazerationsproduktes
f distillation *f* du produit de la macération
p destilação *f* do produto de maceração

1733 **distillation process**
(Prod.)
(Aroma/flavour research and production.)
d Destillationsprozess *m*; Umsiedungsprozess *m*
f procédé *m* par distillation
p processo *m* de destilação

* **distillation tail → 5524**

1734 **distilled essences**
(Prod.)
(Aroma production: e.g. plant essences, fruity essences.)
d destillierte Essenzen *fpl*

f essences *fpl* distillées
p essências *fpl* destiladas

1735 **distilled grape marc**
(Biochem.)
(Nutritional science: enology.)
d destillierter Weintraubenrückstand *m*
f marc *m* de raisin distillé
p bagaço *m* da uva destilado

1736 **distillery**
(Prod.)
(Food processing technology and production, esp.: establishment or production of spirits.)
d Destillatbrennerei *f*
f distillerie *f*
p destilaria *f*

1737 **distribution of agricultural products**
(Agr.)
(Distribution of agricultural produce, marketing.)
d Verteilung *f* der Agrarprodukte; Verteilung *f* von landwirtschaftlichen Produkten
f distribution *f* des produits agricoles
p distribuição *f* dos produtos agrícolas

1738 **distribution of nutrients**
(Biochem.)
(Production of feed, rations, premixes for animal nutrition; nutrients like vitamins, trace elements etc. in the formulation.)
d Verteilung *f* der Nährstoffe
f distribution *f* des nutriments
p distribuição *f* dos nutrientes

1739 **disturbance of the amino acid metabolism**
(Med.)
d Aminosäurestoffwechselstörungen *fpl*; Störungen *fpl* des Aminosäurestoffwechsels
f troubles *mpl* du métabolisme des amino-acides
p perturbações *fpl* do metabolismo dos aminoácidos

1740 **diuresis**
(Med.)
(Urine secretion.)
d Diurese *f*; Harnausscheidung *f*
f diurèse *f*
p diurese *f*

1741 **diuretic**
(Med.)
(Urine-volume increasing medicament; some foods have this property: e.g. coffee and teas.)
d Diuretikum *n*; harntreibendes Mittel *n*
f diurétique *m*
p diurético *m*

1742 **diversification of alimentation**
(Biochem.)
(Nutrition; food biochemistry.)
d Vervielseitigung *f* der Ernährung
f diversification *f* alimentaire
p diversificação *f* da alimentação

1743 **diversified nutrition**
(Biochem.)
(Nutritional science.)
d abwechslungsreiche Ernährung *f*
f alimentation *f* diversifiée
p alimentação *f* diversificada

1744 **diversity of metabolic reactions**
(Biochem.)
(Biochemical research in nutritional science.)
d Mannigfaltigkeit *f* der Stoffwechselreaktionen
f diversité *f* des réactions métaboliques
p diversidade *f* das reações metabólicas

1745 **diversity of products**
(Prod.)
(Food processing technology; foodstuff production and marketing.)
d Produktenmannigfaltigkeit *f*; Mannigfaltigkeit *f* der Produkte
f diversité *f* des produits
p diversidade *f* de produtos

1746 **division** (biology)
(Agr.)
(Botany (flora/fauna). Classification; e.g. animals of similar classes.)
d Stamm *m*
f embranchement *m*
p filo *m*

* **DNA → 1591**

* **docosanoic acid → 585**

1747 **doe**
(Agr.)
(Family "Leporidae", esp. genus "Lepus".)
d Setzhase *m*
f hase *f*
p fêmea *f* de lebre

1748 **dolomite**
(Agr.)
(Biological agriculture: e.g. trace element in fertilizers.)
d Dolomit *m*
f dolomie *f*
p dolomita *f*; dolomia *f*

* **domestically elaborated products → 1751**

1749 **domestic animals**
(Agr.)
(Livestock breeding; tame animals, e.g. as

horses.)
d Haustiere *npl*
f animaux *mpl* domestiques
p animais *mpl* domésticos

1750 **domestic pig**
(Agr.)
(Livestock: Opposed to, e.g., wild boar.)
d Hausschwein *n*
f cochon *m* domestique
p porco *m* doméstico

1751 **domestic products; domestically elaborated products**
(Prod.)
(Gastronomy.)
d hausgemachte Produkte *npl*; selbst gemachte Podukte *npl*
f produits *mpl* élaborés à la maison
p produtos *mpl* feitos em casa; produtos elaborados a domicílio

1752 **dominant gene**
(Biochem.)
(Dominant gene (A) determines dark eyes. Recessive gene (a) determines blue eyes: (Aa) determines dark eyes because (A) is a dominant gene. This example applies to animal and plant growth.)
d dominantes Gen *n*; vorherrschender Erbträger *m*
f gène *m* dominant
p gene *m* dominante

1753 **domination of the fermentation process; mastery of the fermentation process**
(Biochem.)
(Fermentation in nutritional science.)
d Beherrschung *f* des Gärungsprozesses
f maîtrise *f* du processus de la fermentation
p domínio *m* do processo de fermentação

* **donkey → 463**

* **dormant** *adj* **→ 3138**

1754 **dosage of the aroma**
(Prod.)
(Aroma/fragrance research and production.)
d Aromadosierung *f*
f dosage *m* d'arôme
p dosagem *f* do aroma

1755 **double boiler process; water bath**
(Prod.)
(Food processing technology; heating process for heating indirectly and evenly small laboratory vessels by means of hot water. Used also as a cooking method.)
d Wasserbad *n*
f bain-marie *m*
p banho-maria *m*

1756 **double chin**
(Med.)
(Anatomy.)
d Doppelkinn *n*
f double menton *m*
p queixo *m* duplo

1757 **double claw**
(Agr.)
(Apiculture: Bee anatomy: hind leg of a worker bee.)
d Doppelklaue *f*
f griffe *f* double
p garra *f* dupla

1758 **double helix**
(Biochem.)
(Nucleic acid made of two strands wound around each other forming this way a double helix; this structure is the DNA (deoxyribonucleic acid).)
d Doppelwende *f*
f double hélice *f*
p dupla hélice *f*

1759 **dough**
(Prod.)
(Food processing technology: e.g. bakery; mixture of flour and water or milk for pasta preparation.)
d Teig *m*
f détrempe *f*; mélange *m* de farine et d'eau
p massa *f* (*à base de farinha*)

* **dough → 4029**

1760 **dough enriched with baker's yeast**
(Prod.)
(Bakery.)
d mit Backhefe angereicherter Teig *m*
f pâte *f* enrichie de levure de boulanger; pâte *f* enrichie de levure de boulangerie
p massa *f* enriquecida com fermento de panificação

1761 **dough for bread**
(Prod.)
(Bakery product.)
d Brotteig *m*
f pâte *f* à pain
p massa *f* do pão

1762 **dough kneading**
(Prod.)
(Food processing technology, e.g. in bakery.)
d Durchkneten *n* eines Teiges

f pétrissage *m* d'une pâte
p amassadura *f* de uma massa; sova *f*

1763 **doughnut**
(Prod.)
(Cake shop product.)
d Krapfen *m*; Berliner *m*
f boule *f* de Berlin; beignet *m* viennois
p sonho *m*

1764 **doughy** *adj*
(Prod.)
(Food processing technology, e.g. in bakery; characteristic of not thoroughly baked cake.)
d teigig; nicht gut durchbacken
f pâteux; non bien cuit
p pastoso; não bem cozido; meio cru

1765 **dourine; equine syphilis**
(Med.)
(Veterinary.)
d Pferdesyphilis *f*
f syphilis *f* équine
p sífilis *f* eqüina

1766 **draff**
(Prod.)
(Food processing technology; beer brewing process: spent grain.)
d Treber *pl*
f drêche *f*
p resíduo *m* do malte; borra *f* do malte

* **draftbeer → 1774**

1767 **draft horse**
(Agr.)
d Zugpferd *n*
f cheval *m* de trait
p cavalo *m* de tração

1768 **dragging away by vapour**
(Prod.)
(Aroma/flavour research and production: part of separation process type.)
d Mitreißen *n* durch Dampf
f entraînement *m* à la vapeur
p arrasto *m* pelo vapor

* **drainage → 1770**

1769 **drainage layer**
(Agr.)
(Soil preparation; soil treatment.)
d Dränschicht *f*
f couche *f* d'assèchement; strate *f* de drainage
p camada *f* de drenagem

1770 **drainage of water; drainage**
(Agr.)
(Soil treatment; farming land preparations: process of water removal from an area.)
d Wasserableitung *f*, Ableitung *f*
f drainage *m* d'eau; drainage *m*
p drenagem *f* das águas; drenagem *f*

1771 **drainage terrace**
(Agr.)
(Soil treatment: farming land preparations: Water removal by collecting terraces which allow a slow flowing off.)
d Dränterrasse *f*
f terrasse *f* de drainage; terrasse *f* d'écoulement de l'eau
p terraço *m* de drenagem

1772 **drain** *v* **the marc**
(Prod.)
(Enology.)
d den Satz austrocknen lassen; dem Satz die Flüssigkeit entziehen
f assécher le marc
p escoar o bagaço

1773 **drake; male duck**
(Agr.)
(Livestock.)
d Erpel *m*; Enterich *m*
f canard *m* mâle
p pato *m* macho

1774 **draught beer; beer on draught; draftbeer**
(Prod.)
(Food processing technology; beverage: beer type.)
d Bier *n* vom Fass; Fassbier *n*; Schankbier *n*
f bière *f* à la pression; bière *f* pression; bière *f* en tonneau
p chope *m*; cerveja *f* de barril

1775 **draw** *v*; **gut** *v*; **eviscerate** *v*
(Prod.)
(Poultry treatment after slaughter and fish and game.)
d ausnehmen
f vider
p tirar

1776 **draw** *v*; **let** *v* **the tea stand**
(Prod.)
(Gastronomy: tea preparation.)
d ziehen; den Tee ziehen lassen
f faire infuser; laisser le thé infuser
p deixar abrir; deixar o chá abrir; deixar o chá pegar gosto

* **drawing off of the wine → 5435**

* **drawing of the wine → 5435**

1777 **drawn butter; melted butter**
(Prod.)
(Dairy product, e.g. for ice cream production.)
d zerlassene Butter *f*, geschmolzene Butter *f*
f beurre *m* fondu
p manteiga *f* derretida

* **draw *v* off the wine → 5436**

* **draw *v* the wine → 5436**

1778 **dredge *v***
(Prod.)
(Food processing technology and production: to cover food by sprinkling with flour.)
d mit Mehl bestreuen
f saupoudrer de farine
p empanar

1779 **dressing of soils**
(Agr.)
(Soil treatment: addition of macroelements to poor soils: nitrogen (N); phosphorus (P); potassium (K); calcium (Ca); sulphur (S); magnesium (Mg). Microelements: iron (Fe); manganese (Mn), copper (Cu).)
d Aufdüngung *f* der Böden
f fertilisation *f* des sols; amendement *m*
p fertilização *f* dos solos

1780 **dried apricot**
(Agr.)
(Agricultural produce, having undergone a drying process.)
d getrocknete Aprikose *f*
f abricot *m* sec
p damasco *m* seco

1781 **dried cod**
(Prod.)
(Cod family "Gadidae"; processed (dried and salted) codfish; seafood.)
d Stockfisch *m*; Klippfisch *m*
f morue *f* sèche
p bacalhau *m* seco

1782 **dried egg**
(Prod.)
(Dairy plant product; egg in powder form.)
d Trockenei *n*
f œuf *m* en poudre
p ovo *m* em pó

1783 **dried egg products**
(Prod.)
(Dairy plant product of egg powder.)
d Trockeneiprodukte *npl*
f produits *mpl* d'œufs en poudre
p produtos *mpl* de ovo em pó

1784 **dried fig**
(Agr.)
(Agricultural produce, having undergone a drying process.)
d getrocknete Feige *f*
f figue *f* sèche
p figos *mpl* secos

1785 **dried fruits**
(Prod.)
(Food processing technology.)
d Trockenfrüchte *fpl*; Trockenobst *n*; Dörrobst *n*
f fruits *mpl* secs; fruits *mpl* séchés
p frutas *fpl* secas

* **dried milk → 3555**

1786 **dried pasta**
(Prod.)
(Food processing technology; pasta plant product.)
d getrocknete Teigmasse *f*, Trockenteigmasse *f*
f pâte *f* alimentaire sèche
p pasta *f* seca; pasta *f* alimentícia seca

1787 **dried vegetables**
(Prod.)
(Food processing technology.)
d Trockengemüse *n*; Dörrgemüse *n*
f légumes *mpl* séchés
p legumes *mpl* secos

1788 **drink; beverage**
(Prod.)
(Beverages: drinkable liquids.)
d Getränk *n*
f boisson *f*
p bebida *f*

* **drinkable water → 4262**

1789 **drinking trough**
(Agr.)
(Livestock breeding: drinking water supply.)
d Tränke *f*
f abreuvoir *m*
p bebedouro *m*

* **drinking water → 4262**

1790 **drinking water treatment**
(Prod.)
(Water supply treatment; water works processes.)
d Trinkwasseraufbereitung *f*
f traitement *m* d'eau potable
p tratamento *m* da água potável

* **drink powders → 607**

1791 **dripping**
(Prod.)
(Falling of drops: part of an extraction and/or separation process.)
d Abtropfung *f*
f égouttage *m*
p gotejamento *m*

1792 **dripping of white cheese**
(Prod.)
(Dairy products. Dairy plant technology; cheese production.)
d Abtropfen *n* des weißen Käses
f égouttage *m* du fromage blanc
p escorrimento *m* do queijo branco

1793 **drippings**
(Prod.)
(Gastronomy; liquid of the meat occurring during cooking.)
d abtropfendes Bratenfett *n*; Bratensaft *m*
f jus *f* de rôti
p molho *m* de ferrugem

1794 **dripping temperature**
(Prod.)
(Food processing technology: e.g. treatment of fats by heating.)
d Abtropfungstemperatur *f*
f température *f* de suintement; température *f* d'égouttage
p temperatura *f* de gotejamento

1795 **drone**
(Agr.)
(Apiculture: Male of the honey bee.)
d Drohne *f*; Bienenmännchen *n*
f faux bourdon *m*; abeille *m* mâle
p zangão *m*

1796 **droplet**
(Prod.)
(Food processing technology, product characteristic.)
d Tröpfchen *n*
f gouttelette *f*
p gotinha *f*

1797 **droppings; dung**
(Agr.)
(Biological agriculture. Principal source of organic matter for soil fertilization.)
d Tiermist *m*; Tierkot *m*
f déjections *fpl* animaux
p excrementos *mpl* de animais

1798 **drought period; dry season**
(Agr.)
(Climatology: period of lack of rainfall.)
d Trockenperiode *f*, Trockenzeit *f*
f période *f* de sécheresse; période *f* sèche
p período *m* da seca; estiagem *f*

* **drupe → 5246**

* **dry** *v* **→ 1589**

1799 **dry** *adj*
(Prod.)
(Aroma/flavour note; taste quality: Without sweetness; e.g. in the brewery process, after conversion by fermentation of maltose into alcohol and carbonic gas.)
d trocken
f sec
p seco

1800 **dry contents**
(Prod.)
(Food processing technology; product characteristics.)
d Trockengehalt *m*
f teneur *f* en extrait sec
p teor *m* de material seco

1801 **dry culture medium**
(Biochem.)
(Biochemical research in nutritional science; microbiology.)
d Trockennährboden *m*
f milieu *m* de culture sec
p meio *m* seco de cultura

1802 **dry diet**
(Med.)
(Alimentary regimen.)
d trockene Diät *f*, Trockendiät *f*
f diète *f* sèche
p dieta *f* seca

1803 **dry distillation**
(Prod.)
(Food processing technology; separation process type.)
d trockene Destillation *f*, Trockendestillation *f*
f distillation *f* sèche
p destilação *f* seca

1804 **dry extract**
(Prod.)
(Food processing technology and aroma production.)
d Trockenextrakt *m*
f extrait *m* sec
p extrato *m* seco

1805 **dry feed pulp**
(Agr.)
(Cattle breeding; cattle ration: nutrients to be

added are calculated in relation to the dry substance of the ration, e.g.: selenium (Se) between 0.1-0.5 ppm/dry substance.)
d Futtertrockenmasse *f*
f pulpe *f* fourragère sèche
p massa *f* seca de ração animal

1806 dry food products
(Prod.)
(Food processing technology; final consumer goods.)
d trockene Nahrungsmittel *npl*
f produits *mpl* alimentaires secs
p produtos *mpl* alimentícios secos; alimentos *mpl* secos

1807 dry ice
(Prod.)
(Carbon dioxide in solid state; e.g. for refrigeration (at -79° C) of foodstuff, when being transported.)
d Trockeneis *n*
f glace *f* sèche; neige *f* carbonique
p gelo *m* seco

1808 drying of cereal grains
(Agr.)
(Agricultural produce.)
d Getreidekorntrocknung *f*; Trocknung *f* von Getreidekörnern
f séchage *m* de grains de céréales
p secagem *f* de grãos de cereais

1809 drying process
(Prod.)
(Food processing technology; spray-drying, vacuum-drying.)
d Trocknungsvorgang *m*; Trocknungsprozess *m*
f procédé *m* de séchage
p processo *m* de secagem

1810 drying stage
(Prod.)
(Food processing technology; product treatment process, with various (generally three) drying stages.)
d Trocknungsphase *f*
f phase *f* à séchage
p fase *f* de secagem

1811 drying up of the grape by overmaturation
(Agr.)
(Viticulture; ref. to overmaturation sauternes type.)
d Austrocknung *f* der Weinbeeren durch die Edelfäule
f dessèchement *m* des grains de raisin du vin par la pourriture noble
p dessecamento *m* da uva (baga) por sobrematuração nobre; dessecamento *m* da uva (baga) por supermaturação nobre

1812 drying up of the soil
(Agr.)
(Soil; soil erosion.)
d Austrocknung *f* des Bodens
f dessèchement *m* de sol
p dessecamento *m* do solo

1813 drying up of the vegetation
(Agr.)
(Climatology.)
d Austrocknung *f* der Vegetation; Austrocknung *f* des Pflanzenbestandes
f dessèchement *m* de la végétation
p dessecamento *m* da vegetação; dessecação *f* da vegetação

1814 dry malt
(Prod.)
(Food processing technology; prime material for beer production.)
d Darrmalz *n*
f malt *m* sec
p malte *m* seco

1815 dry mustard; mustard powder
(Prod.)
(Gastronomy.)
d Senf *m* in Pulverform; Senfpulver *n*
f moutarde *f* en poudre
p mostarda *f* em pó

1816 dry powder
(Prod.)
(Dairy product: powdered milk.)
d Trockenpulver *n*
f poudre *f* sèche
p pó *m* seco

1817 dry powder coated with gelatine
(Prod.)
(Food processing technology; product characteristic.)
d Trockenpulver *n* mit Gelatine umhüllt
f poudre *f* sèche couverte à gélatine
p pó *m* seco recoberto com gelatina

1818 dry red wine
(Prod.)
(Gastronomy.)
d trockener Rotwein *m*
f vin *m* rouge sec
p vinho *m* tinto seco

1819 dry sausage; hard sausage; chorizo sausage
(Prod.)
(Food processing technology; ref. to meat industrialization; made from pork meat.)
d Hartwurst *f*; Dauerwurst *f*

f saucisse *f* sèche; chorizo *m*
p embutidos *mpl* secos

* **dry season → 1798**

1820 dry sherry
(Prod.)
(Gastronomy.)
d trockener Sherry *m*
f xérès *m* sec
p xerez *m* seco

1821 dry substance
(Prod.)
(Food processing technology.)
d Trockensubstanz *f*
f substance *f* sèche
p substância *f* seca

1822 dry weight
(Prod.)
(Food processing technology.)
d Trockengewicht *n*
f poids *m* sec
p peso *m* seco; peso *m* quando seco

1823 dry white wine
(Prod.)
(Gastronomy.)
d trockener Weißwein *m*
f vin *m* blanc sec
p vinho *m* branco seco

1824 dry wine
(Prod.)
(Gastronomy.)
d trockener Wein *m*
f vin *m* sec
p vinho *m* seco

1825 duck
(Agr.)
(Livestock.)
d Ente *f*
f canard *m*
p pato *m*

1826 duck egg
(Agr.)
(Livestock breeding.)
d Entenei *n*
f œuf *m* de cane
p ovo *m* de pato

1827 dumping syndrome
(Med.)
(Tube-feeding complication.)
d Dumping-Syndrom *n*
f syndrome *m* dumping
p síndrome *m* de dumping; síndrome *m* de esvaziamento rápido

* **dung → 1797**

1828 dung; manure
(Agr.)
(Biological agriculture. Organic fertilizing material; mixed bovine/equine dung contains nitrogen, potassium, zinc, copper, molybdenum. Fowl dung has five times more phosphoric acid and calcium.)
d Dung *m*; Dünger *m*
f fumier *m*
p estrume *m*; esterco *m*

1829 duodenum
(Med.)
(The first of the small intestine parts; the other parts are the jejunum and the ileum.)
d Zwölffingerdarm *m*
f duodénum *m*
p duodeno *m*

* **duration of conservation → 1832**

1830 duration of maturation
(Biochem.)
(Enology.)
d Dauer *f* des Reifeprozesses
f durée *f* de la maturation
p duração *f* da maturação

1831 duration of nursing
(Med.)
(Baby nutrition.)
d Andauern *n* des Stillens
f durée *f* de l'allaitement
p duração *f* da amamentação

1832 duration of preservation; duration of conservation
(Prod.)
(Food processing technology.)
d Dauer *f* der Haltbarkeit; Haltbarkeitsdauer *f*
f durée *f* de conservation
p duração *f* de conservação

* **duration of taste perception → 4114**

1833 durum wheat
(Agr.)
(Agricultural produce; "Triticum durum"; hard wheat with high gluten content used for pasta flour.)
d Hartweizen *m*
f blé *m* dur
p trigo *m* duro

* **dust** *v* **→ 5175**

* **Dutch flecked cattle → 1834**

1834 **Dutch speckled cattle; Dutch flecked cattle**
(Agr.)
(Cattle breeding. Holstein-Friesian cattle breed.)
d holländisches Fleckvieh *n*
f espèce *f* bovine hollandaise à pelage pie
p raça *f* bovina holandesa malhada

1835 **dynamic natural processes; dynamic processes of nature**
(Agr.)
(Biological agriculture and foodstuff production.)
d dynamische Naturprozesse *mpl*
f processus *mpl* dynamiques de la nature
p processos *mpl* dinâmicos da natureza

* **dynamic processes of nature → 1835**

1836 **dyspepsia**
(Med.)
(Indigestion.)
d Dyspepsie *f*; Verdauungsstörung *f*
f dyspepsie *f*
p dispepsia *f*

1837 **dystrophy**
(Med.)
(Tissue disorder due to impaired nourishment.)
d Dystrophie *f*
f dystrophie *f*
p distrofia *f*

E

1838 **ear of rye**
(Agr.)
(Botany; plant part.)
d Roggenähre *f*
f épi *m* du seigle
p espiga *f* do centeio

1839 **earth core; barysphere**
(Agr.)
(Dense interior earth part located below the earth crust.)
d Erdkern *m*; Barysphäre *f*
f noyau *m* central de la Terre; barysphère *f*
p núcleo *m* da Terra; barisfera *f*

* **Earth's crust → 3251**

1840 **earthworm**
(Agr.)
(Biological agriculture: Class "Oligochaeta", family "Lumbricidae"; useful annelid worm in the soil.)
d Regenwurm *m*
f ver *m* de terre
p minhoca *f*

1841 **earthy taste**
(Prod.)
(Faroma/flavour note; e.g. ref. to organoleptic food evaluation.)
d erdiger Geschmack *m*
f saveur *f* terreuse
p sabor *m* de terra

* **easier volatile product → 3632**

1842 **easily digestible diet**
(Med.)
(Alimentary regimen.)
d leichtverdauliche Diät *f*
f diète *f* très digestible
p dieta *f* de fácil digestão

1843 **easily flowing liquid**
(Prod.)
(Food processing technology and flavour research and production.)
d leichtfließende Flüssigkeit *f*
f liquide *m* fluide
p líquido *m* fluido

1844 **easily soluble** *adj*
(Prod.)
(Food processing technology; product characteristic.)
d leicht lösbar; leicht löslich
f facilement soluble
p facilmente solúvel

1845 **eating habits**
(Prod.)
(Gastronomy.)
d Ernährungsgewohnheit *f*; Ernährungsweise *f*
f habitude *f* alimentaire; mode *m* d'alimentation
p costume *m* alimentar; modo *m* de alimentação

1846 **ebullition**
(Prod.)
(Food processing technology.)
d Sieden *n*; Aufkochen *n*
f ébullition *f*
p ebulição *f*; fervura *f*

1847 **echinococcus**
(Med.)
("Echinococcos granulosus", tapeworm, living in the intestine of carnivores; the hydrated form invades the cattle and other animals. Hydatidosis: disease transmitted to men, esp. in rural areas.)
d Echinokokkus *m*
f échinocoque *m*
p equinicoco *m*

1848 **éclair**
(Prod.)
(Cake shop product: Chocolate pastry with cream or custard filling.)
d Schokoladenbombe *f*
f éclair *m* au chocolat
p bomba *f* de chocolate

1849 **ecologic agriculture; ecologic farming**
(Agr.)
(Biological agriculture: organic agriculture; organic farming.)
d ökologische Agrikultur *f*; ökologische Landwirtschaft *f*
f agriculture *f* écologique
p agricultura *f* ecológica

1850 **ecological disequilibrium**
(Agr.)
(Agriculture and agricultural produce.)
d ökologisches Ungleichgewicht *n*; ökologisches Missverhältnis *n*
f déséquilibre *m* écologique
p desequilíbrio *m* ecológico

1851 **ecological zoning**
(Agr.)
(Establishment of agricultural areas as to their production purposes.)

d ökologische Zoneneinteilung *f*
f zones *fpl* d'implantation écologique
p zoneamento *m* ecológico

* **ecologic farming → 1849**

1852 **ecology**
(Agr.)
(Science of the interrelationship between living organisms and the environment.)
d Ökologie *f*
f écologie *f*
p ecologia *f*

* **economic plant → 5642**

1853 **ecoproducts**
(Agr.)
(Biological agriculture, production as to ecologic methods.)
d Ökoprodukte *npl*
f écoproduits *mpl*
p ecoprodutos *mpl*

1854 **ecosystem**
(Agr.)
(Association of the living community and the environment.)
d Ökosystem *n*
f écosystème *m*
p ecossistema *m*

* **edema → 3851**

1855 **edible acids**
(Prod.)
(Adipic acid ($C_6H_{10}O_4$); citric acid ($C_6H_8O_7.H_2O$); prime material.)
d Genusssäuren *fpl*
f acides *mpl* alimentaires
p ácidos *mpl* comestíveis; ácidos *mpl* alimentares

* **edible boletus → 1003**

* **edible fungi → 3654**

1856 **edible oil extraction**
(Prod.)
(Food processing technology; prime material.)
d Speiseölextraktion *f*
f extraction *f* de l'huile alimentaire
p extração *f* de óleo comestível; extração *f* de óleo alimentar

* **edible snail → 1965**

1857 **eel**
(Agr.)
("Anguilla anguilla L." and other species; food fish.)
d Aal *m*
f anguille *f*
p enguia *f*; moréia *f*

1858 **effect of antioxidants on lipid stability**
(Biochem.)
(Nutritional science; ref. to lipid oxidation phenomena in meat.)
d Wirkung *f* von Antioxidantien auf die Lipidstabilität
f effet *m* des antioxydants sur la stabilité des lipides
p efeito *m* de antioxidantes sobre a estabilidade dos lipídios

1859 **effect of vitamin supplementation on swine dysentery**
(Med.)
(Veterinary; ref. to feed supplementation with vitamins etc.)
d Auswirkung *f* der Vitaminsupplementierung auf die Schweineruhr
f effet *m* de la supplémentation vitaminique sur la dysenterie des cochons
p efeito *m* da suplementação vitamínica na disenteria suína

1860 **effervescence**
(Prod.)
(Food processing technology.)
d Schäumen *n*; Sprudeln *n*
f effervescence *f*; bouillonnement *m*
p efervescência *f*

1861 **egg**
(Agr.)
(Poultry farming. Considered to be a rich foodstuff containing proteins, fatty materials, minerals and hydrocarbons.)
d Ei *n*
f œuf *m*
p ovo *m*

* **eggplant → 473**

1862 **egg production**
(Agr.)
(Agricultural produce.)
d Eierproduktion *f*
f production *f* d'œufs
p produção *f* de ovos

1863 **eggshell**
(Prod.)
(Dried egg plant byproduct.)
d Eierschale *f*
f coque *f* d'œuf; coquille *f* d'œuf
p casca *f* do ovo

1864 **egg substitute**
(Prod.)
(Food processing technology.)
d Ei-Austauschprodukt *n*; Eiersatz *m*
f succédané *m* d'œuf
p substituto *m* do ovo; sucedâneo *m* do ovo

1865 **egg white; white of egg**
(Agr.)
(Poultry farming. Egg albumen.)
d Eiweiß *n*; Weiße *n* des Eies
f blanc *m* d'œuf
p clara *f* de ovo

1866 **elaborated finished products**
(Prod.)
(Food processing technology.)
d weiterverarbeitete Fertigprodukte *npl*
f produits *mpl* élaborés
p produtos *mpl* elaborados prontos; produtos *mpl* elaborados acabados

1867 **elderberry**
(Agr.)
(Botany; genus "Sambucus".)
d Holunderbeere *f*
f baie *f* du sureau
p uva *f* do sabugueiro

1868 **electro-ejaculation**
(Med.)
(Veterinary; procedure in cattle breeding; selective and artificial insemination.)
d elektrischer Samenerguss *m*
f éjaculation *f* par la voie électrique
p eltroejaculação *f*

1869 **electrolyte**
(Biochem.)
(Nutritional science: e.g. minerals in foodstuffs, as sodium (Na), potassium (K), chlorine (Cl), for maintaining nutrient exchanges in the cells and fluid balance.)
d Elektrolyt *n*
f électrolyte *m*
p eletrólito *m*

* **elevation of blood sugar → 696**

1870 **elimination by evaporation**
(Prod.)
(Aroma/flavour production: ref. to distillation processes.)
d Elimination *f* durch Verdunstung; Ausscheidung *f* durch Verdunstung
f élimination *f* par évaporation
p eliminação *f* por evaporação

1871 **elimination of particles by decantation**
(Prod.)
(Food processing technology. Separation of liquid from its sediment.)
d Ausscheiden *n* von Teilchen durch Dekantieren; Ausscheiden *n* von Teilchen durch Dekantation
f élimination *f* de particules par décantation
p eliminação *f* de partículas por decantação

1872 **emaciation**
(Med.)
(Body wasting, e.g. due to malnutrition.)
d Abmagerung *f*
f amaigrissement *m*
p emagrecimento *m*; emaciação *f*; definhamento *m*

1873 **embed** *v*
(Biochem.)
(E.g. to enclose in a matrix; to surround, cover (e.g. with a sweet covering, in bakery products, over fruits) etc.)
d einbetten; einführen; überziehen
f incorporer; enrober
p incorporar; cobrir

1874 **embedded in a carbohydrate matrix**
(Biochem.)
(Nutritional science in food biochemistry.)
d eingeführt in eine Matrix aus Kohlenhydraten; eingebettet in eine Kohlenhydratmatrix
f enrobé dans une matrice de glucides; enrobé dans une matrice d'hydrate de carbone
p incorporado numa matriz de carboidratos

1875 **embedded in a gelatin matrix**
(Biochem.)
(Nutritional science in food biochemistry.)
d eingebettet in eine Gelatine-Matrix
f enrobé dans une matrice de gélatine
p encorporado em uma matriz de gelatina

1876 **embryo**
(Agr.)
(Botany; rudimentary plant contained in the seed, bearing nutritive elements for growth of the plant.)
d Keimling *m*
f embryon *m*
p embrião *m*

1877 **embryology**
(Med.)
(Veterinary; ref. to cattle breeding; development of cattle embryos; gestation period approx. 285 days.)
d Embryologie *f*
f embryologie *f*
p embriologia *f*

1878 **emitted vapour**
(Prod.)
(Aroma/flavour research and production:

distillation processes.)
d abgegebener Dampf *m*
f vapeur *f* émise
p vapor *m* emitido

1879 **emitted vapour phase**
(Prod.)
(Aroma/flavour research and addition.)
d abgesonderte Dampfphase *f*
f phase *f* vapeur émise
p fase *f* de vapor emitida

1880 **emmer**
(Agr.)
("Triticum dicoccum"; cereal known for more than 8,000 years.)
d Emmer *m*
f emmer *m*
p emmer *m*

1881 **employment of fungicide**
(Agr.)
(Agricultural activity of fungi destruction.)
d Einsatz *m* von Fungiziden
f emploi *m* de fongicides
p emprego *m* de fungicidas

1882 **emulsification of fats**
(Prod.)
(Food processing technology.)
d Emulgierung *f* von Fetten
f émulsionnement *m* de graisses
p emulsificação *f* de gorduras

1883 **emulsifier**
(Prod.)
(Food processing technology. Auxiliary product.)
d Emulgator *m*
f émulsifiant *m*
p emulsificante *m*; emulgador *m*

1884 **emulsify** *v*
(Prod.)
(Food processing technology.)
d emulgieren
f émulsionner
p emulsionar; emulsificar

1885 **emulsions of various types**
(Prod.)
(Food processing technology.)
d Emulsionen *fpl* unterschiedlicher Art
f émulsions *fpl* de natures différentes
p emulsões *fpl* de vários tipos; emulsões *fpl* de tipos diferentes

1886 **encephalomalacia in chicks**
(Med.)
(Veterinary.)
d Gehirnerweichung *f* der Küken
f encéphalomalacie *f* des poussins
p encefalomalacia *f* nos pintos

1887 **endive; escarole**
(Agr.)
(Agricultural produce. "Cichorium endivia"; chicory relative; salad vegetable.)
d Endivie *f*
f endive *f*
p endívia *f*; escarola *f*

1888 **endocarp; inner layer of the pericarp**
(Agr.)
(Botany; ref. to fruit like apples.)
d Endokarp *n*; innere Schicht *f* der Fruchtwand; innere Schicht *f* des Perikarps
f endocarpe *m*; couche *f* interne du péricarpe
p endocárpio *m*; endocarpo *m*; camada *f* interna do pericarpo

1889 **endogenous** *adj*
(Med.)
(Originated within the body; in nutrition: originated from metabolic processes, the liver etc. and not from the diet.)
d endogen
f endogène
p endógeno

1890 **endogenous protein**
(Biochem.)
(Metabolism: resulting amino acids from protein breakdown.)
d endogenes Protein *n*
f protéine *f* endogène
p proteina *f* endógena

1891 **endogenous synthesis**
(Med.)
(Chemical process by which living cells produce the various substances to cover the necessities of the organism to which they belong.)
d Eigensynthese *f*
f synthèse *f* endogène
p síntese *f* endógena

1892 **endopeptidases**
(Biochem.)
(Peptide bonds breaking enzymes within the proteic molecule; they have specific action: e.g. pepsin, trypsin.)
d Endopeptidasen *fpl*
f endopeptidases *fpl*
p endopeptidases *fpl*

1893 **endoplasmatic reticulum; ER**
(Med.)
(Anatomy: Site of protein synthesis in the cell.)

d endoplasmatisches Retikulum *n*
f réticulum *m* endoplasmatique
p retículo *m* endoplasmático

1894 **endosperm**
(Agr.)
(Botany; plants: nutritive tissue of the seed embryo.)
d Endosperm *n*; Nährgewebe *n*
f endosperme *f*
p endosperma *m*

1895 **endotoxin**
(Biochem.)
(Microbiology in food biochemistry: thermostable toxins, released only after bacteriolysis.)
d Endotoxin *n*
f endotoxine *f*
p endotoxina *f*

1896 **energetic equilibrium**
(Med.)
(Purpose of nutrition.)
d Energiegleichgewicht *n*
f équilibre *m* énergétique
p equilíbrio *m* energético

1897 **energetic metabolism**
(Med.)
d Energiemetabolismus *m*
f métabolisme *m* énergétique
p metabolismo *m* energético

1898 **energetic resource**
(Agr.)
(Water supply; electricity; aeolian energy etc.)
d Energiequelle *f*
f ressource *f* énergétique
p recurso *m* energético

1899 **energizer**
(Prod.)
(Food processing technology: energy supplying product: e.g. glucose.)
d Energiespender *m*
f énergisant *m*
p energizante *m*

* **energizing diet → 1903**

* **energy feeding by heating → 1907**

1900 **energy production**
(Med.)
(Ref. to vitamin activity.)
d Energieaufbau *m*
f production *f* de l'énergie
p produção *f* energética

1901 **energy requirement**
(Med.)
(Total metabolism, 2,200-2,600 kcal daily for men, doing moderate normal work. The result of basal metabolism + occupational metabolism + growth requirements.)
d Energiebedarf *m*
f besoin *m* énergétique
p necessidades *fpl* energéticas

1902 **energy-rich compounds**
(Biochem.)
(Biochemical research in nutritional science. E.g. adenosine triphosphate (ATP).)
d energiereiche Verbindungen *fpl*
f composés *mpl* riches en énergie
p compostos *mpl* ricos em energia

1903 **energy rich diet; energizing diet**
(Med.)
(Alimentary regimen.)
d energiereiche Diät *f*; kräftigende Diät *f*
f diète *f* énergétique; diète *f* fortifiante
p dieta *f* fortificante; dieta *f* tonificante

1904 **energy-rich feedstuff**
(Med.)
(Veterinary: cattle: e.g. cereal grains; maize (corn), wheat subproducts, low in proteins: bran cake, containing fats, Ca, P, dry material; oak: minerals; barley, rye.)
d energiereiche Futtermittel *npl*
f fourrages *mpl* riches en énergie; fourrages *mpl* énergétiques
p forragem *f* energética; rações *fpl* animais energéticas

1905 **energy-rich foods**
(Med.)
(Alimentary regimen.)
d energiereiche Nahrungsmittel *npl*
f aliments *mpl* énergétiques
p produtos *mpl* alimentícios energéticos

1906 **energy supply**
(Med.)
(Alimentary regimen.)
d Energiezufuhr *f*
f apports *mpl* énergétiques
p fornecimento *m* energético

1907 **energy supply by heating; energy feeding by heating**
(Prod.)
(Aroma/flavour research and production processes.)
d Energiezufuhr *f* durch Erhitzung
f apport *m* d'énergie par le chauffage
p alimentação *f* com energia por aquecimento; alimentação *f* energética por aquecimento

1908 **enology**
(Prod.)
(Science which deals with wine and wine production.)
d Önologie *f*
f œnologie *f*
p enologia *f*

1909 **enriched dietary product**
(Prod.)
(Food processing technology; vitamin technology in nutrition.)
d angereichertes Diätprodukt *n*
f produit *m* diététique enrichi
p produto *m* para dieta enriquecido

1910 **enrichment; fortification**
(Prod.)
(Food processing technology; ref. e.g. to vitamin supplementation of margarines (vitamin A and D) and fruit juices (vitamin C).)
d Anreicherung *f*
f enrichissement *m*
p enriquecimento *m*; fortificação *f*

1911 **enrichment by must concentration**
(Prod.)
(Enology; wine improvement process: ref. to increase in sugar contents.)
d Anreicherung *f* durch Mostkonzentrierung
f enrichissement *m* par concentration du moût
p enriquecimento *m* pela concentração do mosto

1912 **enrichment of margarine**
(Prod.)
(Food processing technology: margarine enrichment by vitamins, e.g. vitamin A and vitamin D.)
d Anreicherung *f* von Margarine
f enrichissement *m* de la margarine
p enriquecimento *m* de margarina

1913 **enrichment of mixed feeds**
(Agr.)
(Livestock nutrition: feedstuff preparation e.g. addition of vitamin supplements.)
d Anreicherung *f* von Mischfutter
f enrichissement *m* des fourrages mélangés
p enriquecimento *m* de rações mistas

* **enrichment of the soil with nutritional components → 1914**

1914 **enrichment of the soil with nutritional elements; enrichment of the soil with nutritional components**
(Agr.)
(Soil treatment.)
d Anreicherung *f* des Bodens mit nährenden Komponenten; Bodenanreicherung *f* mit Nährstoffen
f enrichissement *m* du sol en éléments nutritifs
p enriquecimento *m* do solo com elementos nutritivos

1915 **enrichment of the soil with trace elements**
(Agr.)
(Soil treatment.)
d Bodenanreicherung *f* mit Spurenelementen
f enrichissement *m* du sol en oligoéléments
p enriquecimento *m* do solo com microelementos

1916 **enrich *v* the soil with phosphorus**
(Agr.)
(Soil treatment, soil improvement.)
d den Boden mit Phosphor anreichern
f enrichir le sol en phosphore
p enriquecer o solo com fósforo

1917 **enteric absorption; intestinal absorption**
(Med.)
(Veterinary; ref. e.g. to vitamin uptake through supplemented feed.)
d Darmaufnahme *f*; Aufnahme *f* durch den Darm; intestinale Absorption *f*; Aufnahme *f* durch den Verdauungstrakt
f absorption *f* entérique; absorption *f* intestinale
p absorção *f* entérica; absorção *f* intestinal

1918 **enteric absorption of tocopherols; intestinal absorption of tocopherols**
(Med.)
(Veterinary; ref. to vitamin E uptake through supplemented feed.)
d Darmaufnahme *f* von Tocopherolen
f absorption *f* entérique des tocophérols; absorption *f* intestinale des tocophérols
p absorção *f* entérica de tocoferois; absorção *f* intestinal de tocoferois

1919 **enterocolitis of the newborn**
(Med.)
(Baby nutrition. Inflammation of the colon and small intestine of the baby.)
d Dünndarm-Dickdarmentzündung *f* des Neugeborenen
f entérocolite *f* du nouveau-né
p enterocolite *f* do récem-nascido

1920 **enteropathic acrodermatitis**
(Med.)
(Baby nutrition.)
d chronische Kleinkinddermatose *f*
f acrodermatite *f* entéropathique
p acrodermatite *f* enteropática

1921 **entrance of a movable frame hive**
(Agr.)
(Apiculture: Artificial bee-hive construction.)

d Flugloch *n*
f entrée *f m* de vol
p alvado *m*

1922 environmental aspects
(Agr.)
(Preservation of the natural environment, e.g. control of pesticides and other pollution factors.)
d Umweltsaspekte *mpl*
f aspects *mpl* environnementaux
p aspectos *mpl* do meio ambiente

1923 environmental compatible *adj*
(Agr.)
(Biological agriculture.)
d umweltfreundlich
f compatible avec l'environnement
p ambientalmente compatível

1924 environmental factor
(Agr.)
(Ecological relations, the entire collection of mutual interdependent conditions of all beings between themselves and the environment on which they depend.)
d Umweltsfaktor *m*; Umweltsgegebenheit *f*
f donné *f* de l'environnement
p fator *m* ambiental

1925 environmental humidity
(Prod.)
(E.g. in storage, warehouses.)
d Umweltsfeuchtigkeit *f*
f humidité *f* ambiante
p umidade *f* ambiental

1926 environmental impacts
(Agr.)
(Biological agriculture: evaluation of activity, results etc.)
d Umweltseinwirkung *f*; Auswirkung *f* auf die Umwelt
f impacts *mpl* sur l'environnement
p impactos *mpl* sobre o meio ambiente

1927 environmental pollution
(Agr.)
(Main pollution classes: biodegradable pollution and non-biodegradable pollution.)
d Umweltsverschmutzung *f*
f pollution *f* de l'environnement
p poluição *f* ambiental

1928 environmental protection
(Agr.)
(Concern of biological agriculture, organic agriculture; organic farming.)
d Umweltschutz *m*
f protection *f* de l'environnement
p proteção *f* ambiental; proteção *f* do meio ambiente

1929 enzymatic activity
(Biochem.)
(Nutritional science.)
d enzymatische Aktivität *f*; enzymatische Wirksamkeit *f*
f activité *f* enzymatique
p atividade *f* enzimática

1930 enzymatic activity of the proteases; enzymatic activity of the proteolytic enzymes
(Med.)
(Functioning of the digestive enzyme in protein breakdown.)
d enzymatische Wirkung *f* der Proteasen; enzymatische Wirkung *f* der proteolytischen Enzyme
f activité *f* enzymatique des protéases; activité *f* enzymatique des enzymes protéolytiques
p atividade *f* enzimática das proteases; atividade *f* enzimática das enzimas proteolíticas

* **enzymatic activity of the proteolytic enzymes → 1930**

1931 enzymatic alteration
(Med.)
(Enzyme functioning in the body.)
d enzymatische Veränderung *f*
f altération *f* enzymatique
p alteração *f* enzimática

1932 enzymatic catalyzed reactions
(Biochem.)
(Vitamin biochemistry in nutritional science. Ref. to tissue antioxidants.)
d durch Enzyme katalysierte Reaktionen *fpl*
f réactions *fpl* catalysées par les enzymes
p reações *fpl* catalizadas pelas enzimas

1933 enzymatic clarification
(Prod.)
(Food processing technology: e.g. fruit juice treatment.)
d enzymatische Klärung *f*
f clarification *f* enzymatique
p clarificação enzimática

1934 enzymatic deterioration reaction
(Biochem.)
(Food biochemistry.)
d enzymatische Zerfallsreaktion *f*
f réaction *f* enzymatique de détérioration
p reação *f* enzimática de deterioração

1935 **enzymatic digestive activity**
(Med.)
(Nutrition in medicine.)
d enzymatische Wirksamkeit *f* im Verdauungsprozess
f activité *f* enzymatique digestive
p atividade *f* enzimática digestiva

1936 **enzymatic glucose conversion**
(Biochem.)
(Glucose conversion into fructose, in nutritional science.)
d enzymatische Umwandlung *f* der Glykose
f conversion *f* enzymatique du glucose
p conversão *f* enzimática da glicose

1937 **enzymatic lipid peroxidation system**
(Biochem.)
(Nutritional science; ref. to lipid oxidation phenomena in meat.)
d enzymatisches Lipidperoxidationssystem *n*
f système *m* de la peroxydation lipidique enzymatique
p sistema *m* de peroxidação lipídica enzimática

1938 **enzymatic oxidation**
(Biochem.)
(Nutritional science; food biochemistry.)
d enzymatische Oxidation *f*
f oxydation *f* enzymatique
p oxidação *f* enzimática

1939 **enzymatic protection**
(Biochem.)
(Nutritional science.)
d enzymatischer Schutz *m*
f protection *f* enzymatique
p proteção *f* enzimática

1940 **enzymatic reaction**
(Biochem.)
(Nutritional science.)
d enzymatische Reaktion *f*
f réaction *f* enzymatique
p reação *f* enzimática

1941 **enzymatic synthesis**
(Biochem.)
(Nutritional science. Ref. to the elaboration of amino acids.)
d enzymatische Synthese *f*
f synthèse *f* enzymatique
p síntese *f* enzimática

1942 **enzymatic system**
(Biochem.)
(Nutritional science.)
d enzymatisches System *n*
f système *m* enzymatique
p sistema *m* enzimático

1943 **enzymatic treatment**
(Biochem.)
(Process type in nutritional science; also in aroma production.)
d enzymatische Behandlung *f*
f traitement *m* enzymatique
p tratamento *m* enzimático

1944 **enzyme**
(Biochem.)
(Proteic substance which accelerates and catalyzes a specific biochemical reaction: enzyme-ferment-diastase.)
d Enzym *n*
f enzyme *f/m*
p enzima *f*

1945 **enzyme crystallization**
(Biochem.)
(Biochemical research in nutritional science.)
d Enzymkristallierung *f*
f cristallisation *f* des enzymes
p cristalização *f* de enzimas

* **enzyme isolation → 3031**

1946 **enzymes dissolved in the cytoplasm**
(Biochem.)
(Biochemical research in nutritional science.)
d im Cytoplasma gelöste Enzyme *npl*; im Zellplasma gelöste Enzyme *npl*
f enzymes *fpl* dissoutes dans le cytoplasme
p enzimas *fpl* dissolvidas no citoplasma

1947 **enzymes integrated in complex structures**
(Biochem.)
(Biochemical research in nutritional science.)
d in komplexe Systeme integrierte Enzyme *npl*; in komplexe Systeme eingebaute Enzyme *npl*
f enzymes *fpl* intégrées dans des structures complexes
p enzimas *fpl* integradas em estruturas complexas

1948 **enzymology**
(Biochem.)
(Nutritional science of enzymes and fermentation.)
d Zymologie *f*; Wissenschaft *f* der Gärung und der Enzyme
f enzymologie *f*; science *f* traitant de la fermentation et des enzymes
p zimologia *f*; ciência *f* que trata dos fermentos e da fermentação

* **epicarp → 2028**

1949 **epidemic diarrhea of newborns**
(Med.)
(Baby care.)

d epidemischer Säuglingsdurchfall *m*
f diarrhée *f* épidémique des nouveau-nés
p diarréia *f* epidêmica dos récem-nascidos

1950 epiglottis
(Med.)
(Anatomy; body part of the larynx, covering its entrance during swallowing.)
d Kehldeckel *m*
f épiglotte *f*
p epiglote *f*

1951 epigynous ovary
(Agr.)
(Botany; base of the flower carpel; e.g. "superior" and "inferior".)
d oberständiger Fruchtknoten *m*
f ovaire *m* supère
p ovário *m* súpero

1952 epizootic infectious abortion
(Med.)
(Veterinary; ref. e.g. to cattle hogs, sheep: brucellosis, caused by brucellae, genus "Brucella" (Bang's disease).)
d Fehlgeburt *f* durch Brucellose-Infektion
f avortement *m* infectieux épizootique
p aborto *m* infeccioso por brucelose

1953 equilibrium modification
(Prod.)
(Aroma/flavour research and application in food products.)
d Gleichgewichtsveränderung *f*
f modification *f* d'équilibre
p modificação *f* do equilíbrio

1954 equine influenza; pinkeye
(Med.)
(Veterinary; horse disease; ref. to horse breeding on a stud farm; horse treatment.)
d Pferdegrippe *f*
f grippe *f* équine; influenza *f* équine
p gripe *f* eqüina; influenza *f* eqüina

* **equine syphilis → 1765**

* **ER → 1893**

1955 erepsin
(Med.)
(Anatomy: Enzyme-group in the intestine and pancreatic secretion, including aminopeptidases and dipeptidases.)
d Erepsin *n*
f érepsine *f*
p erepsina *f*

1956 ergosterol
(Biochem.)
(Nutritional science: $C_{28}H_{44}O$; ergosterine = phytosterol having the function of provitamin D.)
d Ergosterin *n*
f ergostérol *m*
p ergosterina *f*

1957 erosion
(Agr.)
(Soil; e.g. washing away of arable soil by floodwater.)
d Erosion *f*; Abtragung *f*
f érosion *f*
p erosão *f*

1958 erosion protection
(Agr.)
(Soil treatment.)
d Erosionsschutz *m*
f protection *f* contre l'érosion
p proteção *f* contra a erosão

1959 erosion valley
(Agr.)
(Soil; very profound erosion form.)
d Einbruchstal *n* durch Erosion
f érosion *f* par d'affouillement profond
p erosão *f* em voçorocas

1960 erucic acid
(Prod.)
($C_{22}H_{42}O_2$; unsaturated fatty acid; ingredient in seed oils; limited quantities used in margarines.)
d Erucasäure *f*
f acide *m* érucique
p ácido *m* erúcico

1961 eruptive rock
(Agr.)
(Soil. Igneous or magmatic rock.)
d Eruptivgestein *n*
f roche *f* éruptive
p rocha *f* eruptiva

1962 erythema
(Med.)
(Skin flushing; can be due to niacin (nicotinic acid) deficiency.)
d Erythem *n*; Hautrötung *f*
f érythème *m*
p eritema *m*

* **erythrocytes → 4611**

1963 erythrosine
(Prod.)
($C_{20}H_6I_4Na_2O_5$; FD&C red no. 3: foodstuff colorant.)
d Erythrosin *n*

f érythrosine *f*
p eritrosina *f*

* **escallop → 4856**

1964 **escallop of veal**
(Prod.)
(Gastronomy; veal cutlet.)
d Kalbsschnitzel *n*
f escalope *m* de veau
p escalope *m* de vitela

* **escalope → 4856**

1965 **escargot; edible snail**
(Prod.)
(Gastronomy; edible mollusk.)
d Weinbergschnecke *f*
f escargot *m*; escargot *m* de Bourgogne
p caracol *m* de Borgonha; escargot *m*

* **escarole → 1887**

* **esophagus → 3852**

* **essences → 1968**

1966 **essential amino acids**
(Biochem.)
(Must be present in the diet, supplied e.g. by dietary protein: methionine, valine, tryptophan, threonine, lysine, leucine, isoleucine and phenylalanine.)
d essentielle Aminosäuren *fpl*
f acides *mpl* aminés indispensables; acides *mpl* aminés essentiels
p aminoácidos *mpl* essenciais

1967 **essential fatty acid**
(Biochem.)
(Unsaturated fatty acid: Linoleic acid ($C_{18}H_{32}O_2$), linolenic acid ($C_{18}H_{30}O_2$), arachidonic acid ($C_{20}H_{32}O_2$). Cannot be synthesized by the body, must be supplied by the diet.)
d essentielle Fettsäure *f*
f acide *m* gras essentiel
p ácido *m* graxo essencial

1968 **essential oils; ethereal oils; essences**
(Prod.)
(Volatile oils used in flavourings.)
d ätherische Öle *npl*; Essenzen *fpl*
f huiles *fpl* essentielles; essences *fpl*
p óleos *mpl* essenciais; essências *fpl*

1969 **ester**
(Prod.)
(Compound formed by acid/alcohol reaction. Aroma/fragrance prime material.)
d Ester *m*
f ester *m*
p éster *m*

1970 **esterases**
(Biochem.)
(Enzyme group which breaks down the esters into their specific alcohols and acids.)
d Esterasen *fpl*
f estérases *fpl*
p esterases *fpl*

1971 **esterification**
(Biochem.)
(Nutritional science, food biochemistry.)
d Veresterung *f*
f estérification *f*
p esterificação *f*

1972 **esters of fatty acids**
(Biochem.)
(Nutritional science: e.g. lipids.)
d Fettsäureester *mpl*
f esters *mpl* d'acides gras
p ésteres *mpl* de ácidos graxos

1973 **estrus; heat**
(Med.)
(Veterinary; period of sexual excitability of the female.)
d Brunst *f*
f rut *m*
p estro *m*; cio *m*

* **ethanal → 22**

* **ethanedioic acid → 3952**

* **ethanoic acid → 25**

1974 **ethanol; ethyl alcohol**
(Prod.)
(C_2H_5OH. Alcohol. Prime material for the production of beverages, drinks, produced by sugar fermentation by yeast.)
d Äthanol *m*; Äthylalkohol *m*; Ethanol *m*; Ethylalkohol *m*
f éthanol *m*; alcool *m* éthylique
p etanol *m*; álcool *m* etílico

* **ethereal oils → 1968**

1975 **ethmoid bone**
(Med.)
(Anatomy.)
d Siebbein *n*; Riechbein *n*
f ethmoïde *m*
p etmóide *m*

1976 ethyl acetate
(Prod.)
($C_4H_8O_2$; e.g. used in aroma/fragrance production; prime material.)
d Äthylacetat *n*; Ethylacetat *n*
f acétate *m* d'éthyle
p acetato *m* de etilo

* **ethyl alcohol → 1974**

1977 ethyl butyrate
(Prod.)
($C_6H_{12}O_2$; aroma prime material, e.g. strawberry note; flavour improver.)
d Äthylbutyrat *n*; Ethylbutyrat *n*
f butyrate *m* d'éthyle
p butirato *m* de etila

1978 ethyl caproate
(Prod.)
($C_8H_{16}O_2$. Aroma prime material, e.g. fruit note; flavour improver.)
d Äthylcapronat *n*; Ethylcapronat *n*
f caproate *m* d'éthyle
p capronato *m* de etila

1979 ethyl cellulose
(Prod.)
(Food processing technology: texture improving ingredient.)
d Äthylcellulose *f*; Ethylcellulose *f*
f éthylcellulose *f*
p etilcelulose *f*

1980 ethylene
(Prod.)
(C_2H_4; gaseous unsaturated hydrocarbon, used e.g. in food processing technology: fruit conservation, of fruits with skin.)
d Äthylen *n*; Ethen *n*
f éthylène *f*
p etileno *m*

1981 ethyl formiate
(Prod.)
($C_3H_6O_2$; aroma/flavour prime material, e.g. rum-like flavour.)
d Äthylformiat *n*; Ethylformiat *n*
f éthylformiate *m*
p formiato *m* de etila

1982 ethyl isovalerate; isovaleric acid ethyl ester
(Prod.)
($C_7H_{14}O_2$; aroma prime material, e.g. wine to apple-like flavour; flavour improver.)
d Äthylisovalerianat *n*; Ethylisovalerianat *n*
f isovalérate *m* d'éthyle
p isovalerato *m* de etila

1983 ethyl pelargonate
(Prod.)
($C_{11}H_{22}O_2$; wine ether; flavour chemical, synthetic aroma, e.g. cognac essence.)
d Äthylpelargonat *n*; Ethylpelargonat *n*
f pélargonate *m* d'éthyle
p pelargonato *m* de etila

1984 ethyl propionate
(Prod.)
($C_5H_{10}O_2$; flavour chemical; fruity note.)
d Äthylpropionat *n*; Ethylpropionat *n*
f propionate *m* d'éthyle
p propionato *m* de etila

1985 ethyl vanillin
(Prod.)
($C_9H_{10}O_3$; flavouring prime material.)
d Äthylvanillin *n*; Ethylvanillin *n*
f vanilline *f* d'éthyle
p etilvanilina *f*

1986 eucalyptol; cineol
(Prod.)
($C_{10}H_{18}O$; alpha-pinene derivative; flavour chemical, aroma prime material.)
d Eucalyptol *n*
f eucalyptol *m*
p eucaliptol *m*

1987 eutectic ice
(Prod.)
(Solid mixture of salt and ice, used for conserving fish in fishing boats.)
d eutektisches Eis *n*
f glace *f* eutectique
p gelo *m* eutético

1988 eutrophy
(Med.)
(Nutritional science; state of being well nourished.)
d Eutrophie *f*
f eutrophie *f*
p eutrofia *f*

1989 evaluation of biologic activity of the soil
(Agr.)
(Biological agriculture: soil characteristics.)
d sachgerechte Bewertung *f* der biologischen Bodenaktivität; fachgerechte Bewertung *f* der biologischen Bodenaktivität
f évaluation *f* de l'activité biologique du sol
p avaliação *f* da atividade biológica do solo

1990 evaluation of vitamin activity
(Biochem.)
(Nutritional science: vitamin application research.)
d Bewertung *f* einer Vitaminaktivität

f évaluation *f* d'une activité vitaminique
p avaliação *f* de uma atividade vitamínica

1991 **evaporated milk; condensed milk**
(Prod.)
(Dairy product; tinned milk, thickened by dehydration/evaporation process; with sugar addition.)
d Kondensmilch *f*
f lait *m* condensé
p leite *m* condensado

1992 **evaporation**
(Prod.)
(Aroma/flavour production: ref. to distillation processes.)
d Verdunstung *f*
f évaporation *f*
p evaporação *f*

1993 **evaporation loss**
(Prod.)
(Food processing technology; ref. to thermal treatment.)
d Verdunstungsverlust *m*
f perte *f* par évaporation
p perda *f* por evaporação

1994 **evaporation loss of the wine**
(Biochem.)
(Enology.)
d Verlust *m* des Weines durch Verdunstung; Verdunstungsverlust *m* des Weines
f perte *f* du vin par évaporation
p perda *f* do vinho pela evaporação

1995 **evaporation residue**
(Prod.)
(Aroma/fragrance research and production.)
d Verdampfungsrückstand *m*
f résidu *m* d'évaporation
p resíduo *m* de evaporação

1996 **evaporation start**
(Prod.)
(Aroma/flavour research and production, distillation/extraction processes.)
d Verflüchtigungsbeginn *m*
f début *m* de l'évaporation
p início *m* da evaporação

1997 **evaporation under vacuum**
(Prod.)
(Food processing technology, e.g. of milk.)
d Verdampfung *f* unter Vakuum
f évaporation *f* sous vide
p evaporação *f* sob vácuo

1998 **evening meal; dinner; supper**
(Prod.)
(Gastronomy.)
d Abendessen *n*
f dîner *m*; souper *m*
p jantar *m*; janta *f*

1999 **even number of carbon atoms**
(Biochem.)
(Nutritional science; research.)
d gerade Anzahl *f* von Kohlenstoffatomen
f nombre *m* pair d'atomes de carbone
p número *m* par de átomos de carbono

2000 **everyday diet**
(Med.)
(Alimentary regimen.)
d tägliche Diät *f*
f diète *f* quotidienne
p dieta *f* cotidiana

* **eviscerate** *v* → **1775**

2001 **evocative odour**
(Prod.)
(Aroma/fragrance research and production.)
d evokativer Geruch *m*
f odeur *f* évocatrice
p odor *m* evocativo; cheiro *m* evocativo

2002 **evolution**
(Agr.)
(Botany (fauna/flora): Process of development of plant and animal life from primitive organisms.)
d Evolution *f*; Entwicklung *f*
f évolution *f*
p evolução *f*

2003 **evolution of alimentary technologies**
(Prod.)
(Food processing technology.)
d Evolution *f* der Ernährungstechnologien
f évolution *f* des technologies alimentaires
p evolução *f* das técnologias de alimentação

2004 **evolution of foodstuff consumption**
(Prod.)
(Food processing, research, production and marketing.)
d Evolution *f* des Nahrungsmittelkonsumes; Entwicklung *f* des Nahrungsmittelverbrauches
f évolution *f* de la consommation alimentaire
p evolução *f* do consumo de produtos alimentícios; evolução *f* do consumo de alimentos

2005 **evolution of perception**
(Prod.)
(Physiological phenomena: in aroma/fragrance research and production.)
d Wahrnehmungsentfaltung *f*

f évolution *f* de la perception
p evolução *f* da percepção

2006 **evolution of the blend**
(Prod.)
(In aroma/fragrance research and production; metaphor ref. to aroma composition.)
d Entfaltung *f* der Mischung
f évolution *f* du mélange
p evolução *f* da mistura

2007 **evolution of the ecosystems**
(Agr.)
(Ecology; problems.)
d Entwicklung *f* der Ökosysteme
f évolution *f* des écosystèmes
p evolução *f* dos ecossistemas

2008 **evolution of the wine**
(Biochem.)
(Enology.)
d Entwicklung *f* des Weines
f évolution *f* du vin
p evolução *f* do vinho

2009 **evolution of the wine in the bottle**
(Biochem.)
(Enology.)
d Evolution *f* des Weines in der Flasche; Entwicklung *f* des Weines in der Flasche
f évolution *f* du vin en bouteille
p evolução *f* do vinho na garrafa

2010 **evolution of treatment technics**
(Prod.)
(Food processing technology.)
d Entwicklung *f* der Behandlungsverfahren
f évolution *f* des techniques de traitement
p evolução *f* das técnicas de tratamento

2011 **ewe**
(Agr.)
(Livestock breeding; female sheep of adult age.)
d Mutterschaf *n*; Zippe *f*
f brebis *f*
p ovelha-matriz *f*; carneira-matriz *f*

2012 **examination of soil structure**
(Agr.)
(Biological agriculture: soil treatment.)
d Untersuchung *f* der Bodenstruktur
f examen *m* de la structure du sol
p análise *f* da estrutura do solo

2013 **examine *v* the fermentation**
(Biochem.)
(Ref. to fermentation in nutritional science.)
d Gärungsprozess untersuchen
f rechercher le processus de la fermentation; examiner le processus de la fermentation
p examinar o processo de fermentação

2014 **excessive cholesterol supply**
(Biochem.)
(Nutritional science: incorrect nutritional habits and regimens.)
d übermäßige Cholesterinzufuhr *f*
f apport *m* excessif de cholestérol
p aporte *m* excessivo de colesterol

2015 **excessive heating; overheating**
(Prod.)
(Food processing technology; ref. to research and production processes; flavour production.)
d übermäßige Erhitzung *f*; Übererhitzung *f*
f échauffement *m* excessif; chauffage *m* excessif; surchauffe *f*
p aquecimento *m* excessivo; superaquecimento *m*

2016 **excess of fat; fat surplus**
(Prod.)
(Food processing technology: e.g. meat quality.)
d überschüssiges Fett *n*
f graisse *f* en excès
p gordura *f* em excesso

2017 **exchange surface**
(Prod.)
(Aroma/flavour molecules: in flavour research.)
d Austauschoberfläche *f*
f surface *f* d'échange
p superfície *f* de troca

2018 **exclusion regimen for milk proteins**
(Med.)
(Nutrition.)
d Diätplan *m* bezüglich Milchprotein Ausschlusses; Diätplan *m* mit Milchproteinauschluss
f régime *m* d'exclusion des protéines du lait
p regime *m* de exclusão das proteínas do leite

2019 **excrement**
(Med.)
(Veterinary science; waste matter from animals.)
d Kot *m*; Exkremente *pl*
f excrément *m*
p excremento *m*

2020 **excreted milk volume**
(Med.)
(Baby nutrition.)
d ausgeschiedenes Milchvolumen *n*
f volume *m* de lait excrété
p volume *m* de leite excretado

2021 execution of fertilizing with compost
(Agr.)
(Soil treatment, fertilizing with organic matter; ref. to organic agriculture; organic farming; concern of biological agriculture.)
d Ausübung *f* der Kompostierung
f pratique *f* du compostage
p prática *f* da adubação *f* orgânica

2022 exhausted must
(Biochem.)
(Brewery and enology techniques; food biochemistry.)
d erschöpfter Most *m*
f moût *m* épuisé
p mosto *m* esgotado; mosto *m* exaurido

2023 exhaustion
(Prod.)
(Aroma/flavour research and production: distillation processes.)
d Erschöpfung *f*
f épuisement *m*
p esgotamento *m*; exhaustão *f*

2024 exhaustion by solvents
(Prod.)
(Aroma/flavour production: extraction processes.)
d Erschöpfung *f* durch Lösungsmittel
f épuisement *m* à l'aide de solvants
p esgotamento *m* por solventes

* **exhaustion of nutritional components → 2025**

2025 exhaustion of nutritional elements; exhaustion of nutritional components
(Biochem.)
(Nutritional science; food biochemistry.)
d Erschöpfung *f* an Nahrungsstoffen
f épuisement *m* en éléments nutritifs
p esgotamento *m* de elementos nutritivos; esgotamento *m* de componentes nutritivos

2026 exhaustion of the must
(Biochem.)
(Nutritional science; food biochemistry: e.g. ref. to fermentation processes.)
d Erschöpfung *f* des Mostes
f épuisement *m* du moût
p esgotamento *m* do mosto

2027 exhibitors and products
(Agr.)
(Agricultural marketing; sales procedures of agricultural produce.)
d Aussteller *mpl* und Produkte *npl*
f exposants *mpl* et produits *mpl*
p expositores *mpl* e produtos *mpl*

2028 exocarp; epicarp
(Agr.)
(Botany; outer layer of a pome; surface layer: e.g. the red surface of apples.)
d Exokarp *n*
f épicarpe *m*
p epicarpo *m*

2029 exogenous *adj*
(Med.)
(Originated outside the body; in nutrition: originated from the diet and not from metabolic processes, the liver etc.)
d exogen
f exogène
p exógeno

2030 exopeptidase
(Biochem.)
(Proteolytic enzyme; proteolysis: hydrolysis of proteins and peptides.)
d Exopeptidase *f*
f exopeptidase *f*
p exopeptidase *f*

2031 exotoxin
(Biochem.)
(Microbiology; toxin of microorganisms released into the medium.)
d Exotoxin *n*
f exotoxine *f*
p exotoxina *f*

2032 expeller cake; oil cake
(Agr.)
(Agricultural produce; ref. to oil seed cake after expression: coconut, peanuts etc.)
d Ölkuchen *m*
f tourteau *m*; grignon *m*
p bolo *m* expulsor; torta *f* de sementes oleoginosas

2033 experimental diet
(Med.)
(Veterinary; ref. to nutritional experiments with active principles, e.g. vitamins in feed.)
d Versuchsdiät *f*
f diète *f* expérimentale
p dieta *f* experimental

2034 experimental field cultures
(Biochem.)
(Biochemical research, e.g. in genetic engineering; nutritional science.)
d Versuchskulturen *fpl* des Feldanbaus
f cultures *fpl* expérimentaux en champ
p culturas *fpl* experimentais de campo

2035 expiration
(Med.)
(Flavour perception.)

d Ausatmung *f*
f expiration *f*
p expiração *f*

2036 **exposure to humidity**
(Prod.)
(Food processing technology, food preservation problems.)
d Feuchtigkeitsaussetzung *f*; Aussetzung *f* an die Feuchtigkeit
f exposition *f* à l'humidité
p exposição *f* à umidade

2037 **exposure to light**
(Prod.)
(Food processing technology, food preservation problems.)
d Lichtaussetzung *f*; Aussetzung *f* an das Licht
f exposition *f* à la lumière
p exposição *f* à luz

2038 **exposure to oxygen of the air**
(Prod.)
(Food processing technology, food preservation problems.)
d Aussetzen *n* an den Luftsauerstoff
f exposition *f* à l'oxygène de l'air
p exposição *f* ao oxigênio do ar

* **expression → 4357**

2039 **expression of juice**
(Prod.)
(Food processing technology; aroma/essence production e.g. from fruits.)
d Saftauspressung *f*
f expression *f* de jus
p expressão *f* de suco

2040 **expression under deep temperature**
(Prod.)
(Food processing technology: ref. to cryoextraction; cryoprocess.)
d Auspressen *n* bei tiefer Temperatur
f pressurage *m* à basse température
p expressão *f* sob baixa temperatura; espremedura *f* sob baixa temperatura

2041 **expulsion**
(Med.)
(Veterinary; process of birth: precursory symptoms, contractions, expulsion.)
d Austreibung *f*
f expulsion *f*
p expulsão *f*

* **exquisiteness → 2188**

2042 **exquisite noble vine sort**
(Agr.)
(Viticulture; vine sort quality.)
d edle Rebsorte *f*
f cépage *m* noble
p espécie *f* nobre de cepa

2043 **exquisite wine**
(Agr.)
(Viticulture; ref. to vine quality.)
d edler Wein *m*
f grand cru *m*
p vinho *m* nobre

2044 **extracellular** *adj*
(Biochem.)
(Ref. to cell water as a solvent and transportation agent.)
d extrazellular; extrazellulär
f extracellulaire
p extracelular

2045 **extraction of components of the grape marc**
(Biochem.)
(Nutritional science: enology.)
d Extraktion *f* der Bestandteile des Traubensatzes; Extrahieren *n* der Bestandteile des Traubensatzes
f extraction *f* des constituants du marc de raisin
p extração *f* dos componentes do bagaço da uva

2046 **extraction of fatty matters; fatty body extraction**
(Prod.)
(Food processing technology; prime material processing.)
d Fettkörperextraktion *f*
f extraction *f* des corps gras
p extração *f* de corpos graxos

2047 **extraction of natural aromatic products**
(Prod.)
(Aroma/flavour production.)
d Auszug *m* natürlicher aromatischer Produkte
f extraction *f* des produits aromatiques naturels
p extração *f* dos produtos aromáticos naturais

2048 **extraction of natural tocopherols from vegetable oil**
(Biochem.)
($C_{29}H_{50}O_2$. Vitamin E; antioxidant.)
d Extraktion *f* natürlicher Tocopherole aus Pflanzenölen; Auszug *m* natürlicher Tocopherole aus Pflanzenölen
f extraction *f* des tocophérols naturels de l'huile végétale
p extração *f* de tocoferois naturais do óleo vegetal

2049 **extraction of the must**
(Biochem.)
(Enology.)

d Extraktion *f* des Mostes; Auszug *m* des Mostes
f extraction *f* du moût
p extração *f* do mosto

2050 extraction processes
(Prod.)
(Food processing technology.)
d Extraktionsprozesse *mpl*
f processus *mpl* d'extraction
p processos *mpl* de extração

2051 extraction rate
(Prod.)
(Food processing technology; grain milling processes.)
d Ausmahlungsgrad *m*
f taux *m* d'extraction
p taxa *f* de extração

2052 extraction solvent
(Prod.)
(Food processing technology and flavour research and production.)
d Extraktionslösungsmittel *n*
f solvant *m* d'extraction
p solvente *m* de extração

2053 extraction techniques
(Prod.)
(Food processing technology.)
d Auszugstechniken *fpl*
f techniques *fpl* d'extraction
p técnicas *fpl* de extração

2054 extractive distillation
(Prod.)
(Flavour research and production: extraction/distillation processes.)
d Extrativdestillation *f*
f distillation *f* extractive
p destilação *f* extrativa

2055 extractive starch; free starch
(Prod.)
(Food processing technology: starch type to be extracted by mechanical process only.)
d mechanisch extrahierbare Stärke *f*
f amidon *m* extractible mécaniquement
p amido *m* extraível mecanicamente

2056 extracts of animal tissues
(Biochem.)
(Nutritional science.)
d Auszüge *mpl* tierischer Gewebe
f extraits *mpl* de tissus animaux
p extratos *mpl* de tecidos animais

2057 extracts of plant tissues; extracts of vegetable tissues
(Biochem.)
(Nutritional science.)
d pflanzliche Auszüge *mpl*
f extraits *mpl* de tissus végétaux
p extratos *mpl* de tecidos vegetais

* **extracts of vegetable tissues → 2057**

2058 extruded dough
(Prod.)
(Food processing technology. Pasta plant product.)
d ausgezogener Teig *m*
f pâte *f* extrudée
p massa *f* extrudada

2059 exudation
(Med.)
(Veterinary; normally occurring in presence of an inflammation; the normal defensive mechanism of the body of the animal.)
d Ausschwitzung *f*
f exsudation *f*
p exsudação *f*

2060 exudative diathesis
(Med.)
(Veterinary; predisposition to skin and mucous membrane diseases to be controlled e.g. by selenium supplementation in feed.)
d exudative Diathese *f*
f diathèse *f* exsudative
p diátese *f* exsudativa

2061 eye
(Agr.)
(Botany; undeveloped bud, e.g. potato bud.)
d Auge *n*
f œil *m*; œilleton *m*
p olho *m*

* **eyetooth → 888**

F

2062 **facial muscles**
(Med.)
(Anatomy.)
d Gesichtsmuskeln *mpl*
f muscles *mpl* faciaux
p músculos *mpl* faciais

* **FAD → 2225**

2063 **fallow; fallow field**
(Agr.)
(Soil: unplanted, "reposing"; e.g. moisture and nutrients uptaking land; destined for future cultivation, i.e. agricultural soil working.)
d Brache *f*; Brachfeld *n*; brachliegendes Feld *n*; Brachacker *m*
f terre *f* inculte; friche *f*
p pousio *m*; alqueive *m*; terra *f* baldia; terréu *m*

* **fallow field → 2063**

2064 **family**
(Agr.)
(Botany (flora/fauna): Classification of living organisms; taxonomy: a group of similar families build an order.)
d Familie *f*
f famille *f*
p família *f*

2065 **famine**
(Med.)
(Food scarcity of a population.)
d Hungersnot *f*
f famine *f*
p fome *f*; míngua *f* geral de víveres

* **farce → 5273**

2066 **farm animal**
(Agr.)
(Livestock. Animals raised on the farm for profit, especially cattle.)
d landwirtschaftliches Nutztier *n*
f animal *m* agricole
p animal *m* pecuário

2067 **farming and livestock**
(Agr.)
(Agriculture.)
d Land- und Viehwirtschaft *f*
f agriculture *f* et élevage *m* de bétail
p agropecuária *f*

2068 **farrow** *v*
(Agr.)
(Livestock breeding; bring forth young pigs)
d werfen
f mettre bas
p parir

* **farrow → 3252**

2069 **farrow; farrowing**
(Agr.)
(Livestock breeding; bringing forth of young pigs.)
d Werfen *n*
f mise *f* basse
p parição *f*

* **farrowing → 2069**

2070 **fast; fasting**
(Med.)
(Nutritional abstinence; an absolute diet.)
d Fasten *n*; Nulldiät *f*
f jeûne *m*
p jejum *m*

2071 **fast-food restaurant**
(Prod.)
(Gastronomy.)
d Schnellimbiss *m*; Schnellgaststätte *f*
f restauration *f* rapide
p lanchonete *f*

* **fasting → 2070**

2072 **fat abdomen**
(Med.)
(Anatomy.)
d Fettbauch *m*
f ventre *m* adipeux; abdomen *m* obèse
p ventre *m* adiposo; barriga *f* gorda

2073 **fat accumulation**
(Med.)
(E.g. due to supernutrition.)
d Fettansammlung *f*; Fettübergewicht *n*
f surcharge *f* graisseuse
p acumulação *f* de gorduras; sobrecarga *f* gordurosa

2074 **fat contents**
(Prod.)
(Food processing technology.)
d Fettgehalt *m*
f teneur *f* en graisses; teneur *f* en matières grasses
p teor *m* de gorduras

2075 **fat depot**
(Med.)
(On the walls of the arteries: atheroma formation; e.g. due to incorrect nutrition.)
d Fettdepot *n*
f dépôt *m* graisseux
p depósito *m* gorduroso

* **fat hardening → 2627**

* **fat metabolism → 3210**

2076 **fat oxidation**
(Biochem.)
(Food biochemistry; by vitamin C activity.)
d Fettoxidation *f*
f oxydation *f* de graisse
p oxidação *f* de gordura

2077 **fat-processing industry; oil-processing industry**
(Prod.)
(Food industry.)
d fettverarbeitende Industrie *f*; ölverarbeitende Industrie *f*
f industrie *f* de transformation des graisses; industrie *f* de transformation des huiles
p indústria *f* de transformação de gorduras; indústria *f* de transformação de óleos

2078 **fat richness**
(Med.)
(Nutritional problems of baby nutrition related to human and cow's milk.)
d Reichtum *m* an Fetten
f richesse *f* en graisses
p riqueza *f* de gorduras; riqueza *f* em gorduras

2079 **fats of the food industry**
(Prod.)
(Food processing technology.)
d Fette *npl* der Nahrungsmittelindustrie
f graisses *fpl* de l'industrie alimentaire
p gorduras *mpl* da indústria alimentícia

2080 **fat-soluble** *adj*
(Prod.)
(Food processing technology: product characteristic.)
d fettlöslich
f liposoluble
p lipossolúvel

* **fat-soluble antioxidant → 3233**

2081 **fat-soluble dietary factor**
(Med.)
(Vitamins, e.g. vitamin E found in wheat germs.)
d fettlöslicher Diätfaktor *m*
f facteur *m* diététique liposoluble
p fator *m* dietético lipossolúvel

2082 **fat-soluble dyes**
(Prod.)
(Foodstuff colorants.)
d fettlösliche Farbstoffe *mpl*
f colorants *mpl* liposolubles
p corantes *mpl* lipossolúveis

2083 **fat-soluble vitamins**
(Prod.)
(Vitamins in nutrition; e.g. vitamins A, D, E, K.)
d fettlösliche Vitamine *npl*
f vitamines *fpl* liposolubles
p vitaminas *fpl* lipossolúveis

* **fat surplus → 2016**

2084 **fattened cattle; fattening cattle**
(Agr.)
(Cattle breeding.)
d Mastvieh *n*; Mastrind *n*
f bétail *m* à l'engrais; bétail *m* engraissé; bœufs *mpl* à l'engrais
p rês *f* de engorda; boi *m* de engorda

2085 **fattening; animal fattening**
(Agr.)
(Livestock. Feeding animal for slaughter.)
d Mast *f*; Mästen *n*
f engraissement *m*
p engorda *f*; ceva *f*

* **fattening cattle → 2084**

2086 **fatty**
(Prod.)
(Aroma/flavour note.)
d fettig
f gras
p gorduroso

2087 **fatty acid**
(Prod.)
(Vitamins in nutrition; polyunsaturated essential fatty acids, e.g. linoleic acid.)
d Fettsäure *f*
f acide *m* gras
p ácido *m* graxo

2088 **fatty acid composition of lipids**
(Biochem.)
(Nutritional science; fat biochemistry.)
d Zusammensetzung *f* der Lipide aus Fettsäuren
f composition *f* des lipides en acides gras
p composição *f* dos lipídios por ácidos graxos

2089 fatty alcohol
(Prod.)
(Prime materials in food processing technology.)
d Fettalkohol *m*
f alcool *m* gras
p álcool *m* graxo

2090 fatty body
(Prod.)
(Food processing technology; ref. to prime material processing.)
d Fettkörper *m*
f corps *m* gras
p corpo *m* graxo

* **fatty body extraction → 2046**

2091 fatty body of vegetable origin
(Prod.)
(Food processing technology.)
d Fettkörper *m* pflanzlicher Herkunft
f corps *m* gras d'origine végétale
p corpo *m* graxo de origem vegetal

2092 fatty fishes
(Agr.)
(E.g. tuna; tuna fish.)
d fette Fische *mpl*
f poissons *mpl* gras
p peixes *mpl* gordurosos

2093 fatty foods
(Prod.)
(Food processing technology.)
d fette Nahrungsmittel *npl*
f aliments *mpl* gras
p alimentos *mpl* gordurosos

2094 fatty-green *adj*
(Prod.)
(Product aspect.)
d fettig-grün
f vert-graisseux
p verde-graxo

2095 fatty-green note
(Prod.)
(Taste; aroma/flavour research and production.)
d fettig-grüne Note *f*
f note *f* grasse-verte
p nota *f* verde-graxa

2096 fatty note
(Prod.)
(Taste; aroma/flavour research and production.)
d fettige Note *f*
f note *f* grasse
p nota *f* grodurosa; nota *f* oleosa

2097 fatty particles of the milk
(Prod.)
(Dairy food processing technology.)
d Fettkörperchen *npl* der Milch
f globules *mpl* gras du lait; globules *mpl* graisseux du lait
p partículas *fpl* graxas do leite

2098 fatty phase
(Prod.)
(Food processing technology: e.g. vitamin incorporation into foodstuff.)
d Fettphase *f*
f phase *f* grasse
p fase *f* gordurosa

2099 fawn
(Agr.)
(Game; young female red deer.)
d Hirschkalb *n*
f faon *m*
p enho *m*

2100 FD&C Blue No. 1
(Prod.)
(Foodstuff colorant; colour index: C.I. 42.090.)
d FD&C Blau No. 1
f FD&C Bleu No. 1
p Azul FDC No. 1

* **fecundity → 2151**

* **feeble output → 5853**

2101 feed *v*; **nourish** *v*
(Med.)
(Act of eating, intake of foodstuff, nutrients; to furnish nutriment etc.)
d ernähren; nähren
f alimenter; nourrir
p alimentar; nutrir

2102 feed *v* **cattle**
(Agr.)
(Cattle breeding. Agricultural activity.)
d das Vieh füttern
f affourer les bestiaux
p alimentar o gado

2103 feeding
(Agr.)
(Livestock breeding.)
d Fütterung *f*
f affouragement *m*
p alimentação *f* dos animais

2104 **feeding by tube; gavage**
(Med.)
(Process or direct introduction of alimentary products into the stomach and the small intestine.)
d Sondenernährung *f*
f alimentation *f* par sonde
p alimentação *f* por sonda

* **feeding methods → 2105**

2105 **feeding procedures; feeding methods**
(Agr.)
(Livestock breeding and nutrition.)
d Tierfütterungsverfahren *fpl*; Fütterungsmethoden *fpl*
f méthodes *fpl* d'affouragement
p métodos *mpl* da alimentação animal

2106 **feed phosphate**
(Agr.)
(Livestock; farm animal breeding: animal ration enriched with phosphoric acid.)
d Futterphosphat *n*
f phosphate *m* fourrager
p fosfato *m* para ração

2107 **feedstuff composition**
(Med.)
(Veterinary; analysis stating various types of feedstuff contents, such as dry material, protein ingredients, fibre content, ashes, chemical elements.)
d Futtermittelzusammensetzung *f*
f composition *f* des fourrages
p composição *f* bromatológica da ração animal

2108 **feedstuff ration**
(Agr.)
(Livestock breeding and nutrition.)
d Futtermittelration *f*
f ration *f* fourragère
p ração *f* animal

2109 **feldspar; felspar**
(Agr.)
(Biological agriculture: mineral used in soil treatment compounds.)
d Feldspath *m*
f feldspath *m*
p feldspato *m*

* **felspar → 2109**

2110 **female partridge**
(Agr.)
(Poultry farming. "Perdix". Gallinaceous bird.)
d Rebhuhn *n*
f perdrix *f*
p perdiz *f*

2111 **fennel**
(Agr.)
("Foeniculum vulgare Mill."; Medicinal herb; aromatic seed containing volatile oil.)
d Fenchel *m*
f fenouil *m*
p funcho *m*; anis-doce *m*; erva-doce *f*; maratro *m*

2112 **fennel oil**
(Prod.)
(Volatile oil of the dried fruit of "Foeniculum vulgare Mill."; used e.g. for flavouring; aroma/flavour prime material.)
d Fenchelöl *n*
f essence *f* de fenouil
p essência *f* de funcho

2113 **fennel tea**
(Prod.)
(Herb tea.)
d Fencheltee *m*
f tisane *f* de fenouil
p chá *m* de funcho

2114 **ferment**
(Biochem.)
(Ferment-enzyme-diastase: in nutritional science ferments act in cheese maturation, giving a specific taste by acidifying.)
d Ferment *n*
f ferment *m*
p fermento *m*

2115 **ferment** *v*
(Biochem.)
(Microbiology in foods: undergoing fermentation.)
d fermentieren
f fermenter
p fermentar

2116 **fermentability**
(Biochem.)
(Nutritional science; susceptible to fermentation.)
d Gärfähigkeit *f*
f fermentescibilité *f*
p fermentescibilidade *f*

2117 **fermentable** *adj*
(Biochem.)
(Food processing technology; e.g. capable or susceptible of fermentation.)
d gärfähig
f fermentable; fermentescible
p fermentável

2118 fermentable sugar
(Biochem.)
(Fermentation in nutritional science.)
d gärungsfähiger Zucker *m*
f sucre *m* fermentable; sucre *m* fermentescible
p açúcar *m* fermentável

2119 fermentation
(Biochem.)
(Enzymatic decomposition of carbohydrates to provide chemical energy; biochemical process for aroma development in food.)
d Gärung *f*; Fermentation *f*
f fermentation *f*
p fermentação *f*

2120 fermentation accelerator
(Biochem.)
(Fermentation processes in nutritional science.)
d Gärungsbeschleuniger *m*
f accélérateur *m* de fermentation
p acelerador *m* da fermentação

2121 fermentation alcohol
(Biochem.)
(Fermentation. E.g. in fermented liquors.)
d Fermentationsalkohol *m*
f alcool *m* de la fermentation
p álcool *m* de fermentação

2122 fermentation aromas
(Biochem.)
(Nutritional science; ref. to fermentation processes for elaboration of food aromas.)
d Gärungsaromen *npl*
f arômes *mpl* de fermentation
p aromas *mpl* de fermentação

2123 fermentation byproducts
(Biochem.)
(Nutritional science; ref. to fermentation processes.)
d Gärungsnebenprodukte *npl*
f produits *mpl* secondaires de la fermentation
p subprodutos *mpl* da fermentação

2124 fermentation caused by microorganisms
(Biochem.)
(Nutritional science.)
d von Mikroorganismen verursachte Fermentation *f*; von Mikroorganismen erzeugte Fermentation *f*
f fermentation *f* engendrée par des microorganismes
p fermentação *f* induzida por microorganismos

2125 fermentation conditions
(Biochem.)
(Fermentation processes in nutritional science.)
d Fermentationsbedingungen *fpl*; Gärungsbedingungen *fpl*
f conditions *fpl* de la fermentation
p condições *fpl* de fermentação

2126 fermentation continuation
(Biochem.)
(Fermentation processes in nutritional science.)
d Weitergärung *f*
f continuation *f* de la fermentation
p continuação *f* da fermentação

2127 fermentation interruption by cooling
(Biochem.)
(Nutritional science; food biochemistry: fermentation processes.)
d Abbruch *m* der Gärung durch Abkühlung
f arrêt *m* de la fermentation par refroidissement
p interrupção *f* da fermentação por resfriamento

2128 fermentation of cereals
(Biochem.)
(Brewery processes.)
d Vergärung *f* von Getreide; Getreidevergärung *f*
f fermentation *f* de céréales
p fermentação *f* de cereais

2129 fermentation of germinated barley
(Biochem.)
(Beer production; brewery process.)
d Gärung *f* angekeimter Gerste
f fermentation *f* de l'orge germée
p fermentação *f* da cevada germinada

2130 fermentation of sugar containing solution
(Biochem.)
(Food processing technology: e.g. process part of citric acid production.)
d Vergärung *f* von zuckerhaltiger Lösung
f fermentation *f* d'une solution sucrée
p fermentação *f* de solução contendo açúcar

2131 fermentation of the berry juice
(Biochem.)
(Enology.)
d Gärung *f* des Beerensaftes
f fermentation *f* du jus des baies
p fermentação *f* do sumo das uvas

2132 fermentation of the grape must
(Biochem.)
(Enology; wine production techniques.)
d Gärung *f* des Traubenmostes
f fermentation *f* du moût de raisin
p fermentação *f* do mosto de uvas

2133 **fermentation originated carbon dioxide; carbon dioxide produced by fermentation**
(Biochem.)
(Nutritional science; food biochemistry: fermentation processes, giving rise to CO_2 (carbonic anhydride).)
d gärungsursprüngliches Kohlendioxid *n*
f gaz *m* carbonique d'origine fermentaire; dioxyde *m* de carbone d'origine fermentaire
p gás *m* carbônico originado pela fermentação; dióxido *m* de carbono originado pela fermentação

2134 **fermentation phase**
(Biochem.)
(Fermentation in nutritional science.)
d Gärungsphase *f*
f phase *f* de la fermentation
p fase *f* da fermentação

2135 **fermentation process**
(Biochem.)
(Fermentation. Beer brewery process: First scientific basis was supplied by Louis Pasteur, in 1860.)
d Fermentationsvorgang *m*; Prozess *m* der gesteuerten Gärung; Gärungsprozess *m*
f processus *m* de la fermentation; processus *m* fermentaire
p processo *m* de fermentação

2136 **fermentation realization; carrying out of the fermentation process**
(Biochem.)
(Fermentation in nutritional science.)
d Durchführung *f* der Gärung
f conduite *f* de la fermentation
p condução *f* da fermentação; execução *f* da fermentação

* **fermentation start → 582**

2137 **fermentation temperature**
(Biochem.)
(Fermentation in nutritional science.)
d Gärungstemperatur *f*
f température *f* de fermentation
p temperatura *f* de fermentação

2138 **fermentation under moderate temperature**
(Biochem.)
(Food processing technology.)
d Gärung *f* bei gemäßigter Temperatur
f fermentation *f* à température modérée
p fermentação *f* sob temperatura moderada

2139 **fermentation value**
(Prod.)
(Food processing technology; ref. e.g. to brewery processes: determination of alcohol content in the beer.)
d Vergärungsgrad *m*
f valeur *f* de brassage
p grau *m* da fermentação

2140 **fermentation vat**
(Biochem.)
(Enology; wine production.)
d Gärbottich *m*
f cuve *f* de fermentation
p cuba *f* de fermentação

2141 **fermentation vinegar**
(Biochem.)
(Fermentation: acetic acid obtained through acetic acid fermentation.)
d Gärungsessig *m*
f vinaigre *m* de la fermentation
p vinagre *m* de fermentação

2142 **fermentative bacteria**
(Biochem.)
(Fermentation process bacteria.)
d Gärungsbakterien *fpl*
f bactéries *fpl* de fermentation
p bactérias *fpl* de fermentação

2143 **fermentative force of tissue extracts**
(Biochem.)
(Nutritional science, ref. to enzymes.)
d Fermentationskraft *f* von Gewebsauszügen
f pouvoir *m* de fermentation d'extraits de tissus
p poder *m* de fermentação de extratos de tecidos

2144 **fermented**
(Biochem.)
(Microbiology in foods: having undergone fermentation.)
d fermentiert; gegoren
f fermenté
p fermentado

2145 **fermented beverages; fermented drinks**
(Biochem.)
(Fermentation processes; alcoholic fermentation. Gastronomy.)
d fermentierte Getränke *npl*; Gärungsgetränke *npl*
f boissons *fpl* fermentées
p bebidas *fpl* fermentadas

* **fermented drinks → 2145**

2146 **fermented milk**
(Biochem.)
(Fermentation. Undergoing a pure lactic fermentation process: e.g. yoghurt; lactic fermented milk associated to alcoholic fermented milk: e.g. kefir (Russian product).)
d fermentierte Milch *f*

f lait *m* fermenté
p leite *m* fermentado

2147 fermented products
(Prod.)
(Food processing technology; e.g. cheese, wine.)
d Gärungsprodukte *npl*
f produits *mpl* de fermentation
p produtos *mpl* de fermentação

2148 fermented silage
(Agr.)
(Livestock breeding; animal feeding; a silo-stored foodstuff type.)
d Gärfutter *n*
f ensilage *m* en fermentation
p forragem *f* de fermentação

2149 fermented soya hydrolysate
(Prod.)
(Food processing technology.)
d fermentiertes Sojahydrolysat *n*; vergärtes Sojahydrolysat *n*
f hydrolysat *m* du soja fermenté; produit *m* d'hydrolyse du soja fermenté
p produto *m* de hidrólise da soja fermentada

2150 ferric chlorosis
(Agr.)
(Botany; plant disease; deficiency of nutrients, especially iron.)
d Eisenchlorose *f*
f chlorose *f* ferrique
p clorose *f* férrica

2151 fertility; fecundity
(Agr.)
(Livestock breeding. Characteristic of an animal to be able to reproduce regularly.)
d Fruchtbarkeit *f*; Fertilität *f*; Fekundität *f*
f fertilité *f*; fécondité *f*
p fertilidade *f*; fecundidade *f*

2152 fertilization with compost
(Agr.)
(Soil treatment, fertilizing with organic matter; ref. to organic agriculture; organic farming; concern of biological agriculture.)
d Kompostierung *f*
f compostage *m*; fumure *f* par compost
p adubação *f* orgânica

2153 fertilizer
(Agr.)
(Soil treatment; chemical products to be added to the arable earth layer: synthetic, animal or plant origin, inorganic products.)
d Düngemittel *n*
f fertilisant *m*; engrais *m*
p fertilizante *m*

2154 fertilizer of plant origin; green manure
(Agr.)
(Biological agriculture. Special (plant residual) fertilizer type without containing chemical substances.)
d Gründünger *m*
f engrais *m* vert
p fertilizante *m* vegetal

2155 fertilizing by foliar application
(Agr.)
(Fertilizing process.)
d Blattdüngung *f*
f fertilisation *f* par le feuillage
p adubação *f* foliar

* **fetus → 2289**

2156 fibrous protein
(Biochem.)
(Nutritional science; e.g. long strand proteins, like keratins.)
d fibrilläres Protein *n*
f protéine *f* fibreuse
p proteína *f* fibrilosa

2157 field
(Agr.)
(Soil: land for cultivation.)
d Acker *m*; Feld *n*
f champ *m*
p campo *m*; roça *f*

2158 field crops
(Agr.)
(Agricultural produce.)
d Feldfrüchte *fpl*
f fruits *mpl* des champs
p frutos *mpl* do campo; produtos *mpl* da roça

2159 field vegetables
(Agr.)
(Biological agriculture; horticulture.)
d Feldgemüse *n*
f légumes *mpl* des champs
p hortaliças *fpl* de campo

2160 fig
(Agr.)
(Agricultural produce. "Ficus carica", edible fruit.)
d Feige *f*
f figue *f*
p figo *m*

2161 filament
(Agr.)
(Botany; part of the flower structure: the

filament bears the pollen containing anther, and this entire structure is called stamen.)
d Staubfaden *m*
f filet *m*
p filete *m*

2162 **filamentous mould**
(Biochem.)
(Microbiology.)
d filamentöser Schimmelpilz *m*
f champignon *m* filamenteux
p bolor *m* filamentoso; mofo *m* filamentoso

2163 **filiform papilla**
(Med.)
(Anatomy; kind of tongue protuberance related to the taste buds.)
d fadenförmige Zungenpapille *f*; fadenförmige Geschmacksknospe *f*
f papille *f* filiforme
p papila *f* filiforme

* **filled custard pie → 4541**

2164 **filled pancake**
(Prod.)
(Gastronomy.)
d gefüllter Pfannkuchen *m*
f beignet *m*
p crepe *m* recheado; panqueca *f* recheada

2165 **filled stomach**
(Med.)
(Food intake; nutrition.)
d voller Magen *m*
f estomac *m* rempli
p estômago *m* cheio

2166 **filled tooth**
(Med.)
(Anatomy.)
d gefüllter Zahn *m*; plombierter Zahn *m*
f dent *f* plombée
p dente *m* obturado

2167 **fillet of pork**
(Prod.)
(Butchery; meat part; joint.)
d Schweinefilet *n*
f filet *m* de porc
p filé *m* de porco

2168 **filling; filling up; replenishment**
(Prod.)
(Food processing technology.)
d Füllung *f*; Ausfüllen *n*; Nachfüllen *n*
f remplissage *m*
p enchimento *m*

* **filling up → 2168**

2169 **filter**
(Prod.)
(Food processing technology.)
d Filter *m*
f filtre *m*
p filtro *m*

2170 **filterability**
(Prod.)
(Food processing technology; ref. to prime material characteristics.)
d Filtrierbarkeit *f*
f filtrabilité *m*
p filtrabilidade *f*

2171 **filter bed**
(Prod.)
(Food processing technology; filtering process e.g. in beer, wine and fruit juice production.)
d Filterbett *n*
f couche *f* filtrante
p leito *m* filtrante

* **filter cake → 2174**

2172 **filtered yeast**
(Prod.)
(Yeast production plant product.)
d gefilterte Hefe *f*
f levure *f* filtrée
p fermento *m* filtrado; lêvedo *m* filtrado

2173 **filtering paper**
(Prod.)
(Food processing technology; filtering process accessory.)
d Filterpapier *n*
f papier *m* filtre
p papel *m* de filtrar; papel *m* de filtro

2174 **filtering residue; filter cake**
(Prod.)
(Food processing technology.)
d Filterrückstand *m*; Filterkuchen *m*
f tourteau *m* de filtration; gâteau *m* de filtre
p resíduo *m* de filtração

2175 **filtering surface**
(Prod.)
(Food processing technology; filtering process e.g. in beer, wine and fruit juice production.)
d Oberfläche *f* des Filtermittels
f surface *f* filtrante
p superfície *f* filtrante

2176 **filter material**
(Prod.)
(Food processing technology; filtering process accessory e.g. in beer, wine and fruit juice production.)

d Filtermittel *n*
f matériau *m* de filtration
p material *m* de filtração

2177 **filter press**
(Prod.)
(Food processing technology.)
d Filterpresse *f*; Druckfilter *m*
f filtre-presse *m*
p filtro-prensa *m*

2178 **filtrate**
(Prod.)
(Food processing technology; substance passed through a filter.)
d Filtrat *n*
f filtrat *m*; produit *m* passé; liquide *m* filtré
p líquido *m* filtrado

2179 **filtration aid**
(Prod.)
(Filtering process accessory, e.g. in beer and juice production.)
d Filtrierungshilfsmittel *n*; Filtrierhilfsmittel *n*
f additif *m* de filtration; adjuvant *m* de filtration
p aditivo *m* de filtração; substância *f* auxiliar de filtração

2180 **filtration on infusorial earth**
(Prod.)
(Food processing technology; filtering process e.g. in beer, wine and fruit juice production.)
d Filtration *f* über Infusorienerde
f filtration *f* sur terre d'infusoires
p filtração *f* sobre terra de infusórios

2181 **fin**
(Agr.)
(Fish anatomy.)
d Flosse *f*
f nageoire *f*
p barbatana *f*

2182 **final drying stage**
(Prod.)
(Food processing technology; production process.)
d Endphase *f* des Trocknungsprozesses
f phase *f* finale du séchage
p fase *f* final do processo de secagem

2183 **final maceration**
(Biochem.)
(Enology; technology of wine production.)
d endgültige Mazeration *f*; letztes Ziehenlassen *n*
f macération *f* finale
p maceração *f* final

2184 **final phase of solvent evaporation**
(Prod.)
(Aroma/flavour research and production: solvent extraction processes.)
d Endphase *f* der Lösungsmittelverflüchtigung
f phase *f* finale d'évaporation du solvant
p fase *f* final da evaporação do solvente

2185 **fine grinding**
(Prod.)
(Food processing technology; ref. to flour production.)
d feine Ausmahlung *f*
f mouture *f* fine
p moagem *f* fina

2186 **fine homogenized texture**
(Prod.)
(Baby nutrition; ref. to industrialized baby food composition.)
d feine homogenisierte Textur *f*
f texture *f* fine homogénéisée
p textura *f* fina homogeneizada

2187 **finely grained**
(Prod.)
(Food processing technology: powder aspect definition.)
d feinkörnig
f granulé finement
p granulado de forma fina

2188 **fineness; exquisiteness**
(Prod.)
(Gastronomy; e.g. ref. to the taste, palatability.)
d Feinheit *f*; Erlesenheit *f*
f finesse *f*
p fineza *f*

2189 **fine powder**
(Prod.)
(Food processing technology; product characteristic.)
d Feinpulver *n*; feines Pulver *n*
f poudre *f* fine
p pó *m* fino

2190 **fine powder sodium ascorbate**
(Biochem.)
(Nutritional science: vitamin C, used as an antioxidant.)
d feinpulveriges Natriumascorbat *n*
f ascorbate *m* de sodium en poudre fine
p ascorbato *m* de sódio pó fino

2191 **finest chopping**
(Prod.)
(Food processing technology; ref. to foodstuff industrialization.)
d Feinstzerkleinerung *f*

f coupage *m* extrêmement fin
p corte *m* finíssimo

2192 **fine vine sort**
(Agr.)
(Viticulture; ref. to vine quality.)
d feine Rebsorte *f*
f cépage *m* fin
p espécie *f* de cepa fina

2193 **finished product**
(Prod.)
(Consumer product.)
d Endprodukt *n*
f produit *m* fini
p produto *m* acabado

2194 **fir; silver fir**
(Agr.)
(Botany; "Abies alba". Coniferous tree; cultivated e.g. in Brazil for tannin extraction from the cortex.)
d Tanne *f*; Edeltanne *f*
f sapin *m*; sapin *m* blanc
p abeto *m*; abeto-branco *m*

2195 **fir cone**
(Agr.)
(Botany; "Abies". Evergreen tree, pine family, having female cones.)
d Tannenzapfen *m*; Kienapfel *m*
f pomme *f* de pin
p pinha *f*

2196 **firewood**
(Agr.)
(Agricultural produce; agricultural subproduct.)
d Brennholz *n*
f bois *m* de chauffage
p lenha *f*

2197 **firm abdomen**
(Med.)
(Anatomy.)
d straffer Bauch *m*; fester Bauch *m*
f ventre *m* ferme
p barriga *f* firme

* **firm dough → 1310**

2198 **first fraction of distillation; first runnings; distillation front**
(Prod.)
(Food processing technology: ref. to distillation process: The first dropping of components of low boiling point. Aroma/fragrance research and production.)
d Vorlauf *m* der Destillation; Destillationsvorlauf *m*
f première fraction *f* de la distillation; avant-coulant *m*; eau-de-vie *f* première; tête *f* de distillation
p destilado *m* de cabeça; destilado *m* de flor

* **first runnings → 2198**

2199 **fishbone**
(Med.)
(Veterinary science: anatomy of fishes.)
d Gräte *f*
f arête *f*
p espinha *f*

2200 **fishbone calcium salts**
(Prod.)
(Ref. to tiny fishes eaten entirely: calcium supply; prime material.)
d Calciumsalze *npl* der Gräten
f sels *mpl* de calcium des arêtes
p sais *mpl* de cálcio das espinhas de peixe

2201 **fish consumption**
(Prod.)
(Food processing technology, food marketing.)
d Fischkonsum *m*
f consommation *f* de poisson
p consumo *m* de peixe

2202 **fish dish**
(Prod.)
(Gastronomy.)
d Fischgericht *n*
f plat *m* de poisson
p prato *m* de peixe

* **fish farming → 4193**

2203 **fish hydrolysate**
(Agr.)
(Livestock nutrition; feedstuff ration ingredient.)
d Fischhydrolysat *n*
f hydrolysat *m* de poisson
p produto *m* de hidrólise do peixe

2204 **fishing**
(Agr.)
(Activity of catching fish.)
d Fischfang *m*
f pêche *f*; capture *f* du poisson
p pesca *f*; pescaria *f*

2205 **fish meal**
(Prod.)
(Food processing technology: protein source.)
d Fischmehl *n*
f farine *f* de poisson
p farinha *f* de peixe

2206 **fish meal fertilizer**
(Agr.)
(Biological agriculture; organic fertilizer.)
d Fischmehldüngemittel *n*
f engrais *m* de poudre de poisson
p fertilizante *m* de farinha de peixe

2207 **fish oil**
(Prod.)
(Food processing technology; prime material.)
d Fischöl *n*
f huile *f* de poisson
p óleo *m* de peixe

2208 **fish protein concentrate**
(Prod.)
(Treated fish meal, protein source (ca. 75% in its composition), for low-cost food enrichment; prime material.)
d Fischproteinkonzentrat *n*
f concentré *m* de protéine de poisson
p concentrado *m* protéico de peixe

* **fish salting → 4175**

2209 **fish slice**
(Prod.)
(Gastronomy; thick piece (slice) of a fish.)
d Fischscheibe *f*
f darne *f*
p posta *f* de peixe

2210 **fish soup**
(Prod.)
(Gastronomy.)
d Fischsuppe *f*
f soupe *f* aux poissons
p sopa *f* de peixe

2211 **fish stew**
(Prod.)
(Gastronomy.)
d Fischragout *n*
f matelote *f*
p ragu *m* de peixes; guisado *m* de peixes

* **fission of the chain → 5156**

* **fissured geological bed → 2212**

2212 **fissured geological layer; fissured geological bed; fissured stratum**
(Prod.)
(One possible characteristic of the site of groundwater formation, drinking water source.)
d gespaltene geologische Schicht *f*
f couche *f* géologique fissurée
p camada *f* geológica fissurada; estrato *m* fissurado

* **fissured stratum → 2212**

2213 **fistula**
(Med.)
(Veterinary; e.g. ref. to an abnormal passage linked to an abscess.)
d Fistel *f*
f fistule *f*
p fístula *f*

2214 **fixed acidity**
(Biochem.)
(Enology; wine production, wine characteristic: fraction which cannot be eliminated by distillation.)
d fester Säuregehalt *m*
f acidité *f* fixe
p acidez *f* fixa

2215 **fixing capacity**
(Prod.)
(Flavour particle characteristic and substrate retention: aroma/flavour research.)
d Fixierkapazität *f*
f capacité *f* fixative
p capacidade *f* de fixação

2216 **fizzy drink; soda pop**
(Prod.)
(Soft drink; flavoured, acidulated (citric acid) soda water beverage.)
d Limonadensprudel *m*
f limonade *f* (*gazeuse*)
p limonada *f* (*com gás*)

* **flaky pastry → 4034**

2217 **flaky pastry preparation**
(Prod.)
(Baker's shop process: flaky pastry preparation from puff pastry.)
d Blätterteigzubereitug *f*
f feuilletage *m*
p preparação *f* de massa folhada

2218 **flame** *v*
(Prod.)
(Gastronomy. Ref. to dish preparation: served with flaming liquor.)
d flambieren
f flamber
p flamejar

2219 **flan; fruit flan**
(Prod.)
(Cake shop product.)
d Obstkuchen *m*
f tarte *f* aux fruits
p torta *f* de frutas

2220 **flan case**
(Prod.)
(Baker's packaging material.)
d Tortenplatte *f*
f plat *m* à gâteau
p prato *m* para tortas

2221 **flank**
(Prod.)
(Butchery; meat part; joint; subdivided in thin flank and thick flank.)
d Lappen *m*
f flanchet *m*
p fraldinha *f*

2222 **flanks**
(Agr.)
(Veterinary science; cattle anatomy, lateral part of the animal body: e.g. Holstein-Frisian dairy cattle, showing lean, arch-shaped flanks; the bull, profound arch-shaped flanks.)
d Flanken *fpl*
f flancs *mpl*
p flancos *mpl*

2223 **flash point**
(Prod.)
(Food processing technology; product specification: e.g. of fats and oils: lowest temperature of inflammability.)
d Flammpunkt *m*
f point *m* d'éclair; point *m* d'inflammation
p ponto *m* de inflamação

* **flat** *adj* → **5197**

2224 **flavin**
(Prod.)
(Yellow water-soluble pigment interferes in some biological processes; natural flavin: riboflavin = vitamin B_2, e.g. in cereals.)
d Flavin *n*
f flavine *f*
p flavina *f*

2225 **flavin adenine dinucleotide; FAD**
(Med.)
($C_{27}H_{33}N_9O_{15}P_2$; coenzyme; prosthetic group of certain flavoproteins (flavoenzymes), acts e.g. in the citric acid cycle (metabolism).)
d Flavin-Adenin-Dinucleotid *n*; FAD *n*
f flavine-adénine-dinucléotide *m*; F.A.D. *m*
p dinucleotídeo *m* de flavina-adenina

2226 **flavone; 2-phenylchromone**
(Biochem.)
($C_{15}H_{10}O_2$; see flavonoids.)
d Flavon *n*
f flavone *f*
p flavona *f*

2227 **flavonoids**
(Biochem.)
(Found in nature in vegetable-fruit-etc. pigments; the flavonoids are flavone glycosides.)
d Flavonoide *npl*
f flavonoïdes *mpl*
p flavonoídes *fpl*

2228 **flavoprotein**
(Biochem.)
(Dehydrogenase (an enzyme); in biological oxidation processes.)
d Flavoprotein *n*
f flavoprotéine *f*
p flavoproteína *f*

2229 **flavour assortment**
(Prod.)
(Aroma/flavour production.)
d Geschmacksstoffauswahl *f*
f gamme *f* des flaveurs
p gama *m* dos sabores

2230 **flavour bouquet**
(Prod.)
(Aroma/flavour characteristics; e.g. beer and wine taste qualities.)
d Geschmacksbukett *n*; Blume *f*
f bouquet *m*
p buquê *m*

2231 **flavoured milk**
(Prod.)
(Food processing technology: Sterilized flavoured milk, e.g. with strawberry taste.)
d aromatisierte Milch *f*
f lait *m* aromatisé
p leite *m* aromatizado

2232 **flavoured with caramel**
(Prod.)
(Food processing technology: e.g. milk products.)
d mit Karamel aromatisiert
f aromatisé au caramel
p aromatizado com caramelo

2233 **flavoured with chocolate**
(Prod.)
(Food processing technology: e.g. milk products.)
d mit Schokolade aromatisiert
f aromatisé au chocolat
p aromatizado com chocolate

* **flavoured yoghurt** → **432**

* **flavour extracts** → **414**

2234 **flavour homogeneity**
(Prod.)
(Aroma/fragrance research and production.)
d Homogenität *f* des Geschmacks; Homogenität *f* des Aromas
f homogénéité *f* de la flaveur
p homogeneidade *f* do sabor

2235 **flavouring agents**
(Prod.)
(Flavour chemicals; synthesis products, taste-modifying food additives.)
d Aromastoffe *mpl*; Geschmacksstoffe *mpl*; aromatisches Würzmittel *npl*
f aromatisants *mpl*
p aromatizantes *mpl*; aromatizadores *mpl*

2236 **flavouring ferments**
(Biochem.)
(Nutritional science.)
d Aromafermente *npl*
f ferments *mpl* d'aromatisation
p fermentos *mpl* de aromatização

2237 **flavour modification**
(Prod.)
(Food processing technology; aroma/flavour notes.)
d Geschmacksveränderung *f*
f modification *f* de la flaveur
p modificação *f* do sabor

2238 **flavour modification through foodstuff processing**
(Prod.)
(Food processing technology; aroma/flavour notes.)
d Geschmacksveränderung *f* durch Nahrungsmittelverarbeitung
f modification *f* de la flaveur par la préparation de l'aliment
p modificação *f* do sabor pelo processamento do produto alimentício

2239 **flavour note**
(Prod.)
(Aroma/flavour research and production; flavour chemicals.)
d Geschmacksstoffnote *f*
f note *f* d'arôme
p nota *f* de aroma

2240 **flavour notion**
(Prod.)
(Aroma/flavour research and production.)
d Geschmacksvorstellung *f*
f notion *f* de flaveur
p noção *f* do sabor

2241 **flavour of the mixture**
(Prod.)
(Flavour chemicals, ref. to flavour and fragrance biotechnology in food biochemistry.)
d Geschmack *m* der Mischung
f flaveur *f* du mélange
p sabor *m* da mistura

2242 **flavour particles**
(Prod.)
(Aroma/flavour perception.)
d Geschmackspartikel *fpl*
f corps *mpl* sapides
p corpos *mpl* aromáticos; partículas *fpl* aromáticas

* **flavour potentiating → 417**

2243 **flavour potentiator**
(Prod.)
(E.g. sodium glutamate, $C_5H_8NNaO_4$; Chinese seasoning, to enhance flavour of food, such as meat, fish, vegetables, sauces, soups.)
d Geschmacksverstärker *m*
f agent *m* de sapidité; exhausteur *m* de goût
p realçador *m* de sabor

2244 **flavour prime material**
(Prod.)
(Raw material for the elaboration of synthetic flavours: organic prime material/organic chemistry.)
d Ausgangsmaterial *n* für Aromen
f matière *f* première pour arômes
p matéria *f* prima para aromas

2245 **flavour product compositions**
(Prod.)
(Elaborated synthetic products: e.g. water-soluble: by hydraulic extraction (fruit juices); or fat-soluble: essential oils, extraction by means of organic solvents.)
d Geschmacksstoffzusammenstellungen *fpl*
f compositions *fpl* aromatiques; compositions *fpl* d'arômes
p composições *fpl* de aromas

2246 **flavour recuperation**
(Prod.)
(Aroma/flavour research and production, distillation/extraction processes.)
d Geschmacksstoffrückgewinnung *f*
f récupération *f* d'arôme
p recuperação *f* do aroma

2247 **flavour research**
(Prod.)
(Research of synthetic flavour chemicals and flavour notes.)
d Geschmacksstoffforschung *f*

f recherche *f* de flaveurs
p pesquisa *f* de produtos aromatizantes; pesquisa *f* de aromas

2248 **flavour richness**
(Prod.)
(Aroma/flavour characteristics: flavour research and application in foodstuff processing.)
d Aromafülle *f*; Aromareichhaltigkeit *f*
f richesse *f* aromatique
p riqueza *f* aromática

2249 **flavoxanthin**
(Prod.)
($C_{40}H_{56}O_3$; carotenoid pigment without vitamin A function; foodstuff colorant.)
d Flavoxanthin *n*
f flavoxanthine *f*
p flavoxantina *f*

2250 **flax**
(Agr.)
(Botany; "Linum usitatissimum"; used in crop rotation.)
d Flachs *m*
f lin *m*
p linho *m*

2251 **flaying**
(Prod.)
(Slaughterhouse technology of animals' hide removal after slaughtering.)
d Abhäutung *f*
f procédé *m* d'écorcher
p esfola *f*

2252 **fleece**
(Agr.)
(Livestock. Coat of wool covering a sheep.)
d Schaffell *n*; Schafpelz *m*
f peau *f* de mouton
p tosão *m*; velo *m* de ovelha

2253 **flesh of fish**
(Prod.)
(Veterinary science; anatomy of fishes.)
d Fleisch *n* des Fisches
f chair *f* de poisson
p carne *f* de peixe

2254 **fleshside**
(Agr.)
(Agricultural produce, subproduct from cattle raising: furrier's product: the fleshside is the greasy layer beneath the dermis, which does not undergo tanning treatment.)
d Aasseite *f*
f côté *m* chair; chair *f*
p lado *m* do carnal; carnal *m*; carnaz *m*

* **fleshy fruit → 4497**

2255 **flight board**
(Agr.)
(Apiculture; movable frame hive construction.)
d Flugbrettchen *n*
f planche *f* de vol
p sarrafo *m*

2256 **flitch of bacon**
(Prod.)
(Butchery; meat type.)
d Speckseite *f*
f quartier *m* de lard
p manta *f* de toucinho

2257 **flocculated phenolic compound**
(Biochem.)
(Nutritional science.)
d ausgeflockte Phenolverbindung *f*
f composé *m* phénolique floculé
p composto *m* fenólico floculado

2258 **flocculation**
(Biochem.)
(Nutritional science; food chemistry.)
d Flockung *f*; Flocken *n*; Ausflockung *f*; Ausflocken *n*
f floculation *f*
p floculação *f*

2259 **flocculation of the iron(III)colloid**
(Biochem.)
(Enology.)
d Ausflockung *f* des Eisen(III)kolloides
f floculation *f* du colloïde ferrique
p floculação *f* do colóide férrico

2260 **flocculent sedimentation; flocculent settling**
(Biochem.)
(Nutritional science: ref. to sedimentation processes.)
d flockenförmiger Sedimentationsabsatz *m*; flockiger Niederschlag *m*
f dépôt *m* floconneux sédimentaire; dépôt *m* floconneux de sédimentation
p depósito *m* flocoso de sedimentação; depósito *m* sedimentário em forma de flocos

* **flocculent settling → 2260**

2261 **flock**
(Agr.)
(Livestock breeding; sheep farming: a group of sheep.)
d Schafherde *f*
f troupeau *m* de moutons
p rebanho *m* de ovelhas

2262 floodwater
(Agr.)
(Due to rainfalls; damages the superficial arable soil layer by carrying away nutritive components.)
d Wasserflut *f*
f inondation *f* par les pluies
p enxurrada *f*

2263 floral diagram
(Agr.)
(Botany: schematic representation of the structure of a flower.)
d graphische Darstellung *f* des Blütenaufbaues
f diagramme *m* floral
p diagrama *m* floral

2264 flounder
(Agr.)
("Pleuronectidae"; "Bothidae"; "Paralichthys brasiliensis (Ranz)".)
d Flunder *f*
f flet *m*
p solha *f*

2265 flour beetle; meal beetle
(Agr.)
(Botany. Genus "Tenebrio"; grain products infesting parasite.)
d Mehlkäfer *m*
f ver *m* de farine; ténébrion *m*
p tenebrionídeo *m*

2266 flour handling
(Prod.)
(Bakery technology.)
d Handhabung *f* des Mehles
f manipulation *f* de la farine
p manuseio *m* da farinha

2267 flour improver
(Prod.)
(Additive for improving flour quality: e.g. ascorbic acid (vitamin C).)
d Mehlverbesserer *m*
f améliorant *m* de la farine
p melhorador *m* da farinha

2268 flouring
(Prod.)
(Bakery's process.)
d Bepuderung *f*
f fleurage *m*; saupoudrage *m*
p polvilhação *f*; polvilhamento *m*; pulverização *f*

2269 flour quality
(Prod.)
(Bakery prime material.)
d Mehlqualität *f*
f qualité *f* de la farine
p qualidade *f* da farinha

2270 flour sieving
(Prod.)
(Separation of the flour.)
d Mehlaussiebung *f*
f blutage *m*; tamisage *m* de la farine
p peneiração *f* da farinha; separação *f* da farinha à peneira

2271 flour types for baby nutrition
(Med.)
(Cereal flour, rhizomic flour for baby nutrition.)
d Mehltypen *mpl* für die Kleinkindernährung
f farines *fpl* infantiles; farines *fpl* pour la nutrition infantile
p farinhas *fpl* para nutrição do lactente

2272 floury *adj*
(Prod.)
(Food processing technology: product characteristic.)
d mehlig
f farineux
p farinhoso

2273 flower fertilization
(Agr.)
(Botany.)
d Befruchtung *f* der Blume
f fécondation *f* de la fleur
p fecundação *f* da flor

2274 flower note
(Prod.)
(Taste; aroma research and production: e.g. tea notes.)
d Blütennote *f*
f note *f* florale
p nota *f* de flores

2275 flowing of rainwater
(Agr.)
(Soil treatment.)
d Regenwasserabfluss *m*
f ruissellement *m* pluvial
p escoamento *m* das águas pluviais

2276 fluffy *adj*
(Prod.)
(Food processing technology: product characteristic.)
d locker
f mollet
p fofo

2277 fluid diet; hydropathic diet
(Med.)
(Alimentary regimen; ref. e.g. to

hydrotherapy, use of water in disease treatment.)
d Wasserdiät *f*
f diète *f* hydrique
p dieta *f* hídrica

2278 **fluidity of the oleoresin**
(Prod.)
(Aroma/flavour production: product characteristic.)
d Fließvermögen *n* des Oleoresins; Fließvermögen *n* des Harzöles
f fluidité *f* de l'oléorésine
p fluidez *f* da oleoresina

2279 **fluidized bed process**
(Prod.)
(Type of product processing.)
d Wirbelbettprozess *m*
f procédé *m* en lit fluidisé
p processo *m* de leito fluidizado

2280 **fluorescence**
(Prod.)
(Food processing technology: The fluorescence phenomenon is used in quantitative analysis.)
d Fluoreszenz *f*
f fluorescence *f*
p fluorescência *f*

2281 **fluorescence analysis**
(Prod.)
(Food processing technology: any analytical method for qualitative and quantitative determination of substances in mixtures, by means of their characteristic fluorescence.)
d Fluoreszenzanalyse *f*
f analyse *f* à fluorescence
p análise *f* por fluorescência

2282 **fluoridated table salt**
(Prod.)
(Food processing technology: fluoridation of table salt for caries prevention.)
d fluoridiertes Speisesalz *n*
f sel *m* de cuisine fluoruré
p sal *m* de cozinha fluorado

2283 **fluoridation**
(Prod.)
(Addition of fluorine compounds to foodstuffs (e.g. water), as caries prophylaxis.)
d Fluoridierung *f*
f fluoration *f*
p fluoridação *f*

2284 **fluorine deficiency**
(Med.)
(Veterinary; mineral (F) deficiency causing wear and breaking of the teeth.)
d Fluormangel *m*
f carence *f* en fluor
p deficiência *f* de flúor

2285 **fluviatile erosion**
(Agr.)
(Soil; ref. to ecology problems.)
d fluviatile Erosion *f*
f érosion *f* fluviale
p erosão *f* fluvial

2286 **fly**
(Agr.)
(Order "Diptera"; "Musca domestica L."; problem causing insect in biological agriculture.)
d Fliege *f*
f mouche *f*
p mosca *f*

2287 **fodder**
(Agr.)
(Livestock breeding; e.g. hay, husks, corn chaff; roots; tubers; fermented silage; bran cake, green fodder.)
d Futtermittel *n/npl*
f fourrages *mpl*
p forragem *f*

2288 **fodderplant**
(Agr.)
(Livestock breeding.)
d Futterpflanze *f*
f plante *f* fourragère
p planta *f* forraginosa

2289 **foetus; fetus**
(Agr.)
(Livestock breeding: unborn vertebrate.)
d Fötus *m*; Fetus *m*; Frucht *f*
f fœtus *m*
p feto *m*

2290 **foliage**
(Agr.)
(Botany; representation of leaves.)
d Laub *n*; Laubwerk *n*; Blätterwerk *n*
f feuillage *m*
p folhagen *f*

2291 **foliar fertilizer**
(Agr.)
(Botany; fertilizer applied on the leaves of plants.)
d Blattdünger *m*
f engrais *m* foliaire
p adubo *m* foliáceo

2292 **foliar surface**
(Agr.)
(Botany; surface of the leaves.)
d Blattoberfläche *f*
f surface *f* foliaire
p superfície *f* foliar

2293 **foliate papilla**
(Med.)
(Anatomy; kind of tongue protuberance related to the taste buds.)
d Blätterpapille *f* der Zunge; blätterförmige Geschmacksknospe *f*
f papille *f* foliée
p papila *f* foliata

2294 **folic acid**
(Prod.)
($C_{19}H_{19}N_7O_6$. Belongs to the vitamin B complex.)
d Folsäure *f*
f acide *m* folique
p ácido *m* fólico

2295 **fondant**
(Prod.)
(Food processing technology; sugar mass prepared with addition of colorants and flavour agents, e.g. for chocolate (praliné) production.)
d Fondant *m/n*
f fondant *m*
p fondant *m*

* **fondu → 2296**

2296 **fondue; fondu**
(Prod.)
(Gastronomy.)
d Fondue *n*
f fondue *f*
p fondue *f*

2297 **food; foodstuff; groceries**
(Prod.)
(Product for human nutrition. Alimentary substance in diet compositions which provides energy.)
d Nahrungsmittel *npl*; Lebensmittel *npl*; Esswaren *fpl*; Nährmittel *npl*
f produits *mpl* alimentaires; aliment *m*; vivres *mpl*; comestible *m*; denrée *f*; nourriture *f*
p produtos *mpl* alimentícios; alimento *m*

2298 **food allergy**
(Med.)
(Hypersensitivity to e.g. specific food ingredients.)
d Lebensmittelallergie *f*; Nahrungsmittelallergie *f*; alimentäre Allergie *f*
f allergie *f* alimentaire
p alergia *f* alimentar

2299 **food antioxidant; alimentary antioxidant**
(Prod.)
(Auxiliary products; antioxidants.)
d Nahrungsmittelantioxidant *m*
f antioxydant *m* alimentaire
p antioxidante *m* alimentar

2300 **food assimilation**
(Med.)
(Regimens, diets.)
d Assimilieren *n* von Nahrungsmitteln
f assimilation *f* d'aliments
p assimilação *f* dos alimentos

2301 **food aversion; aversion to a foodstuff**
(Med.)
d Nahrungsmittelaversion *f*; Abneigung *f* gegen ein Nahrungsmittel; Widerwille *m* gegen ein Nahrungsmittel
f aversion *f* pour un aliment
p aversão *f* a um alimento

2302 **food chain**
(Agr.)
(In botany; refers to ecological communities' structures.)
d Nahrungskette *f*
f chaîne *f* alimentaire
p cadeia *f* alimentar

2303 **food colorant**
(Prod.)
(Food processing technology: e.g. beta-carotene.)
d Lebensmittelfarbstoff *m*
f colorant *m* alimentaire
p corante *m* alimentício

2304 **food conservation after heating**
(Prod.)
(Food processing technology; food preservation method.)
d Nahrungsmittelhaltbarmachung *f* nach Erhitzung
f conservation *f* des aliments après chauffage
p conservação *f* dos alimentos após aquecimento

* **food conservation in airtight sealed vessels → 2305**

2305 **food conservation in hermetically sealed vessels; food conservation in airtight sealed vessels**
(Prod.)
(Food processing technology; food preservation method.)

d Nahrungsmittelhaltbarmachung *f* in luftdichten Gefäßen
f conservation *f* des aliments en récipients hermétiques
p conservação *f* de produtos alimentícios em recipientes herméticos

2306 **food containing fatty material; foodstuffs containing fatty material**
(Prod.)
(Food processing technology.)
d Fettstoffe *mpl* enthaltende Lebensmittel
f produits *mpl* alimentaires contenant des matières grasses
p produtos *mpl* alimentícios contendo materiais graxos; alimentos *mpl* contendo gordura

2307 **food dyes range**
(Prod.)
(Foodstuff colorants.)
d Nahrungsmittelfarbstoffpalette *f*
f palette *f* des colorants alimentaires
p sortimento *m* de corantes alimentícios

2308 **food hygiene**
(Prod.)
(Food processing technology.)
d Nahrungsmittelhygiene *f*
f hygiène *f* des denrées
p higiene *f* dos produtos alimentícios; higiene *f* dos alimentos

2309 **food industrialization; foodstuff industrialization**
(Prod.)
(Food processing technology; purpose e.g. time gained for distribution activities.)
d Nahrungsmittelindustrialisierung *f*
f industrialisation *f* de l'alimentation
p industrialização *f* dos produtos alimentícios; industrialização *f* dos aliementos

2310 **food industry**
(Prod.)
(Food processing technology; foodstuff production and marketing.)
d Nahrungsmittelindustrie *f*
f industrie *f* alimentaire
p indústria *f* alimentícia

2311 **food intoxication**
(Med.)
(Microbiology: food poisoning; e.g. a digestive system disease; normally caused by bacteria and toxins.)
d Lebensmittelvergiftung *f*; Nahrungsmittelvergiftung *f*
f intoxication *f* alimentaire
p intoxicação *f* alimentar

2312 **food on the basis of wheat; foodstuff on the basis of wheat**
(Prod.)
(Food processing technology.)
d Nahrungsmittel *npl* auf Weizengrundlage
f aliments *mpl* préparés à base de blé
p produtos *mpl* alimentícios à base de trigo; alimentos *mpl* elaborados à base de trigo

2313 **food pest control**
(Biochem.)
(Food processing technology.)
d Lebensmittelschädlingsbekämpfung *f*
f lutte *f* contre les parasites alimentaires
p controle *m* dos parasitas de alimentos

2314 **food preparation**
(Prod.)
(Food processing technology; food industrialization: ref. in this specific case to the product.)
d Nahrungsmittelpräparat *n*
f préparation *f* alimentaire
p preparado *m* alimentício

2315 **food preparation process; foodstuff preparation process**
(Prod.)
(Food processing technology; industrial phase of preparation.preparation.)
d Nahrungsmittelzubereitung *f*
f préparation *f* de la nourriture
p preparação *f* dos alimentos

2316 **food production; foodstuff production**
(Prod.)
(Food processing technology and production.)
d Nahrungsmittelproduktion *f*
f production *f* des produits alimentaires
p produção *f* de alimentos; produção *f* de produtos alimentícios

2317 **food ration; foodstuff ration**
(Prod.)
(Food processing technology.)
d Nahrungsmittelration *f*
f ration *f* alimentaire
p ração *f* de produtos alimentícios

2318 **food refinement**
(Prod.)
(Food processing technology; food industrialization.)
d Nahrungsmittelveredelung *f*
f affinage *m* alimentaire
p refinação *f* alimentar; refinamento *m* alimentar

2319 **food requirements; demand for foodstuff**
(Med.)
(Food processing technology; foodstuff

production and marketing, e.g. to subsistence diet, minimum diet.)
d Nahrungsmittelbedarf *m*
f besoins *mpl* alimentaires; demande *f* alimentaire
p necessidades *fpl* alimentícias; demanda *f* por produtos alimentícios

2320 food requirements by the consumer
(Prod.)
(Food processing technology; foodstuff production and marketing.)
d Nahrungsmittelbedarf *m* seitens der Verbraucher
f besoins *mpl* alimentaires des consommateurs
p necessidades *fpl* de produtos alimentícios por parte dos consumidores

2321 food research
(Prod.)
(Food processing technology.)
d Nahrungsmittelforschung *f*
f recherche *f* alimentaire
p pesquisas *fpl* alimentícias

* **foodstuff → 2297**

2322 foodstuff analysis
(Med.)
(Veterinary: Analysis e.g. of cattle foodstuff rations.)
d Futtermittelanalyse *f*
f analyse *f* des fourrages
p análise *f* bromatológica

2323 foodstuff consumption
(Prod.)
(Food processing technology; foodstuff production and marketing.)
d Nahrungsmittelkonsum *m*
f consommation *f* alimentaire
p consumo *m* de produtos alimentícios; consumo *m* de alimentos

2324 foodstuff cultures
(Agr.)
(Agricultural produce.)
d nahrungsmittelerzeugende Kulturen *fpl*
f cultures *fpl* vivrières
p culturas *fpl* destinadas à alimentação

* **foodstuff industrialization → 2309**

2325 foodstuff of animal origin
(Prod.)
(Food processing technology.)
d Nahrungsmittel *npl* tierischer Herkunft
f aliments *mpl* d'origine animale
p produtos *mpl* alimentícios de origem animal

* **foodstuff on the basis of wheat → 2312**

* **foodstuff preparation process → 2315**

2326 foodstuff preservation by heat
(Prod.)
(Food processing technology; preservation process.)
d Nahrungsmittelkonservierung *f* durch Hitze
f conservation *f* des comestibles par action de la chaleur
p conservação *f* dos produtos alimentícios pelo calor

* **foodstuff production → 2316**

2327 foodstuff quality
(Agr.)
(Here: ref. to the concerns of biological agriculture and farming.)
d Nahrungsmittelqualität *f*
f qualité *f* de l'alimentation
p qualidade *f* da alimentação

* **foodstuff ration → 2317**

2328 foodstuff ration equilibrium; balance of alimentary ration
(Med.)
(Food processing technology. Important for the human metabolism.)
d Ausgewogenheit *f* der Nahrungsmittelration
f équilibre *m* de la ration des produits alimentaires; équilibre *m* de la ration alimentaire
p equilíbrio *m* da ração de produtos alimentícios; equilíbrio *m* da ração alimentar

* **foodstuffs containing fatty material → 2306**

* **foodstuff taste → 2331**

2329 foodstuff technology
(Prod.)
(Food industrialization; food processing.)
d Lebensmitteltechnologie *f*
f technologie *f* des nutriments
p tecnologia *f* alimentícia; tecnologia *f* dos alimentos

* **foodstuff with a high fat content → 2333**

2330 foodstuff without nutritional value
(Med.)
(Foodstuff research.)
d Nahrungsmittel *n* ohne Nährwert
f aliment *m* dénué de la valeur nutritionnelle
p alimento *m* sem valor nutricional

2331 **food taste; foodstuff taste**
(Prod.)
(Food processing technology, research and production.)
d Geschmack *m* der Nahrungsmittel
f goût *m* des aliments
p gosto *m* dos produtos alimentícios; paladar *m* dos produtos alimentícios

2332 **food technology**
(Prod.)
(Food processing technology.)
d Nahrungsmitteltechnologie *f*
f technologie *f* alimentaire
p tecnologia *f* de alimentação

* **food vitaminization → 5779**

* **food vitaminizing → 5779**

2333 **food with a high fat content; foodstuff with a high fat content**
(Prod.)
(Food processing technology: e.g. margarine.)
d hochfetthaltige Lebensmittel *npl*
f denrées *fpl* alimentaires à forte teneur en graisse
p produtos *mpl* alimentícios com alto teor de gordura

2334 **foot-and-mouth disease; hoof-and-mouth disease**
(Med.)
(Veterinary; febrile virus disease.)
d Maul- und Klauenseuche *f*
f fièvre *f* aphteuse
p aftosa *f*; febre *f* aftosa

2335 **forage culture**
(Agr.)
(Livestock nutrition: Feed for farm animals.)
d Futterpflanzenkultur *f*
f culture *f* fourragère
p cultura *f* forrageira

2336 **fore legs**
(Med.)
(Veterinary; animal anatomy.)
d Vorderbeine *npl*
f jambes *fpl* de devant
p pernas *fpl* dianteiras

2337 **formation of volatile acidity**
(Biochem.)
(Fermentation in nutritional science: e.g. ref. to enology.)
d Bildung *f* flüchtigen Säuregehaltes
f formation *f* d'acidité volatile
p formação *f* de acidez volátil

* **fortification → 1910**

2338 **fortified**
(Prod.)
(Enology: Wine to which alcohol has been added.)
d verstärkt
f fortifié
p fortificado; reforçado

2339 **found** *v* **under decomposition**
(Prod.)
(Food processing technology; ref. to production techniques.)
d schmelzen unter Zersetzung
f fondre avec décomposition
p fundir sob decomposição

* **fowl → 4292**

* **fowl dung → 4298**

2340 **fowl meat**
(Agr.)
(Product poultry farming.)
d Geflügelfleisch *n*
f viande *f* de volaille
p carne *f* de aves

2341 **fowl typhoid**
(Med.)
(Veterinary; typhoid of poultry.)
d Geflügeltyphoid *n*
f typhoïde *f* des volailles
p febre *f* tifóide avícola

2342 **foxglove**
(Agr.)
(Botany. "Digitalis purpurea L."; purple foxglove. Medicinal herb.)
d Fingerhut *m*
f digitale *f*
p dedaleira *f*

2343 **fractional absorption of vitamins**
(Med.)
(Veterinary; ref. to vitamin supplementation to feed and animal metabolism.)
d fraktionelle Aufnahme *f* von Vitaminen; fraktionelle Absorption *f* von Vitaminen
f absorption *f* fractionnelle des vitamines
p absorção *f* fracionada de vitaminas

2344 **fractional distillation; fractionation**
(Prod.)
(Mixture separation by distillation, using a vertical fractionating column.)
d fraktionierte Destillation *f*
f distillation *f* fractionnée
p destilação *f* fracionada

2345 fractional distillation in flavour production
(Prod.)
(Aroma/flavour production. Extraction process.)
d fraktionierte Destillation *f* in der Geschmacksstoffproduktion
f distillation *f* fractionnée pour la production d'arômes
p destilação *f* fracionada na produção de aromas

2346 fractional extraction
(Prod.)
(Food processing technology.)
d fraktionierte Extraktion *f*; fraktionierter Auszug *m*
f extraction *f* fractionnée
p extração *f* fracionada

2347 fractionation
(Prod.)
(Food processing technology: Separation of a substance into different phases.)
d Fraktionierung *f*; Fraktionieren *n*
f fractionnement *m*
p fracionamento *m*

* **fractionation → 2344**

* **fractioning column → 4605**

2348 fractioning of various liquids
(Prod.)
(Aroma/flavour production: ref. to distillation processes.)
d Fraktionierung *f* von mehreren Flüssigkeiten; Fraktionierung *f* mehrerer Flüssigkeiten
f fractionnement *m* de plusieurs liquides
p fracionamento *m* de vários líquidos

2349 fractions
(Biochem.)
(Nutritional science: e.g. ref. to fractional distillation.)
d Fraktionen *fpl*
f fractions *fpl*
p frações *fpl*

2350 fragility of the compound
(Prod.)
(Aroma/fragrance research and production.)
d Empfindlichkeit *f* der Verbindung
f fragilité *f* du composé
p fragilidade *f* do composto

2351 fragrance agents
(Prod.)
(Aroma/flavour/fragrance research and production.)
d Riechstoffe *mpl*
f principes *mpl* odorants
p agentes *mpl* odorantes; princípios *mpl* odoríferos

* **fragrance components → 1259**

2352 framework
(Agr.)
(Agricultural produce, subproduct: Structural timber frame in house building.)
d Balkenwerk *n*; Rahmenwerk *n*
f charpente *f* en bois
p madeiramento *m*; vigamento *m*; travejamento *m*

2353 free acidity
(Prod.)
(Food processing technology; aroma/fragrance research and production.)
d freier Säuregehalt *m*
f acidité *f* libre
p acidez *f* livre; teor *m* de acidez livre

2354 free amino acids
(Biochem.)
(Nutritional science: protein hydrolysis.)
d freie Aminosäuren *fpl*
f acides *mpl* aminés libres
p aminoácidos *mpl* livres

2355 free fatty acid
(Med.)
(Fatty acids dissolved in the blood stream in traces; energy source.)
d freie Fettsäure *f*
f acide *m* gras libre
p ácido *m* graxo livre

2356 free fatty alcohol
(Prod.)
(Food processing technology; prime material.)
d freier Fettalkohol *m*
f alcool *m* gras libre
p álcool *m* graxo livre

2357 free-flowing granules
(Prod.)
(Food processing technology; physical product characteristic/presentation form.)
d freifließendes Granulat *n*
f granulé *m* à écoulement libre
p granulado *m* de fluxo solto

2358 free-flowing powder
(Prod.)
(Food processing technology; physical product characteristic/presentation form.)
d rieselfähiges Pulver *n*
f poudre *f* s'écoulant librement
p pó *m* de livre escorregamento; pó *m* tendo a propriedade de escorregar livremente

2359 **free groundwater surfaces**
(Prod.)
(Water supply; possible situation of groundwater between the geological layers.)
d freie Grundwasserschichten *fpl*; freiliegende Grundwasserschichten *fpl*
f nappes *fpl* libres d'eau souterraines
p lençois *mpl* de água subterrânea livres

2360 **free-living animal; wild-living animal**
(Agr.)
(Livestock as opposed to breed.)
d freilebendes Tier *n*; wildlebendes Tier *n*
f animal *m* sauvage
p animal *m* silvestre

2361 **free radical**
(Biochem.)
(Nutritional science.)
d freies Radikal *n*
f radical *m* libre
p radical *m* livre

2362 **free radical in lipophilic medium**
(Biochem.)
(Nutritional science: Certain vitamins are traps for free radicals.)
d freies Radikal *n* in fettabsorbierendem Medium; freies Radikal *n* in fettabsorbierendem Milieu
f radical *m* libre en milieu lipophile
p radical *m* livre em meio lipófilo

2363 **freesia**
(Prod.)
(Aroma/flavour production. "Narcisus jonquilla"; the iris family, after German physician F.H.Th. Freese. Used for flower essence production.)
d Freesie *f*
f jonquille *f*
p junquilho *m*

* **free starch → 2055**

* **freeze dried lactic bacteria → 3305**

* **freeze-drying → 3303**

2364 **freezing**
(Prod.)
(Food processing technology; refrigeration; every product has its own freezing point, generally between -10° C to -20° C.)
d Gefrieren *n*
f congélation *f*
p congelamento *m*; congelação *f*

2365 **freezing point**
(Prod.)
(Food processing technology.)
d Gefrierpunkt *m*
f point *m* de congélation
p ponto *m* de congelamento; ponto *m* de congelação

2366 **French beans**
(Agr.)
(Horticulture. "Phaseolus vulgaris". Type of beans. Edible: the unripe (green) pod with the seed.)
d grüne Bohnen *fpl*
f haricots *mpl* verts
p vagem *f*; feijão *m* verde

2367 **French loaf; French stick**
(Prod.)
(French white loaf.)
d Stangenweißbrot *n*
f baguette *f*
p baguete *f* (*shorter type*); bisnaga *f* (*longer type*)

* **French stick → 2367**

2368 **frequency of nursing**
(Med.)
(Baby nutrition.)
d Häufigkeit *f* des Stillens
f fréquence *f* de l'allaitement
p freqüência *f* da amamentação

2369 **fresh aroma note**
(Prod.)
(Aroma/flavour note, ref. to flavour chemicals; elaboration of aromas: organic chemistry.)
d frische Geschmacksnote *f*
f note *f* de saveur fraîche
p nota *f* de sabor fresco

2370 **fresh beef**
(Prod.)
(Butchery; cattle meat.)
d frisches Rindfleisch *n*
f viande *f* fraîche bovine
p carne *f* bovina fresca

2371 **fresh-citrus** *adj*
(Prod.)
(Aroma/flavour note.)
d citralig-grün
f frais-citrique
p verde-cítrico

2372 **fresh cream cheese**
(Prod.)
(Dairy product. Cheese type, not having undergone lactic fermentation.)
d Frischkäse *m*

f fromage *m* frais
p queijo *m* cremoso fresco

2373 **fresh dough**
(Prod.)
(Bakery product.)
d frischer Teig *m*
f pâte *f* fraîche
p massa *f* fresca

2374 **fresh fishes**
(Agr.)
(Fish quality.)
d frische Fische *mpl*
f poissons *mpl* frais
p peixes *mpl* frescos

2375 **fresh fruity aroma note**
(Prod.)
(Aroma/flavour note, ref. to flavour chemicals; elaboration of aromas: organic chemistry.)
d frisch-fruchtige Geschmacksnote *f*
f note *f* saveur fraîche-fruitée
p nota *f* fresca de sabor de frutas

2376 **fresh meat**
(Prod.)
(Food processing technology; ref. to meat quality/meat industrialization.)
d Frischfleisch *n*
f viande *f* fraîche
p carne *f* fresca; carne *f* verde

2377 **fresh milk**
(Prod.)
(Dairy product.)
d Frischmilch *f*
f lait *m* frais
p leite *m* fresco

2378 **freshness**
(Agr.)
(Ref. e.g. to the condition of agricultural products.)
d Frische *f*
f fraîcheur *f*
p frescor *m*

2379 **freshness of the fish**
(Agr.)
(Fish quality, e.g. on the market.)
d Frische *f* des Fisches
f fraîcheur *f* du poisson
p frescor *m* do peixe

2380 **fresh products**
(Prod.)
(Food processing technology; e.g. new products, green products.)
d frische Produkte *npl*
f produits *mpl* frais
p produtos *mpl* frescos

2381 **fresh vegetables**
(Agr.)
(Biological agriculture; horticulture.)
d Frischgemüse *n*
f légumes *mpl* frais
p legumes *mpl* frescos; hortaliças *fpl* frescas

2382 **freshwater**
(Prod.)
(Water supply; drinking water source.)
d Süßwasser *n*
f eau *f* douce
p água *f* doce

2383 **freshwater crayfish**
(Prod.)
(Gastronomy. Crustacean; seafood.)
d Flusskrebs *m*
f écrevisse *f*
p camarão *m* de água doce

2384 **freshwater from ground resources**
(Prod.)
(Water supply; e.g. drinking water source.)
d Grundsüßwasser *n*
f eau *f* douce souterraine
p água *f* doce subterrânea

2385 **freshwater reserves from ground resources**
(Prod.)
(Water supply; e.g. drinking water source.)
d Grundsüßwasserreserven *fpl*
f réserves *fpl* d'eau douce souterraines
p reservas *fpl* de água doce subterrâneas

2386 **fresh yeast**
(Prod.)
(Yeast production: yeast separated from the substrate, a sugar-containing wort.)
d frische Hefe *f*
f levure *f* fraîche
p fermento *m* fresco; lêvedo *m* fresco

2387 **fricassee**
(Prod.)
(Gastronomy.)
d Frikassee *n*
f fricassée *f*
p fricassê *m*

2388 **fried deep-frozen potatoes**
(Prod.)
(Food processing technology.)
d gebratene tiefgekühlte Kartoffeln *fpl*; gebratene tiefgefrorene Kartoffeln *fpl*

f pommes *fpl* de terre surgelées
p batatas *fpl* fritas congeladas

* **frosting → 2830**

2389 **froth of beer**
(Prod.)
(Food processing technology; brewery product.)
d Schaum *m* des Bieres; Bierkrone *f*
f mousse *f* de la bière
p espuma *f* da cerveja; colarinho *m* da cerveja

2390 **frozen meat blocks**
(Prod.)
(Food processing technology; ref. to meat industrialization.)
d Gefrierfleischblöcke *mpl*
f blocs *mpl* de viande congelée
p blocos *mpl* de carne congelada

2391 **fructose; fruit sugar; levulose**
(Prod.)
($C_6H_{12}O_6$; Present in fruits and plants, important in energy metabolism. Converted into glycose in the cells of the intestinal mucous membrane.)
d Fructose *f*; Fruchtzucker *m*
f fructose *m*
p frutose *f*

2392 **frugal diet**
(Med.)
(Alimentary regimen; e.g. ref. to plain meals.)
d einfache Diät *f*; Frugaldiät *f*
f diète *f* frugale
p dieta *f* frugal

2393 **frugivore**
(Med.)
(Living being sustained on fruits and vegetables.)
d Früchteesser *m*
f frugivore *m*
p frugívoro *m*; frutívoro *m*

2394 **fruit** *v*; **bear** *v* **fruit**
(Agr.)
(Viticulture; fruit cultures.)
d Früchte tragen
f fructifier; produire des fruits
p frutificar; dar frutos

2395 **fruit additives for milk products**
(Prod.)
(Additives in dairy produce.)
d Fruchtzusätze *mpl* für Milchprodukte
f additifs *mpl* fruités pour produits laitiers
p aditivos *mpl* de frutas para derivados de leite

2396 **fruit concentrate**
(Prod.)
(Food processing technology.)
d Früchtekonzentrat *n*
f concentré *m* de fruit
p concentrado *m* de frutas

2397 **fruit culture**
(Agr.)
(Agricultural produce; horticulture.)
d Obstbau *m*; Obstanbau *m*
f arboriculture *f* fruitière
p fruticultura *f*

2398 **fruit drops**
(Prod.)
(Confectionary.)
d Drops *mpl*; Fruchtdrops *mpl*
f bonbons *mpl* acidulés
p balas *fpl*

2399 **fruit extract**
(Prod.)
(Food processing technology: e.g. yoghurt production.)
d Fruchtextrakt *m*
f extrait *m* de fruits
p extrato *m* de frutas

* **fruit flan → 2219**

2400 **fruit flavour**
(Prod.)
(Aroma/flavour note.)
d Fruchtaroma *n*
f arôme *m* de fruits
p aroma *m* de frutas

2401 **fruit garden**
(Agr.)
(Biological agriculture; horticulture.)
d Obstgarten *m*
f verger *m*
p pomar *m*

2402 **fruit gathering**
(Agr.)
(Horticulture.)
d Pflücken *n* des Obstes; Obsternte *f*
f cueillette *f* des fruits
p colheita *f* das frutas

2403 **fruiting**
(Agr.)
(Botany; period of fruit development and fruit maturation.)
d Fruchtbildung *f*
f fructification *f*
p frutificação *f*; frutescência *f*

2404 **fruit juice; fruit juice beverage**
(Prod.)
(Beverages; e.g. dairy plant distribution product.)
d Fruchtsaft *m*
f jus *m* de fruit
p suco *m* de frutas

* **fruit juice beverage → 2404**

2405 **fruit juice concentrate**
(Prod.)
(Food processing technology.)
d Fruchtsaftkonzentrat *n*
f concentré *m* de jus de fruits
p concentrado *m* de suco de frutas

2406 **fruit juice dilution**
(Prod.)
(Food processing technology.)
d Fruchtsaftverdünnung *f*
f dilution *f* de jus de fruits
p diluição *f* de suco de frutas

2407 **fruit juice stabilization**
(Prod.)
(Food processing technology: e.g. with ascorbic acid (vitamin C).)
d Fruchtsaftstabilisierung *f*
f stabilisation *f* des jus de fruits
p estabilização *f* dos sucos de frutas

2408 **fruit pieces**
(Prod.)
(Food processing technology: e.g. in yoghurt production, as ingredients.)
d Fruchtstücke *npl*
f morceaux *mpl* de fruits
p pedaços *mpl* de frutas

* **fruit pit → 5245**

2409 **fruit production**
(Agr.)
(Horticulture.)
d Produktion *f* von Früchten
f production *f* fruitière
p produção *f* de frutas

2410 **fruit pulp**
(Agr.)
(Botany. Succulent fruit part.)
d Fruchtmark *n*
f pulpe *f* de fruits
p polpa *f* de fruta

2411 **fruit puree**
(Prod.)
(Food processing technology.)
d Obstpüree *n*
f purée *f* de fruits
p purê *m* de frutas

2412 **fruit salad**
(Prod.)
(Gastronomy; cold dish of fresh fruits.)
d Fruchtsalat *m*
f salade *f* de fruits
p salada *f* de frutas

2413 **fruits of the season**
(Agr.)
(Horticulture.)
d Früchte *fpl* der Jahreszeit
f fruits *mpl* de saison
p frutas *fpl* da estação do ano

* **fruit sugar → 2391**

2414 **fruit tree**
(Agr.)
(Botany.)
d Obstbaum *m*
f arbre *m* fruitier
p árvore *f* frutífera; fruteira *f*

2415 **fruity** *adj*
(Prod.)
(Aroma/flavour note.)
d fruchtig
f fruité
p afrutado

2416 **fruity note**
(Prod.)
(Taste; aroma research and production.)
d fruchtige Note *f*
f note *f* fruitée
p nota *f* de frutas

2417 **fruit yoghurt**
(Prod.)
(Food processing technology: e.g. yoghurt production.)
d Fruchtjoghurt *m*
f yaourt *m* aux fruits; yogourt *m* aux fruits
p iogurte *m* de frutas

2418 **fruity wine**
(Prod.)
(Beverages. Wine quality of a new (young) wine: sweet and having a distinct taste of the fruit.)
d fruchtiger Wein *m*
f vin *m* fruité
p vinho *m* afrutado; vinho *m* com sabor da fruta

2419 **fry** *v*
(Prod.)
(Food processing technology (with the use of fat).)

d braten
f frire
p fritar

2420 **frying process**
(Prod.)
(German: das Braten = frying process; der Braten = roast; French: friture = process as well as final product.)
d Braten *n*
f friture *f* (*process as well as final product*)
p fritura *f* (*process as well as final product*)

2421 **fry *v* the fish**
(Prod.)
(Food processing technology: to fry with the use of fat.)
d den Fisch braten
f faire frire du poisson
p fritar o peixe

2422 **full fat cheese**
(Prod.)
(Dairy product.)
d vollfetter Käse *m*
f fromage *m* gras
p queijo *m* de gordura integral

2423 **full fat soft cheese**
(Prod.)
(Dairy product.)
d vollfetter Weichkäse *f*
f fromage *m* gras à pâte molle
p requeijão *m* de gordura integral

2424 **fullness**
(Prod.)
(Aroma/flavour/taste quality, e.g. of wine: full flavour.)
d Abrundung *f*
f rondeur *f*
p corpo *m* (*ser encorpado*)

2425 **functional diversity of the proteins**
(Biochem.)
(Nutritional science: ref. e.g. to active proteins and passive proteins.)
d funktionelle Verschiedenheit *f* der Proteine
f diversité *f* fonctionnelle des protéines
p diversidade *f* funcional das proteínas

2426 **functional trajectory**
(Med.)
(Metabolic pathway of vitamins and enzymes.)
d funktioneller Verlauf *m*
f trajet *m* fonctionnel
p trajeto *m* funcional

2427 **function of vitamins**
(Biochem.)
(Nutritional science.)
d Funktion *f* der Vitamine; Vitaminfunktion *f*
f fonction *f* des vitamines
p função *f* das vitaminas

2428 **function on cell level**
(Biochem.)
(Nutritional science: nutrients, vitamins etc.)
d Funktion *f* auf Zellebene
f fonction *f* au niveau cellulaire
p função *f* ao nível celular

2429 **fungicide**
(Agr.)
(Botany: Fungus-destroying or inhibiting substance.)
d Fungizid *n*
f fongicide *m*
p fungicida *f*

2430 **fungiform papilla**
(Med.)
(Anatomy; kind of tongue protuberance related to the taste buds.)
d pilzförmige Zungenpapille *f*; pilzförmige Geschmacksknospe *f*
f papille *f* fungiforme
p papila *f* fungiforme

2431 **fungus**
(Biochem.)
(Microbiology; Source of antibiotics. Yeast, as vitamin B source. Also harmful species.)
d Pilz *m*; Schwamm *m*; Fungus *m*
f fungus *m*; mycète *m*
p fungo *m*

* **2-furaldehyde → 2433**

2432 **furan**
(Prod.)
(C_4H_4O; furfuran; source of fragrance/aroma prime material.)
d Furan *n*
f furane *m*
p furano *m*

2433 **furfural; 2-furaldehyde**
(Prod.)
($C_5H_4O_2$; source of fragrance/aroma prime material.)
d Furfural *n*; Furfurol *n*
f furfural *m*
p furfural *m*; furfurol *m*; furfuraldeído *m*

2434 **furrow**
(Agr.)
(Soil treatment; soil ditch made by a plough.)
d Ackerfurche *f*

f sillon *m*
p sulco *m*

2435 further processing; subsequent treatment
(Prod.)
(Food processing technology; food production.)
d Weiterbearbeitung *f*; Nachbehandlung *f*
f traitement *m* ultérieur
p processamento *m* posterior; tratamento *m* subseqüente

G

2436 **galactose**
(Biochem.)
($C_6H_{12}O_6$; constituent of milk sugar lactose, i.e. during the enzymatic decomposition of lactose, one molecule of glucose and one of galactose develop, which are converted to glucose in the liver.)
d Galaktose *f*
f galactose *m*
p galactose *f*

2437 **galactosemia**
(Med.)
(Inherited metabolic disease: Absence of the galactose to sugar-converting enzyme.)
d Galaktosämie *f*
f galactosémie *f*
p galactosemia *f*

* **galactosidofructose → 3122**

2438 **galacturonic acid**
(Prod.)
($C_6H_{10}O_7$; e.g. pectin is an ester of polygalacturonic acid, obtained from fruits.)
d Galakturonsäure *f*
f acide *m* galacturonique
p ácido *m* galacturônico

2439 **gallbladder**
(Med.)
(Anatomy. Bile storage organ.)
d Gallenblase *f*
f vésicule *f* biliaire
p vesícula *f* biliar

2440 **gallic acid**
(Prod.)
($C_7H_6O_5$. Production of antioxidants for foods. See Government regulations.)
d Gallussäure *f*
f acide *m* gallique
p ácido *m* gálico

* **gallstone → 614**

2441 **game**
(Agr.)
(Game: Animals hunted for food.)
d Wild *n*
f gibier *m*
p caça *f*

2442 **gamete; sex cell**
(Med.)
(Farm animal breeding: reproductive haploid (containing a single unpaired chromosome set) cell.)
d Keimzelle *f*; Geschlechtszelle *f*
f gamète *m*; cellule *f* reproductrice sexuée
p gameta *f*; célula *f* sexuada

* **gammon → 5015**

2443 **gammon steak**
(Prod.)
(Butchery; meat part; pork joint.)
d Oberschale *f*
f jambon *m* démangé
p gamão *m*; manta *f* de toucinho defumado

2444 **gander**
(Agr.)
(Livestock. Adult male goose.)
d Gänserich *m*
f jars *m*
p ganso *m* macho

2445 **gap in a tooth**
(Med.)
(Anatomy.)
d Zahnlücke *f*
f brèche *f* dentaire
p falha *f* de dente

2446 **garbage fertilizer**
(Agr.)
(Biological agriculture. Fertilizer type, organic (of plant or animal origin) fertilizer.)
d Müllkompost *m*
f engrais *m* à ordures ménagères
p adubo *m* de lixo

2447 **garlic**
(Agr.)
(Botany. "Allium sativum". Cookery ingredient.)
d Knoblauch *m*
f ail *m*
p alho *m*

* **garlic clove → 1166**

2448 **garlic oil**
(Prod.)
("Allium sativum L.". Prime material e.g. in cookery.)
d Knoblauchöl *n*
f huile *f* d'ail
p óleo *m* de alho

2449 **garnish**
(Prod.)
(Gastronomy; product used for food

garnishing, e.g. parsley.)
d Garnierung *f*
f garniture *f*
p guarnição *f*

2450 **gas chromatography**
(Prod.)
(Separation process by vaporization and injection into a carrier gas stream: e.g. in aroma/flavour research and production.)
d Gaschromatographie *f*
f chromatographie *f* en phase gazeuse
p cromatografia *f* em fase gasosa; cromatografia *f* de gases

2451 **gaseous environment**
(Prod.)
(Aroma/flavour research and production.)
d gasförmige Umwelt *f*
f ambiance *f* gazeuse
p ambiente *m* gasoso

2452 **gas phase**
(Biochem.)
(Food biochemistry; chemical state (as e.g. gaseous, aqueous))
d Gasphase *f*
f phase *f* gaz; phase *f* gazeuse
p fase *f* gasosa

2453 **gastric-intestinal disturbance**
(Med.)
(Disturbance of the stomach and the intestine, e.g. due to incorrect nutrition.)
d Magen-Darmstörung *f*
f trouble *m* gastrique-intestinal
p desarranjo *m* gastrintestinal

2454 **gastric-intestinal infection**
(Med.)
(Inflammation process referring to the stomach and the intestines.)
d Magen-Darm-Entzündung *f*
f inflammation *f* gastro-intestinale
p inflamação *f* gastrintestinal

2455 **gastric irrigation; irrigation of the stomach**
(Med.)
(Irrigation process of washing a hollow organ with flow of water.)
d Magenspülung *f*
f irrigation *f* gastrique
p lavagem *f* estomacal

* **gastric juice → 1674**

2456 **gastric mucosa; stomach lining**
(Med.)
(Gastric mucous membrane of the stomach wall.)
d Magenschleimhaut *f*
f muqueuse *f* gastrique; muqueuse *f* de l'estomac
p mucosa *f* gástrica; mucosa *f* do estômago

2457 **gastrin**
(Med.)
(Mucous membrane hormone, stimulated by food intake.)
d Gastrin *n*
f gastrine *f*
p gastrina *f*, gasterina *f*

2458 **gastritis; inflammation of the mucosa of the stomach**
(Med.)
(Due to excessive consumption of alcoholic beverages.)
d Gastritis *f*, Magenschleimhautentzündung *f*
f gastrite *f*, inflammation *f* de la muqueuse de l'estomac
p gastrite *f*, inflamação *f* da mucosa gástrica

2459 **gastroenteritis**
(Med.)
(Baby nutrition; stomach and intestine inflammation.)
d Magen-Darmkatarrh *m*; Gastroenteritis *f*
f gastro-entérite *f*
p gastroenterite *f*, gastrenterite *f*, enterogastrite *f*

2460 **gastrointestinal complaints**
(Med.)
d Beschwerden *fpl* des Magen- und Darmtraktes
f maladies *fpl* gastro-intestinales
p moléstias *fpl* gastrintestinais

2461 **gastropods**
(Agr.)
(Biological agriculture: class of mollusks (Gastropoda): snails.)
d Gastropoden *mpl*
f gastéropodes *mpl*
p gastrópodes *mpl*

2462 **gathered grains**
(Agr.)
(Agricultural produce; ref. in this specific case to cereals.)
d eingesammeltes Korn *n*
f grains *mpl* ramassés
p grãos *mpl* colhidos

2463 **gather *v* grapes after vintage; gather *v* postharvest grapes**
(Agr.)
(Viticulture, winegrowing: postharvest activity.)
d Nachlese halten (*in Weinbergen*)

f grappiller (*dans la vigne*)
p rebuscar nas vinhas

2464 **gathering of fruits**
(Agr.)
(Horticulture; picking up of fruits.)
d Einsammeln *n* der Früchte
f ramassage *m* des fruits
p recolhimento *m* das frutas

* **gather** *v* **postharvest grapes → 2463**

* **gavage → 2104**

2465 **gel**
(Prod.)
(Food processing technology; colloid-like jelly.)
d Gel *n* (*pl Gelen*)
f gel *m*
p gel *m* (*pl géis*; *geles*)

2466 **gelatin; gelatine**
(Prod.)
(Auxiliary products: Colloidal food protein, elaborated from animal tissue by boiling. Alimentary thickening agent.)
d Gelatine *f*
f gélatine *f*
p gelatina *f*

* **gelatine → 2466**

2467 **gelatinization**
(Prod.)
(Food processing technology; product transformation into a gel, having a gelatine-like appearance.)
d Gelatinierung *f*
f gélatinisation *f*
p gelatinização *f*

2468 **gelatinizing agent**
(Biochem.)
(Nutritional science: additive, giving a gel-like appearance and characteristic to a final product; e.g. starch.)
d Geliermittel *n*
f gélifiant *m*; produit *m* de gélatinisation
p agente *m* de gelatinização

2469 **gelding**
(Agr.)
(Livestock breeding: castrated animal, especially a castrated horse.)
d verschnittenes Tier *n*; kastriertes Tier *n*
f animal *m* châtré
p animal *m* castrado

2470 **gel forming; gelling**
(Biochem.)
(Nutritional science: quasi solid form colloid: jelly.)
d Gelbildung *f*
f formation *f* de gel
p formação *f* de gel

* **gelling → 2470**

* **gelose → 122**

2471 **gene**
(Biochem.)
(Genetic material unit localized in the chromosome; e.g. ref. to biochemical research in nutritional science.)
d Gen *n*
f gène *m*
p gene *m*

2472 **general analytic method**
(Biochem.)
(Nutritional science.)
d allgemeine Analysenmethode *f*
f méthode *f* générale d'analyse
p método *m* analítico geral

2473 **genetically modified**
(Biochem.)
(Biochemical plant/vegetable research, e.g. in genetic engineering; nutritional science.)
d erbbiologisch modifiziert; erbbiologisch abgeändert
f modifié génétiquement
p geneticamente modificado

2474 **genetically modified plant**
(Biochem.)
(Biochemistry in agriculture; nutrition.)
d genetisch veränderte Pflanze *f*
f plante *f* modifiée génétiquement
p planta *f* geneticamente modificada

2475 **genetic diversity**
(Biochem.)
(Cattle breeding, plants, etc.)
d genetische Verschiedenheit *f*
f diversité *f* génétique
p diversidade *f* genética

2476 **genetic diversity of agricultural systems**
(Agr.)
(Agriculture.)
d genetische Verschiedenartigkeit *f* der Agrarsysteme
f diversité *f* génétique des systèmes agraires
p diversidade *f* genética dos sistemas agrícolas

2477 **genetic modification**
(Biochem.)
(Biochemical research in nutritional science.)

d genetische Änderung *f*; erblich bedingte Veränderung *f*
f modification *f* génétique
p modificação *f* genética

2478 genetic modifications of soy cultures
(Biochem.)
(Biochemistry in agriculture; nutritional science.)
d genetische Veränderung *f* der Sojakulturen
f modification *f* génétique sur des cultures de soja
p modificação *f* genética das culturas de soja

2479 genetic researches
(Biochem.)
(Food processing technology and research.)
d Vererbungsforschung *f*; genetische Forschung *f*
f recherches *fpl* génétiques
p pesquisas *fpl* genéticas

2480 gentian
(Agr.)
(Botany. Genus "Gentiana"; herb used for flavouring e.g. in some alcoholic beverages.)
d Enzian *m*
f gentiane *f*
p genciana *f*

2481 gentian tincture
(Prod.)
(Aroma/flavour research and production. "Gentiana lutea L.". Extraction process; e.g. for a bitter tonic.)
d Enziantinktur *f*; Enzianauszug *m*
f teinture *f* de gentiane
p tintura *f* de genciana

2482 genus
(Agr.)
(Botany (fauna/flora): Classification of living organisms; taxonomy: a group of similar species; similar genera build a family.)
d Gattung *f*
f genre *m*
p gênero *m*

* **geological bed → 2483**

2483 geological layer; geological bed; stratum
(Prod.)
(Water supply: site of groundwater formation, drinking water source.)
d geologische Schicht *f*
f couche *f* géologique
p camada *f* geológica

2484 geraniol
(Prod.)
($C_{10}H_{18}O$; beta-pinene derivative; flavour chemical, prime material.)
d Geraniol *n*
f géraniol *m*
p geraniol *m*

2485 germ
(Med.)
(Food processing and water treatment.)
d Krankheitserreger *m*; Keim *m*
f germe *m* microbien
p germe *m*; gérmen *m*

2486 germinated barley
(Prod.)
(Beverages: Beer brewing process: green malt.)
d angekeimte Gerste *f*
f orge *f* germée
p cevada *f* germinada

* **germination → 1244**

2487 germination of vegetable tubers
(Prod.)
(Food biochemistry; to be avoided by irradiation processes.)
d Keimung *f* der Gemüseknollen
f germination *f* de tubercules végétaux
p germinação *f* de tubérculos vegetais

2488 germinative power of a grain
(Agr.)
(Botany.)
d Keimkraft *f* eines Samenkornes
f pouvoir *m* germinatif d'une graine
p poder *m* germinativo de uma semente

2489 gestation
(Med.)
(Veterinary; carrying of young in the uterus.)
d Trächtigkeit *f*
f gestation *f*
p prenhez *f*

2490 gestation period
(Med.)
(Veterinary; livestock raising: cows: 283 days; sows: 4 months.)
d Tragezeit *f*
f durée *f* de la gestation
p período *m* de gestação

* **gherkins → 4172**

2491 giblets
(Agr.)
(Poultry farming: Parts of poultry: head, neck, heart etc.)
d Innereien *fpl* vom Geflügel; Geflügelinnereien *fpl*

f abattis *mpl*; abats *mpl* de volaille
p miúdos *mpl* de aves

2492 **gills**
(Agr.)
(Veterinary science; fish anatomy: water oxygen capturing organ.)
d Kiemen *fpl*
f branchies *fpl*; ouïes *fpl* (*orifices externes, sur les côtés de la tête*)
p brânquias *fpl*; guelras *fpl*

2493 **gin**
(Prod.)
(Beverages: distillation of fermented cereal grains together with juniper berries.)
d Gin *m*
f gin *m*
p gim *m*; genebra *f*

2494 **ginger**
(Agr.)
(Botany; "Zingiberaceae"; aromatic rhizome; e.g. used as spice in foods, chocolates and beverages.)
d Ingwer *m*
f gingembre *m*
p gengibre *m*

2495 **ginger biscuit**
(Prod.)
(Confectionary.)
d Ingwerbiskuit *m*
f biscuit *m* au gingembre
p biscoito *m* de gengibre

2496 **gingerbread**
(Prod.)
(Confectionary.)
d Pfefferkuchen *m*
f pain *m* d'épice
p pão *m* de gengibre; broa *f* de Natal

2497 **ginger oil**
(Prod.)
("Zingiber officinale". Flavouring agent e.g. in ginger beverages, biscuits (cookies), chocolates etc. Ingredient.)
d Ingweröl *n*
f huile *f* de gingembre
p óleo *m* de gengibre

2498 **gingivitis**
(Med.)
(Inflammation of the gums.)
d Zahnfleischentzündung *f*
f gingivite *f*
p gengivite *f*

2499 **Glauber's salt; sodium sulphate**
(Med.)
($Na_2SO_4.10H_2O$; laxative effect.)
d Glaubersalz *n*; Natriumsulfat *n*
f sulfate *m* de soude
p sulfato *m* de sódio; sal *m* de Glauber

2500 **glaze** *v*
(Prod.)
(Confectionary; to give a glossy (sugar) surface coating e.g. to cake and fruits.)
d glasieren
f glacer
p cobrir (*com calda de açúcar*)

* **glaze → 2830**

2501 **gliadin**
(Biochem.)
(Protein compound in wheat flower (in gluten). Can be cause of the disease "celiacea", digestive insufficiency of the infant.)
d Gliadin *n*
f gliadine *f*; glutine *f*
p gliadina *f*

2502 **global conformation of proteins**
(Biochem.)
(Nutritional science; ref. to the structures of proteins.)
d globaler Aufbau *m* der Proteine
f conformation *f* globale des protéines
p conformação *f* global das proteínas

2503 **global nutrition**
(Biochem.)
(Nutrition of the population.)
d Allgemeinernährung *f*
f alimentation *f* globale
p alimentação *f* global

2504 **global nutritional approach; global nutritional intervention**
(Med.)
(Nutrition in medicine, treatment.)
d allgemeine nahrungsmittelbezügliche Behandlung *f*; umfassender auf Nahrungsmitteln basierender Eingriff *m*
f approche *f* nutritionnelle globale
p intervenção *f* global pela nutrição

* **global nutritional intervention → 2504**

2505 **globular proteins**
(Biochem.)
(Nutritional science: Formed of rounded water-soluble molecules: e.g. globulins, albumins.)
d globuläre Proteine *npl*

f protéines *fpl* globulaires
p proteínas *fpl* globulares

2506 **globulins**
(Biochem.)
(Proteins formed by a great number of amino acids: e.g. lactoglobulin, ovoglobulin.)
d Globuline *npl*
f globulines *fpl*
p globulinas *fpl*

2507 **glossitis**
(Med.)
(Tongue inflammation, which can be due to niacin deficiency = nicotinic acid deficiency. Niacin belongs to the group of vitamin B. Vitamin B_6 deficiency.)
d Zungenentzündung *f*
f glossite *f*
p glossite *f*

2508 **gluconeogenesis**
(Med.)
(Glucose synthesizing from non-carbohydrate substances.)
d Gluconeogenese *f*; Glykolyseumkehrung *f*
f néoglucogenèse *f*
p gliconeogênese *f*

2509 **gluconic acid; glyconic acid; glycogenic acid**
(Prod.)
($C_6H_{12}O_7$; glucose derivative.)
d Gluconsäure *f*
f acide *m* gluconique
p ácido *m* glucônico; ácido *m* glicônico

* **gluconolactone → 1615**

2510 **glucoproteide**
(Biochem.)
(Nutritional science.)
d Glucoproteid *n*
f glucoprotéide *m*
p glicoproteídeo *m*

2511 **glucosamine**
(Biochem.)
(Nutritional science: $C_6H_{13}NO_5$; amino sugar derived from glucose; constituent of many complex polysaccharides.)
d Glucosamin *n*
f glucosamine *f*
p glicosamina *f*

* **glucose → 2571**

2512 **glucose hydrogenation**
(Prod.)
(Food processing technology: e.g. production of sorbitol.)
d Glucosehydrierung *f*
f hydrogénation *f* de glucose
p hidrogenação *f* de glicose

2513 **glucose intolerance**
(Med.)
(Ref. to diabetes mellitus, carbohydrate-metabolism disorder.)
d Glucoseintoleranz *f*; Glucoseunverträglichkeit *f*
f intolérance *f* au glucose
p intolerância *f* à glicose

2514 **glucose syrup**
(Prod.)
(Confectionary: prime material.)
d Glucosesyrup *m*; Traubenzuckersyrup *m*
f sirop *m* de glucose
p xarope *m* de glicose

2515 **glucose tolerance**
(Med.)
(Glucose tolerance test is used in the diagnosis of diabetes mellitus.)
d Glucosetoleranz *f*; Glucoseverträglichkeit *f*
f tolérance *f* à glucose
p tolerância *f* à glicose

2516 **glutamate; monosodium glutamate**
(Biochem.)
(Nutritional science: $C_5H_8NNaO_4$; food biochemistry: Chinese seasoning: for taste enhancing and especially to give meat flavour to foodstuffs.)
d Glutamat *n*; Mononatriumglutamat *n*
f glutamate *m*; glutamate *m* monosodique
p glutamato *m*; glutamato *m* monossódico

2517 **glutamic acid**
(Biochem.)
(Nutritional science: $C_5H_9NO_4$; non-essential amino acid, basic constituent of proteins. Flavour enhancement additive for food; ingredient in human and in cow's milk.)
d Glutaminsäure *f*
f acide *m* glutamique
p ácido *m* glutâmico

2518 **glutamine**
(Biochem.)
(Nutritional science: $C_5H_{10}N_2O_3$; monoamide of glutamic acid.)
d Glutamin *n*
f glutamine *f*
p glutamina *f*

2519 **glutathione**
(Biochem.)
(Nutritional science: $C_{10}H_{17}N_3O_6S$; peptide; coenzyme; ref. to the oxidation-reduction

processes.)
d Glutathion *n*
f glutathion *m*
p glutationa *f*

2520 **glutathione peroxidase activity**
(Biochem.)
(Vitamin biochemistry.)
d Aktivität *f* der Glutathion-Peroxidase
f activité *f* de la peroxydase de glutathion
p atividade *f* da peroxidase de glutationa

2521 **gluten**
(Biochem.)
(Nutritional science: ref. to protein mixture occurring in cereal grains (wheat). Components: glutenin and gliadin.)
d Gluten *n*; Klebereiweiß *n*
f gluten *m*
p glúten *m*

2522 **gluten enriched dough**
(Prod.)
(Food processing technology.)
d mit Gluten angereicherter Teig *m*; mit Klebereiweiß angereicherter Teig *m*
f pâte *f* enrichie de gluten
p massa *f* enriquecida com glúten

2523 **glutenin**
(Biochem.)
(Plant protein.)
d Glutenin *n*
f gluténine *f*
p glutenina *f*

2524 **glycemia stability**
(Med.)
(Stability of the bloodsugar level; ref. to glucose concentration in the blood; requiring diet.)
d Stabilität *f* der Glykämie
f stabilité *f* de la glycémie
p estabilidade *f* da glicemia

2525 **glyceride**
(Biochem.)
(Nutritional science: glycerol ester; ref. to fatty acid biochemistry.)
d Glycerid *n*
f glycéride *m*
p glicérido *m*

* **glycerin → 2526**

2526 **glycerol; glycerin; propane-1,2,3-triol**
(Biochem.)
($C_3H_8O_3$; fermentation. Also in nutritional science: used in confectionery, liqueurs; sweetening properties; texture improving ingredient.)
d Glycerin *n*
f glycérol *m*; glycérine *f*
p glicerol *m*; glicerina *f*

2527 **glycine; glycocoll**
(Prod.)
($C_2H_5NO_2$; non-essential aminoacetic acid of sweet taste; used, e.g. mixed with saccharin, as sweetening agent; ingredient in human and in cow's milk.)
d Glycin *n*; Glykokoll *n*
f glycine *f*; glycocolle *m*
p glicina *f*; glicocol *m*

* **glycocoll → 2527**

2528 **glycogen; liver starch**
(Biochem.)
($(C_6H_{10}O_5)_n$; animal starch; hydrolysis yields glucose molecules; synthesized by the liver from blood glucose.)
d Glykogen *n*; Leberstärke *f*
f glycogène *m*
p glicogênio *m*

* **glycogenic acid → 2509**

2529 **glycol stearate**
(Prod.)
(Food processing technology: e.g. margarine additive.)
d Glykolstearat *n*
f stéarate *m* de glycol
p estearato *m* de glicol

2530 **glycolysis**
(Biochem.)
(Nutritional science: ref. to glycose decomposition by enzyme-catalyzed process.)
d Glykolyse *f*
f glycolyse *f*
p glicólise *f*

* **glyconic acid → 2509**

2531 **glycoprotein**
(Biochem.)
(Nutritional science.)
d Glucoprotein *n*
f glycoprotéine *f*
p glicoproteína *f*

2532 **glycoside**
(Biochem.)
(Nutritional science: sugar derivative.)
d Glykosid *n*
f glycoside *m*
p glicosido *f*

2533 glycosuria
(Med.)
(Abnormal high presence of glycose in urine; symptom of diabetes mellitus.)
d Glykosurie *f*
f glycosurie *f*
p glicosúria *f*

2534 goat
(Agr.)
(Livestock; farm animal; e.g. milk producer.)
d Ziege *f*; Geiß *f*
f chèvre *f*
p cabra *f*

2535 goat's milk
(Prod.)
(Dairy product.)
d Ziegenmilch *f*
f lait *m* de chèvre
p leite *m* de cabra

* **gobbler → 5597**

2536 goiter; goitre
(Med.)
(Enlargement of the thyroid gland, e.g. due to iodine deficiency, making necessary certain dietary considerations.)
d Kropf *m*
f goitre *m*
p bócio *m*

* **goitre → 2536**

2537 goitrogenic products
(Med.)
(Ref. to the necessity of certain dietary considerations.)
d kropferzeugende Produkte *npl*
f produits *mpl* goitrogènes
p produtos *mpl* capaces de produzir o bócio

2538 gold
(Prod.)
(Au; prime material for food (surface) dye production.)
d Gold *n*
f or *m*
p ouro *m*

2539 gonad
(Med.)
(Veterinary; e.g. ref. to cattle anatomy; reproductive cells (gametes) producing organs; male: trestis; female: ovary.)
d Keimdrüse *f*
f gonade *f*
p gonadia *f*

2540 good colorant distribution
(Prod.)
(Foodstuff colouring processes.)
d gute Farbverteilung *f*
f bonne répartition *f* de la couleur
p boa distribuição *f* da cor

2541 good stability
(Prod.)
(Food processing technology; ref. to product properties.)
d gute Stabilität *f*
f bonne stabilité *f*
p boa estabilidade *f*

2542 goose
(Agr.)
(Poultry farming; "Anatidae". Farm waterfowl.)
d Gans *f*
f oie *f*
p ganso *m*

2543 gooseberry
(Agr.)
(Horticulture. Genus "Ribes"; soft fruit; berry.)
d Stachelbeere *f*
f groseille *f* à maquereau
p uva-espim *f*

2544 goose dripping
(Prod.)
(Gastronomy; goose fat.)
d Gänsefett *n*
f graisse *f* d'oie
p gordura *f* de ganso

2545 goulash
(Prod.)
(Gastronomy; meat stew with paprika; Hungarian dish.)
d Gulasch *n*
f goulasch *m*; goulache *m*
p ensopado *m* de carne; guisado *m*

* **gourd → 4500**

2546 gout
(Med.)
(E.g. due to malfunction of the uric acid metabolism: urates accumulation.)
d Gicht *f*
f goutte *f*
p gota *f*

2547 gouty kidney
(Med.)
d Gichtniere *f*

f rein *m* goutteux
p rim *m* gotoso

2548 **gradual introduction of foodstuffs**
(Med.)
(Nutrition in baby care.)
d graduelle Einfuhr *f* von Nahrungsstoffen; allmähliche Einleitung *f* der Ernährung mit Nahrungsstoffen
f introduction *f* graduelle des aliments
p introdução *f* gradual dos alimentos

* **graft → 2550**

2549 **grafted seedling**
(Agr.)
(Viticulture, ref. to grafting processes.)
d gepfropfter Setzling *m*
f plant *m* greffé
p muda *f* enxertada

2550 **grafting; graft**
(Agr.)
(Botany: method of producing a new plant by joining (growing together) different plants (e.g. in viticulture).)
d Pfropfen *n*; Pfropfung *f*; Okulieren *n*; Okulierung *f*
f greffage *m*
p enxerto *m*; enxertia *f*; enxertadura *f*

2551 **grain; corn**
(Agr.)
(Agricultural produce. Ref. to cereals.)
d Korn *n*
f grain *m*
p grão *m*

2552 **grain alcohol**
(Prod.)
(Prime material; alcohol type.)
d Getreidealkohol *m*
f alcool *m* des grains
p álcool *m* de cereais

2553 **grain harvest**
(Agr.)
(Agricultural produce; cultivation of cereals.)
d Getreideernte *f*
f récolte *f* de céréales
p colheita *f* de cereais

2554 **grain varieties**
(Agr.)
(Agricultural produce.)
d Getreidearten *fpl*
f variétés *fpl* de céréales
p variedades *fpl* de cereais

2555 **grange; aviary**
(Agr.)
(Small farm, especially for poultry farming.)
d Geflügelfarm *f*
f ferme *f* avicole
p granja *f*

2556 **granitic soil**
(Agr.)
(Soil; hard soil, having quartz/feldspar content.)
d granitischer Boden *m*
f sol *m* granitique
p solo *m* granítico

2557 **granular** *adj*
(Prod.)
(Food processing technology; product characteristic.)
d granulös; körnig
f granulaire; granuleux; granulé
p granular; granuloso

2558 **granular powder**
(Prod.)
(Food processing technology; product characteristic.)
d granulöses Pulver *n*; körniges Pulver *n*
f poudre *f* granulaire
p pó *m* granuloso

2559 **granular sodium ascorbate**
(Biochem.)
(Nutritional science: vitamin C, used as an antioxidant.)
d granuliertes Natriumascorbat *n*
f ascorbate *m* de sodium granulaire
p ascorbato *m* de sódio granulado

* **granulated sugar → 1440**

2560 **granulation**
(Prod.)
(Food processing technology.)
d Granulierung *f*
f granulation *f*
p granulação

2561 **granule**
(Prod.)
(Food processing technology; physical product aspect: in form of a grain.)
d Korn *n*
f granule *m*
p grânulo *m*

2562 **grape**
(Agr.)
(Agricultural produce; berry e.g. for wine production.)
d Weinbeere *f*

f grain *m* de raisin
p uva *f*; baga *f*

2563 **grapefruit**
(Agr.)
(Agricultural produce. "Citrus paradisi".)
d Pampelmuse *f*; Grapefruit *f*
f pomélo *m*; pamplemousse *m/f*
p toranja *f*; toronja *f*; grapefruit *m*

2564 **grapefruit juice**
(Prod.)
(Beverages.)
d Pampelmusensaft *m*; Grapefruitsaft *m*
f jus *m* de pomélo; jus *m* de pamplemousse
p suco *m* de toranja; suco *m* de grapefruit

* **grape harvest → 5731**

2565 **grape juice**
(Prod.)
(Beverages.)
d Traubensaft *m*
f jus *m* de raisin
p suco *m* de uva

2566 **grape marc**
(Biochem.)
(Residue after grape expression; e.g. ref. to fermentation in nutritional science; enology.)
d Weintraubensatz *m*; Rückstand *m* der Weintraube
f marc *m* de raisin
p bagaço *m* da uva

2567 **grape must**
(Prod.)
(Food processing technology; grape juice obtained by expression, before finalization of the fermentation process.)
d Traubenmost *m*
f moût *m* de raisin
p mosto *m* de uvas

2568 **grape must undergoing fermentation process**
(Biochem.)
(Fermentation in nutritional science.)
d in Gärung begriffener Traubenmost *m*
f moût *m* de raisin en fermentation
p mosto *m* de uvas em processo de fermentação

2569 **grape of a vine sort**
(Agr.)
(Viticulture; grape selection.)
d Beere *f* einer Rebsorte
f raisin *m* d'un cépage
p uva *f* de uma espécie de cepa

* **grape of quality → 4526**

2570 **grape overmaturation sauternes type**
(Biochem.)
(Enology: ref. to the action of "Botrytis Cinerea".)
d Edelfäule *f* der Weinbeere
f pourriture *f* noble du grain de raisin
p sobrematuração *f* nobre da uva; supermaturação *f* nobre da uva

2571 **grape sugar; glucose; dextrose**
(Prod.)
($C_6H_{12}O_6$; grape/corn sugar)
d Traubenzucker *m*; Glucose *f*; Glukose *f*; Dextrose *f*
f glucose *m*; dextrose *f*
p açúcar *m* de uva; glicose *f*; dextrose *f*

2572 **grape variety**
(Agr.)
(Viticulture.)
d Varietät *f* der Traube; Traubenabart *f*
f variété *f* de raisin
p variedade *f* de cacho de uva

2573 **grasshopper**
(Agr.)
(Botany. Family "Acrididae"; destructive insect to plants.)
d Grashüpfer *m*
f sauterelle *f*
p gafanhoto *m*

2574 **grate** *v*
(Prod.)
(Food processing technology: cheese, bread, vegetable preparation; certain types of oranges e.g. in Brazil for a sweet dessert preparation.)
d raspeln
f râper
p ralar

2575 **gratin**
(Prod.)
(Gastronomy; brown surface crust.)
d Gratin *n*
f gratin *m*
p prato *m* gratinado

2576 **gravel**
(Agr.)
(Soil; soil particles larger than sand.)
d Kies *m*
f gravier *m*
p saibro *m*

2577 **gravy**
(Prod.)
(Gastronomy.)
d Bratensoße *f*; Bratensauce *f*

f sauce *f* de rôti
p molho *m* de carne

2578 great variety
(Prod.)
(Food processing technology, production and marketing.)
d große Auswahl *f*; umfangreiche Auswahl *f*
f vaste sélection *f*
p grande variedade *f*

2579 great variety of
(Agr.)
(Agricultural produce sorts and species etc.)
d verschiedene Abarten *fpl* von
f diverses variétés *fpl* de
p variedades *fpl* diversas de

2580 greaves
(Prod.)
(Gastronomy, lard with bacon lumps.)
d Grieben *fpl*
f rillons *mpl*
p torresmo *m*

*** greenfly → 368**

2581 green fodder
(Agr.)
(Livestock nutrition; vegetable subproducts for animal feeding.)
d Grünfutter *n*
f fourrages *mpl* verts
p forragem *f* verde

2582 green-herbal *adj*
(Prod.)
(Aroma/flavour characteristic.)
d krautartig-grün
f fruité-vert
p verde-herbáceo

2583 green lake
(Prod.)
(Foodstuff colorants. Food dye mixture: E numbers: E 132 + E 104.)
d grüner Farblack *m*; Grünlack *m*
f laque *m* vert
p laca *f* verde

*** green malt → 3352**

*** green manure → 2154**

2584 green peas
(Agr.)
(Horticulture; vegetables.)
d Erbsen *fpl*
f petits pois *mpl*
p ervilhas *fpl*

2585 green pepper
(Agr.)
(Agricultural produce. "Capsicum annuum". Sweet pepper.)
d Paprikaschote *f*
f piment *m*; poivron *m*
p pimentão *m* verde

2586 greens
(Agr.)
(Horticulture: green vegetables: foliage and foliage-bearing stalks.)
d Grüngemüse *n*
f légumes *mpl* verts
p verduras *fpl*

2587 green tea
(Agr.)
(Agricultural produce; "Camellia sinensis". green: made of young dried leaves.)
d grüner Tee *m*
f thé *m* vert
p chá *m* verde

2588 grill
(Prod.)
(Gastronomy; food (e.g. meat) prepared on a grill.)
d Grillade *f*; Gegrilltes *n*
f grillade *f*; grillades *fpl*
p grelhado *m*

2589 grill *v*; **broil** *v*
(Prod.)
(Food processing technology (on a roast).)
d grillen
f griller; rôtir
p grelhar

2590 grilling
(Prod.)
(Food processing technology, broiling on a grill.)
d Grillen *n*
f grillade *f*
p grelhagem *f*

2591 groat
(Prod.)
(Food processing technology; processed agricultural product (e.g. barley/oat grains without hull, for porridge).)
d Grütze *f*; Gerstengrütze *f*
f gruau *m*
p cereais *mpl* em grãos; grão *m* de cevada

2592 groats
(Prod.)
(Gastronomy; prepared from oat grains without its hull.)

d Hafergrütze *f*
f gruau *m* d'avoine
p papa *f* de aveia

* **groceries → 2297**

2593 **ground; wine ground**
(Prod.)
(Food biochemistry; sediments occurring e.g. in vats containing wine. Also other types of fermented drinks, e.g. beer.)
d Satz *m*; Weinsatz *m*
f lie *f*; lie *f* de vin
p borra *f*; lia *f*; borra *f* do vinho; lia *f* do vinho

2594 **ground cereal**
(Prod.)
(The degree of grinding is the base for typifying the flour and meal quality.)
d ausgemahltes Getreide *n*
f céréale *f* broyée
p cereal *m* moído

2595 **ground cinnamon**
(Prod.)
(Food processing technology and production.)
d gemahlener Zimt *m*; gemahlener Kaneel *m*
f cannelle *f* en poudre
p canela *f* em pó

2596 **ground coffee**
(Prod.)
(Food processing technology, gastronomy.)
d gemahlener Kaffee *m*
f café *m* moulu
p café *m* moído

* **ground fodder cereal → 742**

2597 **ground saccharose; ground sugar**
(Prod.)
($C_{12}H_{22}O_{11}$. Sucrose. Sugar. Raw material in the fermentation-based production of alcohol.)
d gemahlene Saccharose *f*; gemahlener Zucker *m*
f saccharose *m* moulu; sucre *m* moulu
p sacarose *f* moída; açucar *m* moído

* **ground sugar → 2597**

2598 **ground to meal**
(Prod.)
(Food processing technology.)
d zu Mehl gemahlen
f moulu en farine
p moído para farinho

2599 **groundwater**
(Prod.)
(Water supply.)
d Grundwasser *n*
f eaux *fpl* souterraines
p água *f* subterrânea; água *f* freática

2600 **growth**
(Agr.)
(Botany; plant development.)
d Wachstum *n*
f croissance *f*
p crescimento *m*

* **grub → 3134, 3323**

2601 **gruel**
(Prod.)
(Food processing technology; processed product of agricultural origin; thin porridge.)
d Haferschleim *m*
f crème *f* d'avoine
p mingau *m* de flocos de aveia

2602 **guava**
(Agr.)
(Botany. Genus "Psidium", esp. "Psidium guajava"; edible fruit.)
d Guajave *f*
f goyave *f*
p goiaba *f*

2603 **guava jam**
(Prod.)
(Confectionary; made from the edible fruit of "Psidium guajava".)
d Guajavenkonfitür *f*
f confiture *f* de goyaves
p doce *m* de goiaba

2604 **guava jelly**
(Prod.)
(Confectionary; made from the edible fruit of "Psidium guajava".)
d Guajavengelee *n/m*
f gelée *f* de goyaves
p geléia *f* de goiaba

2605 **guinea fowl**
(Agr.)
(Poultry farming. "Numida meleagris".)
d Perlhuhn *n*
f pintade *f*
p galinha-d'Angola *f*

* **gum acacia → 2606**

2606 **gum arabic; gum acacia**
(Prod.)
(Acacia sebegal gum; water-soluble: In food processing technology used as thickener and stabilizer; texture improving ingredient.)
d arabisches Gummi *n*; Gummi *n* Arabikum

f gomme *f* arabique
p goma *f* arábica

2607 **gums**
(Med.)
(Anatomy.)
d Zahnfleisch *n*
f gencive *f*
p gengiva *f*

2608 **gum tragacanth; tragacanth**
(Prod.)
(Genus "Astragalus".Thickener and emulsifier in food technology; texture improving ingredient.)
d Tragantgummi *n*; Tragant *n*
f gomme *f* adragante; tragacanthe *f*
p alcatira *f*, tragacanto *m*; adraganta *f*

2609 **gustatory** *adj*
(Med.)
(Related to the sense of taste.)
d geschmacksbezüglich
f gustatif
p gustativo

2610 **gustatory quality; quality of taste**
(Prod.)
(Gastronomy; product characteristic.)
d Geschmacksqualität *f*
f qualité *f* gustative
p qualidade *f* gustativa; qualidade *f* de sabor

* **gut** *v* → **1775**

2611 **gymnosperm**
(Agr.)
(Botany: plant group, generally subdivision of the modern systems, showing ovules and seeds unprotected; gymnosperm = naked seed. E.g. conifers.)
d Nacktsamer *m*
f gymnosperme *f*
p gimnosperma *f*

2612 **gypsum**
(Agr.)
(Soil treatment: inorganic corrective material.)
d Gips *m*
f plâtre *m*
p gesso *m*

H

2613 **haddock**
(Prod.)
("Melanogrammus aeglefinus"; Northern Atlantic precious edible fish.)
d geräucherter Schellfisch *m*
f haddock *m*; aiglefin *m* salé et fumé; églefin *m* salé et fumé
p hadoque *m*

2614 **haeme; heme**
(Med.)
($C_{34}H_{32}N_4O_4Fe$; iron-containing and red colour furnishing prosthetic group of hemoglobin: combination of protoporphyrin and divalent iron.)
d Häm *n*
f hème *m*
p hemo *m*

2615 **haemoglobin; hemoglobin**
(Med.)
(Respiratory pigment of red blood cells associated to the protein: globin, linked to a haeme molecule: oxygen and carbon dioxide transport. See haeme.)
d Hämoglobin *n*
f hémoglobine *f*
p hemoglobina *f*

2616 **haemorrhage; bleeding**
(Med.)
(Veterinary; blood escape, internal or external, from the blood vessels due to their rupture.)
d Hämorrhagie *f*; Blutung *f*
f hémorragie *f*
p hemorragia *f*

2617 **hake**
(Agr.)
(Genus "Merluccius". Fish, related to the Atlantic cod.)
d Seehecht *m*; Dorschfisch *m*
f merlu *m*; colin *m*
p merluza *f*; merlu *f*; merluça *f*; pescada *f* marlonga

2618 **half-a-pound loaf of bread**
(Prod.)
(French fancy bread type, larger and shorter than a baguette.)
d Brotlaib *n* von einem halben Pfund
f pain *m* de bâtard; bâtard *m*
p pão *m* de 250 g tipo francês

2619 **half frozen ice cream**
(Prod.)
(Gastronomy; ice cream type, indicating state of constancy.)
d Halbgefrorenes *n*
f sorbet *m*
p sorvete *m* cremoso; sorvete *m* semi-congelado

2620 **halibut**
(Agr.)
(Atlantic "Hippoglossus hippoglossus". Pacific "Hippoglossus stenolepis", flatfish.)
d Heilbutt *m*
f elbot *m*; flétan *m*
p solha *f* nórdica

2621 **halibut fillet**
(Prod.)
(Gastronomy; smoked flatfish (halibut) fillet.)
d geräucherte Heilbuttfilets *npl*
f filets *mpl* de flétan fumés
p filés *mpl* de solha nórdica defumadas

2622 **ham**
(Prod.)
(Butchery; meat part.)
d Schinken *m*
f jambon *m*
p presunto *m*

2623 **ham hock**
(Prod.)
(Butchery; meat part; e.g. pickled pork joint.)
d Eisbein *n*
f jarret *m* de porc; jambonneau *m*
p joelho *m* de porco; jarrete *m* de porco

2624 **ham on the bone**
(Prod.)
(Butchery; meat type.)
d Knochenschinken *m*; roher Schinken *m* mit Knochen
f jambon *m* cru à l'os
p presunto *m* cru com osso

2625 **hard-boiled egg**
(Prod.)
(Gastronomy.)
d hartgekochtes Ei *n*
f œuf *m* dur
p ovo *m* cozido

2626 **hard dough**
(Prod.)
(Bakery.)
d harter Teig *m*
f pâte *f* dure
p massa *f* dura

2627 **hardening of oils; fat hardening**
(Prod.)
(Food processing technology: transformation of liquid non-saturated fats, oils, into glyceride blends.)
d Ölhärtung *f*, Fetthärtung *f*
f durcissement *m* des huiles; durcissement *m* des matières grasses
p endurecimento *m* de óleos; endurecimento *m* das matérias graxas

2628 **hard granules**
(Prod.)
(Food processing technology: product characteristic.)
d hartes Granulat *n*
f granulé *m* dur
p granulado *m* duro

2629 **hardness**
(Prod.)
(Food processing technology: product characteristic; e.g. water hardness.)
d Härte *f*
f dureté *f*
p dureza *f*

2630 **hardness degree**
(Prod.)
(Water supply; drinking water hardness, determined by calcium salt contents, influencing taste quality.)
d Härtegrad *m*
f degré *m* de dureté
p grau *m* de dureza

2631 **hard palate**
(Med.)
(Anatomy. Roof of the mouth.)
d harter Gaumen *m*
f palais *m*
p pálato *m*; paladar *m*; céu *m* da boca

* **hard sausage → 1819**

2632 **hard solid**
(Prod.)
(Food processing technology: product characteristic.)
d harter Festkörper *m*; harte Festsubstanz *f*
f solide *m* dur
p sólido *m* duro

2633 **hard wheat flour**
(Agr.)
(Agricultural produce. Wheat type for pasta production, having a high content of gluten.)
d Hartweizenmehl *n*
f minot *m*; farine *f* de blé dur
p farinha *f* de trigo duro

2634 **hardwood**
(Agr.)
(Agricultural produce; angiospermous tree wood for construction purposes.)
d Hartholz *n*
f bois *m* dur
p madeira *f* de lei; madeira *f* dura

2635 **hare**
(Agr.)
(Family "Leporidae", esp. genus "Lepus".)
d Hase *m*
f lièvre *m*
p lebre *m*

* **hare meat pate → 2636**

2636 **hare meat pâté; hare meat pate**
(Prod.)
(Gastronomy.)
d Hasenfleischpastete *f*
f pâté *m* de lièvre
p patê *m* de carne de lebre

2637 **haricot beans**
(Agr.)
(Horticulture. "Phaseolus vulgaris"; bean variety.)
d weiße Bohnen *fpl*
f haricots *mpl* blancs
p feijão *m* branco

2638 **harmless** *adj*
(Med.)
d unschädlich
f inoffensif
p inócuo; inofensivo

* **harmlessness of genetic modifications → 2928**

2639 **harmonious blend**
(Prod.)
(Aroma/fragrance research and production.)
d harmonische Mischung *f*
f mélange *m* harmonieux
p mistura *f* harmoniosa

* **hart → 5194**

2640 **harvest from the fields**
(Agr.)
(Agricultural produce; ref. to gathering in a crop.)
d Ernte *f* vom Felde
f récolte *f* des champs
p colheita *f* do campo

2641 harvest moist feed corn
(Agr.)
(Livestock nutrition. Farm cattle forage.)
d erntefeuchtes Futtergetreide *n*
f fourrage *m* vert de céréales
p cereal *m* de forragem úmido da colheita

* **harvest time → 140**

2642 hash
(Prod.)
(Gastronomy; dish made from chopped meat.)
d Haschee *n*
f hachis *m*
p picadinho *m*

2643 hatch *v*
(Agr.)
(Poultry farming.)
d brüten
f couver
p chocar; empolhar; incubar

2644 hatchability
(Agr.)
(Poultry farming.)
d Brütkapazität *f*
f capacité *f* en couver
p capacidade *f* de chocar

2645 hawthorn
(Agr.)
(Botany. Genus "Crataegus"; having berries: haws.)
d Weißdorn *m*
f aubépine *f*
p espinheiro *m* alvar

2646 hay
(Agr.)
(Agricultural produce and subproduct.)
d Heu *n*
f foin *m*
p feno *m*

2647 hay harvest
(Agr.)
(Agricultural produce and subproduct.)
d Heuernte *f*; Heumahd *f*
f fenaison *f*
p sega *f* de feno

2648 hazelnut
(Agr.)
(Agricultural produce; genus "Corylus"; drupe; stone fruit.)
d Haselnuss *f*
f noisette *f*
p avelã *f*

2649 hazelnut roasting
(Prod.)
(Food processing technology.)
d Haselnussröstung *f*
f grillage *m* des noisettes
p torração *f* de avelãs

2650 hazelnut taste
(Prod.)
(Food processing technology; e.g. aroma research.)
d Haselnussgeschmack *m*
f goût *m* de noisette
p gosto *m* de avelã

* **head cheese → 749**

2651 head cheese, Frankfurt style
(Prod.)
(Gastronomy. Alsatian specialty: brawn type, made with knuckle of pork.)
d Frankfurter Sülze *f*
f hure *f* de Francfort
p geléia *f* de carne à moda de Frankfurt

2652 head cheese, Parisian style
(Prod.)
(Gastronomy. Brawn type, Parisian specialty, made with the tongue of pork.)
d Sülze *f* Pariser Art
f hure *f* à la parisienne
p geléia *f* de carne à moda francesa

2653 head note
(Prod.)
(Aroma/fragrance research and production; part of the whole aroma/fragrance note.)
d Kopfnote *f*; Angeruch *m*; Spitze *f*
f note *f* de tête
p nota *f* de cabeça

2654 healthful nutrition
(Med.)
(Ref. to dietary problems.)
d gesunde Ernährung *f*
f alimentation *f* saine
p alimentação *f* saudável; nutrição *f* saudável

2655 healthy bunches of grapes
(Agr.)
(Viticulture; selection of fruits.)
d gesunde Trauben *fpl*
f raisins *mpl* sains; grappes *fpl* de raisin saines
p cachos *mpl* sãos

2656 heart
(Med.)
(Anatomy; blood-pumping muscle.)
d Herz *n*

f cœur *m*
p coração *m*

2657 **heart note; body note**
(Prod.)
(Aroma/fragrance research and production; lasting base of the whole aroma.)
d Herznote *f*; Körper *m*
f note *f* de cœur; note *f* de corps
p corpo *m*

2658 **heart of palm**
(Prod.)
(Gastronomy.)
d Palmherzen *npl*; Palmenherzen *npl*; Palmmark *n*; Palmenmark *n*
f chou *m* palmiste; cœur *m* de palmier
p palmito *m*

* **heat → 1973**

2659 **heat extraction of essential oils**
(Prod.)
(Food processing technology; ref. to prime material processing; also ref. to aroma/flavour research and production.)
d Heißessenzextraktion *f*; Auszug *m* ätherischer Öle auf heißem Wege
f extraction *f* d'essence à chaud
p extração *f* de óleos essenciais sob calor

2660 **heating up of the pressed clusters of grapes**
(Prod.)
(Enology; wine production; bunches of grapes.)
d Erhitzung *f* der gekelterten Weintrauben
f chauffage *m* des raisins foulés
p aquecimento *m* dos cachos de uvas esmagados

2661 **heat regulation**
(Prod.)
(Food processing technology, process control.)
d Wärmeeinstellung *f*; Temperaturregulierung *f*
f régulation *f* thermique
p regulação *f* térmica

2662 **heat resistance**
(Prod.)
(Food processing technology, process control.)
d Wärmebeständigkeit *f*
f résistance *f* à la chaleur
p resistência *f* ao calor

2663 **heat resistance of the aroma**
(Prod.)
(Aroma/flavour research and production; e.g. product property.)
d Hitzestabilität *f* des Aromastoffes
f résistance *f* à la chaleur de l'arôme
p resistência *f* ao calor do aroma

2664 **heat-resistant** *adj*
(Prod.)
(Food processing technology: product property.)
d hitzebeständig
f résistant à la chaleur
p resistente ao calor

2665 **heat-sensitive vitamin**
(Biochem.)
(Vitamin biochemistry in nutritional science.)
d hitzeempfindliches Vitamin *n*
f vitamine *f* sensible à la chaleur
p vitamina *f* sensível ao calor

2666 **heat stabilization**
(Prod.)
(Food processing technology; food preservation method.)
d Wärmestabilisierung *f*
f stabilisation *f* thermique
p estabilização *f* têrmica

2667 **heat sterilization**
(Prod.)
(Food processing technology: In autoclave, sterilizators etc.)
d Hitzesterilisation *f*; Hitzesterilisierung *f*
f stérilisation *f* par le chauffage; appertisation *f*
p esterilização *f* por calor

2668 **heat-sterilized preserve**
(Prod.)
(Food processing technology; food preservation method.)
d Hitzesterilisationskonserve *f*
f conserve *f* appertisée
p conserva *f* de esterilização por calor

2669 **heat transfer**
(Prod.)
(Food processing technology: pasteurization and cooking processes.)
d Hitzeverlagerung *f*
f transfert *m* de chaleur
p transferência *f* de calor

2670 **heat transfer through a large contact surface**
(Prod.)
(Food processing technology; flavour research and production: e.g. in juice concentration processes.)
d Hitzeverlagerung *f* durch eine große Kontaktoberfläche

f transfert *m* de chaleur par une grande surface de contact
p transferência *f* de calor por uma larga superfície de contato

2671 **heat treatment; thermal treatment**
(Prod.)
(Food processing technology.)
d Wärmebehandlung *f*; Hitzebehandlung *f*; Thermalbehandlung *f*; thermische Behandlung *f*
f traitement *m* par la chaleur; traitement *m* thermique
p tratamento *m* por calor; tratamento *m* térmico

2672 **heat treatment in foodstuff processing; thermal treatment in foodstuff processing**
(Prod.)
(Food processing technology: e.g. drying, lyophilization, evaporation.)
d Wärmeverfahren *n* in der Lebensmittelverarbeitung
f traitement *m* thermique dans la transformation des aliments
p tratamento *m* térmico no processamento de alimentos

2673 **heaviest compounds**
(Prod.)
(Aroma/flavour research and production, distillation product.)
d schwerste Bestandteile *fpl*
f composés *mpl* les plus lourds
p compostos *mpl* mais pesados

2674 **heavy fatty acids**
(Biochem.)
(Nutritional science, food research and production.)
d schwere Fettsäuren *fpl*
f acides *mpl* gras lourds
p ácidos *mpl* graxos pesados

2675 **heavy metals**
(Biochem.)
(Of toxicologic importance in nutritional science: lead, mercury, cadmium, arsenic.)
d Schwermetalle *npl*
f métaux *mpl* lourds
p metais *mpl* pesados

* **heel of bread → 1429**

2676 **he-goat; buck; male goat**
(Agr.)
(Livestock breeding. Genus "Capra".)
d Ziegenbock *m*
f bouc *m*
p cabrão; bode *m*

* **heme → 2614**

* **hemoglobin → 2615**

2677 **hen**
(Agr.)
(Poultry farming; female chicken.)
d Henne *f*; Huhn *n*
f poule *f*
p galinha *f*

2678 **heparin**
(Biochem.)
(Heparin sodium; anticoagulant, inhibiting the thrombin enzyme action.)
d Heparin *n*
f héparine *f*
p heparina *f*

2679 **hepatic cirrhosis**
(Med.)
(Caused by chronic and long-term alcohol consumption.)
d Leberzirrhose *f*
f cirrhose *f* hépatique
p cirrose *f* hepática

2680 **hepato-renal metabolism**
(Med.)
(Baby nutrition.)
d Leber-Nieren-Stoffwechsel *m*
f métabolisme *m* hépato-rénal
p metabolismo *m* hepato-renal

2681 **heptanol; n-heptyl alcohol**
(Prod.)
($C_7H_{16}O$; e.g. prime material in aroma production.)
d Heptanol *n*
f heptanol *m*
p heptanol *m*

2682 **herb**
(Agr.)
(Botany; e.g. medicinal herb.)
d Kraut *n*
f herbe *f*
p erva *f*

2683 **herbaceous taste**
(Prod.)
(Aroma note.)
d Kräutergeschmack *m*
f goût *m* herbacé
p gosto *m* herbáceo

2684 **herbal extracts**
(Prod.)
(Aroma/flavour research and production.)
d Kräuterextrakte *mpl*; Kräuterauszüge *mpl*

f extraits *mpl* aux herbes
p extratos *mpl* de ervas

2685 **herbicide**
(Agr.)
(Organic herbicides: mineral oils, phenols, carbamates. Inorganic herbicides: chlorate, cyanate, sodium arsenite. Selective, non-selective, preplanting, preemergence herbicides.)
d Herbizid *n*; Unkrautvertilgungsmittel *n*
f herbicide *m*
p herbicida *f*

2686 **herbs for seasoning; culinary herbs**
(Prod.)
(Ingredient in cookery.)
d Gewürzkräuter *npl*; Küchenkräuter *npl*
f fines herbes *fpl*
p ervas *fpl* finas de tempero

2687 **herb tea**
(Prod.)
(E.g. camomile tea.)
d Kräutertee *m*
f tisane *f*
p chá *m* de ervas

2688 **herd**
(Agr.)
(Livestock breeding; group of animals of the same type.)
d Herde *f*
f troupeau *m*
p rebanho *m*; plantel *m*

2689 **herring**
(Agr.)
("Clupea harengus". Fresh food fish; can be preserved by smoking or by salting.)
d Hering *m*
f hareng *m*
p arenque *m*

2690 **herring fillet**
(Prod.)
(Gastronomy.)
d Heringsfilet *n*
f filet *m* de hareng
p filé *m* de arenque

2691 **hesperidin**
(Biochem.)
($C_{28}H_{34}O_{15}$; glycoside of orange peel and other citric fruits. Acts favourably in the capillaries. Formerly considered to be a vitamin: vitamin P.)
d Hesperidin *n*
f hespéridine *f*
p hesperidina *f*

2692 **hesperidium note; citrus note**
(Prod.)
(Taste; aroma research and production.)
d Zitrusnote *f*
f note *f* hespéridée; note *f* citrique
p nota *f* de hesperídeo; nota *f* cítrica

* **hexadecanoic acid → 3996**

* **hexalin → 1483**

* **hexamethylene → 1482**

2693 **hexane**
(Prod.)
(C_6H_{14}; food processing technology; solvent for oily extractions.)
d Hexan *n*
f hexane *m*
p hexano *m*

2694 **hexanedione**
(Prod.)
($C_6H_{10}O_2$. Natural flavour and fragrant agent, e.g. in coffee, beer.)
d Hexandion *n*
f hexanedione *f*
p hexanodione *f*

* **hexanoic acid → 905**

2695 **hexose**
(Prod.)
(Simple sugar having 6 carbon atoms in the molecule, e.g. glucose ($C_6H_{12}O_6$), fructose ($C_6H_{12}O_6$), galactose ($C_6H_{12}O_6$).)
d Hexose *f*
f hexose *f*
p hexose *f*

2696 **hibernal period**
(Agr.)
(Climatology ref. to the winter period.)
d Überwinterungsperiode *f*
f période *f* hivernale
p período *m* de hibernação; período *m* hibernal

2697 **hide; pelage**
(Med.)
(Veterinary; animal anatomy: hairy covering.)
d Fell *n*; Behaarung *f*
f peau *f*, poils *mpl*
p pêlo *m*; pele *f* de pêlos; pelagem *f*, pelame *m*

2698 **hierarchy of wine quality**
(Prod.)
(Enology: wine production.)
d Qualitätshierarchie *f* des Weines
f hiérarchie *f* de qualité du vin
p hierarquia *f* de qualidade do vinho

2699 high blood pressure; hypertension
(Med.)
(Requiring dietary measures: salt-low (sodium-low) dietary regimen.)
d Bluthochruck *m*; erhöhter Blutdruck *m*
f hypertension *f*
p pressão *f* alta

2700 high caloric diet
(Med.)
(Alimentary regimen.)
d kalorienreiche Diät *f*
f diète *f* riche en calories
p dieta *f* rica em calorias

2701 high contents of oleic acid
(Prod.)
(Food processing technology: e.g. olive oil.)
d hoher Gehalt *m* an Oleinsäure; hoher Gehalt *m* an Ölsäure
f haute teneur *f* en acide oléique
p alto teor *m* de ácido oléico

2702 higher alcohols
(Biochem.)
(Fermentation in nutritional science.)
d höhere Alkohole *mpl*
f alcools *mpl* supérieurs
p álcoois *mpl* superiores

2703 higher esters
(Prod.)
(Aroma prime material.)
d höhere Ester *mpl*
f esters *mpl* supérieurs
p ésteres *mpl* superiores

2704 higher nutritional value
(Agr.)
(Biological agriculture and produce.)
d höherer Nährwert *m*
f valeur *f* nutritionnelle supérieure
p valor *m* nutritivo superior

2705 high fat diet
(Med.)
(Alimentary regimen.)
d fettreiche Diät *f*
f diète *f* grasse
p dieta *f* gordurosa

2706 high level of lipids
(Prod.)
(Nutritional science; ref. to certain plants/fruits.)
d hoher Gehalt *m* an Fettstoffen
f teneur *f* élevée en lipides
p teor *m* elevado de lipídios

2707 highly industrialized basic foodstuffs
(Prod.)
(Food processing technology; foodstuff production and marketing.)
d weitgehend industrialisierte Grundnahrungsmittel *npl*
f produits *mpl* alimentaires de base très industrialisés
p produtos *mpl* alimentícios de base altamente industrializados

2708 highly matured grape
(Agr.)
(Viticulture; grape quality.)
d Beere *f* großer Reife
f raisin *m* d'une grande maturité
p uva *f* de grande maturidade

2709 highly mineralized mineral waters
(Prod.)
(Water supply; mineral waters having a high concentration of minerals.)
d hochmineralisierte Mineralwässer *npl*
f eaux *fpl* minérales fortement minéralisées
p águas *fpl* minerais de alto teor de minerais

2710 highly viscous liquid
(Prod.)
(Food processing technology; product characteristic.)
d hochviskose Flüssigkeit *f*
f liquide *m* de haute viscosité
p líquido *m* de alta viscosidade

2711 high protein diet
(Med.)
(Alimentary regimen.)
d proteinreiche Diät *f*
f diète *f* riche en protéines
p dieta *f* rica em proteínas

2712 high standards of hygiene
(Med.)
d hohe Hygieneansprüche *mpl*
f standard *m* hygiénique élevé
p normas *fpl* elevadas de higiene

2713 high-yield milkers
(Agr.)
(Cattle breeding, milk producing cows.)
d Hochleistungsmilchkühe *fpl*
f vaches *fpl* laitières à haut rendement
p vacas *fpl* leiteiras de alto rendimento

2714 hind
(Agr.)
(Game; adult female red deer.)
d Hirschkuh *f*
f biche *f*
p cerva *f*

2715 **hind brisket**
(Prod.)
(Butchery; meat part; joint.)
d Nachbrust *f*
f poitrine *f* arrière; tendron *m* arrière
p peito *m* posterior

2716 **hind knuckle**
(Prod.)
(Butchery; meat part.)
d Hinterhaxe *f*; Hinterhachse *f*
f jarret *m* de derrière
p mocotó *m* traseiro

2717 **hind legs**
(Med.)
(Veterinary: of animals.)
d Hinterbeine *npl*; Hinterläufe *mpl*
f jambes *fpl* de derrière
p pernas *fpl* traseiras

2718 **histamine releasing action**
(Med.)
d Histamin freisetzende Wirkung *f*
f action *f* libératrice des histamines
p ação *f* de liberação de histaminas

2719 **histidine**
(Biochem.)
($C_6H_9N_3O_2$; essential amino acid; ingredient in human and in cow's milk.)
d Histidin *n*
f histidine *f*
p histidina *f*

* **hive bee → 566**

2720 **hock; white Rhine wine**
(Agr.)
(Viticulture. White wine of the Rhine-river valley.)
d weißer Rheinwein *m*
f vin *m* blanc du Rhin
p vinho *m* branco do Reno

* **hoecake → 1356**

* **hog → 4181**

2721 **hog feeding; pig feeding**
(Agr.)
(Livestock nutrition; hog raising.)
d Schweinefütterung *f*
f affouragement *m* des porcs
p alimentação *f* dos suínos

* **hog for slaughtering → 4182**

2722 **hog raising; pig raising**
(Agr.)
(Livestock raising: animals destined for alimentation.)
d Schweinezucht *f*
f élevage *m* de porcs; élevage *m* porcin
p suinocultura *f*

2723 **Holstein-Frisian dairy cattle**
(Agr.)
(Cattle breeding. Cattle breed. Frisian (North Holland) cattle.)
d holsteinisch-friesische Milchkühe *fpl*
f vache *f* laitière frisonne
p gado *m* leiteiro Friso-Holandês

2724 **home-made bread; cottage loaf**
(Prod.)
(Bakery. Domestically produced bread.)
d hausgebackenes Brot *n*; hausgemachtes Brot *n*
f pain *m* de ménage
p pão *m* feito em casa; pão *m* artesanal

2725 **homeopathy**
(Med.)
(Veterinary; animal treatment option in biologic agriculture.)
d Homöopathie *f*
f homéopathie *f*
p homeopatia *f*

2726 **homogeneity**
(Prod.)
(Food processing technology and flavour research and production: product characteristic.)
d Homogenität *f*
f homogénéité *f*
p homogeneidade *f*

2727 **homogeneous suspension**
(Prod.)
(Food processing technology and flavour research and production: product characteristic.)
d homogene Suspension *f*
f suspension *f* homogène
p suspensão *f* homogênea

2728 **homogenization**
(Prod.)
(Food processing technology; e.g. homogenized milk.)
d Homogenisierung *f*
f homogénéisation *f*
p homogeneização *f*

2729 **homogenization of fatty milk particles**
(Prod.)
(Food processing technology, e.g. of milk.)
d Homogenisierung *f* der Milchfettkörperchen

f homogénéisation *f* des globules gras du lait
p homogeneização *f* das partículas graxas do leite

2730 **homogenize** *v*
(Prod.)
(Food processing technology.)
d homogenisieren
f homogénéiser
p homogeneizar

2731 **homogenized milk**
(Prod.)
(Dairy product; homogenization to avoid cream dissociation within the milk.)
d homogenisierte Milch *f*
f lait *m* homogénéisé
p leite *m* homogeneizado

2732 **homozygous** *adj*
(Med.)
(Veterinary; there are dominant genes (A) and recessive (a) genes. If the genes determining a particular characteristic are identical (AA or aa), the individual is called "pure" or "homozygous".)
d reinerbig; homozygot
f homozygote
p homozigótico

2733 **honey**
(Agr.)
(Apiculture. Flower nectar produced by honeybees.)
d Honig *m*
f miel *m*
p mel *m*

2734 **honey bag; honey sac**
(Agr.)
(Apiculture. Bee anatomy: Part of the bee abdomen.)
d Honigmagen *m*
f jabot *m* d'abeille
p estômago *m* coletor de mel; vesícula *f* melífera

* **honeybee → 566**

2735 **honeycomb**
(Agr.)
(Apiculture. Wax cells where the bees keep the honey and their brood.)
d Wabe *f*; Bienenwabe *f*
f rayon *m* de miel
p favo *m* de mel

2736 **honey enriched milk**
(Prod.)
(Food processing technology; honey as milk ingredient in industrial milk types; ref. to baby nutrition.)
d mit Honig angereicherte Milch *f*
f lait *m* enrichi en miel
p leite *m* enriquecido com mel

2737 **honey-like**
(Prod.)
(Taste note; flavour note.)
d honigartig
f saveur *f* à *f* miel
p sabor *m* de mel

* **honey sac → 2734**

2738 **honey separator**
(Agr.)
(Apiculture. Honey-extraction equipment.)
d Honigschleuder *f*
f extracteur *m* centrifuge de miel
p centrifugador *m* de mel

2739 **honey super**
(Agr.)
(Apiculture. Movable frame hive construction.)
d Honigraum *m*
f magasin *m* à miel
p melgueira *f*

* **hoof-and-mouth disease → 2334**

2740 **hop**
(Agr.)
(Botany. "Humulus lupulus". Used e.g. in beer brewing.)
d Hopfen *m*
f houblon *m*
p lúpulo *m*

2741 **hop culture**
(Agr.)
(Agricultural produce.)
d Hopfenanbau *m*
f culture *f* du houblon
p cultura *f* de lúpolo

2742 **hop field**
(Agr.)
(Agricultural produce; hop culture.)
d Hopfenfeld *n*
f houblonnière *f*; champ *m* de houblon
p campo *m* de cultivo do lúpulo

2743 **hop-like flavour**
(Prod.)
(Aroma/flavour note.)
d hopfiger Geschmack *m*
f saveur *f* à houblon
p sabor *m* de lúpulo

2744 **hopping**
(Prod.)
(Third operation in the beer brewing process: hop addition.)
d Hopfen *n*
f houblonnage *m*
p lupolagem *f*

2745 **hormonal milk composition**
(Med.)
(Baby nutrition: mother's milk composition.)
d hormonale Zusammensetzung *f* der Milch
f composition *f* hormonale du lait
p composição *f* hormonal do leite

2746 **hormones in mother's milk**
(Med.)
(Baby nutrition. E.g. thyroxine, hydrocortisone.)
d Hormone *npl* in der Muttermilch
f hormones *fpl* dans le lait maternel
p hormônios *mpl* no leite maternal

2747 **hornification**
(Med.)
(Pathological skin condition.)
d Verhornung *f*
f kératinisation *f*
p queratinização *f*

2748 **horse**
(Agr.)
(Livestock.)
d Pferd *n*
f cheval *m*
p cavalo *m*

2749 **horse chestnut**
(Agr.)
(Agricultural produce. "Aesculus hippocastanum". Medicinal use.)
d Rosskastanie *f*
f marron *m* d'Inde
p castanha-da-india *f*

2750 **horseradish**
(Agr.)
(Horticulture. "Armoracia lapathifolia", "Nasturtium amoracea". Mustard family.)
d Meerrettich *m*
f raifort *m*
p raiz *f* forte

2751 **hot expression**
(Prod.)
(Food processing technology; separation process.)
d Heißauspressen *n*; Heißauspressung *f*
f pression *f* à chaud
p expressão *f* ao calor

2752 **hot maceration**
(Prod.)
(Food processing technology and processes.)
d heiße Mazeration *f*; Ziehenlassen *n* bei erhöhter Temperatur
f macération *f* à chaud
p maceração *f* sob calor

2753 **human colostrum**
(Med.)
(The first breast secretion containing serum, antibodies etc.; ref. to baby nutrition.)
d Vormilch *f* des Menschen; Humankolostrum *n*
f colostrum *m* humain
p colostro *m* humano

2754 **humanized milk; milk adapted to human necessities**
(Med.)
(Baby nutrition. Industrial milk.)
d humanisierte Milch *f*
f lait *m* humanisé; lait *m* maternisé
p leite *m* humanizado; leite *m* maternizado

2755 **human milk; mother's milk**
(Med.)
(High content of vitamins (C, A, D) of fats and essential amino acids. Lactose content as carbohydrate for the infant. It is considered to be a complete food.)
d Muttermilch *f*; Frauenmilch *f*
f lait *m* de femme; lait *m* maternel
p leite *m* materno

2756 **humbug**
(Prod.)
(Confectionary; hard mint-flavoured candy.)
d Pfefferminzbonbon *m*
f berlingot *m*
p bala *f* de menta

2757 **humidifier**
(Prod.)
(Auxiliary products; additive.)
d Feuchthaltemittel *n*
f humidificateur *m*; humecteur *m*
p umectante *m*; umedecedor *m*

2758 **humidity conditions for yeast drying**
(Prod.)
(Food processing technology; yeast production plant technology: important detail during fluid bed drying.)
d Feuchtigkeitsbedingungen *fpl* für die Hefetrocknung
f conditions *fpl* d'humidité pour le séchage de la levure
p condições *fpl* de umidade para a secagem do fermento; condições *fpl* de umidade para a secagem do lêvedo

2759 humidity of the climate
(Agr.)
(Climatology, e.g. for agricultural purposes.)
d Klimafeuchtigkeit *f*; Feuchtigkeit *f* des Klimas
f humidité *f* du climat
p umidade *f* do clima

2760 humidity rate
(Prod.)
(Dairy plant production processes.)
d Feuchtigkeitsanteil *m*
f taux *m* d'humidité
p taxa *f* de umidade

2761 humidity traces
(Prod.)
(Food processing technology and flavour research and production: product characteristic.)
d Feuchtigkeitsspuren *fpl*
f traces *fpl* d'humidité
p traços *mpl* de umidade

2762 humid starch
(Prod.)
(Food processing technology; raw material in (Brazilian) tapioca production: cassava starch preparation used for puddings. Thickening additive.)
d feuchte Stärke *f*
f fécule *f* humide
p fécula *f* úmida

2763 humid weight
(Prod.)
(Food processing technology.)
d Feuchtgewicht *n*
f poids *m* humide
p peso *m* úmido; peso *m* quando úmido

2764 humus
(Agr.)
(Decomposed plant/animal material, which has turned part of the soil; organic material; due to its colloidal properties it is an important soil component: source of nutrients for plants/vegetables.)
d Humus *m*
f humus *m*
p húmus *m*; humo *m*

2765 humus contents of the soil
(Agr.)
(Biological agriculture. Content of decomposed plant/animal material, which has turned part of the soil; organic material in the soil.)
d Humusgehalt *m* des Bodens
f teneur *f* en humus du sol
p teor *m* de húmus do solo; teor *m* de humo do solo

2766 humus-poor soil
(Agr.)
(Biological agriculture: ref. to soil treatment necessity.)
d humusarmer Boden *m*
f sol *m* pauvre en humus
p solo *m* pobre de húmus; solo *m* pobre de humo

2767 hunger cure; starvation cure
(Med.)
(Slimming treatment.)
d Hungerkur *f*; Fastenkur *f*
f cure *f* de jeûne; cure *f* d'amaigrissement par le jeûne
p tratamento *m* à base de jejum; regime *m* à base de jejum

* **husbandry → 144**

2768 hush puppies
(Prod.)
(Gastronomy; cornmeal dough balls.)
d Maismehlklöße *npl*
f boulette *f* de farine de maïs
p bolinhos *mpl* de fubá

2769 husk; chaff
(Agr.)
(Botany. Corn cover; grain threshing residue.)
d Spreu *f*
f balle *f*
p debulho *m*; moinha *f*

2770 hyaluronic acid
(Prod.)
(Mucopolysaccharide in animal tissue; tissue constituent.)
d Hyaluransäure *f*
f acide *m* hyaluronique
p ácido *m* hialurônico

2771 hybrid
(Agr.)
(Livestock breeding. Animal or plant crossbred, whose parents are different from each other ref. to their hereditary characteristics.)
d Hybrid *n*
f hybride *m*
p híbrido *m*

* **hybridism → 1411**

2772 hydatid
(Med.)
(Larval tapeworm cyst. See Echinococcus.)
d Finne *f*

f hydatide *f*
p hidátide *f*

* **hydrargyria → 3460**

2773 **hydration**
(Biochem.)
(Nutritional science. Combination of ions or polar molecules with water.)
d Hydratation *f*
f hydratation *f*
p hidratação *f*

2774 **hydration capacity**
(Prod.)
(Food processing technology; ref. to product characteristics: water absorption.)
d Wasseraufnahmefähigkeit *f*
f capacité *f* d'hydratation
p capacidade *f* de hidratação

2775 **hydric erosion; water erosion**
(Agr.)
(Soil; soil erosion caused by water.)
d Hydroerosion *f*; Erosion *f* durch Wasser
f érosion *f* hydrique
p erosão *f* hídrica; erosão *f* causada pela água

2776 **hydrocarbons**
(Prod.)
(Ref. to compounds containing only carbon and hydrogen: e.g. a variety of solvents used in extraction processes; prime material for the production of synthetic aroma/fragrance products.)
d Kohlenwasserstoffe *mpl*
f hydrocarbures *mpl*
p hidrocarbonetos *mpl*

2777 **hydrochloric acid**
(Med.)
(HCl; contained in the gastric juice.)
d Salzsäure *f*
f acide *m* chlorhydrique
p ácido *m* clorídrico

2778 **hydro-colloidal system**
(Biochem.)
(Nutritional science: ref. to dispersions: colloidal chemistry.)
d hydrokolloidales System *n*
f système *m* hydrocolloïdal
p sistema *m* hidrocoloidal

2779 **hydrocortisone; cortisol**
(Med.)
($C_{21}H_{30}O_5$; glucocorticoid in human milk, important for the carbohydrate metabolism; ref. to baby nutrition.)
d Hydrokortison *n*
f hydrocortisone *f*
p hidrocortisona *f*

* **hydrocyanic acid → 2784**

2780 **hydrogen**
(Biochem.)
(The elements carbon (C), oxygen (O) and hydrogen (H) form the carbohydrates $C_n(H_2O)_n$, e.g. sugar, starches; constitutional part of odoriferous foodstuff molecules; nutritional science.)
d Wasserstoff *m*
f hydrogène *m*
p hidrogênio *m*

2781 **hydrogenated vegetable oil**
(Prod.)
(Food processing technology; prime material.)
d hydriertes Pflanzenöl *n*
f huile *f* végétale hydrogénée
p óleo *m* vegetal hidrogenado

2782 **hydrogenation**
(Prod.)
(Food processing technology: Food preservation process: e.g. treatment with hydrogen.)
d Hydrierung *f*
f hydrogénation *f*
p hidrogenação *f*

2783 **hydrogenation of fats**
(Prod.)
(Food processing technology, e.g. margarine production.)
d Hydrierung *f* von Fetten
f hydrogénation *f* des graisses
p hidrogenação *f* das gorduras

2784 **hydrogen cyanide; hydrocyanic acid; prussic acid**
(Biochem.)
(Nutritional science. HCN; glycosides containing hydrogen cyanide can be found in seeds of many stone fruits; in larger quantities it is toxic, blocking respiration on cell level.)
d Blausäure *f*
f acide *m* prussique; acide *m* cyanhydrique
p ácido *m* cianídrico

2785 **hydrogen peroxide**
(Prod.)
(H_2O_2; antiseptic; destroys vitamin C.)
d Wasserstoffperoxid *n*; Wasserstoffsuperoxid *n*
f peroxyde *m* d'hydrogène; eau *f* oxygénée
p peróxido *m* de hidrogênio; água *f* oxigenada

2786 **hydrolysate of plant protein**
(Biochem.)
(Nutritional science.)

d Hydrolyseprodukt *n* pflanzlicher Proteine
f hydrolysat *m* de protéines végétales
p produto *m* de hidrólise de proteínas vegetais

2787 **hydrolysis**
(Biochem.)
(A decomposition process.)
d Hydrolyse *f*
f hydrolyse *f*
p hidrólise *f*

2788 **hydrolysis by enzymatic means**
(Biochem.)
(Hydrolysis process type, esp. in aroma production.)
d Hydrolyse *f* auf enzymatischem Wege
f hydrolyse *f* par voie enzymatique
p hidrólise *f* por via enzimática

2789 **hydrolysis of lactose**
(Biochem.)
(Nutritional science.)
d Hydrolyse *f* der Laktose; Milchzuckerhydrolyse *f*
f hydrolyse *f* du lactose
p hidrólise *f* da lactose

2790 **hydrolyzable** *adj*
(Prod.)
(Food processing technology; capable to undergo hydrolysis.)
d spaltbar; hydrolisierbar
f hydrolysable
p hidrolisável

2791 **hydromorphic soil**
(Agr.)
(Soil; one of the principal soils of Brazil, of arenaceous-argillaceous structure; acid soil type, pH inferior than 5. High temporary water content inhibits aerobic factors in soil formation.)
d hydromorpher Boden *m*
f sol *m* hydromorphe
p solo *m* hidromórfico

* **hydropathic diet** → **2277**

2792 **hydroperoxides from lipid oxidation**
(Biochem.)
(Nutritional science; ref. to lipid oxidation in meat; product deterioration.)
d Hydroperoxide *npl* der Lipidoxidation
f hydroperoxydes *mpl* de l'oxydation lipidique
p hidroperóxidos *mpl* da oxidação lipídica

2793 **hydrophile** *adj*; **hydrophilic** *adj*
(Prod.)
(Food processing technology; chemistry: having water affinity.)
d hydrophil; Feuchtigkeit anziehend
f hydrophile
p hidrófilo

* **hydrophilic** *adj* → **2793**

2794 **hydrophilic environment**
(Biochem.)
(Vitamin biochemistry; e.g. vitamin absorption in the body.)
d hydrophiles Umfeld *n*
f environnement *m* hydrophile
p meio *m* hidrófilo

2795 **hydrophobe** *adj*
(Prod.)
(Food processing technology; chemistry: having no affinity to water.)
d hydrophob; Feuchtigkeit abstoßend
f hydrophobe
p hidrófobo

* **hydrophobia** → **4546**

2796 **hydrophobic environment**
(Biochem.)
(Vitamin biochemistry; e.g. vitamin absorption in the body.)
d hydrophobes Umfeld *n*
f environnement *m* hydrophobe
p meio *m* hidrófobo

2797 **hydrophobic substance**
(Prod.)
(Food processing technology; product having no water affinity.)
d hydrophobe Substanz *f*; hydrophober Stoff *m*
f substance *f* hydrophobe
p substância *f* hidrófoba

2798 **hydrosoluble aromas**
(Prod.)
(Flavour chemicals: obtention by extraction, e.g. fruit juice.)
d wasserlösliche Aromen *npl*
f arômes *mpl* hydrosolubles
p aromas *mpl* hidrossolúveis

2799 **hydrosoluble compounds**
(Prod.)
(Aroma/flavour research and production.)
d wasserlösliche Verbindungen *fpl*
f composés *mpl* hydrosolubles
p compostos *mpl* hidrossolúveis

* **hydroxysuccinic acid** → **3346**

2800 **hygienically irrecusable water**
(Prod.)
(Water supply quality, water treatment.)

d hygienisch einwandfreies Wasser *n*
f eau *f* hygiéniquement irrécusable
p água *f* higienicamente irrecusável

2801 **hygroscopicity**
(Prod.)
(Food processing technology; moisture retaining characteristic of a product.)
d Hygroskopizität *f*
f hygroscopicité *f*
p higroscopicidade *f*

2802 **hyoid bone**
(Med.)
(Anatomy; body part; tongue-supporting bone.)
d Zungenbein *n*
f os *m* hyoïde
p hióide *m*

2803 **hyperacid intestinal flora**
(Med.)
d übersäuerte Darmflora *f*
f flore *f* intestinale hyperacide
p flora *f* intestinal hiperácida

2804 **hyperbasic diet**
(Med.)
(Diet as to the Swedish scientist Ragnar Berg (1873-1956), indicating that the nutrition should have more basic than acid nutritional equivalents.)
d basenüberschüssige Kost *f*
f diète *f* hyperbasique
p regime *m* hiperbásico

2805 **hypercalcaemia; hypercalcemia**
(Med.)
(Abnormal high level of blood calcium.)
d Hypercalcämie *f*
f hypercalcémie *f*
p hipercalcemia *f*

* **hypercalcemia → 2805**

2806 **hyperchlorhydria**
(Med.)
(Abnormal hydrochloric acid stomach secretion.)
d Hyperchlorhydrie *f*
f hyperchlorhydrie *f*
p hiperchloridria *f*

2807 **hypercholesterolemia**
(Med.)
(Blood cholesterol excess; can be nutrition-induced; special diets advisable.)
d Hypercholesterinämie *f*
f hypercholestérolémie *f*
p hipercolesterolemia *f*

2808 **hyperglycaemia; hyperglycemia**
(Med.)
(Glucose excess in blood: e.g. diabetes mellitus; special diets advisable.)
d Hyperglykämie *f*
f hyperglycémie *f*
p hiperglicemia *f*

* **hyperglycemia → 2808**

2809 **hyperplasia**
(Med.)
(Baby nutrition. Increased production of normal cells; here: adipocytes: fat cells; in infants.)
d Hyperplasie *f*; Gewebezellvermehrung *f*
f hyperplasie *f*
p hiperplasia *f*

2810 **hyperproteinaceous supply**
(Biochem.)
(Nutrition in medicine.)
d hyperproteinhaltiges Angebot *n*
f apport *m* hyperprotéique
p aporte *m* hiperprotéico

* **hypersensitiveness → 2811**

2811 **hypersensitivity; hypersensitiveness**
(Med.)
d Hypersensibilität *f*; Überempfindlichkeit *f*
f hypersensibilité *f*
p hipersensibilidade *f*

* **hypertension → 2699**

2812 **hyperthyroidism**
(Med.)
(Thyroid gland overactivity with increase of the basal metabolism.)
d Hyperthyreose *f*; krankhaft gesteigerte Schilddrüsensekretionsaktivität *f*
f hyperthyroïdisme *m*; hyperthyroïdie *f*
p hipertiroidismo *m*; hipertiroidia *f*

2813 **hyperuricaemia; hyperuricemia**
(Med.)
(Excess of uric acid in blood; e.g. ref. to gout; special diets advisable.)
d Hyperurikämie *f*
f hyperuricémie *f*
p hiperuricemia *f*

* **hyperuricemia → 2813**

2814 **hypervitaminosis**
(Med.)
(Excessive vitamin intake: Fat-soluble vitamins, taken in excess, are toxic.)
d Hypervitaminose *f*

f hypervitaminose *f*
p hipervitaminose *f*

2815 **hypochlorite**
(Prod.)
(Water supply treatment: chlorine liberating substance.)
d Hypochlorit *n*
f hypochlorite *m*
p hipochlorito *m*

2816 **hypogalactia**
(Med.)
(Reduction of milk secretion in breast feeding.)
d Hypogalaktie *f*
f hypogalactie *f*
p hipogaláctia *f*

2817 **hypoglycaemia; hypoglycemia**
(Med.)
(Insufficiency of glucose in blood, generally accompanied by diabetes mellitus; special diets advisable.)
d Blutzuckerabfall *m*; Hypoglykämie *f*
f hypoglycémie *f*
p hipoglicemia *f*

* **hypoglycemia → 2817**

2818 **hyponatraemic syndrome; hyponatremic syndrome; syndrome of hyponatraemia; syndrome of hyponatremia**
(Med.)
(Salt (NCl) deficiency in blood; cause e.g. dehydration.)
d Salzmangelsyndrom *n*
f syndrome *m* hyponatrémique
p síndrome *m* de hiponatrenia

* **hyponatremic syndrome → 2818**

2819 **hypophysis stimulation**
(Med.)
(Baby nutrition. Lactation stimulation of the mother via hypophysis stimulation through nursing.)
d Hypophysenanregung *f*; Stimulierung *f* der Hirnanhangsdrüse; Stimulieren *n* der Hirnanhangsdrüse
f stimulation *f* de l'hypophyse
p estimulação *f* da hipófise

2820 **hypoproteinaemia; hypoproteinemia**
(Med.)
(Decrease in blood protein: e.g. due to malnutrition.)
d Hypoproteinämie *f*
f hypoprotéinémie *f*
p hipoproteinemia *f*

* **hypoproteinemia → 2820**

2821 **hypothyroid child**
(Med.)
(Hypothyroidism: subnormal activity of the thyroid gland; ref. to baby nutrition.)
d an Hypothyreose leidendes Kind *n*; an Hypothyreoidismus leidendes Kind *n*
f enfant *m* hypothyroïdien
p criança *f* sofrendo de hipotireoidismo

2822 **hypotonia**
(Med.)
(Condition of reduced muscle tension; e.g. due to incorrect baby nutrition.)
d Hypotonie *f*
f hypotonie *f*
p hipotonia *f*

2823 **hypovitaminosis**
(Med.)
(Vitamin deficiency.)
d Hypovitaminose *f*
f hypovitaminose *f*
p hipovitaminose *f*

I

2824 ice cream
(Prod.)
(Gastronomy
d Speiseeis *n*
f glace *f*
p sorvete *m*

2825 ice cream cone
(Prod.)
(Gastronomy; ref. to ice cream form of two-colour products.)
d Speiseeiskegel *m*
f cornet *m* de glace
p cone *m* de sorvete

2826 ice cream cup
(Prod.)
(Gastronomy; ref. to ice cream form of two-colour products.)
d Speiseeistasse *f*
f bol *m* à glace
p copinho *m* de sorvete

2827 ice cream mix
(Prod.)
(Gastronomy; mixture of skim-milk powder, sugar and stabilizer, with water.)
d Speiseeismischung *f*
f mélange *m* de crème glacée
p mistura *f* de sorvete

2828 ice cream production
(Prod.)
(Food processing technology.)
d Speiseeisherstellung *f*
f fabrication *f* de glace
p produção *f* de sorvete

2829 ice-pudding
(Prod.)
(Gastronomy; ref. to ice cream form.)
d Eisbombe *f*; Speiseeisbombe *f*
f bombe *f* glacée
p bola *f* de sorvete

2830 icing; frosting; glaze
(Prod.)
(Bakery; sweet coating of baked products. Confectionary; glossy (sugar) surface coating e.g. for cakes.)
d Zuckerguss *m*; Zuckerüberzug *m*; Glasur *f*; Zuckerglasur *f*
f glace *f*
p glacê *m*; glace *f*; cobertura *f* de açúcar; cobertura *f* de bolo à base de açúcar

2831 icing sugar; confectioner's sugar
(Prod.)
(Food processing technology; very fine sugar type.)
d Puderzucker *m*
f sucre *m* en poudre
p açúcar *m* de confeiteiro

2832 ideal fermentation temperature
(Biochem.)
(Fermentation in nutritional science.)
d Idealtemperatur *f* der Gärung
f température *f* idéale de fermentation
p temperatura *f* ideal de fermentação

2833 identical with the natural product
(Prod.)
(Aroma research and production: aromas of synthetic reaction, having the same chemical structure as the natural product.)
d naturidentisch
f identique au produit naturel
p idêntico com o produto natural

2834 identifiable toxicity
(Med.)
(Food processing technology: that one of known substances in alimentary production and products.)
d identifizierbare Toxizität *f*; feststellbare Giftigkeit *f*
f toxicité *f* identifiable
p toxicidade *f* identifiável

2835 identification threshold
(Med.)
(Aroma/flavour perception.)
d Identifizierungsschwelle *f*
f seuil *m* d'identification
p limiar *m* de identificação

2836 igneous rock
(Agr.)
(Soil; rock formed by the solidification of magma.)
d Erstarrungsgestein *n*
f roche *f* ignée
p rocha *f* ígnea

2837 ileum
(Med.)
(The lowest part of the small intestine.)
d Krummdarm *m*
f iléon *m*
p ileo *m*

2838 illnesses of the cultures
(Agr.)
(Biological agriculture.)
d Krankheiten *fpl* der Kulturen
f maladies *fpl* des cultures
p doenças *fpl* das culturas

* **imidole → 4521**

2839 immerse *v* cheese in tanks
(Prod.)
(Dairy technology of cheese production.)
d Käse in Tanks tauchen
f tremper des fromages dans des cuves
p imergir queijos em tanques

* **immune reaction with supplemental vitamin → 2840**

2840 immune response with supplemental vitamin; immune reaction with supplemental vitamin
(Med.)
(Veterinary; ref. to vitamin supplementation of feed for nutritional veterinary treatment; e.g. ref. to vitamin E.)
d Immunreaktion *f* bei Vitaminsupplementierung
f immunoréponse *f* à la supplémentation vitaminique; immunoréaction *f* à la supplémentation vitaminique
p imunorreação *f* à suplementação vitamínica

2841 immunoglobulins
(Med.)
(As antibody acting proteins.)
d Immunoglobuline *npl*
f immunoglobulines *fpl*
p imunoglobulinas *fpl*

2842 immuno-insufficiency
(Med.)
(Ref. to insufficient defence mechanisms of the body.)
d Immunschwäche *f*
f immunodéficience *f*
p imunodeficiência *f*

2843 immunologic factors
(Med.)
(Baby nutrition. E.g. leucocytes, lysozymes.)
d immunologische Faktoren *mpl*; immunologische Gegebenheiten *fpl*
f facteurs *mpl* immunologiques
p fatores *mpl* imunológicos

2844 immunologic function
(Med.)
(Nutrition: can be prejudiced by subnutrition.)
d Immunfunktion *f*
f fonction *f* immunitaire
p função *f* imunológica

2845 immunopathology of digestion
(Med.)
(Nutrition in medicine.)
d Immunpathologie *f* der Verdauung
f pathologie *f* immunitaire digestive
p patologia *f* imunitária digestiva

2846 immunoreaction
(Med.)
(Ref. to food allergy.)
d Immunreaktion *f*
f immunoréaction *f*
p imunorreação *f*

2847 impact on foodstuff quality
(Agr.)
(Biological agriculture: evaluation of activity, results etc.)
d Auswirkung *f* auf die Qualität der Nahrungsmittel; Auswirkung *f* auf die Nahrungsmittelqualität
f impact *m* sur la qualité des denrées alimentaires
p impacto *m* sobre a qualidade dos gêneros alimentícios

2848 impaired nourishment
(Med.)
d Ernährungsstörung *f*
f désordre *m* d'alimentation
p perturbação *f* da alimentação

2849 impoverishment of the soils
(Agr.)
(Soil destruction, e.g. by mismanagement.)
d Bodenerschöpfung *f*, Bodenmüdigkeit *f*
f appauvrissement *m* des sols; épuisement *m* des sols
p empobrecimento *m* dos solos; esgotamento *m* dos solos

2850 improvement
(Prod.)
(Food processing technology.)
d Verbesserung *f*
f amélioration *f*
p melhoramento *m*; aperfeiçoamento *m*

2851 improvement of digestive symptoms
(Med.)
(Digestive (related to nutrition) disorder improvement.)
d Verbesserung *f* der Verdauungssymptome
f amélioration *f* des symptômes digestifs
p melhoramento *m* dos sintomas digestivos

2852 **improvement of dissolution**
(Prod.)
(Food processing technology.)
d Auflösungsverbesserung *f*
f amélioration *f* de la dissolution
p melhoramento *m* da propriedade de dissolução

2853 **improvement of lipid stability in beef**
(Biochem.)
(Nutritional science; ref. to lipid oxidation phenomena in meat: e.g. cattle dietary treatment with vitamin E.)
d Verbesserung *f* der Lipidstabilität im Rindfleisch
f amélioration *f* de la stabilité des lipides dans le bœuf
p melhoramento *m* da estabilidade dos lipídios na carne bovina

2854 **improvement of nutritional quality**
(Biochem.)
(Nutritional science.)
d Verbesserung *f* der Ernährungsqualität
f augmentation *f* de la qualité nutritionnelle
p aumento *m* da qualidade nutricional

2855 **improvement of nutritional supply**
(Biochem.)
(Nutrition, e.g. in medicine.)
d Verbesserung *f* der Nahrungsmittelzufuhr
f amélioration *f* de l'apport nutritionnel
p melhoramento *m* do aporte nutricional

2856 **improvement of production methods**
(Prod.)
(Food processing technology.)
d Verbesserung *f* der Produktionsverfahren
f amélioration *f* des méthodes de production
p melhoramento *m* dos métodos de produção

2857 **improvement of soil structure**
(Agr.)
(Soil treatment.)
d Verbesserung *f* der Bodenstruktur
f amélioration *f* de la structure du sol
p melhoramento *m* da estrutura do solo

2858 **improvement of the calcium/phosphorus exchange rate in the skeleton**
(Med.)
(Veterinary: Vitamin D_3 in cattle feedstuff is said to regularize this metabolism and to improve intestinal absorption.)
d Verbesserung *f* der Calcium/Phosphoraustauschrate im Skelett
f amélioration *f* de l'équilibre de calcium et phosphore dans le squelette
p melhora *f* no equilíbrio de cálcio/fósforo no esqueleto

2859 **improvement of the taste; taste improvement**
(Prod.)
(Aroma/flavour research and production; one of the flavouring purposes; e.g. ref. to organoleptic food evaluation.)
d Geschmacksverbesserung *f*
f amélioration *f* du goût
p melhoramento *m* do paladar; melhoramento *m* do gosto

2860 **in alcoholic solution**
(Prod.)
(Food processing technology.)
d in alkoholischer Lösung
f en solution alcoolique
p em solução alcoólica

2861 **inanition**
(Med.)
(Exhaustion due to lack of nutrients, caused by malnutrition or absorption diseases.)
d Hungerzustand *m*
f inanition *f*
p inanição *f*

* **inappetence → 3084**

2862 **in aqueous solution**
(Prod.)
(Food processing technology.)
d in wässriger Lösung
f en solution aqueuse
p em solução aquosa

* **in basic environment → 2863**

2863 **in basic milieu; in basic environment**
(Biochem.)
(Food biochemistry.)
d in basischem Milieu; in basischer Umwelt
f en milieu basique
p em ambiente básico

2864 **incisor**
(Med.)
(Anatomy.)
d Schneidezahn *m*
f dent *f* incisive
p dente *m* incisivo

2865 **incorporated in the form of droplets; added in the form of droplets**
(Prod.)
(Food processing technology; process technique.)
d tröpfchenweise eingeführt; in Form von Tröpfchen zugesetzt

f incorporé sous la forme de gouttelettes; additionné goutte à goutte; additionné goutte par goutte
p incorporado em forma de gotinhas; adicionado gota a gota

2866 **incorporation into the phases**
(Prod.)
(Food processing technology: e.g. into oily phases.)
d Einführung *f* in die Phasen
f incorporation *f* aux phases
p incorporação *f* nas fases

2867 **increased vitamin requirements**
(Med.)
d erhöhter Vitaminanspruch *m*
f besoin *m* accru en vitamines
p aumento *m* da necessidade de vitaminas

* **increase in sugar contents → 2868**

2868 **increase in sugar richness; increase in sugar contents**
(Biochem.)
(Enology; wine improvement method.)
d Erhöhung *f* der Zuckerreichhaltigkeit; Erhöhung *f* des Zuckergehaltes
f augmentation *f* de la richesse en sucre
p aumento *m* do teor de açúcar; aumento *m* da riqueza em açúcar

2869 **increase of plant resistance**
(Agr.)
(Biological agriculture: Resistance against insects etc.)
d Verstärkung *f* des Widerstandes der Pflanzen; Erhöhung *f* des Pflanzenwiderstandes
f renforcement *m* de la résistance des plantes
p aumento *m* da resistência das plantas

2870 **increase of the freezing point**
(Prod.)
(Food processing technology.)
d Gefrierpunkterhöhung *f*
f augmentation *f* du point de congélation
p aumento *m* do ponto de congelamento

* **increase of the natural defense mechanism → 4289**

2871 **increase of the sediment volume**
(Prod.)
(Food processing technology.)
d Erhöhung *f* der Sedimentsmenge; Erhöhung *f* des Niederschlagsvolumes
f augmentation *f* du volume du sédiment
p aumento *m* do volume do sedimento; aumento *m* do volume do depósito

2872 **increase *v* the biologic activity of the soils**
(Agr.)
(Aim of biologic agriculture, biologic farming system.)
d die biologische Aktivität des Bodens erhöhen
f augmenter l'activité biologique des sols
p aumentar a atividade biológica dos solos

2873 **increase *v* the protein supply**
(Prod.)
(Food processing technology, research and production.)
d Proteinzufuhr erhöhen
f élever l'apport *m* en protéines
p elevar o aporte *m* protéico; aumentar o fornecimento *m* de proteínas

2874 **in crystalline form**
(Prod.)
(Food processing technology; product characteristic.)
d in kristalliner Form; in Kristallform
f sous forme cristalline
p em forma cristalina

* **index of refraction → 4646**

* **Indian corn → 3339**

* **Indian-corn cake → 3340**

* **Indian-corn dough → 3341**

2875 **indigestion**
(Med.)
(Digestion disorder.)
d Verdauungsbeschwerden *fpl*
f indigestion *f*
p indigestão *f*

2876 **indigestion due to overnutrition; digestive trouble due to overnutrition**
(Med.)
(Dyspepsia type.)
d Verdauungsstörung *f* durch Überernährung
f indigestion *f* par suralimentation
p indigestão *f* por superalimentação

* **indigo → 2877**

2877 **indigotin; indigo**
(Prod.)
($C_{16}H_{10}N_2O_2$; foodstuff colorant, E number: E 132.)
d Indigotin *n*
f indigotine *f*
p indigotina *f*

2878 indirect heating
(Prod.)
(Aroma/flavour research and production: e.g. by means of a distillation flask with double bottom.)
d indirekte Erhitzung *f*
f chauffage *m* indirect
p aquecimento *m* indireto

2879 individual portion
(Prod.)
(Gastronomy.)
d individuelle Portion *f*
f portion *f* individuelle
p porção *f* individual

2880 individual selection
(Med.)
(Veterinary; e.g. ref. to cattle raising; selection of individual animals for improving the forthcoming herds.)
d individuelle Selektion *f*; Einzelauswahl *f*
f sélection *f* individuelle
p seleção *f* individual

2881 individual variations
(Med.)
(Regimens, diets.)
d individuelle Variationen *fpl*; individuelle Abweichungen *fpl*
f variations *fpl* individuelles
p variações *fpl* individuais

2882 indole; 2,3-benzopyrrole
(Prod.)
(C_8H_7N; e.g. in jasmine; orange-blossom oil; source of aroma/fragrance prime material.)
d Indol *n*
f indole *m*
p indol *m*

2883 indoor stable feeding
(Agr.)
(Cattle breeding.)
d Stallfütterung *f*
f affouragement *m* pendant la stabulation
p alimentação *f* durante a estabulação

2884 indoxyl
(Med.)
(C_8H_7NO; auxiliary (urine dosage test) in the intestinal digestion examination.)
d Indoxyl *n*
f indoxyle *m*
p indoxil *m*

2885 industrial byproducts
(Prod.)
(Food processing technology; production processes.)
d industrielle Abfallprodukte *npl*; industrielle Nebenprodukte *npl*
f sous-produits *mpl* industriels
p subprodutos *mpl* industriais

2886 industrial exploitation of microorganisms
(Biochem.)
(Microbiology.)
d industrielle Nutzung *f* von Mikroorganismen
f exploitation *f* industrielle des microorganismes
p exploração *f* industrial de microorganismos

2887 industrial fermentation
(Biochem.)
(Nutritional science; enzymatically controlled transformation processes, basis for baking and for production of beverages (alcohol production).)
d industrielle Fermentation *f*; industrielles Gärungsverfahren *n*
f fermentation *f* industrielle
p fermentação *f* industrial

2888 industrial foodstuff production
(Prod.)
(Food processing technology.)
d industrielle Nahrungsmittelherstellung *f*
f préparation *f* industrielle des aliments
p produção *f* industrial de alimentos

2889 industrialization of agriculture
(Agr.)
(Agricultural branch.)
d landwirtschaftliche Industrialisierung *f*
f industrialisation *f* de l'agriculture
p industrialização *f* da agricultura

2890 industrialized bread
(Prod.)
(Bread produced in an industrial process and scale.)
d industrialisiertes Brot *n*
f pain *m* industriel
p pão *m* industrializado

2891 industrialized enzyme
(Biochem.)
(Food biochemistry; enzyme types.)
d industrialisiertes Enzym *n*
f enzyme *f* industrielle
p enzima *f* industrial

2892 industrialized milk
(Prod.)
(Baby nutrition.)
d industrialisierte Milch *f*
f lait *m* industriel
p leite *m* industrializado

2893 industrialized sweet dessert
(Prod.)
(Food processing technology, research and production; gastronomy.)
d industriell hergestellte Süßspeise *f*
f entremets *m* industriel
p doce *m* de sobremesa industrializado

2894 industrialized vegetable types
(Med.)
(Baby nutrition.)
d industrialisierte Gemüsesorten *fpl*
f légumes *mpl* industriels
p legumes *mpl* industrializados

2895 industrialized yeast
(Biochem.)
(Fermentation in nutritional science.)
d industrialisierte Hefe *f*
f levure *f* industrielle
p fermento *m* industrial

* **industrially prepared afters → 2896**

2896 industrially prepared dessert; industrially prepared afters
(Prod.)
(Food processing technology and production.)
d industriell hergestellte Nachspeisen *fpl*
f desserts *mpl* industriels
p sobremesas *fpl* de fabricação industrial

2897 industrially prepared dough
(Prod.)
(Food processing technology.)
d industriell hergestellter Teig *m*
f pâte *f* préparée industriellement
p massa *f* de preparação industrial

2898 industrially prepared foodstuff
(Prod.)
(Food processing technology and production.)
d industriell hergestellte Lebensmittel *npl*
f aliments *mpl* de préparations industrielles
p produtos *mpl* alimentícios de fabricação industrial

2899 industrial mass production
(Prod.)
(Food processing technology and production.)
d industrielle Massenproduktion *f*
f production *f* industrielle de masse
p produção *f* industrial em massa

2900 industrial methods of conservation; industrial preservation techniques
(Prod.)
(Food processing technology; ref. to food preservation processes.)
d industrielle Konservierungsmethoden *fpl*; industrielle Methoden *fpl* der Haltbarkeitsmachung
f techniques *fpl* de conservation industrielle
p métodos *mpl* da conservação industrial

2901 industrial milk exploitation
(Prod.)
(Food processing technology.)
d industrielle Ausbeute *f* der Milch
f exploitation *f* industrielle du lait
p exploração *f* industrial do leite

2902 industrial panification
(Prod.)
(Food processing technology:)
d industrielle Backwarenherstellung *f*
f panification *f* industrielle
p panificação *f* industrial

2903 industrial pollution
(Agr.)
(Soils; pollution by heavy metals which may enter the food chains.)
d industrielle Umweltsverschmutzung *f*
f pollution *f* industrielle
p poluição *f* industrial

2904 industrial poultry management
(Agr.)
(Poultry farming.)
d Geflügelzuchtsindustrie *f*
f industrie *f* avicole
p indústria *f* avícola

2905 industrial practice
(Prod.)
(Food processing technology.)
d industrielle Praxis *f*
f pratique *f* industrielle
p prática *f* industrial

* **industrial preservation techniques → 2900**

2906 industrial processing
(Prod.)
(Food processing technology.)
d industrielle Umformung *f*; industrielle Verarbeitung *f*
f transformation *f* industrielle
p transformação *f* industrial

2907 industrial products
(Prod.)
(Food processing technology.)
d Industrieprodukte *mpl*; Industrieerzeugnisse *npl*
f produits *mpl* industriels
p produtos *mpl* industriais

2908 **industrial refinement of edible oils**
(Prod.)
(Food processing technology.)
d industrielle Raffination *f* von Speiseölen; Veredelung *f* von Speiseölen
f raffinage *m* industriel des huiles alimentaires
p refinação *f* industrial de óleos comestíveis

2909 **industrial vegetable oil-containing subproducts**
(Agr.)
(Agricultural produce; subproducts are used in animal feedstuff.)
d pflanzliche Öle enthaltende industrielle Nebenprodukte *npl*
f sous-produits *mpl* de la houillification des végétaux
p subprodutos *mpl* da indústria das oleoginosas

2910 **industrial yeast propagation**
(Prod.)
(Food processing technology; Yeast plant technology: Processed in the pre-fermenter unit and in the pure culture vessel.)
d industrielle Fortpflanzung *f* von Hefe; industrielle Hefepropagation *f*
f propagation *f* industrielle de la levure
p propagação *f* industrial do fermento

2911 **industry of agricultural products**
(Prod.)
(Food processing technology.)
d Industrie *f* der Agrarprodukte
f industrie *f* agroalimentaire
p indústria *f* de produtos agro-pastorís

2912 **inert gas**
(Biochem.)
(Enology: preservation agent in wine treatment/preservation.)
d inertes Gas *n*; Schutzgas *n*
f gaz *m* inerte; gaz *m* protecteur
p gás *m* inerte

* **infant → 3725**

2913 **infant food; baby nutrition**
(Prod.)
(Baby nutrition.)
d Säuglingsernährung *f*
f alimentation *f* du nourrisson
p alimentação *f* do récem-nascido; nutrição *f* do récem-nascido

* **infantile dietetics → 1657**

2914 **infantile hypoglycaemia; infantile hypoglycemia**
(Med.)
(Insufficiency of glucose in blood, generally accompanied by diabetes mellitus; special diets advisable.)
d infantile Hypoglykämie *f*; Hypoglykämie *f* des Kindes
f hypoglycémie *f* infantile
p hipoglicemia *f* infantil

* **infantile hypoglycemia → 2914**

2915 **infantile weight surcharge; overweight of the baby**
(Med.)
(Baby nutrition.)
d gewichtsbezogene Überbelastung *f* des Säugling
f surcharge *f* pondérale du nourrisson
p sobrecarga *f* ponderal do récem-nascido

2916 **infestation**
(Agr.)
(Botany; parasitic spreading over plants.)
d Parasitenbefall *m*
f infestation *f*
p infestação *f*

2917 **in fine crystalline form**
(Prod.)
(Food processing technology; product characteristic.)
d in feinkristalliner Form; in Form feiner Kristalle
f sous forme de cristaux fins
p em forma de cristais finos

* **inflammation of the mucosa of the stomach → 2458**

2918 **inflorescence**
(Agr.)
(Botany: Type of arrangement of flowers on an axis, i.e. plant stem.)
d Blütenstand *m*
f inflorescence *f*
p inflorescência *f*

2919 **in form of a powder**
(Prod.)
(Food processing technology; product characteristic.)
d in Pulverform
f en poudre
p em forma de pó

2920 **infusion**
(Prod.)
(Food processing technology; extraction of principles by hot water.)
d Aufguss *m*
f infusion *f*
p infusão *f*

* **infusion of the leaves of wild endive → 5902**

* **infusorial earth → 1631**

2921 **ingredient**
(Prod.)
(Auxiliary products.)
d Zutat *f*
f ingrédient *m*
p ingrediente *m*

2922 **inhibition of enzymes**
(Biochem.)
(Nutritional science; food biochemistry.)
d Enzymhemmung *f*; Hemmung *f* der Enzymwirkung
f inhibition *f* des enzymes
p inibição *f* das enzimas

2923 **initial aroma**
(Biochem.)
(Enology: wine aroma before aging. Also aroma research.)
d Anfangsaroma *n*
f arôme *m* initial
p aroma *m* inicial

2924 **initial mixture**
(Prod.)
(Food processing technology; ref. e.g. to distillation.)
d Ausgangsgemisch *n*
f mélange *m* initial
p mistura *f* inicial

2925 **initiation of biochemical reactions**
(Biochem.)
(Food biochemistry.)
d Beginn *m* biochemischer Reaktionen
f commencement *m* des réactions biochimiques
p início *m* das reações bioquímcas

2926 **injectable vitamin as vaccination adjuvant**
(Med.)
(Veterinary; e.g. vitamin E for improvement of vaccination efficacy in veterinary treatment.)
d injizierbares Vitamin *n* als Impfhilfsmittel
f vitamine *f* injectable comme auxiliaire de la vaccination
p vitamina *f* injetável como auxiliar de vacinação

* **inner layer of the pericarp → 1888**

* **in neutral environment → 2927**

2927 **in neutral milieu; in neutral environment**
(Biochem.)
(Food biochemistry research and production.)
d in neutralem Milieu; in neutraler Umwelt
f en milieu neutre
p em ambiente neutro

2928 **innocuousness of genetic modifications; harmlessness of genetic modifications**
(Biochem.)
(Biochemical research in nutritional science.)
d Unschädlichkeit *f* genetischer Veränderungen; Unschädlichkeit *f* erblich bedingter Veränderungen
f innocuité *f* des modifications génétiques
p inocuidade *f* das modificações genéticas

2929 **inoculated strain**
(Biochem.)
(Yeast: fermentation in nutritional science.)
d inokulierter Strang *m*; eingeimpfter Strang *m*
f souche *f* inoculée
p cepa *f* inoculada; raça *f* inoculada

2930 **inoculation**
(Biochem.)
(Fermentation in nutritional science.)
d Inokulation *f*; Einimpfung *f*
f inoculation *f*
p inoculação *f*

2931 **inoculation with a lactic ferment**
(Biochem.)
(Nutritional science: e.g. in dairy production processes.)
d Einimpfung *f* von Milchsäurefermenten
f ensemencement *m* en ferments lactiques
p inoculação *f* de fermentos lácticos

2932 **inoculum**
(Biochem.)
(Material for inoculation purposes: Food biochemistry.)
d Inokulationsmaterial *n*
f inoculum *m*
p inóculo *m*

2933 **inorganic** *adj*
(Biochem.)
(Nutritional science; ref. to the chemistry branch other than organic, i.e. non-carbon chemistry and compounds.)
d anorganisch
f inorganique
p inorgânico

2934 **inosinic acid**
(Prod.)
($C_{10}H_{13}N_4O_8P$; alimentary additive for taste enhancing.)
d Inosinsäure *f*
f acide *m* inosinique
p ácido *m* inosínico

2935 **inositol**
(Biochem.)
($C_6H_{12}O_6$; meso-Inositol; bios I: ref. to food biochemistry: e.g. growth factor for yeast.)
d Inosit *n*
f inositol *m*
p inositol *m*

* **inositolhexaphosphoric acid → 4164**

2936 **insecticide**
(Agr.)
(Botany. Insect destroying agent.)
d Insektizid *n*; Insektenbekämpfungsmittel *n*; Insektenvertilgungsmittel *n*
f insecticide *m*
p inseticida *m*

2937 **insolubility**
(Prod.)
(Food processing technology; product specification, product characteristic.)
d Unlösbarkeit *f*
f insolubilité *f*
p insolubilidade *f*

2938 **insoluble** *adj*
(Prod.)
(Food processing technology; product specification, product characteristic.)
d unlöslich
f insoluble
p insolúvel

2939 **insoluble in water**
(Prod.)
(Food processing technology: product characteristic.)
d unlöslich in Wasser
f insoluble dans l'eau
p insolúvel na água

2940 **insoluble products**
(Prod.)
(Food processing technology: product characteristic.)
d unlösbare Produkte *npl*; unlösliche Produkte *npl*
f produits *mpl* insolubles
p produtos *mpl* insolúveis

2941 **instant** *adj*
(Prod.)
(Food processing technology: ref. to powdery extracts, immediately dissolved, ready for use by addition of liquids.)
d instant
f instantané
p instantâneo

2942 **instant beverage**
(Prod.)
(Beverages. See instant.)
d Instantgetränk *n*
f boisson *f* instantanée
p bebida *f* instantânea

2943 **instant beverage powder; instant drink powder**
(Prod.)
(Food processing technology.)
d Instanttrinkpulver *n*
f poudre *f* instantanée pour boissons; poudre *f* pour boissons à dissolution instantanée
p pó *m* de refresco instantâneo

2944 **instant cocoa**
(Prod.)
(Food processing technology; See instant.)
d Instantkakao *m*; Kakao instant *m*
f cacao *m* instantané
p chocolate *m* instantâneo

2945 **instant coffee**
(Prod.)
(Food processing technology; See instant.)
d Instantkaffee *m*; Kaffee instant *m*
f café *m* instantané
p café *m* instantâneo

2946 **instant dessert**
(Prod.)
(Food processing technology; dessert product to be turned instantaneously ready for consumption by addition of e.g. milk.)
d Instantnachtisch *m*; Instantnachspeise *f*; Instantdessert *n*
f dessert *m* instantané
p sobremesa *f* instantânea

* **instant drink powder → 2943**

2947 **instant flour**
(Med.)
(Baby nutrition.)
d Instantmehl *n*; sofortgebrauchfertiges Mehl *n*
f farine *f* instantanée
p farinha *f* instantânea

2948 **instantly soluble** *adj*
(Prod.)
(Food processing technology: instant beverages.)
d sofort löslich
f instantanément soluble
p solúvel instantâneamente

2949 **instant milk powder**
(Prod.)
(Dairy product.)

d Instantmilchpulver *n*
f lait *m* en poudre instantané
p pó *m* de leite instantâneo

2950 **instant pudding**
(Prod.)
(Food processing technology; See instant.)
d Instantpudding *m*
f flan *m* instantané
p pudim *m* instantâneo

2951 **instant soup**
(Prod.)
(Food processing technology; See instant.)
d Instantsuppe *f*, Suppe *f* instant
f potage *m* instantané
p sopa *f* instantânea

* **insufficient lactose digestion → 3345**

2952 **insufficient maturity**
(Agr.)
(Botany; biologic constitution of the fruit.)
d ungenügende Reife *f*
f maturité *f* insuffisante
p maturidade *f* insuficiente

2953 **insufficient protein gain**
(Agr.)
(Cattle breeding and nutrition; ref. to quantitative and qualitative makeup of feed ration: e.g. symptom of vitamin B_{12} deficiency.)
d ungenügender Eiweißansatz *m*
f gain *m* protéique insuffisant
p ganho *m* insuficiente de proteína

2954 **insulin**
(Med.)
(Polypeptide hormone, secreted by the Langerhans beta cells in the pancreas: carbohydrate metabolism: regulation of the glucose level in blood; lack of insulin: diabetes mellitus.)
d Insulin *n*
f insuline *f*
p insulina *f*

2955 **insulin resistant diabetes**
(Med.)
(Diabetes type.)
d insulinresistenter Diabetes *m*; insulinresistente Zuckerkrankheit *f*
f diabète *m* résistant à insuline
p diabetes *m* resistente à insulina

2956 **intensify** *v* **the food flavour**
(Prod.)
(Food processing technology; use of natural products as condiments, e.g. mustard.)
d den Geschmack der Nahrungsmittel verstärken
f relever la flaveur d'aliments
p reforçar o paladar dos alimentos

2957 **intensity**
(Prod.)
(Aroma/fragrance research and production. High degree of strength, feeling; olfactory perception.)
d Intensität *f*
f intensité *f*
p intensidade *f*

2958 **intensity of the aroma**
(Prod.)
(Aroma/fragrance research and production; ref. to organoleptic product quality.)
d Aroma-Intensität *f*
f intensité *f* de l'arôme
p intensidade *f* do aroma

2959 **intensive agriculture**
(Agr.)
(Agricultural systems.)
d Intensivanbau *m*; intensiver Anbau *m*
f agriculture *f* intensive
p agricultura *f* intensiva

2960 **intensive exploitation**
(Agr.)
(Agricultural system and management.)
d intensive Nutzung *f*, intensive Ausnutzung *f*
f exploitation *f* intensive
p exploração *f* intensiva

* **intensive industrial livestock raising → 2961**

2961 **intensive industrial livestock rearing; intensive industrial livestock raising**
(Agr.)
(Livestock; ref. to method of farm animal raising.)
d intensive industrielle Züchtung *f*
f élevage *m* industriel intensif
p criação *f* industrial intensiva

2962 **intensive poultry farming**
(Agr.)
(Poultry farming; ref. to intensive farming procedures for productivity increase; raising in henhouses (cage system), not in the open fields.)
d Intensivgeflügelhaltung *f*
f élevage *m* avicole intensif
p avicultura *f* de confinamento

2963 **intensive production system**
(Agr.)
(Farming system.)

d intensives Produktionssystem *n*
f système *m* intensif de production
p sistema *m* intensivo de produção

2964 interaction
(Med.)
(Between medicaments and foodstuff: e.g. milk products inhibit resorption of some antibiotics.)
d Wechselwirkung *f*
f interaction *f*
p interação *f*

2965 interaction of ions
(Biochem.)
(Nutritional science; food biochemistry.)
d Interaktion *f* zwischen Ionen; Wechselwirkung *f* zwischen Ionen
f interaction *f* entre ions
p interação *f* entre íons

2966 interesterification
(Biochem.)
(Nutritional science: Treatment of fats following a glyceride-structure modification: e.g. improving fat cream quality.)
d Interesterifikation *f*
f interestérification *f*
p interesterificação *f*

2967 intermediary metabolism
(Med.)
(Metabolic process between the end of assimilation and the beginning of dissimilation.)
d Intermediärstoffwechsel *m*
f métabolisme *m* intermédiaire
p metabolismo *m* intermediário

2968 intermediate for chemical synthesis
(Prod.)
(Food processing technology.)
d Zwischenprodukt *n* für chemische Synthesen
f produit *m* intermédiaire pour synthèses chimiques
p produto *m* intermediário para sínteses químicas

2969 intermediate host
(Med.)
(Parasitology: e.g. an animal in which the parasite continues its laval phase of existence.)
d Zwischenwirt *m*
f hôte *m* intermédiaire
p hospedeiro *m* intermediário

2970 intermediate notes
(Prod.)
(Aroma/fragrance research and production; ref. to aroma note characteristics.)
d Zwischennoten *fpl*
f notes *fpl* intermédiaires
p notas *fpl* intermediárias

2971 intermediate product in the food industry
(Prod.)
(Food processing technology, e.g. milk powder.)
d Zwischenprodukt *n* in der Nahrungsmittelindustrie
f produit *m* intermédiaire dans les industries alimentaires
p produto *m* intermediário nas indústrias alimentícias

2972 internal organs
(Med.)
(Anatomy; internal parts of the body.)
d innere Organe *npl*
f organes *mpl* internes
p órgãos *mpl* internos; vísceras *fpl*

2973 interruption of fermentation
(Biochem.)
(Fermentation in nutritional science.)
d Gärungsstockung *f*; Gärungsabbruch *m*
f arrêt *m* de la fermentation
p paralização *f* da fermentação

2974 interruptive fermentation
(Biochem.)
(Fermentation in nutritional science.)
d stockende Gärung *f*
f fermentation *f* languissante; fermentation *f* interruptive
p fermentação *f* interruptiva

2975 interrupt *v* wine fermentation; stop *v* wine fermentation
(Biochem.)
(Enology: vinification: conversion of grape fruit into wine by fermentation processes.)
d Weingärung unterbrechen
f muter; arrêter la fermentation du vin
p interromper a fermentação do vinho

2976 intervention by mould growing
(Biochem.)
(Microbiology.)
d Schimmelbefall *m*
f intervention *f* de moisissures
p intervenção *f* do bolor

2977 intervention potential of biological processes
(Biochem.)
(Biochemical research, e.g. in genetic engineering; nutritional science.)
d Potential *n* der biologischen Verfahrenseingriffe

f potentiel *m* d'intervention des procédés biologiques
p potencial *m* de intervenção dos processos biológicos

* **intervention through dietetics → 1650**

* **intestinal absorption → 1917**

* **intestinal absorption of tocopherols → 1918**

2978 **intestinal contents**
(Med.)
(Digestion process.)
d Darminhalt *m*; Inhalt *m* des Darmes
f contenu *m* intestinal
p conteúdo *m* intestinal

2979 **intestinal flora**
(Med.)
(Bacterial flora of the intestinal tract: vitamin K synthesis; faeces production.)
d Darmflora *f*
f flore *f* intestinale
p flora *f* intestinal

2980 **intestinal infection**
(Med.)
(Infection of the intestine.)
d Darminfektion *f*
f infection *f* intestinale
p infecção *f* intestinal

2981 **intestinal irrigation**
(Med.)
(Irrigation process of washing a hollow organ, e.g. with water.)
d Darmspülung *f*; Darmeinlauf *m*; Klistier *n*
f irrigation *f* intestinale
p lavagem *f* intestinal; clister *m*

2982 **intestinal juice**
(Med.)
("Succus entericus".)
d Darmsaft *m*
f suc *m* intestinal
p suco *m* intestinal

2983 **intestinal malabsorption**
(Med.)
(Condition which could lead to subnutrition, deficiencies etc.)
d intestinale Absorptionsstörung *f*; Aufnahmestörung *f* des Darmkanals; Aufnahmestörung *f* des Darmtraktes
f malabsorption *f* intestinale
p má absorção *f* intestinal

2984 **intestinal non-absorption**
(Med.)
(Absorption problems of certain vitamins, causing deficiency problems.)
d Nichtabsorption *f* durch den Darm
f non-absorption *f* intestinale
p não-absorção *f* intestinal

2985 **intestine**
(Med.)
(Anatomy; bowel; gut; alimentary canal section, extending from the stomach to the anus.)
d Darm *m*
f intestin *m*
p intestino *m*

2986 **in the form of the pure substance**
(Prod.)
(Vitamins in nutrition; vitamin presentation form.)
d in Form der Reinsubstanz
f sous la forme de la substance pure
p em forma de substância pura

2987 **intima**
(Med.)
(Anatomy; tuna intima; inner layer of the wall of blood vessels.)
d Intima *f*
f intima *f*
p íntima *f*

2988 **intolerance against cow's milk**
(Med.)
(Nutrition in medicine.)
d Intoleranz *f* gegen Kuhmilch; Unverträglichkeit *f* der Kuhmilch
f intolérance *f* au lait de vache
p intolerância *f* ao leite de vaca

2989 **intolerance against gluten**
(Med.)
(Metabolic disturbance.)
d Intoleranz *f* gegen Gluten; Intoleranz *f* gegen Klebereiweiß
f intolérance *f* au gluten
p intolerância *f* ao glúten

2990 **intolerance to proteins of cow's milk**
(Med.)
(Especially ref. to baby nutrition.)
d Kuhmilchproteinintoleranz *f*; Kuhmilchproteinunverträglichkeit *f*
f intolérance *f* aux protéines du lait de vache
p intolerância *f* às proteínas do leite de vaca

2991 **intracellular** *adj*
(Biochem.)
(Nutritional science: e.g. ref. to cell water, contained within the cell as a cell compound.)
d intrazellular; intrazellulär

f intracellulaire
p intracelular

2992 **intracellular localization of vitamins**
(Biochem.)
(Veterinary; ref. to certain vitamins in the cells of the animal body.)
d intrazelluläre Lokalisierung *f* von Vitaminen; intrazelluläre Zuordnung *f* von Vitaminen
f localisation *f* intracellulaire des vitamines
p localização *f* intracelular de vitaminas

2993 **intracellular respiration**
(Med.)
(Vitamin functions within the cells: e.g. ref. to vitamin E.)
d intrazelluläre Atmung *f*
f respiration *f* intratissulaire
p respiração *f* intracelular

2994 **introduction of strange genes**
(Biochem.)
(Biochemical research in nutritional science.)
d Einführung *f* von Fremdgenen
f introduction *f* de gènes étrangers
p introdução *f* de genes estranhos

2995 **introduction of truck farming**
(Agr.)
(Biological agriculture; vegetable gardening; horticulture.)
d Einführung *f* des Gemüseanbaues
f implantation *f* de cultures maraîchères
p introdução *f* da horticultura

2996 **inversion**
(Biochem.)
(Food biochemistry. Decomposition of saccharose, into a mixture of glucose and fructose, related to plane rotation of polarized light, from dextrorotatory to levorotatory.)
d Inversion *f*
f inversion *f*
p inversão *f*

* **invertase → 4775**

2997 **invert sugar**
(Prod.)
(Food processing technology; dextrose/levulose mixture.)
d Invertzucker *m*
f sucre *m* inverti
p açúcar *m* invertido

2998 **"in vitro" behaviour**
(Biochem.)
(Microbiology: research.)
d "In-vitro"-Verhalten *n*
f comportement *m* "in vitro"
p comportamento *m* "in vitro"

2999 **iodine**
(Med.)
(Symbol: I. E.g. necessary for the synthesis of the thyroid hormone.)
d Jod *n*
f iode *m*
p iodo *m*

3000 **iodine contents**
(Prod.)
(Food processing technology: addition of iodine in foodstuffs.)
d Jodgehalt *m*
f teneur *f* en iode
p teor *m* de iodo

3001 **iodine deficiency**
(Prod.)
(Food processing technology: nutritional problem, goitre risk.)
d Jodmangel *m*
f carence *f* en iode
p deficiência *f* de iodo

* **iodine number → 3004**

3002 **iodine-poor nutrition**
(Med.)
(Goitre risk.)
d jodarme Ernährung *f*
f alimentation *f* pauvre en iode
p alimentação *f* pobre em iodo

3003 **iodine-rich fishes**
(Agr.)
(Saltwater fish quality.)
d jodreiche Fische *mpl*
f poissons *mpl* riches en iode
p peixes *mpl* ricos de iodo

3004 **iodine value; iodine number**
(Prod.)
(Food processing technology; ref. to the quantity of iodine (expressed in gram) which can be fixed on the double bonds of unsaturated fatty acids, within 100 g of lipids.)
d Jodnummer *f*, Jodwert *m*
f indice *m* d'iode
p número *m* de iodo

3005 **iodized milk**
(Med.)
(Regimens, diets; hyperthyroidism prevention.)
d jodierte Milch *f*
f lait *m* iodé
p leite *m* iodado

3006 **iodized table salt**
(Prod.)
(Regimens, diets; e.g. to avoid goitre; hyperthyroidism prevention.)
d jodiertes Speisesalz *n*; Jodspeisesalz *n*
f sel *m* de table iodé
p sal *m* de cozinha iodado

3007 **ion-exchange chromatography**
(Biochem.)
(Amino acids/protein analysis in nutritional science.)
d Ionenaustauschchromatographie *f*
f chromatographie *f* d'échange d'ions
p cromatografia *f* de intercâmbio de íons; cromatografia *f* de intercâmbio iônico

3008 **ion-exchange resins**
(Biochem.)
(Food processing technology: used e.g. in water treatment: water softening.)
d Ionenaustauscher *mpl*; Ionenaustauschharz *n*
f résines *fpl* échangeuses d'ions
p resinas *fpl* trocadoras de íons

3009 **ionization**
(Biochem.)
(Nutritional science; the degree of ionization determines the strength of an acid: pH value.)
d Ionisation *f*
f ionisation *f*
p ionisação *f*

3010 **ionizing foodstuff irradiation**
(Biochem.)
(Food biochemistry: e.g. ionizing irradiation of foodstuffs: treatment for microorganism elimination; preservation process.)
d ionisierende Nahrungsmittelbestrahlung *f*
f irradiation *f* ionisante des aliments
p irradiação *f* ionizante dos produtos alimentícios; irradiação *f* ionizante dos alimentos

3011 **ionone**
(Prod.)
($C_{13}H_{20}O$; prime material for aroma/fragrance production.)
d Jonon *n*
f ionone *f*
p ionona *f*

3012 **iron**
(Biochem.)
(Fe. Trace element activity e.g. within enzymes and respiratory pigments, esp. hemoglobin.)
d Eisen *n*
f fer *m*
p ferro *m*

3013 **iron(III) colloid**
(Biochem.)
(Nutritional science. Enology.)
d Eisen(III)kolloid *n*
f colloïde *m* ferrique
p colóide *m* férrico

3014 **iron complex salt**
(Prod.)
(Food processing technology.)
d Eisenkomplexsalz *n*
f sel *m* de complexe de fer
p sal *m* de complexo de ferro

3015 **iron deficiency**
(Med.)
(Veterinary; mineral (Fe) deficiency, causing e.g. anaemia, growth reduction, decrease in fattening and milk production.)
d Eisenmangel *m*
f carence *f* en fer
p deficiência *f* de ferro

3016 **iron-deficiency anaemia**
(Med.)
(Nutritional anaemia: iron deficiency.)
d Eisenmangelblutarmut *f*; Eisenmangelanämie *f*
f anémie *f* par carence en fer
p anemia *f* ferropriva

* **iron-enriched milk → 3548**

3017 **iron oxides**
(Prod.)
(Prime material for food (surface) dyes. Foodstuff colorants.)
d Eisenoxide *npl*
f oxydes *mpl* de fer
p óxidos *mpl* de ferro

3018 **iron oxides of high analytical purity**
(Prod.)
(Food colorants; food dyes; insoluble pigment forms.)
d Eisenoxide *npl* hoher analytischer Reinheit
f oxydes *mpl* de fer d'une pureté analytique élevée
p óxidos *mpl* de ferro de pureza analítica elevada

3019 **iron-related catalysis**
(Biochem.)
(Nutritional science; ref. to lipid oxidation in meat.)
d mit Eisen verbundene Katalyse *f*; eisenbedingte Katalyse *f*
f catalyse *f* dépendante du fer
p catálise *f* relacionada ao ferro

3020 **iron resorption**
(Med.)
(Ref. to assimilation of iron.)
d Eisenresorption *f*
f résorption *f* du fer
p ressorção *f* do ferro; reabsorção *f* do ferro

3021 **irradiation**
(Biochem.)
(Microbiology; e.g. ionizing irradiation of foodstuffs: treatment of microorganism elimination. Ultraviolet irradiation: superficial treatment of mould prevention.)
d Irradiation *f*; Bestrahlung *f*
f irradiation *f*
p irradiação *f*

3022 **irreversible biochemical process**
(Biochem.)
(Food biochemistry.)
d irreversibler biochemischer Prozess *m*; nicht umkehrbarer biochemischer Vorgang *m*
f processus *m* biochimique irréversible
p processo *m* bioquímico irreversível

3023 **irreversible reaction**
(Biochem.)
(Food biochemistry.)
d irreversible Reaktion *f*; nicht umkehrbare Reaktion *f*
f réaction *f* irréversible
p reação *f* irreversível

* **irrigation of the stomach → 2455**

3024 **irrigation water; sprinkling water**
(Agr.)
(Biological agriculture: Soil/culture treatment.)
d Besprengungswasser *n*; Berieselungswasser *n*
f eau *f* d'arrosage
p água *f* de irrigação; água *f* de rega

3025 **ischaemic cardiopathy; ischemic cardiopathy**
(Med.)
(Heart disease by blood vessel obstruction, e.g. due to incorrect nutritional habits.)
d ischämisches Herzleiden *n*
f cardiopathie *f* ischémique
p cardiopatia *f* isquémica

* **ischemic cardiopathy → 3025**

3026 **isoamyl acetate; 3-methylbutyl acetate**
(Prod.)
($C_7H_{14}O_2$. Amylacetic ester. Aroma/flavouring agent, fruity, pear-like note.)
d Isoamylacetat *n*; 3-Methylbutylacetat *n*
f acétate *m* d'isoamyle; acétate *m* de méthyle-3-butyle
p acetato *m* de iso-amila; acetato *m* de metil-3-butila

3027 **isoamyl butyrate**
(Prod.)
($C_9H_{18}O_2$; aroma/fragrance prime material; sweet-fruity, e.g. apricot-like flavours.)
d Isoamylbutyrat *n*
f butyrate *m* d'isoamyle
p butirato *m* de iso-amila

3028 **isoamyl isovalerate; isoamyl valerianate**
(Prod.)
($C_{10}H_{20}O_2$; flavouring prime material e.g. for baker's shop products, in liqueurs: apple note.)
d Isoamylisovalerat *n*
f isovalérate *m* d'isoamyle
p isovalerato *m* de isoamila

* **isoamyl valerianate → 3028**

3029 **isoascorbic acid**
(Prod.)
($C_6H_8O_6$; erythorbic acid; isovitamin C; ascorbic acid isomer, having only faible vitamin C activity; antioxidant.)
d Isoascorbinsäure *f*
f acide *m* isoascorbique
p ácido *m* isoascórbico

3030 **isobutyric acid; isopropylformic acid**
(Prod.)
($C_4H_8O_2$; fragrance/flavour prime material.)
d Isobuttersäure *f*
f acide *m* isobutyrique
p ácido *m* isobutírico

3031 **isolation of enzymes; enzyme isolation**
(Biochem.)
(Nutritional science.)
d Enzymisolierung *f*
f isolement *m* d'enzymes
p isolamento *m* das enzimas

3032 **isoleucine**
(Biochem.)
($C_6H_{13}NO_2$. Essential dietary amino acid and essential amino acid ingredient in human and cow's milk.)
d Isoleucin *n*
f isoleucine *f*
p isoleucina *f*

3033 **isomer**
(Biochem.)
(Nutritional science: Compounds having the same number of atoms however different structural arrangements: glucose and fructose: $C_6H_{12}O_6$.)

d Isomer *n*
f isomère *m*
p isômero *m*

* **isopropylbenzene → 1450**

* **isopropylformic acid → 3030**

3034 **isotonic** *adj*
(Biochem.)
(Nutritional science: Characteristic of two solutions having the same concentration and thus the same osmotic pressure.)
d isotonisch
f isotonique
p isotônico

3035 **isotope**
(Biochem.)
(Atoms having the same atomic number (atomic weight): Nutritional science: Isotopes accompany the elements during metabolism; they are detectable due to their irradiation: used for tracing.)
d Isotop *n*
f isotope *m*
p isótopo *m*

* **isovaleral → 3036**

3036 **isovaleraldehyde; isovaleric aldehyde; isovaleral**
(Prod.)
($C_5H_{10}O$; flavour prime material.)
d Isovaleraldehyd *n*
f isovaléraldéhyde *m*
p aldeído *m* iso-valérico

* **isovalerianic acid → 3037**

3037 **isovaleric acid; isovalerianic acid**
(Prod.)
($C_5H_{10}O_2$; flavour prime material; in rum, butter, cheese etc. notes.)
d Isovaleriansäure *f*
f acide *m* isovalérianique
p ácido *m* isovalérico

* **isovaleric acid ethyl ester → 1982**

* **isovaleric aldehyde → 3036**

3038 **Italian bread stick**
(Prod.)
(Italian bread type, crisp, dry, biscuit consistency.)
d italienisches knuspriges Stangenbrot *n*
f gressin *m*
p baguete *f* italiana

J

* **jackass → 463**

3039 **jackfruit** (close to breadfruit)
(Agr.)
("Artocarpus integrifolia", "Artocarpus heterophyllus", "Artocarpus integra". Huge fruits with edible pulp. Origin: Asia; very common in Brazil.)
d Brotfrucht *f*
f fruit *m* du jaquier; fruit *m* du jacquier (*proche du fruit de pain*)
p jaca *f* (*próxima à fruta-pão*)

* **jam → 3389**

3040 **jasmine**
(Prod.)
(Flavour note: natural: flower of "Jasmina grandiflorum"; can be artificially obtained by synthesis from organic intermediates.)
d Jasmin *m*
f jasmin *m*
p jasmim *m*

3041 **jaw**
(Med.)
(Anatomy.)
d Kinnlade *f*, Kinnbacken *m*
f mâchoire *f*
p maxila *f*, queixada *f*

3042 **jejunum**
(Med.)
(Small intestine section.)
d Leerdarm *m*
f jéjunum *m*
p jejuno *m*

3043 **jellied dessert**
(Prod.)
(Gastronomy.)
d gelierter Dessert *m*; gelierter Nachtisch *m*
f dessert *m* gélifié
p sobremesa *f* gelificada

3044 **jellied milk**
(Prod.)
(Gastronomy.)
d gelierte Milch *f*
f lait *m* gélifié
p leite *m* gelificado

3045 **jellied sweets**
(Prod.)
(Gastronomy.)
d gelierte Süßigkeiten *fpl*
f confiserie *f* gélifiée
p doce *mpl* gelificado

3046 **jellification**
(Prod.)
(Food processing technology; ref. to an accidental viscosity alteration of frozen eggs: accident during freezing processes.)
d Gelierung *f*
f gélification *f*
p aparência *f* gelatiniforme

3047 **jelly roll**
(Prod.)
(Confectionary.)
d Biskuitrolle *f*
f biscuit *m* roulé
p rocambole *m*

3048 **jennet**
(Agr.)
(Livestock: female donkey; female ass. A hinny is a hybrid between a stalion and a jennet.)
d Eselin *f*
f ânesse *f*
p jumenta *f*

* **jerked beef → 1030**

* **joints → 443**

3049 **joule**
(Prod.)
((J). Unit of work/energy (English physicist J. Joule, 1818-1889); 1000 J = 1 kJ = 0.239 kcal; 1 calorie = 4.1868 J.)
d Joule *n*
f joule *m*
p joule *m*

3050 **jugged hare**
(Prod.)
(Gastronomy; culinary preparation with stew of hare innards.)
d Hasenpfeffer *m*
f civet *m*; lièvre *m* en civet
p miúdos *mpl* guisados de lebre

3051 **juice concentrate**
(Prod.)
(Food processing technology.)
d Saftkonzentrat *n*
f jus *m* concentré
p suco *m* concentrado

3052 **juice in fermentation; juice in the state of fermentation**
(Biochem.)
(Enology; ref. to fermentation processes.)
d Saft *m*, in Gärung begriffen; in Gärung begriffener Saft *m*
f jus *m* en fermentation
p suco *m* em fermentação

* **juice in the state of fermentation → 3052**

3053 **juice obtained by dripping process**
(Prod.)
(Food processing technology; juice production method.)
d Tropfsaft *m*; abgetropfter Saft *m*
f jus *m* de goutte
p sumo *m* de gotejamento; sumo *m* obtido por gotejamento

3054 **juice of the fruit pulp**
(Agr.)
(Ref. to fruit treatment.)
d Saft *m* des Fruchtmarks
f jus *m* de la pulpe de fruits
p sumo *m* da polpa de frutas; suco *m* da polpa de frutas

3055 **juice recuperated by expression**
(Prod.)
(Aroma production.)
d Saft *m* angefallen durch Auspressen; durch Auspressen angefallener Saft *m*
f jus *m* récupéré par pressurage
p suco *m* recuperado por expressão; suco *m* recuperado por espremedura

3056 **juiciness; succulence**
(Prod.)
(Food processing technology; product characteristic; e.g. meat characteristic.)
d Saftigkeit *f*
f jutosité *f*; succulence *f*
p suculência *f*

* **juicy** *adj* **→ 5295**

3057 **julienne soup**
(Prod.)
(Gastronomy. Consommé made of vegetables sliced into strips (julienned vegetables).)
d Gemüsesuppe *f* à Julienne
f julienne *f*; julienne *f* de légumes
p sopa *f* de legumes Juliana

3058 **juniper**
(Agr.)
(Botany. "Juniperus communis"; Juniper berry. Used in gin preparation, flavouring of smoked meat and canned food.)
d Wacholder *m*
f genièvre *m*
p zimbro *m*; junípero

3059 **juniper berry oil**
(Prod.)
("Juniperus communis L."; Used e.g. as prime material for the production of liqueurs.)
d Wacholderbeerenöl *n*
f huile *f* de la baie de genièvre
p óleo *m* de bago de zimbro

* **junket → 1462**

K

* **kabob → 3061**

3060 **kale; curly kale**
(Agr.)
(Horticulture; "Brassica oleracea acephala"; cabbage.)
d Grünkohl *m*
f chou *m* vert
p couve *f* verde; couve *f* galega

3061 **kebab; kebob; kabob**
(Prod.)
(Gastronomy; spit with pieces of meat: lamb, beef and mutton.)
d Kebab *m*; Kebabbratspieß *m*
f chiche-kebab *m*
p espetinho *m* de carne

* **kebob → 3061**

3062 **kefir drink**
(Prod.)
(Beverages. Drink of the Balkans made from fermented milk (streptococcus, lactobacillus and yeast) with low content of alcohol.)
d Kefir *m*
f képhir *m*; kéfir *m*
p kefir *m*

* **kelp → 4872**

3063 **ketchup; catsup**
(Prod.)
(Gastronomy; seasoned sauce made from tomatoes.)
d Ketschup *n/m*; Ketchup *n/m*
f ketchup *m*
p ketchup *m*

3064 **ketogenesis**
(Med.)
(Lipid metabolism: ketone body production; energy source.)
d Ketonbildung *f*
f cétogenèse *f*
p cetogênese *f*

3065 **ketone bodies**
(Med.)
(Acetone bodies; produced during fat metabolism.)
d Ketonkörper *mpl*
f corps *mpl* cétoniques
p corpos *mpl* cetônicos

3066 **ketones**
(Med.)
(Ketone bodies are substances of the ultimate phase of fatty acid degradation (fat metabolism). Increased ketone levels in the tissues = ketosis (metabolism deficiency).)
d Ketone *npl*
f cétones *fpl*
p cetonas *fpl*

3067 **ketonuria**
(Med.)
(Diabetes mellitus consequence: Presence of ketone bodies in the urine.)
d Ketonurie *f*
f cétonurie *f*
p cetonúria

3068 **ketosis**
(Med.)
(Increased level of ketone bodies in the organism: fat metabolism deficiency.)
d Ketose *f*
f cétose *f*
p cetose *f*

3069 **ketosis syndrome**
(Med.)
(Symptom group occurring together with ketonuria and/or ketonaemia (Diabetes mellitus).)
d Ketosesyndrom *n*
f syndrome *m* de cétose
p síndrome *m* de cetose

* **kid → 5966**

3070 **kid glove leather**
(Agr.)
(Agricultural industrial product.)
d Glacéleder *n*
f chevreau *m* glacé
p couro *m* de cabra tipo "megis"

3071 **kidney**
(Med.)
(Anatomy; pair of blood-filtration organs.)
d Niere *f*
f rein *m*
p rim *m*

* **kieselguhr → 1631**

3072 **kinds of bread; types of bread**
(Prod.)
(Bakery.)
d Brotsorten *fpl*

f sortes *fpl* de pain
p tipos *mpl* de pães; qualidades *fpl* de pães

3073 **kipper**
(Agr.)
(Fish. Kippered (salted and smoked) herring.)
d gesalzener Räucherhering *m*
f kipper *m*
p arenque *m* salgado defumado

3074 **knead** *v*
(Prod.)
(Food processing technology. Working process for dough and cake mixture treatment, to render the product firm.)
d kneten; durchkneten
f pétrir; malaxer
p amassar; sovar

3075 **kneading of a mixture**
(Prod.)
(Food processing technology, e.g. in bakery.)
d Durchkneten *n* einer Mischung
f pétrissage *m* d'un mélange
p amassadura *f* de uma mistura

3076 **knuckle of veal; osso bucco**
(Prod.)
(Gastronomy; generally braised shank of the veal. Italian dish when the bone is served with marrow and tomatoes, prepared with white wine.)
d Kalbshachse *f*; Kalbshaxe *f*
f jarret *m* de veau; osso buco *m*
p pernil *m* de vitela; osso buco *m*

3077 **kohlrabi**
(Agr.)
(Horticulture. "Brassica oleracea var. gongylodes", cabbage.)
d Kohlrabi *m*
f chou-rave *m*
p couve-rábano *m*

3078 **kosher** *adj*
(Prod.)
(Food processing technology. Foodstuffs prepared as to the Hebraic law.)
d koscher
f kasher; casher
p kosher

3079 **Kreb's cycle; citric acid cycle**
(Biochem.)
(As to the English biochemist Sir H. A. Krebs (1900-1981). Ref. to reactions within the cells, of enzymatic degradation of glucides and lipids etc.: cellular respiration and source of biologic energy.)
d Krebszyklus *m*; Zitronensäurezyklus *m*
f cycle *m* de Krebs; cycle *m* de l'acide citrique
p ciclo *m* de Krebs; ciclo *m* do ácido cítrico

3080 **kryptoxanthin**
(Prod.)
($C_{40}H_{56}O_2$: xanthophyll. Carotenoid dyestuff. No. CEE: E 161. Foodstuff colorant.)
d Kryptoxanthin *n*
f kryptoxanthine *f*
p criptoxantina *f*

***kümmel → 3081**

3081 **kümmel liqueur; kümmel**
(Prod.)
(Alcoholic beverage (a liqueur), flavoured with caraway seeds etc.; alcohol content: around 70%. Origin: Germany, Russia.)
d Kümmellikör *m*; Kümmel *m*
f kummel *m*; liqueur *f* de kummel
p licor *m* de kummel; licor *m* de cúmel

3082 **kumquat**
(Agr.)
(Horticulture. Genus "Fortunella"; of the rue family; small citrus fruit/orange from East Asia.)
d Kumquatorange *f*; Kumquatapfelsine *f*
f kumquat *m*; orange *f* du kumquat
p kumquat *m*

L

3083 **labiates**
(Agr.)
(Botany; family of flower plants with labiate corolla; essential oil bearing, ornamental and plenty of them for medical use.)
d Lippenblüter *mpl*
f labiées *fpl*
p labiadas *fpl*

* **labour → 1334**

3084 **lack of appetite; inappetence**
(Med.)
d Appetitlosigkeit *f*
f manque *m* d'appétit; inappétence *f*
p falta *f* de apetite; inapetência *f*

3085 **lack of movement**
(Med.)
(One of the causes of high blood pressure.)
d Bewegungsmangel *m*
f manque *m* de mouvement
p falta *f* de movimento

3086 **lactalbumin**
(Biochem.)
(Protein of high nutritional value present in milk. Food processing technology: milk whey contains lactalbumin and lactoglobulin; their precipitation is e.g. part of the cheese making process.)
d Laktalbumin *n*
f lactalbumine *f*
p lactalbumina *f*

3087 **lactase**
(Biochem.)
(Occurs in yeast; also pancreatic lactose hydrolyzing enzyme, yielding glucose and galactose.)
d Laktase *f*
f lactase *f*
p lactase *f*

3088 **lactase activity**
(Biochem.)
(Nutritional science. Lactose hydrolyzing enzyme.)
d Laktasewirksamkeit *f*; Laktaseaktivität *f*
f activité *f* lactasique
p atividade *f* da lactase

3089 **lactation**
(Agr.)
(Cattle breeding: releasing of milk e.g. by the cow.)
d Laktation *f*; Milchabsonderung *f*
f lactation *f*
p lactação *f*

3090 **lactic acid**
(Prod.)
($C_3H_6O_3$; e.g. used in formulas for infant-feeding products; e.g. food preservative.)
d Milchsäure *f*
f acide *m* lactique
p ácido *m* láctico; ácido *m* lático

3091 **lactic acid diet**
(Med.)
(Alimentary regimen.)
d Milchsäurediät *f*
f diète *f* d'acide lactique
p dieta *f* de ácido láctico

3092 **lactic acid fermentation**
(Biochem.)
($C_3H_6O_3$; alpha-hydroxypropanoic acid. Characteristic product of sour milk. Acidulant additive in wort (brewing process), in yeast production (bacteria removal); beverages; cheese; confectionary etc.)
d Milchsäuregärung *f*; Milchsäurefermentation *f*
f fermentation *f* d'acide lactique
p fermentação *f* de ácido lático

3093 **lactic acidification**
(Prod.)
(Dairy plant technology: Acidification of cheese by lactic starting material.)
d laktische Säuerung *f*
f acidification *f* lactique
p acidificação *f* lática

3094 **lactic bacteria**
(Biochem.)
(Fermentation in nutritional science: enology.)
d laktische Bakterien *fpl*
f bactéries *fpl* lactiques
p bactérias *fpl* láticas

3095 **lactic dietetic infantile aliment; lactic dietetic infantile nutriment**
(Med.)
(Diets. Special food developed for children of very young age.)
d laktische dietätische Kindernahrung *f*
f aliment *m* lacté diététique infantile
p alimento *m* láctico dietético infantil

* **lactic dietetic infantile nutriment → 3095**

3096 **lactic drink; milk drink**
(Prod.)
(Dairy product; milk-based drink.)
d laktisches Getränk *n*; Milchgetränk *n*
f boisson *f* lactée
p bebida *f* láctica; bebida *f* à base de leite

3097 **lactic ferment**
(Biochem.)
(Saprophytic bacteria of the milk, involved in the process of milk fermentation and cheese production.)
d Milchsäureferment *n*
f ferment *m* lactique
p fermento *m* lático

3098 **lactic fermentation**
(Biochem.)
(Nutritional science; fermentation produced by lactic bacteria.)
d laktische Gärung *f*
f fermentation *f* lactique
p fermentação *f* lática; fermentação *f* láctica

3099 **lactic fermentation in saline medium**
(Biochem.)
(Nutritional science; fermentation produced by lactic bacteria.)
d Milchsäuregärung *f* in salzigem Medium; Milchsäuregärung *f* in salzhaltigem Milieu
f fermentation *f* lactique en milieu salé
p fermentação *f* lática em meio salino

3100 **lactic ion**
(Biochem.)
(Enology: wine fermentation in nutritional science.)
d laktisches Ion *n*
f ion *m* lactique
p íon *m* láctico

3101 **lactic nutriment**
(Med.)
(Regimens, diets.)
d laktisches Nahrungsmittel *n*
f aliment *m* lacté
p alimento *m* lácteo

3102 **lactic nutrition; nutrition based on milk**
(Med.)
(Baby nutrition.)
d Milchnahrung *f*; Ernährung *f* auf Basis von Milch
f alimentation *f* lactée
p alimentação *f* láctica

3103 **lactic secretion**
(Med.)
(Baby nutrition. Ref. to nursing.)
d laktische Sekretion *f*; Milchabsonderung *f*
f sécrétion *f* lactée
p secreção *f* láctea

3104 **lactic streptococcus**
(Biochem.)
(Microbiology: "Streptococcus lactis".)
d laktischer Streptokokkus *m*
f streptocoque *m* lactique
p estreptococo *m* láctico

3105 **lactobacillus**
(Biochem.)
(Microbiology. Lactic-acid producing (from lactose and other types of carbohydrates) bacteria.)
d Laktobazille *f*; Laktobazillus *m*
f lactobacille *m*
p lactobacilo *m*

3106 **lactobacillus acidophilus**
(Biochem.)
(Microbiology: used in the production of fermented milk and milk drinks and in white cheese.)
d Milchsäurebazillus *m*; Milchsäurebakterie *f*
f lactobacille *m* acidophilus
p lactobacilo *m* acidófilo

3107 **lactobacillus casei**
(Biochem.)
(Microbiology: bacterium used in cheese maturation.)
d Laktobazillus *m* casei
f lactobacille *m* casei
p lactobacilo *m* casei

3108 **lactobacillus helveticus**
(Biochem.)
(Microbiology: Ingredient in the production process of cooked white cheese. Also used in "Emmenthaler" type of cheese.)
d Laktobazillus *m* helveticus; helvetische Milchsäurebakterie *f*
f lactobacille *m* helveticus; lactobacille *m* helvétique
p lactobacilus *m* helveticus; lactobacilo *m* helvécio

* **lactofiltration → 3549**

3109 **lactoflavin**
(Biochem.)
($C_{17}H_{20}N_4O_6$. Riboflavin: Vitamin B_2.)
d Laktoflavin *n*
f lactoflavine *f*
p lactoflavina *f*

3110 **lactoglobulin**
(Biochem.)
(Nutritional science; protein present in milk

whey; e.g. cheese making; see: lactalbumin.)
d Laktoglobulin *n*; Lactoglobulin *n*
f lactoglobuline *f*
p lactoglobulina *f*

3111 **lactoprotein**
(Biochem.)
(Nutritional science: constituent of the proteic milk fraction: used in meat treatment: structural and maturation improvement, promotes emulsion of fats.)
d Laktoprotein *n*
f lactoprotéine *f*
p lactoproteína *f*

3112 **lactose; milk sugar**
(Prod.)
($C_{12}H_{22}O_{11}$. Used e.g. for infant feeding; in caloric diets. Baby nutrition.)
d Laktose *f*; Milchzucker *m*
f lactose *f*
p lactose *f*

3113 **lactose compounds**
(Biochem.)
(Food biochemistry: e.g. carbohydrates of the milk.)
d Laktoseverbindungen *fpl*
f composés *mpl* de lactose
p compostos *mpl* de lactose

3114 **lactose digestibility**
(Med.)
(Regimens, diets and eventually to nutritional diseases.)
d Laktoseverdaulichkeit *f*; Laktoseverdaubarkeit *f*
f digestibilité *f* du lactose
p digestibilidade *f* da latose

* **lactose elimination → 3117**

3115 **lactose intolerance**
(Med.)
(Due to the absence of the enzyme, denominated "lactase" in the body.)
d Laktoseunverträglichkeit *f*; Laktoseintoleranz *f*; Milchzuckerunverträglichkeit *f*
f intolérance *f* au lactose
p intolerância *f* à lactose

3116 **lactose monohydrate**
(Biochem.)
($C_{12}H_{22}O_{11}.H_2O$; Food biochemistry.)
d Laktosemonohydrat *n*
f monohydrate *m* de lactose
p monoidrato *m* de lactose

3117 **lactose removal; lactose elimination**
(Prod.)
(Dairy technology: cheese production: elimination of lactose from the product, occurring by dripping.)
d Laktoseabsonderung *f*; Laktoseentfernung *f*
f délactosage *m*
p remoção *f* da lactose; eliminação *f* da lactose

3118 **lactoserum; whey**
(Prod.)
(Dairy product; milk water (milk serum) separated from the coagulable milk part: Cheese production.)
d Laktoserum *m*; Molke *f*
f lactosérum *m*; petit-lait *m*
p lacto-soro *m*; soro *m* de leite

3119 **lactosuria; presence of lactose in the urine**
(Med.)
(May happen during breast feeding.)
d Laktosurie *f*; Laktoseausscheidung *f* mit dem Harn
f lactosurie *f*; présence *f* de lactose dans les urines
p lactosúria *f*; presença *f* de lactose na urina

3120 **lactovegetarian diet**
(Med.)
(Alimentary regimen; certain type of vegetarianism; ref. to dairy products and vegetables.)
d laktovegetabile Diät *f*
f diète *f* lactovégétarienne
p dieta *f* lactovegeteriana

3121 **lactovovegetable diet**
(Med.)
(Alimentary regimen; certain type of vegetarianism; ref. to dairy products (including eggs), vegetables and cereals.)
d ovolaktovegetabile Diät *f*
f diète *f* lactovovégétale
p dieta *f* lactovovegetal

3122 **lactulose; galactosidofructose**
(Med.)
(Activator of the bifid intestinal flora.)
d Laktulose *f*; Galaktosidfruktose *f*
f lactulose *f*
p lactulose *f*; galactosidefrutose *f*

3123 **lacustrine soil**
(Agr.)
(Soil. Lake soil, formed from sediments deposited by lakes.)
d Seeboden *m*
f sol *m* lacustre; sol *m* de lac
p solo *m* de lago

3124 **lager beer**
(Prod.)
(Food processing technology; beer type; denomination refers to the fermentation process type.)
d untergäriges Bier *n*
f bière *f* de fermentation en submersion; bière *f* basse
p cerveja *f* de baixa fermentação

* **lagering of the beer → 3412**

3125 **lake**
(Agr.)
(Soil; ref. to earth science.)
d See *m*
f lac *m*
p lago *m*

3126 **lamb** *v*
(Med.)
(Veterinary science; to bring forth a lamb.)
d lammen
f mettre bas un agneau
p parir um carneiro; parir um borrego

3127 **lamb; yearling lamb**
(Agr.)
(Livestock. Young sheep. Sheep less than one year old.)
d Lamm *n*
f agneau *m*
p cordeiro *m*; anho *m*; borrêgo *m*

3128 **lamb shoulder**
(Prod.)
(Butcher's product; meat joint.)
d Schulter *f* des Lammes; Schulterstück *n* des Lammes
f épaule *f* d'agneau
p paleta *f* do cordeiro

3129 **langouste; spiny lobster; crayfish**
(Prod.)
(Gastronomy. Marine crustacean; seafood.)
d Languste *f*
f langouste *f*
p lagosta *f*

3130 **lard** *v*
(Prod.)
(Food processing technology: process of introducing small pieces of bacon into the meat.)
d spicken
f larder
p lardear

3131 **lard**
(Prod.)
(Butchery.)
d Schweineschmalz *m*; Schweinefett *n*
f saindoux *m*; axonge *f*; graisse *f* de porc fondue
p banha *f*; gordura *f* de porco

3132 **large intestine**
(Med.)
(Anatomy; activity: e.g. water absorption of the content delivered from the small intestine.)
d Dickdarm *m*
f gros intestin *m*
p intestino *m* grosso

3133 **large-scale production**
(Agr.)
(Agricultural production system, agricultural yield.)
d Produktion *f* in großem Maßstab; Großproduktion *f*
f production *f* sur grande échelle
p produção *f* em grande escala; produção *f* em massa

3134 **larva; grub**
(Agr.)
(Apiculture: larva of the bee.)
d Larve *f*
f larve *f*
p larva *f*

3135 **larynx**
(Med.)
(Anatomy; body part: e.g. for air passage and voice production.)
d Kehlkopf *m*
f larynx *m*
p laringe *f*

3136 **lasagna noodles; lasagne noodles**
(Prod.)
(Food processing technology. Noodles in broad ribbon form, and a baked dish of these boiled noodles together with cheese etc.; Italian type.)
d Bandnudeln *fpl* (*Lasagne-Art*)
f lasagne *f*
p lasanha *f*

* **lasagne noodles → 3136**

3137 **lasting taste**
(Prod.)
(Aroma/flavour research and production.)
d anhaltender Geschmack *m*
f saveur *f* persistante
p gosto *m* persistente; sabor *m* prolongado

3138 **latent** *adj*; **dormant** *adj*
(Agr.)
(Botany; inactive now, but capable of growth

later on.)
d latent
f latent
p latente

3139 latent diabetes
(Med.)
(Diabetes mellitus type.)
d latenter Diabetes *m*; latente Zuckerkrankheit *f*
f diabète *m* latent
p diabetes *m* latente

3140 late vine sort; maturing vine sort
(Agr.)
(Climatology in winegrowing.)
d späte Rebsorte *f*
f cépage *m* tardif
p espécie *f* de cepa tardia

3141 late vintage wine
(Agr.)
(Viticulture.)
d Spätlese *f*
f vin *m* tardif; vin *m* de vendanges tardives
p vinho *m* de vindima tardia

3142 laurel; bay
(Agr.)
(Botany. "Laurus nobilis L.".)
d edler Lorbeer *m*
f laurier *m*
p louro *m*

3143 laurel leaves
(Agr.)
(Botany. "Lauraceae". Aromatic leaves used as condiment.)
d Lorbeerblätter *fpl*
f feuilles *fpl* de laurier
p folhas *fpl* de louro

3144 laurel oil
(Agr.)
("Laurus nobilis L."; Oil from the fruits of the laurel.)
d Lorbeeröl *n*
f huile *f* de laurier
p óleo *m* do louro

3145 lauric acid
(Prod.)
($C_{12}H_{24}O_2$; occurs in certain vegetable fats, in coconut oil in form of a glyceride, also in butter; e.g. in fatty acid synthesis: prime material for aroma/fragrance production.)
d Laurinsäure *f*
f acide *m* laurique
p ácido *m* láurico

3146 lauter process for draff settling
(Prod.)
(Food processing technology; Beer brewery process: clarification process.)
d Läutern *n*; Klären *n*
f processus *m* de rectification; processus *m* de clarification
p clarificação *f* por separação do líquido e dos resíduos

3147 laxative *adj*
(Med.)
(Foodstuff characteristic: intestinal peristaltic activation promoting the elimination of salts; e.g. plums. Cellulose-containing food, due to water retention/volume increase.)
d mild abführend
f laxatif
p laxativo

3148 laxative effect
(Med.)
(Ref. to e.g. sorbitol.)
d laxierende Wirkung *f*; abführende Wirkung *f*
f effet *m* laxatif
p efeito *m* laxativo

*** layer → 3149**

*** layer cakes → 5443**

3149 laying hen; layer
(Agr.)
(Poultry raising: hen raised to produce eggs.)
d Legehenne *f*
f pondeuse *f*; poule *f* pondeuse
p poedeira *f*; galinha *f* poedeira

3150 laying of eggs
(Agr.)
(Poultry farming.)
d Eierlegen *n*
f ponte *f*
p postura *f*

3151 leaf stalk; petiole
(Agr.)
(Botany; the leaf stalk supports the leaf; the rhubarb leaf stalk is edible (when cooked).)
d Blattstiel *m*; Blattstengel *m*
f pétiole *m*
p pecíolo *m*

3152 lean *adj*
(Prod.)
(Food processing technology; e.g. meat piece characteristics.)
d mager
f maigre
p magro

3153 lean meat
(Prod.)
(Food processing technology; e.g. meat piece characteristics.)
d Magerfleisch *n*
f viande *f* maigre
p carne *f* magra

3154 lean part of meat
(Prod.)
(Food processing technology; e.g. meat piece characteristics.)
d Stück *n* Mageres
f morceau *m* de maigre
p peça *f* de carne magra

3155 leather
(Agr.)
(Agricultural produce; agricultural industrial product.)
d Leder *n*
f cuir *m*
p couro *m*

3156 leaven; sourdough
(Prod.)
(Food processing technology; fermentation producing substance, e.g. baking powder etc.)
d Sauerteig *m*
f levain *m*
p massa *f* azeda

* **leaven-raised bread → 5115**

3157 lecithin
(Prod.)
(Ca. $C_{43}H_{88}NO_9P$; vitellin; e.g. phosphorus containing emulsifier: in margarines. Used e.g. in chocolates; food antioxidant. In medicine: e.g. treatment of hypercholesterolemia and sprue (psilosis).)
d Lezithin *n*
f lécithine *f*
p lecitina *f*

3158 leek; scallion
(Agr.)
(Horticulture. "Allium porrum".)
d Porree *m*; Lauch *m*
f poireau *m*
p alho-porro *m*; alho-poró *m*; porro *m*

3159 leftover food
(Prod.)
(Gastronomy; later warmed up meal.)
d Speisereste *npl*; aufgewärmtes Essen *n*
f rogatons *mpl*
p sobejos *mpl* de comida

3160 leg
(Prod.)
(Butchery; meat part; joint.)
d Keule *f*
f cuisse *f*
p pernil *m*

3161 leg of mutton
(Prod.)
(Gastronomy.)
d Hammelkeule *f*
f gigot *m* de mouton; cuisse *f* de mouton
p pernil *m* de carneiro; perna *f* de carneiro

3162 legume; pod
(Agr.)
(Botany; plant seed casing, e.g. as with beans.)
d Hülse *f*; Schote *f*
f cosse *f*; gousse *f*; enveloppe *f*
p vagem *f*; folhelho *m*; folhato *m*

3163 leguminous plant
(Agr.)
(Horticulture: "Leguminosae". Legumes.)
d Hülsenfrucht *f*
f légumineuse *f*
p leguminosa *f*

3164 lemon
(Agr.)
(Agricultural produce. "Citrus limonum"; edible acid fruit.)
d Zitrone *f*
f citron *m*
p limão *m*

3165 lemon drink
(Prod.)
(Alcohol-free, carbonic acid gas (carbon dioxide: CO_2) containing beverage, made of fruit juice or essences, sugar and water.)
d Limonade *f*
f citronnade *f*
p refresco *m* de limão

3166 lemon flavours
(Prod.)
(Flavouring product.)
d Zitronenaromen *npl*
f arômes *mpl* de citron
p aromas *mpl* de limão

3167 lemon juice
(Prod.)
(Beverages.)
d Zitronensaft *m*
f jus *m* de citron
p suco *m* de limão

3168 **lemon-like note**
(Prod.)
(Taste; aroma research and production.)
d Zitronennote *f*
f note *f* de citron
p nota *f* de limão

3169 **lemon-like taste**
(Prod.)
(Taste; aroma research and production.)
d Zitronengeschmack *m*
f saveur *f* citron
p sabor *m* de limão

3170 **lemon oil**
(Prod.)
("Citrus limonum L."; peel oil; used for flavouring foods, beverages, pastry etc.)
d Zitronenöl *n*
f essence *f* de citron
p essência *f* de limão

3171 **lemon-peel aroma note**
(Prod.)
(Flavour chemicals; citral: $C_{10}H_{16}O$; ref. to elaboration of aromas: organic chemistry.)
d Zitronenschalengeschmacksnote *f*
f note *f* saveur zeste de citron
p sabor *m* de casca de limão

3172 **lemon-peel note**
(Prod.)
(Taste; aroma research and production.)
d Zitronenschalennote *f*
f note *f* de zeste de citron
p nota *f* de casca de limão

3173 **lemon sole**
(Agr.)
("Pleuronectidae "; edible flatfish.)
d Rotzunge *f*
f limande *f*
p linguado *m*

3174 **lentil**
(Agr.)
(Horticulture; "Lens culinaris"; edible seeds of the leguminous plant.)
d Linse *f*
f lentille *f*
p lentilha *f*

3175 **less hygroscopic** *adj*
(Biochem.)
(Food biochemistry; product characteristic: easily taking up humidity; moisture retaining.)
d weniger hygroskopisch
f moins hygroscopique
p menos higroscópico

3176 **less prestigious wine sorts**
(Prod.)
(Gastronomy; wine quality.)
d weniger renommierte Weine *mpl*
f vins *mpl* moins prestigieux
p vinhos *mpl* menos prestigiados; vinhos *mpl* menos renomeados

3177 **less processed products**
(Prod.)
(Food processing technology and production.)
d weniger weiterverarbeitete Produkte *npl*
f produits *m* peu élaborés
p produtos *mpl* menos transformados

3178 **less volatile product**
(Prod.)
(Aroma/flavour production: ref. to distillation processes.)
d am wenigsten verdunstbares Produkt *n*; am wenigsten flüchtiges Produkt *n*
f produit *m* le moins volatil
p produto *m* menos volátil

* **let** *v* **the tea stand → 1776**

* **lettuce → 829**

3179 **leucine**
(Biochem.)
(Nutritional science: $C_6H_{13}NO_2$; essential amino acid and essential amino acid-ingredient in human and in cow's milk; a nutrient.)
d Leucin *n*
f leucine *f*
p leucina *f*

3180 **leveling**
(Agr.)
(Soil treatment, giving the terrain a horizontal form.)
d Einebnung *f*
f nivellement *m*; aplainissement *m*
p nivelamento *m*; nivelação *f*

3181 **level of odour sensibility thresholds**
(Med.)
(Flavour/fragrance production and research.)
d Ebene *f* der Geruchsempfindlichkeitsschwellen; Niveau *n* der Geruchsempfindlichkeitsschwellen
f niveau *m* des seuils de sensibilité aux odeurs
p nível *m* dos limiares de sensibilidade *f* aos odores

3182 **level of supplementation**
(Med.)
(Veterinary: ref. to vitamin supplementation of feedstuffs and in the animal body.)

d Supplementierungshöhe *f*; Supplementierungsniveau *n*
f niveau *m* de supplémentation
p nível *m* de suplementação

* **levulose → 2391**

3183 **liberate *v* the flavour progressively; release *v* the flavour progressively**
(Prod.)
(Aroma/flavour research and application.)
d Geschmacksstoffe allmählich freisetzen; Geschmacksstoffe progressiv freisetzen
f libérer progressivement les flaveurs
p liberar progressivamente os aromas

3184 **liberation of carbon dioxide**
(Biochem.)
(Enology: wine production; fermentation process.)
d Freiwerden *n* von Kohlendioxid
f dégagement *m* de gaz carbonique; dégagement de dioxyde de carbone
p liberação *f* de gás carbônico; liberação *f* de dióxido de carbone

3185 **liberation of gases**
(Biochem.)
(Fermentation in nutritional science.)
d Bildung *f* von Gasen; Freiwerden *n* von Gasen; Freisetzen *n* von Gasen
f dégagement *m* gazeux
p liberação *f* de gases

* **lice → 3272**

* **licorice → 3248**

3186 **lie *v* fallow**
(Agr.)
(Soil: plowing and leaving untilled.)
d brachlegen; brachliegen
f mettre en jachère; être en friche
p alqueivar; lavrar a terra e deixá-la de pouso

3187 **light diet**
(Med.)
(Alimentary regimen.)
d leichte Diät *f*
f diète *f* légère
p dieta *f* leve

3188 **light sensitive vitamin**
(Biochem.)
(Vitamin biochemistry in nutritional science.)
d lichtempfindliches Vitamin *n*
f vitamine *f* sensible à la lumière
p vitamina *f* sensível à luz

3189 **light wine**
(Prod.)
(Gastronomy: Wine with reduced contents of alcohol.)
d leichter Wein *m*
f vin *m* léger
p vinho *m* leve

* **ligneous *adj* → 5932**

3190 **lignoceric acid**
(Prod.)
($C_{24}H_{48}O_2$; tetracosanoic acid; saturated fatty acid; constituent of most natural fats; prime material.)
d Lignocerinsäure *f*
f acide *m* lignocérique
p ácido *m* lignocérico

3191 **lime**
(Agr.)
(Horticulture; "Citrus aurantifolia"; small greenish fruit with acid pulp, like a small lemon; very common e.g. in Brazil.)
d Limetta *f*; Limette *f*
f limette *f*
p lima *f*

3192 **lime-blossom tea**
(Prod.)
(Genus "Tilia", family "Tiliaceae": linden.)
d Lindenblütentee *m*
f tisane *f* des fleurs du tilleul; infusion *f* de tilleul
p chá *m* da flor da tília; chá *m* de tília

3193 **lime fertilizer**
(Agr.)
(Soil treatment.)
d Kalkdünger *m*
f engrais *m* de chaux
p fertilizante *m* de cálcio

3194 **liming**
(Agr.)
(Leather treatment; application of the liming paste on the fleshside yields wool of improved quality; application on the hairy coat side destroys fur of inferior quality.)
d Schwöden *n*
f plamage *m*; pelainage *m*
p depilamento *m* por meio de pasta

3195 **limiting value**
(Biochem.)
(Nutritional science.)
d Grenzwert *m*
f valeur *f* limite
p valor *m* limite

3196 limit *v* the energy ration
(Med.)
(Alimentary regimen.)
d die Energieration begrenzen
f limiter la ration énergétique
p limitar a ração energética

3197 limonene
(Prod.)
($C_{10}H_{16}$; hydrocarbon of the terpene family; occurs in various ethereal oils; e.g. in lemon essence; aroma/fragrance prime material.)
d Limonen *n*
f limonène *m*
p limoneno *m*

3198 linalool
(Prod.)
($C_{10}H_{18}O$; aroma prime material, flavour chemical; e.g. herbaceous flavour, bergamot-similar aroma.)
d Linalool *n*
f linalol *m*
p linalol *m*

3199 linalyl acetate
(Prod.)
($C_{12}H_{20}O_2$; aroma prime material, e.g. fresh, bergamot flavour.)
d Linalylacetat *n*
f acétate *m* de linalyle
p acetato *m* de linalila

3200 lindane
(Agr.)
($C_6H_6Cl_6$ (T. van der Linden; Dutch chemist, born 1949) hexachlorocyclohexane; insecticide; parasiticide.)
d Lindan *n*
f lindane *m*
p lindano *m*

3201 lineage; pedigree
(Agr.)
(Cattle breeding; genealogy.)
d Stammbaum *m*
f lignage *m*
p linhagem *m*

3202 linoleic acid
(Prod.)
($C_{18}H_{32}O_2$; linolic acid; e.g. as pharmaceutical dietary supplement; e.g. against hypercholesterolemia.)
d Linolsäure *f*
f acide *m* linoléique
p ácido *m* linoléico

3203 linolenic acid
(Prod.)
($C_{18}H_{30}O_2$; multiple unsaturated fatty acid; prime material.)
d Linolensäure *f*
f acide *m* linolénique
p ácido *m* linolênico

3204 lipases
(Biochem.)
(Nutritional science: enzyme, having the property to break down fats, releasing fatty acids.)
d Lipasen *fpl*
f lipases *fpl*
p lipases *fpl*

3205 lipid
(Biochem.)
(Food biochemistry; nutrition; dietary constituents as e.g. fats and substances similar to fats.)
d Lipid *n*; Fettstoff *m*
f lipide *m*
p lipídio *m*

3206 lipid contents
(Prod.)
(Food processing technology, meat quality.)
d Fettstoffgehalt *m*
f teneur *f* en lipides
p teor *m* de lipídio

3207 lipid droplets
(Biochem.)
(Vitamin biochemistry in nutritional science.)
d Lipidtröpfchen *npl*
f gouttelettes *fpl* lipidiques
p gotinhas *fpl* de lipídios

3208 lipid fraction
(Biochem.)
(Nutritional science.)
d Lipidfraktion *f*
f fraction *f* lipidique
p fração *f* lipídica

3209 lipid-free radicals
(Biochem.)
(Food processing technology; ref. to oxidation processes in uncooked meat.)
d lipidfreie Radikale *npl*
f radicaux *mpl* libres de lipides
p radicais *mpl* isentos de lipídios

3210 lipid metabolism; fat metabolism
(Med.)
(Decomposition of the fat-intake by nutrition. A high fat concentration in blood causes hyperlipemia, clouding of the blood plasma.)
d Fettstoffwechsel *m*; Fettmetabolismus *m*
f métabolisme *m* de lipides

p metabolismo *m* dos lipídios; metabolismo *m* das gorduras

3211 **lipid metabolism disturbance**
(Med.)
(One of the causes of overweight; increase of blood-serum level of fats.)
d Fettstoffwechselstörung *f*; Störung *f* des Fettmetabolismus
f trouble *m* du métabolisme des lipides
p deficiência *f* do metabolismo dos lipídios; perturbação *f* do metabolismo dos lipídios

3212 **lipid oxidation in meat**
(Biochem.)
(Nutritional science: quality-reducing factor in meat processing.)
d Lipidoxidation *f* des Fleisches
f oxydation *f* lipidique de la viande
p oxidação *f* lipídica da carne

3213 **lipid oxidation in uncooked meat**
(Biochem.)
(Phenomena in biochemistry, e.g. nutritional science.)
d Lipidoxidation *f* in ungekochtem Fleisch; Lipidoxidation *f* in nicht gekochtem Fleisch
f oxydation *f* lipidique dans la viande non-cuite
p oxidação *f* lipídica *f* na carne não cozida

* **lipid peroxidation → 4105**

3214 **lipids in meat**
(Biochem.)
(Food biochemistry.)
d Fettstoffe *mpl* des Fleisches
f lipides *mpl* présents dans les viandes
p lipídios *mpl* presentes nas carnes

3215 **lipids in poultry products**
(Biochem.)
(Nutritional science: Lipids contribute to some characteristics as flavour/aroma enhancing, tenderness improvement etc.)
d Lipide *npl* in Geflügelprodukten
f lipides *mpl* dans les produits avicoles
p lipídios *mpl* nos produtos avícolas

3216 **lipid stability**
(Biochem.)
(Nutritional science; ref. to lipid oxidation phenomena in meat.)
d Lipidstabilität *f*
f stabilité *f* des lipides
p estabilidade *f* dos lipídios

3217 **lipid supply by nutrition**
(Med.)
(Regimens, diets.)
d Lipidzufuhr *f* durch Ernährung
f apport *m* lipidique alimentaire
p aporte *m* lipídico alimentar

3218 **lipid suspensions**
(Biochem.)
(Food biochemistry.)
d lipidische Suspensionen *fpl*
f suspensions *fpl* lipidiques
p suspensões *f* lipídicas

3219 **lipocardia**
(Med.)
(Cardiac adiposis.)
d Herzverfettung *f*
f lipocardie *f*
p lipocardia *f*; adipose *f* cardíaca

3220 **lipoid** *adj*; **lipoidal** *adj*
(Biochem.)
(Nutritional science: fat-resembling characteristic of a substance.)
d lipoid; fettähnlich
f lipoïde
p lipóide

* **lipoidal** *adj* **→ 3220**

3221 **lipoids**
(Biochem.)
(Nutritional science: e.g. phospholipids and cholesterol: fat-resembling products.)
d Lipoide *npl*
f lipoïdes *mpl*
p substância *f* lipóide

3222 **lipolysis**
(Biochem.)
(Nutritional science: Lipolysis: Hydrolysis of fat; transformation of lipids into fatty acids by the enzyme lipase.)
d Lipolyse *f*
f lipolyse *f*
p lipólise *f*

3223 **lipolytic** *adj*
(Biochem.)
(Nutritional science: ref. to lipolysis, fat hydrolysis.)
d fettspaltend
f lipolytique
p lipolítico

3224 **lipolytic activity**
(Biochem.)
(Nutritional science: Lipolysis: Hydrolysis of fat; transformation of lipids into fatty acids by the enzyme lipase.)
d lipolytische Aktivität *f*; lipolytische Wirksamkeit *f*

f activité *f* lipolytique
p atividade *f* lipolítica

3225 **lipolytic enzymes**
(Biochem.)
(Nutritional science.)
d fettspaltende Enzyme *npl*
f enzymes *fpl* lipolytiques
p enzimas *fpl* lipolíticas

3226 **lipolytic rancidity; lipolytic rancidness**
(Biochem.)
(Food biochemistry; due to fat-hydrolyzing enzymes in stored fatty foodstuff; these enzymes are destroyed by heating the product.)
d lipolytische Ranzigkeit *f*
f rance *m* lipolytique
p ranço *m* lipolítico

* **lipolytic rancidness → 3226**

* **lipoma → 94**

3227 **lipophilic** *adj*
(Biochem.)
(Food biochemistry: Characteristic of showing affinity to fats.)
d fettabsorbierend; fettaufnehmend
f lipophile
p lipófilo

3228 **lipoprotein**
(Med.)
(Vehicle for e.g. cholesterol in blood circulation; a protein/lipid complex.)
d Lipoprotein *n*
f lipoprotéine *f*
p lipoproteína *f*

3229 **lipoprotein carrier; lipoprotein vehicle**
(Biochem.)
(Vitamin biochemistry: ref. to cellular uptake of certain vitamins into cells from its carrier lipoproteins.)
d Lipoproteinträger *m*
f support *m* lipoprotéique; véhicule *m* lipoprotéique
p suporte *m* lipoprotéico

3230 **lipoprotein complex**
(Med.)
(Veterinary; e.g. ref. to vitamin transport in the animal body.)
d Lipoproteinkomplex *m*
f complexe *m* lipoprotéique
p complexo *m* lipoprotéico

3231 **lipoprotein lipase**
(Biochem.)
(Nutritional science: glycerides hydrolyzing enzyme.)
d Lipoproteinlipase *f*
f lipase *f* lipoprotéique
p lipase *f* lipoprotéica

3232 **lipoprotein-receptor**
(Med.)
(Anatomy. Ref. to vitamin biochemistry, vitamin uptake in the body; also veterinary.)
d Lipoproteinrezeptor *m*
f récepteur *m* des lipoprotéines
p receptores *mpl* das lipoproteína

* **lipoprotein vehicle → 3229**

3233 **liposoluble antioxidant; fat-soluble antioxidant**
(Prod.)
(Auxiliary products: Antioxidant.)
d fettlösliches Antioxidant *n*
f antioxydant *m* liposoluble
p antioxidante *m* lipossolúvel

3234 **liposoluble aromas**
(Prod.)
(Flavour chemicals: their characteristics and their production process.)
d fettlösliche Aromen *npl*
f arômes *mpl* liposolubles
p aromas *mpl* lipossolúveis

* **lipuria → 99**

* **liquefied carbon dioxide → 3235**

3235 **liquefied carbonic acid gas; liquefied carbon dioxide**
(Prod.)
(CO_2; used as solvent in extraction processes; e.g. in aroma/flavour research and production: coffee extraction.)
d verflüssigtes Kohlendioxid *n*
f gaz *m* carbonique liquéfié; dioxyde *m* de carbone liquéfié
p gás *m* carbônico liquefeito; dióxido *m* de carbono liquefeito

3236 **liqueur**
(Prod.)
(Alcoholic beverage.)
d Likör *m*
f liqueur *f*
p licor *m*

3237 **liquid base of the aroma**
(Prod.)
(Aroma/fragrance research and production.)
d flüssige Basis *f* des Aromas

f base *f* liquide de l'arôme
p base *f* líquida do aroma

3238 **liquid chromatographic method**
(Prod.)
(Food processing technology; chromatographic analysis: Analytical method in biochemistry (e.g. in nutritional science) for identifying the composition of substances.)
d Methode *f* der Flüssigkeitschromatographie
f méthode *f* chromatographique liquide
p método *m* por cromatografia líquida

3239 **liquid chromatography**
(Prod.)
(Separation process for analysis, e.g. in aroma/flavour research and production.)
d Flüssigkeitschromatographie *f*
f chromatographie *f* liquide
p cromatografia *f* líquida

3240 **liquid culture medium**
(Biochem.)
(Microbiology: for microorganisms or tissue growth; e.g. ref. to biochemical research in nutritional science.)
d flüssiger Nährboden *m*
f milieu *m* nutritif liquide
p meio *m* nutritivo líquido

3241 **liquid dough**
(Prod.)
(Bakery.)
d flüssiger Teig *m*
f pâte *f* liquide
p massa *f* líquida

3242 **liquid fatty component**
(Prod.)
(Food processing technology.)
d flüssige Fettkomponente *f*
f composant *m* gras liquide
p componente *m* graxo líquido

3243 **liquid foodstuff**
(Prod.)
(Food processing technology; food characteristic.)
d flüssiges Nahrungsmittel *n*
f aliment *m* liquide
p alimento *m* líquido

* **liquid foodstuff thickener → 3246**

3244 **liquid manure**
(Agr.)
(Biological agriculture. Manure made of urine and the decomposition of solid dung.)
d Jauche *f*
f purin *m*
p fertilizante *m* orgânico líquido

3245 **liquid nutrition**
(Med.)
(Nutrition form, ref. e.g. to normal food intake problems.)
d flüssige Ernährung *f*
f nutrition *f* liquide
p nutrição *f* líquida

3246 **liquid thickening agent for foodstuff; liquid foodstuff thickener**
(Prod.)
(Food processing technology.)
d flüssiger Nahrungsmittelverdicker *m*
f épaississant *m* liquide alimentaire
p espessante *m* alimentício líquido

3247 **liquid under environmental temperature** *adj*
(Prod.)
(Food processing technology.)
d flüssig bei Umweltstemperatur
f liquide à la température environnementale
p líquido à temperatura ambiental

3248 **liquorice; licorice**
(Prod.)
(Confectionary made of "Glycyrrhiza glabra"-extract (leguminous plant).)
d Lakritze *f*
f réglisse *f*
p alcaçuz *m*

3249 **lithium**
(Biochem.)
(Food biochemistry: Li; one of the trace element ingredients in table salt.)
d Lithium *n*
f lithium *m*
p lítio *m*

3250 **lithium fluoride**
(Prod.)
(LiF; element eventually contained in form of traces in mineral water.)
d Lithiumfluorid *n*
f fluorure *m* de lithium
p fluoreto *m* de lítio

3251 **lithosphere; Earth's crust**
(Agr.)
(Soil; outer layer of the Earth.)
d Lithosphäre *f*; Erdkruste *f*
f lithosphère *f*; couche *f* externe de la croûte terrestre
p litosfera *f*; crosta *f* terrestre

3252 **litter; farrow**
(Agr.)
(Livestock breeding: group of young animals; farrow: a litter of pigs.)

d Wurf *m*
f portée *f*
p cria *f*

3253 **liver**
(Med.)
(Anatomy. The largest gland of the human body; e.g. carbohydrate storage; regulation of the protein metabolism; conversion of haemoglobin into bile pigments.)
d Leber *f*
f foie *m*
p fígado *m*

3254 **liver necrosis**
(Med.)
(Veterinary; ref. to cell death of the liver; to be controlled e.g. by selenium supplementation in feed.)
d Lebernekrose *f*
f nécrose *f* hépatique
p necrose *f* hepática

3255 **liver pâté**
(Prod.)
(Gastronomy.)
d Leberpastete *f*
f pâté *m* de foie gras
p patê *m* de fígado

3256 **liver sausage; liverwurst**
(Prod.)
(Gastronomy.)
d Leberwurst *f*
f saucisse *f* de foie; saucisse *f* de pâté de foie
p embutido *m* de fígado

* **liver starch → 2528**

* **liverwurst → 3256**

3257 **living upper surface layer**
(Agr.)
(Soil treatment; biological agriculture.)
d lebende Oberbodenfläche *f*
f couche *f* vivante de la surface
p camada *f* viva da superfície

3258 **lixiviation**
(Prod.)
(Aroma/flavour production: extraction processes: separation by extraction.)
d Auslaugung *f*; Auslaugen *n*
f lixiviation *f*; lessivage *m*
p lixiviação *f*

3259 **loaf of bread**
(Prod.)
(Bakery; bread not sliced.)
d Brotlaib *m*
f miche *f* de pain
p pão *m* inteiro

3260 **loam**
(Agr.)
(Soil type consisting of clay, sand and silt.)
d Lehm *m*
f glaise *f*
p argila *f*

3261 **lobster**
(Prod.)
(Gastronomy; e.g. "Scyllarides brasiliensis". Seafood.)
d Hummer *m*
f homard *m*
p lagostim *m*

3262 **local biologic resource**
(Agr.)
(Biological agriculture.)
d örtliche biologische Quelle *f*
f ressource *f* biologique locale
p recurso *m* biológico local

3263 **localized treatment**
(Agr.)
(Biological agriculture.)
d ortsgebundene Behandlung *f*; örtlich bestimmte Behandlung *f*
f traitement *m* localisé
p tratamento *m* localizado

* **locust bean → 949**

3264 **loin; sirloin**
(Prod.)
(Gastronomy; cut of meat, beef.)
d Lende *f*; Lendenstück *n*
f aloyau *m*
p lombo *m*; lombo *m* de boi

3265 **long chained fatty acids**
(Biochem.)
(Nutritional science: e.g. chains of 20 or more carbons.)
d langkettige Fettsäuren *fpl*
f acides *mpl* gras à chaîne longue
p ácidos *mpl* graxos de cadeia comprida

* **long cut pasta → 5702**

3266 **long grain rice**
(Agr.)
(Agricultural produce; ref. to rice type.)
d langkörniger Reis *m*
f riz *m* à grains longs
p arroz *m* de grão longo

3267 long-term supplementation
(Med.)
(Veterinary; ref. to ration supplementation (enrichment; fortification) with vitamins etc. in cattle dietary treatment.)
d langanhaltende Supplementierung *f*
f supplémentation *f* de longue durée
p suplementação *f* de longa duração

3268 loosening of the soil
(Agr.)
(Soil treatment.)
d Auflockerung *f* des Bodens
f ameublissement *m* du sol
p afofamento *m* do solo; revolvimento *m* do solo

3269 loosen *v* up
(Agr.)
(Soil treatment; biological agriculture.)
d auflockern
f ameublir
p afofar

3270 loose *v* weight
(Med.)
(Due to insufficient nutrition.)
d abmagern
f maigrir
p emagrecer

3271 losses of nutrient
(Prod.)
(Food processing technology: food conservation process.)
d Nährstoffverluste *npl*
f pertes *fpl* de nutriments
p perdas *fpl* de nutrientes

3272 louse; lice (*pl*)
(Med.)
(Veterinary science; insects which feed on animals and plants.)
d Laus *f*; Läuse *fpl*
f pou *m*; poux *mpl*
p piolho *m*; piolhos *mpl*

3273 low-amino acids diet
(Med.)
(Alimentary regimen.)
d Aminosäurenmangeldiät *f*; Diät *f* arm an Aminosäuren
f diète *f* pauvre en acides aminés
p dieta *f* pobre em aminoácidos

3274 low-caloric diet
(Med.)
(Alimentary regimen.)
d kalorienarme Diät *f*
f diète *f* pauvre en calories
p dieta *f* de baixo teor calórico

3275 low-caloric foodstuff
(Med.)
(Regimen: dietary products.)
d kalorienarme Nahrungsmittel *npl*
f produits *mpl* alimentaires pauvres en calories
p produtos *mpl* alimentícios pobres em calorias; produtos alimentícios de baixo teor de calorias

3276 low-dusting granules
(Prod.)
(Food processing technology; physical product presentation form.)
d Granulat *n* mit geringer Staubentwicklung
f granulé *m* à faible teneur en poussière
p granulado *m* de pouco desenvolvimento de poeira

3277 lower abdomen
(Med.)
(Anatomy.)
d Unterleib *m*
f bas-ventre *m*
p baixo-ventre *m*

*** lower jaw → 3369**

3278 lower lip
(Med.)
(Anatomy.)
d Unterlippe *f*
f lèvre *f* inférieure
p lábio *m* inferior

3279 low-fat curd cheese
(Prod.)
(Dairy product.)
d Magerquark *m*
f caillebotte *f* peu gras
p ricota *f* de baixo teor de gordura

3280 low-fat diet
(Med.)
(Alimentary regimen.)
d fettarme Diät *f*, Magerdiät *f*
f diète *f* maigre
p dieta *f* pobre em gorduras

3281 low-fat fish
(Agr.)
(Fish-meat quality.)
d magerer Fisch *m*
f poisson *m* maigre
p peixe *m* magro

3282 low-histidine diet
(Med.)
(Special diet type; see histidine.)
d Histidinmangelernährung *f*
f régime *m* pauvre en histidine
p regime *m* com baixo teor de histidina

3283 **low leucine diet**
(Med.)
(Alimentary regimen; essential amino acid, $C_6H_{13}NO_2$, obtained by the body from food proteins.)
d leucinarme Diät *f*
f diète *f* pauvre en leucine
p dieta *f* pobre em leucinas

3284 **low-oxalic acid diet**
(Med.)
(Alimentary regimen. $H_2C_2O_4$; present in some plants in the form of oxalates; low oxalate diet.)
d oxalsäurearme Diät *f*
f diète *f* pauvre en acide oxalique
p dieta *f* pobre em ácido oxálico

3285 **low pressure**
(Prod.)
(Food processing technology; ref. to certain processes.)
d Unterdruck *m*
f pression *f* basse
p baixa pressão *f*; subpressão *f*

3286 **low-protein diet**
(Med.)
(Alimentary regimen.)
d proteinarme Diät *f*
f diète *f* pauvre en protéines
p dieta *f* pobre em proteínas

3287 **low-salt diet**
(Med.)
(Alimentary regimen; low contents of sodium chloride (NaCl); table salt; e.g. treatment of high blood pressure.)
d salzarme Diät *f*
f diète *f* pauvre en sel
p dieta *f* pobre de sal

3288 **low-sodium diet**
(Med.)
(Alimentary regimen.)
d natriumarme Diät *f*
f diète *f* pauvre en sodium
p dieta *f* pobre de sódio

3289 **low-sugar** *adj*
(Prod.)
(Food processing technology; dietetic product.)
d zuckerarm
f pauvre en sucre
p com pouco açúcar

3290 **low-temperature vinification**
(Biochem.)
(Enology.)
d Weinbereitung *f* unter tiefer Temperatur
f vinification *f* à basse température
p vinificação *f* sob baixa temperatura

3291 **low viscosity**
(Prod.)
(Food processing technology; substance characteristic.)
d niedrige Viskosität *f*
f viscosité *f* basse
p viscosidade *f* baixa

3292 **lox**
(Prod.)
(Gastronomy; smoked salmon.)
d Räucherlachs *m*; geräucherter Lachs *m*
f saumon *m* fumé
p salmão *m* defumado

3293 **lucern; lucerne; alfalfa**
(Agr.)
(Botany: "Medicago sativa"; leguminous forage plant and used as green manure (biological agriculture).)
d Luzerne *f*
f luzerne *f*
p alfafa *f*; luzerna *f*

* **lucerne → 3293**

3294 **lukewarm** *adj*; **tepid** *adj*
(Prod.)
(Food processing technology: moderately warm temperature.)
d lauwarm; lau
f tiède
p morno

3295 **lukewarm coffee; tepid coffee**
(Prod.)
(Gastronomy, moderately warm; also ref. to dishes etc.)
d lauwarmer Kaffee *m*
f café *m* tiède
p café *m* morno; café *m* frio

* **lump sugar → 1441**

* **lumpy jaw → 66**

3296 **lunch**
(Prod.)
(Gastronomy.)
d Mittagessen *n*
f déjeuner *m*
p almoço *m*

3297 **lung**
(Med.)
(Anatomy; respiratory organ.)

d Lunge *f*
f poumon *m*
p pulmão *m*

3298 **lupine**
(Agr.)
(Botany: "Lupinus albus"; "Lupinus luteus"; leguminous forage herbs, also used as green manure (biological agriculture); having edible seeds.)
d Lupine *f*
f lupin *m*
p tremoçeiro *m*; tremoço *m*

3299 **lupulin**
(Prod.)
(Food processing technology; hop part with essential oil content; brewery prime material.)
d Lupolin *n*
f lupoline *f*
p lupolina *f*

3300 **lupulon; beta-lupulic acid**
(Prod.)
($C_{26}H_{38}O_4$; antibiotic contained in hop.)
d Lupolon *n*
f lupolone *f*
p lupulona *f*

3301 **lutein**
(Prod.)
(Additive. Vegetable lutein, vegetable luteol: xanthophyll ($C_{40}H_{56}O_2$); carotenoid alcohol; foodstuff colorant (CEE No. E 161) in leaves and plants and in the yellow of eggs.)
d Lutein *n*
f lutéine *f*
p luteína *f*

3302 **lymphocytes**
(Med.)
(Baby nutrition. Immunity involved, antibodies producing white blood cells, e.g. in human milk.)
d Lymphozyten *mpl*
f lymphocytes *mpl*
p linfócitos *mpl*

3303 **lyophilization; freeze-drying**
(Prod.)
(Drying and elimination process for volatile substances at low temperatures under reduced pressure. Vacuum-sublimation process, resulting in excellent product keeping quality; in foodstuff production.)
d Gefriertrocknung *f*; Lyophilisation *f*
f lyophilisation *f*; dessiccation *f* par congélation
p liofilização *f*

3304 **lyophilization auxiliary**
(Prod.)
(Food processing technology. Lyophilization: Preservation process, consisting of rapid freezing followed by dehydration.)
d Lyophilisationshilfsmittel *n*
f produit *m* auxiliaire de lyophilisation
p auxiliar *m* de liofilização

3305 **lyophilized lactic bacteria; freeze dried lactic bacteria**
(Biochem.)
(Microbiology.)
d lyophilisierte Milchsäurebakterien *fpl*; der Gefriertrocknung unterzogene Milchsäurebakterien *fpl*
f bactéries *fpl* lactiques lyophilisées
p bactérias *fpl* lácticas liofilizadas

3306 **lysine**
(Prod.)
($C_6H_{14}N_2O_2$; auxiliary product; essential amino acid; used for food enrichment: e.g. nutritive quality improver of proteins in wheat dough products (e.g. bread) promoting growth.)
d Lysin *n*
f lysine *f*
p lisina *f*

3307 **lysozyme**
(Biochem.)
(Globulin G 1; a hydrolytic enzyme. Found in certain human secretions (e.g. tears) and in the white of eggs. (2.5% of total solids). Used in sterilization processes; antibiotic properties.)
d Lysozym *n*
f lysozyme *m*
p lisozima *f*

M

3308 macaroni
(Prod.)
(Food processing technology; pasta plant product: tubular pasta type.)
d Makkaroni *pl*
f macaroni *mpl*
p macarrão *m*

3309 macaroon
(Prod.)
(Confectionary; small cookies produced from almonds, egg white and sugar.)
d Makrone *f*
f macaron *m*
p bolinho *m* de amêndoa; suspiro *m*

3310 macédoine of fruits
(Prod.)
(Gastronomy; fruit salad made of small cut fruit parts.)
d Obstsalat *m*
f macédoine *f* de fruits
p macedônia *f* de frutas

3311 macédoine of vegetables
(Prod.)
(Gastronomy; vegetable mixture, e.g. as salad or as a garnish.)
d Gemüsegarnierung *f* Gärtnerinnen-Art; gemischtes Gemüse *n*; Gemüseplatte *f*
f macédoine *f* de légumes; jardinière *f*
p macedônia *f* de legumes

3312 maceration
(Prod.)
(Food processing technology: soaking process, steeping of raw material: e.g. in fruit juice and cheese production.)
d Mazeration *f*; Ziehenlassen *n*; Einweichung *f*; Einlegen *n*
f macération *f*
p maceração *f*

3313 maceration in wine
(Prod.)
(Food processing, food aromatization/preservation.)
d Einlegen *n* in Wein
f macération *f* dans le vin
p maceração *f* em vinho

3314 maceration of the grape skin
(Biochem.)
(Enology: technology of wine production; e.g. ref. to red wine types.)
d Mazeration *f* der Beerenhaut; Ziehenlassen *n* der Beerenhaut
f macération *f* de la peau de raisin; macération *f* pelliculaire
p maceração *f* da pele da uva

3315 maceration with different liquids
(Prod.)
(Aroma/flavour research and production: extraction process.)
d Mazeration *f* in verschiedenen Flüssigkeiten
f macération *f* dans différents liquides
p maceração *f* sob líquidos diferentes

3316 mackerel
(Prod.)
(Gastronomy; "Scomber scombrus"; North Atlantic bony edible fish.)
d Makrele *f*
f maquereau *m*
p cavala *f*

3317 maconnais cheese
(Prod.)
(Dairy product; goat's cheese.)
d Ziegenmilchkäse *m*
f mâconnais *m*; fromage *m* au lait de chèvre
p queijo *m* de leite de cabra

3318 macrobiotics
(Med.)
(Ref. to a whole grain diet. Highest stage of macrobiotic method of nutrition of whole grains, containing 79% of carbohydrates; as to Christoph Wilhelm Hufeland (1762-1836), German physician.)
d Makrobiotik *f*
f macrobiotique *f*
p macrobiótica *f*

3319 macromolecular component
(Biochem.)
(Nutritional science.)
d makromolekularer Bestandteil *m*
f constituant *m* macromoléculaire
p componente *m* macromolecular

3320 macronutritional subdeficiency
(Biochem.)
(Nutritional science.)
d Submangel *m* an Makronahrungsmittelkomponenten
f subcarence *f* macronutritionnelle
p subcarência *f* macronutricional

3321 macronutritional supplementation
(Biochem.)
(Miscibility with edible oils in food stuff

processing.)
d Makrosupplementation *f*
f supplémentation *f* macronutritionnelle
p suplementação *f* macronutricional

3322 **madeleine**
(Prod.)
(Bakery: small cake.)
d Sandplätzchen *n*
f madeleine *f*
p biscoitinho *m* confeitado

3323 **maggot; grub**
(Agr.)
(Biological agriculture. Fruit-destructive (apples etc.) larva of dipterous (flies etc.) insects.)
d Made *f*
f asticot *m*
p verme *m*; bicho *m*

3324 **magmatic rock**
(Agr.)
(Soil. Molten rock of the earth's interior, from which originates the igneous rock by cooling and posterior solidification.)
d magmatisches Gestein *n*
f roche *f* magmatique
p rocha *f* magmática

* **magnesia → 3330**

3325 **magnesium**
(Biochem.)
(Nutritional science: Mg. Trace element, promoting enzymatic reaction in urea production in the liver.)
d Magnesium *n*
f magnésium *m*
p magnésio *m*

3326 **magnesium bicarbonate**
(Prod.)
($Mg(HCO_3)_2$; element eventually contained in form of traces in mineral water.)
d Magnesiumbicarbonat *n*
f bicarbonate *m* de magnésium
p bicarbonato *m* de mangésio

3327 **magnesium carbonate**
(Prod.)
($MgCO_3$; antihygroscopic additive.)
d Magnesiumcarbonat *n*
f carbonate *m* de magnésium
p carbonato *m* de magnésio

3328 **magnesium chloride**
(Prod.)
($MgCl_2.6H_2O$; element eventually contained in form of traces in mineral water.)
d Magnesiumchlorid *n*
f chlorure *m* de magnésium
p cloreto *m* de magnésio

3329 **magnesium nitrate**
(Prod.)
($Mg(NO_3)_2.6H_2O$; element eventually contained in form of traces in mineral water.)
d Magnesiumnitrat *n*
f nitrate *m* de magnésium
p nitrato *m* de magnésio

3330 **magnesium oxide; magnesia**
(Prod.)
(MgO; water treatment: water hardening agent; deacidifying additive.)
d Magnesiumoxid *n*; Magnesia *n*
f oxyde *m* de magnésium; magnésie *f*
p óxido *m* de magnésio; magnésia *f*

3331 **magnesium-rich fertilizer**
(Agr.)
(Biological agriculture: soil treatment.)
d magnesiumhaltiges Düngemittel *n*
f fertilisant *m* riche en magnésium
p fertilizante *m* enriquecido de magnésio

3332 **magnesium stearate**
(Prod.)
(Approx. $Mg\ (C_{18}H_{35}O_2)_2$; e.g. baker's additive.)
d Magnesiumstearat *n*
f stéarate *m* de magnésium
p estearato *m* de magnésio

3333 **magnesium sulphate**
(Prod.)
($MgSO_{4\cdot 7}H_2O$; element eventually contained in form of traces in mineral water.)
d Magnesiumsulfat *n*
f sulfate *m* de magnésium
p sulfato *m* de magnésio

3334 **Maillard products**
(Biochem.)
(Nutritional science: e.g. by Maillard reaction formed aromas and browning substances.)
d Maillardprodukte *npl*
f produits *mpl* de Maillard
p produtos *mpl* de Maillard

3335 **Maillard reaction**
(Biochem.)
(Nutritional science: reaction between amino acids and sugars, with decrease of protein value. Non-enzymatic browning reaction.)
d Maillardreaktion *f*
f réaction *f* de Maillard
p reação *f* de Maillard

3336 main cereals
(Agr.)
(Agricultural produce; e.g. wheat; Indian corn.)
d Hauptgetreidearten *fpl*; hauptsächliche Getreidearten *fpl*
f céréales *fpl* principales
p cereais *mpl* principais

3337 maintain *v* **the fertility of the soils**
(Agr.)
(Aim of biologic agriculture, biologic farming system.)
d die Fruchtbarkeit des Bodens erhalten; die Bodenfruchtbarkeit erhalten
f maintenir la fertilité des sols
p manter a fertilidade dos solos

3338 maintain *v* **the temperature necessary for the process**
(Prod.)
(Food processing technology.)
d die für den Prozess notwendige Temperatur aufrechterhalten; die für den Prozess notwendige Temperatur bestehen lassen
f maintenir la température nécessaire du processus
p manter a temperatura necessária para o processo

3339 maize; Indian corn
(Agr.)
(Agricultural produce. "Zea mays"; Indian corn.)
d Mais *m*
f maïs *m*
p milho *m*

3340 maize cake; Indian-corn cake
(Prod.)
(Confectionary.)
d Maiskuchen *m*
f galette *f* de maïs
p bolo *m* de milho; bolo *m* de fubá

3341 maize dough; Indian-corn dough
(Prod.)
(Food processing technology. Used for the preparation of the Brazilian "pamonha" cake type and "polenta" dough.)
d Maisteig *m*
f pâte *f* de maïs
p massa *f* de milho

3342 maize pap
(Prod.)
(Gastronomy. "Zea mays"; Indian corn.)
d Maisbrei *m*
f bouillie *f* de maïs
p angú *m* de fubá

3343 maize seed oil
(Prod.)
(Prime material. "Zea mays"; Indian corn.)
d Maiskeimöl *n*
f huile *f* de germe de maïs
p óleo *m* da semente do milho; óleo *m* do germe do milho

3344 malabsorption syndrome
(Med.)
(Reduced small intestine absorption of nutrients, occurring with various deficiencies, e.g. vitamin deficiency.)
d Malabsorptionssyndrom *n*
f syndrome *m* de malabsorption
p síndrome *m* de malabsorção

3345 maldigestion of lactose; insufficient lactose digestion
(Med.)
(Milk intolerance, esp. in baby nutrition.)
d unzureichende Laktoseverdauung *f*
f maldigestion *f* du lactose
p má digestão *f* da lactose

*** male duck → 1773**

*** male goat → 2676**

3346 malic acid; apple acid; hydroxysuccinic acid
(Prod.)
($C_4H_6O_5$; prime material; organic acid which occurs in apples and some other fruits.)
d Apfelsäure *f*; Äpfelsäure *f*; Hydroxybernsteinsäure *f*
f acide *m* malique
p ácido *m* málico

3347 malic acid decomposition
(Biochem.)
(Nutritional science; selected yeast strains in fermentation; e.g. wine production.)
d Apfelsäureabbau *m*; Äpfelsäureabbau *m*; Hydroxybernsteinsäureabbau *m*
f décomposition *f* de l'acide malique
p decomposição *f* do ácido málico

3348 malic acid of the wine
(Biochem.)
(Enology. $C_4H_6O_5$.)
d Apfelsäure *f* des Weines; Äpfelsäure *f* des Weines; Hydroxybernsteinsäure *f* des Weines
f acide *m* malique du vin
p ácido *m* málico do vinho

3349 malnutrition
(Med.)
(Causing e.g. deficiencies in vitamins and trace elements.)

d Fehlernährung *f*
f malnutrition *f*
p subalimentação *f*

3350 malolactic fermentation
(Biochem.)
(Fermentation in nutritional science: e.g. ref. to enology: the bacterial conversion of malic acid to lactic acid in wine biochemistry.)
d malolaktische Gärung *f*
f fermentation *f* malolactique
p fermentação *f* malolática

3351 malt *v*
(Prod.)
(Food production technology; beer brewing: transforming barley into malt; treating with malt: to malt the beer.)
d mälzen
f malter
p maltar

3352 malt; green malt
(Agr.)
(Agricultural produce; used in brewery: Beer production: Germinated barley grain.)
d Malz *n*
f malt *m*
p malte *m*

* **Malta fever → 793**

3353 maltase
(Biochem.)
(Nutritional science: catalytic enzyme that acts in the hydrolysis process of maltose (malt sugar, $C_{12}H_{22}O_{11}.H_2O$), forming glucose.)
d Maltase *f*
f maltase *f*
p maltase *f*

3354 malted barley
(Prod.)
(Food processing technology: malt extract for brewing processes.)
d Malzgerste *f*; gemälzte Gerste *f*
f orge *f* maltée
p cevada *f* maltada

3355 malted milk
(Prod.)
(Food processing technology, dairy produce.)
d Malzmilch *f*
f lait *m* malté
p leite *m* maltado

3356 malt extract
(Prod.)
(Food processing technology; prepared from wheat and barley, containing maltose i.e. malt sugar.)
d Malzextrakt *m*
f extrait *m* de malt
p extrato *m* de malte

3357 malt flour
(Prod.)
(Food processing technology: made of germinated barley or wheat; rich in diastase, used with common flour for bread baking.)
d Malzmehl *f*
f farine *f* du malt; farine *f* d'orge
p farinha *f* de malte

3358 malt germs
(Prod.)
(Food processing technology: Beer brewing process: malt prepared from barley; raw material for brewing.)
d Malzkeime *mpl*
f germes *mpl* du malt
p radículus *mpl* do malte

3359 malt industry
(Prod.)
(Malt production industry: raw material production for brewing processes.)
d Mälzerei *f*
f malterie *f*; industrie *f* du malt
p indústria *f* de malte

3360 malting
(Prod.)
(First phase of the beer brewing process. Malt preparation.)
d Mälzen *n*
f maltage *m*
p maltagem *f*; malteação *f*

3361 malting barley
(Prod.)
(Raw material for the beer brewing process.)
d Braugerste *f*; Brauereigerste *f*
f orge *m* pour maltage
p cevada *f* para maltagem; cevade *f* para malteação

3362 malting tower
(Prod.)
(Food processing technology; unit for drying of germinated barley to stop the germination process: brewing activity.)
d Mälzturm *m*
f touraille *f* de la malterie
p torre *f* de maltagem

3363 maltose; malt sugar
(Prod.)
($C_{12}H_{22}O_{11}$; prime material; nutrient and sweetener.)

d Maltose *f*; Malzzucker *m*
f maltose *m*; sucre *m* de malt
p maltose *f*; açúcar *m* do malte

3364 **malt preparation**
(Prod.)
(Food processing technology: First phase of the brewery process.)
d Malzbereitung *f*
f préparation *f* du malt
p preparação *f* do malte

3365 **malt production process**
(Prod.)
(Food processing technology: Beer brewery process.)
d Malzproduktion *f*
f production *f* de malt
p processo *m* de malteação

* **malt sugar → 3363**

3366 **mamma**
(Med.)
(Anatomy. Breast.)
d Brüste *f*; Mutterbrust *f*
f mamelle *f*; sein *m*
p seio *m*; mama *f*

3367 **mammal**
(Agr.)
(Livestock. Warm-blooded vertebrates (class Mammalia), having mammary glands for milk secretion.)
d Säugetier *n*
f mammifère *m*
p mamífero *m*

* **mammilla → 3736**

3368 **mandarin; tangerine**
(Agr.)
(Agricultural produce. "Citrus reticulata"; mandarin orange.)
d Mandarine *f*
f mandarine *f*
p tangerina *f*; bergamota *f*; mexerica

3369 **mandible; lower jaw**
(Med.)
(Anatomy. The lower jawbone.)
d Unterkiefer *m*; Unterkieferknochen *n*
f mandibule *f*; mâchoire *f* inférieure
p mandíbula *f*; maxilar *m* inferior

3370 **manganese**
(Biochem.)
(Nutritional science; Mn. Trace element, activator and cofactor of enzymes.)
d Mangan *n*
f manganèse *m*
p manganês *m*

* **mange → 4850**

3371 **mango**
(Agr.)
(Fruit of "Mangifera indica". Horticulture; a tropical fruit.)
d Mango *f*
f mangue *f*
p manga *f*

3372 **manifestation of alimentary allergy**
(Med.)
(Nutritional disorder.)
d Manifestwerden *n* einer Nahrungsmittelallergie; Anzeichen *n/npl* einer Nahrungsmittelallergie
f manifestation *f* allergique alimentaire
p manifestação *f* alérgica alimentar

3373 **manioc; cassava**
(Agr.)
(Horticulture. "Manihot utilissima"; tupi "mãdi'og": edible rootstock; source of starch.)
d Maniok *m*
f manioc *m*
p mandioca *f*; aipim *m*

3374 **manna**
(Agr.)
(Lichen "Lecanora esculenta", used as foodstuff as in biblical times.)
d Manna *n/f*
f manne *f*
p mana *m*

* **mannite → 3375**

3375 **mannitol; mannite**
(Prod.)
($C_6H_{14}O_6$; food processing technology: e.g. texture improving ingredient; sweetening agent: polyalcohol.)
d Mannit *n*
f mannitol *m*
p manitol *m*; manita *f*

3376 **manual kneading**
(Prod.)
(Food processing technology, e.g. in bakery.)
d Handkneten *n*; manuelles Durchkneten *n*
f pétrissage *m* à main
p amassamento *m* manual; sova *f* manual

3377 **manual milking**
(Agr.)
(Cattle breeding.)
d Handmelken *n*

f traite *f* manuelle; mulsion *f* manuelle
p ordenha *f* manual

3378 manual weeding
(Agr.)
(Manual removal of weeds, e.g. in biological agriculture.)
d manuelle Unkrautvertilgung *f*
f désherbage *m* manuel
p remoção *f* manual de ervas daninhas

* **manure → 1828**

3379 maple
(Agr.)
(Botany; Genus "Acer"; Family "Aceraceae"; deciduous tree.)
d Ahorn *m*
f érable *m*
p ácer *m*; bordo *m*

3380 maple syrup
(Prod.)
(Canadian syrup type of "Acer saccharinum".)
d Ahornsyrup *m*
f tire *f*
p xarope *m* de bordo de Canadá

3381 maraschino
(Prod.)
(Beverages. Sweet liqueur from the Dalmation sour cherry.)
d Maraschino *m*
f marasquin *m*
p marasquino *m*

3382 marbled
(Prod.)
(Dairy product. Blue cheese characteristic, having internal mould.)
d marmorisiert
f persillé
p marmorizado

3383 marc
(Prod.)
(Food processing technology; residue after fruit expression; residue of extraction processes.)
d Satz *m*; Bodensatz *m*
f marc *m*
p bagaço *m*

3384 mare
(Agr.)
(Livestock; female horse.)
d Stute *f*
f jument *f*
p égua *f*

3385 margarine partially hydrogenated
(Prod.)
(Food processing technology.)
d zum Teil gehärtetes Pflanzenfett *n*
f margarine *f* végétale partiellement hydrogénée
p margarina *f* vegetal parcialmente hidrogenada

3386 marinade
(Prod.)
(Gastronomy. Souce type, made of vinegar, garlic, onion, bay leaves etc., for fish and meat preparation; salad dressing.)
d Marinade *f*
f marinade *f*
p marinada *f*; vinha-d'alhos *f*

3387 marinated sardines
(Prod.)
(Gastronomy.)
d marinierte Sardinien *fpl*
f escabèche *f* de sardines
p escabeche *m* de sardinhas

3388 marjoram
(Prod.)
(Genus "Origanum majorana"; aromatic herbs in gastronomy.)
d Majoran *m*
f marjolaine *f*
p manjerona *f*

3389 marmalade; jam
(Prod.)
(Confectionary. Marmalade: esp. made of oranges. Jam: consisting of any kind of boiled fruit.)
d Marmelade *f*
f marmelade *f*; confiture *f*; gelée *f*
p marmelada *f*; geléia *f*

* **marron → 1073**

3390 marrowbone
(Prod.)
(Butchery.)
d Markknochen *m*
f os *m* à moelle
p osso *m* com tutano

3391 marsh hen; mud hen
(Agr.)
(Poultry farming. "Laterallus Gray".)
d Wasserhuhn *n*
f poule *f* d'eau
p frango-d'água *m*

3392 marshmallow
(Prod.)
(Confectionary; sweet consisting of an aerated mixture of gelatine, albumin sugar and starch

syrup. Originally made from the marshmallow Althaea-root.)
d Mohrenkopf *m*
f nègre *m* en chemise
p nhabenta *f*

3393 **marzipan**
(Prod.)
(Confectionary; made of almonds, almond paste; ref. to food processing technology.)
d Marzipan *n*
f pâte *f* d'amandes
p maçapão *m*

* **mash** *v* **→ 1423**

3394 **mash**
(Prod.)
(Food processing technology. Mashing process in beer brewing.)
d Maische *f*
f trempe *f*
p empastagem *f*

3395 **mash; purée**
(Prod.)
(Gastronomy.)
d Püree *n*
f purée *f*
p purê *m*

3396 **mashed potatoes**
(Prod.)
(Gastronomy.)
d Kartoffelpüree *n*; Kartoffelbrei *m*
f purée *f* de pommes de terre
p purê *m* de batatas

3397 **mashing process**
(Prod.)
(Food processing technology. Beer brewery process.)
d Sudprozess *m*
f processus *m* de cuisson *f* du moût
p processo *m* de cozimento do mosto de cerveja; processo *m* de mostura; processo *m* de empastagem

* **mash** *v* **until the obtention of flour → 1427**

3398 **masking power**
(Prod.)
(Aroma/fragrance research and production: related to taste: aroma characteristic.)
d Maskierungskraft *f*; Maskierkraft *f*; Überdeckungskraft *f*
f pouvoir *m* masquant
p poder *m* de mascarar

3399 **masking unpleasant taste**
(Prod.)
(Flavouring purpose; food processing technology; e.g. ref. to organoleptic food evaluation.)
d Geschmacksmaskierung *f*
f masquage *m* du goût
p mascaração *f* do paladar

3400 **masseter**
(Med.)
(Anatomy; muscle; "Musculus masseter".)
d großer Kaumuskel *m*
f masséter *m*
p masseter *m*

3401 **master brewer**
(Prod.)
(Beer brewery: masher master.)
d Braumeister *m*; Biersieder *m*
f maître-brasseur *m*; brasseur *m*
p mestre-cervejeiro *m*

* **mastery of the fermentation process → 1753**

3402 **mastication**
(Med.)
(Food crushing with the teeth before swallowing.)
d Kauen *n*; Zerkauen *n*
f mastication *f*
p mastigação *f*

3403 **mastitis**
(Med.)
(Veterinary; bovine mastitis: dairy cattle: inflammation of the mammal glands by streptococci "Streptococcus pyogenes" and by staphylococci "Staphylococcus aureus".)
d Mastitis *f*; Brustdrüsenentzündung *f*
f mastite *f*
p mastite *f*

3404 **mate; maté**
(Agr.)
(Agricultural produce. "Ilex paraguariensis"; Quechua language; tea-like South American beverage.)
d Mate *m*
f maté *m*; thé *m* du Brésil
p mate *m*; chá-mate *m*

* **maté → 3404**

3405 **material equilibrium**
(Med.)
(Purpose of nutrition.)
d materielles Gleichgewicht *n*
f équilibre *m* matériel
p equilíbrio *m* material

3406 mating
(Med.)
(Veterinary; controlled mating: permits to avoid loss of the rutting season (heat of the female) and control of the consanguinity of the herd by selection of reproducers.)
d Paarung *f*
f accouplement *m*
p acasalamento *m*

3407 maturation
(Prod.)
(Food processing technology: e.g. fruits when growing until the very final stage. Wine: develops maturation in the barrels. Cheese kept in the cellar called "cave de maturation".)
d Reifung *f*; Ausreifung *f*; Ausreifen *n*
f maturation *f*
p maturação *f*

3408 maturation evolution of vine
(Agr.)
(Viticulture: vine maturity.)
d Reifungsentwicklung *f* des Weinstocks
f évolution *f* de la maturation de la vigne
p evolução *f* de maturação da vinha

3409 maturation of fruits
(Agr.)
(Horticulture; plant growth.)
d Reifung *f* der Früchte; Ausreifung *f* der Früchte
f maturation *f* des fruits
p maturação *f* das frutas

3410 maturation of meat; ripening of meat
(Prod.)
(Food processing technology, meat quality.)
d Ausreifung *f* des Fleisches
f maturation *f* de la viande
p maturação *f* da carne

3411 mature human milk
(Med.)
(Baby nutrition.)
d reife Humanmilch *f*
f lait *m* humain mature
p leite *m* humano maduro

3412 maturing of the beer; lagering of the beer
(Prod.)
(Food processing technology. Beer production, after the pasteurization process.)
d Lagern *n* des Bieres
f maturation *f* de la bière
p maturação *f* da cerveja

3413 maturing process
(Prod.)
(Food processing technology, beer and wine production and maturing.)
d Reifungsprozess *m*; Alterungsprozess *m*
f processus *m* de mûrissement
p processo *m* de amadurecimento; processo *m* de envelhecimento

* **maturing vine sort → 3140**

* **maturity → 4720**

3414 maturity of the vine
(Agr.)
(Viticulture; ripeness of a fruit, its full development; e.g. ref. to viticulture.)
d Reife *f* der Weinrebe
f maturité *f* de la vigne
p maturidade *f* da videira

3415 maturity of the vintage
(Agr.)
(Viticulture; harvest(ed) quality.)
d Reife *f* der geerntete Weintrauben
f maturité *f* des vendanges
p maturidade *f* das vindimas

3416 maxilla; upper jawbone; upper jaw
(Med.)
(Anatomy; bones; "Maxilla".)
d Oberkieferbein *n*
f maxillaire *m* supérieur; mâchoire *f* supérieure
p maxila *f* superior; maxilar *m*

3417 maxillary bone
(Med.)
(Veterinary science; ref. to cattle breeding; quality of the cattle can be determined by its head formation.)
d Kieferknochen *m*
f os *m* maxillaire
p maxilar *m*; osso *m* maxilar

3418 maximum vitamin supply
(Med.)
(Veterinary; e.g. ref. farm animal raising, fodder composition.)
d Vitaminoptimalversorgung *f*
f approvisionnement *m* vitaminique optimal
p suprimento *m* máximo de vitaminas

3419 mayonnaise
(Prod.)
(Gastronomy; type of dressing, based on egg yolks, prepared with vinegar and vegetable oils.)
d Majonäse *f*
f mayonnaise *f*
p maionese *f*

3420 May woodruff punch
(Prod.)
(Beverages; German drink on "Asperula odorata" herb.)

d Maibowle *f* mit Waldmeister
f punch *m* de mai à base d'aspérule
p ponche *m* de maio à base de aspérula

* **meal → 1708**

* **meal beetle → 2265**

3421 measured weight
(Prod.)
(Food processing technology.)
d gemessenes Gewicht *n*
f poids *m* mesuré
p peso *m* medido

3422 meatball
(Prod.)
(Gastronomy.)
d Fleischkloß *m*; Frikadelle *f*; Klops *m*
f godiveau *m*; quenelle *f* de viande; boulette *f*
p almôndega *f*

3423 meatballs made of minced meat
(Prod.)
(Butchery.)
d Hackfleischklößchen *npl*
f boulettes *fpl* de la viande hachée
p almôndegas *fpl* de carne picada

* **meat conservation by heat treatment → 3424**

3424 meat conservation by thermal treatment; meat conservation by heat treatment
(Prod.)
(Food processing technology; meat industrialization; preservation process.)
d Fleischkonservierung *f* durch Wärmebehandlung
f conservation *f* de la viande par traitement thermique
p conservação *f* de carne por tratamento térmico

3425 meat consumption
(Prod.)
(Food processing technology, food marketing.)
d Fleischkonsum *m*
f consommation *f* de viande
p consumo *m* de carne

3426 meat-curing salt
(Prod.)
(Food industry: E.g. meat conservation process: salt meat production.)
d Pökelsalz *n*
f sel *m* pour la salaison des viandes
p sal *m* de salmoura para a conservação de carne

3427 meat cuts for boiling
(Prod.)
(Butchery. Meat type of poorer quality.)
d Kochfleisch *n*
f viande *f* à bouillir; morceaux *m* à bouillir
p carne *f* para cozinhar; carne *f* para cozer

3428 meat diet
(Med.)
(Alimentary regimen.)
d Fleischdiät *f*
f diète *f* carnée
p dieta *f* de carne

3429 meat dish
(Prod.)
(Gastronomy.)
d Fleischgericht *n*
f plat *m* de viande
p prato *m* de carne

3430 meat extract; beef extract
(Prod.)
(Food processing technology, meat industrialization product: thickened aqueous extraction of meat, used for flavouring soups etc.)
d Fleischextrakt *m*
f extrait *m* de viande
p extrato *m* de carne

* **meat/fish dumpling → 4540**

3431 meat from herbivores
(Prod.)
(Butchery; meat from plant-eating animals.)
d Fleisch *n* pflanzenfressender Tiere
f viande *f* d'herbivores
p carne *f* de herbívoros

3432 meat inspection
(Prod.)
(Food processing technology; product examination.)
d Fleischbeschau *f*; Fleischinspektion *f*
f inspection *f* des viandes
p inspeção *f* da carne

3433 meat joints
(Prod.)
(Butchery.)
d Schlachttierteile *fpl*
f morceaux *mpl* de viande de boucherie
p cortes *mpl* de carne

3434 meat of nervous tissue
(Prod.)
(Butchery; meat quality.)
d Fleisch *n* mit Nerven
f morceaux *mpl* de viande tendineuse
p carne *f* com nervos

3435 **meat-poultry**
(Agr.)
(Poultry farming; poultry type.)
d Fleischgeflügel *n*
f volaille *f* de chair
p aves *fpl* de carne

3437 **meat products**
(Prod.)
(Butchery.)
d Fleischprodukte *npl*
f produits *mpl* carnés
p produtos *mpl* de carne

3436 **meat products; pork products**
(Prod.)
(Charcuterie: French butcher, specialized in pork products.)
d Fleischwurstwaren *fpl*; Schweinefleischwurstwaren *fpl*
f charcuterie *f*
p carnes *fpl*; carne *f* do proco

3438 **meat proteins**
(Prod.)
(Food processing technology: e.g. meat quality.)
d Fleischproteine *npl*
f protéines *fpl* de la viande
p proteínas *fpl* da carne

3439 **meat salad**
(Prod.)
(Gastronomy.)
d Fleischsalat *m*
f salade *f* de viande
p salada *f* de carne

* **meat salting → 4176**

3440 **meaty chicken**
(Agr.)
(Poultry farming; chicken farming, chicken type.)
d fleischiges Hühnchen *n*
f poulet *m* de chair
p frango *m* carnudo

3441 **mechanical kneading**
(Prod.)
(Bakery.)
d mechanisches Kneten *n*
f pétrissage *m* mécanique
p amassamento *m* mecânico; sova *f* mecânica

3442 **mechanical means of separation for clarification processes**
(Prod.)
(Food processing technology: ref. to the clarification of beer, juices, wine etc.)
d mechanische Trennungsmittel *npl* für Klärungsprozesse
f moyens *mpl* mécaniques de séparation destinés à la clarification
p meios *mpl* mecânicos de separação destinados à clarificação

3443 **mechanical method**
(Prod.)
(Aroma/flavour production: type of separation process.)
d mechanisches Verfahren *n*
f méthode *f* mécanique
p método *m* mecânico

3444 **mechanism of fermentation**
(Biochem.)
(Nutritional science.)
d Gärungsmechanismus *m*
f mécanisme *m* de la fermentation
p mecanismo *m* da fermentação

* **mechanized grape harvest → 3445**

3445 **mechanized vintage; mechanized grape harvest**
(Agr.)
(Viticulture, winegrowing.)
d mechanisierte Weinernte *f*
f vendange *f* mécanique
p vindima *f* mecânica

3446 **medicinal plant**
(Agr.)
(Botany.)
d Heilpflanze *f*
f plante *f* médicinale
p planta *f* medicinal

3447 **medicinal virtue**
(Med.)
(Medicinal properties of certain herbs.)
d medizinische Eigenschaften *fpl*
f vertu *m* médicinale
p virtudes *fpl* medicinais; propriedades *fpl* medicinais

* **Mediterranean fever → 793**

3448 **Mediterranean fish stew**
(Prod.)
(Gastronomy.)
d Mittelmeerfischragout *n*
f matelote *f* de poissons méditerranéens; bouillabaisse *f*
p ragu *m* de peixes do Mediterrâneo; guisado *m* de peixes do Mediterrâneo

3449 **medium concentration**
(Biochem.)
(Nutritional science.)

d Konzentration *f* des Mediums
f concentration *f* du milieu
p concentração *f* do meio

3450 medium-fat fishes
(Agr.)
(Edible fish; e.g. a carp.)
d halbfette Fische *mpl*
f poissons *mpl* demi-gras
p peixes *mpl* de pouca gordura

3451 medlar
(Agr.)
(Horticulture; "Mespilus germanica". Edible fruit.)
d Mispel *f*
f nèfle *f*
p nêspera *f*

* **meiosis → 4628**

3452 melissa tea
(Prod.)
(Herb tea of "Melissa officinalis".)
d Melissentee *m*
f tisane *f* de mélisse
p chá *m* de erva-cidreira

3453 melon
(Agr.)
(Agricultural produce. "Cucumis melo".)
d Melone *f*
f melon *m*
p melão *m*

3454 melt *v*
(Prod.)
(Food processing technology.)
d zerlassen
f fondre; fair fondre
p derreter

* **melted butter → 1777**

3455 melt extrusion
(Prod.)
(Food processing technology, processing form.)
d Schmelzextrusion *f*
f extrusion *f* par fusion; filature *f* à chaud
p extrusão *f* por fusão

3456 melting point
(Prod.)
(Food processing technology, temperature at which a solid matter melts.)
d Schmelzpunkt *m*
f point *m* de fusion
p ponto *m* de fusão

3457 membrane differentiation
(Biochem.)
(Biochemical research in nutritional science.)
d Membrandifferenzierung *f*
f différenciation *f* des membranes
p diferenciação *f* das membranas

3458 membrane filtration
(Prod.)
(Food processing technology: separation process.)
d Membranfiltration *f*; Membranverfahren *n*
f filtration *f* à diaphragme; filtration *f* microporeuse
p filtração *f* por membrana; filtração *f* por diafragma

3459 menthol
(Prod.)
($C_{10}H_{20}O$; peppermint oil aroma; alpha-pinene derivative; flavour chemical.)
d Menthol *n*
f menthol *m*
p mentol *m*

3460 mercurialism; hydrargyria
(Med.)
(Mercury poisoning.)
d Quecksilbervergiftung *f*
f hydrargyrisme *m*; intoxication *f* par le mercure
p hidrargirismo *m*; hidrargirose *f*; hidrargíria *f*; intoxicação *f* por mercúrio

3461 meringue
(Prod.)
(Confectionary; made of sugar and egg white whipped together.)
d Baiser *n*; Meringe *f*
f meringue *f*
p merengue *m*

3462 merino breed
(Agr.)
(Livestock; ref. to sheep raising: good wool producing sheep breed.)
d Merino-Rasse *f*
f race *f* de mérinos
p raça *f* merina

3463 mesocarp
(Agr.)
(Botany; part of the pericarp of the fruit: e.g. the pulp, i.e. the succulent fruit part.)
d Mesokarp *n*; Mesokarpium *n*
f mésocarpe *m*
p mesocarpo *m*

3464 messenger RNA
(Med.)
(Anatomy. mRNA, transports the genetic code transcribed from DNA to the ribosomes.)

d Botschafter-RNS *f*
f A.R.N. messager *m*
p RNA mensageiro *m*

3465 **metabolic disease**
(Med.)
(Regimens, diets.)
d Stoffwechselkrankheit *f*
f maladie *f* métabolique
p doença *f* metabólica

3466 **metabolic disequilibrium**
(Med.)
(Metabolic disorders.)
d metabolisches Missverhältnis *n*
f déséquilibre *m* métabolique
p desequilíbrio *m* metabólico

3467 **metabolic disorders**
(Med.)
(E.g. due to vitamin deficiencies.)
d metabolische Störungen *fpl*; Stoffwechselstörungen *fpl*
f perturbations *fpl* métaboliques
p perturbações *fpl* metabólicas

3468 **metabolic intermediate**
(Med.)
(Anatomy.)
d Vermittler *m* im Stoffwechselprozess
f intermédiaire *m* métabolique
p intermediário *m* metabólico

3469 **metabolic nutritional approach; metabolic nutritional intervention**
(Med.)
(Regimens, diets in therapy.)
d Eingriff *m* in den Stoffwechsel durch Nahrungsmittel; metabolischer Eingriff *m* durch Nahrungsmittel
f approche *f* nutritionnelle métabolique
p intervenção *f* no metabolismo pela nutrição

* **metabolic nutritional intervention → 3469**

3470 **metabolic optimization**
(Med.)
(Nutrition in medicine.)
d Optimierung *f* des Stoffwechsels; Stoffwechseloptimierung *f*
f optimisation *f* métabolique
p otimização *f* metabólica

3471 **metabolic pathology**
(Med.)
(Ref. to diabetes etc.)
d Stoffwechselpathologie *f*
f pathologie *f* métabolique
p patologia *f* metabólica

3472 **metabolism**
(Med.)
(Total of the body's chemical, biochemical and physical processes.)
d Stoffwechsel *m*; Metabolismus *m*
f métabolisme *m*
p metabolismo *m*

3473 **metabolism of animal cells**
(Biochem.)
(Biochemical research, e.g. in genetic engineering; nutritional science.)
d Stoffwechsel *m* der tierischen Zelle
f métabolisme *m* des cellules animales
p metabolismo *m* das células animais

3474 **metabolism of plant cells**
(Biochem.)
(Biochemical research, e.g. in genetic engineering; nutritional science.)
d Stoffwechsel *m* der pflanzlichen Zellen
f métabolisme *m* des cellules végétales
p metabolismo *m* das células vegetais

3475 **metabolism of the living cells**
(Biochem.)
(Genetic engineering, e.g. nutritional science.)
d Stoffwechsel *m* der lebenden Zellen
f métabolisme *m* des cellules vivantes
p metabolismo *m* das células vivas

3476 **metabolite**
(Med.)
(Metabolism product.)
d Metabolit *n*; Stoffwechselprodukt *n*
f métabolite *m*
p metabólito *m*

3477 **metabolizable** *adj*
(Med.)
(Able to undergo metabolization.)
d metabolisierbar; stoffwechselfähig
f métabolisable
p metabolizável

3478 **metabolizable energy**
(Med.)
(Difference between total energy and the losses through faeces and urine.)
d für den Stoffwechsel verwertbare Energie *f*
f énergie *f* métabolisable
p energia *f* metabolisável; energia *f* digestiva

3479 **metabolize** *v*
(Med.)
(Act of performing metabolism.)
d metabolisieren; im Stoffwechselprozess umsetzen
f métaboliser
p metabolizar

3480 metaldehyde
(Agr.)
(Biological agriculture; $(C_2H_4O)_n$; acetaldehyde polymer of human toxicity: e.g. used for snail destruction.)
d Metaldehyd *n*
f métaldéhyde *m*
p metaldeída *f*

3481 metamorphic rock
(Agr.)
(Soil. Rock derived from a pre-existing rock by the metamorphism process, which results e.g. in a structural change through heat and pressure.)
d metamorphes Gestein *n*
f roche *f* métamorphique
p rocha *f* metamórfica

3482 methionine
(Biochem.)
($C_5H_{11}NO_2S$. Dietary supplement, produced by vitamin B_{12} activity and essential amino acid ingredient in human and in cow's milk.)
d Methionin *n*
f méthionine *f*
p metionina *f*

* **method of fruit tree culture → 402**

3483 methodology
(Biochem.)
(Nutritional science.)
d Methodologie *f*
f méthodologie *f*
p metodologia *f*

3484 methods of biological supervision
(Biochem.)
(Nutritional science.)
d Methoden *fpl* biologischer Überwachung
f méthodes *fpl* de surveillance biologique
p métodos *mpl* de supervisão biológica

3485 methods of deep-freezing
(Prod.)
(Food processing technology; food preservation processes.)
d Tiefkühlmethoden *fpl*; Methoden *fpl* der Tiefkühlung
f techniques *fpl* de surgélation
p técnicas *fpl* de congelamento

3486 methods of therapeutics in dietetics
(Med.)
(Nutrition.)
d diätetisch-therapeutische Methoden *fpl*
f méthodes *fpl* thérapeutiques diététiques
p métodos *mpl* terapêutico-dietéticos

3487 methods of weeding; methods of weed killing
(Agr.)
(Weed removal, e.g. in biological agriculture.)
d Unkrautvertilgungsmethoden *fpl*
f techniques *fpl* de désherbage
p técnicas *fpl* herbicidas

* **methods of weed killing → 3487**

* **1-methoxy-4-methylbenzene → 4048**

* **4-methoxybenzyl alcohol → 300**

3488 methyl anthranilate
(Prod.)
($C_8H_9NO_2$; artificial neroli oil; synthetic aroma prime material, e.g. grape flavour; flavour chemical.)
d Anthranilsäure-Methylester *m*
f anthranilate *m* de méthyle
p antranilato *m* de metila

* **2-methylbutanoic acid → 3489**

* **3-methylbutyl acetate → 3026**

3489 methylbutyric acid; 2-methylbutyric acid; 2-methylbutanoic acid
(Prod.)
($C_5H_{10}O_2$; aroma prime material, e.g. cheese-like (Roquefort-type) flavour; flavour chemical.)
d Methylbuttersäure *f*
f acide *m* méthylbutyrique
p ácido *m* metilbutírico

* **2-methylbutyric acid → 3489**

3490 methylcellulose
(Prod.)
(Food processing technology: e.g. texture improving ingredient.)
d Methylcellulose *f*
f méthylcellulose *f*
p metilcelulose *f*

3491 methyl cinnamate
(Prod.)
($C_{10}H_{10}O_2$; aroma prime material, e.g. flavour improver; in butter and cream aromas and in some fruity notes; in confectionary, due to its strawberry-like aroma; flavour chemical.)
d Methylcynnamat *n*
f cinnamate *m* de méthyle
p metilcinamato *m*

3492 methylene blue
(Biochem.)
($C_{16}H_{18}ClN_3S.3H_2O$; oxidation-reduction indicator, stain in biochemistry: as such used

as bacteriological quality indicator in milk: colour change speed indicates bacteria conc.: dye-reduction test.)
d Methylenblau *n*
f bleu *m* de méthylène
p azul *m* de metileno

3493 **methylene chloride; dichloromethane**
(Prod.)
(CH_2Cl_2; solvent in oil extraction processes. Auxiliary product.)
d Methylenchlorid *n*
f chlorure *m* de méthylène
p cloreto *m* de metileno

3494 **methylionone**
(Prod.)
($C_{14}H_{22}O$; irone; prime material for aroma/fragrance production; flavour chemical.)
d Methyljonon *n*
f méthylionone *f*
p metilionona *f*

* **methyl nonyl acetaldehyde → 170**

* **methyl octyl acetaldehyde → 169**

* **2-methyl-undecanal → 170**

3495 **metritis**
(Med.)
(Veterinary; ref. to dairy cattle breeding: uterus inflammation.)
d Gebärmutterentzündung *f*
f métrite *f*
p metrite *f*

3496 **mevalonic acid**
(Prod.)
($C_6H_{12}O_4$; ref. to the synthesis of terpene compounds; aroma/fragrance prime material.)
d Mevalonsäure *f*
f acide *m* mévalonique
p ácido *m* mevalônico

3497 **micellar dispersion**
(Med.)
(Veterinary; ref. e.g. to absorption of liposoluble vitamins in the animal body, animal metabolism.)
d mizelläre Dispersion *f*
f dispersion *f* micellaire
p dispersão *f* micelar

3498 **micellar solubilization of vitamins**
(Med.)
(Veterinary; ref. to vitamin supplementation to feed, vitamin absorption and animal metabolism.)
d mizelläre Löslichmachung *f* von Vitaminen; mizelläre Solubilisierung *f* von Vitaminen
f solubilisation *f* micellaire des vitamines
p solubilização *f* micelar de vitaminas

3499 **micelle**
(Biochem.)
(Nutritional science; molecular aggregate; colloidal particle.)
d Mizelle *f*; Mizell *n*
f micelle *f*
p micela *f*

3500 **microbe**
(Biochem.)
(Microbiology.)
d Mikrobe *f*
f microbe *m*
p micróbio *m*

3501 **microbes of contamination**
(Biochem.)
(Microbiology; food spoiling microorganisms.)
d Kontaminationsmikroben *fpl*; kontaminierende Mikroben *fpl*
f microbes *mpl* de contamination
p micróbios *mpl* de contaminação

3502 **microbial accident**
(Biochem.)
(Food biochemistry.)
d mikrobieller Unfall *m*
f accident *m* microbien
p acidente *m* microbial; acidente *m* microbiano

3503 **microbial activity**
(Biochem.)
(Food biochemistry.)
d mikrobielle Aktivität *f*; mikrobielle Wirksamkeit *f*
f activité *f* microbienne
p atividade *f* microbial; atividade *f* microbiana

3504 **microbial activity of the soil**
(Agr.)
(Soil treatment.)
d mikrobielle Bodenaktivität *f*
f activité *f* microbienne du sol
p atividade *f* microbial do solo; atividade *f* microbiana do solo

3505 **microbial fermentation**
(Biochem.)
(Food biochemistry.)
d mikrobielle Gärung *f*
f fermentation *f* microbienne
p fermentação *f* microbial; fermentação *f* microbiana

3506 microbial flora
(Med.)
(Intestinal flora, e.g. lactobacillus bifidus.)
d mikrobielle Flora *f*
f flore *f* microbienne
p flora *f* microbial; flora *f* microbiana

* **microbial phenomena → 3507**

3507 microbial phenomenons; microbial phenomena
(Biochem.)
(Microbiology in food biochemistry.)
d mikrobielle Erscheinungen *fpl*
f phénomènes *mpl* microbiens
p fenômenos *mpl* microbianos

3508 microbial proliferation
(Biochem.)
(Food biochemistry.)
d mikrobielle Vermehrung *f*; mikrobielle Proliferation *f*
f prolifération *f* microbienne
p proliferação *f* microbial; proliferação *f* microbiana

3509 microbial stability
(Biochem.)
(Microbiology; fermentation.)
d mikrobielle Stabilität *f*
f stabilité *f* microbienne
p estabilidade *f* microbiana

3510 microbicidal effect
(Biochem.)
(Microbiology; food conservation; food preservative.)
d mikrobizide Wirkung *f*
f effet *m* microbicide
p efeito *m* microbicida; efeito *m* germicida

3511 microbiological control
(Biochem.)
(Microbiology.)
d mikrobiologische Kontrolle *f*
f contrôle *m* microbiologique
p controle *m* microbiológico

3512 microbiological purity
(Biochem.)
(Microbiology in food biochemistry.)
d mikrobiologische Reinheit *f*
f pureté *f* microbiologique
p pureza *f* microbiológica

3513 microbiologic contamination
(Biochem.)
(Microbiology in food biochemistry.)
d mikrobiologische Kontamination *f*; mikrobiologische Verseuchung *f*
f contamination *f* microbienne
p contaminação *f* microbiológica

3514 microbiologic treatment
(Biochem.)
(Microbiology; process type, e.g. in aroma production.)
d mikrobiologische Behandlung *f*
f traitement *m* microbiologique
p tratamento *m* microbiológico

3515 microbiology
(Biochem.)
(Science of microorganisms e.g. in food biochemistry.)
d Mikrobiologie *f*
f microbiologie *f*
p microbiologia *f*

3516 microbiology of wine
(Biochem.)
(Microbiology ref. to enology.)
d Mikrobiologie *f* des Weines
f microbiologie *f* du vin
p microbiologia *f* do vinho

3517 microcrystalline *adj*
(Biochem.)
(Food biochemistry; product characteristic.)
d mikrokristallin
f microcristallin
p microcristalino

3518 microcrystalline beta-carotene
(Prod.)
(Food processing technology: product characteristic.)
d mikrokristallines Beta-Carotin *n*
f bêta-carotène *m* microcristallin
p beta-caroteno *m* microcristalino

3519 microdispersible vitamin formulation
(Med.)
(Veterinary; formulations for the absorption (promotion) of certain vitamins by the animal body.)
d mikrodispergierbare Vitaminformulierung *f*
f formulation *f* vitaminique microdispersible
p formulação *f* vitamínica microdispersível

3520 microdistillation
(Prod.)
(Aroma/flavour production: ref. to distillation process types.)
d Mikrodestillation *f*
f microdistillation *f*
p microdestilação *f*

3521 microfauna
(Agr.)
(Soil; e.g. insects in the soil, ref. to arable soil formation and natural cycles.)
d Mikrofauna *f*
f microfaune *f*
p microfauna *f*

3522 microflora
(Agr.)
(Soil; e.g. bacteria; algae in the soils; ref. to arable soil formation and natural cycles.)
d Mikroflora *f*
f microflore *f*
p microflora *f*

3523 micronutrient
(Biochem.)
(Nutritional science.)
d Mikronährstoff *m*
f micronutriment *m*
p micronutriente *m*

3524 micronutritional antioxidant equilibrium
(Biochem.)
(Nutritional science.)
d antioxidierende Ausgeglichenheit *f* der Mikronahrungsmittelkomponenten
f équilibre *m* micronutritionnel antioxydant
p equilíbrio *m* micronutricional antioxidante

3525 micronutritional disequilibrium
(Biochem.)
(Nutritional science.)
d Missverhältnis *n* an Mikronahrungsmittelkomponenten; Unausgeglichenheit *f* an Mikronahrungsmittelkomponenten
f déséquilibre *m* micronutritionnel
p desequilíbrio *m* micronutricional

3526 micronutritional equilibrium
(Biochem.)
(Nutritional science.)
d Ausgeglichenheit *f* der Mikronahrungsmittelkomponenten
f équilibre *m* micronutritionnel
p equilíbrio *m* micronutricional

3527 micronutritional subdeficiency
(Biochem.)
(Nutritional science.)
d Submangel *m* an Mikronahrungsmittelkomponenten
f subcarence *f* micronutritionnelle
p subcarência *f* micronutricional

3528 micronutritional supplementation
(Biochem.)
(Nutritional science: ref. to regimens, diets.)
d Mikrosupplementierung *f*
f supplémentation *f* micronutritionnelle
p suplementação *f* micronutricional

3529 microwaves
(Prod.)
(Food processing technology: microwave heating, rapid foodstuff heating.)
d Mikrowellen *fpl*
f micro-ondes *fpl*
p microondas *fpl*

3530 microwave treatment
(Prod.)
(Food processing technology: preservation process.)
d Mikrowellenbehandlung *f*
f traitement *m* par micro-ondes
p tratamento *m* por microondas

3531 middle brisket
(Prod.)
(Butchery; meat part; joint.)
d Mittelbrust *f*
f poitrine *f* intermédiaire; tendron *m* intermédiaire
p peito *m*

3532 middle rib and chuck
(Agr.)
(Butchery; meat part; joint.)
d Fehlrippe *f*; Rindlendenstück *n*; Schulterstück *n*
f surlonge *f*; paleron *m*
p agulha *f*; cernelha *f*

3533 middlings
(Prod.)
(Food processing technology; Obtained by milling coarse cereal grains: the meal adherent to the bran and to be extracted by a second milling process; prime material.)
d Schrotmehl *n*; kleiehaltiges Mehl *n*
f remoulage *m*; recoupe *m*; rebulet *m*
p farinha *f* de farelo; farinha *f* grossa

3534 migration
(Prod.)
(Aroma/flavour molecules.)
d Migration *f*, Auswanderung *f*
f migration *f*
p migração *f*

3535 migration facility in foodstuff
(Prod.)
(Aroma/flavour particle property: flavour research.)
d Leichtigkeit *f* des Migrierens im Nahrungsmittel

f facilité *f* à migrer dans l'aliment
p facilidade *f* de migrar dentro do alimento

3536 mild blue cheese
(Prod.)
(Dairy plant product, penicillium roqueforti cheese.)
d milder blauer Käse *m*
f bleu *m* à pâte molle
p queijo *m* azul suave

3537 mildew
(Agr.)
(Biological agriculture; fungus and its whitish growth on plants.)
d Mehltau *m*
f mildiou *m*
p alforra *f*; míldio

3538 milieu acidification; acidification of the medium
(Biochem.)
(Synthesis condition e.g. in nutritional science.)
d Ansäuerung *f* des Mediums
f acidification *f* du milieu
p acidificação *f* do meio

3539 milk
(Prod.)
(Dairy product which has to contain more than 3% of fats and more than 85% of other types of solids.)
d Milch *f*
f lait *m*
p leite *m*

* **milk adapted to human necessities → 2754**

3540 milk analysis
(Prod.)
(Dairy product examination.)
d Milchanalyse *f*
f analyse *f* du lait
p análise *f* do leite

3541 milk carton
(Prod.)
(Dairy package made of cardboard or plastics.)
d Milchpackung *f*
f berlingot *m* de lait
p caixinha *f* de leite

3542 milk clodding; milk curdling
(Prod.)
(Dairy product.)
d Milchgerinnung *f*
f caillage *f* du lait
p coalhadura *f* do leite

* **milk conservation by heat treatment → 3543**

3543 milk conservation by thermal treatment; milk conservation by heat treatment
(Prod.)
(Dairy plant technology; milk industrialization.)
d Milchkonservierung *f* durch Wärmebehandlung
f conservation *f* du lait par traitement thermique
p conservação *f* do leite por tratamento térmico

* **milk cow → 1500**

* **milk curdling → 3542**

3544 milk decomposition
(Biochem.)
(Food biochemistry.)
d Milchzersetzung *f*
f décomposition *f* de lait
p decomposição *f* do leite

3545 milk diet
(Med.)
(Alimentary regimen.)
d Milchdiät *f*
f diète *f* lactée
p dieta *f* láctea

* **milk drink → 3096**

3546 milk dyspepsia
(Med.)
(Indigestion caused by exclusive cow-milk feeding: malnutrition type.)
d Milchdyspepsie *f*, milchernährungsbedingte Verdauungsstörung *f*
f dyspepsie *f* du lait de vache
p dispepsia *f* de leite de vaca

3547 milk-enriched dough
(Prod.)
(Bakery.)
d milchangereicherter Teig *m*
f pâte *f* enrichie de lait
p massa *f* enriquecida com leite

3548 milk enriched with iron; iron-enriched milk
(Med.)
(Baby nutrition.)
d eisenangereicherte Milch *f*, mit Eisen angereicherte Milch *f*
f lait *m* enrichi en fer
p leite *m* enriquecido com ferro

* **milk enriched with vitamin D → 5761**

* **milker → 1500**

3549 **milk filtration; lactofiltration**
(Prod.)
(Dairy process. Milk filtration process on cotton wool: Cleanness test.)
d Milchfiltrierung *f*; Laktofiltration *f*
f filtration *f* du lait; lactofiltration *f*
p filtração *f* du leite; lactofiltração *f*

3550 **milking**
(Agr.)
(Agricultural activity: ref. to dairy cattle breeding.)
d Melken *n*
f traite *f*
p ordenha *f*

3551 **milk lipids**
(Biochem.)
(Food biochemistry.)
d Milchfettstoffe *mpl*; Milchlipide *npl*
f lipides *mpl* du lait
p lipídios *mpl* do leite

3552 **milk of the ruminants**
(Med.)
(E.g. cow's milk; different in composition from human milk; ref. to baby nutrition.)
d Milch *f* der Wiederkäuer
f lait *m* des ruminants
p leite *m* dos ruminantes

3553 **milk pap**
(Prod.)
(Gastronomy.)
d Milchbrei *m*
f bouillie *f* au lait
p papa *f* de leite; mingau *m* de leite

3554 **milk pasteurization**
(Prod.)
(Food processing technology. Normal low-temperature: ca. 62°; High temperature short time (HTST): 72°-15 s; high temperature: 95°.)
d Milchpasteurisieren *n*; Pasteurisieren *n* von Milch
f pasteurisation *f* du lait
p pasteurização *f* do leite

3555 **milk powder; powder milk; dried milk**
(Prod.)
(Dairy final consumer product.)
d Trockenmilch *f*; Milchpulver *n*
f lait *m* en poudre
p leite *m* em pó

3556 **milk powder particles**
(Prod.)
(Dairy plant technology, milk powder production.)
d Trockenmilchteilchen *npl*
f particules *fpl* du lait en poudre
p partículas *fpl* de leite em pó

3557 **milk preparation**
(Prod.)
(Dairy process for cheese making.)
d Milchvorbereitung *f*
f préparation *f* du lait
p preparação *f* de leite

3558 **milk product**
(Prod.)
(Dairy product; product obtained from milk, e.g. cheese, butter; cream etc.)
d Milchprodukt *n*; Milchspeise *f*
f laitage *m*
p produto *m* à base de leite

3559 **milk production**
(Prod.)
(Dairy activity.)
d Milcherzeugung *f*; Milchproduktion *f*
f production *f* laitière
p produção *f* de leite

3560 **milk proteins**
(Biochem.)
(Food biochemistry. Proteins of high biological value, e.g. important for dairy products.)
d Milchproteine *npl*
f protéines *fpl* du lait
p proteínas *fpl* do leite

3561 **milk stabilized by acidification**
(Prod.)
(Dairy processing technology.)
d durch Säuerung stabilisierte Milch *f*
f lait *m* stabilisé par acidification
p leite *m* estabilizado por acidificação

3562 **milk substitutes**
(Prod.)
(Food processing technology.)
d Milchaustauschprodukte *npl*; Milchaustauscher *mpl*; Milchersatz *m*
f succédanés *mpl* du lait
p sucedâneos *mpl* do leite; substitutos *mpl* de leite

* **milk sugar → 3112**

3563 **milk sweetened with saccharose**
(Prod.)
(Baby nutrition. Milk ingredient in industrial milk types.)
d mit Saccharose gesüßte Milch *f*
f lait *m* sucré au saccharose
p leito *m* adoçado com sacarose

3564 milk tooth
(Med.)
(Anatomy.)
d Milchzahn *m*
f dent *f* de lait
p dente *m* de leite

3565 mill
(Prod.)
(Food processing technology; establishment for grinding grain into flour.)
d Müllerei *f*
f meunerie *f*
p moinho *m*

3566 mill *v*
(Prod.)
(Food processing technology.)
d mahlen
f moudre
p moer

3567 mille-feuille cake; puff pastry cake
(Prod.)
(Confectionary.)
d Blätterteigkuchen *m*
f mille-feuille *m*
p bolo *m* de mil-folhas

3568 millet
(Agr.)
(Agricultural produce. "Panicum miliaceum". Cereal.)
d Hirse *f*
f millet *m*
p painço *m*; milho *m* miúdo

3569 milling process
(Prod.)
(Food processing technology.)
d Mahlen *n*
f mouture *f*
p moedura *f*; moagem *f*

3570 mince *v*
(Prod.)
(Butchery; meat treatment.)
d zerhacken
f hacher
p picar

3571 minced meat
(Prod.)
(Butchery; chopped meat.)
d Hackfleisch *n*; Gehackte *n*
f viande *f* hachée
p carne *f* picada

3572 mincing
(Prod.)
(Butchery; meat industrialization; meat treatment.)
d Wolfen *n*
f hachage *m*
p processo *m* de picar

3573 mineral complements
(Agr.)
(Livestock; ref. to feedstuff ration.)
d Mineralzusatzstoffe *mpl*
f compléments *mpl* minéraux
p complementos *mpl* minerais

3574 mineral deficiency of the soil
(Agr.)
(Soils; soil treatment; e.g. phosphorus addition.)
d Mineralienmangel *m* des Bodens
f carence *f* minérale du sol
p carência *f* mineral do solo

3575 mineral elements
(Biochem.)
(Food biochemistry: Essential elements are taken in, together with foodstuff; essential for growth etc.: sodium (Na); potassium (Ka); calcium (Ca); magnesium (Mg); chlorine (Cl) and others.)
d Mineralstoffe *mpl*
f éléments *mpl* minéraux
p elementos *mpl* minerais

3576 mineral fertilizer
(Agr.)
(Biological agriculture. Auxiliary fertilizers, completing the organic fertilizing material with components like potassium, calcium etc.)
d Mineraldünger *m*
f engrais *m* minéral
p fertilizante *m* mineral

3577 mineralizing agent
(Agr.)
(Supplementation of animal ration with mineral components: calcium (Ca), iodine (I), iron (Fe), magnesium (Mg), phosphorus (P), zinc (Zn), selenium (Se), potassium (K), fluorine (F).)
d Mineralisierungsmittel *n*
f agent *m* de minéralisation
p mineralizante *m*

3578 mineral nitrogen
(Agr.)
(Biological agriculture: fertilization.)
d Mineralstickstoff *m*
f azote *m* minéral
p nitrogênio *m* mineral

3579 **mineral-poor flour**
(Prod.)
(Food processing technology; ref. to flour types like e.g. buckwheat flour. Prime material.)
d mineralstoffarmes Mehl *n*
f farine *f* pauvre en éléments minéraux
p farinha *f* pobre de elementos minerais

* **mineral reserves of the soil → 4677**

* **mineral resources → 3695**

3580 **mineral salts**
(Med.)
(Veterinary: indispensable elements for the maintenance of the animal body; to be found e.g. in tissues and vital for the skeletal and cartilage formation.)
d Mineralsalze *npl*
f sels *mpl* minéraux
p sais *mpl* minerais

3581 **mineral salts in milk grades**
(Med.)
(Baby nutrition.)
d Mineralsalze *npl* in den Milchsorten
f sels *mpl* minéraux dans les laits
p sais *mpl* minerais nos leites

3582 **minerals of fresh vegetables**
(Agr.)
(Horticulture. Mineral plant constituents important for the human body.)
d Mineralien *fpl* des Frischgemüses
f minéraux *mpl* des légumes frais
p minerais *mpl* dos legumes frescos; minerais *mpl* das hortaliças frescas

3583 **mineral supply**
(Agr.)
(Botany; mineral plant constituents important for the human body.)
d Mineralienzufuhr *f*
f apport *m* en minéraux
p aporte *m* de minerais; fornecimento *m* de minerais

3584 **mineral water**
(Prod.)
(Water supply; therapeutic fountain water types, containing carbon dioxide (CO_2) and mineral salts.)
d Mineralwasser *n*
f eau *f* minérale
p água *f* mineral

3585 **mineral water containing carbon dioxide**
(Prod.)
(Water supply; CO_2; carbonic anhydride.)
d kohlensäurehaltiges Mineralwasser *n*
f eau *f* minérale contenant de gaz carbonique
p água *f* mineral contendo gás carbônico

3586 **mineral waters cure**
(Med.)
(Health treatment based on therapeutic fountain waters.)
d Brunnentrinkkur *f*
f cure *f* d'eau minérale
p tratamento *m* á base de água mineral

3587 **minimum vitamin supply**
(Med.)
(Veterinary e.g. ref. farm animal raising, fodder composition.)
d Minimalvitaminversorgung *f*
f approvisionnement *m* vitaminique minimal
p suprimento *m* mínimo de vitaminas

3588 **mint**
(Agr.)
(Genus "Mentha"; an aromatic plant, e.g. used in confection production, as flavour and in cookery.)
d Minze *f*
f menthe *f*
p menta *f*; hortelã *f*; levante *m*

3589 **mint essence tincture**
(Prod.)
(Aroma/flavour research and production: extraction process. Genus "Mentha", "Mentha piperita".)
d Minzessenztinktur *f*; Auszug *m* des Minzenöles
f teinture *f* d'essence de menthe
p tintura *f* da essência da hortelã

3590 **mint flavour**
(Prod.)
(Aroma/flavour note.)
d minziger Geschmack *m*
f saveur *f* de menthe
p sabor *m* de menta

3591 **mint note**
(Prod.)
(Taste; aroma research and production, e.g. tea flavour.)
d Minzennote *f*
f note *f* de menthe
p nota *f* de hortelã; nota *f* de menta

3592 **mirabelle; yellow plum**
(Agr.)
(Horticulture. "Kochia scoparia"; plum; edible fruit.)
d Mirabelle *f*

f mirabelle *f*
p mirabela *f*

* **miscarriage → 2**

3593 **miscibility degree of liquids**
(Prod.)
(Aroma/flavour research and production: distillation processes.)
d Mischbarkeitsgrad *m* von Flüssigkeiten
f degré *m* de miscibilité des liquides
p grau *m* de miscibilidade dos líquidos

3594 **miscible with edible oils**
(Prod.)
(Vitamins in nutrition; e.g. ref. to vitamin blends in food stuff processing.)
d mischbar mit Speiseölen
f miscible aux huiles alimentaires
p miscível com óleos alimentícios

3595 **miscible with fats**
(Prod.)
(Vitamins in nutrition; e.g. ref. to vitamin blends in food stuff processing.)
d mischbar mit Fetten
f miscible aux graisses
p miscíveis às gorduras

3596 **mixed diet; combined diet**
(Med.)
(Alimentary regimen.)
d Mischdiät *f*
f diète *f* mêlée
p dieta *f* mista

3597 **mixture of saccharose and dextrin-maltose**
(Prod.)
(Baby nutrition. Milk ingredient in industrial milk types.)
d Mischung *f* von Saccharose und Dextrinmaltose
f mélange *m* saccharose et dextrine-maltose
p mistura *f* de sacarose e dextrina-maltose

3598 **models of foodstuff consumption**
(Prod.)
(Food processing, research, production and marketing.)
d Modelle *npl* des Nahrungsmittelkonsums
f modèles *mpl* de consommation alimentaire
p modelos *mpl* do consumo alimentício

3599 **modernization of agriculture**
(Agr.)
(Agriculture.)
d Modernisierung *f* der Agrikultur; Modernisierung *f* des landwirtschaftlichen Betriebes
f modernisation *f* de l'agriculture
p modernização *f* da agricultura

3600 **modification of blood coagulation**
(Med.)
(Nutrition in medicine; e.g. thrombogenic processes.)
d Änderung *f* der Blutgerinnung
f modification *f* de la coagulation sanguine
p modificação *f* da coagulação do sangue

3601 **modification of foodstuff consumption**
(Prod.)
(Food processing, research, production and marketing.)
d Änderung *f* des Nahrungsmittelverbrauches
f modification *f* de la consommation alimentaire
p modificação *f* do consumo alimentício

3602 **modification of nutriments; alteration of nutriments**
(Biochem.)
(Nutritional science.)
d Veränderung *f* der Nahrungsmittel
f modification *f* des aliments
p modificação *f* dos alimentos

3603 **modification of nutritional custom**
(Biochem.)
(Nutritional science.)
d Änderung *f* der Ernährungsgewohnheiten
f modification *f* des habitudes alimentaires
p modificação *f* dos hábitos de alimentação; modificação *f* dos costumes de alimentação

3604 **modifications of vegetable consistency**
(Prod.)
(Food processing technology: cooking and boiling processes.)
d Konsistenzveränderungen *fpl* des Gemüses
f modifications *fpl* de consistance des végétaux
p modificações *fpl* da consistência dos vegetais

3605 **modified proteins**
(Biochem.)
(Nutritional science.)
d modifizierte Proteine *npl*; veränderte Proteine *npl*
f protéines *fpl* modifiées
p proteínas *fpl* modificadas

3606 **modified starch**
(Biochem.)
(Food biochemistry; product having undergone chemical treatment for property improvement: e.g. swelling characteristics.)
d modifizierte Stärke *f*
f amidon *m* modifié; fécule *f* modifiée
p amido *m* modificado

3607 moisture contents
(Prod.)
(Food processing technology.)
d Feuchtgehalt *m*; Feuchtigkeitsgehalt *m*
f teneur *f* en humidité
p teor *m* de umidade

3608 moisture resistance
(Prod.)
(Food processing technology; product characteristic.)
d Feuchtigkeitsbeständigkeit *f*
f résistance *f* à l'humidité
p resistência *f* à umidade

3609 moisture-saturated atmosphere
(Prod.)
(Food processing technology. Pasta plant: Drying equipment characteristic: short drying: moisture saturated at 105°C.)
d Feuchtatmosphäre *f*; feuchtigkeitsangereicherte Atmosphäre *f*
f atmosphère *f* humide
p atmosfera *f* húmida; ambiente *m* húmido

3610 molar fraction
(Biochem.)
(Nutritional science; ref. to aroma/fragrance molecules.)
d molare Fraktion *f*
f fraction *f* molaire
p fração *f* molar

3611 molasses; treacle
(Agr.)
(Agricultural produce and byproduct of sugar production.)
d Melasse *f*
f mélasse *f*
p melaço *m*

3612 molasses clarification
(Prod.)
(Food processing technology: Yeast plant production process: Molasse is a substrate for yeast propagation.)
d Melasseklärung *f*
f clarification *f* de la mélasse
p clarificação *f* do melaço

3613 molasses preparation
(Prod.)
(Food processing technology; ref. to yeast production technology.)
d Aufbereitung *f* der Melasse
f préparation *f* de la mélasse
p preparação *f* do melaço

3614 molasses pretreatment
(Prod.)
(Food processing technology. Yeast production phase: dilution of yeast, clarification, sterilization and final cooking.)
d Hefevorbehandlung *f*
f prétraitement *m* de la mélasse
p pré-tratamento *m* do melaço

3615 molasses storage
(Prod.)
(Foodstuff and prime material storage technology)
d Einlagerung *f* der Melasse
f emmagasinage *m* de la mélasse; entreposage *m* de la mélasse
p armazenamento *m* do melaço

3616 mold *v* the curd
(Prod.)
(Dairy plant process.)
d den Quark formen
f mouler la caillebotte
p moldar a ricota

3617 molecular distillation
(Prod.)
(Aroma/flavour research and production.)
d Molekulardestillation *f*
f distillation *f* moléculaire
p destilação *f* molecular

3618 molecule availability
(Biochem.)
(Food biochemistry.)
d Verfügbarkeit *f* der Moleküle
f disponibilité *f* des molécules
p disponibilidade *f* das moléculas

3619 molluscs
(Agr.)
(Agricultural produce. "Phylum Mollusca".)
d Weichtiere *npl*
f mollusques *mpl*
p moluscos *mpl*

3620 molten cheese
(Prod.)
(Dairy product; soft cheese type.)
d Schmelzkäse *m*
f fromage *m* fondu
p queijo *m* fundido

3621 molten product
(Prod.)
(Food processing technology; product aspect.)
d geschmolzenes Produkt *n*
f produit *m* fondu
p produto *m* fundido

3622 molybdenum deficiency
(Med.)
(Veterinary; mineral (Mo) deficiency: metabolic disequilibrium.)

d Molybdänmangel *m*
f carence *f* en molybdène
p deficiência *f* de molibdênio

3623 **monoaminoxydase inhibitor**
(Biochem.)
(Nutritional science: MAO inhibitor; e.g. ref. to cheese disease: In case of MAO-inhibition in cheese-tyramine degradation: provokes high blood pressure, headache etc.)
d Monoaminoxidasehemmer *m*
f inhibiteur *m* de mono-amino-oxydase
p inibidor *m* da monoamino-oxidase

* **monocotyledon → 3624**

3624 **monocotyledonous angiosperm; monocotyledon**
(Agr.)
(Botany. "Angiospermae" having one seed leaf.)
d einkeimblättriger Decksamen *m*
f angiosperme *f* monocotylédone; monocotylédone *f*
p angiosperma *f* monocotiledônea

* **monocropping → 3625**

3625 **monoculture; monocropping**
(Agr.)
(Agricultural system; continuous planting of the same single crop.)
d Monokultur *f*
f monoculture *f*
p monocultura *f*

3626 **monocyclic monoterpenes**
(Prod.)
($C_{10}H_{16}$; e.g. limonene; source of aroma/fragrance prime material.)
d monozyklische Monoterpene *npl*
f monoterpènes *mpl* monocycliques
p monoterpenos *mpl* monocíclicos

3627 **monosaccharide**
(Prod.)
(Monosaccharose; $C_n(H_2O)_n$; simple sugar, not further hydrolyzable.)
d Monosaccharid *n*
f monosaccharide *m*; ose *m*
p monossacarídeo *m*

* **monosodium glutamate → 2516**

3628 **monosodium salt of glutamic acid**
(Biochem.)
($C_5H_8O_4NaN$; see glutamate.)
d Mononatriumsalz *n* der Glutaminsäure
f sel *m* monosodique de l'acide glutamique
p sal *m* monossódico do ácido glutâmico

3629 **mono-unsaturated fatty acid**
(Biochem.)
(E.g. oleic acid ($C_{18}H_{34}O_2$).)
d einfach ungesättigte Fettsäure *f*
f acide *m* gras mono-insaturé
p ácido *m* graxo mono-insaturado

3630 **Monterey jack**
(Prod.)
(Dairy product; semisoft whole-milk cheese.)
d halbweicher Vollmilchkäse *m*
f fromage *m* semi-mol à lait non-écrémé
p queijo *m* semi-mole de leite integral

3631 **moor; moorland**
(Agr.)
(Soil. Uncultivated boggy land type; e.g. used for cattle breeding.)
d Moor *n*
f marais *m*; marécage *m*
p pântano *m*

* **moorland → 3631**

* **morass → 5370**

3632 **more volatile product; easier volatile product**
(Prod.)
(Aroma/flavour research and production: distillation processes.)
d leichter verdunstbares Produkt *n*; schneller flüchtiges Produkt *n*
f produit *m* plus volatil
p produto *m* mais volátil

3633 **mortadella**
(Prod.)
(Butchery. Seasoned sausage, Italian type.)
d Mortadella *f*
f mortadelle *f*
p mortadela *f*

3634 **moss**
(Agr.)
(Botany. Class "Musci"; e.g. peat moss is used for ground covering around the plant for protection purposes.)
d Moos *n*
f mousse *f*
p musgo *m*

3635 **most volatile compounds**
(Prod.)
(Aroma/flavour research and production, distillation product.)
d flüchtigste Bestandteile *fpl*
f composés *mpl* les plus volatils
p compostos *mpl* mais volátis

* **mother's milk → 2755**

3636 **mother's milk substitute**
(Med.)
(Baby nutrition; industrialized milk.)
d Muttermilchersatz *m*; Muttermilchaustauschprodukt *n*
f substitut *m* du lait maternel
p substituto *m* do leite maternal

* **mother's milk sugar → 5321**

3637 **mother suspension**
(Biochem.)
(Food biochemistry.)
d Muttersuspension *f*
f suspension-mère *f*
p suspensão-mãe *f*

3638 **mould-growing prevention**
(Biochem.)
(Nutritional science.)
d Schimmelbildungsvorbeugung *f*; Vorbeugung *f* gegen den Schimmelbefall
f prévention *f* de la formation de moisissure
p prevenção *f* de formação de bolor

3639 **moulding**
(Prod.)
(Food processing technology: e.g. cheese production.)
d Formen *n*; Formgebung *f*
f moulage *m*
p moldagem *f*

* **mounting → 3679**

3640 **mouth**
(Med.)
(Anatomy.)
d Mund *m*
f bouche *f*
p boca *f*

3641 **mozzarella type cheese**
(Prod.)
(Dairy product: Italian salt-free cheese type of unripened constitution. Made of cow milk or buffalo milk.)
d Mozzarella-Käse *m*
f mozzarella *f*
p queijo *m* tipo mozarela

3642 **mucilage**
(Biochem.)
(Food biochemistry; gelatinous plant substance; plant gum.)
d Pflanzenschleim *m*
f mucilage *m*
p mucilagem *f*

3643 **mucilaginous** *adj*
(Biochem.)
(Food biochemistry. Ref. to gelatinous plant substance; plant gum.)
d schleimig
f mucilagineux
p mucilaginoso

3644 **mucous membrane**
(Med.)
(Anatomy; mucosa.)
d Schleimhaut *f*
f muqueuse *f*
p mucosa *f*

* **mud hen → 3391**

3645 **mulberry**
(Agr.)
(Horticulture. Genus "Morus"; berry.)
d Maulbeere *f*
f mûre *f*
p amora *f*

3646 **mule**
(Agr.)
(Livestock. Result of mating a mare and a jackass (male ass), a (male) donkey and a mare: a horse/donkey hybrid.)
d Maulesel *m*; Maultier *n*
f petit mulet *m*; bardot *m*
p mulo *m*; muar *m*

* **mulled claret → 3647**

3647 **mulled wine; mulled claret**
(Prod.)
(Beverages.)
d Glühwein *m*
f vin *m* chaud
p vinho *m* quente

3648 **multienzymatic systems**
(Biochem.)
(Nutritional science.)
d vielfältig-enzymatische Systeme *npl*
f systèmes *mpl* multienzymatiques
p sistemas *mpl* multienzimáticos

3649 **multiple vitamin E-nature**
(Biochem.)
(Nutritional science: Vitamin E activity: eight natural compounds.)
d vielfache natürliche Beschaffenheit *f* des Vitamins E
f constitution *f* naturelle multiple de la vitamine E
p natureza *f* múltipla da vitamina E; constituição *f* múltipla da vitamina E

3650 multivitamin drink granulate
(Prod.)
(Vitamin in nutrition; ref. to instant drink preparation.)
d Multivitamingetränkgranulat *n*
f granulés *mpl* buvables polyvitaminés
p granulado *m* bebível polivitamínico

3651 multivitamin instant drink granulate
(Prod.)
(Vitamin in nutrition; ref. to instant drink preparation.)
d Multivitaminsofortgetränkgranulat *n*; Multivitamininstantangetränkgranulat *n*
f granulés *mpl* buvables instantanés polyvitaminés
p granulado *m* de refresco instantâneo polivitamínico

3652 muscular dystrophy
(Med.)
(Veterinary; muscle degeneration of the animal, e.g. due to nutritional deficiencies.)
d Muskeldystrophie *f*
f dystrophie *f* musculaire
p distrofia *f* muscular

3653 mushroom-like *adj*
(Prod.)
(Aroma/flavour note.)
d pilzartig
f note *f* de champignon
p nota *f* de cogumelo

3654 mushrooms; edible fungi
(Agr.)
(Agricultural produce.)
d echte Pilze *mpl*
f champignons *mpl* comestibles
p cogumelos *mpl* comestíveis

* **mushy diet → 4496**

3655 mussel
(Agr.)
(Genus "Mytilus", an edible marine mollusk.)
d Miesmuschel *f*
f moule *f*
p mexilhão *m*

3656 mustard
(Prod.)
("Brassica hirta", "Brassica nigra"; spice made of the seeds.)
d Senf *m*
f moutarde *f*
p mostarda *f*

* **mustard powder → 1815**

3657 mustard seeds
(Agr.)
(Botany. "Brassica hirta".)
d Senfkörner *mpl*
f graines *fpl* de moutarde
p sementes *mpl* da mostadeira; mostarda *f*

3658 must fermentability
(Biochem.)
(Brewery and enology techniques; food biochemistry.)
d Gärfähigkeit *f* des Mostes
f fermentescibilité *f* du moût
p fermentescibilidade *f* do mosto

3659 must of white vintages
(Agr.)
(Viticulture; must quality.)
d Most *m* weißer Weintrauben
f moût *m* de vendanges blanches
p mosto *m* de vindimas brancas

3660 must stabilization
(Biochem.)
(Food biochemistry: fruit processing.)
d Stabilisierung *f* des Mostes
f stabilisation *f* du moût
p estabilização *f* do mosto

3661 mutagenicity
(Med.)
(Toxicological foodstuff tests: e.g. animal experiments.)
d Mutagenität *f*; Mutationsfähigkeit *f*
f mutagénicité *f*; capacité *f* de mutagenèse
p mutagenicidade *f*; capacidade *f* mutagênica

3662 mutation
(Med.)
(Veterinary; change in the DNA of a cell.)
d Mutation *f*; Veränderung *f* im Erbgefüge
f mutation *f*
p mutação *f*

3663 mutton
(Prod.)
(Butchery. Meat of the wether; a cut of mutton: chop.)
d Hammelfleisch *n*
f viande *f* du mouton mâle
p carne *f* de carneiro

3664 mutton chop
(Prod.)
(Butchery; mutton cut.)
d Hammelkotelett *n*
f côtelette *f* de mouton
p costeleta *f* de carneiro

3665 mycotoxin
(Biochem.)
(Food biochemistry: Mycotoxin (produced by

fungus and mould) is capable of food contamination.)
d Mykotoxin *n*; Pilzgift *n*
f mycotoxine *f*; toxine *f* de champignon
p micotoxina *f*; veneno *m* de cogumelo

3666 **myrcene**
(Prod.)
($C_{10}H_{16}$; occurs in hop, verbena etc. oils; terpene family, origin ß-pinene; aroma/fragrance prime material.)
d Myrcen *n*
f myrcène *m*
p mircena *f*

3667 **myristic acid**
(Prod.)
($C_{14}H_{28}O_2$; long chained saturated fatty acid in animal and vegetable fats; in milk fats; in butter; in nutmeg butter.)
d Myristinsäure *f*
f acide *m* myristique
p ácido *m* mirístico

3668 **myxoedema**
(Med.)
(Thyroid disease, hypothyroidism, e.g. due to deficient iodine assimilation.)
d Myxödem *n*
f myxœdème *m*
p mixedema *m*

N

3669 naphthalene; naphthalin; tar camphor
(Prod.)
($C_{10}H_8$; prime material for aroma/fragrance production.)
d Naphthalin *n*
f naphtalène *m*
p naftaleno *m*

* **naphthalin → 3669**

3670 narine
(Med.)
(Anatomy, part of the nose.)
d Nasenloch *n*
f narine *f*
p narina *f*

3671 nasal bone
(Med.)
(Anatomy; bones; "Os nasale".)
d Nasenbein *n*
f os *m* nasal
p nasal *m*; osso *m* nasal

3672 nasal cavity
(Med.)
(Anatomy; body part of the skull.)
d Nasenhöhle *f*
f fosse *f* nasale
p fossa *f* nasal

3673 nasal feeding
(Med.)
(Artificial feeding through the nose.)
d nasale Ernährung *f*
f alimentation *f* nasale
p alimentação *f* nasal

3674 nasal granuloma
(Med.)
(Veterinary; snoring disease due to inflamed tissue with granulation process: a cattle disease.)
d Nasengranulationsgeschwulst *f*
f granulome *m* nasal
p granuloma *m* nasal

3675 nasal mucous membrane
(Med.)
(Anatomy.)
d Nasenschleimhaut *f*
f muqueuse *f* nasale
p mucosa *f* nasal

3676 nasal tube feeding
(Med.)
d nasale Sondenernährung *f*
f alimentation *f* nasale par sonde
p alimentação *f* nasal por sonda

3677 natural agriculture; natural farming
(Agr.)
(See organic agriculture; organic farming; biological agriculture.)
d natürliche Agrikultur *f*; natürliche Landwirtschaft *f*
f agriculture *f* naturelle
p agricultura *f* natural

3678 natural aroma
(Prod.)
(Aroma research and production: aroma of vegetable and/or plant origin.)
d natürliches Aroma *n*
f arôme *m* naturel
p aroma *m* natural

3679 natural covering; mounting
(Agr.)
(Biological agriculture.)
d natürliche Befruchtung *f*; natürliches Decken *n*
f monte *f* naturelle
p cobertura *f* natural; fecundação *f* natural

3680 natural defense mechanism of the animal
(Med.)
(Veterinary; ref. to immune system, immune response.)
d natürliches Abwehrsystem *n* des Tieres
f défense *f* naturelle de l'animal
p sistema *m* de defesa natural do animal

3681 natural deficiency symptoms
(Med.)
(Vitamin deficiency.)
d natürliche Mangelerscheinungen *fpl*
f effets *mpl* de carence naturelle
p efeitos *mpl* de carência natural

3682 natural deposits
(Agr.)
(Soil; ref. to minerals, chemical raw material etc.)
d natürliche Vorkommen *mpl*
f gisements *mpl* naturels
p depósitos *mpl* naturais

3683 natural drying up
(Prod.)
(Food processing technology; ref. to fruits, grapes.)
d natürliche Austrocknung *f*
f dessèchement *m* naturel
p dessecamento *m* natural

3684 **natural dry substance**
(Prod.)
(Food processing technology.)
d natürliche Trockensubstanz *f*
f substance f sèche naturelle
p substância f seca natural

3685 **natural dyestuff**
(Prod.)
(Foodstuff colorants.)
d Naturfarbstoff *m*
f colorant *m* naturel
p corante *m* natural

3686 **natural enemies**
(Agr.)
(Biological agricultural pest control method: use of antagonistic insects etc.)
d natürliche Feinde *mpl*
f ennemis *mpl* naturels
p inimigos *mpl* naturais

3687 **natural enzyme**
(Biochem.)
(Food biochemistry; enzyme types.)
d natürliches Enzym *n*
f enzyme *f* naturelle
p enzima *f* natural

* **natural farming → 3677**

3688 **natural honeycombs**
(Agr.)
(Apiculture.)
d Naturwabe *f*
f rayon *m* naturel
p favo *m* natural

3689 **naturally pure** *adj*
(Prod.)
(The German adjective indicates wine quality: a wine without sugar addition.)
d naturrein
f naturellement pur
p naturalmente puro

3690 **natural molecule**
(Biochem.)
(Food biochemistry: aroma/fragrance research and production.)
d natürliches Molekül *n*
f molécule *f* naturelle
p molécula *f* natural

3691 **natural phenolic antioxidant**
(Biochem.)
(Nutritional science; ref. to restructured meat in meat processing.)
d natürliches phenolisches Antioxidant *n*
f antioxydante *m* phénolique naturel
p antioxidante *m* fenólico natural

3692 **natural phosphates**
(Agr.)
(Element for soil enrichment, soil treatment.)
d Naturphosphate *npl*
f phosphates *mpl* naturels
p fosfatos *mpl* naturais

3693 **natural polypeptides**
(Biochem.)
(Food biochemistry: research in nutritional science.)
d natürliche Polypeptide *npl*
f polypeptides *mpl* naturels
p polipeptídeos *mpl* naturais

3694 **natural purity**
(Prod.)
(Mineral water quality.)
d natürliche Reinheit *f*
f pureté *f* naturelle
p pureza *f* natural

3695 **natural resources; mineral resources**
(Agr.)
(Soil.)
d Bodenschätze *mpl*
f richesses *fpl* naturelles; richesses *fpl* du sol; ressources *fpl* minérales
p recursos *mpl* naturais; recursos *mpl* minerais; riquezas *fpl* do solo

3696 **natural rice**
(Prod.)
(Gastronomy.)
d natürlicher Reis *m*
f riz *m* nature
p arroz *m* natural

3697 **natural selection**
(Med.)
(Veterinary; ref. to evolution as to Darwinism.)
d natürliche Auslese *f*
f sélection *f* naturelle
p seleção *f* natural

3698 **natural yeast**
(Biochem.)
(Fermentation in nutritional science.)
d natürliche Hefe *f*
f levure *f* naturelle
p fermento *m* natural

3699 **natural yoghurt flavour**
(Prod.)
(Food processing technology: e.g. yoghurt production.)

d natürliches Joghurtaroma *n*
f arôme *m* naturel du yaourt
p aroma *m* natural do iogurte

3700 nature of perceived sensation
(Prod.)
(Aroma/flavour research and application in food products.)
d Natur *f* der wahrgenommenen Empfindung; Art *f* der wahrgenommenen Empfindung
f nature *f* de la sensation perçue
p natureza *f* da sensação percebida

3701 nature of the odoriferous molecule
(Biochem.)
(Olfactory stimulation, nervous cells system: aroma/flavour research: ref. to odoriferous molecules.)
d Art *f* des Riechstoffmoleküles
f nature *f* de la molécule odorante
p natureza *f* da molécula odorífera

3702 nature of vitamin E structures
(Biochem.)
(Nutritional science: Vitamin E activity: eight natural compounds.)
d natürliche Vitamin-E-Strukturen *fpl*
f structures *fpl* naturelles de la vitamine E
p estruturas *fpl* naturais de vitamina E

3703 navel bleeding in piglets
(Med.)
(Veterinary; haemorrhage type which can be due to vitamin K deficiency in fodder ration.)
d Nabelbluten *n* bei Ferkeln
f hémorragie *f* ombilicale du goret
p hemorragia *f* umbilical do leitão

3704 nearly inodorous *adj*
(Prod.)
(Food processing technology; product characteristic.)
d fast geruchlos
f presque inodore
p quase inodoro

3705 nearly neutral reaction in aqueous solution
(Biochem.)
(Production techniques in food biochemistry.)
d fast neutrale Reaktion in wässriger Lösung
f réaction *f* presque neutre en solution aqueuse
p reação *f* quase neutra em solução aquosa

3706 necessary nutrients; nutrients
(Prod.)
(Food processing technology and human nutritional necessities.)
d notwendige Nährstoffe *mpl*; Nahrungsstoffe *mpl*
f nutriments *mpl* nécessaires; nutriments *mpl*
p nutrientes *mpl* necessários; nutrientes *mpl*

3707 neck
(Agr.)
(Butchery; meat part; joint.)
d Kamm *m*
f collier *m*
p pescoço *m*

3708 necrosis of the gums
(Med.)
(Due to certain vitamin deficiencies.)
d Zahnfleischnekrose *f*
f nécrose *f* des gencives
p necrose *f* das gengivas

3709 necrotizing enteritis
(Med.)
(Veterinary; e.g. ref. to hogs: intestinal inflammation.)
d nekrosierende Dünndarmentzündung *f*
f entérite *f* nécrotisante
p enterite *f* necrotizante

3710 nectar
(Prod.)
(Here: a beverage made from fruit juice and fruit pulp.)
d Nektar *m*
f nectar *m*
p néctar *m*

3711 nectarine
(Agr.)
(Horticulture. Peach; the French "brugnon" is a nectarine variety; the nectarine is a stone fruit.)
d Nektarine *f*
f nectarine *f*; brugnon *m*
p nectarina *f*

3712 nephelometry; tyndallometry
(Prod.)
(Analytical process using the Tyndall effects for turbidity determination, used in the production of beverages.)
d Nephelometrie *f*; Streulichtmessung *f*
f néphélométrie *f*
p nefelometria *f*

3713 nephrosclerosis
(Med.)
(Consequence of hypertension.)
d Nephrosklerose *f*
f néphrosclérose *f*
p nefroesclerose *f*

3714 nerolidol; peruviol
(Prod.)
($C_{15}H_{26}O$; acetylene derivative; ref. to aroma

synthesis, prime material.)
d Nerolidol *n*
f nérolidol *m*
p nerolidol *m*

3715 neroli oil
(Prod.)
(Volatile oil distilled from orange flowers. Flavour prime material, aroma.)
d Neroliöl *n*
f néroli *m*; essence *f* de néroli; huile *f* essentielle de fleurs d'oranger
p óleo *m* néroli; óleo *m* da flor da laranjeira

3716 nerve cells
(Med.)
(Veterinary; ref. to animal anatomy, e.g. nervous tissue as the neurons.)
d Nervenzellen *fpl*
f cellules *fpl* nerveuses
p células *fpl* nervosas

3717 nerve of a tooth
(Med.)
(Anatomy.)
d Zahnnerv *m*
f nerf *m* dentaire
p nervo *m* do dente

3718 nervous system
(Med.)
(Veterinary.)
d Nervensystem *n*
f système *m* nerveux
p sistema *m* nervoso

3719 nervure; rib; vein of the leaf
(Agr.)
(Botany; leaf structure.)
d Blattader *f*; Blattnerv *m*
f nervure *f* de la feuille; charpente *f* de la feuille
p nervura *f* da folha

3720 nest
(Agr.)
(Shelter-like constructions made of wood in form of batteries or series; contain the bird's nests; for bird breeding.)
d Nest *n*
f nid *m*
p ninho *m*

3721 neurologic aging due to glycemia
(Med.)
(Nutrition.)
d Alterung *f* des Nervensystemes bedingt durch die Glykämie
f vieillissement *m* neurologique par la glycémie
p envelhecimento *m* neurológico pela glicemia

3722 neurologic metabolism
(Med.)
(Nutrition.)
d neurologischer Stoffwechsel *m*
f métabolisme *m* neurologique
p metabolismo *m* neurológico

3723 neurotransmitter
(Biochem.)
(Aroma/flavour research and production. Chemical nerve impulses transmitting substance.)
d Neurotransmitter *m*
f neurotransmetteur *m*
p neurotransmissor *m*

3724 neutral fat
(Med.)
(Fat type in nutrition.)
d neutrales Fett *n*
f graisse *f* neutre; corps *m* gras neutre
p gordura *f* neutra; corpo graxo *m* neutro

3725 newborn; baby; infant
(Med.)
(Recently born child.)
d Neugeborene *n*; Säugling *m*
f nouveau-né *m*; nouveau-née *f*; nourrisson *m*; bébé *m*
p récem-nascido *m*; bebê *m*; nenê *m*; lactente *m*

3726 Newcastle disease
(Med.)
(Veterinary; poultry virus disease.)
d Newcastle-Krankheit *f*
f maladie *f* de Newcastle
p doença *f* de Newcastle

* **new foodstuff generations → 3727**

3727 new generations of foodstuffs; new foodstuff generations
(Prod.)
(Food processing technology; foodstuff production and marketing.)
d neue Generationen *fpl* von Nahrungsmitteln
f nouvelles générations *fpl* de produits alimentaires
p novas gerações *fpl* de produtos alimentícios

3728 new potatoes
(Agr.)
(Agricultural produce; precociously harvested, before fully mature.)
d neue Kartoffeln *fpl*
f pommes *fpl* de terre nouvelles
p batatas *fpl* novas

3729 new wine
(Biochem.)
(Enology, ref. to wine type.)

d neuer Wein *m*
f vin *m* nouveau
p vinho *m* novo

* **n-heptyl alcohol → 2681**

* **n-hexanal → 172**

* **niacin → 3732**

3730 **niacin-poor** *adj*
(Biochem.)
(Food biochemistry; certain agricultural products like maize, Indian corn.)
d niacinarm; arm an Niacin
f pauvre en niacine
p pobre de niacina

3731 **nicotinamide**
(Prod.)
(Vitamins in nutrition; nicotinic acid amide; vitamin B_3. $C_6H_6N_2O$. Constituent of co-enzymes. PP-factor (Pellagra preventing factor).)
d Nicotinsäureamid *n*
f nicotinamide *m*
p nicotinamida *f*

3732 **nicotinic acid; niacin**
(Prod.)
(Vitamin B_3. $C_6H_5NO_2$. Used like nicotinamide.)
d Nicotinsäure *f*; Niacin *n*
f acide *m* nicotinique; niacine *f*
p ácido *m* nicotínico; niacina *f*

3733 **night blindness**
(Med.)
(Can be caused by dietary deficiency of vitamin.)
d Nachtblindheit *f*
f héméralopie *f*
p cegueira *f* noturna

* **nightly alimentary requirement → 3753**

3734 **nimbostratus**
(Agr.)
(Climatology; dark rainy cloud in layer form; less than 2,500 m high.)
d Nimbostratus *m*; Regenschichtwolke *f*
f nimbostratus *m*; couche *f* nuageuse de pluie
p nimbo-estrato *m*; estrato-nimbo *m*

3735 **nimbus; rain cloud**
(Agr.)
(Climatology; low cloud: precipitation of rain or snow.)
d Nimbus *m*; Regenwolke *f*
f nimbus *m*; nuage *m* porteur de pluie
p nimbo; nuvem *f* de chuva

3736 **nipple; mammilla**
(Med.)
(Anatomy; body part; "papilla".)
d Brustwarze *f*
f mamelon *m*; bout *m* de sein
p mamilo *m*; bico *m* do peito

3737 **nitrate concentration**
(Agr.)
(Biological agriculture: soil composition.)
d Nitratkonzentration *f*
f concentration *f* en nitrate
p concentração *f* de nitrato

3738 **nitrification**
(Agr.)
(Biological agriculture: Oxidation of ammonium salts to nitrites (e.g. by bacteria) and further oxidation process of nitrites to nitrates.)
d Salpeterbildung *f*
f nitrification *f*; salpêtrisation *f*
p nitrificação *f*

3739 **nitrifying bacteria**
(Biochem.)
(Microbiology. "Nitrobacteraceae"; soil bacteria.)
d nitrifizierende Bakterien *fpl*
f bactéries *fpl* nitrifiantes
p bactérias *fpl* nitrificantes

3740 **nitrogen absorption by the plants**
(Agr.)
(Botany; biologic agriculture.)
d Stickstoffaufnahme *f* der Pflanzen; Stickstoffabsorption *f* der Pflanzen
f absorption *f* d'azote par les plantes
p absorção *f* de nitrogênio pelas plantas

3741 **nitrogen contents**
(Agr.)
(Nitrogen: N. Botany.)
d Stickstoffgehalt *m*
f teneur *f* en azote
p teor *m* de nitrogênio

3742 **nitrogen cycle in nature**
(Agr.)
(Soil; soil fertilization technology.)
d Stickstoffkreislauf *m* in der Natur
f cycle *m* d'azote dans la nature
p ciclo *m* de nitrogênio na natureza

3743 **nitrogen fertilization**
(Agr.)
(Soil; soil fertilization type.)
d Stickstoffdüngung *f*

f fertilisation *f* azotée
p fertilização *f* nitrogenada

3744 nitrogen insufficiency
(Agr.)
(Biological agriculture.)
d Unzulänglichkeit *f* an Stickstoff
f insuffisance *f* d'azote organique
p insuficiência *f* de nitrogênio

3745 nitrogen loss by lixiviation
(Agr.)
(Soil treatment.)
d Stickstoffverlust *m* durch Auslaugung
f perte *f* d'azote par lessivage; perte *f* d'azote par lixiviation
p perda *f* de nitrogênio por lixiviação

3746 nitrogenous *adj*
(Prod.)
(Nitrogen containing: e.g. fertilizers.)
d stickstoffhaltig
f azoté
p nitrogenado

3747 nitrogenous fertilizer
(Agr.)
(Botany. Fertilizer type containing nitrogen (N). Nitrification is part of the nitrogen cycle.)
d Salpeterdünger *m*
f engrais *m* azoté; engrais *m* azotique
p adubo *m* nítrico; adubo *m* nitrogenado

3748 nitrogenous fertilizer with long-lasting effect
(Agr.)
(Soil. Fertilizer type with long-lasting action, based on nitrogen (N).)
d nachhaltigwirkender Stickstoffdünger *m*
f engrais *m* azoté à effet prolongé
p fertilizante *m* nitrogenado de ação prolongada

3749 nitrogenous one-element fertilizer
(Agr.)
(Soil. Fertilizer type, based on only one component part containing nitrogen (N).)
d Stickstoffeinzeldünger *m*
f engrais *m* azotique à un composant
p fertilizante *m* nitrogenado de composto único

3750 nitrogen requirement
(Agr.)
(Botany; synthetic fertilizer for plants containing nitrogen; formula: N-P-K (nitrogen, phosphorus, potassium).)
d Stickstoffanspruch *m*
f exigence *f* en azote
p demanda *f* de nitrogênio

3751 nitrosamine
(Biochem.)
(Food biochemistry; group NNO; carcinogen; reaction product between nitrites and amines present in nitrite-treated foodstuffs, e.g. meat conservation.)
d Nitrosamin *n*
f nitrosamine *f*
p nitrosamina *f*

3752 nitrosamine formation
(Prod.)
(Food processing technology: see nitrosamine; Vitamin C (sodium ascorbate) is used e.g. for nitrosamine reduction in meat products.)
d Nitrosaminbildung *f*
f formation *f* de nitrosamines
p formação *f* de nitrosaminas

3753 nocturnal alimentary requirement; nightly alimentary requirement
(Med.)
(Baby nutrition.)
d nächtliches Ernährungsbedürfnis *n*
f besoin *m* alimentaire nocturne
p necessidade *f* de alimentação noturna

* **non-alcoholic beer → 573**

* **non-alcoholic beverage → 3754**

3754 non-alcoholic drink; non-alcoholic beverage
(Prod.)
(Beverages.)
d alkoholfreies Getränk *n*
f boisson *f* non-alcoolique
p bebida *f* sem álcool; bebida *f* isenta de álcool

* **nonanoic acid → 4069**

3755 non-caloric *adj*
(Biochem.)
(Food biochemistry.)
d nicht kalorienhaltig
f non-calorique
p não calórico

3756 non-chemical treatment
(Agr.)
(Biological agriculture, biologic farming system.)
d nicht chemische Behandlung *f*
f traitement *m* non-chimique
p tratamento *m* não-químico

3757 non-energetic nutrient
(Biochem.)
(Food biochemistry: e.g. ref. to vitamins and minerals.)
d nicht energetischer Nährstoff *m*

f nutriment *m* non-énergétique
p nutriente *m* não-energético

3758 **non-enzymatic browning**
(Biochem.)
(Nutritional science: Maillard reaction: reaction between amino acids and reducing sugars, changing the colour of foodstuffs. This reaction diminishes the nutritional value of the product.)
d nicht enzymatische Bräunung *f*
f brunissement *m* non-enzymatique
p escurecimento *m* não-enzimático; reação *f* marrom não-enzimática

3759 **non-enzymatic lipid oxidation**
(Biochem.)
(Nutritional science; ref. to restructured meat in meat processing.)
d nicht enzymatische Lipidoxidation *f*
f oxydation *f* lipidique non-enzymatique
p oxidação *f* lipídica não enzimática

3760 **non-essential amino acids**
(Biochem.)
(Synthesized by the body. Constituents of protein: alanine. arginine, asparagine, aspartic acid, cysteine, glutamic acid, glutamine, glycine, histidine, proline, serine, tyrosine.)
d nicht essentielle Aminosäuren *fpl*
f acides *mpl* aminés secondaires
p aminoácidos *mpl* não essenciais

3761 **non-nutritious sweetener; non-nutritive sweetener**
(Prod.)
(Food processing technology: e.g. synthetic sweeteners, aspartame, cyclamate, saccharine.)
d nicht nährstoffhaltiges Süßungsmittel *n*
f produit *m* sucrant exempt de nutriments
p edulcorante *m* sem nutrientes

* **non-nutritive sweetener → 3761**

3762 **non-polar lipids**
(Biochem.)
(Nutritional science. E.g. fat-soluble vitamins.)
d unpolare Lipide *npl*; homöopolare Lipide *npl*
f lipides *mpl* homopolaires
p lipídios *mpl* homopolares

* **nonylic acid → 4069**

3763 **noodles; tubular pasta products**
(Prod.)
(Macaroni-type pasta products.)
d Nudeln *fpl*; röhrenförmige Teigwaren *fpl*
f nouilles *fpl*; pâte *f* alimentaire de longueur moyenne
p massas *fpl*; pasta *f* tipo macarrão; produtos *mpl* tubulares de pasta

* **Norfolk Island pine → 401**

3764 **normal intestinal flora**
(Med.)
(Containing e.g. lactobacillus bifidus.)
d normale Darmflora *f*
f flore *f* intestinale normale
p flora *f* intestinal normal

3765 **normal weight**
(Med.)
(Avoiding obesity by dietary methods.)
d Normalgewicht *n*
f poids *m* normal
p peso *m* normal

3766 **nose**
(Med.)
(Anatomy; olfactory organ.)
d Nase *f*
f nez *m*
p nariz *m*

3767 **nose root**
(Med.)
(Anatomy.)
d Nasenwurzel *f*
f racine *f* du nez
p raiz *f* do nariz

3768 **nostrils**
(Med.)
(Veterinary; animal anatomy: nasal cavity.)
d Nüstern *fpl*
f naseaux *mpl*
p ventas *fpl*

* **not-durable character → 3771**

3769 **note of red fruits**
(Prod.)
(Taste; aroma research and production, e.g. tea flavour.)
d Note *f* roter Früchte
f note *f* de fruits rouges
p nota *f* de frutas vermelhas

3770 **not-miscible phases**
(Prod.)
(Aroma/flavour research and production: distillation processes.)
d nicht mischbare Phasen *fpl*
f phases *fpl* non-miscibles
p fases *fpl* não miscíveis

3771 **not-remaining property; not-durable character**
(Agr.)
(Ref. to certain types of insecticides authorized in biological agriculture.)
d nicht zurückbleibende Eigenschaft *f*; nicht andauernde Eigenschaft *f*
f propriété *f* non-rémanente
p propriedade *f* não permanente; caráter *m* não contínuo

3772 **nougat**
(Prod.)
(Confectionary with nuts as an ingredient.)
d Nugat *n*
f nougat *m*
p nugá *m*; nogado *m*

* **nourish** *v* → **2101**

3773 **nourishing** *adj*
(Biochem.)
(Nutritional science.)
d nährend
f nourrissant
p nutriente; nutritivo

3774 **nucleic acid**
(Biochem.)
(Nutritional science. Ribonucleic acid (RNA) and desoxyribonucleic acid (DNA).)
d Nukleinsäure *f*
f acide *m* nucléique
p ácido *m* nucléico

3775 **nucleotides**
(Biochem.)
(DNA and RNA structural units, purine or pyrimidine base, linked to one of the sugars, ribose or desoxyribose and to phosphoric acid. DNA and RNA are made of long nucleotide chains.)
d Nucleotide *mpl*
f nucléotides *mpl*
p nucleotídeos *mpl*

3776 **nurse** *v*; **breast-feed** *v*
(Med.)
(Baby feeding from a mother's breast.)
d stillen
f allaiter
p amamentar

3777 **nursing**
(Med.)
(Here: to nourish a baby at the breast.)
d Stillen *n*
f allaitement *m*; allaitement *m* maternel; tétée *f*
p amamentação *f*; aleitamento *f*; aleitação *f*

3778 **nut kernel**
(Agr.)
(Botany; inner part of the nut.)
d Nusskern *m*
f amande *f* de noix
p miolo *m* da noz

3779 **nutmeg**
(Agr.)
(Botany. "Myristica fragrans"; aromatic seed used as spice.)
d Muskatnuss *f*
f muscade *f*, noix *f* muscade
p noz-moscada *f*

3780 **nutmeg oil**
(Prod.)
("Myristica fragrans Houtt". Volatile oil of myristica. The seed is used as spice; the oil as flavouring agent.)
d Muskatöl *n*
f essence *f* de muscade
p essência *f* de noz-moscada

3781 **nutrient**
(Prod.)
(Food processing technology.)
d Nährstoff *m*
f nutriment *m*
p nutriente *m*; substância *f* nutriente

3782 **nutrient containing sweetener**
(Prod.)
(Food processing technology: e.g. sugar, glucose, lactose, maltose.)
d nährstoffhaltige Süßungsmittel *n*
f produit *m* sucrant contenant de nutriments
p edulcorante *m* contendo nutrientes

3783 **nutrient hydrolyzer**
(Biochem.)
(Nutritional science; vitamin/enzyme biochemistry.)
d Nährstoffspalter *m*
f hydroliseur *m* de nutriments
p hidrolisador *m* de nutrientes

* **nutrients** → **3706**

3784 **nutrient salts**
(Prod.)
(Additives for molasse treatment, as substrate for yeast cell production.)
d Nährsalze *npl*
f sels *mpl* nutritifs
p sais *mpl* nutritivos; sais-nutrientes *mpl*

3785 **nutrient substance**
(Biochem.)
(Food biochemistry.)

d nahrhafte Substanz *f*
f substance *f* nutritive
p substância *f* nutritiva

3786 **nutriments necessary for development**
(Med.)
(Baby nutrition.)
d zur Entwicklung notwendige Nahrungsstoffe *mpl*; zu der Entwicklung erforderliche Nährstoffe *mpl*
f nutriments *mpl* nécessaires au développement
p nutrimentos *mpl* necessários para o desenvolvimento

3787 **nutritiological toxicology**
(Med.)
(Food processing technology.)
d Nahrungsmitteltoxikologie *f*
f toxicologie *f* nutritiologique
p toxicologia *f* nutricional

3788 **nutritional achromotrichia**
(Med.)
(Capilary (hair) pigmentation absence.)
d ernährungsbedingte Grauhaarigkeit *f*
f achromotrichie *f* nutritive
p acromotriquía *f* nutricional

3789 **nutritional alteration**
(Med.)
(Modification in nutrition, regimens, diets.)
d Ernährungsveränderung *f*
f altération *f* nutritionnelle
p alteração *f* nutricional

3790 **nutritional approach; nutritional intervention**
(Med.)
(Nutritional therapy, regimens, diets.)
d Behandlung *f* durch Nahrungsmitteln; Eingriff *m* durch Nahrungsmitteln
f approche *f* nutritionnelle
p intervenção *f* pela nutrição

3791 **nutritional balance**
(Med.)
(Nutrition, regimens, diets.)
d Ausgeglichenheit *f* der Ernährung
f équilibre *m* nutritionnel
p equilíbrio *m* nutriticional

* **nutritional behaviour correction → 583**

3792 **nutritional characteristics**
(Prod.)
(Food processing technology, research and production: product characteristic.)
d Nähreigenschaft *f*
f caractéristique *f* nutritionnelle
p caraterística *f* nutricional

3793 **nutritional component**
(Biochem.)
(Food biochemistry.)
d Nahrungsmittelkomponente *f*
f constituant *m* alimentaire
p componente *m* nutricional; componente *m* nutritivo

3794 **nutritional composition**
(Med.)
(Ref. e.g. to alimentary regimens.)
d Zusammensetzung *f* der Ernährung
f composition *f* de la nourriture
p composição *f* da alimentação

3795 **nutritional conditions**
(Biochem.)
(Nutritional science. ref. to nutrition e.g. of the concerning population.)
d Ernährungsbedingungen *fpl*
f condition *f* alimentaire
p condição *f* alimentar

3796 **nutritional deficiency**
(Med.)
(Nutrition in medicine, regimens, diets.)
d Nährstoffmangel *m*
f carence *f* nutritionnelle
p carência *f* nutricional

3797 **nutritional deficiency of proteins**
(Med.)
(Nutrition in medicine, regimens, diets.)
d Proteinnährstoffmangel *m*; Nahrungsstoffmangel *m* bezüglich Proteinzufuhr
f carence *f* nutritionnelle en protéines
p carência *f* nutricional relacionada às proteínas

3798 **nutritional density; nutritional richness**
(Biochem.)
(Food biochemistry; food composition.)
d Nahrungsreichhaltigkeit *f*, gehaltvolle Ernährung *f*
f densité *f* nutritionnelle
p densidade *f* nutricional; riqueza *f* nutricional

3799 **nutritional diseases**
(Med.)
(Caused by erroneous diets, as high-saturated fats diets, refined nutrition without roughage etc.)
d Nahrungsmittelkrankheiten *fpl*
f maladies *fpl* alimentaires
p doenças *fpl* nutricionais

3800 **nutritional disequilibrium**
(Med.)
(Nutrition in medicine; nutritional diseases.)
d nahrungsbezogenes Missverhältnis *n*

f déséquilibre *m* nutritionnel
p desequilíbrio *m* nutricional

3801 **nutritional disorders**
(Biochem.)
(Nutrition in medicine; nutritional diseases.)
d Ernährungsstörungen *fpl*
f perturbations *fpl* nutritionnelles; désordres *mpl* nutritionnels
p perturbações *fpl* nutricionais

3802 **nutritional education**
(Med.)
(Nutrition; correct nutritional habits.)
d Ernährungserziehung *f*
f éducation *f* nutritionnelle
p educação *f* nutricional

3803 **nutritional elements**
(Agr.)
(Botany; plant life and growth.)
d nährende Bestandteile *npl*
f éléments *mpl* nutritifs
p elementos *mpl* nutritivos

3804 **nutritional energetic value**
(Prod.)
(1 kcal - 4185 kJ (kilojoule). 1 kJ (kilojoule) = 0.239 kcal (kilocalorie).)
d Nahrungsmittelenergiewert *m*; Energiewert *m* der Nahrungsmittel
f valeur *f* énergétique des aliments
p valor *m* energético dos produtos alimentícios

3805 **nutritional factor**
(Med.)
(Nutritional science.)
d Ernährungsfaktor *m*
f facteur *m* nutritionnel
p fator *m* nutricional

3806 **nutritional interest**
(Prod.)
(Food processing technology: e.g. paradigm of valuation.)
d ernährungswissenschaftliches Interesse *n*
f intérêt *m* nutritionnel
p interesse *m* do ponto de vista nutricional

3807 **nutritional interrelationship of selenium and vitamin E**
(Biochem.)
(Nutritional science.)
d ernährungsbezogene Wechselbeziehungen *fpl* zwischen Selen und Vitamin E
f rapport *m* nutritionnel entre sélénium et vitamine E
p interrelação *f* nutricional entre selênio e vitamina E

* **nutritional intervention → 3790**

3808 **nutritional muscular dystrophy in chicks**
(Med.)
(Veterinary; ref. to nutritional myopathy in chicks; prevention e.g. vitamin E supplementation of feed ration.)
d ernährungsbezügliche Muskeldystrophie *f* der Küken
f dystrophie *f* musculaire nutritionnelle des poussins
p distrofia *f* muscular nutricional dos pintos

3809 **nutritional myopathy in chicks**
(Med.)
(Veterinary; prevention e.g. vitamin E supplementation of feed ration.)
d ernährungsbezügliches Muskelleiden *n* der Küken
f myopathie *f* nutritionnelle des poussins
p miopatia *f* nutricional dos pintos

3810 **nutritional necessities**
(Med.)
(Ref. to motivation for foodstuff choice.)
d Ernährungsbedürfnisse *fpl*
f besoins *mpl* nutritionnels
p necessidades *fpl* nutricionais

3811 **nutritional optimization**
(Med.)
(Nutrition in medicine; regimens, diets.)
d Ernährungsoptimierung *f*
f optimisation *f* nutritionnelle; optimisation *f* de la nutrition
p otimização *f* nutricional; otimização *f* da nutrição

3812 **nutritional origin**
(Med.)
(Nutrition in medicine; nutritional diseases, regimens, diets.)
d ernährungsbezüglicher Ursprung *m*
f origine *f* nutritionnelle
p origem *f* nutricional

3813 **nutritional pancreatic atrophy**
(Med.)
(Veterinary; cell degeneration of the pancreas due to deficient nutrition.)
d ernährungsbedingte Pankreasatrophie *f*
f atrophie *f* pancréatique nutritionnelle
p atrofia *f* pancrática nutricional

3814 **nutritional problems**
(Prod.)
(Food processing, research, production and marketing.)
d Ernährungsprobleme *npl*

f problèmes *mpl* nutritionnels
p problemas *mpl* de alimentação; problemas *mpl* de nutrição

3815 nutritional quality
(Prod.)
(Food processing technology, research and production.)
d Qualität *f* des Nährwertes
f qualité *f* nutritionnelle
p qualidade *f* nutricional

3816 nutritional requirements of the child
(Med.)
(Baby nutrition.)
d Nahrungsbedarf *m* des Kindes
f besoins *mpl* nutritifs infantiles
p necessidades *fpl* relacionadas à nutrição infantil

*** nutritional richness → 3798**

3817 nutritional source
(Biochem.)
(Ref. to new sources of nutrients: purpose of nutritional science.)
d Nahrungsmittelquelle *f*
f source *f* de nourriture
p fonte *f* de nutrição

3818 nutritional state of the population
(Med.)
(Nutrition in medicine; nutritional diseases, regimens, diets.)
d Ernährungszustand *m* der Bevölkerung
f statut *m* nutritionnel de la population
p estado *m* nutricional do povo

3819 nutritional superiority
(Prod.)
(Food processing technology, food characteristics.)
d Überlegenheit *f* bezogen auf den Nährwert; nährwertbezügliche Überlegenheit *f*
f supériorité *f* nutritionnelle
p superioridade *f* nutricional

3820 nutritional supplementation
(Biochem.)
(Nutritional science; food biochemistry.)
d Nahrungsmittelergänzung *f*; Nahrungsmittelzuschuss *m*
f supplémentation *f* nutritionnelle
p suplementação *f* nutricional

3821 nutritional supply of micronutrients
(Biochem.)
(Nutritional science; food biochemistry.)
d Zufuhr *f*, über den Nahrungsmittelweg, von Mikronährstoffen
f apport *m* nutritionnel des micronutrients
p aporte *m* nutricional dos micronutrientes

3822 nutritional tendencies
(Prod.)
(Food processing, research, production and marketing.)
d Ernährungstendenzen *fpl*
f tendances *fpl* nutritionnelles
p tendências *fpl* da alimentação

3823 nutritional tolerance
(Med.)
(Nutrition in medicine; nutritional diseases, regimens, diets.)
d Nahrungstoleranz *f*; Nahrungsmittelverträglichkeit *f*
f tolérance *f* nutritionnelle
p tolerância *f* nutricional

3824 nutritional treatment; treatment based on nutrition
(Med.)
(Nutrition in medicine.)
d ernährungsbezogene Behandlung *f*; Behandlung *f* durch Ernährung
f traitement *m* nutritionnel; traitement *m* basé sur la nutrition
p tratamento *m* nutricional; tratamento *m* à base de nutrição

3825 nutritional value; physicochemical nutritional value
(Biochem.)
(Nutritional science; ref. to energetic properties; protein quality; foodstuff quantity/nutritional energy ratio; food digestibility; nutrient disponibility etc.)
d Nährwert *m*; ernährungsphysiologischer Wert *m*
f valeur *f* nutritive; valeur *f* physico-chimique nutritive
p valor *m* nutritivo; valor *m* físico-químico nutricional

3826 nutritional value of cow's milk
(Biochem.)
(Food biochemistry; important factor e.g. in dairy products.)
d Nährwert *m* der Kuhmilch
f valeur *f* nutritionnelle du lait de vache
p volar *m* nutricional do leite de vaca

*** nutrition based on milk → 3102**

3827 nutrition by duodenal sound; alimentation by duodenal tube
(Med.)
(Artificial alimentation methods in medicine.)

d duodenale Sondenernährung *f*; Duodenalsondenernährung *f*
f alimentation *f* par sonde duodénale
p alimentação *f* por sonda duodenal

* **nutrition of the brain → 1013**

3828 **nutrition research**
(Prod.)
(Food processing technology; foodstuff research.)
d Ernährungsforschung *f*
f recherche *f* de nutrition
p pesquisa *f* de nutrição

3829 **nutrition rich in antioxidants**
(Biochem.)
(Nutritional science.)
d antioxidantreiche Ernährung *f*
f alimentation *f* riche en antioxydants
p alimentação *f* rica em antioxidantes

3830 **nutritive liquid for cell culture; nutritive solution for cell culture**
(Biochem.)
(Aroma production from plant prime material.)
d Nährlösung *f* für die Zellenkultur
f liquide *m* nutritif pour la culture de cellules
p líquido *m* nutritivo para a cultura de células; solução *f* nutritiva para a cultura de células

3831 **nutritive solution**
(Med.)
(For feeding by tube; gavage.)
d Nährlösung *f*
f solution *f* nutritive
p solução *f* nutritiva

* **nutritive solution for cell culture → 3830**

3832 **nut shell**
(Agr.)
(Botany; protective covering of the nut kernel.)
d Nussschale *f*
f coquille *f* de noix
p casca *f* da noz

3833 **nutty** *adj*
(Prod.)
(Aroma/flavour note; food processing technology.)
d nussartig
f à saveur de noix
p de sabor de noz

* **n-valeraldehyde → 171**

* **n-valeric acid → 5652**

O

3834 **oak**
(Agr.)
(Botany. Genus "Quercus"; deciduous hardwood tree.)
d Eiche *f*
f chêne *m*
p carvalho *m*

3835 **oak barrel**
(Prod.)
(Ref. e.g. to wine preservation, wine storage.)
d Fass *n* aus Eichenholz
f fût *m* de chêne
p barril *m* de carvalho; pipa *f* de carvalho

3836 **oat**
(Agr.)
(Agricultural produce. Genus "Avena"; cereal.)
d Hafer *m*
f avoine *f*
p aveia *f*

3837 **oatfield**
(Agr.)
(Agriculture.)
d Haferfeld *n*
f champ *m* d'avoine
p aveal *m*

3838 **oatmeal**
(Agr.)
(Agricultural produce. "Avena sativa"; meal type made from oats.)
d Hafermehl *n*
f farine *f* d'avoine
p farinha *f* de aveia

3839 **obesity**
(Med.)
(Excess of fat accumulation due to higher fat consumption than necessary for energy production. Accumulation takes place by hyperplasia (increase of cells) and by hypertrophy (cell enlargement).)
d Fettleibigkeit *f*
f obésité *f*
p obesidade *f*

3840 **obligatory vaccination; required vaccination**
(Med.)
(Veterinary; ref. to farm animal vaccination.)
d Zwangsimpfung *f*
f vaccination *f* obligatoire
p vacinação *f* obrigatória

* **obstipation → 1312**

* **obstruct** *v* **→ 4218**

3841 **occupational metabolism**
(Med.)
(Metabolism due to manual activity.)
d Arbeitsumsatz *m* des Stoffwechsels; Leistungszuwachs *m* des Stoffwechsels
f métabolisme *m* occupationnel; métabolisme *m* par le travail
p metabolismo *m* ocupacional; metabolismo *m* pelo trabalho

3842 **octanal**
(Prod.)
(n-Octanal; $C_8H_{16}O$; caprylic aldehyde; flavour prime material; e.g. fatty, sweet note.)
d Octanal *n*
f octanal *m*
p octanal *m*

* **1,8-octanedicarboxylic acid → 4873**

* **octanoic acid → 907**

3843 **octyl gallate**
(Biochem.)
(Food biochemistry: foodstuff antioxidant.)
d Octylgallat *n*
f gallate *m* d'octyle
p galato *m* de octila

3844 **odd-pinnate leaf**
(Agr.)
(Botany; leaf type.)
d unpaarig gefiedertes Blatt *n*
f feuille *f* imparipennée
p folha *f* imparipenada

3845 **odoriferous characteristic; odour characteristic**
(Prod.)
(Aroma/flavour research.)
d Duftcharakteristik *f*; Dufteigenschaft *f*
f caractéristique *f* odorante
p caraterística *f* odorífera

3846 **odoriferous foodstuff molecules**
(Prod.)
(Aroma/fragrance research and elaboration for foodstuff production.)
d Nahrungsmittelriechstoffmoleküle *npl*
f molécules *fpl* odorantes des aliments
p moléculas *fpl* odoríferas dos alimentos

3847 odoriferous fraction
(Prod.)
(Aroma/flavour research and production.)
d Riechstofffraktion *f*
f fraction *f* odorante
p fração *f* odorante

3848 odoriferous molecules
(Prod.)
(Ref. to the research of synthetic flavour chemicals and flavour notes.)
d Riechstoffmoleküle *fpl*
f molécules *fpl* odorantes
p moléculas *fpl* odoríferas

3849 odoriferous particles
(Med.)
(Aroma/flavour prime material.)
d Riechpartikel *fpl*
f corps *mpl* odorants
p partículas *fpl* odoríferas

* **odour characteristic → 3845**

3850 odour sensibility
(Med.)
(Flavour/fragrance production and research.)
d Geruchsempfindlichkeit *f*
f sensibilité *f* aux odeurs
p sensibilidade *f* aos odores

3851 oedema; edema
(Med.)
(Veterinary; pathologic liquid accumulation in the tissues.)
d Ödem *n*; Gewebewassersucht *f*
f œdème *m*
p edema *m*

3852 oesophagus; esophagus
(Med.)
(Anatomy; gullet; food passage from the mouth to the stomach.)
d Speiseröhre *f*
f œsophage *m*
p esôfago *m*

3853 off-white powder
(Prod.)
(Food processing technology; product characteristic.)
d beinahe weißes Pulver *n*
f poudre *f* presque blanche
p pó *m* quase branco

* **oil cake → 2032**

3854 oil corn bran; oil grain bran
(Agr.)
(Cattle breeding and nutrition: feedstuff raw material.)
d Ölschrot *m*
f son *m* huileux
p farelo *m* oleoso

3855 oiled cheese rind
(Prod.)
(Dairy technology. Rind ointment method for hard cheeses, for desiccation/dehydration prevention.)
d eingefettete Käserinde *f*, ölige Käserinde *f*
f croûte *f* du fromage huilée
p crosta *f* engordurada de queijo; casca *f* oleosa de queijo

3856 oil from the seed of grapes
(Prod.)
(Food processing technology: gastronomy.)
d Weintraubenkernöl *n*
f huile *f* de pépins de raisins
p óleo *m* dos sementes da uva; óleo *m* do caroço da uva

* **oil grain bran → 3854**

3857 oil-in-water emulsions; o/w emulsions
(Prod.)
(Food processing technology; e.g. milk, dressings etc.)
d Öl/Wasser-Emulsionen *fpl*
f émulsions *fpl* huile/eau; émulsions *fpl* H/E
p emulsões *fpl* óleo/água; emulsões *fpl* o/a

3858 oil of cardamom
(Prod.)
(Essential oil from the seeds of "Elettaria cardamomum". Used in confectionary, curry sauces, flavouring of liqueurs etc. Flavour prime material.)
d Kardamomöl *n*
f essence *f* de cardamome
p essência *f* de cardamomo

3859 oil of neutral taste
(Prod.)
(Food processing technology; organoleptic food evaluation.)
d Öle *npl* neutralen Geschmackes
f huiles *fpl* à goût neutre
p óleos *mpl* de paladar neutro

* **oil-processing industry → 2077**

3860 oil seed bran
(Agr.)
(Cattle breeding and nutrition: feedstuff raw material; animal ration component part.)
d Ölsaatschrot *m*
f son *m* des semences huileuses
p farelo *m* de sementes oleosas

3861 oil seed extraction bran
(Agr.)
(Cattle breeding and nutrition: feedstuff raw material; feedstuff basis.)
d Ölsaatextraktionsschrot *m*
f son *m* de l'extraction des semences huileuses
p farelo *m* de extração de sementes oleosas

3862 oils of the food industry
(Prod.)
(Food processing technology.)
d Öle *npl* der Nahrungsmittelindustrie
f huiles *fpl* de l'industrie alimentaire
p óleos *mpl* para a indústria alimentícia

3863 oil vitamin-carrier
(Biochem.)
(Food biochemistry; peanut oil for oily vitamin blends in foodstuff processing.)
d Öl-Vitaminträger *m*
f support *m* vitaminique huileux
p base *f* vitamínica de óleo; suporte *m* vitamínico de óleo

3864 oil-water interface
(Biochem.)
(Nutritional science; surface forming a common boundary between e.g. phases.)
d Öl/Wasser-Schnittfläche *f*
f interface *f* huile-eau
p interface *f* óleo-água

3865 oily *adj*
(Prod.)
(Food processing technology; product characteristic.)
d ölig
f huileux
p oleoso

3866 oily liquid
(Prod.)
(Food processing technology; product characteristic.)
d ölige Flüssigkeit *f*
f liquide *m* huileux
p líquido *m* oleoso

3867 oily phase
(Biochem.)
(Food biochemistry.)
d Ölphase *f*
f phase *f* huileuse
p fase *f* oleosa

3868 oily suspension
(Prod.)
(Food processing technology.)
d ölige Suspension *f*
f suspension *f* huileuse
p suspensão *f* oleosa

3869 oily vitamin blend
(Prod.)
(Food processing technology: vitamins in nutrition.)
d öliges Vitamingemisch *n*
f mélange *m* huileux de vitamines
p mistura *f* oleosa de vitaminas

3870 oily vitamin preparation
(Prod.)
(Vitamins in nutrition.)
d öliges Vitaminpräparat *n*
f préparation *f* huileuse de vitamines
p preparado *m* oleoso de vitaminas

3871 oleaginous fruit
(Agr.)
(Horticulture. Oil-rich fruits.)
d ölhaltige Frucht *f*
f fruit *m* oléagineux
p fruta *f* oleaginosa

3872 oleaginous plant
(Agr.)
(Agricultural produce. Plants containing or producing oil or used for oil extraction.)
d Ölpflanze *f*
f plante *f* oléagineuse
p planta *f* oleaginosa

* **olefines → 213**

* **olefins → 213**

3873 oleic acid
(Prod.)
($C_{18}H_{34}O_2$; e.g. in fatty acid synthesis: prime material for aroma/fragrance production.)
d Ölsäure *f*; Oleinsäure *f*
f acide *m* oléique
p ácido *m* oléico

3874 oleoresin
(Prod.)
(Aroma/flavour research and production: e.g. natural flavouring material in the nutmeg.)
d Oleoresin *n*; Harzöl *n*
f oléorésine *f*
p oleorresina *f*

3875 oleoresin extraction
(Prod.)
(Aroma/flavour research and production.)
d Oleoresinextraktion *f*; Harzölextraktion *f*
f extraction *f* d'oléorésines
p extração *f* de oleorresina

3876 olfaction
(Med.)
(Smelling process.)
d Riechen *n*
f olfaction *f*
p olfação *f*

3877 olfacto-gustatory sensation
(Med.)
(Aroma/flavour perception.)
d Riech- und Geschmacksempfindung *f*; riech- und geschmacksbezügliche Empfindung *f*
f sensation *f* olfacto-gustative
p sensação *f* olfato-gustativa

3878 olfactory *adj*
(Med.)
(Ref. to the sense of smell.)
d geruchsbezüglich
f olfactif
p olfativo

3879 olfactory bulb
(Med.)
(Anatomy; ref. olfactory stimulation, nervous cells system: aroma/flavour research: ref. to odoriferous molecules perceptivity and perceptibility.)
d Anschwellung *f* der Riechhirnstränge
f bulbe *m* olfactif
p bulbo *m* olfativo

3880 olfactory organ
(Med.)
(Anatomy.)
d Riechorgan *n*
f organe *m* olfactif
p órgão *m* olfativo

3881 olfactory sensations
(Med.)
(Ref. to the sense of smell.)
d Geruchswahrnehmungen *fpl*
f sensations *fpl* olfactives
p sensações *fpl* olfativas

3882 olfactory stimulation
(Biochem.)
(Aroma/flavour research and production.)
d Geruchswahrnehmungsanregung *f*; Anregung *f* der Geruchswahrnehmung
f stimulation *f* olfactive
p estimulação *f* olfativa

3883 olfactory sulcus
(Med.)
(Anatomy. "Sulcus olfactorius".)
d Geruchsfurche *f*
f sillon *m* olfactif
p sulco *m* olfativo

3884 oligopeptide
(Biochem.)
(Food biochemistry; containing up to 10 amino acids.)
d Oligopeptid *n*
f oligopeptide *m*
p oligopeptídio *m*

3885 oligosaccharide
(Biochem.)
(Food biochemistry; indigestible ingredient of legumes, containing up to eight hydrocarbon residues.)
d Oligosaccharid *n*
f oligosaccharide *m*
p oligossacarídeo *m*

3886 olive
(Agr.)
(Agricultural produce. "Olea europaea"; tree. Its fruit is e.g. salad oil source.)
d Ölbaum *m*
f olivier *m*
p oliveira *f*

3887 olive (the fruit)
(Agr.)
(Agricultural produce. "Olea europaea"; the fruit is e.g. salad oil source.)
d Olive *f*
f olive *f*
p azeitona *f*

3888 olive oil
(Prod.)
(Food processing technology.)
d Olivenöl *n*
f huile *f* d'olives
p azeite *m* de olivas

3889 omelette with chanterelle
(Prod.)
(Gastronomy. "Cantharellus cibarius"; edible mushroom. In Brazil: omelete; in Portugal: omeleta.)
d Pfifferlingsomelett *n*
f omelette *f* aux girolles
p omelete *f* de cantarelo

3890 omelette with chervil
(Prod.)
(Gastronomy; dish of beaten cooked eggs with chervil herb; in Brazil: omelete; in Portugal: omeleta.)
d Kerbelomelett *n*
f omelette *f* au cerfeuil
p omelete *f* de cerefólio

3891 one day's chick
(Agr.)
(Poultry farming.)
d Eintagsküken *n*
f poussin *m* d'un jour
p pinto *m* de um dia

3892 onion
(Agr.)
(Horticulture. "Allium cepa".)
d Zwiebel *f*
f oignon *m*
p cebola *f*

3893 onions browned in butter
(Prod.)
(Gastronomy.)
d Zwiebeln *fpl* in Butter gebräunt
f oignons *mpl* revenus au beurre
p cebolas *fpl* douradas na manteiga

* **O.P. → 3935**

3894 optical rotatory power
(Biochem.)
(Nutritional science; ref. to polarization; e.g. ref. to processes of analysis.)
d optische Drehkraft *f*; optisches Drehvermögen *n*
f pouvoir *m* rotatoire optique
p poder *m* ótico de rotação; poder *m* óptico de rotação

3895 optimal maturity condition
(Agr.)
(Botany; biologic constitution of the fruit.)
d optimaler Reifezustand *m*
f état *m* de maturité optimum; état *m* de maturité optimal
p estado *m* ótimo de *m* maturidade

3896 optimization of cell nutrition
(Med.)
(Ref. to therapy of nutritional diseases.)
d Optimierung *f* der Zellernährung
f optimisation *f* de la nutrition cellulaire
p otimização *f* da nutrição celular

3897 optimization of vitamin absorption
(Med.)
(Veterinary; ref. to vitamin supplementation to feed and animal metabolism.)
d Optimierung *f* der Vitaminaufnahme
f optimisation *f* de l'absorption vitaminique
p otimização *f* da absorção vitamínica

3898 oral moment
(Med.)
(Ref. to the touch of the food through the mouth, with the mucosae.)
d oraler Moment *m*
f étape *f* buccale
p momento *m* oral

3899 oral supplementation
(Med.)
(Veterinary; e.g. ref. to feed supplementation with vitamins etc.)
d orale Supplementierung *f*; mündliche Ergänzungszufuhr *f*
f supplémentation *f* orale
p suplementação *f* oral

3900 oral touch
(Med.)
(Ref. to the touch of the food through the mouth, with the mucosae.)
d mündliche Berührung *f*
f touche *f* buccale
p toque *m* oral

3901 orange
(Agr.)
(Agricultural produce. Citrus fruit.)
d Apfelsine *f*; Orange *f*
f orange *f*
p laranja *f*

3902 orange essence
(Prod.)
(Aroma/flavour research and production; essence note.)
d Orangenessenz *f*; Apfelsinenessenz *f*
f essence *f* d'orange
p essência *f* de laranja

3903 orange juice
(Prod.)
(Food processing technology.)
d Apfelsinensaft *m*
f jus *m* d'oranges
p suco *m* de laranja

3904 orange-like aroma note
(Prod.)
(Flavour note, flavour chemicals; elaboration of aromas: organic chemistry.)
d orangenartige Geschmacksnote *f*; apfelsinenartige Geschmacksnote *f*
f note *f* de saveur orange
p nota *f* de sabor laranja

3905 orange note
(Prod.)
(Taste; aroma research and production.)
d Apfelsinennote *f*
f note *f* d'orange
p nota *f* de laranja

3906 orange oil
(Prod.)
(Flavouring agent. "Citrus aurantium".)
d Apfelsinenöl *n*
f huile *f* d'orange
p óleo *m* de laranja

3907 orange-peel flavour note
(Prod.)
(Flavour note, flavour chemicals; elaboration of aromas.)
d Orangenschalengeschmacksnote *f*; Apfelsinenschalengeschmacksnote *f*
f note *f* de saveur zeste d'orange
p nota *f* de sabor casca de laranja

3908 orange tree-leaf infusion
(Prod.)
(Herb tea.)
d Tee *m* der Blätter des Apfelsinenbaumes
f tisane *f* des feuilles d'oranger
p chá *m* das folhas da laranjeira

3909 orbicularis oris
(Med.)
(Anatomy; circular muscle around the mouth; "Musculus orbicularis oris".)
d Ringmuskel *m* des Mundes; Mundringmuskel *m*
f orbiculaire *m* des lèvres
p músculo *m* orbicular dos lábios

3910 order
(Agr.)
(Botany (flora/fauna). Classification of living organisms; taxonomy: a group of similar families build an order; a group of similar orders build a class.)
d Ordnung *f*
f ordre *m*
p ordem *f*

3911 ordinary wine
(Prod.)
(Wine quality.)
d gewöhnlicher Wein *m*; mittelmäßiger Wein *m*
f vin *m* ordinaire
p vinho *m* comum; vinho *m* de mesa corrente

3912 oreganum
(Prod.)
(Food processing technology. "Origanum vulgare"; seasoning agent; aromatic oil.)
d Oregano *m*; Origano *m*
f origan *m*
p orégano *m*

3913 organelles
(Biochem.)
(Cell constituents, cell structure: specialized cellular organs; e.g. in genetic engineering; nutritional science.)
d Zellorganellen *fpl*
f organelles *mpl* de la cellule
p organelas *fpl* celulares

3914 organic *adj*
(Biochem.)
(Organic chemistry in nutritional science: carbon compound chemistry.)
d organisch
f organique
p orgânico

3915 organic acid
(Biochem.)
(Nutritional science.)
d organische Säure *f*
f acide *m* organique
p ácido *m* orgânico

3916 organic agriculture; organic farming
(Agr.)
(Biological agriculture: without using synthetic fertilizers, herbicides; utilization of fertilizers only of plant and animal origin.)
d organische Agrikultur *f*; organisch-biologische Landwirtschaft *f*
f agriculture *f* organique
p agricultura *f* orgânica

* **organic farming → 3916**

3917 organic nitrogen
(Agr.)
(Biological agriculture: fertilization.)
d organischer Stickstoff *m*
f azote *m* organique
p nitrogênio *m* orgânico

3918 organic soil
(Agr.)
(Soil type with more than 20% of organic material, i. e. of animal or vegetable matter.)
d organischer Boden *m*
f sol *m* organique
p solo *m* orgânico

3919 organic soil substance
(Agr.)
(Soil; consisting of animal and vegetable residues incorporated into the soil surface: humus.)
d organische Bodensubstanz *f*
f matières *fpl* organiques du sol
p substâncias *fpl* orgânicas do solo

3920 organic solvent
(Prod.)
(Flavour research and production: essence fractioning.)

d organisches Lösungsmittel *n*
f solvant *m* organique
p solvente *m* orgânico

3921 organization chart
(Agr.)
(Poultry farming: ref. to the agricultural organizational diagram of avian production and respective branches of activity.)
d Organogramm *n*; Organisationsplan *m*
f organigramme *m*
p organograma *m*

3922 organoleptic character of the wine
(Biochem.)
(Enology: ref. to elaboration of wine quality.)
d organoleptischer Charakter *m* des Weines
f caractère *m* organoleptique du vin
p caráter *m* organoléptico do vinho

* **organoleptic choice → 3927**

3923 organoleptic consequence; organoleptic effect
(Biochem.)
(Enology: wine treatment.)
d organoleptische Konsequenz *f*; organoleptische Auswirkung *f*
f incidence *f* organoleptique; conséquence *f* organoleptique
p conseqüência *f* organoléptica

3924 organoleptic drinking water quality
(Prod.)
(Drinking water (tap water) production: characteristics referring to smell and taste.)
d organoleptische Qualität *f* des Trinkwassers
f qualité *f* organoleptique de l'eau potable
p qualidade *f* organoléptica da água potável

* **organoleptic effect → 3923**

3925 organoleptic homogeneity
(Prod.)
(Food processing technology and flavour research and production: product characteristic.)
d organoleptische Homogenität *f*
f homogénéité *f* organoleptique
p homogeneidade *f* organoléptica

3926 organoleptic quality
(Prod.)
(Food processing technology: Quality of the final consumer product, pleasant to the sense, as e.g. taste.)
d organoleptische Qualität *f*
f qualité *f* organoleptique
p qualidade *f* organoléptica

3927 organoleptic selection; organoleptic choice
(Med.)
(Psychology: motivation for foodstuff choice by the final consumer.)
d organoleptische Auswahl *f*
f choix *f* organoleptique
p seleção *f* organoléptica

3928 origin of breed
(Agr.)
(Cattle breeding.)
d Ursprung *m* der Rasse; Rassenursprung *m*
f provenance *f* de la race
p origem *f* da raça

3929 origin of the wine
(Agr.)
(Viticulture.)
d Ursprung *m* des Weines; Herkunft *f* des Weines
f origine *f* du vin
p origem *f* do vinho

3930 ornithine; alfa,delta-diaminovaleric acid
(Biochem.)
($C_5H_{12}N_2O_2$; participates in the urea cycle. Nutritional science: Participation in the formation of glutamic acid.)
d Ornithin *n*; 2,5-Diaminovaleriansäure *f*
f ornithine *f*; acide *m* 2,5 diamiovalérianique
p ornitina *f*; ácido *m* 2,5 amino-valeriânico

* **ornithosis → 4487**

3931 orotic acid
(Biochem.)
(Nutritional science; $C_5H_4N_2O_4$; whey factor. Intermediate in the biosynthesis of the pyrimidines; growth factor for certain microorganisms; also called vitamin B_{13}.)
d Orotsäure *f*
f acide *m* orotique
p ácido *m* orótico

3932 orthophosphates
(Prod.)
(Acïdifying agents, promoting anti-oxidative effect of other auxiliaries, used in bakery and dessert products: Calcium o. (CEE No. 341); Potassium o. (CEE No. 340); Sodium o. (CEE No. 339).)
d Orthophosphate *npl*
f orthophosphates *mpl*
p ortofosfatos *mpl*

3933 orthophosphoric acid
(Prod.)
(H_3PO_4; antioxidant additive. In caffeine containing refrigerants (E 338).)

d Orthophosphorsäure *f*
f acide *m* orthophosphorique
p ácido *m* orto-fosfórico

3934 **osmosis**
(Prod.)
(Passage process of ions through a semi-permeable membrane. In food processing technology osmosis process is used in industrial form for juice concentration.)
d Osmose *f*
f osmose *f*
p osmose *f*

3935 **osmotic pressure; O.P.**
(Prod.)
(Solution characteristic; depends on solution particles concentration. Osmosis process is used in industrial form for juice concentration. Food processing technology.)
d osmotischer Druck *m*
f pression *f* osmotique
p pressão *f* osmótica

3936 **ossein**
(Prod.)
(By hydrolysis yields gelatine, prime material for the foodstuff industry.)
d Ossein *n*; Eiweißsubstanz *f* des Knochengerüstes
f osséine *f*; substance *f* protéique des os
p osseína *f*; osteína *f*

* **osso bucco → 3076**

3937 **osteoichtyes**
(Agr.)
(Bony fish type.)
d Knochenfische *mpl*
f ostéichtyens *mpl*; poisson *m* osseux
p osteíctios *mpl*

3938 **osteomalacia; softening of the bones**
(Med.)
(Veterinary; softening of the skeleton due to insufficient calcification, e.g.: vitamin D deficiency.)
d Osteomalazie *f*; Knochenerweichung *f*
f ostéomalacie *f*; ramollissement *m* des os
p osteomalacia *f*; amolecimento *m* ósseo

3939 **ovalbumin; albumin of white of egg**
(Med.)
(Egg albumin.)
d Eiweißalbumin *n*
f ovalbumine *f*; albumine *f* du blanc d'œuf
p ovalbumina *f*; albumina *f* de branca do ovo

3940 **ovary position**
(Agr.)
(Botany. Base of the flower carpel; e.g. "superior" and "inferior".)
d Stellung *f* des Fruchtknotens
f position *f* d'ovaire
p altura *f* de ovário; posição *f* do ovário

* **overburn** *v* **→ 809**

3941 **overdose**
(Prod.)
(Aroma/fragrance research and production: related to taste.)
d Überdosis *f*
f surdose *f*
p dose *f* excessiva

* **overflow** *v* **→ 772**

3942 **overgrowing by undesirable herbs**
(Agr.)
(Biological agriculture: Soil treatment.)
d Unkrautüberwucherung *f*; Überwucherung *f* durch unerwünschte Gräser
f envahissement *m* d'herbes indésirables
p invasão *f* por ervas indesejáveis

* **overhead distillate → 5524**

3943 **overheat** *v*
(Prod.)
(Aroma/food processing technology; excessive heating.)
d überhitzen
f surchauffer
p sobreaquecer

* **overheating → 2015**

3944 **overmaturation**
(Agr.)
(Viticulture: characteristic of grapes.)
d Überreifung *f*
f surmaturation *f*
p sobrematuração *f*; supermaturação *f*

3945 **overnutrition**
(Med.)
(Due to eating to excess.)
d Überernährung *f*
f suralimentation *f*
p superalimentação *f*

3946 **overperoxidation**
(Biochem.)
(Nutritional science; e.g. ref. to certain vitamins in contact with certain minerals.)
d Überperoxidation *f*
f surperoxydation *f*
p sobre-peroxidação *f*

3947 **overpressure; superpressure**
(Prod.)
(Food processing technology; ref. to processes.)
d Überdruck *m*
f surpression *f*
p superpressão *f*; sobrepressão *f*

3948 **overproduction**
(Prod.)
(Food processing technology: production and marketing problems.)
d Überproduktion *f*
f surproduction *f*
p superprodução *f*

3949 **oversalt** *v*
(Prod.)
(Gastronomy.)
d versalzen
f saler trop
p salgar demais; salgar em excesso

3950 **overweight**
(Med.)
(Obesity; origin: positive energy balance.)
d Übergewicht *n*
f surpoids *m*; excédent *m* de poids
p sobrepeso *m*; excesso *m* de peso

* **overweight of the baby → 2915**

3951 **ovulation**
(Med.)
(Veterinary; ref. to cattle breeding, cattle reproduction: release of a mature ovum from the Graaf follicle.)
d Ovulation *f*, Eisprung *m*
f ovulation *f*
p ovulação *f*

* **o/w emulsions → 3857**

* **ox → 5222**

3952 **oxalic acid; ethanedioic acid**
(Prod.)
($H_2C_2O_4.2H_2O$; present in chocolate; excretion via urine, increased in case of diabetes.)
d Oxalsäure *f*, Äthandisäure *f*, Ethandisäure *f*
f acide *m* oxalique
p ácido *m* oxálica

3953 **oxidants**
(Biochem.)
(Food biochemistry.)
d Oxidationsmittel *n/npl*; Oxidans *n*
f oxydants *mpl*
p oxidantes *mpl*

3954 **oxidation by polyunsaturated fatty acids**
(Biochem.)
(Oxidation phenomena in nutrients, e.g. of vitamins.)
d Oxidation *f* durch mehrfach ungesättigte Fetssäuren
f oxydation *f* par des acides gras polyinsaturés
p oxidação *f* pelos ácidos graxos poliinsaturados

3955 **oxidation enzyme; oxidizing enzyme**
(Biochem.)
(Food biochemistry. Oxidative enzyme.)
d Oxidationsenzym *n*
f enzyme *f* d'oxydation
p enzima *f* de oxidação

3956 **oxidation of the wine**
(Biochem.)
(Enology; wine defect by treatment error, e.g. may cause microbial development.)
d Oxidation *f* des Weines
f oxydation *f* du vin
p oxidação *f* do vinho

3957 **oxidation reactions in meat products**
(Prod.)
(Food processing technology.)
d Oxidationsreaktionen *fpl* in Fleischprodukten
f réactions *fpl* d'oxydation dans des produits de viande
p reações *fpl* oxidativas em produtos de carne

3958 **oxidation-reduction**
(Biochem.)
(Food biochemistry: redox.)
d Oxidationsreduktion *f*
f oxydoréduction *f*
p óxido-redução *f*, oxi-redução *f*

3959 **oxidation-sensitive** *adj*
(Prod.)
(Food processing technology. Product characteristics.)
d oxidationsempfindlich
f sensible à l'oxydation
p sensível à oxidação

3960 **oxidation stability**
(Prod.)
(One of the major problems of vitamin and food processing technology.)
d Oxidationsstabilität *f*
f stabilité *f* à l'oxydation
p estabilidade *f* à oxidação

3961 **oxidative aging of wine**
(Biochem.)
(Enology.)
d oxidative Alterung *f* des Weines

f vieillissement *m* oxydatif du vin
p envelhecimento *m* oxidante do vinho; envelhecimento *m* do vinho oxidação

3962 oxidative cell membrane degradation
(Biochem.)
(Nutritional science; it is said that vitamin E and selenium (Se) together protect the membrane against oxidative degradation. Selenium acts as a coenzyme.)
d oxidativer Abbau *m* der Zellmembrane
f dégradation *f* oxydative de la membrane cellulaire
p degradação *f* oxidativa da membrana celular

3963 oxidative changes in meat
(Biochem.)
(Nutritional science; e.g. phenomenon development during cold storage.)
d oxidative Veränderungen *fpl* des Fleisches
f modifications *fpl* oxydatives de la viande
p modificações *fpl* oxidativas da carne

3964 oxidative decomposition of fats
(Biochem.)
(Food biochemistry; by drying.)
d oxidative Zersetzung *f* der Fette
f décomposition *f* oxydative des graisses
p decomposição *f* oxidativa das gorduras

3965 oxidative degradation
(Biochem.)
(Vitamin/food biochemistry. Ref. to tissue oxidation processes and antioxidant activity.)
d oxidativer Abbau *m*
f dégradation *f* oxydative
p degradação *f* oxidativa

3966 oxidative deterioration of meat lipids
(Biochem.)
(Nutritional science; ref. to restructured meat in meat processing.)
d oxidativer Verderb *m* von Fleischlipiden
f détérioration *f* oxydative des lipides de la viande
p deterioração *f* oxidativa dos lipídios da carne

3967 oxidative phenomenon
(Biochem.)
(Nutritional science; food biochemistry.)
d Oxidationsphänomen *n*; Oxidationserscheinung *f*
f phénomène *m* oxydatif
p fenômeno *m* de oxidação

3968 oxidative rancidity
(Biochem.)
(Food biochemistry.)
d oxidative Ranzigkeit *f*
f rancissement *m* oxydatif
p rancidez *f* oxidativa

3969 oxidative rancidity in cooked meat
(Biochem.)
(Nutritional science; quality reducing factor in meat processing.)
d oxidative Ranzigkeit *f* gekochten Fleisches
f rancissement *m* oxydatif de la viande cuite
p rancidez *f* oxidativa da carne cozida

3970 oxidative rancidity in raw meat
(Biochem.)
(Nutritional science; quality reducing factor in meat processing.)
d oxidative Ranzigkeit *f* rohen Fleisches
f rancissement *m* oxydatif de la viande non cuite
p rancidez *f* oxidativa da carne não cozida

3971 oxidative stability of meat
(Biochem.)
(Nutritional science; ref. to restructured meat in meat processing.)
d Oxidationsstabilität *f* des Fleisches
f stabilité *f* de la viande à l'oxydation
p estabilidade *f* da carne á oxidação

3972 oxidizable substrate
(Biochem.)
(Food biochemistry.)
d oxidierbares Substrat *n*
f substrat *m* oxydable
p substrato *m* oxidável

* **oxidizing enzyme → 3955**

3973 oxidoreductases
(Biochem.)
(Nutritional science; class of enzymes.)
d Oxidoreduktasen *fpl*; Oxidoreductasen *fpl*
f oxydoréductases *fpl*
p óxidoreductases *fpl*

3974 oxtail soup
(Prod.)
(Gastronomy.)
d Ochsenschwanzsuppe *f*
f potage *m* oxtail; potage *m* de queue de bœuf
p sopa *f* de rabada de boi

3975 ox tongue
(Prod.)
(Butchery.)
d Ochsenzunge *f*
f langue *f* de bœuf
p língua *f* de boi

3976 oxygen
(Prod.)
(O; Aromas: e.g. constitutional part of odoriferous foodstuff molecules.)

d Sauerstoff *m*
f oxygène *m*
p oxigênio *m*

3977 **oxygenated compounds**
(Prod.)
(Aroma/flavour research and production, distillation product.)
d sauerstoffangereicherte Verbindungen *fpl*
f composés *mpl* oxygénés
p compostos *mpl* oxigenados

3978 **oxygenated free radical**
(Biochem.)
(Nutritional science.)
d oxigenangereichertes freies Radikal *n*; sauerstoffangereichertes freies Radikal *n*
f radical *m* libre oxygéné
p radical *m* livre oxigenado

3979 **oxygen content of the water**
(Prod.)
(Water supply; water treatment.)
d Sauerstoffgehalt *m* des Wassers
f concentration *f* d'oxygène d'eau
p concentração *f* de oxigênio na água

* **oxygen feeding → 3981**

3980 **oxygen sensitive vitamin**
(Biochem.)
(Vitamin biochemistry in nutritional science.)
d sauerstoffempfindliches Vitamin *n*
f vitamine *f* sensible à l'oxygène
p vitamina *f* sensível ao oxigênio

3981 **oxygen supply; oxygen feeding**
(Biochem.)
(Microbiology. O; vital atmospheric element for organisms of aerobic respiration. 28% of the atmosphere's volume.)
d Sauerstoffzuführung *f*; Sauerstoffversorgung *f*
f alimentation *f* en oxygène; oxygénation *f*
p admissão *f* de oxigênio; abastecimento *m* de oxigênio; oxigenação *f*

3982 **oyster**
(Agr.)
(Family "Ostreidae"; edible marine mollusk.)
d Auster *f*
f huître *f*
p ostra *f*

3983 **oyster shells**
(Agr.)
(Biological agriculture: Soil treatment. The ground shells, containing calcium, are used for soil improvement.)
d Austernschalen *fpl*
f écailles *fpl* d'huîtres
p cascas *fpl* de ostra

3984 **ozonation; ozonization**
(Prod.)
(Food processing technology: treatment for disinfection purposes e.g. of water.)
d Ozonisierung *f*
f ozonisation *f*
p ozonização *f*; ozonificação *f*

* **ozonation of drinking water → 3986**

3985 **ozone**
(Prod.)
(O_3; Used as disinfectant due to its oxidizing characteristics. Auxiliary.)
d Ozon *n/m*
f ozone *m*
p ozônio *m*

* **ozonization → 3984**

3986 **ozonization of tap water; ozonation of drinking water**
(Prod.)
(Water supply; water (tap water) treatment with ozone (O_3), an oxygen form.)
d Ozonisierung *f* von Leitungswasser; Ozonisierung *f* von Trinkwasser
f ozonisation *f* de l'eau du robinet; ozonisation *f* de l'eau potable
p ozonização *f* da água da bica; ozonificação *f* da água encanada; ozonificação *f* da água potável

3987 **ozonization of the water**
(Prod.)
(Water supply treatment.)
d Ozonisierung *f* des Wassers
f ozonisation *f* de l'eau
p ozonização *f* da água

P

3988 **packaged curd cheese**
(Prod.)
(Dairy product.)
d abgepackter Quark *m*
f caillebotte *f* empaquetée
p ricota *f* empacotada

3989 **packaged in plastic bags**
(Prod.)
(Dairy plant packing system.)
d in Plastiksäcken abgepackt
f empaqueté en sac plastique
p empacotado em sacos plásticos

3990 **packaged into portions**
(Prod.)
(Food processing technology, meat industrialization and marketing.)
d portionsweise abgepackt
f conditionné en portions
p acondicionado em porções

3991 **packaging material**
(Prod.)
(Foodstuff packaging technology.)
d Verpackungsmaterial *n*
f matériau *m* d'emballage
p material *m* de embalagem

3992 **pack animal; beast of burden**
(Agr.)
(Livestock. Animals used in agriculture e.g. for carrying burdens, traction of vehicles.)
d Lasttier *n*; Tragtier *n*; Packtier *n*
f bête *f* de somme
p animal *m* de carga

3993 **paddy**
(Agr.)
(Agricultural produce. Untreated rice.)
d ungeschälter Reis *m*
f riz *m* non-décortiqué; riz *m* en paille
p arroz *m* em casca

3994 **palatability**
(Prod.)
(Gastronomy; e.g. ref. to savouriness of a dish, of food, of a product.)
d Schmackhaftigkeit *f*
f palatabilité *f*
p palatabilidade *f*

* **palatable** *adj* → **379**

3995 **palatine bone**
(Med.)
(Anatomy. Facial bone.)
d Gaumenbein *n*
f os *m* palatin; palatin *m*
p osso *m* palatino; palatino *m*

3996 **palmitic acid; hexadecanoic acid**
(Prod.)
($C_{16}H_{32}O_2$; saturated fatty acid (prime material) present in the tissue of mammals)
d Palmitinsäure *f*; Hexadecansäure *f*
f acide *m* palmitique
p ácido *m* palmítico

3997 **palm kernel oil**
(Prod.)
(Food processing technology; extracted from the seed of the nut; e.g. for margarine production.)
d Palmkernfett *n*
f huile *f* de palmiste
p óleo *m* de semente da palmeira

3998 **palm oil**
(Prod.)
(Food processing technology: extracted from the pulp of the nut. Edible fat; e.g. margarine production.)
d Palmfett *n*; Kokosfett *n*
f huile *f* de palme
p óleo *m* de palma; óleo *m* de coco

3999 **pancreas**
(Med.)
(Anatomy; e.g. site of the Langerhans islets: insulin secretion.)
d Bauchspeicheldrüse *f*
f pancréas *m*
p pâncreas *m*

4000 **pancreas juice**
(Med.)
(One of the digestive juices; see gastric juice.)
d Bauchspeicheldrüsensaft *f*
f suc *m* pancréatique
p suco *m* do pâncreas

4001 **pancreatic amylases**
(Med.)
(Pancreas enzyme: starch digestion.)
d Pankreasamylasen *fpl*
f amylases *fpl* pancréatiques
p amilíases *fpl* pancreáticas

4002 **pancreatic lipase**
(Med.)
(Veterinary; important for digestion of alimentary fat.)
d Pankreaslipase *f*

f lipase *f* pancréatique
p lipase *f* pancreática

4003 pangamic acid
(Biochem.)
(Nutritional science; $C_{10}H_{19}NO_8$; vitamin B_{15}; derivative of glucuronic acid; occurs e.g. in brewer's yeast; related to the activation of cell respiratory process.)
d Pangamsäure *f*
f acide *m* pangamique
p ácido *m* pangâmico

* **pantothenic acid → 5747**

4004 papain
(Prod.)
(Papayotin; vegetable pepsin; proteolytic enzyme of the papaw fruit "Carica papaya". Food processing technology: e.g. meat treatment-tenderness improvement.)
d Papain *n*
f papaïne *f*
p papaína *f*

4005 papaya
(Prod.)
(Edible sweet fruit of "Carica papaya L.", very common in Brazil; used as a dessert fruit; also papain production, a protease, used as meat tenderizer. Food processing technology.)
d Papaya *f*
f papaye *f*
p papaia *f*

4006 paprika
(Prod.)
(Gastronomy; red fruit of "Capsicum annuum". Used e.g. in salads.)
d Paprika *n*
f paprika *m*
p páprica *f*

* **paraffins → 212**

4007 parasite
(Med.)
(Veterinary science. Organism which attaches itself to a plant or animal (the hosts) to obtain food from it.)
d Schmarotzer *m*; Parasit *m*
f parasite *m*
p parasita *m*

4008 parboiled
(Prod.)
(Food processing technology: preliminary incomplete cooking process.)
d halbgekocht
f étuvé préliminairement; semi-cuit
p parboilizado; semi-cozido

* **parboiling process → 4009**

4009 parboil procedure; parboiling process
(Prod.)
(Food processing technology; preliminary process of semi-cooking, in a closed vessel under high temperature.)
d Parboilprozess *m*
f étuvage *m*
p processo *m* de escaldadura; processo *m* de parboilizar

4010 parboil rice
(Prod.)
(Food processing technology. Rice treated as to the parboil method.)
d halbekochter Reis *m*; parboilisierter Reis *m*
f riz *m* étuvé; riz *m* précuit; riz *m* parboilisé
p arroz *m* parboilizado

4011 parenteral feeding
(Med.)
(Food intake by any way other than the mouth: generally administered by intravenous injection, in form of solutions.)
d parenterale Ernährung *f*
f alimentation *f* parentérale
p alimentação *f* parenteral

4012 parodontitis
(Med.)
(Inflammation around a tooth.)
d Zahnbettentzündung *f*
f parodontite *f*
p parodontite *f*; periodontite *f*

4013 parodontium
(Med.)
(Anatomy. Tooth socket.)
d Zahnbett *n*
f parodontium *m*
p parodôncio *m*; parodôntio *m*

4014 parodontosis
(Med.)
(Disease without inflammation.)
d Zahnbetterkrankung *f*
f parodontose *f*
p parodeontose *f*

* **parrot fever → 4487**

4015 parsley
(Agr.)
(Horticulture. "Petroselinum crispum", "Petroselinum sativum"; culinary and garnish herb.)
d Petersilie *f*

f persil *m*
p salsa *f*

4016 **part dry** *adj*
(Prod.)
(Food processing technology: product characteristic, e.g. wine.)
d halbtrocken
f demi-sec
p meio seco

4017 **partial condensation**
(Prod.)
(Aroma/flavour research and production: distillation processes.)
d Teilkondensation *f*
f condensation *f* partielle
p condensação *f* parcial

4018 **partial destruction of important active principles**
(Prod.)
(Production and research problem for food processing technology.)
d teilweise Zerstörung *f* wichtiger Wirkstoffe
f destruction *f* partielle des principes actifs importants
p destruição *f* parcial de princípios ativos importantes

4019 **partial fermentation**
(Biochem.)
(Fermentation, e.g. beer production, wine production; fermentation process type.)
d Teilgärung *f*
f fermentation *f* partielle
p fermentação *f* parcial

4020 **partially crystallized**
(Prod.)
(Food processing technology. Physical product presentation form.)
d teilkristallisiert; teilweise kristallisiert
f partiellement cristallisé
p parcialmente cristalizado

4021 **partial maceration**
(Prod.)
(Enology.)
d partielle Mazeration *f*; teilweises Ziehenlassen *n*
f macération *f* partielle
p maceração *f* parcial

4022 **partial scumming**
(Prod.)
(Dairy plant technology for milk processing: separation of the cream from the milk.)
d Teilentrahmung *f*
f écrémage *m* partiel
p separação *f* parcial do creme

4023 **particle in suspension**
(Biochem.)
(Food biochemistry.)
d Suspensionsteilchen *n*; in Suspension befindliches Teilchen *n*
f particule *f* en suspension
p partícula *f* em suspensão

4024 **partridge**
(Agr.)
(Poultry farming. "Perdix". Here: male partridge; gallinaceous game bird.)
d Rebhahn *m*
f perdrix *m* mâle
p perdigão *m*

4025 **passion flower**
(Agr.)
(Horticulture. Genus "Passiflora"; tropical fruit: maracujá. Very common in Brazil.)
d Passionsblume *f*
f fleur *f* de la Passion
p passiflora *f*

4026 **passion fruit**
(Agr.)
(Horticulture. Edible fruit of the passion flower. Very common in Brazil.)
d Passionsfrucht *f*
f fruit *m* de la passion
p maracujá *m*

4027 **passive proteins**
(Biochem.)
(Nutritional science: Having a structural function: e.g. the fibrous protein collagen, in the connective skin tissue.)
d passive Proteine *npl*
f protéines *fpl* passives
p proteínas *fpl* passivas

4028 **pass** *v* **through a sieve; sieve** *v*; **sift** *v*
(Prod.)
(Food processing technology. Process form.)
d durch ein Sieb geben; sieben
f passer au tamis; tamiser
p passar pela peneira; tamisar; peneirar

4029 **pasta; dough**
(Prod.)
(Food processing technology. Alimentary, processed, paste products, e.g. like spaghetti.)
d Teigwaren *fpl*
f pâtes *fpl* alimentaires
p massas *fpl* alimentícias; pasta *f* alimentícia

4030 **paste-like concentrate**
(Prod.)
(Aroma/flavour research: fruit juice concentrate.)
d pastenförmiges Konzentrat *n*
f concentré *m* pâteux
p concentrado *m* pastoso

4031 **pasteurization**
(Prod.)
(Heating process for foodstuff conservation, with temperatures under 100°C; over this limit: sterilization. Pasteurization is used in milk treatment, fruit juice production, brewing process etc.)
d Pasteurisierung *f*; Pasteurisieren *n*
f pasteurisation *f*
p pasteurização *f*

4032 **pasteurized cream**
(Prod.)
(Dairy product e.g. butter production.)
d pasteurisierte Creme *f*
f crème *f* pasteurisée
p creme *m* pasteurizado

4033 **pasteurized milk**
(Prod.)
(Dairy product; partial sterilization of the milk.)
d pasteurisierte Milch *f*
f lait *m* pasteurisé
p leite *m* pasteurizado

4034 **pastry; flaky pastry; puff paste; puffy paste**
(Prod.)
(Confectionary; flaky pastry, short pastry; sweet, made of dough.)
d Feingebäck *n*; Blätterteig *m*
f pâtisserie *f*; pâte *f* feuilletée
p massa *f* folhada

4035 **pastry filling; sponge cake filling**
(Prod.)
(Confectionary.)
d Biskuitfüllung *f*
f fourrage *m* de biscuits
p recheio *m* de biscoitos

4036 **pasturage**
(Agr.)
(Cattle breeding; taking livestock out for grazing.)
d Weidegang *m*
f pâturage *m*
p pastoreio *m*; pastorejo *m*

4037 **pasturage of cattle; pasture of cattle**
(Agr.)
(Biological agriculture.)
d Weidegang *m* des Viehes
f pâturage *m* des bestiaux
p pastoreio *m* do gado

4038 **pasture**
(Agr.)
(Soil. Land destined for cattle grazing.)
d Weideland *n*; Weide *f*
f pâture *f*
p pastagem *f*

* **pasture of cattle → 4037**

* **patch → 4216**

* **pâté → 4039**

4039 **pate; pie; pâté**
(Prod.)
(Gastronomy.)
d Pastete *f*
f pâté *m*
p pastel *m*; empada *f*; rissole *m*

4040 **patent blue**
(Prod.)
(Foodstuff colorants. Food dye: E number: E 131.)
d Patentblau *n*
f bleu *m* patente
p azul *m* patente

4041 **patent flour**
(Prod.)
(Food processing technology: High-grade wheat flour.)
d Qualitätsweizenmehl *n*
f fleur *f* de farine; fine fleur *f* de froment
p farinha *f* especial de trigo

4042 **pathogenic** *adj*
(Med.)
(Disease causing: ref. to bacteria, chemical substances etc.)
d pathogen; krankmachend; Krankheit erregend
f pathogène
p patogênico; patógeno

4043 **pathogenic agent**
(Med.)
(Bacteria, microbes, chemical substances.)
d krankheitserregendes Agens *n*; pathogenes Agens *n*
f agent *m* pathogène
p agente *m* patogênico

4044 **pathogenic bacterium**
(Med.)
(E.g. those parasitic in nutrition.)
d krankheitsverursachende Bakterie *f*

f bactérie *f* pathogène
p bactéria *f* patogênica

4045 **pathogenic for animals**
(Med.)
(Veterinary; ref. to certain substances, microbes, bacteria, plants etc.)
d krankheitserregend für Tiere; pathogen für Tiere
f pathogène pour les animaux
p patógeno para os animais

4046 **pathogenic for men**
(Med.)
(Ref. to certain substances, microbes, bacteria etc.)
d krankheitserregend für Menschen; pathogen für Menschen
f pathogène pour les hommes
p patogênico para os homens

4047 **patient on diet**
(Med.)
(Nutrition in medicine.)
d Diätpatient *m*
f patient *m* à la diététique
p paciente *m* de dieta

4048 **p-cresyl methyl ether; 1-methoxy-4-methylbenzene**
(Prod.)
(Aroma prime material.)
d p-Cresylmethyläther *m*
f éther *m* p-crésyl-métylique
p éter *m* p-cresilmetílico

4049 **pea**
(Agr.)
(Horticulture. "Pisum sativum"; leguminous plant.)
d Erbse *f*
f pois *m*
p ervilha *f*

4050 **peach**
(Agr.)
(Horticulture. "Prunus persica"; drupe (stone fruit).)
d Pfirsich *m*
f pêche *f*
p pêssego *m*

4051 **peach flan**
(Prod.)
(Confectionary; fruit flan.)
d Pfirsichtorte *f*
f tarte *f* aux pêches
p torta *f* de pêssegos

4052 **peach tree**
(Agr.)
(Horticulture. "Prunus persica".)
d Pfirsichbaum *m*
f pêcher *m*
p pessegueiro *m*

4053 **peach tree borer**
(Agr.)
(Biologic agriculture; "Synanthedon exitiosa", aphid; ref. to destruction of stone fruit tree cultures by this insect.)
d Blattlaus *f* des Pfirsichbaumes
f puceron *m* des pêchers
p pulgão *m* do pessegueiro; afídio *m* do pessegueiro

4054 **peanut**
(Agr.)
(Agricultural produce. "Arachis hypogaea". With edible oily seeds.)
d Erdnuss *f*
f arachide *f*; cacahuète *f*
p amendoim *m*

4055 **peanut butter**
(Prod.)
(Food processing technology. Spread (as on bread) made of ground peanuts.)
d Erdnussbutter *f*
f beurre *f* d'arachide; beurre *f* de cacahuète
p manteiga *f* de amendoim

4056 **peanut oil; arachis oil**
(Prod.)
("Arachis hypogaea". Margarine additive, used e.g. as cooking oil; in salad preparations; in oily vitamin preparations.)
d Erdnussöl *n*
f huile *f* d'arachide
p óleo *m* de amendoim

4057 **pear**
(Agr.)
(Horticulture. Genus "Pyrus"; pome.)
d Birne *f*
f poire *f*
p pêra *f*

4058 **pearl barley**
(Prod.)
(Food processing technology.)
d Graupen *fpl*; Perlgraupen *fpl*
f orge *m* perlé; orge *m* mondé
p cevadinha *f*

4059 **pear-like flavour note**
(Prod.)
(Prime material; flavour chemical e.g. isoamyl acetate ($C_7H_{14}O_2$). Flavour note, elaboration of aromas: organic chemistry.)

d birnenartige Geschmacksnote *f*
f note *f* saveur de poire
p nota *f* de sabor de pera

4060 pear-like taste
(Prod.)
(Aroma chemicals, ref. to the taste of isoamyl acetate.)
d birnenartiger Geschmack *m*
f saveur *f* poire
p sabor *m* de pêra

* **peasant bread → 1175**

4061 pea soup
(Prod.)
(Gastronomy.)
d Erbsensuppe *f*
f soupe *f* de pois
p sopa *f* de ervilhas

4062 peat
(Agr.)
(Soil; partly decomposed and compressed plant residues under water; a bog after a long time forms peat.)
d Torf *n*
f tourbe *f*
p turfa *f*

4063 pectic acid
(Prod.)
(Organic acids which are present in ripe fruits, due to pectin transformation by an enzyme. Prime material.)
d Pektinsäure *f*
f acide *m* pectique
p ácido *m* péctico

4064 pectin
(Prod.)
(Food processing technology: Used for the production of fruit gelly gel; texture improving ingredient.)
d Pektin *n*
f pectine *f*
p pectina *f*

4065 pectinase
(Biochem.)
(Food biochemistry; Diastase hydrolyzes pectic substances, resulting in gel-like material.)
d Pektinase *f*
f pectinase *f*
p pectinase *f*

4066 pectin destruction
(Biochem.)
(Nutritional science: e.g. due to the influence of enzymes.)
d Pektinzerstörung *f*
f destruction *f* des pectines
p destruição *f* das pectinas

4067 pectization
(Biochem.)
(Food biochemistry.)
d Pektinisierung *f*
f pectisation *f*
p pectinização *f*; formeção *f* de pectinas

* **pedigree → 3201**

4068 peel *v*
(Prod.)
(Food processing technology: ref. to fruit and vegetable treatment.)
d schälen
f éplucher
p descascar

* **peel → 4986**

* **peeling → 4986**

* **pelage → 2697**

4069 pelargonic acid; nonanoic acid; nonylic acid
(Prod.)
($C_9H_{18}O_2$; prime material for flavour additive.)
d Pelargonsäure *f*; Nonansäure *f*
f acide *m* pélargonique; acide *m* nonanoïque; acide *m* nonylique
p ácido *m* pelargônico; ácido *m* nonóico; ácido *m* nonílico

4070 pellagra
(Med.)
(Ref. to vitamin B_3 (nicotinic acid) deficiency disease.)
d Pellagra *f*
f pellagre *f*
p pelagra *f*

4071 pellagra-preventive vitamin
(Med.)
(Ref. to vitamin PP (niacin). Pellagra: deficiency disease due to niacin deficient diet.)
d Pellagra vorbeugendes Vitamin *n*; Pellagra verhütendes Vitamin *n*
f vitamine *f* préventive de la pellagre
p vitamina *f* preventiva da pelagra

4072 pellagra risk
(Med.)
(Due to niacin (vitamin PP) poor foodstuff intake, e.g. nutrition based only on maize; Indian corn.)

d Pellagrarisiko *n*
f risque *m* de pellagre
p risco *m* de pelagra

4073 **pelvis**
(Med.)
(Veterinary e.g. cattle anatomy: the sexual organs of the cow are in the pelvis and within the abdominal cavity.)
d Becken *n*; Pelvis *f*
f bassin *m*; pelvis *m*
p bacia *f*; pelve *f*

4074 **penicillin**
(Med.)
(Antibiotic from the mould "Penicillium chrysogenum".)
d Penicillin *n*
f pénicilline *f*
p penicilina *f*

4075 **penis**
(Med.)
(Veterinary; animal anatomy of the male: e.g. of the bull.)
d Penis *m*
f pénis *m*; verge *f*
p pênis *m*; verga *f*; vara *f*

* **pentamethylene → 1486**

4076 **pentane**
(Prod.)
(C_5H_{12}; aroma/flavour research and production in extraction processes.)
d Pentan *n*
f pentane *m*
p pentano *m*

4077 **pentose**
(Biochem.)
(Nutritional science. $C_5H_{10}O_5$; monosaccharide.)
d Pentose *f*
f pentose *m*
p pentose *f*

4078 **peppermint**
(Agr.)
(Botany. "Mentha piperita L.". The menthol-containing oil is used as flavouring agent e.g. in liqueurs.)
d Pfefferminze *f*
f menthe *f* poivrée
p hartelã-pimenta *f*

4079 **peppermint oil**
(Prod.)
(Flavouring auxiliary. "Mentha piperita L.".)
d Pfefferminzöl *n*
f huile *f* de menthe
p óleo *m* de hortelã; óleo *m* de menta

4080 **peptide**
(Biochem.)
(Nutritional science; amide.)
d Peptid *n*
f peptide *m*
p peptídeo *m*

4081 **peptide bond**
(Biochem.)
(Nutritional science. Bonds between amino acids: the most important covalent bond type in peptides and proteins.)
d Peptidbindung *f*
f liaison *f* peptidique
p ligação *f* peptídica

4082 **peptide group**
(Biochem.)
(Food/protein biochemistry: group of organic compounds with one or more amino acids linked by peptide bonds.)
d Peptidgruppe *f*
f groupe *m* peptidique
p grupo *m* peptídico

4083 **peptides of short chains**
(Biochem.)
(Nutritional science. ref. to protein hydrolyzation.)
d kurzkettige Peptide *npl*
f peptides *mpl* à courtes chaînes
p peptídeos *mpl* de cadeia curtas

4084 **peptidic structure**
(Biochem.)
(Nutritional science. ref. to amides derived from amino acids.)
d Peptidstruktur *f*
f structure *f* peptidique
p estrutura *f* peptídica

4085 **peptone**
(Biochem.)
(Nutritional science; polypeptide, originated by partial hydrolysis of a proteide.)
d Pepton *n*
f peptone *f*
p peptona *f*

4086 **perceived sensations**
(Biochem.)
(Nutritional science: Olfactory stimulation, nervous cells system: aroma/flavour research: ref. to odoriferous molecules.)
d wahrgenommene Empfindungen *fpl*
f sensations *fpl* perçues
p sensações *fpl* percebidas

4087 percentage of protein binding
(Biochem.)
(Nutritional science.)
d Prozentsatz *m* der Proteinbindung
f pourcentage *m* de fixation aux protéines
p percentagem *f* da fixação protéica

4088 perception of food
(Med.)
(Physiological phenomena.)
d Nahrugsmittelwahrnehmung *f*
f perception *f* d'un aliment
p percepção *f* de un produto alimentício; percepção *f* de un alimento

4089 perch
(Agr.)
("Perca fluviatilis", small edible freshwater fish.)
d Barsch *m*; Flussbarsch *m*
f perche *f*
p perca *f*

4090 percolation
(Prod.)
(Flavour production: extraction process.)
d Perkolation *f*; Durchsickerung *f*
f percolation *f*
p percolação *f*

4091 pericarp
(Agr.)
(Botany: walls of a plant ovary.)
d Fruchthülle *f*; Samengehäuse *n*
f péricarpe *m*
p pericarpo *m*

4092 periodic ophthalmia
(Med.)
(Veterinary; moon blindness of horses: recurrent eye inflammation.)
d periodische Augenentzündung *f*
f ophtalmie *f* périodique
p oftalmia *f* periódica

4093 periodic structure of fibrous proteins
(Biochem.)
(Food biochemistry. Following the fibre axis.)
d periodische Struktur *f* der fibrillären Proteine
f structure *f* périodique des protéines fibreuses
p estrutura *f* periódica das proteínas fibrilosas

4094 periosteum
(Med.)
(Veterinary; ref. animal anatomy: connective tissue layer of the bones.)
d Periost *n*; Knochenhaut *f*
f périoste *m*
p periósteo *m*

4095 perishable consumer goods
(Prod.)
(Food processing technology, research and production and conservation techniques.)
d leichtverderbliche Konsumgüter *npl*
f biens *mpl* de consommation périssables
p bens *mpl* de consumo perecíveis

4096 perishable food
(Prod.)
(Food processing technology, food characteristics.)
d leichtverderbliche Lebensmittel *npl*
f denrées *fpl* périssables
p produtos *mpl* alimentícios perecíveis; alimentos *mpl* perecíveis

4097 peristalsis
(Med.)
(Ref. to the wavelike intestinal movement; intestinal resorption of nutrients.)
d Peristaltik *f*
f péristaltisme *m*
p peristaltismo *m*; peristalse *f*

4098 peritoneum
(Med.)
(Anatomy; membrane of the abdominal cavity.)
d Bauchfell *n*
f péritoine *m*
p peritônio *m*

4099 permanent stabling
(Agr.)
(Cattle breeding: for this kind of cattle confinement the biggest and tallest animals are preferred, as they will have a better development, weight-gain and conversion of nutrients.)
d Dauerstallhaltung *f*
f stabulation *f* permanente
p estabulação *f* permanente

4100 permeability of the soil
(Agr.)
(Soils; soil treatment.)
d Permeabilität *f* des Bodens; Durchlässigkeit *f* des Bodens
f perméabilité *f* du sol
p permeabilidade *f* do solo

4101 permit *v* maturation
(Prod.)
(Dairy technology, ref. e.g. cheese etc.)
d reifen lassen; die Reifung gewährleisten
f permettre la maturation
p permitir a maturação

* **permitted fungicide → 5513**

4102 **pernicious anaemia**
(Med.)
(Ref. to vitamin B_{12} (cyanocobalamin) deficiency disease.)
d perniziöse Anämie *f*
f anémie *f* pernicieuse
p anemia *f* perniciosa

4103 **peroxidase**
(Biochem.)
(Nutritional science. Hydrogen peroxide (H_2O_2) decomposing enzyme: e.g. present in milk.)
d Peroxidase *f*
f peroxydase *f*
p peroxidase *f*

4104 **peroxidation**
(Biochem.)
(Nutritional science; ref. to peroxide: hydrogen containing oxide.)
d Peroxidation *f*
f peroxydation *f*
p peroxidação *f*

4105 **peroxidation of lipids; lipid peroxidation**
(Biochem.)
(Nutritional science; ref. to lipid oxidation phenomena in meat.)
d Peroxidation *f* der Lipide; Lipidperoxidation *f*
f peroxydation *f* des lipides; peroxydation *f* lipidique
p peroxidação *f* dos lipídios; peroxidação *f* lipídica

4106 **peroxidation process**
(Biochem.)
(Nutritional science.)
d Peroxidationsprozess *m*
f processus *m* peroxydant
p processo *m* de peroxidação

* **peroxided component → 4107**

4107 **peroxided constituent; peroxided component**
(Biochem.)
(Nutritional science.)
d peroxidierter Bestandteil *m*
f constituant *m* peroxydé
p constituinte *m* peroxidado

4108 **peroxide determination**
(Prod.)
(Food processing technology; aroma/fragrance research and production.)
d Peroxidbestimmung *f*
f détermination *f* des peroxydes
p determinação *f* dos peróxidos

4109 **peroxide formation of a lipid**
(Biochem.)
(Vitamin/food biochemistry. Ref. to tissue antioxidants.)
d Peroxidbildung *f* eines Lipides
f formation *f* des peroxydes d'un lipide
p formação *f* de peróxidos de um lipídio

4110 **peroxide level**
(Biochem.)
(Nutritional science, ref. to tissular oxidation reactions, requiring tissue antioxidants, e.g. certain vitamins and trace elements.)
d Peroxidhöhe *f*; Peroxidniveau *n*
f niveau *m* des peroxydes
p nível *m* dos peróxidos

4111 **peroxide radical**
(Biochem.)
(Nutritional science, ref. to tissular oxidation processes and antioxidant activity, e.g. in vitamin/food biochemistry.)
d Peroxidradikal *n*
f radical *m* du peroxyde
p radical *m* do peróxido

4112 **perry**
(Prod.)
(Beverages. Fermented pear juice.)
d Birnenmost *m*
f poiré *m*
p mosto *m* de pêra

4113 **persimmon**
(Agr.)
(Horticulture; "Diospyros kaky"; edible persimmon berry, common in Brazil.)
d Persimone *f*
f kaki *m*
p caqui *m*; dióspiro *m*

4114 **persistence of taste perception; duration of taste perception; continuity of taste perception**
(Biochem.)
(Enology; ref. to wine degustation, wine quality evaluation.)
d Andauer *f* der Geschmackswahrnehmung; Andauer *f* der Geschmacksempfindung
f persistance *f* de la sensation gustative
p persistência *f* da sensação gustativa

* **peruviol → 3714**

4115 **pesticidal pollution**
(Agr.)
(Agriculture. Environmental pollution by pesticides which may enter the food chains.)
d Umweltsbeschmutzung *f* durch Schädlingsbekämpfungsmittel

f pollution *f* pesticide
p poluição *f* por pesticida

4116 **pesticide**
(Agr.)
(Agriculture. Crop protection chemical.)
d Schädlingsbekämpfungsmittel *n*
f pesticide *m*
p pesticida *f*

4117 **petal**
(Agr.)
(Botany; flower: part of the corolla.)
d Blütenblatt *n*
f pétale *m*
p pétala *f*

* **petiole → 3151**

4118 **petroleum ether; benzine**
(Prod.)
(Aroma/flavour research and production: used in extraction processes.)
d Petroläther *m*; Petrolether *m*; Benzin *n*
f éther *m* de pétrole
p éter *m* de petróleo; benzina *f*

4119 **pH**
(Biochem.)
(Nutritional science. Acidity/alkalinity measure of a solution, indicating the no.7 the state of neutrality, lower nos. increasing acidity.)
d pH-Wert *m*; pH *m*
f pH *m*; potentiel *m* hydrogène
p pH *m*; valor *m* pH

4120 **pharynx**
(Med.)
(Anatomy; e.g. passage way for food.)
d Pharynx *m*
f pharynx *m*
p faringe *f*

4121 **pheasant**
(Agr.)
(Poultry farming. Family "Phasianidae"; ornamental gallinaceous bird.)
d Fasan *m*
f faisan *m*
p faisão *m*

4122 **phenol**
(Prod.)
(C_6H_6O; benzene derivative; ref. to aroma synthesis; prime material.)
d Phenol *n*
f phénol *m*
p fenol *m*

4123 **phenol derivate; phenolic derivate**
(Biochem.)
(Enology: agent of bad taste.)
d Phenolderivat *n*
f dérivé *m* du phénol; dérivé *m* phénolique
p derivado *m* do fenol; derivado *m* fenólico

4124 **phenolic compound**
(Prod.)
(Flavour chemicals.)
d Phenolverbindung *f*
f composé *m* phénolique
p composto *m* fenólico

* **phenolic derivate → 4123**

4125 **phenolic vine cycle**
(Agr.)
(Viticulture; winegrowing; cultivation of wine grapes.)
d Phenol-Zyklus *m* der Weinrebe
f cycle *m* phénolique de la vigne
p ciclo *m* fenólico da videira

* **phenomena of erosion → 4127**

* **phenomena of esterification → 4128**

4126 **phenomenon of oxidoreduction**
(Biochem.)
(Enology.)
d Erscheinung *f* des Oxidations-Reduktions-Prozesses
f phénomène *m* de l'oxydoréduction; phénomène *m* oxydoréducteur
p fenômeno *m* da oxido-redução

4127 **phenomenons of erosion; phenomena of erosion**
(Agr.)
(Soil; soil treatment.)
d Erosionserscheinungen *fpl*
f phénomènes *mpl* d'érosion
p manifestações *fpl* de erosão

4128 **phenomenons of esterification; phenomena of esterification**
(Biochem.)
(Nutritional science, food biochemistry.)
d Veresterungserscheinungen *fpl*
f phénomènes *mpl* d'estérification
p fenômenos *mpl* de esterificação

4129 **phenylalanine**
(Biochem.)
(Nutritional science; $C_9H_{11}NO_2$; essential amino acid, indispensable in nutrition and essential amino acid ingredient in human and in cow's milk.)
d Phenylalanin *n*

f phénylalanine *f*
p fenilalanina *f*

* **2-phenylchromone → 2226**

* **2-phenylethanol → 4130**

4130 **phenylethyl alcohol; 2-phenylethanol**
(Prod.)
($C_8H_{10}O$; benzene derivative; ref. to aroma synthesis; prime material.)
d Phenyläthylalkohol *m*; Phenylethylalkohol *m*
f alcool *m* phényléthylique
p álcool *m* feniletílico

4131 **phenylketonuria**
(Med.)
(Protein-metabolism disease, causing an increase of phenylalanine in the blood; result: mental retardation.)
d Phenylketonurie *f*
f phénylcétonurie *f*
p fenilcetonuria *f*

4132 **phosphatase**
(Biochem.)
(Nutritional science; phosphatic esters hydrolyzing enzyme; phosphatase exists in milk. The phosphatase test of milk assures the destruction of the enzyme after pasteurization.)
d Phosphatase *f*
f phosphatase *f*
p fosfatase *f*

4133 **phosphatase test**
(Biochem.)
(The phosphatase test of milk assures its destruction by heating.)
d Phosphatasetest *m*
f test *m* à la phosphatase
p teste *m* de fosfatase

4134 **phosphate**
(Prod.)
(Food processing technology; salt or ester of phosphoric acid; in milk are present: calcium phosphate, magnesium phosphate and potassium phosphate.)
d Phosphat *n*
f phosphate *m*
p fosfato *m*

4135 **phosphate requirements**
(Agr.)
(Botany: synthetic fertilizer for plants is used to enrich the soils.)
d Phosphatanspruch *m*
f exigence *f* en phosphate
p demanda *f* de fosfato

4136 **phosphatides**
(Biochem.)
(Nutritional science; same as phospholipids.)
d Phosphatides *n*
f phosphatides *m*
p fosfátides *mpl*

4137 **phosphatized flour**
(Med.)
(Baby nutrition.)
d phosphatiertes Mehl *n*
f farine *f* phosphatée
p farinha *f* fosfatada

4138 **phospholipid**
(Biochem.)
(Nutritional science; ref. to a phosphate group containing lipid; e.g. lecithins; constituent of all kind of tissues, e.g. of the brain.)
d Phospholipid *n*
f phospholipide *m*
p fosfolipído *m*

4139 **phospholipid composition of fatty acid**
(Biochem.)
(Nutritional science; fat biochemistry.)
d Zusammensetzung *f* der Fettsäuren an Phospholipiden
f composition *f* phospholipidique des acides gras
p composição *f* fosfolipídica dos ácidos graxos

4140 **phosphoric acid**
(Prod.)
(H_3PO_4; food processing technology; e.g. used in flavoured soft drinks, as e.g. in fizzy drinks, soda pops.; present in foodstuffs as e.g. milk and cheese products, cereals, meat and fishes.)
d Phosphorsäure *f*
f acide *m* phosphorique
p ácido *m* fosfórico

4141 **phosphorized insecticide**
(Agr.)
(Agriculture. Phosphorus-based insecticide.)
d phosphoresziertes Schädlingsbekämpfungsmittel *n*; phosphoresziertes Insektizid *n*
f insecticide *m* phosphoré
p inseticida *m* fosforado

4142 **phosphorprotein**
(Biochem.)
(Nutritional science; e.g. casein: phosphorprotein of milk.)
d Phosphorprotein *n*
f phosphoprotéine *f*
p fosfoproteína *f*

4143 phosphorus
(Agr.)
(Livestock nutrition; animal ration: phosphorus (P) is a macromineral, necessary for vitamin D fixation in the organism.)
d Phosphor *m*
f phosphore *m*
p fósforo *m*

4144 phosphorus cycle
(Agr.)
(Contained in the composition of various types of rocks; absorbed by plants for use in organic synthesis; e.g. the guano is one of the forms of how the sea returns the phosphates to the land.)
d Phosphorkreislauf *m*
f cycle *m* de phosphore
p ciclo *m* de fósforo

4145 phosphorus deficiency
(Agr.)
(Livestock nutrition; feedstuff ration deficiency.)
d Phosphormangel *m*
f carence *f* en phosphore
p deficiência *f* de fósforo; carência *f* de fósforo

4146 phosphorus-rich fishes
(Agr.)
(Fishes are a phosphorus source.)
d phosphorreiche Fische *mpl*
f poissons *mpl* riches en phosphore
p peixes *mpl* ricos de fósforo

4147 phosphorylation
(Biochem.)
(Biochem. process of introducing or combining a chemical substance with phosphoric acid or a phosphorous group; also enzymatic conversion of carbohydrates into their phosphoric esters, in metabolism.)
d Phosphorylierung *f*
f phosphorylation *f*
p fosforilação *f*

4148 photosynthesis
(Agr.)
(Botany; plant process of synthesizing (in the presence of sunlight), organic compounds from carbon dioxide and water.)
d Photosynthese *f*
f photosynthèse *f*
p fotossíntese *f*

4149 phylloxera
(Agr.)
(Viticulture: "Phylloxera vitifoliae". Vine (plant) lice.)
d Phylloxera *f*; Reblaus *f*
f phylloxéra *m*
p filoxera *f*

4150 phylum (zoology)
(Agr.)
(Botany (flora/fauna). Classification; e.g. animals of similar classes.)
d Phylum *n*
f phylum *m*
p filo *m*

4151 physical preservation processes
(Prod.)
(Food processing technology: e.g. dehydration, heating.)
d physikalische Konservierungsverfahren *npl*
f traitements *mpl* préservatifs physiques
p processos *mpl* físicos de conservação

4152 physical properties
(Prod.)
(Food processing technology; ref. to product characteristics.)
d physikalische Eigenschaften *fpl*
f propriétés *fpl* physiques
p propriedades *fpl* físicas

4153 physical soil characteristics
(Agr.)
(Soil; e.g. for agricultural purposes.)
d physikalische Bodenbeschaffenheit *f*
f caractéristiques *fpl* physiques du sol
p caraterísticas *fpl* físicas do solo

4154 physical state
(Prod.)
(Food processing technology; e.g. substance quality.)
d physikalischer Zustand *m*
f état *m* physique
p estado *m* físico

4155 physical state of the foodstuff
(Prod.)
(Food processing technology: e.g. foodstuff quality.)
d physikalischer Zustand *m* des Nahrungsmittels
f état *m* physique de l'aliment
p estado *m* físico do alimento

4156 physico-chemical interaction
(Prod.)
(Food processing technology and flavour research and production.)
d physikochemische Wechselwirkung *f*
f interaction *f* physico-chimique
p interação *f* físico-química

4157 physico-chemical method
(Prod.)
(Food processing technology.)

d physikalisch-chemische Methode *f*
f méthode *f* physico-chimique
p método *m* físico-químico

* **physicochemical nutritional value → 3825**

4158 **physiological condition**
(Prod.)
(Food processing technology; product quality.)
d physiologische Beschaffenheit *f*; physiologischer Zustand *m*
f condition *f* physiologique
p condição *f* fisiológica

4159 **physiological equilibrium**
(Med.)
(Purpose of nutrition.)
d physiologisches Gleichgewicht *n*
f équilibre *m* physiologique
p equilíbrio *m* fisiológico

4160 **physiologic dose**
(Med.)
(Nutrition in medicine.)
d physiologische Dosis *f*
f dose *f* physiologique
p dose *f* fisiologógica

4161 **physiologic necessities of the animals; physiologic requirements of the animals**
(Agr.)
(Biological agriculture. Raising of farm animals.)
d physiologische Bedürfnisse *npl* der Tiere
f besoins *mpl* physiologiques des animaux
p necessidades *fpl* fisiológicas dos animais

* **physiologic requirements of the animals → 4161**

4162 **physiology of nursing**
(Med.)
(Ref. to the science of functioning of the nursing process.)
d Physiologie *f* des Stillens
f physiologie *f* de l'allaitement
p fisiologia *f* do aleitamento; fisiologia *f* da amamentação

4163 **physiology of nutrition**
(Med.)
(Physiology: Science of function of life, organs, chemical and physical phenomena; in this case related to the nutritional area.)
d Ernährungsphysiologie *f*
f physiologie *f* nutritionnelle
p fisiologia *f* da nutrição

4164 **phytic acid; inositolhexaphosphoric acid**
(Prod.)
($H_{18}O_{24}P_6$; food processing technology: occurs e.g. in some types of nuts, in cereal husks.)
d Phytinsäure *f*
f acide *m* phytique
p ácido *m* fítico

4165 **phytoestrogen**
(Biochem.)
(Food biochemistry; plant hormone in nutrition.)
d Phytoöstrogen *n*
f phytoestrogène *m*; phyto-œstrogène *m*
p fitoestrogênio *m*

4166 **phytohormone**
(Med.)
(Plant hormone.)
d Phytohormon *n*; Pflanzenhormon *n*
f phytohormone *f*
p fitohormônio *m*

4167 **phytophagous insects**
(Agr.)
(Biological agriculture: insects feeding on plants.)
d phytophage Insekten *npl*; Pflanzen fressende Insekten *npl*
f insectes *mpl* phytophages
p insetos *mpl* fitófagos

4168 **phytosterols**
(Prod.)
(Sterols derived from plants; e.g. additive in certain dietary margarine types.)
d Phytosterine *npl*
f phytostérols *mpl*
p fitoesteróis *npl*

4169 **phytotherapy**
(Med.)
(Veterinary; animal treatment by plant substances, in biologic agriculture.)
d Phytotherapie *f*; pflanzliche Heilbehandlung *f*
f phytothérapie *f*
p fitoterapia *f*

4170 **phytotoxicity**
(Agr.)
(Biological agriculture: Characteristic of substances poisonous to plants.)
d Phytotoxizität *f*
f phytotoxicité *f*
p fitotoxicidade *f*

4171 **pickle** *v*
(Prod.)
(Food processing technology: e.g. to pickle food in vinegar.)
d einlegen in Essig

f confire dans le vinaigre
p conservar em vinagre; pôr de conserva em vinagre

* **pickle** *v* → **5117**

* **pickle → 4172**

* **pickled cabbage → 4842**

4172 **pickled cucumbers; pickle; gherkins**
(Prod.)
(Ref. to preservation method in vinegar or salt water. Cucumber-type conserve.)
d Essiggurken *fpl*; Gewürzgurken *fpl*
f cornichons *mpl* au vinaigre; cornichons *mpl*
p pepinos *mpl* em vinagre

4173 **pickled meat**
(Prod.)
(Butchery.)
d eingelegtes Fleisch *n*
f viande *f* marinée
p carne *f* marinada; carne *f* pôsto em vinha-d'alhos

4174 **pickled preserves**
(Prod.)
(Food processing technology; mixed vegetables bottled and preserved in vinegar.)
d mixed Pickles *pl*
f conserves *fpl* acides
p conservas *fpl* de picles

4175 **pickling of fish; fish salting**
(Prod.)
(Food processing technology e.g. fish preservation.)
d Pökeln *n* des Fisches; Einpökeln *n* des Fisches; Einsalzen *n* des Fisches
f salaison *f* du poisson
p salga *f* do peixe; salgação *f* do peixe; salgadura *f* do peixe

4176 **pickling of the meat; meat salting**
(Prod.)
(Butchery; meat preservation.)
d Pökeln *n* des Fleisches; Einpökeln *n* des Fleisches; Einsalzen *n* des Fleisches
f salaison *f* des viandes
p salga *f* da carne; salgação *f* da carne; salgadura *f* da carne

4177 **pickling with brine; salting with brine**
(Prod.)
(Food processing technology.)
d Pökeln *n* mit Hilfe von Salzlake; Einsalzen *n* in Salzlake
f salaison *f* par l'emploi de saumure; salaison *f* par l'emploi d'eau saline
p salga *f* com salmoura; salgação *f* por intermédio de salmoura; salgadura *f* por água salina

4178 **pick** *v* **the currants from the shrub**
(Agr.)
(Horticulture; ref. to the harvest of red or black currants.)
d abbeeren von Johannisbeeren; Johannisbeeren vom Strauch abbeeren
f égrapper des groseilles
p desbagoar; esbagoar; desengaçar; separar a groselha da groselheira

4179 **pick** *v* **the grape from the bunch**
(Agr.)
(Viticulture; grape harvest.)
d abbeeren von Weinbeeren; die Weinbeeren aus den Trauben lösen
f égrapper des raisins; égrapper des raisins du vin
p desbagoar as uvas; desengaçar as uvas; colher as uvas do cacho; tirar as uvas do cacho

4180 **pick** *v* **the grapes selecting from the vine**
(Agr.)
(Viticulture; fruit selection.)
d die Beeren am Rebstock verlesen; die Beeren am Rebstock aussortieren
f trier les raisins à la vigne
p escolher as uvas na cepa

* **pie → 4039**

4181 **pig; hog**
(Agr.)
(Livestock. Sow, boar, barrow (castrated male), gilt (young sow), boar (male hog). Another word for pig is swine (not used in British English !).)
d Schwein *n*
f porc *m*; cochon *m*
p porco *m*; suíno *m*

* **pig feeding → 2721**

4182 **pig for slaughter; hog for slaughtering**
(Agr.)
(Livestock.)
d Schlachtschwein *n*
f cochon *m* de boucherie
p suíno *m* de abate

4183 **piglet; shoat**
(Agr.)
(Livestock. Very young hog; young female pig: gilt.)
d Ferkel *n*; Läufer *m*
f porcelet *m*; goret *m*; cochonnet *m*
p leitão *m*; leitoa *f*; bácaro *m* de mama; bácara *f* de mama

4184 **pig livestock**
(Agr.)
(Livestock; a castrated male hog is called "barrow".)
d Borstenvieh *n*
f espèce *f* porcine
p cerdo *m*; porco *m*

4185 **pigmentation**
(Med.)
(Veterinary; e.g. ref. to poultry treatment: colour deficiency can eventually be a sign of disease like avitaminosis, verminous disease, coccidiosis.)
d Pigmentierung *f*
f pigmentation *f*
p pigmentação *f*

* **pig raising → 2722**

* **pig's foot → 5574**

4186 **pig's head**
(Prod.)
(Butchery; meat part.)
d Schweinskopf *m*
f tête *f* de porc
p cabeça *f* de porco

4187 **pike**
(Agr.)
("Esox lucius L."; fish of European rivers.)
d Süßwasserhecht *m*
f brochet *m*
p lúcio *m*

* **pinch → 1508**

4188 **pinch of salt**
(Prod.)
(Gastronomy.)
d Prise *f* Salz
f prise *f* de sel
p pitada *f* de sal

4189 **pine**
(Agr.)
(Botany; Genus "Pinus", Family "Pinaceae"; coniferous evergreen tree.)
d Kiefer *f*; Föhre *f*
f pin *m*; pin *m* sylvestre
p pinheiro *m*

4190 **pineapple**
(Agr.)
(Horticulture. "Ananas sativus Schult", Family "Bromeliaceae".)
d Ananas *f*
f ananas *m*
p abacaxi *m*; ananás *m*

4191 **pinene**
(Prod.)
($C_{10}H_{16}$; occurring in essential oils; e.g. aroma/fragrance prime material.)
d Pinen *n*
f pinène *m*
p pineno *m*

* **pinkeye → 1954**

4192 **pink powder**
(Prod.)
(Vitamin in nutrition: e.g. aspect of vitamin B_{12}.)
d rosafarbiges Pulver *n*
f poudre *f* rose
p pó *m* cor de rosa

4193 **pisciculture; fish farming**
(Agr.)
(Fish culture.)
d Fischzucht *f*
f pisciculture *f*
p piscicultura *f*

* **p-isopropylbenzaldehyde → 1452**

4194 **pistachio**
(Agr.)
(Botany. "Pistacia vera; Pistacia lentiscus"; cashew family. Tree and seed. In Brazil: tree = pistácia. In Portugal: plant and fruit: pistácia.)
d Pistazie *f*
f pistache *f*
p pistácio *m*

4195 **pistil; carpel**
(Agr.)
(Botany; flower structure: the female reproductive organ.)
d Stempel *m*
f pistil *m*
p pistilo *m*; gineceu *m*

4196 **pit** *v*; **stone** *v*
(Agr.)
(Horticulture. Stone fruit preparation: to core (ref. to apples).)
d entkernen; entsteinen
f ôter les pépins; ôter les noyaux
p descaroçar; tirar o caroço; tirar os caroços

4197 **placenta**
(Agr.)
(Veterinary science; cattle raising: e.g. nourishment (for the fetus) providing and respiratory organ. Cattle expel the placenta after birth of the fetus.)
d Plazenta *f*; Mutterkuchen *m*

f placenta *m*
p placenta *f*

4198 **placenta retention**
(Med.)
(Veterinary; pathological condition; normally the cow expels the placenta 3 to 12 hours after giving birth.)
d Plazenta-Einbehaltung *f*; Einbehaltung *f* des Mutterkuchens
f rétention *f* placentaire
p retenção *f* da placenta

4199 **plaice**
(Agr.)
("Pleuronectes platessa", a flatfish.)
d Scholle *f*
f plie *f*
p solho *m*

* **plains of cereal cultivation → 1007**

4200 **plaited bun**
(Prod.)
(Bakery.)
d Hefezopf *m*
f tresse *f*
p trança *f*

4201 **planarian**
(Agr.)
(Veterinary science. Genus "Planaria"; flatworms; some are parasites.)
d Planarie *f*
f planaire *f*
p planária *f*

4202 **plantain**
(Agr.)
(Horticulture; "Musa paradisiaca"; banana plant and its fruit (used as food when cooked).)
d Plantainbanane *f*
f banane *f* plantain
p pacova *f*; pacoba *f*; banana *f* de cozinhar

4203 **plant antioxidant**
(Biochem.)
(Nutritional science.)
d Antioxidant *n* pflanzlicher Herkunft
f antioxydant *m* d'origine végétal
p antioxidante *m* de origem vegetal

4204 **plant aroma extracts; plant flavour extracts**
(Prod.)
(Aroma/flavour research and production.)
d pflanzliche Aromaextrakte *mpl*; pflanzliche Geschmacksstoffauszüge *mpl*
f extraits *mpl* aromatiques de végétaux
p extratos *mpl* aromáticos de vegetais

4205 **plant cell**
(Agr.)
(Botany. Unit of plant structure.)
d Pflanzenzelle *f*
f cellule *f* végétale
p célula *f* vegetal

4206 **plant cell culture**
(Biochem.)
(Biochemical research in nutritional science.)
d Kultur *f* pflanzlicher Zellen; Pflanzenzellenkultur *f*
f culture *f* de cellules végétales
p cultura *f* de células vegetais

4207 **plant cover of the soil**
(Agr.)
(Biological agriculture.)
d pflanzliche Bodendecke *f*
f couverture *f* végétale du sol
p cobertura *f* vegetal do solo

* **plant flavour extracts → 4204**

4208 **plant immunity**
(Agr.)
(Botany; condition when plants are not susceptible to infesting pathogens and diseases.)
d Pflanzenimmunität *f*
f immunité *f* des plantes
p imunidade *f* das plantas

4209 **plant lipids**
(Biochem.)
(Food biochemistry; dietary constituents: e.g. margarine.)
d Pflanzenfettstoffe *mpl*; pflanzliche Lipide *npl*
f lipides *mpl* végétaux
p lipídios *mpl* vegetais

4210 **plant protection**
(Agr.)
(Aim of biologic agriculture, biologic farming system.)
d Pflanzenschutz *m*
f protection *f* des plantes
p proteção *f* das plantas

4211 **plant rests**
(Agr.)
(Biological agriculture; used for soil treatment.)
d Pflanzenreste *mpl*
f débris *mpl* végétaux
p restos *mpl* de plantas; restos *mpl* vegetais

4212 **plant tissues; vegetable tissues**
(Prod.)
(Basis of flavour prime material.)

d Pflanzengewebe *npl*; pflanzliche Gewebe *npl*
f tissus *mpl* végétaux
p tecidos *mpl* vegetais

* **plant toxin → 5686**

* **plasmalemma → 4213**

4213 **plasma membrane; cell membrane; plasmalemma**
(Biochem.)
(Cell constituents, cell structure; cell membrane; e.g. in genetic engineering; nutritional science.)
d Zellmembran *f*
f membrane *f* plasmatique
p membrana *f* plasmática

4214 **plasma tocopherols in a weanling pig**
(Med.)
(Veterinary; ref. to treatment of young pigs with vitamin E.)
d Plasmatocopherole *npl* in einem entwöhnten Ferkel; Plasmatocopherole *npl* in einem abgesetzten Ferkel
f tocophérols *mpl* plasmatiques dans le porcelet sevré
p tocoferois *mpl* plasmáticos num leitão desmamado

4215 **platyhelminthes**
(Med.)
(Veterinary; flatworm; parasite.)
d Plattwürmer *mpl*
f plathelminthes *mpl*
p platelmintos *mpl*

4216 **plot; bed; patch**
(Agr.)
(Horticulture: small planted area, as e.g. a vegetable plot.)
d Beet *n*
f planche *f*
p canteiro *m*

* **ploughable land → 134**

* **plowable land → 134**

4217 **pluck**
(Prod.)
(Butchery; heart, lungs etc. of a slaughtered animal, prepared as food.)
d Innereien *fpl*
f fressure *f*
p miúdos *mpl*

4218 **plug** *v*; **obstruct** *v*
(Prod.)
(Production processes: machines, systems etc.)
d verstopfen; zustopfen; zupfropfen
f colmater; boucher
p entupir; obstruir

4219 **plum**
(Agr.)
(Horticulture. Genus "Prunus"; fruit; drupe.)
d Pflaume *f*; Zwetsche *f*
f prune *f*; quetsche *f*
p ameixa *f*

* **pneumatic separation → 150**

4220 **pneumococcus**
(Med.)
(Baby nutrition: there have been identified specific antibodies in human milk, e.g. against pneumococcus.)
d Pneumokokkus *m*
f pneumocoque *m*
p pneumococo *m*

4221 **poaching**
(Prod.)
(Food processing technology: Boiling in salty water with vinegar addition.)
d Pochieren *n*
f pochage *m*
p escaldadura *f*; escaldamento *m*

* **pod → 3162**

* **podsol → 4222**

4222 **podzol; podsol**
(Agr.)
(Soil; podzolic soil is a not very rich moist-climate soil, having a thin organic-mineral surface layer.)
d Podsol *m*; podsolierter Boden *m*
f podzol *m*; sol *m* podzolique
p solo *m* podsólico

4223 **poison gland of the bee**
(Agr.)
(Apiculture: Bee anatomy.)
d Giftdrüse *f* der Biene
f glande *f* à venin d'abeille
p glândula *f* de veneno da abelha

4224 **poisoning by heavy metals**
(Med.)
(Principally ref. to lead, mercury, cadmium, arsenic.)
d Schwermetallvergiftung *f*
f empoisonnement *m* par des métaux lourds
p envenenamento *m* por metais pesados; intoxicação *f* por metais pesados

4225 **polenta**
(Prod.)
(Gastronomy; made in various ways as to the country where it is served: paste of maize flour and parmesan-type cheese in Brazil and Italy, Corsica: chestnut meal; USA also: semolina.)
d Polenta *f*
f polenta *f*
p polenta *f*

4226 **polished rice**
(Prod.)
(Food processing technology: Treated rice.)
d polierter Reis *m*
f riz *m* poli; riz *m* glácé
p arroz *m* polido

4227 **polishing processes**
(Prod.)
(Food processing technology, e.g. rice treatment.)
d Polierprozesse *mpl*
f techniques *fpl* de polissage
p métodos *mpl* de polimento

4228 **pollen basket**
(Agr.)
(Apiculture: Bee anatomy: hind leg of a worker bee.)
d Pollenkörbchen *n*; Blütenstaubkörpchen *n*
f corbeille *f* à pollen
p cestinha *f* coletora de pólen

4229 **pollen brush; pollen comb**
(Agr.)
(Apiculture: Bee anatomy: hind leg of a worker bee.)
d Pollenbürste *f*; Blütenstaubbürste *f*
f brosse *f* à pollen
p pente *m* limpador do pólen

* **pollen comb → 4229**

4230 **pollination**
(Agr.)
(Botany; pollen transfer.)
d Pollenübertragung *f*, Blütenstaubübertragung *f*
f pollinisation *f*
p polinização *f*

4231 **polyalcohol**
(Prod.)
(Food processing technology: natural prime material for sweetening agents, e.g. sorbitol ($C_6H_{14}O_6$).)
d Polyalkohol *m*
f polyalcool *m*; polyol *m*
p poliálcool *m*

4232 **polyethylene foil bag**
(Prod.)
(Foodstuff packaging technology.)
d Polyäthylenfoliensack *m*; Polyethylenfoliensack *m*
f sac *m* en feuilles de polyéthylène
p saco *m* de folhas de polietileno

4233 **polymer**
(Biochem.)
(Nutritional science: polysaccharides.)
d Polymer *n*
f polymère *m*
p polímero *m*

4234 **polymerization**
(Biochem.)
(Nutritional science, food biochemistry; combination reaction of two or more molecules, forming a larger molecule.)
d Polymerisation *f*
f polymérisation *f*
p polimerização *f*

4235 **polyneuritis**
(Med.)
(Veterinary; e.g. poultry disease which can be due to vitamin B_1 (thiamin) deficiency.)
d Polyneuritis *f*
f polynévrite *f*
p polineurite *f*

4236 **polypeptide**
(Biochem.)
(Nutritional science; molecular amino acid chain.)
d Polypeptid *n*
f polypeptide *m*
p polipeptídio *m*

4237 **polypeptides resulting from protein digestion**
(Med.)
(Regimens, diets.)
d Polypeptide *npl*, die sich aus der Proteinverdauung ergeben; aus der Proteinverdauung sich ergebene Polypeptide *npl*
f polypeptides *mpl* résultant de la digestion des protéines
p polipeptídeos *mpl* resultantes da digestão protéica

4238 **polypeptidic synthesis**
(Biochem.)
(Nutritional science.)
d polypeptidische Synthese *f*
f synthèse *f* polypeptidique
p síntese *f* polipeptídica

4239 **polyphosphates**
(Prod.)
(Alkaline salts of the polyphosphoric acid. In food processing technology: Improving meat (ham) cut tenderness; in soft cheese. CEE No. E 450.)
d Polyphosphate *mpl*
f polyphosphates *mpl*
p polifosfatos *mpl*

4240 **polysaccharide**
(Biochem.)
(Nutritional science; carbohydrates of long (sugar) molecular chains.)
d Polysaccharid *n*
f polysaccharide *m*
p polissacarideo *m*

4241 **polysaccharide matrix**
(Biochem.)
(Food biochemistry; active substance-embedding material.)
d Polysaccharidmatrix *f*
f matrice *f* de polysaccharide
p matriz *f* de polissacarídeo

4242 **polyunsaturated** *adj*
(Biochem.)
(Nutritional science; constituted of many double or triple bonds in the molecule; e.g. ref. to fats.)
d mehrfach ungesättigt
f poly-insaturé
p poliinsaturado

4243 **polyunsaturated fatty acid**
(Biochem.)
(Food biochemistry; arachidonic acid ($C_{20}H_{32}O_2$).)
d mehrfach ungesättigte Fettsäure *f*
f acide *m* gras poly-insaturé
p ácido *m* graxo poliinsaturado

4244 **polyvitamin supplementation**
(Biochem.)
(Food biochemistry.)
d Polyvitaminzuschuss *m*; Polyvitaminergänzungszufuhr *f*; Polyvitaminsupplementierung *f*
f supplémentation *f* polyvitaminique
p suplementação *f* polivitamínica

4245 **pome**
(Agr.)
(Horticulture. Fruits with a core containing seeds: e.g. apple.)
d Kernobst *n*
f fruits *mpl* à pépins
p fruta *f* de caroço principal

4246 **pomegranate; pomegranate berry**
(Agr.)
(Horticulture. "Punica granatum"; fruit of the pomegranate tree.)
d Granatapfel *m*
f grenade *f*
p romã *f*

* **pomegranate berry → 4246**

4247 **pomegranate tree**
(Agr.)
(Horticulture. "Punica granatum"; tree and berry of the same name.)
d Granatapfelbaum *m*
f grenadier *m*
p romeira *f*; romãzeira *f*

4248 **ponceau colorant**
(Prod.)
(Food processing technology: Food colorant e.g. in preserved fruits (e.g. strawberries), for sweets and beverages, subject to Government regulations. No. CEE E 126.)
d Ponceau-Farbstoff *m*
f matière *f* colorante ponceau
p corante *m* ponceau

4249 **pony**
(Agr.)
(Livestock. Small horse.)
d Pony *n*
f poney *m*
p pônei *m*

4250 **poorly mineralized mineral waters**
(Prod.)
(Mineral waters having a low concentration of minerals.)
d wenig mineralisierte Mineralwässer *npl*
f eaux *fpl* minérales peu minéralisées
p águas *fpl* minerais de baixo teor de minerais

4251 **popcorn**
(Prod.)
(Food processing technology. "Zea mays praecox"; bursting maize grains when exposed to heat.)
d Puffmais *m*
f pop-corn *m*; grains *mpl* de maïs soufflés
p pipoca *f*

4252 **poppy-seed oil**
(Prod.)
(Poppy seeds are used also in bread etc: flavouring product; auxiliary.)
d Mohnsamenöl *n*; Mohnöl *n*
f huile *f* de la semence de l'œillette
p óleo *m* da semente da papoula

4253 pork
(Prod.)
(Butchery; meat of the pig.)
d Schweinefleisch *n*
f viande *f* de porc
p carne *f* de porco

4254 pork blood
(Prod.)
(Gastronomy: blood of the pork prepared with meat and acidulated with vinegar: North German dish called "das Schwarzsauer".)
d Schweineblut *n*
f sang *m* de porc
p sangue *m* de porco

* **pork products → 3436**

4255 pork rib
(Prod.)
(Gastronomy; meat joint; butcher's product.)
d Schweinerippchen *npl*
f côtes *fpl* de porc
p costeleta *f* de porco

4256 porosity of the soil
(Agr.)
(Soil condition: porosity through which air and water can pass.)
d Bodenporosität *f*; poröse Beschaffenheit *f* des Bodens
f porosité *f* du sol; constitution *f* poreuse du sol
p porosidade *f* do solo; consituição *f* porosa do solo

* **porous geological bed → 4257**

4257 porous geological layer; porous geological bed; porous stratum
(Prod.)
(One possible characteristic of the site of groundwater formation, drinking water source.)
d poröse geologische Schicht *f*
f couche *f* géologique poreuse
p camada *f* geológica porosa; estrato *m* poroso

4258 porous quality
(Prod.)
(Food processing technology: e.g. cooky and pastry quality.)
d poröse Beschaffenheit *f*
f qualité *f* poreuse
p qualidade *f* porosa

* **porous stratum → 4257**

4259 porridge
(Prod.)
(Farinaceous food brought to the boil; generally oat meal.)
d Brei *m*; Haferbrei *m*
f bouillie *f*; bouillie *f* d'avoine
p mingau *m* de aveia

4260 port
(Prod.)
(Sweet wine made in Portugal.)
d Portwein *m*
f vin *m* de Porto; porto *m*
p vinho *m* do Porto

4261 posterior contamination; subsequent contamination
(Biochem.)
(Food biochemistry.)
d Nachverseuchung *f*; Nachkontamination *f*
f contamination *f* postérieure
p contaminação *f* posterior

* **potable → 163**

4262 potable water; drinkable water; drinking water
(Prod.)
(Water supply: As to its origin it contains underground water, sea water, river water, spring water; containing dissolved salts (and fluorine addition).)
d Trinkwasser *n*
f eau *f* potable
p água *f* potável

* **potash → 4267**

4263 potassium acetate
(Prod.)
($C_2H_3KO_2$; conservation agent. Additive.)
d Kaliumacetat *n*
f acétate *m* de potassium
p acetato *m* de potássio

4264 potassium alginate
(Prod.)
(Food processing technology: e.g. texture improving ingredient.)
d Kaliumalginat *n*
f alginate *m* de potassium
p alginato *m* de potássio

4265 potassium benzoate
(Prod.)
($C_7H_5KO_2$; food preservative. Additive.)
d Kaliumbenzoat *n*
f benzoate *m* de potassium
p benzoato *m* de potássio

4266 potassium bitartrate; potassium hydrogen tartrate
(Prod.)
($C_4H_5KO_6$; cremor tartari; e.g. baking powder ingredient.)

d Kaliumhydrogentartrat *n*; Weinstein *m*
f tartrate *m* double de potassium; hydrogénocarbonate *m* de potassium
p bitartrato *m* de potássio; cremor *m* de tártaro

4267 potassium carbonate; potash
(Prod.)
(K_2CO_3; auxiliary substance.)
d Kaliumcarbonat *n*; Pottasche *f*
f carbonate *m* de potassium; potasse *f*
p carbonato *m* de potássio; potassa *f*

4268 potassium chloride
(Prod.)
(KCl; element eventually contained in traces in mineral water.)
d Kaliumchlorid *n*
f chlorure *m* de potassium
p cloreto *m* de potássio

4269 potassium citrate
(Prod.)
($K_3C_6H_5O_7$; potassium salt of citric acid: foodstuff additive.)
d Kaliumcitrat *n*
f citrate *m* de potassium
p citrato *m* de potássio

4270 potassium deficiency
(Med.)
(Regimens, diets: Potassium (K) is one of the minerals and electrolytes in the body; promotes exchanges of nutrients between body fluid and cell membranes; maintains fluid balance.)
d Kaliummangel *m*
f manque *m* de potassium
p deficiência *f* de potássio

4271 potassium ferrocyanide
(Biochem.)
($K_4Fe(CN)_6.3H_2O$. Used e.g. in enology.)
d Kaliumeisenzyanür *n*
f ferrocyanure *m* de potassium; prussiate *m* jaune
p ferro *m* cianeto de potássio; prussiato *m* amarelo

4272 potassium fertilizer
(Agr.)
(Soil treatment. Potassium (K) is absorbed by the plants and deposited within the cells. Soil rich in potassium yields higher quality of fruits and shows an increase in soil conservation.)
d Kalidünger *m*
f engrais *m* potassique
p fertilizante *m* de potássio

* **potassium hydrogen tartrate → 4266**

4273 potassium metabisulphite
(Prod.)
($K_2S_2O_5$; e.g. brewery and wine production: antifermentative and antioxidant auxiliary; food preservative.)
d Kaliummetabisulfit *n*
f métabisulfite *m* de potassium
p metabissulfito *m* de potássio

4274 potassium nitrate
(Prod.)
(KNO_3; saltpeter. No. CEE: E 252. Used as preservation agent in some foodstuffs, e.g. meat. Subject to Government regulations.)
d Kaliumnitrat *n*
f nitrate *m* de potassium
p nitrato *m* de potássio

4275 potassium phosphate
(Prod.)
(Additive in the production of e.g. meat products. E Number: E 340.)
d Kaliumphosphat *n*
f phosphate *m* de potassium
p fosfato *m* de potássio

4276 potassium sorbate
(Prod.)
($C_6H_7KO_2$; sorbic acid potassium salt; No. CEE: E 202. Food preservative, e.g. in yoghurts; yeast/mould inhibitor.)
d Kaliumsorbat *n*
f sorbate *m* de potassium
p sorbato *m* de potássio

4277 potassium sulphate
(Agr.)
(K_2SO_4; soil; e.g. plant fertilizer.)
d Kalksulfat *n*
f sulfate *m* de potassium
p sulfato *m* de potássio

4278 potassium sulphite
(Prod.)
(K_2SO_3. Auxiliary in food processing technology.)
d Kaliumsulfit *n*
f sulfite *m* de potassium
p sulfito *m* de potássio

4279 potassium tartrate
(Prod.)
($C_4H_4O_6K_2$; additive in confectionary, as to No. CEE: E 336.)
d Kaliumtartrat *n*
f tartrate *m* de potassium
p tartarato *m* de potássio

4280 **potato**
(Agr.)
(Agricultural produce; "Solanum tuberosum"; tuberous plant.)
d Kartoffel *f*
f pomme *f* de terre
p batata *f*

4281 **potato flakes for mash preparation; potato flakes for puree preparation**
(Prod.)
(Food processing technology.)
d Kartoffellflocken *fpl* für die Zubereitung von Brei
f flocons *mpl* de pommes de terre pour la préparation de purée
p flocos *mpl* de batata para a preparação de purê

* **potato flakes for puree preparation → 4281**

4282 **potato flour**
(Agr.)
(Agricultural produce, subproduct; starch flour production derivative: high water content with starch flour in suspension.)
d Kartoffelmehl *n*
f fécule *f* verte
p farinha *f* de batata

4283 **potato flour fermentation**
(Biochem.)
(Food biochemistry; process part of lactic acid production.)
d Kartoffelmehlvergärung *f*
f fermentation *f* de la fécule verte
p fermentação *f* da farinha de batata

4284 **potato starch**
(Agr.)
(Agricultural produce, subproduct. Starch compound extracted from potatoes which contain between 12-20%.)
d Kartoffelstärke *f*
f fécule *f* de pomme de terre
p fécula *f* de batata; amido *m* de batata

4285 **potato sugar**
(Prod.)
($C_6H_{12}O_6$. D-glucose.)
d Kartoffelzucker *m*
f sucre *m* de fécule de pommes de terre
p açúcar *m* de batata

4286 **potato tuber**
(Agr.)
(Botany; tuber: fleshy rhizome or root type, containing reserve food for the plant.)
d Kartoffelknolle *f*
f tubercule *m* de la pomme de terre
p tubérculo *m* da batata

4287 **potentiality of solar energy**
(Agr.)
(Botany; agriculture and soils.)
d Potentialität *f* der Sonnenenergie
f potentialité *f* de l'énergie solaire
p potencialidade *f* da energia solar

4288 **potentiality of the agricultural area; potentiality of the arable land**
(Agr.)
(Soil; ref. to the possibility of the soil, yielding good crops.)
d Ackerbodenpotentialität *f*
f potentialité *f* des terroirs
p potencialidade *f* da terra de planta

* **potentiality of the arable land → 4288**

4289 **potentiation of the natural defense mechanism; increase of the natural defense mechanism**
(Med.)
(Veterinary; ref. to immune system, immune response.)
d Anhebung *f* des natürlichen Abwehrsystems; Verstärkung *f* des natürlichen Abwehrsystems
f renforcement *m* des défenses naturelles
p aumento *m* do sistema de defesa natural

4290 **potherb**
(Prod.)
(Ingredient in gastronomy.)
d Suppenkraut *n*; Suppengrün *n*
f herbes *fpl* potagères
p ervas *fpl* para tempero de sopa

4291 **poulard; poularde**
(Agr.)
(Poultry farming. Fattened hen, fattening pullet; broiler: young chicken ready for broiling.)
d Masthuhn *n*
f poularde *f*
p galinha *f* de engorda

* **poularde → 4291**

4292 **poultry; fowl; birds**
(Agr.)
(Poultry farming.)
d Geflügel *n*
f volaille *f*
p aves *fpl* domésticas

4293 **poultry farming; poultry raising**
(Agr.)
(Livestock.)
d Geflügelzucht *f*
f aviculture *f*
p avicultura *f*

4294 poultry feed-ration handling
(Agr.)
(Poultry farming, poultry nutrition.)
d Handhabung *f* der Geflügelfuttermittelration
f manipulation *f* de la ration fourragère avicole
p manejo *m* da ração para aves

4295 poultry for slaughtering
(Agr.)
(Poultry farming.)
d Schlachthühner *npl*
f poulets *mpl* d'abattage
p frangos *mpl* de corte

4296 poultry handling
(Agr.)
(Poultry farming and treatment.)
d Handhabung *f* des Geflügels; Umgang *m* mit dem Geflügel
f manipulation *f* de la volaille
p manejo *m* das aves

4297 poultry litter feed
(Agr.)
(Poultry farming: feed type.)
d Geflügelstrohfuttermittel *n*
f ration *f* avicole à paille
p ração *f* de palha das aves

4298 poultry manure; fowl dung
(Agr.)
(Soil. Phosphoric acid and calcium-rich organic fertilizing material.)
d Geflügelmist *m*
f fumier *m* de volaille
p esterco *m* de aves

4299 poultry manure utilization
(Agr.)
(Soil. This manure type contains e.g. 0.5% of nitrogen (N); 0.25% phosphoric anhydride; 0.5% potassium (K).)
d Hühnerdungausnutzung *f*
f utilisation *f* du fumier de volaille
p aproveitamento *m* de esterco

4300 poultry meat consumption in several countries
(Agr.)
(Poultry farming and industrialization and food marketing.)
d Geflügelfleischkonsum *m* in verschiedenen Ländern
f consommation *f* de viande de volaille sur les diverses nations
p consumo *m* de carne de aves em diversos países

4301 poultry nutrition
(Agr.)
(Poultry farming.)
d Geflügelernährung *f*
f nutrition *f* de la volaille
p nutrição *f* das aves; alimentação *f* das aves

4302 poultry processing
(Agr.)
(Poultry farming and food industrialization.)
d Geflügelverarbeitung *f*
f transformation *f* industrielle de la volaille
p processamento *m* de aves

* **poultry raising → 4293**

4303 poultry slaughtering
(Agr.)
(Poultry farming.)
d Geflügelschlachtung *f*
f abattage *m* de volailles
p abate *m* de aves domésticas

4304 poultry waste recycling in feed
(Agr.)
(Poultry farming; process type of ration preparation.)
d Geflügelabfallprodukte *npl* zur Wiederverarbeitung in Futtermitteln
f sous-produit *m* avicole pour recyclage fourrager
p material *m* residual da avicultura para reciclagem em rações

4305 powder behaviour
(Prod.)
(Food processing technology.)
d Verhalten *n* des Puders
f comportement *m* des poudres
p comportamento *m* dos pós

4306 powder behaviour testing
(Prod.)
(Food processing technology.)
d Untersuchung *f* des Verhaltens des Puders
f recherche *f* sur le comportement des poudres
p pesquisa *f* do comportamento dos pós

4307 powder contents
(Prod.)
(Food processing technology; ref. e.g. to substance composition.)
d Pulveranteil *m*
f part *f* en poudre
p teor *m* em pó

* **powder milk → 3555**

4308 powder with a characteristic odour
(Prod.)
(Food processing technology; product characteristic.)

d Pulver *n* mit einem charakteristischen Geruch
f poudre *f* à odeur spécifique
p pó *m* de um odor específico

4309 **powder with a week odour**
(Prod.)
(Food processing technology.)
d Pulver *n* mit einem schwachen Geruch
f poudre *f* à odeur faible
p pó *m* de um odor fraco

4310 **powdery aroma base**
(Prod.)
(Aroma/fragrance research and production.)
d pulverige Aromabasis *f*; pulvrige Aromabasis *f*
f base *f* pulvérulente de l'arôme
p base *f* de aroma em forma de pó; base *f* pulvérea do aroma

4311 **practically insoluble** *adj*
(Biochem.)
(Food biochemistry; product characteristic.)
d praktisch unlösbar; praktisch unlöslich
f pratiquement insoluble
p praticamente insolúvel

* **prawn → 4963**

4312 **prebetalipoprotein**
(Med.)
(VLDL, very low density lipoproteins.)
d Präbetalipoprotein *n*
f prébêtalipoprotéine *f*
p prebetalipoproteína *f*

4313 **precipitate**
(Biochem.)
(Nutritional science: solid separated substance out of a solution/suspension.)
d Präzipitat *n*
f précipité *m*
p precipitado *m*

4314 **precipitated protein**
(Biochem.)
(Nutritional science.)
d präzipitiertes Protein *n*; ausgefälltes Protein *n*
f protéine *f* précipitée
p proteína *f* precipitada

4315 **precipitation of instable salts**
(Biochem.)
(Food biochemistry.)
d Niederschlag *m* unstabiler Salze
f précipitation *f* des sels instables
p precipitação *f* dos sais instáveis

4316 **precipitation process**
(Prod.)
(Aroma/flavour production: separation procedure.)
d Ausfällungsprozess *m*; Fällungsprozess *m*
f processus *m* de précipitation
p processo *m* de precipitação

4317 **precipitation reaction**
(Prod.)
(Food processing technology.)
d Fällungsreaktion *f*
f réaction *f* de précipitation
p reação *f* de precipitação

4318 **preclarification**
(Biochem.)
(Food biochemistry; enology, brewery processes, also fruit juice production.)
d Vorklärung *f*
f préclarification *f*
p pré-clarificação *f*

4319 **precocious fruits**
(Agr.)
(Horticulture.)
d frühreife Früchte *fpl*
f fruits *mpl* précoces
p frutos *mpl* temporões

* **precocious maturation → 4320**

4320 **precociousness of maturation; precocious maturation**
(Agr.)
(Botany.)
d vorzeitige Reifung *f*; vorzeitige Ausreifung *f*
f précocité *f* de la maturation
p precocidade *f* da maturação

4321 **precocious vine sort**
(Agr.)
(Viticulture.)
d frühreife Rebsorte *f*
f cépage *m* précoce
p espécie *f* precoce de cepa; espécie *f* temporã de cepa

4322 **precooked**
(Prod.)
(Food processing technology; ref. e.g. to pasta plant process.)
d vorgekocht
f précuit
p pré-cozido

4323 **precooked flour types**
(Med.)
(Baby nutrition.)
d vorgekochte Mehlsorten *fpl*
f farines *fpl* précuites
p farinhas *fpl* précozidas

4324 **precooked vegetables**
(Prod.)
(Food processing technology.)
d vorgekochtes Gemüse *n*
f légumes *mpl* précuits
p legumes *mpl* pré-cozidos

4325 **precursor**
(Biochem.)
(Nutritional science; e.g. beta-carotene is a precursor of vitamin.)
d Vorstufe *f*
f précurseur *m*
p precursor *m*

4326 **pre-cutting process**
(Prod.)
(Food processing technology; ref. to meat industrialization process; sausage production.)
d Vorschneideverfahren *n*; Vorzerkleinerung *f*
f précoupage *m*
p processo *m* de pré-corte

4327 **predominance of a strain**
(Biochem.)
(Yeast: in fermentation in nutritional science.)
d Vorherrschen *n* eines Stranges; Überwiegen *n* eines Stranges
f prédominance *f* d'une souche
p predominância *f* de uma cepa; predominância *f* de uma raça

4328 **pre-dried pasta product**
(Prod.)
(Food processing technology; pasta plant product.)
d vorgetrocknetes Teigprodukt *n*
f pâte *f* alimentaire préséchée
p produto *m* de pasta pré-secado

4329 **predrying**
(Prod.)
(Food processing technology and processes.)
d Vortrocknung *f*
f préséchage *f*; séchage *f* préalable
p pré-secagem

4330 **preemergence herbicide**
(Agr.)
(Application after sowing, before emerging of the plant.)
d Vorauflaufmittel *n* zur Unkrautbekämpfung
f herbicide *m* préémergence
p herbicida *f* pré-emergência

4331 **prefermentative maceration**
(Prod.)
(Food processing technology; ref. to certain maceration and fermentation processes.)
d Vorgärungsmazeration *f*
f macération *f* préfermentaire
p maceração *f* pré-fermentante

4332 **pregnancy diet**
(Med.)
(Alimentary regimen.)
d Schwangerschaftsdiät *f*
f diète *f* de grossesse
p dieta *f* de gravidez

4333 **premature; premature baby**
(Med.)
(Premature birth: e.g. a baby weighing less than 2500 g at birth.)
d frühgeborenes Kind *n*; vorzeitig geborenes Kind *n*
f prématuré *m*; prématurée *f*
p prematuro *m*

4334 **premature aging of the wine**
(Biochem.)
(Enology; e.g. depending on environmental storage temperatures.)
d verfrühte Alterung *f* des Weines; vorzeitige Alterung *f* des Weines
f vieillissement *m* prématuré du vin
p envelhecimento *m* prematuro do vinho

* **premature baby → 4333**

4335 **premature interruption of fermentation**
(Biochem.)
(Fermentation in nutritional science.)
d vorzeitige Stockung *f* der Gärung; vorzeitiger Gärungsabbruch *m*
f arrêt *m* prématuré de la fermentation
p paralização *f* prematura da fermentação

4336 **premature start of fermentation**
(Biochem.)
(Fermentation in nutritional science.)
d vorzeitiger Gärungsbeginn *m*
f départ *m* prématuré de la fermentation
p começo *m* prematuro da fermentação

4337 **premolar tooth**
(Med.)
(Anatomy; bicuspid; body part.)
d vorderer Backenzahn *m*
f prémolaire *f*
p dente *m* pré-molar

4338 **pre-packed meat joints**
(Prod.)
(Butchery. Ref. to industrialized packaging type of meat products.)
d abgepacktes Fleisch *n*
f viande *f* préemballée
p corte *m* de carne pré-embalado

4339 preparation
(Prod.)
(Food processing technology; e.g. alimentary preparations: flavour ingredients.)
d Zubereitung *f*
f préparation *f*
p preparação *f*

4340 preparation of fruit juices
(Prod.)
(Food processing technology; flavour research and production.)
d Fruchtsaftzubereitung *f*
f préparation *f* des jus de fruits
p preparação *f* de sucos de frutas

4341 preparation of new derivates
(Biochem.)
(Nutritional science.)
d Präparierung *f* neuer Derivate; Zubereitung *f* neuer Derivate
f préparation *f* de nouveaux dérivés
p preparação *f* de novos derivados

4342 prepared food
(Prod.)
(Gastronomy. Food ready for consumption.)
d Fertiggericht *n*
f mets *m* tout préparé
p prato *m* feito

4343 prepared products
(Prod.)
(Food processing technology.)
d zubereitete Produkte *npl*
f produits *mpl* préparés
p produtos *mpl* preparados

* **presence of lactose in the urine → 3119**

4344 presence of pesticidal residues
(Agr.)
(Agriculture.)
d Gegenwart *f* von Rückständen der Schädlingsbekämpfungsmittel; Gegenwart *f* der Schädlingsbekämpfungsmittelrückstände
f présence *f* de résidus de pesticides
p presença *f* de resíduos de pesticidas

4345 presence of vitamins in feed
(Med.)
(Veterinary; ref. to chemical assay (analysis) of the feed (see entry).)
d Gegenwart *f* von Vitaminen in Futtermitteln
f présence *f* de vitamines dans les fourrages
p presença *f* de vitaminas nas forragens

4346 preservation of organoleptic quality
(Prod.)
(Food processing technology: Quality of the final consumer product, pleasant to the sense, as e.g. to taste.)
d Erhaltung *f* der organoleptischen Qualität
f conservation *f* de la qualité organoleptique
p conservação *f* da qualidade organolé(p)tica

4347 preservation technique
(Prod.)
(Food processing technology.)
d Konservierungsverfahren *n*; Konservierungstechnik *f*
f technique *f* de conservation
p técnica *f* de conservação

4348 preservative
(Prod.)
(Food processing technology: e.g. sorbic acid; sodium sorbate, benzoic acid etc.)
d Konservierungsmittel *n*
f agent *m* de conservation
p conservante *m*

4349 preserve *v* by boiling down
(Prod.)
((Domestic) food processing technology: Preservation of fruits, vegetables by boiling and air sealing.)
d einkochen
f confire par cuisson
p fazer conservas

4350 preserve *v* by cooking
(Prod.)
((Domestic) food processing technology; e.g. for fruits and vegetables.)
d einmachen
f conserver par cuisson
p conservar por cozimento

4351 preserved food
(Prod.)
(Food processing technology. Perishable food conservation by thermal treatment (sterilization:100-130°C) or sterile packaging and addition of preservatives.)
d Vollkonserve *f*; Lebensmittelvollkonserve *f*
f conserve *f*
p conserva *f*

4352 press *v*
(Agr.)
(Viticulture; treatment of grapes for wine production.)
d keltern
f fouler
p espremer; esmagar

4353 pressed bunch of grapes
(Agr.)
(Viticulture; wine production.)

d gekelterte Weintraube *f*
f raisin *m* foulé
p cacho *m* de uva esmagado; cacho *m* de uva espremido

4354 **pressed out vintage**
(Agr.)
(Viticulture: technology of wine production.)
d gekelterte Weinlese *f*
f vendange *f* foulée
p vindima *f* expremida; vindima *f* esmagada

4355 **pressing of grapes; squeezing out of grapes; pressing of the bunch of grapes; squeezing out of the bunch of grapes**
(Agr.)
(Viticulture; technology of wine production.)
d Keltern *n* der Beeren; Keltern *n* der Traube
f foulage *m* des grains de raisin; foulage *m* de la grappe de raisin
p esmagamento *m* das uvas; espremedura *f* do cacho de uvas

* **pressing of the bunch of grapes → 4355**

4356 **pressure extraction**
(Prod.)
(Aroma/flavour production: extraction by pressure.)
d Druckextraktion *f*
f extraction *f* par pression
p extração *f* por pressão

4357 **pressure method; expression**
(Prod.)
(Aroma/flavour production: separation processes.)
d Auspressungsmethode *f*; Auspressen *n*; Auspressung *f*
f méthode *f* par expression; expression *f*
p método *m* por pressão; expressão

4358 **presugared products**
(Prod.)
(Food processing technology and production, e.g. yoghurts.)
d vorgezuckerte Produkte *npl*
f produits *mpl* présucrés
p produtos *mpl* pré-açucarados

4359 **presumed long-term toxicity; supposed toxicity over a long period**
(Med.)
(Food processing technology: toxicological long term studies.)
d für langzeitig möglich gehaltene Toxizität *f*; mutmaßliche Giftigkeit *f* über längeren Zeitraum
f toxicité *f* supposée à long terme
p toxicidade *f* presumida sobre períodos prolongados; toxicidade *f* suspeitada a longo termo

4360 **pretreatment**
(Prod.)
(Food processing technology.)
d Vorbehandlung *f*
f prétraitement *m*
p pré-tratamento *m*

4361 **pretzel**
(Prod.)
(Bakery product.)
d Bretzel *f*
f bretzel *m*
p rosca *f*

4362 **prevent *v* flocculation**
(Biochem.)
(Enology.)
d das Ausflocken verhindern
f empêcher la floculation
p impedir a floculação; evitar a floculação

4363 **prevention**
(Agr.)
(Agriculture; advanced measures e.g. in crop protection.)
d Vorbeugung *f*
f prévention *f*
p prevenção *f*

4364 **prevention against infectious diseases by nutrition**
(Med.)
(Nutrition in medicine.)
d Vorbeugung *f* gegen Infektionskrankheiten durch Ernährung
f prévention *f* des maladies infectieuses par la nutrition
p prevenção *f* das doenças infecciosas pela nutrição

4365 **prevention of aging through nutrition**
(Biochem.)
(Nutritional science in medicine.)
d Alterungsvorbeugung *f* durch Ernährung
f prévention *f* du vieillissement par l'alimentation
p prevenção *f* do envelhecimento pela alimentação

4366 **prevention of enteropathic acrodermatitis**
(Med.)
(Baby nutrition: Zn present in human milk: important e.g. for the prevention of enteropathic acrodermatitis.)
d Vorbeugung *f* der chronischen Kleinkinddermatose

f prévention *f* de l'acrodermatite entéropathique
p prevenção *f* da acrodermatite enteropática

4367 prevention of fermentation interruption
(Biochem.)
(Fermentation in nutritional science.)
d Vorbeugungsmaßnahmen *fpl* gegen Gärungsstockungen; Vorbeugungsmaßnahmen *fpl* gegen Gärungsabbrüchen
f préventions *fpl* des arrêts de la fermentation; mesures *fpl* préventives contre des arrêts de la fermentation
p medidas *fpl* preventivas contra a interrupção de fermentação; medidas *fpl* de prevenção contra a interrupção de fermentação

4368 prevention of illnesses due to surcharge
(Med.)
(Baby nutrition: ref. to nutritional equilibrium.)
d Vorbeugung *f* der Überbelastungskrankheiten; Vorbeugung *f* der auf Überbelastung beruhenden Krankheiten
f prévention *f* des maladies de surcharge
p prevenção *f* das doenças por sobrecarga

* **preventive alimentation → 4369**

4369 preventive nutrition; preventive alimentation
(Biochem.)
(Nutritional science in medicine.)
d vorbeugende Ernährung *f*; Präventivernährung *f*
f nutrition *f* préventive; alimentation *f* préventive
p nutrição *f* preventiva; alimentação *f* preventiva

4370 preventive treatment
(Agr.)
(Biological agriculture; e.g. ref. to plant protection.)
d Präventivbehandlung *f*
f traitement *m* préventif
p tratamento *m* preventivo

4371 primary obesity
(Med.)
(Baby nutrition.)
d primäre Fettleibigkeit *f*; Primärfettsucht *f*
f obésité *f* primaire
p obesidade *f* primária

4372 primary structure of the protein
(Biochem.)
(Nutritional science; certain sequence of polypeptide chains of amino acids.)
d Primärstruktur *f* des Proteins
f structure *f* primaire de la protéine
p estrutura *f* primária da proteína

4373 procedures of vinification
(Agr.)
(Viticulture; wine production.)
d Weinbereitungsverfahren *npl*; Verfahren *npl* der Weinbereitung
f procédés *mpl* de vinification
p processos *mpl* de vinificação

* **process** *v* **→ 5558**

4374 processed cheese
(Prod.)
(Dairy product.)
d Käsezubereitung *f*
f préparation *f* à base de fromage
p preparado *m* à base de queijo

4375 processed foodstuffs
(Prod.)
(Food processing technology.)
d weiterverarbeitete Nahrungsmittel *npl*
f produits *mpl* alimentaires transformés
p produtos *mpl* alimentícios de transformação

4376 processed milk
(Prod.)
(Dairy product.)
d aufbereitete Milch *f*
f lait *m* traité
p leite *m* beneficiado

* **processed water → 5559**

4377 processes of food fermentation
(Biochem.)
(Nutritional science.)
d Nahrungsmittelgärungprozesse *mpl*; Nahrungsmittelfermentationsprozesse *mpl*
f fermentations *fpl* alimentaires
p fermentações *fpl* alimentares

4378 processing
(Prod.)
(Food processing technology.)
d Verarbeitung *f*; Weiterverarbeitung *f*
f transformation *f*
p transformação *f*; processamento *m*

4379 processing industry
(Prod.)
(Food processing technology; foodstuff production.)
d weiterverarbeitende Industrie *f*
f industrie *f* de transformation
p indústria *f* de transformação

4380 **processing of agricultural products**
(Agr.)
(Agricultural produce (food) processing technology.)
d Verarbeitung *f* von Agrarprodukten; Weiterverarbeitung *f* landwirtschaftlicher Produkte
f transformation *f* des produits agricoles
p transformação *f* dos produtos agrícolas

* **processing of essential oils → 5561**

4381 **processing of vitamins in feeds**
(Agr.)
(Livestock nutrition elaboration.)
d Verarbeitung *f* von Vitaminen in Futtermitteln
f manipulation *f* des vitamines dans des fourrages
p manipulação *f* de vitaminas em rações

4382 **process of mechanical pressure**
(Prod.)
(Food processing technology: separation process.)
d mechanisches Druckverfahren *n*
f procédé *m* de pressage mécanique
p processo *m* de pressão mecânica

* **producing toxin** *adj* **→ 5536**

4383 **product conservation**
(Prod.)
(Food processing technology of food preservation.)
d Produktkonservierung *f*; Konservierung *f* des Produktes
f conservation *f* du produit
p conservação *f* do produto

4384 **product homogeneity**
(Prod.)
(Food processing technology and flavour research and production: product characteristic.)
d Produkthomogenität *f*
f homogénéité *f* du produit
p homogeneidade *f* do produto

4385 **production of aperitifs**
(Prod.)
(Beverages.)
d Aperitifherstellung *f*
f fabrication *f* d'apéritifs
p produção *f* de aperitivos

4386 **production of beverages**
(Prod.)
(Beverages.)
d Getränkeherstellung *f*
f fabrication *f* de boissons
p produção *f* de bebidas

4387 **production of fresh grapes**
(Agr.)
(Viticulture; e.g. grapes for wine production.)
d Produktion *f* frischer Trauben
f production *f* de raisins frais; production *f* de grappes de raisin fraîches
p produção *f* de cachos frescos de uva

* **production of liquor → 4390**

4388 **production of low intensity**
(Agr.)
(Biological agriculture.)
d Produktion *f* geringer Intensität
f production *f* peu intensive
p produção *f* pouco intensiva

4389 **production of semolina**
(Prod.)
(Food processing technology.)
d Grießproduktion *f*
f fabrication *f* de la semoule
p produção *f* de sêmola

4390 **production of spirits; production of liquor**
(Prod.)
(Beverages.)
d Spirituosenherstellung *f*
f fabrication *f* de spiritueux
p produção *f* de bebidas alcoólicas

4391 **production technique**
(Prod.)
(Food processing technology.)
d Herstellungstechnik *f*; Produktionsverfahren *n*
f technique *f* de production
p técnica *f* de produção; processo *m* de produção

4392 **product qualification**
(Agr.)
(As to the rules of biologic agriculture.)
d Qualifikation *f* des Produktes
f qualification *f* du produit
p qualificação *f* do produto

4393 **product quality improvement**
(Prod.)
(Food processing technology.)
d Qualitätsverbesserung *f* der Produkte
f amélioration *f* de la qualité des produits
p melhoramento *m* da qualidade dos produtos; aperfeiçoamento *m* da qualidade dos produtos

4394 **product quality of biologic agriculture**
(Agr.)
(Biologic agriculture and its production.)
d Qualität *f* der Produkte der biologischen Landwirtschaft; Produktenqualität *f* der biologischen Agrikultur

f qualité *f* des produits de l'agriculture biologique
p qualidade *f* dos produtos da agricultura biológica

4395 product range
(Prod.)
(Food processing technology.)
d Sortimentspalette *f*; Produktensortiment *n*
f tableau *m* de l'assortiment; assortiment *m* de produits
p paleta *f* de sortimento; sortimento *m* dos produtos

4396 products conform to specifications
(Prod.)
(Food processing technology.)
d Produkte *npl* gemäß den Spezifikationen
f produits *mpl* conformes aux spécifications
p produtos *mpl* conforme as especificações

4397 products excreted into mother's milk
(Med.)
(Ref. e.g. to toxic products of pharmaceutical origin.)
d in die Muttermilch ausgeschiedene Produkte *npl*
f produits *mpl* excrétés dans le lait maternel
p produtos *mpl* excretados no leite maternal

4398 products of biotechnological origin
(Biochem.)
(Nutritional science; ref. to genetic engineering.)
d Produkte *npl* biotechnologischer Herkunft
f produits *mpl* d'origine biotechnologique
p produtos *mpl* de origem biotecnológica

4399 products unsuitable for nutrition
(Prod.)
(Baby nutrition.)
d Produkte *npl* untauglich für die Ernährung; ernährungsuntaugliche Produkte *npl*
f produits *mpl* inaptes à l'alimentation
p produtos *mpl* inadequados para a alimentação

4400 products without fat contents
(Prod.)
(Food processing technology.)
d fettlose Produkte *npl*
f produits *mpl* ne contenant pas de graisse
p produtos *mpl* isentos de gorduras

4401 product valorization
(Prod.)
(Value valorizing of a product, e.g. ref. to agricultural foodstuff production and marketing.)
d Produktwertsteigerung *f*
f valorisation *f* du produit
p valorização *f* do produto

4402 profound erosion; depth erosion
(Agr.)
(Soil; causing profound furrows, fall in of ravines; erosion valleys.)
d Tiefenerosion *f*
f érosion *f* profonde
p erosão *f* profunda

* **profound geological bed → 4403**

4403 profound geological layer; profound geological bed; profound stratum
(Prod.)
(One possible characteristic of the site of groundwater formation, drinking water source.)
d tiefe geologische Schicht *f*; tiefliegende geologische Schicht *f*
f couche *f* géologique profonde
p camada *f* geológica profunda; estrato *m* profundo

* **profound stratum → 4403**

4404 progressive decomposition
(Biochem.)
(Nutritional science; e.g. ref. to vitamin modification in the presence of humidity etc.)
d progressive Dekomposition *f*; allmählicher Zerfall *m*
f décomposition *f* progressive
p decomposição *f* progressiva

* **progressive degradation of the soil → 4405**

4405 progressive wear of the soil; progressive degradation of the soil
(Agr.)
(Soil; soil treatment.)
d progressive Bodenabnutzung *f*
f usure *f* progressive du sol
p desgaste *m* progressivo do solo; degradação *f* progressiva do solo

* **prolamines → 4406**

4406 prolamins; prolamines
(Biochem.)
(Nutritional science; plant proteins present in the seed of cereals.)
d Prolamine *npl*
f prolamines *fpl*
p prolaminas *fpl*

4407 proliferation of parasites
(Agr.)
(Biological agriculture.)
d Wucherung *f* von Schädlingen

f prolifération *f* de ravageurs
p proliferação *f* de parasitas

4408 **proline**
(Biochem.)
(Nutritional science; $C_5H_9NO_2$; 2-pyrrolidine-carboxylic acid. Non-essential heterocyclic amino acid; ingredient in human and in cow's milk.)
d Prolin *n*
f proline *f*
p prolina *f*

4409 **pro-oxidative effect**
(Biochem.)
(Phenomena in food biochemistry.)
d prooxidative Wirkung *f*
f effet *m* pro-oxydatif
p efeito *m* pro-oxidante

4410 **propagation**
(Agr.)
(Botany (flora/fauna); ref. to the reproduction and multiplication processes of plants and animals; also the increase in numbers.)
d Fortpflanzung *f*
f propagation *f*
p propagação *f*

4411 **propagation of biochemical reactions**
(Biochem.)
(Food biochemistry.)
d Vermehrung *f* biochemischer Reaktionen
f propagation *f* des réactions biochimiques
p propagação *f* das reações bioquímicas

* **1,2-propanediol → 4418**

* **propane-1,2,3-triol → 2526**

* **1-propanol → 4417**

* **2-propanone → 31**

* **2-propenal → 63**

4412 **properties of dissolution**
(Prod.)
(Aroma/flavour research and production, ref. to solvent characteristics, solvent qualities.)
d Auflösungseigenschaften *fpl*
f propriétés *fpl* dissolvantes
p propriedades *fpl* de dissolução

4413 **prophylactic measures**
(Agr.)
(Livestock breeding, esp. poultry farming: cleaning procedures, disinfection; hygienic controls etc.)
d vorbeugende Maßnahmen *fpl*
f mesures *fpl* prophylactiques
p medidas *fpl* profiláticas

4414 **prophylactic use in case of hypovitaminosis**
(Med.)
(Use of vitamins and vitaminized food.)
d prophylaktischer Einsatz *m* im Falle von Hypovitaminose
f emploi *m* prophylactique en cas d'hypovitaminose
p emprego *m* profilático em caso de hipovitaminose

4415 **prophylaxis**
(Med.)
(Veterinary; disease prevention in livestock raising.)
d Prophylaxe *f*
f prophylaxie *f*
p profilaxia *f*

4416 **propionic acid**
(Prod.)
($C_3H_6O_2$; fatty acid e.g. found in milk; used in foodstuff preservation as an ingredient.)
d Propionsäure *f*
f acide *m* propionique
p ácido *m* propiônico

4417 **propyl alcohol; 1-propanol; propylic alcohol**
(Prod.)
(C_3H_8O; prime material for aroma/fragrance production.)
d Propylalkohol *m*; 1-Propanol *n*
f alcool *m* propylique; 1-propanol *m*
p álcool *m* propílico; 1-propanol *m*

4418 **propylene glycol; 1,2-propanediol**
(Prod.)
($C_3H_8O_2$; solvent; prime material for aroma/fragrance production.)
d Propylenglykol *m*; 1,2-Propandiol *m*
f propylène-glycol *m*; propanédiol-1,2 *m*
p propilenoglicol *m*; 1,2 propanodiol *m*

4419 **propylene glycol alginate**
(Prod.)
(Food processing technology: e.g. texture improving ingredient.)
d Propylenglykolalginat *n*
f alginate *m* de propylène-glycol
p alginato *m* de propilenoglicol

4420 **propyl gallate**
(Biochem.)
($C_{10}H_{12}O_5$; food biochemistry: foodstuff antioxidant (observe Government regulations).)
d Propylgallat *n*

f gallate *m* de propyle
p galato *m* de propila

* **propylic alcohol → 4417**

4421 **prostaglandins**
(Med.)
(Hormone; produced by the body from essential fatty acids.)
d Prostaglandine *npl*
f prostaglandines *fpl*
p prostaglandinas *fpl*

4422 **prosthetic group**
(Biochem.)
(Nutritional science; non-proteic enzyme fraction.)
d prosthetische Gruppe *f*
f groupe *m* prosthétique
p grupo *m* prostético

4423 **protamines**
(Biochem.)
(Highly basic proteins, with high arginine content, associated to the DNA.)
d Protamine *npl*
f protamines *fpl*
p protaminas *fpl*

4424 **protease; proteolytic enzyme**
(Biochem.)
(Nutritional science; ref. to digestive enzyme in protein breakdown.)
d Protease *f*; proteolytisches Enzym *n*
f protéase *f*; enzyme *f* protéolytique
p protease *f*; enzima *f* proteolítica

4425 **protect *v* against oxidation**
(Biochem.)
(Nutritional science; ref. to auxiliaries in processes and products.)
d gegen Oxidation schützen
f protéger de l'oxydation
p proteger contra a oxidação

4426 **protecting nutrient**
(Med.)
(Nutrition in medicine.)
d Schutznahrungsstoff *m*; schützender Nährstoff *m*
f nutriment *m* protecteur
p nutriente *m* protetor

4427 **protection from lipid oxidation**
(Biochem.)
(Nutritional science; e.g. ref. to the activity of selenium and vitamin E.)
d Schutz *m* vor der Lipidoxidation
f protection *f* contre l'oxydation lipidique
p proteção *f* contra a oxidação lipídica

4428 **protection of the wine against oxidation; wine protection against oxidation**
(Biochem.)
(Enology.)
d Oxidationsschutz *m* des Weines
f protection *f* du vin contre l'oxydation
p proteção *f* do vinho contra a oxidação

4429 **protective colloid**
(Biochem.)
(Food biochemistry.)
d Schutzkolloid *n*
f colloïde *m* protecteur
p colóide *m* protetor

4430 **protective effect**
(Biochem.)
(Nutritional science, ref. to certain nutrients.)
d Schutzeffekt *m*; Schutzwirkung *f*
f effet *m* protecteur
p efeito *m* protetor

4431 **protective effect of fish oils**
(Biochem.)
(Nutritional science.)
d Schutzeffekt *m* der Fischöle; Schutzwirkung *f* der Fischöle
f effet *m* protecteur des huiles de poisson
p efeito *m* protetor dos óleos de peixe

4432 **protective wood impregnation**
(Agr.)
(Agricultural produce; agricultural activity: wood treatment for timber production.)
d Holzschutzimprägnierung *f*
f imprégnation *f* protectrice du bois
p impregnação *f* de proteção da madeira

4433 **protect *v* livestock against climatic extremes**
(Agr.)
(Biological agriculture.)
d die Tiere vor den Extremen des Klimas schützen
f protéger les animaux des excès climatiques
p proteger os animais dos extremos climáticos

4434 **proteide**
(Biochem.)
(Nutritional science; combination of a protein molecule and a prosthetic group: milk ingredient.)
d Proteid *n*
f protéide *m*
p proteídeo *m*

4435 **protein**
(Biochem.)
(Nutritional science; group of organic compounds of amino acid chain(s), essential constituent of the body.)

d Protein *n*; Eiweiß *n*
f protéine *f*
p proteína *f*

4436 **proteinaceous breakfast supply**
(Med.)
(Regimens, diets.)
d Proteinversorgung *f* zum Frühstuck; morgendliche Proteinversorgung *f*
f apport *m* protéique matinal
p aporte *m* protéico matinal

4437 **proteinaceous composition**
(Biochem.)
(Nutritional science.)
d Proteinkomposition *f*; proteinbezügliche Zusammensetzung *f*
f composition *f* protéique
p composição *f* protéica

* **proteinaceous contents → 4448**

4438 **proteinaceous dish**
(Biochem.)
(Nutritional science.)
d proteinhaltiges Gericht *n*
f repas *m* protéique
p refeição *f* protéica

4439 **proteinaceous hypercatabolism**
(Med.)
(Catabolism dysfunction in nutritional disorder and nutritional diseases.)
d Proteinhyperkatabolismus *m*
f hypercatabolisme *m* protéique
p hipercatabolismo *m* protéico

4440 **proteinaceous malnutrition**
(Med.)
(Nutritional protein deficiency in regimens, diets.)
d Proteinfehlernährung *f*
f malnutrition *f* protéinique
p subalimentação *f* protéica

4441 **proteinaceous nutrients**
(Biochem.)
(Nutritional science.)
d proteinartige Nährstoffe *mpl*
f nutriments *mpl* de nature protéique
p nutrientes *mpl* protéicos; nutrientes *mpl* de natura protéica

4442 **proteinaceous polypeptidic hormones**
(Biochem.)
(Biochemical research, e.g. in genetic engineering; nutritional science.)
d polypeptidische Proteohormone *npl*
f hormones *fpl* protéiniques polypeptidiques
p hormônios *mpl* protéicos polipeptídicos

4443 **proteinaceous soy derivative**
(Biochem.)
(Nutritional science.)
d proteinhaltiges Sojaderivat *n*
f dérivé *m* protéique du soja
p derivado *m* protéico da soja

4444 **protein assimilation**
(Med.)
(Pepsin, an enzyme of the mucous membrane of the stomach, hydrolyzes peptide compounds. This process is called protein assimilation.)
d Eiweißverdauung *f*
f assimilation *f* de protéine
p assimilação *f* protéica; assimilação *f* de proteínas

4445 **protein biosynthesis**
(Med.)
(Regimens, diets; occurs in the human body, starting from amino acids.)
d Proteinbiosynthese *f*
f biosynthèse *f* de protéines
p biossíntese *f* das proteínas

4446 **protein break**
(Biochem.)
(Nutritional science.)
d Proteinbruch *m*
f casse *f* protéique
p quebra *f* protéica

4447 **protein compound**
(Biochem.)
(Nutritional science.)
d Eiweißverbindung *f*; Proteinverbindung *f*
f composé *m* protéique
p composto *m* protéico

4448 **protein contents; proteinaceous contents**
(Biochem.)
(Food biochemistry; foodstuff composition.)
d Proteingehalt *m*; Eiweißgehalt *m*
f teneur *f* en protéines
p teor *m* de proteínas

4449 **protein decomposition product**
(Biochem.)
(Nutritional science.)
d Eiweißabbauprodukt *n*
f produit *m* de décomposition protéique
p produto *m* de decomposição da proteína

4450 **protein deficiency**
(Biochem.)
(Nutritional science.)
d Proteinmangel *m*
f carence *f* en protéines; carence *f* protéique
p deficiência *f* de proteínas; carência *f* de proteínas; carência *f* protéica

4451 **protein depletion**
(Biochem.)
(Nutritional science; harmful reduction, impoverishment.)
d Proteindezimierung *f*
f déplétion *f* protéique
p depleção *f* protéica

4452 **protein digestibility**
(Biochem.)
(Nutritional science.)
d Proteinverdaulichkeit *f*, Proteinverdaubarkeit *f*
f digestibilité *f* des protéines
p digestibilidade *f* das proteínas

4453 **protein elimination**
(Biochem.)
(Nutritional science; ref. to the production of beer, wine and juices in clarification processes.)
d Proteinausscheidung *f*
f élimination *f* des protéines
p eliminação *f* das proteínas

4454 **protein factor**
(Biochem.)
(Nutritional science.)
d Proteinfaktor *m*; Eiweißfaktor *m*
f facteur *m* protéique
p fator *m* protéico

4455 **protein feedstuffs**
(Agr.)
(Livestock nutrition.)
d proteinreiche Futtermittel *npl*
f fourrages *mpl* protéiques
p forragens *fpl* protéicas

4456 **protein fermentation**
(Biochem.)
(Food processing technology; food decomposition; putrefaction.)
d Eiweißgärung *f*
f fermentation *f* protéique
p fermentação *f* protéica

4457 **protein fibres**
(Med.)
(Anatomy; e.g. ref. to the nervous system and the bloodsugar level; related to nutritional problems.)
d Proteinfasern *fpl*
f fibres *fpl* protéiques
p fibras *fpl* de proteínas

4458 **protein inactivation**
(Biochem.)
(Nutritional science; ref. to the production of beer, wine and juices in clarification processes.)
d Inaktivierung *f* der Proteine; Unwirksammachung *f* der Proteine
f inactivation *f* des protéines
p inativação *f* das proteínas

4459 **protein intolerance**
(Med.)
(Baby nutrition. Ref. to intolerance type esp. against cow's milk.)
d Proteinintoleranz *f*, Proteinunverträglichkeit *f*
f intolérance *f* aux protéines
p intolerância *f* às proteínas

4460 **protein metabolism**
(Med.)
(Proteins, being built up from amino acids, are structural elements of the body. There exists a balance between the protein built up, synthesization in the body, and its breakdown.)
d Proteinstoffwechsel *m*; Eiweißstoffwechsel *m*
f protéométabolisme *m*
p metabolismo *m* protéico

4461 **protein of lactic origin**
(Biochem.)
(Nutritional science.)
d Protein *n* laktischen Ursprunges
f protéine *f* d'origine lactée
p proteína *f* de origem láctica

4462 **protein of the egg**
(Prod.)
(Food processing technology.)
d Eiprotein *n*
f protéine *f* de l'œuf
p proteína *f* do ovo

4463 **protein poor flour**
(Prod.)
(Food processing technology; ref. to special flour types like e.g. buckwheat flour.)
d proteinarmes Mehl *n*; Mehl *n* arm an Proteinen
f farine *f* pauvre en protéines
p farinha *f* pobre de proteínas

4464 **protein requirement**
(Med.)
(Proteins are essential body constituents; they are synthesized in the body and are obtained from diet.)
d Eiweißbedarf *m*; Proteinbedarf *m*
f besoin *m* de protéine
p necessidades *fpl* protéicas

4465 **protein-rich food**
(Biochem.)
(Nutritional science.)
d proteinreiche Nahrungsmittel *npl*

f aliments *mpl* riches en protéines
p alimentos *mpl* ricos em proteínas

4466 **protein-rich yeast**
(Biochem.)
(Nutritional science.)
d proteinreiche Hefen *fpl*.
f levures *fpl* riches en protéines
p leveduras *fpl* ricas em proteínas

4467 **proteins contained in food**
(Prod.)
(Food processing technology.)
d Nahrungsmittelproteine *npl*; in Nahrungsmitteln *npl* enthaltene Proteine
f protéines *fpl* contenues dans les aliments
p proteínas *fpl* contidas nos alimentos

4468 **proteins of excellent biological value**
(Biochem.)
(Food biochemistry; proteins of dairy products.)
d Proteine *npl* hohen biologischen Wertes
f protéines *fpl* d'excellente valeur biologique
p proteínas *fpl* de alto valor biológico

4469 **protein source**
(Prod.)
(Food processing technology: e.g. eggs.)
d Proteinquelle *f*
f source *f* de protéines
p fonte *f* de proteínas

4470 **protein specificity**
(Biochem.)
(Nutritional science: Olfactory stimulation, nervous cells system: aroma/flavour research: ref. to odoriferous molecules.)
d Proteinspezifität *f*
f spécificité *f* des protéines
p especificidade *f* das proteínas

4471 **protein strands wound around each other into a helix**
(Biochem.)
(The two strands of nucleic acid, forming the DNA.)
d schraubenförmig verwundene Eiweißkette *f*; Eiweißkettenhelixmodell *n*
f hélice *f* des protéines; conformation *f* tridimensionnelle en hélice des protéines
p hélice *f* protéica enovelade sobre si

4472 **protein substance**
(Prod.)
(Food processing technology. Alimentary substance.)
d Proteinsubstanz *f*
f substance *f* protéique
p substância *f* protéica

4473 **protein supply**
(Prod.)
(Food processing technology.)
d Proteinzufuhr *f*
f apport *m* en protéines; apport *m* protéique
p aporte *m* protéico; fornecimento *m* de proteínas

4474 **protein synthesis**
(Med.)
(In the human body.)
d Proteinsynthese *f*; Eiweißsynthese *f*
f synthèse *f* de protéine
p síntese *f* das proteínas

4475 **protein synthesis of the nervous system**
(Med.)
(Nutrition in medicine.)
d Proteinsynthese *f* des Nervensystemes
f synthèse *f* des protéines du système nerveux
p síntese *f* das proteínas do sistema nervoso

4476 **proteolysis**
(Biochem.)
(Nutritional science; protein or peptide hydrolysis, forming simpler substances.)
d Proteolyse *f*
f protéolyse *f*
p proteólise *f*

* **proteolytic cellular enzyme → 989**

4477 **proteolytic diastase**
(Biochem.)
(Nutritional science; contained in fishes and hydrolyzing the proteins during digestion.)
d proteolytische Diastase *f*
f diastase *f* protéolytique
p diástase *f* proteolítica

* **proteolytic enzyme → 4424**

4478 **proteose**
(Biochem.)
(Nutritional science. Water-soluble derivatives of protein decomposition: Decomposition sequence: proteins-proteoses-peptones-polypeptides-amino acids.)
d Proteose *f*
f protéose *f*
p proteose *f*

4479 **protozoan; protozoon** (*pl* protozoa)
(Med.)
(Veterinary; any of a phylum or subkingdom Protozoa, e.g. amoebas, trypanosomes; pathogenic parasites.)
d Protozoon *n* (*pl Protozoen*)
f protozoaire *m*
p protozoário *m*

* **protozoon → 4479**

4480 **protuberant abdomen**
(Med.)
(Anatomy.)
d Spitzbauch *m*
f ventre *m* protubérant
p ventre *m* protuberante; barriga *f* saliente

4481 **provitamin**
(Prod.)
(Vitamins in nutrition; vitamin precursor, convertible into a vitamin in the human body.)
d Provitamin *n*
f provitamine *f*
p provitamina *f*

* **provitamin A → 600**

4482 **proximate analysis**
(Prod.)
(Food processing technology; analytical method.)
d Näherungsanalyse *f*
f analyse *f* immédiate
p análise *f* aproximada

4483 **prune**
(Prod.)
(Food processing technology; dried plum.)
d Backpflaume *f*; Dörrpflaume *f*; gedörrte Pflaume *f*; getrocknete Pflaume *f*
f pruneau *m*; prune *f* séchée
p ameixa *f* seca

4484 **prune** *v*; **trim** *v*
(Agr.)
(Horticulture. Cutting, clipping unfavourable, useless plant parts.)
d beschneiden; ausputzen
f tailler
p podar

* **prussic acid → 2784**

4485 **pseudocarp**
(Agr.)
(Botany; false fruit.)
d Scheinfrucht *f*
f pseudocarpe *m*
p pseudofruto *m*

4486 **pseudopernicious anaemia**
(Med.)
(Due to vitamin B_{12} deficiency in nutrition or absorption disturbances of this vitamin.)
d pseudoperniziöse Anemie *f*; pseudobösartige Blutarmut *f*
f anémie *f* pseudopernicieuse
p anemia *f* pseudoperniciosa

* **psilosis → 5180**

4487 **psittacosis; ornithosis; parrot fever**
(Med.)
(Veterinary; communicable disease (zoonosis: from animals to humans), caused by virus.)
d Papageienkrankheit *f*; Psittakose *f*
f psittacose *f*; ornithose *f*
p psitacose *f*; ornitose *f*

4488 **psychrobacteria; psychrophylic bacteria**
(Biochem.)
(Microbiology; bacteria which develop under low temperatures: 0-5°C, e.g. genus "Penicillum".)
d Psychrobakterien *fpl*; Kältebakterien *fpl*
f psychrobactéries *fpl*; bactéries *fpl* psychrophiliques
p psicrobactérias *fpl*; bactérias *fpl* psicrofílicas

* **psychrophylic bacteria → 4488**

4489 **pteroylglutamic acid**
(Biochem.)
(Nutritional science; $C_{19}H_{19}N_7O_6$; PGA; Folic acid; liver Lactobacillus casei factor; occurs in the liver and in yeast, mushrooms and green leaves etc.)
d Pteroylglutaminsäure *f*
f acide *m* ptéroylglutamique
p ácido *m* pteroilglutâmico

4490 **ptomaine**
(Med.)
(Protein-decomposition product: nitrogenous-substance decomposition by putrefactive bacteria, resulting in e.g. cadaverine ($C_5H_{14}N_2$); putrescine ($C_4H_{12}N_2$) etc; found in the intestine, often toxic.)
d Ptomain *n*
f ptomaïne *f*
p ptomaína *f*

4491 **ptyalin**
(Med.)
(Amylolytic enzyme from salivary glands hydrolyzing starch into dextrin and maltose, for starch conversion: beginning of the chemical digestion process.)
d Ptyalin *n*
f ptyaline *f*
p ptialina *f*

* **puff paste → 4034**

* **puff pastry cake → 3567**

* **puffy paste → 4034**

4492 **pullet; young chicken**
(Agr.)
(Poultry farming. "Gallus gallus".)
d Hühnchen *n*
f poulette *f*
p franga *f*

4493 **pulmonary congestion**
(Med.)
(Veterinary; especially important disease relating to one day's chicks from hatcheries, exposed to heat and cold; symptoms: dispnoea, lack of appetite, ruffled up feathers; diarrhoea.)
d Lungenkongestion *f*
f congestion *f* pulmonaire
p congestão *f* pulmonária

4494 **pulmonary hypotonia of the premature**
(Med.)
(Pediatrics.)
d Lungenschwäche *f* des Frühgeborenen
f hypotonie *f* du prématuré
p hipotonia *f* do récem-nascido

4495 **pulp**
(Agr.)
(Botany; soft inner part of the fruit.)
d Fruchtfleisch *n*
f pulpe *f*
p polpa *f*

4496 **pulpy diet; mushy diet**
(Med.)
(Alimentary regimen.)
d Breidiät *f*; breiige Diät *f*
f diète *f* pulpeuse; diète *f* en bouillie
p dieta *f* de papas; dieta *f* pastosa

4497 **pulpy fruit; fleshy fruit**
(Agr.)
(Botany. Succulent part of a fruit.)
d fleischige Frucht *f*
f fruit *m* charnu
p fruta *f* carnosa

4498 **pulse**
(Agr.)
(Horticulture. Edible seed of various leguminous crops, e.g. beans, peas, lentils.)
d getrocknete Hülsenfrüchte *fpl*
f légumes *mpl* secs
p grãos *mpl* de leguminosa

4499 **pulverization over the product surface**
(Prod.)
(Food processing technology; vitamin application.)
d Versprühung *f* auf die Produktoberfläche; Besprühung *f* der Produktoberfläche
f pulvérisation *f* à la surface du produit
p pulverização *f* da superfície do produto

4500 **pumpkin; squash; cucurbit; gourd**
(Agr.)
(Agricultural produce; "Cucurbitaceae"; gourd family.)
d Kürbis *m*; Riesenkürbis *m*
f citrouille *f*; courge *f*; potiron *m*; giraumont *m*
p abóbora *f*; jerimum *m*

4501 **pumpkin seeds**
(Prod.)
(Gastronomy; e.g. in sauce preparation.)
d Kürbissamen *m/mpl*
f graines *fpl* de courges
p sementes *mpl* da abóbora

4502 **punch**
(Prod.)
(Gastronomy, alcoholic beverage made of rum, sugar, lemon, water, red wine and spices.)
d Punsch *m*
f punch *m*
p ponche *m*

4503 **pungent odour**
(Prod.)
(Food processing technology; product characteristic: e.g. hot to the taste like sauces made from peppers.)
d stechender Geruch *m*
f odeur *m* âcre
p cheiro *m* penetrante

4504 **pungent taste**
(Prod.)
(Food processing technology; product characteristic: e.g. hot to the taste like sauces made from peppers.)
d stechender Geschmack *m*
f goût *m* âcre
p gosto *m* penetrante

4505 **pupa; chrysalis**
(Agr.)
(Apiculture. Bee anatomy: Pupa of the honeybee: intermediate phase, between the larva and the adult insect.)
d Puppe *f*
f nymphe *f*; chrysalide *f*
p crisálida *f*; pupa *f*

* **pure alcohol → 5**

4506 **pure fraction**
(Prod.)
(Aroma/flavour research and production: ref. to product quality.)

d Reinfraktion *f*
f fraction *f* pure
p fração *f* pura

* **pure must → 1155**

4507 **pure substance**
(Prod.)
(Food processing technology.)
d Reinsubstanz *f*
f substance *f* pure
p substância *f* pura

4508 **pure vine sort**
(Agr.)
(Viticulture; ref. winegrowing and selection.)
d pure Rebsorte *f*
f cépage *m* pur
p espécie *f* de cepa pura

4509 **pure yeast culture**
(Biochem.)
(Food biochemistry, ref. to yeast production, preparation of yeast material in the laboratory.)
d reine Hefekultur *f*
f culture *f* pure en levure
p cultura *f* pura de fermento

4510 **purification**
(Prod.)
(Food processing technology.)
d Reinigung *f*; Purifikation *f*
f purification *f*; épuration *f*
p purificação *f*

4511 **purified honey**
(Agr.)
(Apiculture; honey quality.)
d gereinigter Honig *m*
f miel *m* blanc; miel *m* purifié
p mel *m* purificado

4512 **purine base**
(Biochem.)
(Nitrogenous compound occurring in nucleic acids.)
d Purinbase *f*
f base *f* purique
p base *f* púrica

4513 **purine poor diet**
(Med.)
(Alimentary regimen; ref. to purine base; $C_5H_4N_4$, e.g. occurring in uric acid. DNA constituent. Diet in cases of rheumatism and gout.)
d purinarme Diät *f*
f diète *f* pauvre en purine
p dieta pobre em purina

* **purée → 3395**

4514 **putrescent clostridium**
(Biochem.)
(Microbiology. Anaerobic protein-decomposing bacteria.)
d Eiweißfäulnisclostridium *n*
f clostridium *m* putrescent
p clostridium *m* putrefaciente

* **pyloric sphinctor → 4515**

4515 **pylorus; pyloric sphinctor**
(Med.)
(Anatomy. The food passes from the stomach through the pylorus into the duodenum; lower stomach connection to the duodenum)
d Pylorus *m*; Pförtner *m*; Pförtnerschließmuskel *m*
f pylore *m*; sphincter *m* pylorique
p piloro *m*; esfíncter *m* pilórico

4516 **pyrazine**
(Prod.)
($C_4H_4N_2$; 1,4-diazine; source of aroma/fragrance prime material.)
d Pyrazin *n*
f pyrazine *m*
p pirazina *f*

4517 **pyridine**
(Prod.)
(C_5H_5N; food processing technology; occurs in coffee roasting processes.)
d Pyridin *n*
f pyridine *f*
p piridina *f*

* **pyridoxine → 5748**

4518 **pyrimidine**
(Biochem.)
($C_4H_4N_2$; 1,3-diazine; a base, constituent of DNA, RNA.)
d Pyrimidin *n*
f pyrimidine *m*
p pirimidina *f*

4519 **pyrimidine base**
(Biochem.)
(Nitrogenous compound occurring in nucleic acids.)
d Pyrimidinbase *f*
f base *f* pyrimidique
p base *f* pirimídica

4520 **pyrolysis**
(Biochem.)
(Food biochemistry; chemical decomposition by heat.)

d Pyrolyse *f*; Zersetzung *f* durch Hitze
f pyrolyse *f*
p pirólise *f*

4521 pyrrole; imidole
(Prod.)
(C_4H_5N; food processing technology; occurs in coffee roasting processes.)
d Pyrrol *n*
f pyrrol *m*; pyrrole *m*
p pirrol *m*

4522 pyruvic acid
(Med.)
($C_3H_4O_3$; 2-oxopropanoic acid; intermediate product in metabolism; ref. to the cycle of carbohydrate catabolism and the citric acid Krebs cycle.)
d Brenztraubensäure *f*
f acide *m* pyruvique
p ácido *m* pirúvico

4523 pyruvic acid fermentation
(Biochem.)
(Fermentation; ref. to pyruvic acid, 2-oxopropanoic acid; $C_3H_4O_3$.)
d Brenztraubensäuregärung *f*; Brenztraubensäurefermentation *f*
f fermentation *f* d'acide pyruvique
p fermentação *f* do ácido pirúvico

Q

4524 **quail**
(Agr.)
(Poultry farming; "Coturnix coturnix"; gallinaceous bird.)
d Wachtel *f*
f caille *f*
p codorna *f*; codorniz *f*

4525 **quality control**
(Prod.)
(Food processing technology.)
d Qualitätskontrolle *f*
f contrôle *m* de qualité
p controle *m* de qualidade

4526 **quality grape; grape of quality**
(Agr.)
(Viticulture; wine production.)
d Qualitätstraube *f*
f grappe *f* de raisin de qualité
p cacho *m* de uva de qualidade

4527 **quality improvement**
(Prod.)
(Food processing technology.)
d Qualitätsverbesserung *f*
f amélioration *f* de la qualité
p melhoramento *m* de qualidade; aperfeiçoamento *m* da qualidade

4528 **quality of agricultural products**
(Agr.)
(Agricultural produce.)
d Qualität *f* der Agrarprodukte
f qualité *f* des produits agricoles
p qualidade *f* dos produtos agrícolas

4529 **quality of being appetizing**
(Prod.)
(Gastronomy.)
d Appetitlichkeit *f*
f qualité *f* d'être appétissant
p qualidade *f* de ser apetitoso

4530 **quality of potable water**
(Prod.)
(Water supply.)
d Trinkwasserqualität *f*
f qualité *f* d'eau potable
p qualidade *f* da água potável

* **quality of taste → 2610**

4531 **quality-tested wine**
(Prod.)
(Enology.)
d Qualitätswein *m*
f vin *m* de qualité
p vinho *m* de qualidade

4532 **quantitative analysis**
(Biochem.)
(Nutritional science.)
d Mengenanalyse *f*; quantitative Analyse *f*
f analyse *f* quantitative
p análise *f* quantitativa

4533 **quantitative thin-layer chromatography**
(Biochem.)
(Nutritional science; ref. to process of analysis.)
d quantitative Dünnschichtchromatographie *f*
f chromatographie *f* quantitative sur couche mince
p cromatografia *f* quantitativa de camada fina

4534 **quarter of a beef**
(Agr.)
(Cattle breeding. Quarter of an ox.)
d Rinderviertel *n*
f quartier *m* de bœuf
p quarto *m* de carcaça do boi

4535 **quartz crystals**
(Agr.)
(Biological agriculture: used in soil treatment compounds.)
d Quartzkristalle *npl*
f cristaux *mpl* de quartz
p cristais *mpl* de quartzo

4536 **quassia tincture; tincture of bitter wood**
(Med.)
("Picrasma excelsa"; "Quassia amara L." (Origin: Brazil); used as oral stimulant in indigestion; as rectal injection (enema) as enterobiasis (oxyuriasis) treatment.)
d Quassietinktur *f*; Auszug *m* der Quassie
f teinture *f* de quassia
p tintura *f* de quassia

4537 **quaternary structure of the protein**
(Biochem.)
(Polypeptide chains of amino acids: Specification of the structural relationship of these polypeptides.)
d Quaternärstruktur *f* des Proteins
f structure *f* quaternaire de la protéine
p estrutura *f* quaternária da proteína

4538 **queen bee**
(Agr.)
(Apiculture. Fertile female bee.)

d Bienenkönigin *f*; Weisel *m*
f reine *f*; mère *f* des abeilles; reproductrice *f* des abeilles
p rainha *f* das abelhas; abelha-mestra *f*

4539 **queen excluder**
(Agr.)
(Apiculture: Movable comb construction.)
d Absperrgitter *n*; Schied *m*
f grille *f* à reine; grille *f* à reproductrice
p tela *f* excluidora de rainha

4540 **quenelle; meat/fish dumpling**
(Prod.)
(Gastronomy; made of forcemeat, often e.g. pike.)
d Fleisch/Fischknödel *m*
f quenelle *f*
p bolinho *m* de carne/peixe

4541 **quiche; filled custard pie**
(Prod.)
(Gastronomy; filling: e.g. spinach; bacon etc.)
d Quiche *f*; Mürbeteigspeckkuchen *m*
f quiche *f*; tourte *f* à pâte brisée
p quiche *f*

4542 **quince**
(Agr.)
(Horticulture; "Cydonia oblonga"; edible fruit.)
d Quitte *f*
f coing *m*
p marmelo *m*

4543 **quinoline; chinoleine**
(Prod.)
(C_9H_7N; foodstuff colorant prime material: chinoleine yellow is a food dye.)
d Chinolin *n*
f quinoléine *f*
p quinolina *f*; quinoleína *f*

R

4544 **rabbit**
(Agr.)
(Family "Laporidae", genus "Oryctolagus cuniculus L."; Livestock: domestic rabbits.)
d Kaninchen *n*
f lapin *m*
p coelho *m*

4545 **rabbit fricassee**
(Prod.)
(Gastronomy; rabbit meat, prepared in white wine.)
d Kaninchenfrikassee *n* in Weißwein
f gibelotte *f* de lapin; lapin *m* en gibelotte
p fricassê *m* de carne de coelho

4546 **rabies; hydrophobia**
(Med.)
(Veterinary; virus disease of the nervous system.)
d Tollwut *f*
f rage *f*
p raiva *f*

* **race horse → 4717**

4547 **racemic mixture**
(Biochem.)
(Vitamin food/biochemistry: A not optically active mixture of equal quantities of dextrorotatory and levorotatory aspects of the same compound.)
d razemische Mischung *f*
f mélange *m* racémique
p mistura *f* racêmica

4548 **rachitogenic diet**
(Med.)
(Alimentary regimen: Vitamin D deficiency food intake.)
d Rachitis verursachende Diät *f*
f diète *f* rachitique
p dieta *f* raquítica; dieta *f* causadora de raquitismo

4549 **radicals**
(Biochem.)
(Nutritional science: Group of atoms.)
d Radikale *npl*
f radicaux *mpl*
p radicais *mpl*

4550 **radioactive at the well**
(Prod.)
(Water supply; ref. to well water characteristic.)
d radioaktiv an der Quelle
f radioactif à la fontaine
p radioativo na fonte

* **radioactive nuclide → 4552**

4551 **radioactivity**
(Med.)
(Nutritiological toxicology, due to the intake of radionuclides (radioactive nuclides) through foodstuffs and its chronicle radiation effects on the body.)
d Radioaktivität *f*
f radioactivité *f*
p radioatividade *f*

4552 **radionuclide; radioactive nuclide**
(Med.)
(Nutritiological toxicology: ref. to the intake of radionuclides through foodstuffs and its chronicle radiation effects on the body.)
d Radionuklid *n*; radioaktives Nuklid *n*
f radionucléide *m*; nucléide *m* radioactif
p radionuclídeo *m*; nuclídeo *m* radioativo

4553 **radish**
(Agr.)
(Horticulture. "Raphanus satius"; pungent short red root.)
d Radieschen *n*
f radis *m* rose
p rabanete *m*

4554 **ragout**
(Prod.)
(Gastronomy.)
d Ragout *n*
f ragoût *m*
p ragu *m*

* **rain cloud → 3735**

4555 **raised oyster**
(Agr.)
(Agricultural produce. Family "Ostreidae"; edible marine mollusk; raised in special basins/tanks for quality-increasing treatment.)
d Zuchtauster *f*
f fine *f* de claire; huître *f* de claire
p ostra *f* de criação

* **raisin → 5335**

4556 **raisin flavour note**
(Prod.)
(Aroma/flavour chemical: methyl anthranilate: $C_8H_9NO_2$; ref. to elaboration of aromas: organic chemistry.)

d Weinbeerengeschmacksnote *f*
f note *f* saveur de raisins
p nota *f* de sabor de uvas

* **raising → 4592**

4557 **raisin note**
(Prod.)
(Flavour note: flavour taste of methyl-anthranilate.)
d Weinbeerengeschmack *m*
f saveur *f* raisin
p sabor *m* de uva

4558 **ram**
(Agr.)
(Livestock. Male sheep.)
d Widder *m*; Schafbock *m*
f bélier *m*
p carneiro *m*; bode *m*

4559 **ram foot**
(Prod.)
(Butchery; meat part.)
d Spitzbein *n* des Schafbocks
f pied *m* de bélier
p pé *m* de carneiro

4560 **rancid flavour in processed meat**
(Biochem.)
(Nutritional science; ref. to restructured meat in meat processing.)
d ranzige Geschmacksstoffe *mpl* in verarbeitetem Fleisch
f flaveur *f* rance dans la viande transformée
p sabor *m* rançoso na carne processada

4561 **rancid flavours in processed meat systems**
(Biochem.)
(Nutritional science; ref. to lipid oxidation phenomena in meat.)
d ranziger Geschmack *m* in Systemen weiterverarbeiteten Fleisches
f flaveurs *mpl* rances dans les systèmes des viandes transformées
p sabores *mpl* rançosos em sistemas de carnes processados

4562 **rancidity; rancidness**
(Prod.)
(Food processing technology: Certain product characteristic.)
d Ranzigkeit *f*
f rance *m*
p ranço *m*

4563 **rancidity due to acid formation by air contact**
(Biochem.)
(Nutritional science; quality reducing factor in meat processing.)
d Ranzigwerden *n* durch Säureentstehung bei Luftkontakt
f rancissement *m* dû à la formation d'acides au contact de l'air
p rancificação *f* devida à formação de ácidos ao contato com o ar

* **rancidity in fowl meat → 4564**

4564 **rancidity in poultry meat; rancidity in fowl meat**
(Biochem.)
(Nutritional science; quality reducing factor in meat processing.)
d Ranzigkeit *f* in Geflügelfleisch
f rancissement *m* dans la viande de volaille
p rancidez *f* na carne das aves

* **rancidness → 4562**

4565 **rape; canola**
(Agr.)
(Agricultural produce; "Brassica napus"; canola is an improved rape variety, canola oil is an edible vegetable oil.)
d Raps *m*
f colza *m*
p colza *f*

4566 **rape oil; canola oil**
(Agr.)
(Agricultural produce. Canola is an improved rape variety, canola oil is an edible vegetable oil.)
d Rapsöl *n*
f huile *f* de colza
p óleo *m* de colza

4567 **rapid decomposition**
(Biochem.)
(Food biochemistry; product characteristic.)
d schnelle Dekomposition *f*; schneller Zerfall *m*
f décomposition *f* rapide
p decomposição *f* rápida

* **rapid filtration → 14**

4568 **rapidly growing plant**
(Agr.)
(Botany.)
d schnellwachsende Pflanze *f*; Pflanze *f* schnellen Wuchses
f plante *f* à croissance rapide
p planta *f* de crescimento rápido

4569 **raspberry**
(Agr.)
(Horticulture. Genus "Rubus"; soft fruit; berry.)

d Himbeere *f*
f framboise *f*
p framboesa *f*; amora-vermelha *f*

4570 **raspberry aroma note**
(Prod.)
(Flavour note, flavour chemicals; elaboration of aromas: organic chemistry.)
d Himbeergeschmacksnote *f*
f note *f* saveur framboise
p nota *f* sabor de framboesa

4571 **raspberry ketone**
(Prod.)
(Flavouring agent; application e.g. in fruit flavours for milk products, soft drinks and sweets.)
d Himbeerketon *n*
f cétone-framboise *f*
p cetona-framboesa *f*

* **rate of dry matter → 1324**

4572 **rate of phenolic compounds; value of phenolic compounds**
(Prod.)
(Enology, nutritional science of wine production.)
d Wert *m* der Phenol-Verbindungen
f taux *m* de composés phénoliques
p taxa *f* de compostos fenólicos

4573 **rational livestock nutrition**
(Agr.)
(Livestock breeding.)
d rationelle Ernährung *f* des Viehes; rationelle Viehernährung *f*
f alimentation *f* rationnelle du bétail
p alimentação *f* racional do gado

* **ravage of the culture → 1603**

4574 **raw essence**
(Prod.)
(Aroma/flavour research and production.)
d Rohessenz *f*
f essence *f* brute
p essência *f* bruta

4575 **raw milk**
(Prod.)
(Dairy plant product.)
d Rohmilch *f*
f lait *m* cru
p leite *m* cru

4576 **raw milk cost**
(Prod.)
(Dairy prime material cost.)
d Rohmilchkosten *pl*
f coût *m* du lait cru
p custo *m* do leite cru

4577 **raw milk quality**
(Prod.)
(Characteristic of dairy prime material.)
d Rohmilchqualität *f*
f qualité *f* du lait cru
p qualidade *f* do leite cru

4578 **raw molasses**
(Biochem.)
(Food biochemistry; sugar-containing substrate for yeast inoculation, obtaining the production of yeast cells and, this way, the production of yeast.)
d Rohmelasse *f*
f mélasse *f* crue
p melaço *m* cru

4579 **raw vegetables and fruits**
(Prod.)
(Gastronomy.)
d Rohkost *f*
f crudités *fpl*
p alimentos *mpl* crus

4580 **raw vegetables-and-fruits diet**
(Med.)
(Ref. to Maximilian Oskar Bircher-Benner-raw-food diet; Swiss physician (1867-1939): vegetables, milk products and eggs.)
d Rohkostdiät *f*
f diète *f* de crudités
p dieta *f* de alimentos crus

4581 **ray**
(Agr.)
(Fish: marine rays and sweetwater rays; there are approx. 30 species in Brazil.)
d Rochen *m*
f raie *f*
p raia *f*; arraia *f*

4582 **reaction**
(Biochem.)
(Nutritional science; relating to enzymes: catalyzing specific biochemical reactions.)
d Reaktion *f*
f réaction *f*
p reação *f*

4583 **reaction mechanisms**
(Prod.)
(Food processing technology.)
d Reaktionsmechanismen *mpl*
f mécanismes *mpl* réactionnels
p mecanismos *mpl* reactionais; mecanismos *mpl* de reação

4584 reaction of plasmatic coagulation
(Med.)
(Degenerative diseases e.g. due to incorrect nutritional habits.)
d Reaktion *f* der plasmatischen Koagulation; Reaktion *f* der Plasmakoagulation
f réaction *f* de coagulation plasmatique
p reação *f* de coagulação plasmática

4585 reaction product
(Prod.)
(Synthesis: aroma/flavour research and production.)
d Reaktionsprodukt *n*; Umsetzungsprodukt *n*
f produit *m* de réaction
p produto *m* de reação

4586 reactivation phase
(Biochem.)
(Food biochemistry: e.g. ref. to bacteria, fermentation processes.)
d Reaktivierungsphase *f*; Wiederbelebungsphase *f*
f phase *f* de réactivation
p fase *f* de reativação

4587 reactive groups
(Biochem.)
(Biochemical synthesis, e.g. nucleic acids, in nutritional science.)
d reaktive Gruppen *fpl*
f groupements *mpl* réactifs
p grupamentos *mpl* reativos

4588 reactivity
(Biochem.)
(Nutritional science; ref. to reaction intensity.)
d Reaktivität *f*
f réactivité *f*
p reatividade *f*

4589 ready portions for sale
(Prod.)
(Food processing technology, e.g. meat etc.)
d zum Verkauf bestimmte Fertigportionen *fpl*
f portions *fpl* prêtes à la vente
p porções *fpl* prontas para venda

4590 ready poultry-ration in bulk
(Agr.)
(Poultry farming and nutrition.)
d loses Geflügelfertigfutter *n*
f ration *f* avicole prête en vrac
p ração *f* pronta a granel para aves

4591 ready-to-use suspension
(Prod.)
(Food processing technology.)
d verbrauchsfertige Suspension *f*
f suspension *f* prête à l'emploi
p suspensão *f* pronta para utilização

* **real coffee → 1198**

4592 rearing; raising
(Agr.)
(Livestock breeding; raising of farm animals.)
d Zucht; Züchten *n*; Züchtung *f*
f élevage *m*
p criação *f*

* **reason for the interruptions of fermentation → 979**

4593 receptors
(Med.)
(Ref. to the research of synthetic flavour chemicals and flavour notes: sense organ constituent.)
d Rezeptoren *mpl*; Zellrezeptoren *mpl*; Aufnahmezellen *fpl*
f cellules *fpl* réceptrices; récepteurs *mpl*
p receptores *mpl*; células *fpl* receptoras

4594 recessive gene
(Biochem.)
(Dominant gene (A) determines dark eyes. Recessive gene (a) determines blue eyes: (Aa) determines dark eyes because (A) is a dominant gene. This example applies to animal and plant growth.)
d rezessives Gen *n*; zurücktretender Erbträger *m*
f gène *m* récessif
p gene *m* recessivo

4595 reciprocal exhaustion
(Prod.)
(Aroma/flavour research and production: distillation processes.)
d gegenseitige Erschöpfung *f*
f épuisement *m* réciproque
p esgotamento *m* recíproco; exhaustão *f* recíproca

4596 recognition
(Med.)
(Flavour research. Related to sensory message reception and passage.)
d Erkennen *n*
f reconnaissance *f*
p reconhecimento *m*

* **recommencement of fermentation → 4688**

4597 recommendation for vitamin E supplements
(Med.)
(Veterinary; ref. to livestock ration composition. In food, tocopherol is an important antioxidant.)

d Vitamin E- Zusatzempfehlung *f*
f recommandation *f* pour supplémenter en vitamine E
p recomendação *f* de suplementação com vitamina E

4598 **recomposition**
(Prod.)
(Food processing technology.)
d Wiederzusammensetzung *f*
f recomposition *f*
p recomposição *f*

4599 **reconstitute *v* the aromas**
(Prod.)
(Aroma/fragrance production.)
d Aroma wieder erneuern; Aroma neu hervorbringen
f reconstituer les arômes
p reconstituir os aromas

4600 **reconstitution**
(Prod.)
(Food processing technology: dairy product techniques.)
d Rekonstitution *f*
f reconstitution *f*
p reconstituição *f*

4601 **reconstitution of milk**
(Prod.)
(Food processing technology, to restore (e.g. milk) to its former condition.)
d Milchrekonstitution *f*
f reconstitution *f* du lait
p reconstituição *f* do leite

4602 **recontamination**
(Prod.)
(Water supply; drinking water (tap water) production.)
d Nachverkeimung *f*
f recontamination *f*
p recontaminação *f*

4603 **recovery of biologic functions through nutrition**
(Med.)
(Nutrition in therapy.)
d Wiederherstellung *f* der biologischen Funktionen durch die Ernährung
f restauration *f* des fonctions biologiques par la nutrition
p restauração *f* das funções biológicas pela nutrição

4604 **rectal feeding**
(Med.)
(Artificial feeding method.)
d rektale Ernährung *f*
f alimentation *f* rectale
p alimentação *f* retal

4605 **rectification column; fractioning column; stripper column**
(Prod.)
(Food processing technology. Distillation installation.)
d Rektifiziersäule *f*; Rektifizierkolonne *f*; Strippersäule *f*
f tour *f* de fractionnement; tour *f* de rectification; colonne *f* de distillation
p coluna *f* retificadora; coluna *f* de retificação

4606 **rectification of essences**
(Prod.)
(Aroma/flavour research and production: repeated distillation of essences as purifying treatment.)
d Rektifikation *f* von Essenzen
f rectification *f* des essences
p retificação *f* de essências

4607 **rectified alcohol**
(Prod.)
(Food processing technology; ref. to alcohol purified by a second distillation.)
d gereinigter Alkohol *m*; rektifizierter Alkohol *m*; doppeltdestillierter Alkohol *m*
f alcool *m* rectifié
p álcool *m* retificado; álcool *m* redestilado

4608 **rectum**
(Med.)
(Anatomy. Final part of the large intestine.)
d Mastdarm *m*
f rectum *m*
p reto *m*

4609 **recycling**
(Agr.)
(Biological agriculture.)
d Recycling *n*; Wiederverarbeitung *f*; Aufbereitung *f* und Wiederverwendung *f*
f recyclage *m*
p reciclagem *f*

4610 **recycling of nutritional elements**
(Agr.)
(Biological agriculture.)
d Recycling *n* von Nährstoffen; Aufbereitung *f* und Wiederverwendung *f* von Nährstoffen
f recyclage *m* des éléments nutritifs
p reciclagem *f* dos elementos nutritivos

4611 **red blood cells; erythrocytes**
(Med.)
d rote Blutkörperchen *npl*; Erythrozyten *mpl*
f globules *mpl* rouges; érythrocytes *mpl*
p glóbulos *mpl* vermelhos; eritrócitos *mpl*

4612 **red cabbage**
(Agr.)
(Horticulture. "Brassica oleracea var. capitata".)
d Rotkohl *m*; Rotkraut *n*
f chou *m* rouge
p repolho *m* roxo

4613 **red currant**
(Agr.)
(Horticulture; "Ribes rubrum", "Ribes sativum"; soft fruit; berry.)
d rote Johannisbeere *f*
f groseille *f*; groseille *f* rouge
p groselha *f* vermelha

4614 **red deer**
(Agr.)
(Game. Stag: adult male red deer.)
d Rotwild *n*
f bêtes *fpl* fauves
p caça *f* de veação; veado *m*

4615 **rediluted concentrate**
(Prod.)
(Aroma/flavour production.)
d wiederverdünntes Konzentrat *n*
f concentré *m* redilué
p concentrado *m* rediluído; concentrado *m* novamente diluído

4616 **redilution**
(Prod.)
(Food processing technology: e.g. fruit juice treatment.)
d Rückverdünnung *f*
f redilution *f*
p rediluição *f*

4617 **redispersibility**
(Biochem.)
(Nutritional science.)
d Wiederdispergierbarkeit *f*
f remise *f* en dispersion
p redispersão *f*

4618 **redistribution of the vitamin**
(Med.)
(Veterinary; e.g. ref. to vitamin transport in the animal body.)
d Vitaminwiederverteilung *f*
f redistribution *f* de la vitamine
p redistribuição *f* da vitamina

4619 **red meat**
(Prod.)
(Butchery; cattle meat, poultry meat.)
d rotes Fleisch *n*
f viande *f* rouge
p carne *f* vermelha

4620 **red mullet**
(Agr.)
(Family "Mugilidae", edible marine fish.)
d Plötze *f*; Rotauge *n*
f gardon *m*
p pargo *m*

4621 **redox-decomposition**
(Biochem.)
(Vitamin-enzyme biochemistry. Food biochemistry.)
d Redox-Abbau *m*
f dégradation *f* oxydo-réductrice
p degradação *f* de óxido-redução

4622 **redox reaction**
(Biochem.)
(Nutritional science; oxidation-reduction processes; oxidation means loss of electrons, reduction means gain of electrons.)
d Redox-Reaktion *f*
f réaction *f* oxydoréductrice
p reação *f* de óxido-redução

4623 **redox reaction by trace minerals**
(Biochem.)
(Production of feed, rations, premixes for animal nutrition: problems of vitamin stability.)
d Redox-Reaktion *f* durch Spurenmineralien
f réaction *f* oxydoréductrice par des minéraux de trace
p reação *f* de óxido-redução pelos microminerais

4624 **reduced hatchability**
(Agr.)
(Poultry farming; reduced fertility of poultry, generally due to vitamin B_{12} deficiency.)
d verringerte Brütkapazität *f*
f capacité *f* d'incubation réduite; fertilité *f* réduite
p capacidade *f* incubadora reduzida; capacidade *f* de chocar reduzida

4625 **reducing agent; reductant**
(Biochem.)
(Food biochemistry e.g. of aroma synthesis: an electron donating substance.)
d Reduktor *m*
f réducteur *m*; agent *m* de réduction
p redutor *m*; agente *m* redutor

* **reductant → 4625**

4626 **reduction**
(Biochem.)
(Chemical process of transfer of electrons; e.g. in aroma biosynthesis; food biochemistry.)
d Reduktion *f*

f réduction *f*
p redução *f*

4627 **reduction catalyst**
(Biochem.)
(Food biochemistry.)
d Reduktionskatalysator *m*
f catalyseur *m* de réduction
p catalisador *m* de redução

4628 **reduction division; meiosis**
(Med.)
(Ref. to certain type of cell division, showing the resulting daughter cells half of the chromosome quantity.)
d Reduktionsteilung *f*
f réduction *f* méiotique; méiose *f*
p meiose *f*

* **reduction of blood glucose concentration → 698**

4629 **reduction of microorganism load**
(Biochem.)
(Food biochemistry e.g. result of pasteurization process.)
d Abbau *m* des Mikroorganismen-Anfalles; Abbau *m* der Mikroorganismen-Ladung
f réduction *f* de la charge de microorganismes
p redução *f* da carga de microorganismos

4630 **reduction of the sedimentation rate**
(Prod.)
(Food processing technology.)
d Verminderung *f* der Sedimentationsrate; Verringerung *f* der Niederschlagsrate
f réduction *f* de la vitesse de sédimentation
p redução *f* do tempo de sedimentação

4631 **reduction power; reductive power**
(Biochem.)
(Nutritional science; e.g. addition of electrons to an atom; ref. to aroma biochemistry.)
d Reduktionskraft *f*
f pouvoir *m* réducteur
p poder *m* redutor; poder *m* de redução

4632 **reductive** *adj*
(Biochem.)
(Food biochemistry; aroma synthesis: characteristic of a reducing agent.)
d reduzierend
f réducteur
p redutor

* **reductive power → 4631**

4633 **reductive substance**
(Biochem.)
(Ref. to nicotinamide adenine diphosphate; e.g. ref. to biochemical research in nutritional science.)
d reduzierende Substanz *f*
f substance *f* réductrice
p substância *f* redutora

4634 **red vine sort**
(Agr.)
(Viticulture; grape selection)
d rote Rebsorte *f*
f cépage *m* rouge
p espécie *f* de cepa vermelha

4635 **red wine**
(Prod.)
(Beverages; colour occurs naturally during fermentation of dark-coloured grapes.)
d Rotwein *m*
f vin *m* rouge
p vinho *m* tinto

4636 **red wine vinification**
(Agr.)
(Viticulture.)
d Rotweinbereitung *f*
f vinification *f* en rouge
p vinificação *f* de vinhos tintos

4637 **reequilibration of the metabolism**
(Med.)
(Ref. to dietetics in medicine.)
d Wiederherstellung *f* der Ausgeglichenheit des Stoffwechsels
f rééquilibrage *m* du métabolisme
p reequilibração *f* do metabolismo

4638 **refermentation**
(Biochem.)
(Enology: e.g. a fermentation accident.)
d Wiedervergärung *f*
f refermentation *f*
p refermentação *f*

4639 **refined crystal sugar**
(Prod.)
(Food processing technology: Sugar treatment.)
d Kristallraffinade *f*
f sucre *m* en cristaux raffiné
p açúcar *m* em cristais refinado

4640 **refined ground sugar**
(Prod.)
(Food processing technology: Sugar treatment.)
d gemahlene Raffinade *f*
f sucre *m* raffiné moulu
p açúcar *m* refinado e moído

4641 **refined sugar**
(Prod.)
(Food processing technology.)
d Raffinade *f*; raffinierter Zucker
f sucre *m* raffiné
p açúcar *m* refinado

4642 **refinement**
(Prod.)
(Food processing technology: e.g. of sugar, obtaining white saccharose crystals.)
d Raffination *f*
f raffinage *m*
p refinação *f*

4643 **refining process**
(Prod.)
(Food processing technology: e.g. sugar refining for the yield of white saccharose crystals, having a purity of 99.95%.)
d Veredlungsverfahren *n*
f procédé *m* d'affinage; procédé *m* de raffinage
p processo *m* de refinamento

4644 **reflux condenser**
(Prod.)
(Food processing technology; ref. to distillation process.)
d Rückflussverdichter *m*; Rückflusskondensator *m*
f condenseur *m* de reflux; condenseur *m* à refluement
p condensador *m* de refluxo

4645 **refraction**
(Biochem.)
(Nutritional science; deflection of a light ray under certain conditions; e.g. ref. to processes of analysis.)
d Refraktion *f*; Brechung *f*
f réfraction *f*
p refração *f*

4646 **refractive index; index of refraction**
(Prod.)
(Food processing technology; product specification.)
d Brechungsindex *m*
f indice *m* de réfraction
p índice *m* de refração

4647 **refrigeration of the must; cooling of the must**
(Prod.)
(Food processing technology; food preservation.)
d Kühlung *f* des Mostes; Abkühlung *f* des Mostes
f réfrigération *f* du moût
p refrigeração *f* do mosto

4648 **regeneration; renewal; restoration**
(Biochem.)
(Ref. e.g. to treatment of plants, tissues etc.; in biochemical research of nutritional science.)
d Regeneration *f*; Wiederherstellung *f*; Rückgewinnung *f*
f régénération *f*; réactivation *f*
p regeneração *f*; recuperação *f*; restauração *f*; reativação *f*

* **regimen → 1636**

4649 **regional enteritis**
(Med.)
(Crohn's disease; enteritis regionalis; Morbus Crohn; inflammation and ulceration of the ileum. Consequence: malabsorption of nutrients.)
d regionäre Enteritis *f*; regionäre Dünndarmentzündung *f*
f entérite *f* régionale
p enterite *f* regional

4650 **regional wine**
(Agr.)
(Viticulture. Wine types produced and consumed locally in the region of origin.)
d regionaler Wein *m*
f vin *m* de pays
p vinho *m* regional

4651 **regulation of renal excretion of calcium and phosphorus**
(Med.)
(Veterinary; e.g. ref. to the physiological importance of vitamin D_3, which regulates the calcium and phosphorus metabolism and intestinal absorption of these elements.)
d Regulierung *f* der Calcium- und Phosphorausscheidung über die Niere
f régulation *f* de l'excrétion rénale de calcium et phosphore
p regulação *f* da excreção renal de cálcio e fósforo

4652 **reindeer**
(Agr.)
(Livestock; "Rangifer tarandus"; beast of burden in the northern parts of the world; also a milk producer.)
d Ren *n*; Rentier *n*
f renne *m*
p rena *f*; rangífer *m*

4653 **reinforce** *v* **vinosity; strengthen** *v* **vinosity**
(Biochem.)
(Enology: wine fermentation in nutritional science.)
d Weingehalt verstärken

f renforcer la vinosité
p reforçar a vinosida

4654 **relation between stimulus and response**
(Biochem.)
(Food biochemistry; olfactory stimulation: aroma/flavour research and production.)
d Verhältnis *n* zwischen Anregung und Reaktion
f relation *f* entre le stimulus et la réponse
p relação *f* entre o estímulo e a resposta

4655 **relation between sugar and acidity**
(Agr.)
(Viticulture: vine maturity indication.)
d Zucker-Säure-Verhältnis *n*; Verhältnis *n* zwischen Zucker- und Säuregehalt
f rapport *m* sucre sur acidité
p relação *f* entre açúcar e acidez

4656 **relation odour/taste**
(Prod.)
(Aroma/fragrance research and production.)
d Verhältnis *n* Geruch/Geschmack
f rapport *m* odeur/saveur
p relação *f* odor/paladar

4657 **relative density**
(Prod.)
(Food processing technology; product specification.)
d relative Dichte *f*
f densité *f* relative
p densidade *f* relativa

* **release** *v* **the flavour progressively → 3183**

4658 **remelting**
(Prod.)
(Food processing technology: e.g. sugar treatment.)
d Wiedereinschmelzung *f*
f refonte *f*
p refusão *f*

4659 **removal of sludge; sludgy sediment removal**
(Prod.)
(Food processing technology. Fruit treatment processes.)
d Entschlämmung *f*
f débourbage *m*
p remoção *f* da lama de sedimentação; remoção *f* do lodo de sedimentação

4660 **renal calculus**
(Med.)
(Stones in the kidney: e.g. in form of mineral salt concretions; formation can be inhibited by alimentary regimen.)
d Nierenstein *m*
f calcul *m* rénal
p cálculo *m* renal

4661 **renal calyx**
(Med.)
(Anatomy; division type of the kidney.)
d Nierenkelch *m*
f calice *m* du rein
p cálice *m* renal

4662 **renewable energetic resources**
(Agr.)
(Soil.)
d erneuerungsfähige Energiequellen *fpl*
f ressources *fpl* énergétiques renouvelables
p recursos *m* energéticos renováveis

* **renewal → 4648**

4663 **renewal of the groundwater level**
(Prod.)
(Water supply; renewal by precipitations.)
d Erneuerung *f* des Grundwasserspiegels
f renouvellement *m* de la nappe d'eau souterraine
p renovação *f* do lençol de água subterrânea

4664 **rennet**
(Prod.)
(Dairy. Milk curdling ferment.)
d Lab *n*
f présure *f*
p coalho *m*; coalheira *f*; coagulador *m*

4665 **rennin**
(Prod.)
(Dairy. Milk coagulating enzyme (diastase) used in cheese production.)
d Rennin *n*; Labferment *n*; Chymosin *n*
f labferment *m*
p renina *f*; quimosina *f*

4666 **reoxidation**
(Biochem.)
(Nutritional science.)
d Reoxidation *f*; Wiederoxidieren *n*
f réoxydation *f*
p reoxidação *f*

* **repair** *v* **soil deficiencies → 1372**

4667 **repeated contamination**
(Prod.)
(Drinking water; ref. e.g. to drinking water (tap water) production.)
d Neuinfektion *f*; wiederholte Kontamination *f*
f contamination *f* répétée
p contaminação *f* repetida

4668 **repeating structures in the fibrous proteins**
(Biochem.)
(Protein food biochemistry: ref. to protein structure.)
d wiederholte Strukturen *fpl* in den fibrillären Proteinen
f structures *fpl* répétitives dans les protéines fibreuses
p estruturas *fpl* repetitivas nas proteínas fibrilosas

* **replenishment → 2168**

4669 **repletion**
(Med.)
(Feeling of the satisfied stomach, which depends on the individual satisfaction properties of the foodstuff.)
d Völlegefühl *n*; Magenüberfüllung *f*
f réplétion *f*
p saciedade *f*; repleção *f*

4670 **reproductive system**
(Med.)
(Veterinary; ref. to animal anatomy.)
d Fortpflanzungssystem *n*
f système *m* de reproduction
p sistema *m* de reprodução

* **required vaccination → 3840**

4671 **requirement of the suckling**
(Med.)
(Baby nutrition.)
d Bedarf *m* des Säuglings
f besoin *m* de nourrisson
p necessidade *f* do lactente

4672 **requirements**
(Med.)
(Quantitative nutrient requirements.)
d Bedürfnisse *npl*
f besoins *mpl*
p necessidades *fpl*

4673 **requiring trace elements**
(Med.)
(Veterinary; vital for animal development: e.g. iron, copper, manganese, iodine, zinc, cobalt, molybdenum, fluorine, selenium (selenium deficiency e.g. causes "white muscle disease").)
d spurenelementbedürftig
f pauvre en oligo-éléments
p carente de microelementos

4674 **research of chords**
(Prod.)
(Aroma/fragrance research and production; metaphor ref. to aroma composition.)
d Erforschung *f* von Akkorden
f recherche *f* d'accords
p pesquisa *f* de acordes

4675 **research of prime material**
(Prod.)
(Aroma/fragrance research and production.)
d Erforschung *f* der Grundstoffe
f recherche *f* des matières premières
p pesquisa *f* das matérias primas

4676 **resecretion of the vitamin**
(Med.)
(Veterinary; e.g. ref. to vitamin transport in the animal body.)
d Resekretion *f* des Vitamins; Wiederabsonderung *f* des Vitamins
f resécrétion *f* de la vitamine
p ressecreção *f* da vitamina

4677 **reserves of soil minerals; mineral reserves of the soil**
(Agr.)
(Soil; soil characteristics and quality.)
d Bodenmineralienbestand *m*; Reserven *fpl* von Bodenmineralien
f réserves *fpl* minérales du sol
p reservas *fpl* minerais do solo

4678 **residual permanence of the pesticide**
(Agr.)
(Problem in biological agriculture.)
d Rückstand *m* des Schädlingsbekämpfungsmittels
f rémanence *f* du pesticide
p permanência *f* residual da pesticida

4679 **residual solvent**
(Prod.)
(Aroma/flavour research and production: in extraction processes.)
d Rückstandslösungsmittel *n*; Lösungsmittel *n* als Rückstand vorhanden
f solvant *m* résiduel
p solvente *m* residual

4680 **residual sugar in the grape marc; contents of residual sugar in the grape marc**
(Biochem.)
(Enology: wine fermentation.)
d restlicher Zuckerbestand *m* im Rückstand der Weintraube; Zuckerrückstand *m* im Weintraubensatz
f sucre *m* résiduel dans le marc de raisin; teneur *m* de sucre résiduel dans le marc de raisin
p açúcar *m* residual no bagaço de uva; teor *m* de açúcar residual no bagaço de uva

4681 **residue**
(Prod.)
(Food processing technology.)
d Rückstand *m*; Rest *m*; Abfall *m*
f résidu *m*
p resíduo *m*

4682 **resistance of the plant**
(Agr.)
(Biological agriculture: against insects etc.)
d Widerstand *f* der Pflanze
f résistance *f* de la plante
p resistência *f* da planta

4683 **resistance to ethanol**
(Biochem.)
(Nutritional science; selected yeast strains in fermentation; e.g. wine production.)
d Äthanolwiderstandsfähigkeit *f*; Ethanolwiderstandsfähigkeit *f*
f résistance *f* à l'éthanol
p resistência *f* ao etanol

4684 **resistance to pesticides**
(Agr.)
(In agriculture, horticulture etc.)
d Widerstand *m* gegen Schädlingsbekämpfungsmittel
f résistance *f* aux pesticides
p resistência *f* aos pesticidas

* **resistant against drought → 4685**

4685 **resistant against dryness; resistant against drought**
(Agr.)
(Plant characteristic.)
d widerstandsfähig gegen die Trockenheit; widerstandsfähig gegen die Dürre
f résistant à la sécheresse
p resistente à seca

* **restoration → 4648**

4686 **restrictive regimen**
(Med.)
(Systematic diet plan, e.g. a hypoglycemic regimen.)
d Einschränkungsdiät *f*; restriktiver Diätplan *m*
f régime *m* restrictif
p regime *m* restritivo

4687 **restructured meat products**
(Prod.)
(Food processing technology.)
d restrukturierte Fleischprodukte *npl*
f produits *mpl* de la viande restructurés
p produtos *mpl* de carne reestruturados

4688 **resumption of fermentation; recommencement of fermentation**
(Biochem.)
(Nutritional science; fermentation process.)
d Wiederaufnahme *f* der Gärung
f reprise *f* de la fermentation
p recomeço *m* da fermentação

4689 **retailer**
(Prod.)
(Food processing technology and marketing.)
d Kleinhändler *m*
f détaillant *m*
p varejista *m*

4690 **retain *v* the amorphous form**
(Biochem.)
(Food biochemistry. Physical product presentation.)
d die amorphe Form bewahren
f maintenir la forme amorphe
p manter a forma amorfa

4691 **retarded boiling**
(Prod.)
(Food processing technology.)
d Siedeverzug *m*
f ébullition *f* retardée
p retardação *f* de ebulição; retardamento *m* da ferrura

4692 **retention force**
(Prod.)
(Aroma/flavour particle characteristic and substrate retention: flavour research.)
d Zurückhaltevermögen *n*; Einbehaltungskraft *f*
f pouvoir *m* de rétention
p força *f* de retenção

4693 **retention period in blood**
(Med.)
(Veterinary; ref. to active principles, e.g. vitamins.)
d Verbleibsdauer *f* im Blut
f période *f* de rétention dans le sang
p período *m* de retenção no sangue

4694 **rheology**
(Prod.)
(Science which deals with the deformation and flow of matter; in food processing technology refers to elasticity and viscosity e.g. of fats etc.)
d Rheologie *f*; Fließkunde *f*
f rhéologie *f*
p reologia *f*

4695 **rheumatism diet**
(Med.)
(Alimentary regimen: non-acidifying food intake.)

d Rheumadiät *f*
f diète *f* rhumatique
p dieta *f* de reumatismo

4696 **rhizome**
(Agr.)
(Botany; underground root, e.g. rootstock.)
d Rhizom *n*; Wurzelstock *m*
f rhizome *m*
p rizoma *m*

4697 **rhodopsin**
(Med.)
(Photosensitive retina pigment: Vitamin A is a part of this pigment and thus important for the process of vision.)
d Rhodopsin *n*
f rhodopsine *f*
p rodopsina *f*

4698 **rhubarb**
(Agr.)
(Horticulture. Genus "Rheum"; vegetable plant of the buckwheat family with edible leafstalks and poisonous leaves.)
d Rhabarber *m*
f rhubarbe *f*
p ruibarbo *m*

4699 **rhythms of nature**
(Agr.)
(Biological agriculture.)
d Naturrythmen *mpl*
f rythmes *mpl* de la nature
p ritmos *mpl* da natureza

4700 **rhythms of the seasons**
(Agr.)
(Biological agriculture.)
d Jahreszeitenrythmen *mpl*
f rythmes *mpl* des saisons
p ritmos *mpl* das estações do ano

4701 **rib**
(Med.)
(Veterinary; ref. to cattle anatomy.)
d Rippe *f*
f côte *f*
p costela *f*

* **rib → 3719**

4702 **rib of beef**
(Prod.)
(Gastronomy; meat piece.)
d Rippenstück *f*
f entrecôte *f*
p entrecosto *m*

* **riboflavin → 5746**

4703 **riboflavin as drinking powder colorant**
(Prod.)
($C_{17}H_{20}N_4O_6$. Vitamins in nutrition; application of vitamin B_2 in food production. Foodstuff colorants.)
d Riboflavin *n* als Farbstoff für Trinkpulver
f riboflavine *f* comme colorant de poudres à boire
p riboflavina *f* como corante para pós de bebida

4704 **ribose**
(Biochem.)
($C_5H_{10}O_5$; monosaccharide of the ribonucleic acid within the cellular plasma.)
d Ribose *f*
f ribose *m*
p ribose *f*

4705 **ribosomes**
(Med.)
(Site of protein synthesis within the cell.)
d Ribosome *npl*
f ribosomes *mpl*
p ribossomos *mpl*

4706 **rice**
(Agr.)
(Agricultural produce. "Oryza sativa"; cereal grass.)
d Reis *m*
f riz *m*
p arroz *m*

4707 **rice alcohol**
(Agr.)
(Agricultural produce, subproduct.)
d Reisalkohol *m*
f alcool *m* de riz
p álcool *m* do arroz

4708 **rice blanching**
(Prod.)
(Food processing technology.)
d Blanchieren *n* des Reises
f blanchiment *m* du riz
p branqueamento *m* do arroz por escaldadura

4709 **rice bran**
(Agr.)
(Livestock nutrition; feedstuff ingredient.)
d Reisschrot *m*
f riz *m* égrugé
p farelo *m* de arroz

4710 **rice pudding**
(Prod.)
(Gastronomy.)
d Milchreis *m*
f riz *m* au lait
p arroz *m* doce

4711 **rice wine vinegar**
(Prod.)
(Food condiment, food preservative; obtained by alcoholic fermentation.)
d Reisweinessig *m*
f vinaigre *m* de vin de riz
p vinagre *m* de vinho de arroz; vinagre *m* de aroz

4712 **rich in starch**
(Agr.)
(Agricultural produce, subproduct. Starch compound extracted from potatoes which contain between 12-20%.)
d reich an Stärke
f riche en fécule
p rico em amido

4713 **richness of lipids in fatty acids**
(Biochem.)
(Food biochemistry, research and production.)
d Reichhaltigkeit *f* der Fettstoffe an Fettsäuren; Reichhaltigkeit *f* der Lipide an Fettsäuren
f richesse *f* des lipides en acides gras
p riqueza *f* dos lipidios em ácidos graxos

4714 **richness of minerals**
(Agr.)
(Biological agriculture; ref. to certain vegetables, greens etc.)
d Mineralienreichtum *m*
f richesse *f* minérale; richesse *f* minéralogique
p riqueza *f* de minerais

4715 **ricinoleic acid**
(Prod.)
($C_{18}H_{34}O_3$; e.g. in fatty acid synthesis: prime material for aroma/fragrance production.)
d Rizinusölsäure *f*; Ricinolsäure *f*
f acide *m* ricinoléique
p ácido *m* ricinoléico

4716 **rickets**
(Med.)
(Children's bone disease due to vitamin D deficiency disease.)
d Rachitis *f*; englische Krankheit *f*
f rachitisme *m*; maladie *f* anglaise
p raquitismo *m*

4717 **riding horse; saddle horse; race horse**
(Agr.)
(Livestock.)
d Reitpferd *n*; Rennpferd *n*
f cheval *m* de selle; cheval *m* de course; coureur *m*
p cavalo *m* de montaria; cavalo *m* de corridas

4718 **ring cake**
(Prod.)
(Confectionary.)
d Topfkuchen *m*; Puffer *m*; Gugelhupf *m*; Napfkuchen *m*
f kouglof *m*
p bolo *m* de forma

4719 **ripe bunches of grapes**
(Agr.)
(Viticulture; fruit selection.)
d reife Trauben *fpl*
f raisins *mpl* mûrs; grappes *fpl* de raisin mûres
p cachos *mpl* maduros

4720 **ripeness; maturity**
(Agr.)
(Horticulture; ref. to fruit/plant development.)
d Reife *f*
f maturité *f*
p madureza *f*

4721 **ripening of ice cream mix**
(Prod.)
(Food processing technology. The mix is ripened in insulated tanks under cooling with chilled water. Addition of colours, flavours etc.)
d Reifung *f* der Speiseeismischung *f*
f maturation *f* du mélange de crème glacée
p amadurecimento *m* da mistura de sorvete

* **ripening of meat → 3410**

4722 **ripening phase**
(Prod.)
(Dairy process of cheese production.)
d Phase *f* der Reifung; Reifungsphase *f*
f phase *f* de maturation
p fase *f* de maturação

4723 **river water**
(Prod.)
(Water supply; drinking water (tap water) source.)
d Flusswasser *n*
f eau *f* de rivière; eau *f* fluviale
p água *f* de rio; água *f* fluvial

4724 **roast**
(Prod.)
(Gastronomy.)
d Braten *m*
f rôti *m*
p assado *m*

4725 **roast** *v*
(Prod.)
(Food processing technology; e.g. coffee treatment.)
d rösten
f torréfier
p torrar

4726 **roast beef**
(Prod.)
(Butchery; beef for roasting.)
d Rinderbraten *m*; Rindsbraten *m*; Roastbeef *n*
f rosbif *m*
p rosbife *m*

4727 **roast chicken; roaster; broiler**
(Prod.)
(Gastronomy.)
d gebratenes Hähnchen *n*; gebratenes Hühnchen *n*; Brathuhn *n*
f poulet *m* rôti; poulet *m* à rôtir
p frango *m* assado

4728 **roast duck**
(Prod.)
(Gastronomy.)
d Entenbraten *m*
f canard *m* rôti
p pato *m* assado

4729 **roasted products**
(Prod.)
(Food processing technology: e.g. almonds, malt, peanuts.)
d Röstprodukte *npl*
f produits *mpl* torréfiés
p produtos *mpl* torrados

* **roaster → 4727**

4730 **roast hare**
(Prod.)
(Dish, hare meat.)
d Hasenbraten *m*
f rôti *m* de lièvre
p lebre *f* assada

4731 **roasting of cacao beans**
(Prod.)
(Food processing technology.)
d Kakaobohnenröstung *f*
f torréfaction *f* d'amandes de cacao
p torrefação *f* da semente do cacau

4732 **roasting of cereal products**
(Prod.)
(Food processing technology.)
d Rösten *n* von Getreideprodukten
f grillage *m* de produits céréaliers
p torração *f* de produtos cereais; torrefação *f* de produtos cereais

4733 **robust vine sort**
(Agr.)
(Viticulture; ref. to the biologic constitution of the plant.)
d robuste Rebsorte *f*
f cépage *m* rustique
p espécie *f* rústica de cepa

4734 **rock**
(Agr.)
(Soil; large stone mass; also the solid part of the earth's crust.)
d Gestein *n*
f roche *f*
p rocha *f*

4735 **rock salt**
(Prod.)
(Common solid mineral salt; occurring e.g. in salt mines; prime material.)
d Steinsalz *n*
f sel *m* gemme
p sal *m* gema

4736 **rodent**
(Agr.)
(Culture destroying animal, esp. in biological agriculture.)
d Nagetier *n*
f rongeur *m*
p roedor *m*

4737 **rod-shaped bacteria; bacilli**
(Med.)
(Usually in form of spores in the soil and air.)
d Stäbchenbakterien *fpl*; Bacilli *mpl*
f bactérie *f* en forme de bâtonnet; bacilles *mpl*
p bactérias *fpl* em forma de bastonete; bacilos *mpl*

4738 **roe**
(Agr.)
(Edible fish eggs.)
d Rogen *m*
f rogue *f*, œufs *mpl* de poisson
p ovas *fpl* de peixe

4739 **roebuck**
(Agr.)
(Game.)
d Rehbock *m*
f brocard *m*; jeune chevreuil *m* mâle
p corço *m*

4740 **roe deer**
(Agr.)
(Game.)
d Rehwild *n*
f chevreuil *m*
p veado *m* de pequeno porte

4741 **roll**
(Prod.)
(Bakery; bread type.)
d Brötchen *n*; Rundstück *n*; Semmel *m*; Wecken *n*

f petit pain *m*
p pãozinho *m*

4742 rolled oats
(Prod.)
(Food processing technology.)
d Haferflocken *fpl*
f flocons *mpl* d'avoine
p flocos *mpl* de aveia

4743 roll *v* out
(Prod.)
(Bakery; ref. to the treatment of dough.)
d ausrollen
f abaisser
p abrir a massa com rolo; estender a massa com rolo

4744 Roman chamomile
(Agr.)
(Botany; "Anthemis nobilis". Used as bitter flavouring agent in drinks.)
d römische Kamille *f*
f camomille *f* romaine
p camomila *f* Romana

4745 root hairs
(Agr.)
(Botany.)
d Wurzelhaare *npl*
f poils *mpl* de la racine
p pêlos *mpl* radicais

4746 roothold
(Agr.)
(Botany; plant fixation to the soil through root spreading.)
d Verwurzelung *f*
f enracinement *m*
p enraizamento *m*

4747 root of the tooth
(Med.)
(Anatomy; tooth-body part.)
d Zahnwurzel *f*
f racine *f* de dent
p raiz *f* do dente

4748 rosé
(Biochem.)
(Enology: technology of wine production, ref. to a pink wine type, made from red grapes by removal of the grape skin at the beginning of the fermentation process.)
d Roseewein *m*; Roséwein *m*
f vin *m* rosé
p vinho *m* rosé

4749 rose hip
(Agr.)
(Botany.)
d Hagebutte *f*
f fruit *m* de l'églantier
p pseudofruto *m* da roseira brava

4750 rosemary
(Agr.)
(Botany; "Rosmarinus officinalis"; used for flavouring and seasoning purposes. Also medicinal plant.)
d Rosmarin *m*
f romarin *m*
p alecrim *m*

4751 rotatory power
(Biochem.)
(Nutritional science; ref. to polarization in biochemistry.)
d Rotationskraft *f*; Drehvermögen *n*
f pouvoir *m* rotatoire
p poder *m* rotatório

4752 roughage
(Med.)
(Residual dietary fibres; ref. to alimentary regimen, promoting normal evacuation (defecation).)
d Ballaststoffe *mpl*; Schlackenstoffe *mpl*
f matières *fpl* aliments de lest
p matérias *fpl* alimentícias fibrosas; fibras *fpl*

4753 roughage of vegetable fibres
(Med.)
(For promotion of normal evacuation (defecation).)
d Nahrungsmittelballaststoffe *mpl* aus Pflanzenfasern
f fibres *fpl* alimentaires végétaux de lest
p fibras *mpl* alimentícias végetais

4754 roughage-rich diet
(Med.)
(Ref. to alimentary regimen, promoting normal evacuation (defecation).)
d ballaststoffreiche Diät *f*
f diète *f* riche en lest
p dieta *f* rica em fibras

4755 roughage supply
(Med.)
(For promotion of normal evacuation (defecation).)
d Ballaststoffzufuhr *f*
f apport *m* en fibres alimentaires
p aporte *m* de fibras

4756 roulade
(Prod.)
(Gastronomy: stuffed meat roll.)
d Roulade *f*

f roulade *f*; paupiette *f*
p rolinho *m* de carne

4757 **roulades of calf-meat**
(Prod.)
(Gastronomy.)
d Kalbfleischrouladen *fpl*
f paupiettes *fpl* de veau
p rolinhos *mpl* de carne de vitela

4758 **round *v* off an aroma**
(Prod.)
(Aroma/fragrance research and production; ref. to aroma note characteristics.)
d Aroma abrunden
f arrondir un arôme
p arredondar o aroma; dar o último toque ao aroma

4759 **round timber**
(Agr.)
(Agricultural produce, subproduct; log.)
d Rundholz *n*
f bois *m* rond
p madeira *f* em toras

4760 **roux**
(Prod.)
(Gastronomy; flour cooked in butter etc. (e.g. with olives and prepared in Dendê-oil (a palm oil); Brazilian gastronomic specialty.)
d Mehlschwitze *f*
f roux *m*
p farofa *f*

4761 **rue**
(Agr.)
(Botany."Ruta graveolens"; medicinal herb with leaves of bitter taste.)
d Raute *f*
f rue *f*
p arruda *f*

4762 **rum**
(Prod.)
(Alcoholic beverage made e.g. from cane sugar molasses.)
d Rum *m*
f rhum *m*
p rum *m*

4763 **rumen**
(Med.)
(Veterinary; ruminant's first stomach compartment for cellulose digestion.)
d Pansen *m*
f rumen *m*; panse *f*
p rúmen *m*

4764 **ruminant**
(Agr.)
(Livestock. Cud chewing animal, having a stomach with four chambers: the rumen; reticulum; omasum; abomasum.)
d Wiederkäuer *m*
f ruminant *m*
p ruminante *m*

* **rump → 4765**

4765 **rump steak; rump**
(Prod.)
(Butchery.)
d Rumpsteak *n*
f romsteck *m*; romsteak *m*
p alcatra *f*

4766 **runner bean**
(Agr.)
(Horticulture; "Phaseolus coccineus"; scarlet runner bean.)
d Stangenbohne *f*
f haricot *m* à rames; haricot *m* grimpant
p fava *f* de estaca

* **run of fermentation → 1384**

4767 **rusk**
(Prod.)
(Bakery; dry and crisp bread product and sliced form.)
d Zwieback *m*
f biscotte *f*; pain *m* braisé
p torrada *f*

4768 **Russia leather**
(Agr.)
(Agricultural produce, subproduct.)
d Juchtenleder *n*
f cuir *m* de Russie
p couro *m* da Rússia; moscóvia *f*

4769 **rusticity**
(Prod.)
(Gastronomy: wine character, wine quality.)
d Rustikalität *f*; rustikaler Typ *m*
f rusticité *f*
p rusticidade *f*; rustiquez *f*

4770 **rust of the leaves**
(Agr.)
(Botany; rust: plant disease caused by fungi; also denomination of the fungus.)
d Rost *m* der Blätter
f rouille *f* des feuilles
p ferrugem *f* das folhas

* **rutabaga → 5372**

4771 **rye**
(Agr.)
(Agricultural produce. "Secale cereale"; the grain is widely used in bread production, beverages (whiskey).)
d Roggen *m*
f seigle *m*
p centeio *m*

4772 **rye bread**
(Prod.)
(Bakery; rye flour bread.)
d Roggenbrot *n*
f pain *m* de seigle
p pão *m* de centeio

4773 **rye-bread roll**
(Prod.)
(Bakery; bread type.)
d Roggenbrötchen *n*
f petit pain *m* en seigle
p pãozinho *m* de centeio

4774 **rye bread with caraway seeds**
(Prod.)
(Bakery; rye flour bread with caraway seeds.)
d Graubrot *n* mit Kümmel
f pain *m* bis au cumin
p pão *m* de centeio com cominho

S

4775 **saccharase; invertase**
(Biochem.)
(Nutritional science; enzyme which promotes the hydrolyzation of saccharose into glucose and fructose.)
d Saccharase *f*; Glykosidhydrolase *f*
f saccharase *f*
p sacarase *f*

4776 **saccharic acid**
(Prod.)
($C_6H_{10}O_8$; glucose derivative; prime material.)
d Rohrzuckersäure *f*
f acide *m* saccharique
p ácido *m* sacárico

4777 **saccharification**
(Prod.)
(Food processing technology; beer brewery process phase: transformation of malt starch into maltose during wort boiling.)
d Saccharifikation *f*
f saccharification *f*
p sacarificação *f*

4778 **saccharin**
(Prod.)
($C_7H_5O_3NS$; food processing technology: non-caloric sweetening synthetic agent.)
d Saccharin *n*
f saccharine *f*
p sacarina *f*

4779 **saccharin sodium; saccharin soluble**
(Prod.)
($C_7H_4NNaO_3S.2H_2O$; non-caloric sweetening agent.)
d Saccharinnatrium *n*
f saccharine *f* sodique; saccharine *f* soluble
p sacarina *f* sódica

* **saccharin soluble → 4779**

4780 **saccharolytic** *adj*
(Biochem.)
(Nutritional science; ref. to decomposition of sugar.)
d zuckerspaltend
f saccharolytique
p sacarolítico

4781 **saccharose**
(Prod.)
($C_{12}H_{22}O_{11}$; Food processing technology; sucrose. Cane sugar, beet sugar: extraction and refining, obtaining table sugar.)
d Saccharose *f*; Rohrzucker *m*
f saccharose *f*
p sacarose *f*

4782 **saccharose crystalline**
(Prod.)
($C_{12}H_{22}O_{11}$; food processing technology; presentation form of saccharose (sucrose).)
d kristalline Saccharose *f*
f saccharose *m* cristallin
p sacarose *f* cristalina

4783 **saccharose excess**
(Prod.)
(Food processing technology; milk ingredient in excess in industrial milk types; ref. to baby nutrition.)
d Saccharoseüberschuss *m*
f excès *m* de saccharose
p excesso *m* de sacarose

* **saddle → 322**

* **saddle horse → 4717**

4784 **saffron; crocus**
(Agr.)
(Botany; "Crocus sativus L."; flavouring agent; foot dye; Natural Yellow 6; C.I. No. 75.100.)
d Safran *m*
f safran *m*
p açafrão *m*; urucu *m*

4785 **sage**
(Agr.)
(Botany; "Salvia officinalis"; aromatic mint, e.g. used in meat flavouring.)
d Salbei *f*
f sauge *f*
p salva *f*; salveta *f*

4786 **sago**
(Prod.)
(Food processing technology: starch prepared from the sago palm pit.)
d Sago *m*
f sagou *m*
p sagu *m*

4787 **salad**
(Agr.)
(Green vegetables, e.g. lettuce.)
d Salat *m*
f salade *f*
p salada *f*

4788 salad dressing
(Prod.)
(Type of dressing in form of a sauce; gastronomy.)
d Salatsoße *f*; Salattunke *f*
f sauce *f* à salade
p molho *m* de salada; tempero *m* de salada

4789 salad oil
(Prod.)
(Food processing technology.)
d Salatöl *n*; Tafelöl *n*
f huile *f* de table
p óleo *m* para salada

4790 sales period of agricultural products
(Agr.)
(Agricultural produce marketing.)
d Verkaufssaison *f* der Agrarprodukte
f saison *f* de vente de produits agro-alimentaires
p época *f* do ano de venda de produtos agro-pastorís

4791 sales period of fattened cattle
(Agr.)
(Marketing of livestock.)
d Verkaufssaison *f* des gemästeten Viehes
f saison *f* de vente de bétail à l'engrais
p época *f* do ano de vendas de gado gordo

4792 salicylaldehyde; salicylic aldehyde
(Prod.)
($C_7H_6O_2$; source of fragrance/aroma prime material.)
d Salicylaldehyd *n*; 2-Hydroxybenzaldehyd *n*
f salicylaldéhyde *m*; aldéhyde *m* salicylique; salicylal *m*
p salicilaldeído *m*; aldeído *m* salicílico; salicilal *m*

4793 salicylic acid
(Prod.)
($C_7H_6O_3$; food product preservative in some countries.)
d Salicylsäure *f*
f acide *m* salicylique
p ácido *m* salicílico

* **salicylic aldehyde → 4792**

4794 saliferous *adj*
(Prod.)
(Food processing technology: containing salt.)
d salzhaltig
f salifère
p salífero

4795 salinity
(Prod.)
(Food processing technology, concentration of salt in a substance.)
d Salzigkeit *f*
f salinité *f*
p salinidade *f*

4796 salivary amylases
(Med.)
(Saliva enzyme: starch digestion.)
d Speichelamylasen *fpl*
f amylases *fpl* salivaires
p amilíases *fpl* salivares

4797 salivary secretion
(Med.)
(Stimulated by flavour and fragrance emission from foodstuff.)
d Speichelsekretion *f*; Speichelabsonderung *f*
f sécrétion *f* de salive; sécrétion *f* salivaire
p secreção *f* de saliva

4798 salivation; sialorrhoea
(Med.)
(Ptyalism; denoting excessive saliva production.)
d Speichelvermehrung *f*
f salivation *f*; sialorrhée *f*
p salivação *f*; sialorréia *f*

4799 salmon
(Agr.)
("Salmo salar"; edible fish.)
d Lachs *m*
f saumon *m*
p salmão *m*

4800 salmonella
(Med.)
(Bacteria. As to the American bacteriologist Daniel E. Salmon (1850-1914). Food poisoning in foods of animal origin.)
d Salmonelle *f*
f salmonelle *f*
p salmonela *f*

4801 salmonellosis
(Med.)
(Food intoxication by bacteria of the genus "Salmonella", affecting the digestive system.)
d Salmonellose *f*
f salmonellose *f*
p salmonelose *f*; salmonelíase *f*

4802 salmon smoking
(Prod.)
(Food processing technology; fish preparation, fish treatment.)
d Lachsräucherung *f*
f fumaison *f* du saumon
p defumação *f* do salmão

4803 salt; table salt
(Prod.)
(NaCl; common salt for food seasoning.)
d Salz *n*; Tafelsalz *n*; Küchensalz *n*; Kochsalz *n*; Speisesalz *n*
f sel *m*; sel *m* commun; sel *m* de cuisine
p sal *m*; sal *m* de cozinha

4804 salt addition
(Prod.)
(Gastronomy.)
d Salzzusatz *m*
f addition *f* de sel
p adição *f* de sal

4805 salt-catalyzed lipid oxidation in processed meat systems
(Biochem.)
(Nutritional science; ref. to restructured meat in meat processing.)
d salz-katalysierte Lipidoxidation *f* in Systemen verarbeiteter Fleischprodukte
f oxydation *f* lipidique catalysée par le sel dans les systèmes des viandes transformées
p oxidação *f* lipídica catalizada pelo sal nos sistemas de carnes processadas

4806 salt contents
(Prod.)
(Food processing technology; product characteristic.)
d Salzgehalt *m*
f teneur *f* en sel
p teor *m* de sal

4807 salted cheese
(Prod.)
(Dairy product, cheese type.)
d gesalzter Käse *m*
f fromage *m* salé
p queijo *m* salgado

4808 salted crackers
(Prod.)
(Confectionary.)
d gesalzene Kekse *mpl*
f crackers *mpl* salés; biscuits *mpl* salés
p crackers *m* de sal; biscoitos *mpl* de sal; bolachas *fpl* salgadas

4809 salted herring
(Agr.)
("Clupe harengus". Food fish preserved by salting.)
d gesalzener Hering *m*
f hareng *m* salé
p arenque *m* salgado

4810 salt-free diet
(Med.)
(Alimentary regimen without sodium chloride (NaCl), table salt; e.g. treatment of high blood pressure.)
d salzfreie Diät *f*; salzlose Diät *f*
f diète *f* sans sel
p dieta *f* sem sal

4811 salt-free rusk
(Prod.)
(Bakery.)
d salzfreier Zwieback *m*
f biscotte *f* sans sel
p torrada *f* sem sal

4812 salting
(Prod.)
(Food processing technology: foodstuff salting: e.g. in cheese production.)
d Einsalzen *n*
f salage *m*
p salga *f*; salgação *f*; salgadura *f*

* **salting with brine → 4177**

4813 salt meat
(Prod.)
(Food processing technology.)
d Pökelfleisch *n*
f viande *f* salée; salaisons *fpl*
p carne *f* salgada

4814 salt-soluble proteins
(Biochem.)
(Nutritional science; ref. to restructured meat in meat processing.)
d salzlösliche Proteine *npl*
f protéines *fpl* solubles dans le sel
p proteínas *fpl* solúveis em sal

4815 saltwater fish
(Agr.)
(Fishes living in the open sea.)
d Seefisch *m*
f poisson *m* de mer
p peixe *m* de mar

4816 salty *adj*
(Prod.)
(Aroma/flavour note.)
d salzig
f salé
p salgado

4817 salty aroma
(Prod.)
(Aroma/flavour research and production: e.g. onion, garlic.)
d salziges Aroma *n*
f arôme *m* salé
p aroma *m* salgado

4818 salty condiment
(Prod.)
(Gastronomy; ref. to spices, e.g. macerated vegetable preparation in vinegar.)
d salziges Gewürz *n*
f condiment *m* salé
p condimento *m* salgado

4819 salty solution
(Prod.)
(Food processing technology; product characteristic.)
d salzige Lösung *f*; salzhaltige Lösung *f*
f solution *f* saline
p solução *f* salgada

4820 salty taste
(Prod.)
(Flavour note; e.g. ref. to organoleptic food evaluation.)
d salziger Geschmack *m*
f goût *m* salé; saveur *f* salée
p gosto *m* salgado; sabor *m* salgado

4821 sample
(Prod.)
(Food processing technology; substance sample.)
d Muster *n*
f échantillon *m*
p amostra *f*

4822 sampling techniques
(Prod.)
(Food processing technology.)
d Verfahren *npl* der Musterentnahme
f techniques *fpl* de prélèvement
p técnicas *fpl* de amostragem

4823 sandy soil
(Agr.)
(Soil; this soil contains more than 50% of sand in its composition; permeable, dry, light and movable.)
d Sandboden *m*
f sol *m* sablonneux
p solo *m* arenoso

4824 sanitation
(Med.)
(Execution of measures which eliminate diseases, thus providing sanitary conditions. Animal sanitation is important for the reduction of zoonoses.)
d Sanierung *f*
f assainissement *m*
p saneamento *m*

4825 saponification
(Biochem.)
(Nutritional science; decomposition of fats by hydrolysis.)
d Verseifung *f*
f saponification *f*
p saponificação *f*

4826 saponins
(Prod.)
(Nutritional science. Sapogenin glycosides; e.g. constituent of raw sugar; non-toxic by oral intake (e.g. with food), but having a strong hemolytic effect when introduced into the bloodstream.)
d Saponine *npl*
f saponines *fpl*
p saponinas *fpl*

4827 sardine
(Agr.)
("Sardina pilchardus" and other small fishes; canned and preserved in oil.)
d Sardine *f*
f sardine *f*
p sardinha *f*

4828 sardine in oil
(Prod.)
(Food processing technology.)
d Ölsardine *f*
f sardine *f* à l'huile
p sardinha *f* em óleo

4829 satisfaction of protein requirements
(Med.)
(Food processing technology, research and production.)
d Befriedigung *f* des Proteinbedarfs
f satisfaction *f* du besoin en protéines
p satisfação *f* das necessidades protéicas

4830 satisfactory production yield
(Agr.)
(Here: examination of agricultural produce.)
d ausreichendes Produktionsergebnis *n*
f rendement *m* satisfaisant de la production
p rendimento *m* satisfatório da produção

4831 saturated *adj*
(Biochem.)
(Nutritional science; organic compound without double or triple bonds between carbon atoms.)
d gesättigt
f saturé
p saturado

4832 saturated fatty acids
(Biochem.)
(Food biochemistry; foodstuffs with saturated fatty acids have an increased cholesterol level.

There should not be more than 30% in the food, calculated over the total fat supply.)
d gesättigte Fettsäuren *fpl*
f acides *mpl* gras saturés
p ácidos *mpl* graxos saturados

4833 saturated fatty alcohols
(Biochem.)
(Food biochemistry.)
d gesättigte Fettalkohole *mpl*
f alcools *mpl* gras saturés
p álcoois *mpl* graxos saturados

4834 saturated steam
(Prod.)
(Aroma/flavour research and production: distillation processes.)
d Sattdampf *m*; gesättigter Dampf *m*
f vapeur *f* saturée
p vapor *m* saturado

4835 saturated water vapour
(Prod.)
(Food processing technology.)
d gesättigter Wasserdampf *m*
f vapeur *f* d'eau saturée
p vapor *m* de água saturado

4836 saturation
(Prod.)
(Food processing technology; chemistry, e.g. ref. to the hydrogenation process.)
d Sättigung *f*
f saturation *f*
p saturação *f*

4837 saturation vapour
(Prod.)
(Aroma/fragrance research and production.)
d Sättigungsdampf *m*
f vapeur *f* saturante
p vapor *m* de saturação

4838 saturation vapour pressure
(Prod.)
(Aroma/fragrance research and production.)
d Sättigungsdampfdruck *m*
f pression *f* de vapeur saturante
p pressão *f* do vapor de saturação

4839 sauce; dip
(Prod.)
(Gastronomy.)
d Soße *f*; Tunke *f*
f sauce *f*
p molho *m*

4840 sauce preparation
(Prod.)
(Gastronomy.)
d Soßenzubereitung *f*; Zubereitung *f* von Tunken
f préparation *f* des sauces
p preparação *f* de molhos

4841 sauerbraten
(Prod.)
(Gastronomy; e.g. pot-roasted marinated beef cooked in vinegar.)
d Sauerbraten *m*
f viande *f* marinée et cuite au vinaigre
p assado *m* avinagrado

4842 sauerkraut; pickled cabbage
(Prod.)
(Food processing technology; salted and fermented cabbage, German style.)
d Sauerkraut *n*
f choucroute *f*
p chucrute *m*

4843 sausage; sausages
(Prod.)
(Butchery.)
d Wurst *f*; Wurstwaren *fpl*
f saucisse *f*; saucisson *m*
p salsicha *f*; lingüiça *f*

4844 sausage meat
(Prod.)
(Butchery. Sausage manufacturer's raw material.)
d Wurstmasse *f*; Brät *n*
f hachis *m* à saucisse
p carne *f* para lingüiça

* **sausages → 4843**

4845 saute *v*; **sauté** *v*
(Prod.)
(Food processing technology: to fry briefly (with swinging movements) in a pan, e.g. frying briefly again an already fried fish in hot fat.)
d sautieren
f sauter; faire sauter
p sauté

* **sauté** *v* **→ 4845**

4846 saute *v* **potatoes**
(Prod.)
(Food processing technology: brief frying with some swinging movements in hot fat.)
d Kartoffeln sautieren
f faire sauter des pommes de terre
p sauté as batatas

4847 savory; savoury
(Agr.)
(Horticulture; "Satureja hortensis" (summer savory) and "Satoreja montana" (winter savory); aromatic mint.)
d Bohnenkraut *n*
f sarriette *f*
p segurelha *f*; alfavaca-do-campo *f*

* **savoury → 4847**

4848 Savoy cabbage
(Agr.)
(Horticulture.)
d Wirsingkohl *m*
f chou *m* de Milan
p couve *f* lombarda

4849 sawdust liver
(Med.)
(Veterinary; type of hepatic necrosis of the cattle and sheep e.g. due to nutritional deficiencies, as lack of vitamin E and selenium (Se).)
d Sägespänleber *f*
f nécrose *f* hépatique avitaminique
p necrose *f* hepática avitamínica

4850 scabies; mange
(Med.)
(Veterinary; skin infection by "Sarcoptes scabiei".)
d Räude *f*
f gale *f*
p sarna *f*; escabiose *f*; pereba *f*

4851 scald *v*
(Prod.)
(Food processing technology e.g. to subject the food to hot-water treatment, just below the boiling point.)
d brühen; abkochen
f échauder; ébouillanter
p escaldar

4852 scalded sausage
(Prod.)
(Butchery.)
d Brühwürstchen *n*
f petite saucisse *f* à bouillir
p salsicha *f* fervida; salsicha *f* a ferrer

* **scald** *v* **the milk → 714**

4853 scale
(Med.)
(Veterinary science; ref. to fish anatomy.)
d Fischschuppe *f*
f écaille *f* de poisson
p escama *f* de peixe

4854 scale; boiler scale
(Prod.)
(Food processing technology; ref. to water treatment: carbonate sediments formed by boiling water e.g. from calcium and magnesium.)
d Kesselstein *m*
f tartre *m* de la bouilloire; incrustations *fpl* de la bouilloire
p pedra *f* da chaleira; incrustações *fpl* da chaleira

4855 scale of the identification threshold
(Biochem.)
(Nutritional science; aroma/flavour perception: using a scale of comparison.)
d Maßstab *m* der Identifizierungsschwelle
f mesures *fpl* du seuil d'identification
p escala *f* do limiar de identificação

* **scallion → 3158**

4856 scallop; escallop; escalope
(Prod.)
(Gastronomy.)
d Schnitzel *n*
f escalope *f*
p escalope *m*

* **Schwyz breed → 5325**

4857 scion
(Agr.)
(Ref. to grafting process: the shoot (scion) of the desired variety is grafted into the stock.)
d Edelreis *n*
f greffon *m*; greffe *f*
p garfo *m*

* **scleroprotein → 157**

4858 sclerosis
(Med.)
(Tissue hardening after inflammation: e.g. arteriosclerosis, atherosclerosis.)
d Sklerose *f*
f sclérose *f*
p esclerose *f*

4859 scorbutogenic diet
(Med.)
(Alimentary regimen: vitamin C deficiency food intake.)
d Skorbut verursachende Diät *f*
f diète *f* scorbutique
p dieta *f* escorbútica

* **scorch** *v* **→ 4976**

4860 Scotch whisky
(Prod.)
(Alcoholic distilled beverage (40-50% of alcohol) made from fermented grain mash, e.g. barley.)
d schottischer Whisky *m*; Scotch *m*
f whisky *m* écossais
p uísque *m* escocês

* **S.C.P. → 4977**

4861 scrap grinding
(Prod.)
(Food processing technology; pasta plant technology.)
d Mahlen *n* des Rückstandes
f mouture *f* des résidus
p moagem *f* dos resíduos

4862 scumming
(Prod.)
(Dairy plant technology for milk processing: separation of the cream from the milk.)
d Abkremen *n*; Entrahmen *n*
f écrémage *f*
p separação *f* do creme

4863 scumming by centrifugation; centrifugal scumming
(Prod.)
(Food processing technology, separation process.)
d Abkremen *n* der Milch durch Schleudern; Entrahmen *n* der Milch durch Zentrifugierung
f écrémage *f* du lait par centrifugation
p separação *f* do creme do leite por centrifugação; centrifugação *f* do leite para separação do crème

4864 scurvy
(Med.)
(Ref. to vitamin B_1 (thiamin deficiency) disease.)
d Skorbut *m*
f scorbut *m*
p escorbuto *m*

4865 sea
(Agr.)
(Soil; ref. to earth science.)
d See *f*
f mer *f*
p mar *m*

4866 sea bream; chrysophrys
(Agr.)
("Chrysophrys aurata"; also family "Sparidae"; edible fish.)
d Goldmakrele *f*; Dorade *f*; Goldbrasse *f*
f dorade *f*; daurade *f*
p dourada *f*

4867 sea food
(Prod.)
(Gastronomy.)
d Meeresfrüchte *fpl*
f produits *mpl* de la mer
p frutos *mpl* do mar

4868 sealing process of the bottles
(Prod.)
(Food processing technology; ref. to bottles containing beer, wine or juices etc.)
d Abdichtung *f* der Flaschen
f bouchage *m* des bouteilles
p vedação *f* das garrafas

4869 sea perch
(Agr.)
("Centropomus undecimalis (Bloch)"; An edible fish.)
d Seebarsch *m*
f perche *f* de mer; serran *m*
p robalo *m*; robalão *m*

4870 sea salt
(Prod.)
(Sea water evaporated in saltworks produce this type of salt; prime material.)
d Meersalz *n*
f sel *m* marin
p sal *m* marinho

4871 seasonal plant
(Agr.)
(Botany; e.g. the rape plant: source of edible rape oil; canola oil.)
d Saisonpflanze *f*
f plante *f* saisonnière
p planta *f* pendente da estação do ano

* **seasoned timber → 151**

* **seasoning → 1294**

* **seasoning mix → 688**

* **seasoning mix ready for use → 689**

4872 seaweed; kelp
(Agr.)
(Soil treatment. Organic mineral and nitrogen supplying fertilizer.)
d Seetang *m*; Braunalge *f*
f varech *m*; algue *f* brune
p sargaço *m*

4873 sebacic acid; 1,8-octanedicarboxylic acid
(Prod.)
($C_{10}H_{18}O_4$; prime material in aroma production.)

d Sebacinsäure *f*; 1,8-Octandicarbonsäure *f*
f acide *m* sébacique
p ácido *m* sebácico

4874 secondary structure of the protein
(Biochem.)
(Nutritional science; certain sequence of polypeptide chains of amino acids: coiling or pleating of the polypeptides results in secondary structure.)
d Sekundärstruktur *f* des Proteins
f structure *f* secondaire de la protéine
p estrutura *f* segundária da proteína

4875 second dentition
(Med.)
(Anatomy.)
d Zahnwechsel *m*
f seconde dentition *f*
p segunda dentição *f*

4876 second fermentation
(Biochem.)
(Fermentation e.g. in enology.)
d zweite Gärung *f*; zweiter Gärungsgang *m*
f deuxième fermentation *f*; seconde fermentation *f*
p segunda fermentação *f*

4877 sedimentary rocks
(Agr.)
(Soil. Rock formed by rock fragments and minerals etc.)
d Sedimentgesteine *npl*; Schichtgesteine *npl*
f roches *fpl* sédimentaires
p rochas *fpl* sedimentares

4878 sedimentary soil
(Agr.)
(Soil, formed from sediments.)
d sedimentärer Boden *m*
f sol *m* sédimentaire
p solo *m* sedimentar

4879 sedimentation; settling
(Prod.)
(Food processing technology.)
d Sedimentation *f*; Niederschlag *m*
f sédimentation *f*
p sedimentação *f*

4880 sedimentation deposit; settling deposit
(Prod.)
(Food processing technology.)
d Sedimentationsabsatz *m*
f dépôt *m* sédimentaire; dépôt *m* de sédimentation
p depósito *m* de sedimentação

4881 sedimentation rate
(Prod.)
(Food processing technology.)
d Sedimentationsgeschwindigkeit *f*; Niederschlagsgeschwindigkeit *f*
f vitesse *f* de sédimentation
p tempo *m* de sedimentação; velocidade *f* de sedimentação

4882 seed
(Agr.)
(Botany; grains for sowing.)
d Samen *m*; Saatgut *n*
f semence *f*
p semente *m*

4883 seedbed preparation
(Agr.)
(Horticulture; work in the fields.)
d Saatbettbereitung *f*
f préparation *f* du sol pour l'ensemencement; préparation *f* du champ pour l'ensemencement
p preparação *f* do solo para a semeadura; preparação *f* do solo para a semeação

4884 seeding time
(Agr.)
(Climatology; agricultural activity.)
d Aussaatzeit *f*; Zeit *f* der Aussaat
f période *f* d'ensemencement
p tempo *m* da semeação; tempo *m* da semeadura

* **seed leaf → 1378**

4885 seedling; seedling plant
(Agr.)
(Botany. Young plant originated from seed.)
d Sämling *m*; Trieb *m*; Schössling *m*
f pousse *f*
p broto *m*

4886 seedling box
(Agr.)
(Horticulture; ref. to planting techniques: seed preparation for posterior planting in arable land.)
d Aussaatkasten *m*; Setzkasten *m*
f boîte *f* partoir de semis
p caixa *f* de sementeira

* **seedling plant → 4885**

* **seed lobe → 1378**

* **select *v* → 1446**

4887 selected bacteria mixture
(Prod.)
(Dairy plant technology: Starter for injection into milk and cream to increase acidity.)
d Mischung *f* ausgesuchter Bakterien

f mélange *m* sélectif de bactéries
p mistura *f* de bactérias selecionadas

4888 **selected lactic ferments**
(Biochem.)
(Food biochemistry; in dairy production processes.)
d ausgewählte Milchsäurefermente *npl*
f ferments *mpl* lactiques sélectionnés
p fermentos *mpl* láticos selecionados

4889 **selected yeast**
(Biochem.)
(Fermentation in nutritional science.)
d ausgewählte Hefesorten *f*
f levure *f* sélectionnée
p lêvedo *m* selecionado; levedura *f* selecionada

4890 **selection**
(Med.)
(Veterinary; e.g. ref. to cattle raising, cattle type selection, for obtaining specific productivities, as e.g. milk production, meat production of the animals.)
d Selektion *f*; Auswahl *f*
f sélection *f*
p seleção *f*

4891 **selection of agricultural prime material**
(Agr.)
(Agricultural produce; e.g. for processing, treatment purposes.)
d Auswahl *f* landwirtschaftlicher Rohprodukte; Selektion *f* von Agrarrohprodukten
f sélection *f* de matières premières agricoles
p seleção *f* de matérias primas agrícolas

4892 **selection of varieties**
(Biochem.)
(Food biochemistry; plant, vegetable, fruit etc. varieties for human consumption.)
d Varietätenauswahl *f*; Auswahl *f* von Abarten
f sélection *f* des variétés
p seleção *f* das variedades

* **selection of vine sorts → 1109**

4893 **selective adsorption of polyphenols**
(Prod.)
(Food processing technology; beer brewing process.)
d selektive Adsorption *f* von Polyphenolen
f adsorption *f* sélective des polyphénols
p adsorção *f* seletiva de polifenóis

4894 **selective degradation**
(Biochem.)
(Nutritional science; food biochemistry.)
d selektiver Abbau *m*
f dégradation *f* sélective
p degradação *f* seletiva

4895 **selective effect**
(Biochem.)
(Nutritional science; ref. to auxiliaries, bacteria etc. in processes.)
d selektive Wirkung *f*; auswählende Wirkung *f*
f effet *m* sélectif
p efeito *m* seletivo

4896 **selective fermentation**
(Biochem.)
(Nutritional science.)
d selektive Fermentation *f*
f fermentation *f* sélective
p fermentação *f* seletiva

4897 **selective modification**
(Prod.)
(Food processing technology.)
d selektive Modifikation *f*; auswählende Abänderung *f*
f modification *f* sélective
p modificação *f* seletiva

4898 **selective permeability**
(Biochem.)
(Nutritional science; ref. to olfactory stimulation, nervous cells system: aroma/flavour research: ion transfer.)
d selektive Permeabilität *f*; selektive Durchlässigkeit *f*
f perméabilité *f* sélective
p permeabilidade *f* seletiva

4899 **selective separation**
(Prod.)
(Food processing technology; production process: in control processes.)
d selektive Trennung *f*
f séparation *f* sélective
p separação *f* seletiva

4900 **selective treatment**
(Agr.)
(Biological agriculture.)
d zielgerichtete Behandlung *f*; selektive Behandlung *f*
f traitement *m* sélectif
p tratamento *m* seletivo

4901 **selenium deficiency**
(Med.)
(Veterinary; mineral (Se) deficiency: WMD-disease (White Muscle Disease).)
d Selenmangel *m*
f carence *f* en sélénium
p deficiência *f* de selênio

4902 **self raising flour**
(Prod.)
(Bakery.)
d hefehaltiges Mehl *n*
f farine *f* contenant de levure
p farinha *f* contendo fermento

4903 **semicontinuous cheese-making process**
(Prod.)
(Dairy plant technology.)
d halbkontinuierliches Käseherstellungsverfahren *n*
f procédé *m* de fabrication semi-continuée de fromage
p processo *m* semi-contínuo de produção de queijo

4904 **semidry wine**
(Biochem.)
(Enology; wine type.)
d halbtrockener Wein *m*
f vin *m* semi-sec
p vinho *m* meio seco

4905 **semifinished product**
(Prod.)
(Food processing technology, food industrialization: partially processed product.)
d halbfertiges Produkt *n*
f produit *m* semi-fini
p produto *m* semi-acabado

4906 **semihard cheese**
(Prod.)
(Dairy product.)
d halbharter Käse *f*
f fromage *m* semi-dur
p queijo *m* semi-endurecido

4907 **semihard dough**
(Prod.)
(Bakery.)
d halbharter Teig *m*
f pâte *f* semi-dure
p massa *f* meio-dura

4908 **semipreserved food**
(Prod.)
(Food processing technology: pasteurized (less than 100°C) food conservation.)
d Halbkonserve *f*
f semi-conserve *f*
p semiconserva *f*

4909 **semiskinned industrialized cow's milk**
(Med.)
(Baby nutrition.)
d industrialisierte halbentrahmte Kuhmilch *f*
f lait *m* de vache industriel demi-écrémé
p leite *m* de vaca industrializado semi-desnatado

4910 **semiskinned milk**
(Prod.)
(Dairy product, food processing technology.)
d teilentrahmte Milch *f*
f lait *m* demi-écrémé
p leite *m* semi-desnatado

4911 **semiskinned powdered milk**
(Med.)
(Baby nutrition.)
d teilentrahmtes Vollmilchpulver *n*
f lait *m* demi-écrémé en poudre
p leite *m* em pó semi-desnatado

4912 **semisolid** *adj*
(Prod.)
(Food processing technology; product characteristic.)
d halbfest
f semi-solide
p semi-sólido

4913 **semolina**
(Agr.)
(Agricultural produce; hard wheat, used for the production of e.g. pasta. Also semolina pudding.)
d Grieß *m*
f semoule *f*
p sêmola *f*; semolina *f*

4914 **senile intestinal flora**
(Med.)
(Containing e.g. less lactobacillus and increased contents of coli (colon bacillus).)
d senile Darmflora *f*
f flore *f* intestinale sénile
p flora *f* intestinal senil

* **senna leaves → 962**

4915 **sensation intensity**
(Biochem.)
(Nutritional science; olfactory stimulation, nervous cells system: aroma/flavour research; ref. to odoriferous molecules.)
d Wahrnehmungsintensität *f*; Wahrnehmungsstärke *f*
f intensité *f* de la sensation
p intensidade *f* da sensação

4916 **sensation of alimentary lack; sensation of lack of foodstuff intake**
(Med.)
(Condition of having appetite.)
d Empfindung *f* unzureichender Nahrungsmitteleinnahme
f sensation *f* de manque d'aliment
p sensação *f* de falta de alimentos

* **sensation of lack of foodstuff intake → 4916**

4917 **sense of smell**
(Med.)
(Enabling the smelling process.)
d Geruchssinn *m*
f odorat *m*
p olfato *m*; faro *m*

4918 **sensitive to heavy metals**
(Prod.)
(Food processing technology; product characteristic.)
d schwermetallempfindlich; empfindlich gegenüber Schwermetallen
f sensible aux métaux lourds
p sensível aos metais pesados

4919 **sensitive to impregnation with strange odours**
(Biochem.)
(Enology: ref. to wine quality.)
d empfindlich gegen die Aufnahme von Fremdgerüchen
f sensible à l'imprégnation d'odeurs étrangères
p sensível à impregnação com odores estranhos

4920 **sensitive to light**
(Prod.)
(Food processing technology; product characteristic.)
d lichtempfindlich
f sensible à la lumière
p sensível à luz

4921 **sensitive to microbial contamination**
(Biochem.)
(Enology.)
d empfindlich gegen mikrobielle Kontamination; empfindlich gegen mikrobielle Verseuchung; empfindlich gegen mikrobielle Verunreinigung
f sensible à la contamination microbienne
p sensível à contaminação microbiana; sensível à contaminação microbial

4922 **sensitive to substances of alcaline/acid reaction**
(Prod.)
(Food processing technology; product characteristic.)
d empfindlich gegenüber alkalisch/sauer reagierender Substanzen
f sensible aux substances de réaction alcaline/acide
p sensível às substâncias de reação álcalina/ácida

4923 **sensorial analysis; sensory analysis**
(Med.)
(Aroma/flavour perception.)
d Empfindungsanalyse *f*; sensorische Analyse *f*
f analyse *f* sensorielle
p análise *f* sensorial

* **sensory analysis → 4923**

4924 **sepal**
(Agr.)
(Botany; flower parts forming the calyx.)
d Kelchblatt *n*
f sépale *m*
p sépala *f*

4925 **separation**
(Prod.)
(Food processing technology; aroma/flavour research and production: Separation of different materials, phases etc.)
d Trennung *f*
f séparation *f*
p separação *f*

4926 **separation by density-difference**
(Prod.)
(Food processing technology; aroma/flavour research and production: Separation procedure of liquid phases.)
d Trennung *f* durch Dichteunterschied
f séparation *f* par différence de densité
p separação *f* por diferença na densidade

4927 **separation by retention**
(Prod.)
(Food processing technology; research and production: Separation procedure.)
d Trennung *f* durch Zurückhalten; Trennung *f* durch Retention
f séparation *f* par rétention
p separação *f* por retenção

4928 **separation methods**
(Prod.)
(Food processing technology: separation processes.)
d Trennungsmethoden *fpl*
f méthodes *fpl* de séparation
p métodos *mpl* de separação

4929 **separation of constituents**
(Prod.)
(Aroma/flavour research and production: distillation processes.)
d Trennung *f* der Bestandteile
f séparation *f* des constituants
p separação *f* dos componentes

4930 **separation of impurities**
(Prod.)
(Food processing technology.)

d Abtrennung *f* von Fremdstoffen
f séparation *f* des impuretés
p separação *f* das impurezas

4931 **separation of the mixture**
(Prod.)
(Food processing technology.)
d Mischungstrennung *f*
f séparation *f* du mélange
p separação *f* da mistura

4932 **separation process**
(Prod.)
(Food processing technology; processes for separating substance mixtures and for purification of single substances on the basis of the physical/chemical properties of their components.)
d Trennverfahren *n*
f opération *f* de séparation
p operação *f* de separação

4933 **separation stage**
(Prod.)
(Food processing technology; ref. to the distillation process.)
d Trennstufe *f*
f phase *f* séparative
p etapa *f* de separação

4934 **sequence of the bases**
(Med.)
(In genetics ref. to the replication reproduction of the DNA.)
d Basenreihenfolge *f*
f séquence *f* des bases
p seqüência *f* das bases

4935 **sequential structure of proteins**
(Biochem.)
(Nutritional science; ref. to protein biochemistry, organic compounds as enzymes, hormones, immunoglobulins.)
d sequentielle Struktur *f* des Proteins; sequentielle Struktur *f* des Eiweißes
f structure *f* séquentielle des protéines
p estrutura *f* seqüencial das proteínas

4936 **serine**
(Biochem.)
($C_3H_7NO_3$; ß-hydroxylalanina; non-essential amino acid. Participates in the protein construction, and is an important intermediate product in the intermediary metabolism; milk ingredient.)
d Serin *n*
f sérine *f*
p serina *f*

4937 **serve *v* an exquisite wine**
(Prod.)
(Gastronomy.)
d einen edlen Wein servieren
f servir un grand cru
p servir un vinho nobre

4938 **sesame**
(Agr.)
(Horticulture; "Sesamum indicum"; the seeds are an oil source and prime material for aroma/flavouring agents.)
d Sesam *m*
f sésame *m*
p gergelim *m*; sésamo *m*

4939 **sesame oil**
(Prod.)
(Horticulture; "Sesamum indicum"; the seeds are an oil source and prime material for aroma/flavouring agents.)
d Sesamöl *n*
f huile *f* de sésame
p óleo *m* de gergelim; óleo *m* de sésamo

4940 **sesame seed**
(Prod.)
(Horticulture. "Sesamum indicum"; the seeds are an oil source and prime material for aroma/flavouring agents.)
d Sesamsamen *m*
f graine *f* de sésame
p semente *m* de gergelim; semente *m* de sésamo

4941 **sesquiterpenes**
(Prod.)
($C_{15}H_{24}$; e.g. caryophyllene; source of aroma/fragrance prime material.)
d Sesquiterpene *npl*
f sesquiterpènes *mpl*
p sesquiterpenos *mpl*

4942 **set period**
(Prod.)
(Dairy plant technology of cheese production.)
d Ruheperiode *f*
f période *f* de repos
p período *m* de descanso

* **settling → 4879**

* **settling deposit → 4880**

4943 **settling tendency**
(Prod.)
(Food processing technology; solution.)
d Absetzungstendenz *f*, Absetzungsneigung *f*
f tendance *f* à former un dépôt
p tendência *f* de formar depósitos

4944 sewage sludge
(Agr.)
(Waste water treatment.)
d Klärschlamm *m*
f boues *fpl* de curage
p lama *f* de decantação de águas servidas; lodo *m* de decantação de águas servidas

* **sex cell → 2442**

4945 sex chromosome
(Med.)
(Also in veterinary; ref. to sex-determining chromosomes x and y; e.g. one x and one y give a male; two "x" give a female.)
d Geschlechtschromosom *n*
f chromosome *m* sexuel
p cromossomo *m* sexual

4946 shallow groundwater levels; shallow groundwater surfaces
(Prod.)
(Water supply; ref. in this case to not very profound layers of water (drinking water) source.)
d untiefe Grundwasserschichten *fpl*; untiefer Grundwasserspiegel *m*
f nappes *fpl* phréatiques
p lencois *mpl* freáticos

* **shallow groundwater surfaces → 4946**

4947 shear *v*; **clip** *v*; **cut** *v*
(Agr.)
(Veterinary science; to cut the hair of an animal, e.g. of a goat.)
d scheren
f tondre
p tosquiar; tosar

4948 shearing
(Agr.)
(Veterinary science; cutting of the hair of an animal, e.g. of a ewe.)
d Schur *f*
f tonte *f*
p tosquia *f*; tosa *f*; tosadura *f*

4949 shed *v*
(Agr.)
(Ref. to an animal loosing its hair.)
d haaren
f perdre son poil
p estar na muda

4950 sheep
(Agr.)
(Livestock; ref. to sheep raising: Adult female sheep. British English: hogg for a young sheep.)
d Schaf *n*
f mouton *m*
p ovelha *f*

4951 sheep raising; sheep rearing
(Agr.)
(Livestock breeding.)
d Schafzucht *f*
f élevage *m* de moutons
p ovinocultura *f*

* **sheep rearing → 4951**

4952 sheep's milk
(Agr.)
(Agricultural produce.)
d Schafsmilch *f*; Schafmilch *f*
f lait *m* de brebis
p leite *m* de ovelha

4953 shell *v*
(Prod.)
(Food processing technology: e.g. opening of a nut, chestnut, peanuts.)
d enthülsen
f écaler
p quebrar a casca

4954 shell egg
(Agr.)
(Poultry farming; egg type.)
d Schalenei *n*
f œuf *m* à coquille
p ovo *m* de casca

4955 shell-fish soup
(Prod.)
(Gastronomy; dish.)
d Krebssuppe *f*
f bisque *f*
p sopa *f* de frutos do mar; caldeirada *f* de frutos do mar; sopa *f* Leão Veloso (*regional*)

4956 sherbet
(Prod.)
(Gastronomy; sorbet: e.g. half-frozen ice cream (das Halbgefrorene) prepared with sweet wine or spirits (liquor); or an ice-cold drink, made of sweet fruit juice or wine.)
d Sorbet *m/n*; Sorbett *m/n*; Scherbett *m/n*
f granité *m*; sorbet *m* granuleux; sorbet *m* mousseux
p sorbet *m*

* **shoat → 4183**

4957 shortage effect of vitamin
(Med.)
(Vitamin deficiencies.)
d Auswirkung *f* eines Vitaminmangels

f effet *m* d'un défaut en vitamine
p efeito *m* de uma carência de vitamina

4958 short-chained fatty acids
(Biochem.)
(Nutritional science; e.g. chains of 4 carbons.)
d kurzkettige Fettsäuren *fpl*
f acides *mpl* gras à chaîne courte
p ácidos *mpl* graxos de cadeia curta

4959 short-cut pasta
(Prod.)
(Food processing technology; pasta plant product, raw macaroni form.)
d kurzgeschnittene Teigmasse *f*
f pâte *f* alimentaire découpée
p pasta *f* cortada em comprimento curto

4960 shortenings
(Prod.)
(Food processing technology; fats for baked goods to make them tender.)
d Küchenfette *npl* für Teigwaren
f graisses *fpl* de cuisine pour pâtes alimentaires
p gorduras *fpl* de cozinha para massas

4961 short paste
(Prod.)
(Bakery; similar to flaky pastry, but without flake forming characteristics.)
d Mürbeteig *m*
f pâte *f* brisée
p massa *f* brisé

4962 short-term supplementation
(Med.)
(Veterinary; ref. to ration supplementation (enrichment; fortification) with vitamins etc. in cattle dietary treatment.)
d kurzandauernde Supplementierung *f*
f supplémentation *f* de courte durée
p suplementação *f* de curta duração

4963 shrimp; prawn
(Prod.)
(Gastronomy; marine crustacean; seafood.)
d Garnele *f*
f crevette *f*
p camarão *m*

4964 shrub
(Agr.)
(Botany. Low woody plant type.)
d Busch *m*; Strauch *m*
f arbuste *m*; arbrisseau *m*
p subarbusto *m*

4965 sial; surface of the lithosphere
(Agr.)
(Soil; surface of the earth crust.)
d Erdoberkruste *f*; Sial *n*
f sial *m*; couche *f* superficielle de la lithosphère
p sial *m*; camada *f* superior da crosta terrestre; camada *f* superior da litosfera

* **sialorrhoea → 4798**

4966 side graft
(Agr.)
(Botany (viticulture); grafting method: insertion of the scion between the bark and the alburnum (sapwood).)
d seitliche Pfropfung *f*; Einsatz *m* des Edelreises zwischen Rinde und Splintholz
f greffage *m* latéral; insertion *f* de la greffe entre l'écorce et l'aubier
p enxerto *m* lateral; enxertia *f* lateral; enxertadura *f* lateral; inserção *f* do garfo entre a casca e o alburno

4967 side of pork
(Agr.)
(Livestock breeding. Half of a pork.)
d Schweinehälfte *f*
f demi-porc *m*
p meia carcaça *f* do suíno

* **sieve** *v* **→ 4028**

* **sift** *v* **→ 4028**

4968 silage additive
(Agr.)
(Livestock nutrition: Fodder additive.)
d Silagemittel *n*; Ensilagemittel *n*
f additif *m* d'ensilage
p aditivo *m* de silagem

4969 silicon
(Biochem.)
(Si; essential trace element, in food biochemistry.)
d Silicium *n*; Silizium *n*
f silicium *m*
p silício *m*

4970 silver
(Prod.)
(Ag; prime material for food (surface) dye production.)
d Silber *n*
f argent *m*
p prata *f*

* **silver fir → 2194**

4971 sima
(Agr.)
(Soil. Layer subjacent to the surface of the earth crust; rich in silicium and magnesium compounds.)

d Sima *n*; unterer Teil *m* der Erdkruste
f sima *m*; couche *f* intermédiaire de l'écorce terrestre
p sima *m*; camada *f* subjacente ao sial

4972 **Simmental breed; Simmental flecked breed**
(Agr.)
(Cattle breed of German and Swiss origin.)
d Simmentaler Fleckvieh *n*
f bétail *m* Simmental à pelage pie
p raça *f* Simmental; raça *f* Simmental malhada

* **Simmental flecked breed → 4972**

4973 **simmer** *v*
(Prod.)
(Food processing technology; (1) to bubble e.g. (in) hot water; stewing process; (2) to cook slowly.)
d brodeln; langsam kochen lassen
f bouillonner; mitonner
p fervilhar; cozer a fogo lento

4974 **simple proteins**
(Biochem.)
(Nutritional science; Single proteins: constituted only of amino acids. Conjugated proteins: constituted of amino acid and other substances.)
d einfache Proteine *npl*
f protéines *fpl* simples
p proteínas *fpl* simples

4975 **simultaneous determination of traces**
(Biochem.)
(Food biochemistry.)
d gleichzeitige Spurenfeststellung *f*
f détermination *f* simultanée de traces
p determinação *f* simultânea de traços

4976 **singe** *v*; **scorch** *v*
(Prod.)
(Food processing technology; In this case more to remove the feathers of the fowl, poultry.)
d ansengen; versengen; abbrennen
f roussir; brûler
p chamuscar; queimar penugens

4977 **single cell proteins; S.C.P.**
(Biochem.)
(Microbiology; proteins produced by means of unicellular organisms: e.g. yeast cultivated on molasses; source of dietetic proteins.)
d Proteine *npl* einzelliger Herkunft
f protéines *fpl* d'origine unicellulaire; P.O.U. *fpl*
p proteínas *fpl* de origem unicelular

* **sirloin → 3264**

4978 **sitting hen**
(Agr.)
(Poultry farming.)
d Glucke *f*; Bruthenne *f*
f couveuse *f*
p galinha *f* choca

* **situation of defective nutrition → 4979**

4979 **situation of nutritional deficiency; situation of defective nutrition**
(Med.)
(Regimens, diets.)
d Zustand *m* der Fehlernährung
f situation *f* nutritionnelle défectueuse; situation *f* de carence nutritionnelle
p situação *f* de carência nutricional

4980 **skewer**
(Prod.)
(Gastronomy: spit for holding meat pieces etc.; barbecue roasting.)
d Bratspieß *m*
f broche *f*
p espeto *m*

4981 **skim** *v*
(Prod.)
(Food processing technology: to remove froth from boiling food.)
d abschäumen; abschöpfen; entrahmen
f écumer
p tirar a espuma; desnatar

4982 **skimmed** *adj*
(Prod.)
(Food processing technology: e.g. dairy product treatment.)
d entrahmt
f écrémé
p desnatado

* **skimmed milk → 4983**

* **skimmed milk powder → 4985**

4983 **skim-milk; skimmed milk**
(Prod.)
(Dairy product; food industrialization.)
d Magermilch *f*
f lait *m* écrémé
p leite *m* desnatado; leite *m* magro

4984 **skim-milk cheese**
(Prod.)
(Dairy product; quality characteristic of cheese prepared from skimmed milk.)
d Magerkäse *m*
f fromage *m* maigre
p queijo *m* magro

4985 skim-milk powder; skimmed milk powder
(Prod.)
(Dairy product for ice cream production.)
d Magermilchpulver *n*
f lait *m* écrémé en poudre; lait *m* en poudre écrémé
p leite *m* em pó desnatado

4986 skin; peel; peeling
(Agr.)
(Botany; fruits: the exocarp; e.g. orange; peel, peeling: the skin (e.g. of an orange) when stripped off.)
d Schale *f*
f zeste *m*
p casca *f*; pele *f* (*very thin*)

4987 skin disease
(Med.)
(Dermatosis.)
d Hautkrankheit *f*
f maladie *f* de la peau
p enfermidade *f* cutânea; enfermidade *f* da pele

4988 skin of fruits
(Agr.)
d Obstschale *f*
f peau *f* des fruits; pelure *f* des fruits
p pele *f* das frutas; casca *f* das frutas

4989 skin of the fish
(Med.)
(Veterinary science; ref. to fish anatomy.)
d Fischhaut *f*
f peau *f* de poisson
p pele *f* de peixe

4990 slab cake with chocolate icing
(Prod.)
(Confectionary.)
d Kastenkuchen *m* mit Schokoladenüberzug
f gâteau *m* moulé enrobé de chocolat
p bolo *m* gelado com cobertura de chocolate

4991 slaughter *v*
(Prod.)
(Butchery; slaughterhouse technology: butchering of animals for alimentation purpose.)
d schlachten
f abattre
p abater

4992 slaughter; slaughtering
(Prod.)
(Butchery; slaughterhouse activity; meat production.)
d Schlachten *n*; Schlachtung *f*
f abattage *m*
p abate *m*

4993 slaughterhouse offals
(Agr.)
(Biological agriculture: used for organic fertilization.)
d Schlachthofabfälle *mpl*
f déchets *mpl* d'abattoirs
p restos *mpl* dos matadouros

* **slaughtering → 4992**

4994 slaw; coleslaw
(Prod.)
(Gastronomy. Raw chopped cabbage salad.)
d roher Kohlsalat *m*
f salade *f* de chou cru
p salada *f* de repolho cru

4995 slice of bread
(Prod.)
(Bakery.)
d Brotscheibe *f*; Brotschnitte *f*
f tranche *f* de pain
p fatia *f* de pão

4996 slicer knife
(Prod.)
(Butchery: equipment.)
d Aufschnittmesser *n*
f couteau *m* à découper
p faca *f* para frios

* **slicing → 1471**

4997 slight characteristic odour
(Prod.)
(Flavour notes.)
d schwacher charakteristischer Geruch *m*
f odeur *f* spécifique faible
p odor *m* específico fraco

4998 slightly acidified dietetic milk
(Med.)
(Baby nutrition.)
d angesäuerte Diätmilch *f*
f lait *m* diététique acidifié (*légèrement*)
p leite *m* dietético acidulado

4999 slightly fruity *adj*
(Prod.)
(Flavour note, flavour chemicals; elaboration of aromas: organic chemistry.)
d leicht fruchtig
f légèrement fruité
p leve nota *f* de frutas

5000 slightly opalescent; slightly turbid
(Biochem.)
(Food biochemistry.)
d leicht trüb
f faiblement opalescent
p ligeiramente turvo

* **slightly turbid → 5000**

5001 **slime soil**
(Agr.)
(Soil type.)
d Schlammboden *m*
f sol *m* de boue
p solo *m* limoso

5002 **slimming diet**
(Med.)
(Nutrition.)
d Abmagerungskur *f*
f cure *f* d'amaigrissement
p tratamento *m* de emagrecimento; cura *f* de emagrecimento

5003 **slow *v* down maturity**
(Agr.)
(Fruit culture, viticulture etc.)
d die Reife verlangsamen
f ralentir la maturité
p retardar a maturidade

5004 **slow *v* down the course of fermentation**
(Biochem.)
(Fermentation in nutritional science.)
d den Gärungsverlauf verlangsamen
f ralentir la marche de la fermentation; ralentir le cours de la fermentation
p retardar o curso da fermentação

5005 **slowing down of the reaction**
(Biochem.)
(Food biochemistry.)
d Verlangsamung *f* der Reaktion
f ralentissement *m* de la réaction; décélération *f* de la réaction
p desaceleração *f* da reação

5006 **slowly growing plant**
(Agr.)
(Biology.)
d langsam wachsende Pflanze *f*; Pflanze *f* langsamen Wuchses
f plante *f* à croissance lente
p planta *f* de crescimento lento

5007 **slow release fertilizer**
(Agr.)
(Soil. Synthetic fertilizer which releases the nutrients slowly.)
d Kunstdünger *m* langsamer Freigabe
f engrais *m* synthétique à libération progressive
p fertilizante *m* sintético de liberação progressiva

5008 **sludge; sludgy sediment**
(Prod.)
(Food processing technology; ref. to fruit treatment processes.)
d Absatzschlamm *m*
f bourbe *f* de la sédimentation
p lama *f* de sedimentação; lodo *m* de sedimentação

* **sludgy sediment → 5008**

* **sludgy sediment removal → 4659**

5009 **slug**
(Agr.)
(Biological agriculture: gastropod; pest.)
d Nacktschnecke *f*
f limace *f*
p lesma *f*

5010 **small agricultural industries**
(Agr.)
(Agribusiness.)
d landwirtschaftliche Betriebe *mpl*
f petites industries *fpl* ruraux
p pequenas indústrias *fpl* agrícolas

* **small cod → 1194**

5011 **small intestine**
(Med.)
(Anatomy; intestinal part consisting of duodenum, jejunum, ileum.)
d Dünndarm *m*
f intestin *m* grêle
p intestino *m* delgado

5012 **small loaf of bread**
(Prod.)
(French fancy bread type: semi-baguette.)
d kleines Stangenbrot *n*
f ficelle *f*
p meia-baguete *f*

* **small round loaf → 532**

5013 **small test portions**
(Prod.)
(Food processing technology.)
d kleine Testportionen *fpl*; kleine Testmengen *fpl*
f prises *fpl* d'essai réduites
p pequenas porções *fpl* de teste

5014 **smoked fish**
(Prod.)
(Gastronomy.)
d Räucherfisch *m*
f poisson *m* fumé
p peixe *m* defumado

5015 **smoked ham; gammon**
(Prod.)
(Food processing technology:)

d geräucherter Schinken *m*
f jambon *m* fumé
p presunto *m* defumado

5016 **smoked herring**
(Agr.)
("Clupea harengus". Food fish preserved by smoking.)
d Bückling *m*
f hareng *m* fumé; gendarme *m*; hareng *m* saur
p arenque *m* defumado

5017 **smoked meat**
(Prod.)
(Butchery; meat type.)
d Rauchfleisch *n*
f viande *f* fumée; viande *f* boucanée
p carne *f* defumada

5018 **smoke-dry** *adj*
(Prod.)
(Ref. to the taste of the smoked-out meat or fish product.)
d geräuchert
f boucané
p defumado

5019 **smoked sausage**
(Prod.)
(Butchery.)
d Räucherwurst *f*; geräucherte Wurst *f*
f saucisse *f* fumée
p lingüiça *f* defumada

5020 **smoked trout**
(Prod.)
(Gastronomy.)
d geräucherte Forelle *f*
f truite *f* fumée
p truta *f* defumada

5021 **smoking**
(Prod.)
(Food processing technology: fish and meat are, in some cases, smoked out, after having been salted. This method preserves the organoleptic qualities of the product.)
d Räuchern *n*
f boucanage *m*; fumage *m*; fumaison *f*
p defumação *f*

5022 **smoky-dry streaky bacon**
(Prod.)
(Food processing technology; bacon-type.)
d Dörrfleisch *n*
f lard *m* maigre fumé
p toucinho *m* entremeado defumado

5023 **snipe**
(Agr.)
(Genus "Gallinago".)
d Schnepfe *f*
f bécasse *f*
p galinhola *f*

5024 **soaking of rice**
(Prod.)
(Food processing technology.)
d Einweichung *f* des Reises; Einweichen *n* des Reises
f trempage *m* du riz
p ensopamento *m* do arroz; remolho *m* do arroz

5025 **soaking water**
(Prod.)
(Food processing technology: cooking processes.)
d Einweichwasser *n*
f eau *f* de trempage
p água *f* de ensopamento; água *f* de remolho

* **soda pop → 2216**

5026 **sodium**
(Biochem.)
(Na. Trace element in food biochemistry.)
d Natrium *n*
f sodium *m*
p sódio *m*

5027 **sodium alginate**
(Prod.)
(Food processing technology: e.g. texture improving ingredient.)
d Natriumalginat *n*
f alginate *m* de sodium
p alginato *m* de sódio

5028 **sodium ascorbate**
(Prod.)
(Vitamins in nutrition; vitamin C form. $C_6H_7O_6Na$. E.g. used in meat curing. Antioxidant.)
d Natriumascorbat *n*
f ascorbate *m* de sodium
p ascorbato *m* de sódio

5029 **sodium benzoate**
(Prod.)
($C_7H_5NaO_2$; food preservative.)
d Natriumbenzoat *n*
f benzoate *m* de sodium
p benzoato *m* de sódio

5030 **sodium bicarbonate; sodium hydrogen carbonate**
(Prod.)
($NaHCO_3$; baking soda; additive in baking powders, beverages, effervescent compounds, for its CO_2 release.)

d Natriumbicarbonat *n*; Natriumhydrogencarbonat *n*; Natron *n*
f bicarbonate *m* de sodium; hydrogénocarbonate *m* de sodium; sel *m* de Vichy
p bicarbonato *m* de sódio

5031 **sodium bisulphite**
(Prod.)
($NaHSO_3$. Additive for foodstuff preservation; antioxidant.)
d Natriumdisulfit *n*; Natriumbisulfit *n*
f bisulfite *m* de sodium
p bissulfito *m* de sódio

5032 **sodium carbonate**
(Prod.)
(Na_2CO_3; neutralizing auxiliary; e.g. in dairy products.)
d Natriumcarbonat *n*
f carbonate *m* de sodium
p carbonato *m* de sódio

5033 **sodium chloride**
(Prod.)
(NaCl salt; table salt; auxiliary product.)
d Natriumchlorid *n*
f chlorure *m* de sodium
p cloreto *m* de sódio

5034 **sodium chlorite**
(Prod.)
($NaClO_2$; used in treatment processes e.g. of oils (oxidizing effect); auxiliary.)
d Natriumchlorit *n*
f chlorite *m* de sodium
p clorito *m* de sódio

5035 **sodium citrate**
(Prod.)
($C_6H_5Na_3O_7$; additive: e.g. in cheese preparation.)
d Natriumcitrat *n*
f citrate *m* de sodium
p citrato *m* de sódio

5036 **sodium deficiency**
(Biochem.)
(Food biochemistry; provoking cramps. This type of deficiency is unlikely to occur as table salt is composed of sodium and chloride.)
d Natriummangel *m*
f carence *f* en sodium
p deficiência *f* de sódio; carência de sódio

5037 **sodium diacetate**
(Prod.)
($CH_3COONa.CH_3COOH$; sodium salt of acetic acid, used as conservation auxiliary; e.g. inhibits moulds in bread.)
d Natriumdiacetat *n*
f diacétate *m* de sodium
p diacetato *m* de sódio

* **sodium dithionite → 5047**

5038 **sodium fluoride**
(Prod.)
(NaF; element eventually contained in form of traces in mineral water.)
d Natriumfluorid *n*
f fluorure *m* de sodium
p fluoreto *m* de sódio

5039 **sodium-free salt**
(Prod.)
(Food processing technology: e.g. salt type for dietary purposes.)
d natriumfreies Salz *n*
f sel *m* exempt de sodium
p sal *m* isento de sódio

* **sodium hydrogen carbonate → 5030**

* **sodium hydrosulphite → 5047**

5040 **sodium lactate**
(Prod.)
($C_3H_5NaO_3$; synthetic sodium salt of lactic acid, used as antioxidant additive in foodstuff, e.g. in certain cheese preparations (E 325).)
d Natriumlaktat *n*
f lactate *m* de sodium
p lactato *m* de sódio

5041 **sodium metabisulphite**
(Prod.)
($Na_2S_2O_5$; e.g. antioxidant auxiliary in food processing technology.)
d Natriummetabisulfit *n*
f métabisulfite *m* de sodium
p metabissulfito *m* de sódio

5042 **sodium nitrate; Chile salpetre**
(Agr.)
($NaNO_3$; fertilizing agent; food preservative.)
d Natriumnitrat *n*; salpetersaures Natron *n*
f nitrate *m* de sodium; salpêtre *m* du Chili
p nitrato *m* de sódio; nitro *m* de Chile

5043 **sodium nitrite**
(Prod.)
($NaNO_2$; e.g. in meat-curing processes; food preservative. See Government regulations.)
d Natriumnitrit *n*
f nitrite *m* de sodium
p nitrito *m* de sódio

5044 **sodium phosphate**
(Prod.)
(Na_2HPO_4; sodium salt of phosphoric acid; auxiliary as antioxidant additive, stabilizer and

anticoagulant in dairy products; also baking powder ingredient.)
d Natriumphosphat *n*
f phosphate *m* de sodium
p fosfato *m* de sódio

5045 **sodium propionate**
(Prod.)
($C_3H_5NaO_2$; sodium salt of propionic acid: mould prevention additive; conservation auxiliary.)
d Natriumpropionat *n*
f propionate *m* de sodium
p propionato *m* de sódio

* **sodium sulphate → 2499**

5046 **sodium sulphite**
(Prod.)
(Na_2SO_3; e.g. antioxidant; auxiliary.)
d Natriumsufit *n*
f sulfite *m* de sodium
p sulfito *m* de sódio

5047 **sodium sulphoxylate; sodium hydrosulphite; sodium dithionite**
(Prod.)
($Na_2S_2O_4$; auxiliary in sugar treatment: bleaching additive.)
d Natriumdithionit *n*
f sulfoxylate *m* de sodium
p sulfoxilato *m* de sódio; hidrossulfito *m* de sódio

5048 **sodium tartrate**
(Prod.)
($Na_2C_4H_4O_6$; sodium salt of tartaric acid; e.g. antioxidant auxiliary.)
d Natriumtartrat *n*
f tartrate *m* de sodium
p tartarato *m* de sódio

5049 **sodium thiosulphate**
(Prod.)
($Na_2S_2O_3$; auxiliary e.g. in bleaching of oils.)
d Natriumthiosulfat *n*
f thiosulfate *m* de sodium
p tiossulfato *m* de sódio

5050 **sodium tripolyphosphate**
(Prod.)
($Na_5P_3O_{10}$; sodium triphosphate; water softening auxiliary; auxiliary in cake and dairy production.)
d Natriumtripolyphosphat *n*; Natriumtriphosphat *n*
f tripoliphosphate *m* de sodium
p tripolifosfato *m* de sódio

5051 **soft-boiled egg**
(Prod.)
(Gastronomy.)
d weichgekochtes Ei *n*
f œuf *m* à la coque
p ovo *m* quente

5052 **soft cheese**
(Prod.)
(Dairy product.)
d Weichkäse *m*
f fromage *m* mou; fromage *m* à pâte molle
p requeijão *m*

5053 **soft cheese with external mould**
(Prod.)
(Dairy plant technology: cheese with external mould covering: e.g. Camembert-type.)
d Weichkäse *m* mit äußerlichem Schimmelpilzbefall
f fromage *m* à pâte molle avec moisissures extérieures
p requeijão *m* com bolor externo

5054 **soft dough**
(Prod.)
(Bakery.)
d weicher Teig *m*
f pâte *f* molle
p massa *f* mole

5055 **soft drinks**
(Prod.)
(Beverages.)
d Erfrischungsgetränke *npl*; alkoholfreie Getränke *npl*
f boissons *fpl* non-alcoolisées; boissons *fpl* rafraîchissantes sans alcool
p refrescos *mpl*; refrigerantes *mpl*

5056 **soften** *v*
(Prod.)
(Water supply; e.g. ref. to water treatment; water quality.)
d enthärten
f adoucir
p descalcificar

* **softening of the bones → 3938**

5057 **soft fruits**
(Agr.)
(Horticulture.)
d Beerenobst *n*
f baies *fpl*
p fruta *f* de bagos

5058 **soft palate**
(Med.)
(Anatomy. Posterior part of the palate.)
d weicher Gaumen *m*; Gaumensegel *n*

f voile *m* du palais
p vela *f* palatina; véu *m* do paladar

* **soil → 134**

5059 soil acidification
(Agr.)
(Soil; ref. to agricultural soil characteristics.)
d Bodenversauerung *f*
f acidification *f* du sol
p acidificação *f* do solo

5060 soil-adapted varieties; varieties adapted to the soil
(Agr.)
(Biological agriculture.)
d bodenangepasste Arten *fpl*; dem Boden angepasste Arten *fpl*
f variétés *fpl* adaptées au sol
p variedades *fpl* adaptadas ao solo

5061 soil analysis
(Agr.)
(Soil; ref. to the upper earth layer for plowing and plant growing.)
d Bodenanalyse *f*
f analyse *f* des sols
p análise *f* dos solos

5062 soil conditioner
(Agr.)
(Soil treatment: material used for soil improvement; e.g. gypsum.)
d Bodenkonditionierungsmaterial *n*; Bodenkonditionierungsmittel *n*
f agent *m* de conditionnement du sol
p material *m* condicionador do solo

5063 soil constitution
(Agr.)
(Soil; soil consists of two parts: a mineral part (including water and air) and an organic part (organic complex).)
d Bodenzusammensetzung *f*
f constitution *f* du sol
p constituição *f* do solo

5064 soil covering
(Agr.)
(Horticulture: covering up of the soil against erosion.)
d Abdeckung *f* des Bodens
f couverture *f* du sol
p cobertura *f* do solo

* **soil cultivation → 5499**

* **soil deficiencies → 1534**

5065 soil disinfection
(Agr.)
(Soil treatment, conservation of arable land.)
d Bodenentseuchung *f*
f désinfection *f* du sol
p desinfecção *f* do solo

5066 soil fertility
(Agr.)
(Soil; soil capacity for plant nourishing.)
d Bodenfruchtbarkeit *f*
f fécondité *f* du sol
p fertilidade *f* do solo

5067 soil formation
(Agr.)
(Soil; soils are formed by disintegration of rocks, chemical processes and enrichment by organic material due to the action of animal and vegetal organisms.)
d Bodenbildung *f*
f formation *f* du sol
p formação *f* do solo

5068 soil improvement
(Agr.)
(Soil; improvement of arable land.)
d Bodenverbesserung *f*
f amélioration *f* du sol; amendement *m*
p melhoramento *m* do solo; correção *f* do solo

5069 soil low in phosphates
(Agr.)
(Soil; natural phosphates are found e.g. in form of mineral mixtures (apatite and phosphorite in the North of Brazil).)
d phosphatarmer Boden *m*
f sol *m* pauvre en phosphate
p solo *m* pobre em fosfatos

5070 soil potentiality
(Agr.)
(Soil treatment.)
d Potentialität *f* des Bodens
f potentialité *f* du sol
p potencialidade *f* do solo

5071 soil preservation
(Agr.)
(Soil; protective farmland treatment.)
d Erhaltung *f* des Erdbodens
f conservation *f* du sol
p conservação *f* do solo

5072 soil profile
(Agr.)
(Soil; the soil profile is a cross section of the soil structure.)
d Bodenprofil *n*
f profil *m* du sol
p perfil *m* do solo

5073 soil regeneration
(Agr.)
(Soil treatment.)
d Bodenregeneration *f*; Bodenerneuerung *f*
f régénération *f* des sols
p regeneração *f* dos solos

5074 soil settlement
(Agr.)
(Soil treatment; conservation method: certain forms of planting e.g. crop rotation.)
d Bodenfestigung *f*
f stabilisation *f* du sol
p estabilização *f* do solo

5075 soils subject to erosion
(Agr.)
(Soil; erosion process is e.g. the washing away of the fertile soil surface by moving water, the dragging along of soil particles, ruining the land.)
d erosionsgefährdete Böden *mpl*
f sols *mpl* exposés à l'érosion
p solos *mpl* sujeitos à erosão

5076 soil structure
(Agr.)
(Soil; A horizon: topsoil with humus. B horizon: subsoil of clay. C horizon: rock stratum.)
d Bodenstruktur *f*; Bodengefüge *n*
f structure *f* du sol
p estrutura *f* do solo

5077 soil waste
(Agr.)
(Soil; the rich superficial soil layer is washed away by rain falls, together with the seeds, fertilizing elements etc.; loss of fertility; loss of value: Erosion.)
d Bodenverwitterung *f*
f effritement *m* du sol
p desgaste *m* do solo

5078 solanum
(Agr.)
(Horticulture. Genus "Solanum"; nightshade family: vegetables, herbs and shrubs; e.g. aubergine (eggplant), tomato, potato.)
d Nachtschattengewächs *n*
f solanacée *f*
p solanácea *f*

5079 solar energy
(Agr.)
(Climatology.)
d Sonnenenergie *f*
f énergie *f* solaire
p energia *f* solar

5080 sole
(Agr.)
("Solea solea"; edible flatfish.)
d Seezunge *f*
f sole *f*
p linguado *m*

* **solid → 5081**

5081 solid body; solid
(Prod.)
(Food processing technology.)
d fester Körper *m*; Festkörper *m*
f corps *m* solide; solide *m*
p corpo *m* sólido; sólido *m*

5082 solid diet; solid food diet
(Med.)
(Alimentary regimen.)
d feste Diät *f*; Diät *f* fester Nahrung
f diète *f* solide; alimentation *f* d'une diète solide
p dieta *f* sólida; dieta *f* de alimentação sólida

* **solid food diet → 5082**

5083 solid foods; solid foodstuff
(Prod.)
(Food processing technology; food characteristic.)
d feste Nahrungsmittel *npl*
f produits *mpl* alimentaires solides; aliments *m* solides
p alimentos *mpl* sólidos

* **solid foodstuff → 5083**

5084 solidify *v*
(Biochem.)
(Food biochemistry: product characteristic.)
d erstarren
f solidifier
p solidificar

5085 solidify *v* **as gel**
(Biochem.)
(Food biochemistry; product characteristic.)
d gelartig erstarren
f solidifier en formant un gel
p solidificar sob formação de gel

5086 solids content
(Prod.)
(Food processing technology; e.g. of an aqueous solution.)
d Feststoffgehalt *m*
f teneur *f* en matières solides
p teor *m* sólido

5087 solids in suspension
(Prod.)
(Water supply treatment. Suspension of

solids.)
d Schwebestoffe *mpl*
f corps *mpl* solides en suspension
p corpos *mpl* sólidos em suspensão

5088 **solid state**
(Prod.)
(Food processing technology; ref. to product characteristic.)
d Festkörperzustand *m*
f état *m* solide
p estado *m* sólido

5089 **solid under environmental temperature**
(Prod.)
(Food processing technology: certain fats, e.g. margarine.)
d fest bei Umweltstemperatur
f solide à la température environnementale
p sólido à temperatura ambiental

5090 **solubility**
(Prod.)
(Aroma/fragrance research and production; ref. to food processing technology; product specification: product characteristic.)
d Löslichkeit *f*
f solubilité *f*
p solubilidade *f*

5091 **solubilization**
(Prod.)
(Food processing technology.)
d Löslichmachung *f*; Solubilisierung *f*
f solubilisation *f*
p solubilização *f*

5092 **solubilizer**
(Prod.)
(Food processing technology; auxiliary product.)
d Lösungsvermittler *m*
f solubilisant *m*
p solubilizante *m*

5093 **soluble** *adj*
(Prod.)
(Food processing technology; product characteristic.)
d löslich; lösbar
f soluble
p solúvel

5094 **soluble colorants**
(Prod.)
(Foodstuff colorants.)
d lösliche Farbstoffe *mpl*
f colorants *mpl* solubles
p corantes *mpl* solúveis

5095 **soluble fertilizers**
(Agr.)
(Agriculture.)
d lösliche Düngemittel *npl*
f engrais *mpl* solubles
p fertilizantes *mpl* solúveis

5096 **soluble in alcohol; alcohol-soluble** *adj*
(Prod.)
(Food processing technology.)
d alkohollöslich; löslich in Alkohol
f alcoolosoluble; soluble dans l'alcool
p solúvel em álcool

5097 **soluble in hydrocarbon**
(Prod.)
(Food processing technology: e.g. product characteristic.)
d löslich in Kohlenhydraten
f soluble dans les hydrocarbures
p solúvel em hidrocarbonetos

5098 **soluble in the nasal mucous membrane**
(Med.)
(Physicochemical characteristic of odoriferous particles.)
d löslich in der Nasenschleimhaut
f soluble dans le mucus nasal
p solúvel na mucosa nasal

5099 **soluble products**
(Prod.)
(Food processing technology.)
d lösbare Produkte *npl*; lösliche Produkte *npl*
f produits *mpl* solubles
p produtos *mpl* solúveis

5100 **solution**
(Biochem.)
(Food biochemistry; a homogenous mixture: a liquid system of a single phase.)
d Lösung *f*
f solution *f*
p solução *f*

* **solution via dietetics → 1658**

5101 **solvent**
(Prod.)
(Food processing technology; auxiliary products.)
d Lösungsmittel *n*
f solvant *m*
p solvente *m*

5102 **solvent extraction**
(Prod.)
(Aroma/flavour research and production; extraction process of plant products.)
d Lösungsmittelextraktion *f*

f extraction *f* au moyen de solvants
p extração *f* por solventes

5103 **solvent penetration**
(Prod.)
(Aroma/flavour research and production, ref. to extraction processes.)
d Lösungsmittelpenetration *f*; Eindringung *f* des Lösungsmittels
f pénétration *f* du solvant
p penetração *f* do solvente

5104 **sorbic acid**
(Prod.)
($C_6H_8O_2$, used in food preservation.)
d Sorbinsäure *f*
f acide *m* sorbique
p ácido *m* sórbico

* **sorbit → 5105**

5105 **sorbitol; sorbit**
(Prod.)
($C_6H_{14}O_6$; e.g. texture improving ingredient; sweetening agent: polyalcohol.)
d Sorbit *n*
f sorbitol *m*
p sorbitol *m*

5106 **sorghum**
(Agr.)
(Agricultural produce. Genus "Sorghum"; economically important tropical/subtropical, esp. African, grass.)
d Sorgho *m*; Sorghum *n*; Durra *f*; Mohrenhirse *f*
f sorgho *m*; sorgo *m*
p sorgo *m*

5107 **sorrel**
(Agr.)
(Horticulture; "Rumex acetosella"; plant with edible leaves (potherb) containing oxalic acid, used against scurvy; the seed gives starch, used for bread and biscuit baking.)
d Sauerampfer *m*
f oseille *f*
p azeda-miúda *f*, azeda *f*, azedinha *f*

5108 **soufflé**
(Prod.)
(Gastronomy.)
d Auflauf *m*; Soufflee *n*
f soufflé *m*
p suflê *m*

5109 **sound tooth**
(Med.)
(Anatomy.)
d gesunder Zahn *m*
f dent *f* saine
p dente *m* sadio

5110 **soup**
(Prod.)
(Gastronomy.)
d Suppe *f*
f potage *m*
p sopa *f*

5111 **soup powders**
(Prod.)
(Food processing technology.)
d Suppenpulver *n*
f poudre *f* pour potages
p pó *m* de sopas

5112 **soup seasoning**
(Prod.)
(Food processing technology: soup ingredient.)
d Suppenwürze *f*
f arôme *m* pour potages
p condimentos *mpl* para sopa

5113 **sour cherry**
(Agr.)
("Prunus cerasus"; edible acid fruit.)
d Sauerkirsche *f*
f griotte *f*
p cereja *f* ácida

5114 **sour cream**
(Prod.)
(Dairy product; cream soured by lactobacillus.)
d saure Sahne *f*, Sauerrahm *m*
f crème *f* acide
p creme *m* de leite ácido

* **sourdough → 3156**

5115 **sourdough bread; leaven-raised bread**
(Prod.)
(Bakery; leaven; ref. to certain type of baker's mixture for bread making: fermenting dough.)
d Sauerteigbrot *n*
f pain *m* au levain
p pão *m* lêvedo; pão *m* de massa lêveda

5116 **sour solution; acid solution**
(Prod.)
(Food processing technology: product characteristic.)
d saure Lösung *f*, Säurelösung *f*
f solution *f* acide; solution *f* d'acide
p solução *f* ácida; solução *f* de ácido

5117 **souse** *v*; **pickle** *v*
(Prod.)
(Food processing technology.)

d marinieren
f mariner
p marinar; pôr de escabeche

5118 soused herring
(Prod.)
(Pickeld herring; Rollmops: soused herring fillet, sometimes rolled around a gherkin.)
d marinierter Hering *m*; Rollmops *m*
f hareng *m* mariné; rollmops *m*
p arenque *m* marinado; arenque *m* à escabeche; arenque *m* à escabeche enrolado

5119 sow
(Agr.)
(Livestock; hog raising; an adult female hog.)
d Sau *f*
f femelle *f* du porc; truie *f*
p porca *f*

5120 sowing
(Agr.)
(Agriculture; scattering of seeds for planting purposes.)
d Aussaat *f*
f ensemencement *m*; semailles *fpl*; semis *m*
p semeadura *f*; semeação *f*

5121 sowing of cereals
(Agr.)
(Agriculture; cultivation of cereals.)
d Getreideaussaat *f*
f emblavage *m*
p semeadura *f* de cereais; semeação *f* de cereais

* **soya bean oil → 5124**

* **soya bean seed → 5122**

5122 soybean; soya bean seed
(Agr.)
(Agricultural produce. "Glycine max". Proteinaceous seeds, rich in oil contain soybean oil, used e.g. as food and are source of fatty acids.)
d Sojabohne *f*; Samen *m* der Sojabohne
f soja *m*; graine *f* de soja
p soja *f*; feijão *m* de soja

5123 soybean extraction bran
(Agr.)
(Cattle breeding and nutrition; feedstuff basis.)
d Sojaextraktionsschrot *m*
f son *m* de l'extraction de soja
p farelo *m* de extração da soja

5124 soybean oil; soya bean oil
(Prod.)
(The most important vegetable oil in human nutrition, prime material obtained from soybeans by extraction or expression; used in the production of shortenings and margarines.)
d Sojaöl *n*
f huile *f* de soja
p óleo *m* de soja

5125 soy bread
(Prod.)
(Bakery.)
d Sojabrot *n*
f pain *m* de soja
p pão *m* de soja

5126 soy flour
(Prod.)
(Food processing technology.)
d Sojamehl *n*
f farine *f* de soja
p farinha *f* de soja

5127 soy sauce
(Prod.)
(Food processing technology.)
d Sojasoße *f*
f sauce *f* de soja
p molho *m* de soja

5128 soy shoot
(Prod.)
(Gastronomy: edible young shoots e.g. in salads.)
d Sojaspross *m*
f pousse *f* de soja
p broto *m* de soja

5129 spaghetti
(Prod.)
(Food processing technology; pasta plant product.)
d Spaghetti *pl*
f spaghetti *mpl*
p espaguete *m*

5130 spare rib
(Prod.)
(Butchery; meat part; joint.)
d Schweinekamm *m*
f échine *m* de porc
p ponta *f* de costeleta de porco

5131 sparingly soluble *adj*
(Prod.)
(Food processing technology; product specification.)
d schwerlöslich
f difficilement soluble
p pouco solúvel

5132 **sparingly soluble in ethanol**
(Biochem.)
(Food biochemistry; product characteristic.)
d wenig lösbar in Äthanol; wenig löslich in Äthanol
f peu soluble dans l'éthanol
p pouco solúvel em etanol

5133 **sparkling** *adj*
(Biochem.)
(Enology; characteristic of a certain white wine type.)
d spritzig
f effervescent
p efervescente

5134 **sparkling wine**
(Prod.)
(Enology; wine type: effervescent table wine.)
d Perlwein *m*
f vin *m* perlant; vin *m* pétillant
p vinho *m* frisante

5135 **sparkling wine stabilization**
(Biochem.)
(Enology; e.g. with ascorbic acid.)
d Schaumweinstabilisierung *f*
f stabilisation *f* du mousseux; stabilisation *f* du vin mousseux
p estabilização *f* do vinho *m* espumante

5136 **spasm**
(Med.)
(Veterinary; involuntary muscular contraction.)
d Spasmus *m*; Krampf *m*
f spasme *m*; crampe *f*
p espasmo *m*

5137 **species**
(Agr.)
(Botany (flora/fauna). Classification category: similar individuals enabled to produce fertile offsprings; similar species are classified as genus.)
d Art *f*
f espèce *f*
p espécie *f*

5138 **specific deficiency of nutrients**
(Med.)
(Nutrition in medicine; regimens, diets.)
d spezifischer Mangel *m* an Nährstoffen; spezifischer Nahrungsstoffmangel *m*
f carence *f* spécifique en nutriments
p carência *f* específica de nutrientes

5139 **specific diet**
(Med.)
(Diet for special purposes.)
d spezifische Diät *f*
f diète *f* spécifique
p dieta *f* específica

5140 **specific enzyme activity**
(Biochem.)
(Biochemical research in nutritional science.)
d spezifische Enzymwirksamkeit *f*; spezifische Enzymaktivität *f*
f activité *f* spécifique des enzymes
p atividade *f* específica das enzimas

* **specific flavour of a food → 5142**

5141 **specific strain**
(Biochem.)
(Fermentation; yeast strains of specific qualities, e.g. in brewery processes.)
d spezifischer Strang *m*
f souche *f* spécifique
p cepa *f* específica; raça *f* específica

5142 **specific taste of a food; specific flavour of a food**
(Biochem.)
(Characteristic given to the food by flavouring ferments; nutritional science, ref. to organoleptic food evaluation.)
d spezifischer Geschmack *m* eines Nahrungsmittels
f goût *m* spécifique d'un aliment
p gosto *m* específico de um alimento

5143 **specific volume**
(Biochem.)
(Nutritional science; v = V/m, v = quotient of the volume v and mass m; value inversely related to "density".)
d spezifisches Volumen *n*; massenbezogenes Volumen *n*
f volume *m* spécifique; densité *f* réciproque
p volume *m* específico

5144 **spectrometric method**
(Biochem.)
(Nutritional science; ref. to analytical method.)
d spektrometrische Methode *f*
f méthode *f* spectrométrique
p método *m* espectrométrico

5145 **spectrophotometric detection**
(Biochem.)
(Food biochemistry; analysis process.)
d spektrophotometrische Feststellung *f*
f détection *f* spectrophotométrique
p detecção *f* espectrofotométrica

* **speed *v* up maturity → 15**

* **spherical bacteria → 1183**

5146 sphincter
(Med.)
(Anatomy; orifice-surrounding ring muscle, e.g. anal sphincter.)
d Schließmuskel *m*
f sphincter *m*
p esfíncter *m*

5147 spice
(Prod.)
(Here: natural (plant) additives for taste accentuation; promotion of appetite, stimulation of salivary glands and the secretion of gastric juices. This way spices promote the resorption of nutrients.)
d Gewürz *n*
f épice *f*; aromate *m*
p tempero *m*; especiarias *fpl*

5148 spicy note
(Prod.)
(Aroma/flavour note.)
d würzige Note *f*
f note *f* aromatique; saveur *f* aromatique
p sabor *m* picante

5149 spicy taste
(Prod.)
(Aroma/flavour note; e.g. ref. to organoleptic food evaluation.)
d würziger Geschmack *m*
f saveur *f* épicée
p sabor *m* aromático

5150 spinach
(Agr.)
(Horticulture. "Spinacia oleracea".)
d Spinat *m*
f épinard *m*
p espinafre *m*

5151 spinal column; vertebral column; backbone
(Med.)
(Veterinary; anatomic part of animals (of a vertebrate).)
d Rückgrat *n*
f épine *f* dorsale; colonne *f* vertébrale
p espinha *f* dorsal; coluna *f* vertebral

* **spiny lobster → 3129**

5152 spirits
(Prod.)
(Alcoholic beverage.)
d Spirituosen *fpl*
f spiritueux *mpl*
p bebidas *fpl* alcoólicas

5153 spirochaetes; spirochetes
(Med.)
(Order "Spirochaetales"; e.g. "Treponema pallidum", syphilis causing bacterium.)
d Spirochäten pl; Schraubenbakterien *fpl*
f spirochètes *mpl*
p espirilos *mpl*

* **spirochetes → 5153**

5154 splayed-legs disease
(Med.)
(Veterinary; ref. to bone and articulation deformation in piglets; manifestation of avitaminosis, e.g. choline chloride.)
d Spreizbeinigkeitskrankheit *f*
f maladie *f* des jambes écartées
p doença *f* das patas divergentes

5155 spleen
(Med.)
(Anatomy: lien. Activity: e.g. blood filtration and production of lymphocytes.)
d Milz *f*
f rate *f*
p baço *m*

5156 splitting of the chain; fission of the chain
(Biochem.)
(Food biochemistry of aroma chemicals; aroma synthesis.)
d Spaltung *f* der Kette
f scission *f* de la chaîne; fission *f* de la chaîne
p quebra *f* de cadeia

5157 split *v* up
(Biochem.)
(Nutritional science; e.g. ref. to chemical reactions.)
d spalten; aufspalten
f dédoubler
p desdobrar

5158 split *v* up into glucose and galactose
(Med.)
(E.g. carbohydrates of the milk during metabolizing process.)
d aufspalten in Glykose und Galaktose
f dédoubler en glucose et galactose
p desdobrar em glicose e galactose

5159 split *v* up the essence into different fractions
(Prod.)
(Aroma/flavour research and production: by means of solvents and countercurrent process.)
d Essenzen in verschiedene Fraktionen aufteilen
f partager l'essence en différentes fractions
p partir as essências em diferentes frações

* **spoilage → 1596**

5160 **spoiled bunches of grapes**
(Agr.)
(Viticulture; selection of fruits.)
d verdorbene Trauben *fpl*
f grappes *fpl* altérées
p cachos *mpl* estragados

5161 **sponge cake**
(Prod.)
(Bakery product.)
d Biskuitkuchen *m*
f génoise *f*
p pão-de-ló *m*

* **sponge cake filling → 4035**

5162 **spongy gums**
(Med.)
(Anatomy.)
d schwammiges Zahnfleisch *n*
f gencives *fpl* spongieuses
p gengivas *fpl* esponjosas

5163 **spontaneous fermentation**
(Biochem.)
(Fermentation.)
d spontane Gärung *f*
f fermentation *f* spontanée
p fermentação *f* espontânea

5164 **spontaneous malolactic fermentation**
(Biochem.)
(Enology.)
d spontane malolaktische Gärung *f*; malolaktische Spontangärung *f*
f fermentation *f* malolactique spontanée
p fermentação *f* espontânea malolática

5165 **spores**
(Biochem.)
(Microbiology; environmentally resistant (e.g. temperature elevation) form of microorganisms)
d Sporen *fpl*
f spores *fpl*
p esporos *mpl*

5166 **sporulation**
(Biochem.)
(Microbiology; formation of spores by microorganisms: conservation purpose.)
d Sporenbildung *f*
f sporulation *f*
p esporulação *f*

5167 **sprat; brisling**
(Prod.)
(Gastronomy; "Sprattus sprattus"; small edible fish, related to the herring.)
d Sprotte *f*
f sprat *m*; anchois *m* de Norvège; harenguet *m*
p pequeno arenque *m*

5168 **spray-drying**
(Prod.)
(Food processing technology; processing method.)
d Sprühtrocknung *f*
f séchage *m* par pulvérisation
p secagem *f* por pulverização

5169 **spray-drying process**
(Prod.)
(Dairy plant process. After evaporation the milk enters the spray dryer in which the concentrate is sprayed: Powder milk production.)
d Trockensprühverfahren *n*
f procédé *m* de séchage par vaporisation
p processo *m* de secagem por pulverização

5170 **spread** *v*
(Prod.)
(Gastronomy; to spread butter on a slice of bread.)
d streichen
f tartiner
p passar

5171 **spreadability**
(Prod.)
(Dairy technology; butter quality, indicating its characteristic of being spread on a slice of bread.)
d Verstreichbarkeit *f*
f tartinabilité *f*; étalement *m*
p espalhabilidade *f*; caraterística *f* de espalhamento

5172 **spreading of organic material**
(Agr.)
(Biological agriculture: application of fertilizers only of plant and animal origin.)
d Ausstreuen *n* organischen Dunges
f épandage *m* de matières organiques
p espalhamento *m* de material orgânico

5173 **spring frost**
(Agr.)
(Climatology; sudden frost during springtime.)
d Frühjahrsfrost *m*
f gelées *fpl* de printemps
p geadas *fpl* primeverís; geadas *fpl* primaverais

5174 **spring water**
(Prod.)
(Mineral waters are spring water containing

mineral salts and free carbon dioxide i.e. carbon dioxide gas (O_2).)
d Quellwasser *n*
f eau *f* de source
p água *f* de fonte

5175 **sprinkle** *v*; **dust** *v*
(Prod.)
(Food processing technology: e.g. salt, sugar.)
d streuen
f saupoudrer
p polvilhar

5176 **sprinkling capacity of the salt**
(Prod.)
(Food processing technology: product property/quality.)
d Streufähigkeit *f* des Salzes
f capacité *f* de saupoudrage du sel
p capacidade *f* de polvilhamento do sal

* **sprinkling water → 3024**

5177 **sprout**
(Agr.)
(Botany; ref. to a shoot for planting at a definitive site.)
d Steckling *m*
f bouture *f*
p muda *f*

5178 **sprout** *v*
(Agr.)
(Botany; plants.)
d treiben
f pousser
p brotar

* **sprouting → 1244**

5179 **spruce**
(Agr.)
(Botany. Genus "Picea"; evergreen tree of the pine family. The Portuguese "abeto; abete " designs likewise the genus "Abies" and "Picea".)
d Fichte *f*
f épicéa *m*
p abeto *m*; abete *m*

5180 **sprue; psilosis**
(Med.)
(Deficient food absorption related to diseased small intestine; deficiency of vitamin B, D, K.)
d Sprue *f*
f sprue *f*
p espru *m*

* **squash → 4500**

5181 **squeezed-out juice**
(Prod.)
(Food processing technology; juice production method.)
d ausgepreßter Saft *m*
f jus *m* de presse
p sumo *m* de expressão

* **squeezing out of grapes → 4355**

* **squeezing out of the bunch of grapes → 4355**

* **squid → 1475**

5182 **stability of genetic modifications**
(Biochem.)
(Biochemical research in nutritional science.)
d Stabilität *f* der genetischen Veränderungen; Stabilität *f* der erblich bedingten Veränderungen
f stabilité *f* des modifications génétiques
p estabilidade *f* das modificações genéticas

5183 **stabilization of enzymes**
(Biochem.)
(Biochemical research in nutritional science.)
d Enzymstabilisierung *f*
f stabilisation *f* des enzymes
p estabilização *f* de enzimas

5184 **stabilization of fatty matters**
(Prod.)
(Food processing technology.)
d Fettkörperstabilisierung *f*
f stabilisation *f* des matières grasses
p estabilização *f* dos corpos graxos

5185 **stabilization of vitamins; vitamin stabilization**
(Biochem.)
(Vitamin/food biochemistry.)
d Stabilisierung *f* von Vitaminen; Vitaminstabilisierung *f*
f stabilisation *f* des vitamines
p estabilização *f* de vitaminas

5186 **stabilization process**
(Biochem.)
(Nutritional science, e.g. ref. to a process or a product (wine stabilization).)
d Stabilisierungsprozess *m*
f procédé *m* de stabilisation
p processo *m* de estabilização

5187 **stabilize** *v*
(Biochem.)
(Nutritional science, e.g. ref. to a process or a product (wine stabilization).)
d stabilisieren

f stabiliser
p estabilizar

5188 **stabilized**
(Prod.)
(Food processing technology.)
d stabilisiert
f stabilisé
p estabilizado

5189 **stabilized beta-carotene**
(Prod.)
(Food processing technology, product characteristic.)
d stabilisiertes Beta-Carotin *n*
f bêta-carotène *m* stabilisé
p beta-caroteno *m* estabilizado

5190 **stabilized form**
(Prod.)
(Food processing technology; product characteristic.)
d stabilisierte Form *f*
f forme *f* stabilisée
p forma *f* estabilizada

5191 **stabilizer**
(Prod.)
(Additive which stabilizes emulsions, e.g. of fat and water.)
d Stabilisator *m*
f stabilisant *m*
p estabilizante *m*

5192 **stable on air contact**
(Biochem.)
(Food biochemistry: product characteristic.)
d stabil bei Luftkontakt
f stable au contact de l'air
p estável ao contato com o ar

5193 **stable to oxygen**
(Biochem.)
(Food biochemistry: product characteristic.)
d oxigenstabil
f stable à l'oxygène
p estável ao oxigênio

5194 **stag; hart**
(Agr.)
(Game. Stag: adult male red deer.)
d Hirsch *m*
f cerf *m*
p veado *m*

5195 **stake**
(Agr.)
(Vine post e.g. in viticulture.)
d Weinpfahl *m*; Stickel *m*
f paisseau *m*; échalas *m*
p tutor *m*

5196 **stale** *adj*
(Prod.)
(Bakery; bread which is no more fresh, but dry and getting hard.)
d altbacken
f rassis
p duro

5197 **stale** *adj*; **flat** *adj*
(Biochem.)
(Enology; taste quality; e.g. of wine: tasteless.)
d schal; abgestanden; flach
f éventé
p choco; insípido; vinhado (*only for wine*)

5198 **staling**
(Prod.)
(Bakery; bread: softening of the bread crust from the inside (crumb) to the exterior, with taste modification by diffusion of the volatile particles of the crust into the interior of the bread.)
d Altbackenwerden *n*
f rassissement *m*
p ficar *m* amanhecido; ficar *m* duro

5199 **stallion**
(Agr.)
(Livestock raising. Male horse for breeding purposes.)
d Zuchthengst *m*
f étalon *m*
p garanhão *m*

5200 **standardization according to analysis**
(Prod.)
(Food processing technology; food industrialization; quality control techniques.)
d Standardisierung *f* laut Analyse
f standardisation *f* selon analyse
p padronização *f* conforme análise

5201 **staphylococcus**
(Med.)
(Foodstuff intoxication.)
d Staphylokokkus *m*
f staphylocoque *m*
p estafilococo *m*

5202 **staple food; basic food; basic foodstuffs**
(Agr.)
(Principal food of a region: e.g. in Germany: potatoes, cereal; e.g. in Brazil: rice, dark brown/black beans; in the Orient: e.g. rice.)
d Hauptnahrungsmittel *n*; Grundnahrungsmittel *n*

f aliment *m* de base; produits *mpl* alimentaires de base
p alimento *m* principal; produtos *mpl* alimentícios de base

5203 **starch; starch flour**
(Prod.)
($(C_6H_{10}O_5)_x$. Complex carbohydrate; foodstuff; prime material.)
d Stärke *f*; Stärkemehl *n*
f fécule *f*; amidon *m*
p fécula *f*; amido *m*

5204 **starch-containing foodstuffs**
(Agr.)
(Agricultural produce, agricultural raw material.)
d stärkehaltige Nahrungsmittel *npl*
f aliments *mpl* féculents
p produtos *mpl* alimentícios contendo amido

5205 **starch dyspepsia**
(Med.)
(Indigestion caused by protein deficiency.)
d Mehldyspepsie *f*; durch Mehlnährschaden bedingte Verdauungsstörung *f*
f dyspepsie *f* alimentaire par les farineux
p dispepsia *f* alimentar por farinhas

5206 **starch employment in the food industry**
(Prod.)
(Food processing technology.)
d Stärkeeinsatz *m* in der Nahrungsmittelindustrie
f emploi *m* de la fécule dans l'industrie alimentaire
p emprego *m* do amido na indústria alimentícia; emprego *m* da fécula na indústria alimentícia

5207 **starch employment in the kitchen**
(Prod.)
(Gastronomy; e.g. in soup preparation.)
d Stärkeeinsatz *m* in der Küche
f emploi *m* de la fécule en cuisine
p emprego *m* do amido na cozinha; emprego *m* da fécula na cozinha

* **starch flour → 5203**

5208 **starch gelatinization**
(Biochem.)
(Food biochemistry.)
d Stärkegelatinisierung *f*
f gélatinisation *f* de l'amidon
p gelatinização *f* do amido

* **starch gum → 1613**

5209 **starch hydrolyzate**
(Biochem.)
(Food biochemistry.)
d Hydrolysat *n* der Stärke; der Stärke Hydrolyseprodukt *n*
f hydrolysat *m* d'amidon; produit *m* d'hydrolyse d'amidon
p produto *m* de hidrólise do amido

5210 **starch-rich foodstuffs**
(Prod.)
(Food processing technology, research; e.g. potato-based food.)
d stärkereiche Nahrungsmittel *npl*
f aliments *mpl* riches en amidon; aliments *mpl* riches en fécule
p produtos *mpl* alimentícios ricos em amido; alimentos *mpl* ricos em amido

5211 **starter**
(Prod.)
(Gastronomy. The Portuguese "acepipe" is used in Portugal, not in Brazil.)
d Vorspeise *f*
f entrée *f*
p entrada *f*; acepipe *m*

5212 **starting components**
(Prod.)
(Aroma/flavour/fragrance research and production.)
d Ausgangsbestandteile *mpl*
f constituants *mpl* du départ
p componentes *mpl* primários

5213 **starting material**
(Prod.)
(Aroma/flavour research and production.)
d Ausgangsprodukt *n*
f produit *m* du départ
p matéria *f* prima

* **start of grape harvest → 581**

* **starvation cure → 2767**

5214 **steam** *v*
(Prod.)
(Treatment process.)
d dünsten; dämpfen
f étuver
p estufar

5215 **steam condensation**
(Prod.)
(Food processing technology; ref. to thermal treatment. Change of phases: Vapour into a liquid.)
d Verdichtung *f* des Dampfes; Dampfkondensation *f*
f condensation *f* de la vapeur
p condensação *f* de vapor

5216 **steam distillation**
(Prod.)
(Food processing technology; distillation process. Distillation of liquids, inmiscible with water, by steam addition.)
d Wasserdampfdestillation *f*
f distillation *f* à vapeur
p destilação *f* a vapor

5217 **steamed meat**
(Prod.)
(Gastronomy.)
d gedünstetes Fleisch *n*
f viande *f* cuite à la vapeur; viande *f* cuite à l'étuvée
p carne *f* cozida no vapor

5218 **steaming**
(Prod.)
(Food treatment by vapour, specially referring to meat processing.)
d Dünsten *n*; Dämpfen *n*
f ébouillantage *f*; étuvée *f*
p estufagem *f*

5219 **steam sterilization**
(Prod.)
(Food processing technology. Sterilization process for tins, cans etc.)
d Dampfsterilisation *f*
f stérilisation *f* à vapeur
p esterilização *f* a vapor

5220 **stearic acid**
(Prod.)
($C_{18}H_{36}O_2$; long chained fatty acid of 18 carbon atoms; glyceride in animal fats, animal oil and some vegetable oils; e.g. in fatty acid synthesis: prime material for aroma/fragrance production.)
d Stearinsäure *f*
f acide *m* stéarique
p ácido *m* esteárico

5221 **steatosis of the liver**
(Med.)
(Fatty liver disease.)
d Leberverfettung *f*
f maladie *f* foi de gras; stéatose *f* du foie
p esteatose *f* hepática

5222 **steer; ox**
(Agr.)
(Cattle breeding: Castrated males of the cow family: Ox generally used as beast of burden; steer is raised for beef.)
d Ochse *m*
f bœuf *m*
p boi *m*

* **step** *v* **up fermentation** → 720

5223 **stepwise reduction of oxygen in tissues**
(Biochem.)
(Vitamin/food biochemistry; ref. to tissue antioxidants, vitamin functions, e.g. of vitamin E.)
d stufenweise Reduktion *f* von Gewebssauerstoff
f réduction *f* graduelle d'oxygène tissulaire
p redução *f* gradual do oxigênio tissular

5224 **sterilization**
(Prod.)
(Food processing technology: Elimination of all microorganism: Foodstuff treatment principally by heat sterilization: over 100° C.)
d Sterilisation *f*; Sterilisierung *f*
f stérilisation *f*
p esterilização *f*

5225 **sterilization in biochemistry**
(Biochem.)
(Microbiology; process of elimination of living microorganisms.)
d biochemische Sterilisation *f*; biochemische Sterilisierung *f*
f stérilisation *f* en biochimie
p esterilização *f* na bioquímica

5226 **sterilization with simultaneous aseptic filling up**
(Prod.)
(Food processing technology.)
d Sterilisierung *f* mit gleichzeitiger keimfreier Nachfüllung
f stérilisation *f* avec remplissage aseptique
p esterilização *f* junto com enchimento asséptico

5227 **sterilized milk**
(Prod.)
(Dairy product. Milk prepared and conserved at 100° C.)
d sterilisierte Milch *f*
f lait *m* stérilisé
p leite *m* esterilizado

5228 **steroids**
(Biochem.)
(Nutritional science; here are included: vitamin D, feminine and masculine sex hormones and those of the adrenal cortex etc; group of biologically important organic compounds.)
d Steroide *npl*
f stéroïdes *mpl*
p esteróides *mpl*

5229 **sterols**
(Biochem.)
(Natural substances, either free sterols or fatty

acid esters; e.g. ergosterol of yeast is a precursor of vitamin D.)
d Sterine *npl*; Sterole *npl*
f stérols *mpl*
p esteróis *npl*

5230 **sterol synthesis**
(Biochem.)
(Natural substances, either free sterols or fatty acid esters; e.g. ergosterol of yeast is a precursor of vitamin D.)
d Sterolsynthese *f*; Sterinsynthese *f*
f synthèse *f* du stérol
p síntese *f* do esterol

5231 **stew**
(Prod.)
(Gastronomy; culinary preparation with vegetables, and meat.)
d Eintopf *m*
f potée *f*
p ensopado *m*

5232 **stew** *v*
(Prod.)
(Food processing technology: gastronomy; culinary preparation method.)
d schmoren
f mijoter
p guisar

* **stigma of the carpel → 5233**

5233 **stigma of the pistil; stigma of the carpel**
(Agr.)
(Botany; pollen-receiving top part of a flower carpel.)
d Narbe *f* des Stempels; Narbe *f* des Fruchtblattes
f stigmate *m* du pistil
p estigma *m* do pistilo

5234 **stimulate** *v* **digestion**
(Med.)
(Property of certain food products like roughage: food containing fibre material.)
d Verdauung fördern
f favoriser la digestion
p favorecer a digestão; beneficiar a digestão

5235 **stimulation of microbial life**
(Agr.)
(Soil treatment.)
d Anregung *f* des mikrobiellen Lebens
f stimulation *f* de la vie microbienne
p estimulação *f* da vida microbial; estimulação *f* da vida microbiana

5236 **stimulation of the hypothalamus**
(Med.)
(Baby nutrition. Lactation stimulation of the mother via hypothalamus stimulation through nursing.)
d Hypothalamusanregung *f*; Stimulierung *f* des Hypothalamus; Stimulieren *n* des Hypothalamus
f stimulation *f* de l'hypothalamus
p estimulação *f* do hipotálamo

5237 **stinging nettle**
(Agr.)
(Biological agriculture. Genus "Urtica"; used in soil treatment compounds.)
d Brennessel *f*
f ortie *f*
p urtiga *f*

5238 **sting of the bee**
(Agr.)
(Apiculture: Stinging organ of the bee, of the female (worker) bee.)
d Stachel *m* der Biene
f aiguillon *m* d'abeille
p ferrão *m* da abelha

5239 **stirred curd cheese**
(Prod.)
(Dairy product.)
d geschlagener Quark *m*
f caillebotte *f* fouettée
p ricota *f* batida

* **St.John's bread → 949**

5240 **stock**
(Agr.)
(Viticulture; ref. to grafting process: the shoot (scion) of the desired variety is grafted into the stock, which is the rooted member of the graft.)
d Wildling *m*
f porte-greffe *m*
p porta-enxerto *m*

5241 **stock cube; bouillon cube**
(Prod.)
(Food processing technology.)
d Brühwürfel *m*
f tablette *f* de bouillon concentré; cube *m* de consommé
p cubo *m* de caldo

5242 **stomach**
(Med.)
(Anatomy.)
d Magen *m*
f estomac *m*
p estômago *m*

* **stomach lining → 2456**

5243 **stomatic flora**
(Med.)
(Flora of the mouth.)
d Mundflora *f*
f flore *f* stomatique
p flora *f* estomática

5244 **stomatitis**
(Med.)
(Mouth inflammation; can be due to niacin (nicotinic acid) and vitamin B_2 deficiency. Vitamin B_6 deficiency.)
d Stomatitis *f*; Mundentzündung *f*
f stomatite *f*
p estomatite *f*

5245 **stone; fruit pit**
(Agr.)
(Botany; endocarp of stone fruit, e.g. plum, peach.)
d Stein *m*
f noyau *m*
p caroço *m*

* **stone** *v* → **4196**

5246 **stone fruit; drupe**
(Agr.)
(Botany; fruit that develops from a cell ovar and is surrounded by a hard endocarp, called stone or pit. The endocarp is surrounded by the fleshy edible fruit part, called mesocarp; e.g. peaches.)
d Steinobst *n*
f fruits *mpl* à noyau; drupe *f*
p drupa *f*

* **stop** *v* **wine fermentation** → **2975**

5247 **storage loss**
(Prod.)
(Food processing technology and marketing.)
d Lagerungsverlust *m*
f perte *f* par stockage
p perda *f* por armazenamento

5248 **storage under deep temperatures**
(Prod.)
(Food processing technology and marketing.)
d Kälteeinlagerung *f*
f stockage *m* à basse température
p armazenamento *m* a baixas temperaturas

5249 **store** *v* **in the barn**
(Agr.)
(Agricultural produce. Storage.)
d in die Scheune bringen; in die Scheune einfahren
f engranger; mettre en grange
p pôr no celeiro; armanezar na granja

5250 **strain adapted to the wine types**
(Biochem.)
(Enology; yeast strains of specific qualities in fermentation, in wine production.)
d den Weintypen angepasster Strang *m*
f souche *f* adaptée aux types de vin
p cepa *f* adaptada aos tipos de vinho; raça *f* adaptada aos tipos de vinho

5251 **strained honey**
(Agr.)
(Apiculture. Honey elaboration process. Honey type.)
d Schleuderhonig *m*
f miel *m* extrait par centrifugation
p mel *m* centrifugado

5252 **strains**
(Biochem.)
(Microbiology; microorganisms: lineage.)
d Stränge *mpl*
f souches *fpl*
p cepas *fpl*; raças *fpl*

5253 **strains of selected microorganisms**
(Biochem.)
(Microbiology.)
d Stränge *mpl* von ausgewählten Mikroorganismen; Stränge *mpl* ausgewählter Mikroorganismen
f souches *fpl* de microorganismes sélectionnés
p cepas *fpl* de microorganismos selecionados

* **stratum** → **2483**

5254 **stratus**
(Agr.)
(Climatology; 600-2,100 m high (2,000-7,000 feet).)
d Schichtwolke *f*
f stratus *m*; nuage *m* en nappe
p estrato *m*

5255 **strawberry**
(Agr.)
(Horticulture. Genus "Fragaria"; soft fruit.)
d Erdbeere *f*
f fraise *f*
p morango *m*

5256 **strawberry flan**
(Prod.)
(Confectionary; fruit flan.)
d Erdbeertorte *f*
f tarte *f* aux fraises
p torta *f* de morangos

5257 **streaky bacon**
(Prod.)
(Butchery; bacon-type.)

d durchwachsener Speck *m*
f lard *m* maigre
p toucinho *m* entremeado

* **strengthen** *v* **vinosity → 4653**

5258 streptococcus
(Med.)
(Baby nutrition: there have been identified specific antibodies in human milk, e.g. against streptococcus, staphylococcus etc.)
d Streptokokkus *m*
f streptocoque *m*
p estreptococo *m*

* **stripper column → 4605**

5259 stripping of leaves
(Agr.)
(Botany. Plant culture process.)
d Entblätterung *f*; Entblättern *n*
f effeuillage *m*
p desfolhamento *m*

5260 strong acid
(Biochem.)
(Food biochemistry; almost completely dissociated in water: e.g. sulphuric acid (H_2SO_4).)
d starke Säure *f*
f acide *m* fort
p ácido *m* forte

5261 strontium sulphate
(Prod.)
($SrSO_4$; element eventually contained in form of traces in mineral water.)
d Strontiumsulfat *n*
f sulfate *m* de strontium
p sulfato *m* de estrôncio

5262 structural elements of the cells
(Biochem.)
(Biochemical research in nutritional science.)
d Zellbausteine *mpl*; Strukturelemente *npl* der Zelle
f éléments *mpl* structuraux des cellules
p elementos *mpl* estruturais das células

5263 structural modification of the nutrient
(Biochem.)
(Food biochemistry.)
d Strukturänderung *f* des Nahrungsmittels
f modification *f* structurale du nutriment
p modificação *f* estrutural do nutriente

5264 structural study
(Biochem.)
(Food biochemistry.)
d Strukturuntersuchung *f*
f étude *f* structurale
p estudos *fpl* estruturais

5265 structural variety of the proteins
(Biochem.)
(Nutritional science; this variety is the cause of their functional diversity. See: active proteins and passive proteins.)
d strukturelle Vielfalt *f* der Proteine
f variété *f* structurelle des protéines
p variedade *f* estrutural das proteínas

5266 structure of agricultural exploitation
(Agr.)
(Biological agriculture.)
d Struktur *f* der landwirtschaftlichen Nutzung
f structure *f* de l'exploitation agricole
p estrutura *f* da exploração agrícola

5267 structure of enzymes
(Biochem.)
(Biochemical research in nutritional science.)
d Struktur *f* der Enzyme
f structure *f* des enzymes
p estrutura *f* das enzimas

5268 structure of the flavouring agent
(Prod.)
(Aroma/fragrance research and production.)
d Geschmacksstoffstruktur *f*
f structure *f* de l'aromatisant
p estrutura *f* de aromatizante

5269 structure of the phospholipid
(Biochem.)
(Nutritional science; ref. to a phosphate group-containing lipid; e.g. lecithins; constituent of all kind of tissues, e.g. of the brain.)
d Struktur *f* des Phospholipides
f structure *f* du phospholipide
p estrutura *f* do fosfolipídio

5270 stubble field
(Agr.)
(Soil; field characteristic.)
d Stoppelfeld *n*
f champ *m* en chaume
p restolhal *m*

5271 stuffed dough
(Prod.)
(Bakery. Confectionary.)
d gefüllter Teig *m*
f pâte *f* farcie
p massa *f* recheada

5272 stuffed olive
(Prod.)
(Gastronomy.)

d gefüllte Olive *f*
f olive *f* farcie
p aceitona *f* recheiada

5273 **stuffing; farce**
(Prod.)
(Gastronomy; forcemeat type of meat or fish.)
d Füllung *f*; Farce *f*
f farce *f*
p recheio *m*

5274 **stump**
(Med.)
(Anatomy; ref. to tooth condition.)
d Zahnstumpf *m*; Zahnstummel *m*
f chicot *m*; dent *f* cessée
p caco *m* (*de dente*)

5275 **sturgeon**
(Agr.)
(Family "Acipenseridae"; Fish. The roe is a caviar source.)
d Stör *m*
f esturgeon *m*
p esturjão *m*

* **style of the carpel → 5276**

5276 **style of the pistil; style of the carpel**
(Agr.)
(Botany; stalk of the pistil, of the carpel.)
d Griffel *m* des Stempels
f style *m* du pistil
p estilete *m* do pistilo

5277 **subcutaneous haemorrhage**
(Med.)
(Veterinary; subcutaneous bleeding.)
d subkutane Blutung *f*; unter der Haut befindliche Blutung *f*
f hémorragie *f* sous-cutanée
p hemorragia *f* subcutânea

5278 **subdivision**
(Agr.)
(Botany (flora/fauna). Ref. to taxonomic classification of organism, category between division and class.)
d Unterreich *n*
f sous-division *f*
p subreino *m*

5279 **subject *v* to drying; submit *v* to the drying process**
(Prod.)
(Food processing technology.)
d der Trocknung unterziehen; dem Trocknungsprozess unterziehen
f subir un séchage; soumettre au séchage
p sofrer secagem; submeter à secagem

5280 **submerge culture**
(Biochem.)
(Fermentation; brewery process, ref. to the submerged collocation of yeast, sedimented to the bottom of the fermentation tank.)
d Submersverfahren *n*; untergäriges Verfahren *n*
f culture *f* de submersion; fermentation *f* par culture de submersion
p processo *m* de baixa fermentação

5281 **submerge fermentation**
(Biochem.)
(Fermentation process type in beer brewing.)
d Submersgärung *f*
f fermentation *f* en submersion
p processo *m* de baixa fermentação

* **submit *v* to the drying process → 5279**

5282 **subnutrition**
(Med.)
d Unterernährung *f*
f sous-alimentation *f*; dénutrition *f*
p subnutrição *f*; desnutrição *f*

5283 **sub-optimal supply**
(Prod.)
(Vitamins in nutrition; e.g. of vitamins.)
d Unterversorgung *f*
f sous-entretien *m*
p suplementação *f* deficiente

5284 **sub-optimal vitamin supply**
(Med.)
(Veterinary e.g. ref. farm animal raising, fodder composition.)
d suboptimale Vitaminversorgung *f*
f approvisionnement *m* vitaminique sous-optimal
p suprimento *m* subótimo de vitaminas

5285 **subphylum**
(Agr.)
(Botany (flora/fauna). Ref. to taxonomic classification of organism, category between phylum and class.)
d Unterstamm *m*
f sous-phylum *m*
p subfilo *m*

5286 **subproducts of fish-processing industry**
(Prod.)
(Livestock nutrition; food industrialization: subproducts used in feedstuff.)
d Nebenprodukte *fpl* der fischverarbeitenden Industrie
f sous-produits *mpl* de l'industrie de transformation des poissons; sous-produits *mpl* de l'industrie de la pêche
p subprodutos *mpl* da indústria de peixes

5287 **subproducts of meat-processing industry**
(Agr.)
(Livestock nutrition; food industrialization: subproducts used in feedstuff.)
d Nebenprodukte *fpl* der fleischverarbeitenden Industrie
f sous-produits *mpl* de l'industrie de transformation de la viande
p subprodutos *mpl* da indústria de carnes

* **subsequent contamination → 4261**

* **subsequent treatment → 2435**

5288 **subsoil**
(Agr.)
(Soil; "B" horizon profile, under the "A" topsoil, not used for tillage purposes.)
d Untergrund *m*
f sous-sol *m*
p subsolo *m*

5289 **substance with a high boiling point**
(Prod.)
(Food processing technology; substance characteristic.)
d schwer siedende Substanz *f*; Substanz *f* hohen Siedepunktes
f substance *f* de point élevé d'ébullition
p substância *f* de alto ponto de ebulição

5290 **substance with a low boiling point**
(Prod.)
(Food processing technology.)
d leichtsiedende Substanz *f*; Substanz *f* niedrigen Siedepunktes
f substance *f* de point bas d'ébullition
p substância *f* de baixo ponto de ebulição

5291 **substantial** *adj*
(Prod.)
(Food processing technology; food quality.)
d gehaltvoll
f substantiel; nutritif; nourissant
p substancial; substancioso; nutritivo

5292 **substrate**
(Biochem.)
(Food biochemistry; basis material for biochemical enzyme reaction.)
d Substrat *n*; Keimboden *m*; Nährboden *m*
f substrat *m*
p substrato *m*

5293 **successive steps**
(Prod.)
(Food production technology.)
d aufeinanderfolgende Etappen *fpl*
f étapes *fpl* successives
p etapas *fpl* sucessivas

5294 **succinic acid**
(Med.)
($C_4H_6O_4$; amber acid present in the Krebs cycle (citric acid cycle): reaction sequence in the body.)
d Bernsteinsäure *f*
f acide *m* succinique
p ácido *m* succínico

* **succulence → 3056**

5295 **succulent** *adj*; **juicy** *adj*; **tasty** *adj*
(Prod.)
(Gastronomy.)
d saftig; schmackhaft
f succulent; délicieux
p suculento; sucoso

5296 **sucking pig**
(Agr.)
(Livestock. Very young pig.)
d Spanferkel *n*
f cochon *m* de lait
p leitão *f*

5297 **suckle** *v*
(Med.)
(Baby nutrition.)
d saugen
f téter
p sugar

5298 **sucklings dyspepsia**
(Med.)
(Alimentary indigestion of babies.)
d Säuglingsdyspepsie *f*; ernährungsbedingte Verdauungstörung *f* des Säuglings
f dyspepsie *f* alimentaire des nourrissons
p dispepsia *f* alimentar do lactente

5299 **suction**
(Med.)
(Baby nutrition. Act of sucking.)
d Saugen *n*
f succion *f*
p sucção *f*; sução *f*

5300 **suctorial ped**
(Agr.)
(Apiculture: Bee anatomy: hind leg of a worker bee.)
d Haftballen *m*
f pelote *f* adhésive
p ventosa *f* da pata

5301 **sudden drop in temperature**
(Agr.)
(Climatology.)
d Temperatursturz *m*
f chute *f* de température
p queda *f* de temperatura

5302 **suet**
(Prod.)
(Butchery; animal fat (kidney and loins); tallow source.)
d Talg *m*; Nierenfett *n*
f suif *m*
p sebo *m*

5303 **sugar**
(Agr.)
(($C_{12}H_{22}O_{11}$); Refined sucrose; main source is sugar cane.)
d Zucker *m*
f sucre *m*
p açúcar *m*

5304 **sugar beet**
(Agr.)
("Beta vulgaris"; Horticulture; sugar source in the temperate zones.)
d Zuckerrübe *f*
f betterave *f* à sucre
p beterraba *f* doce

5305 **sugar candy**
(Prod.)
(Confectionary; crystallized sugar; also a confection.)
d Kandiszucker *m*
f sucre *m* candi
p açúcar-cande *m*

5306 **sugarcane**
(Agr.)
(Agricultural produce. "Saccharum officinarum"; sugar source: saccharose; sucrose; refined for table sugar; at 200°C it becomes caramel.)
d Zuckerrohr *n*
f canne *f* à sucre
p cana *m* de açúcar

5307 **sugarcane bagasse; crushed sugarcane husks**
(Agr.)
(Livestock nutrition; feedstuff basis: The entire sugar cane has ca. 15% of fibre, produces ca. 90% of syrup and furnishes 500 kg of husks per t (1,000 kg) with humidity content of 50%.)
d Zuckerrohrbagasse *f*; Bagasse *f*
f bagasse *f*; résidu *m* des tiges de canne à sucre
p bagaço *m* da cana-de-açúcar

5308 **sugarcane brandy**
(Prod.)
(Alcoholic beverage made from sugar cane or cane molasses.)
d Zuckerrohrschnaps *m*
f guildive *f* de canne à sucre
p cachaça *f*; pinga *f*

* **sugarcane juice → 885**

5309 **sugarcane products**
(Agr.)
(Agricultural produce; sugar source.)
d Zuckerrohrprodukte *npl*
f produits *mpl* de canne à sucre
p produtos *mpl* de cana-de-açúcar

5310 **sugar-coated** *adj*
(Prod.)
(Confectionary; ref. to sweets, cakes etc.)
d zuckerübergossen
f saupoudré de sucre
p coberto com açúcar

5311 **sugar contents of the grape must**
(Prod.)
(Enology; wine production techniques.)
d Zuckergehalt *m* des Traubenmostes
f teneur *f* en sucre du moût de raisin
p teor *m* de açúcar do mosto de uvas

5312 **sugar culture medium**
(Biochem.)
(Fermentation: carbohydrate fermentation control.)
d Zuckernährboden *m*
f milieu *m* de culture sucré
p meio *m* de cultura de·açúcar

5313 **sugar degradation**
(Biochem.)
(Fermentation; enology.)
d Zuckerabbau *m*
f dégradation *f* du sucre
p degradação *f* de açúcar

5314 **sugared almond**
(Prod.)
(Confectionary.)
d Konfekt *n*; Zuckerwerk *n*
f dragées *fpl*
p confeito *m*

5315 **sugared aroma**
(Prod.)
(Aroma/flavour research and production: e.g. fruit aromas of red fruits: strawberries.)
d gezuckertes Aroma *n*
f arôme *m* sucré
p aroma *m* açucarado

5316 **sugared unskimmed milk**
(Med.)
(Baby nutrition: milk with saccharose addition.)
d gesüßte Vollmilch *f*, mit Zucker gesüßte Vollmilch *f*

f lait *m* entier sucré
p leite *m* integral açucarado

5317 **sugar factory**
(Prod.)
(Food processing technology and production: raw sugar treatment and transformation.)
d Zuckerfabrik *f*; Zuckerindustrie *f*
f sucrerie *f*
p usina *f* de açúcar; indústria *f* açucareira

5318 **sugar fermentation**
(Biochem.)
(Fermentation. Monosaccharides are the simplest sugar types.)
d Zuckerfermentation *f*
f fermentation *f* du sucre
p fermentação *f* de açúcar

5319 **sugar-free diet**
(Med.)
(Alimentary regimen; e.g. in the case of diabetes mellitus.)
d zuckerfreie Diät *f*
f diète *f* sans sucre; diète *f* exempte de sucre
p dieta *f* isenta de açúcar

5320 **sugaring of the must**
(Biochem.)
(Enology: wine production; adding of sugar before fermentation.)
d Zusetzen *n* von Zucker zum Most; Zuckerzusatz *m* zum Most
f sucrage *m* du moût; chaptalisation *f*
p adicionação *f* de açúcar ao mosto; adicionamento *m* de açúcar ao mosto

5321 **sugar of human milk; mother's milk sugar**
(Med.)
(Baby nutrition: lactose.)
d Zucker *m* der Muttermilch
f sucre *m* du lait maternel
p açúcar *m* do leite maternal

5322 **sugar-rich grape**
(Agr.)
(Viticulture; grape quality.)
d zuckerreiche Beere *f*
f grain *m* de raisin riche en sucre
p uva *f* rica em açúcar

5323 **sugar richness of the grape**
(Agr.)
(Viticulture; grape quality.)
d Zuckerreichhaltigkeit *f* der Weinbeere
f richesse *f* en sucre du grain de raisin
p riqueza *f* do teor de açúcar da uva do vinho

5324 **sugar succedaneum**
(Biochem.)
(Nutritional science: e.g. fructose, mannitol, sorbitol, xylitol (polyalcohols).)
d Zuckeraustauschstoff *m*
f succédané *m* du sucre
p sucedâneo *m* do açúcar

5325 **Suiss breed; Schwyz breed**
(Agr.)
(Cattle breeding; cattle of Swiss origin.)
d schweizer Braunvieh *n*
f bétail *m* suisse brun
p raça *f* Pardo-Suiça

5326 **sulphates**
(Prod.)
(Salts and esters of sulphuric acid (H_2SO_4); e.g. auxiliary in caramel production.)
d Sulfate *npl*
f sulfates *mpl*
p sulfatos *mpl*

5327 **sulphur**
(Biochem.)
(Vitamin/food biochemistry: S. Present in the structure of vitamin B_1 and in biotin.)
d Schwefel *m*
f soufre *m*
p enxofre *m*

5328 **sulphur deficiency**
(Med.)
(Veterinary; S-deficiency; a rare mineral deficiency; generally abundant within the organism, especially in the rumen.)
d Schwefelmangel *m*
f carence *f* en soufre
p deficiência *f* de enxofre; carência *f* de enxofre

5329 **sulphur dioxide; sulphurous anhydride**
(Prod.)
(SO_2; sulphúrous oxide. Food preservative. Fermentation control agent in wine production. Acid-adjusting agent of the extraction water in sugar factories, bacteria-growth prevention; antioxidant.)
d Schwefeldioxid *n*; Schwefligsäureanhydrid *n*
f dioxyde *m* de sulfure; anhydride *m* sulfureux
p dióxido *m* de enxofre; anidrido *m* sulfuroso

5330 **sulphuric acid**
(Prod.)
(H_2SO_4; starch-syrup production process. Oil purification. Auxiliary.)
d Schwefelsäure *f*
f acide *m* sulfurique
p ácido *m* sulfúrico

* **sulphuring → 5331**

* **sulphuring of the vintage → 5332**

5331 **sulphurization; sulphuring; sulphurizing process**
(Prod.)
(Food processing technology; food conservation; wine treatment.)
d Schwefelung *f*
f soufrage *m*; sulfuration *f*
p sulfuração *f*; sulfurização *f*; enxoframento *m*

5332 **sulphurization of the vintage; sulphuring of the vintage; sulphurizing of the vintage**
(Agr.)
(Viticulture, winegrowing.)
d Schwefelung *f* der Weinernte
f soufrage *m* de la vendange
p sulfuração *f* da vindima; sulforização *f* da vindima

* **sulphurizing of the vintage → 5332**

* **sulphurizing process → 5331**

5333 **sulphurous** *adj*
(Prod.)
(Food processing technology; see sulphurous acid.)
d schwefligsauer
f sulfureux
p sulfuroso

5334 **sulphurous acid**
(Prod.)
(H_2SO_3; conservation auxiliary for foodstuff; in wine: for stabilization, acetaldehyde neutralization, wild-fermentation inhibitor.)
d schweflige Säure *f*
f acide *m* sulfureux
p ácido *m* sulfuroso

* **sulphurous anhydride → 5329**

5335 **sultana; raisin**
(Prod.)
(Dried seedless grape, used as baking ingredient.)
d Sultanine *f*; Rosine *f*
f raisin *m* sec
p uva-passa *f*; passa *f*

* **summer squash → 1383**

5336 **sun-dried green forage**
(Agr.)
(Livestock nutrition: specially processed (open-air dried) vegetable material for animal feeding.)
d sonnengetrocknetes Grünfutter *n*
f fourrage *m* vert séché au soleil
p forragem *f* verde secada ao sol

5337 **sunflower**
(Agr.)
(Horticulture. "Helianthus". The seeds yield an edible oil by milling, used in foodstuff elaboration, as salad oil, in certain margarine types and in the production of candies.)
d Sonnenblume *f*
f tournesol *m*
p girassol *m*

5338 **sunflower oil**
(Prod.)
(Food processing technology.)
d Sonnenblumenöl *n*
f huile *f* de tournesol
p óleo *m* de girassol

5339 **sunflower-oil margarine**
(Prod.)
(Food processing technology; food industrialization.)
d Sonnenblumenölmargarine *f*
f margarine *f* du tournesol
p margarina *f* de óleo de girassol

5340 **superconsummation**
(Med.)
(Nutrition.)
d Überkonsum *m*; übertriebener Verzehr *m*
f surconsommation *f*
p superconsumação *f*

5341 **supercooled; undercooled**
(Prod.)
(Food processing technology: supercooled food (below the freezing point, however without solidification).)
d unterkühlt
f rafraîchi
p resfriado

5342 **supercooled foodstuffs; undercooled foodstuffs**
(Prod.)
(Food processing technology: cooling process below the freezing point.)
d unterkühlte Nahrungsmittel *npl*
f produits *mpl* alimentaires surrefroidis
p produtos *mpl* alimentícios superrefrigerados; alimentos *mpl* superesfriados

5343 **superficial erosion**
(Agr.)
(Soil; extensive superficial floodwater-erosion of the soil; a laminar (layer-form) erosion.)
d Oberflächenerosion *f*
f érosion *f* superficielle
p erosão *f* superficial; erosão *f* laminar

5344 **superficial soil aeration and loosening-up**
(Agr.)
(Soil treatment; biological agriculture.)
d Wiederauflockerung *f* des Bodens; Wiederpflügen *n*
f binage *m*; rélabourage *m*
p reaeração *f* do solo

5345 **superficial soil layer**
(Agr.)
(Soil.)
d Bodenoberfläche *f*
f couche *f* superficielle du sol
p camada *f* superficial do solo

5346 **superphosphate**
(Agr.)
(Soil treatment; monobasic calcium phosphate/calcium sulphate based fertilizer type.)
d Superphosphat *n*
f superphosphate *m*
p superfosfato *m*

* **superpressure → 3947**

* **supper → 1998**

5347 **supplementary addition**
(Prod.)
(Vitamins in nutrition; vitamin addition in food.)
d Supplementierung *f*
f addition *f* supplémentaire
p suplementação *f*

5348 **supplementation of antioxidant factors**
(Biochem.)
(Food biochemistry.)
d Ergänzungszufuhr *f* an Antioxidantienfaktoren; Supplementierung *f* an Antioxidantienfaktoren
f supplémentation *f* en facteurs antioxydants
p suplementação *f* de fatores antioxidantes

5349 **supplementation with a trace mineral salt**
(Med.)
(Veterinary; ref. to feed supplementation.)
d Supplementierung *f* an einem Spurenmineraliensalz
f supplémentation *f* en un sel de minéral de trace
p suplementação *f* por um sal de um micromineral

* **supposed toxicity over a long period → 4359**

5350 **suppress *v* lipid oxidation**
(Biochem.)
(Nutritional science; ref. to restructured meat in meat processing.)
d Lipidoxidation unterdrücken
f supprimer l'oxydation lipidique
p suprimir a oxidação lipídica

5351 **suprarenal gland**
(Med.)
(Anatomy; two adrenal glands, on the upper surface of the kidney.)
d Nebenniere *f*
f capsule *f* surrénale
p cápsula *f* supre-renal

5352 **surface-culture brewery technique; surface fermentation**
(Biochem.)
(Fermentation. Brewery process: surface collocation of yeast, upon the liquid in the fermentation tank.)
d Oberflächengärung *f*
f culture *f* en surface; fermentation *f* par culture en surface
p processo *m* de alta fermentação

5353 **surface dehydration**
(Prod.)
(Food processing technology: treatment of slaughtered poultry: conservation technique.)
d Oberflächendehydratation *f*; Oberflächendehydratisierung *f*
f déshydratation *f* de surface
p desidratação *f* de superfície

5354 **surface drying**
(Prod.)
(Food processing technology. Pasta plant technology for pasta drying, to prevent from sticking together.)
d Oberflächentrocknung *f*
f séchage *m* de surface
p secagem *f* superficial

* **surface fermentation → 5352**

5355 **surface fertilization with compost**
(Agr.)
(Biological agriculture.)
d Oberflächenkompostierung *f*
f compostage *m* en surface
p adubação *f* orgânica de superfície

5356 **surface losses**
(Agr.)
(Livestock nutrition; animal ration production: losses that can occur during the conservation period of rations.)
d Oberflächenverluste *mpl*
f pertes *fpl* de la surface
p perdas *fpl* de superfície

5357 **surface mold of cheese**
(Prod.)
(Dairy product; cheese component.)
d Oberflächenschimmelpilz *m* des Käses
f moisissures *fpl* en surface de fromage
p bolor *m* superficial do queijo

* **surface of the lithosphere → 4965**

5358 **surface renewal**
(Prod.)
(Aroma/flavour research and production.)
d Oberflächenerneuerung *f*
f renouvellement *m* des surfaces
p renovação *f* da superfície

5359 **surface treatment of food**
(Prod.)
(Food processing technology. Conservation methods: conservation products which are not incorporated into foodstuff, e.g. sulphur dioxide (SO_2) in treatment of dried fruits.)
d Oberflächenbehandlung *f* von Lebensmitteln
f traitement *m* de surfaces de denrées alimentaires
p tratamento *m* da superfície de alimentos

5360 **surface water**
(Prod.)
(Origin: A superficial freshwater surface. Drinking water source.)
d Oberflächenwasser *n*
f eau *f* douce superficielle; eau *f* de ruissellement; eau *f* de surface
p água *f* doce superficial

5361 **surplus chlorine**
(Prod.)
(Ref. to drinking water, tap water treatment.)
d überschüssiges Chlor *n*
f chlore *m* excédent
p cloro *m* em excesso

5362 **surplus of agricultural products**
(Agr.)
(Agricultural produce.)
d Überschuss *m* an Agrarprodukten
f surplus *m* agricole
p excedente *m* agrícola

5363 **surplus production**
(Agr.)
(Biological agriculture.)
d Überschussproduktion *f*; überschüssige Produktion *f*
f production *f* excédentaire
p produção *f* excedente

5364 **surplus supply of vitamins**
(Agr.)
(Livestock nutrition: Excess supply of vitamins in animal rations, which can turn out to be harmful.)
d Vitaminüberangebot *n*
f surplus *m* vitaminique; surabondance *f* de vitamines
p fornecimento *m* superavitário de vitaminas

5365 **susceptibility to disease**
(Med.)
(Veterinary; e.g. ref. to livestock and poultry diseases.)
d Krankheitsanfälligkeit *f*
f susceptibilité *f* aux maladies
p suscetibilidade *f* para doenças

5366 **susceptibility to oxidative deterioration**
(Biochem.)
(Nutritional science; ref. to meat products, poultry products.)
d Anfälligkeit *f* gegen oxidativen Verderb
f susceptibilité *f* à la détérioration oxydative
p suscetibilidade *f* para deterioração oxidativa

5367 **susceptible culture**
(Agr.)
(Biological agriculture.)
d anfällige Kultur *f*; empfindliche Kultur *f*
f culture *f* vulnérable
p cultura *f* vulnerável; cultura *f* suscetível

5368 **suspension stabilizer**
(Prod.)
(Food processing technology.)
d Suspensionsstabilisator *m*
f stabilisant *m* de suspensions
p estabilizante *m* de suspensões

5369 **swallow** *v*
(Med.)
(Food transfer from the mouth through the oesophagus into the stomach: deglutition.)
d schlucken
f avaler; déglutir
p engolir; deglutir

5370 **swamp; swamp land; morass**
(Agr.)
(Soil; soil formation: wetland.)
d Sumpf *m*; Sumpfland *n*; Verwässerungszone *f*
f sol *m* marécageux
p charco *m*; atoleiro *m*; brejo *m*

* **swamp land → 5370**

5371 **swarm of bees**
(Agr.)
(Apiculture: emigrating bees; colony of bees.)
d Bienenschwarm *m*

f essai *m* d'abeilles
p enxame *m* de abelhas

5372 **Swede; rutabaga**
(Agr.)
(Horticulture. "Brassica napus napobrassica". Having a yellowish edible root.)
d Kohlrübe *f*; Steckrübe *f*
f chou-navet *m*; rutabaga *m*
p nabo *m*; rutabaga *f*

* **sweet → 1593**

* **sweet basil → 555**

5373 **sweet bread**
(Prod.)
(Bakery.)
d Einback *m*
f pain *m* de mie
p pão *m* doce

5374 **sweet butter; unsalted butter**
(Prod.)
(Dietetic dairy product.)
d nicht gesalzene Butter *f*; ungesalzene Butter *f*; salzfreie Butter *f*
f beurre *m* doux
p manteiga *f* sem sal

5375 **sweet cherry**
(Agr.)
("Prunus avium"; fruit.)
d Süßkirsche *f*
f guigne *f*
p cereja *f* doce

5376 **sweeten** *v*
(Prod.)
(Food processing technology: taste modification/product improvement.)
d süßen
f sucrer; édulcorer
p adoçar

5377 **sweetener**
(Prod.)
(Food processing technology; edulcorant: non-nutritive sweetening auxiliary, can be of natural or artificial origin.)
d Süßstoff *m*
f édulcorant *m*
p adoçante *m*; edulcorante *m*

5378 **sweetening additive**
(Prod.)
(Additives; e.g. for bakery.)
d süßende Zusatzstoffe *mpl*
f matières *fpl* sucrantes
p aditivos *mpl* edulcorantes

5379 **sweetening of dishes; sweetening of the meal**
(Prod.)
(Gastronomy.)
d Süßen *n* von Speisen; Süßen *n* von Gerichten
f sucrage *m* des plats; édulcoration *f* des mets
p adoçamento *m* dos pratos; adoçamento *m* da comida

* **sweetening of the meal → 5379**

5380 **sweetening power**
(Prod.)
(Food processing technology: ref. to artificial sweetening agents.)
d Süßkraft *f*
f pouvoir *m* édulcorant; pouvoir *m* sucrant
p poder *m* edulcorante; intensidade *f* adoçante

5381 **sweet flaky biscuits**
(Prod.)
(Confectionary.)
d süßes Blätterteiggebäck *n*
f biscuits *mpl* feuilletés sucrés
p biscoitos *mpl* folhados doces

5382 **sweet-fruity** *adj*
(Prod.)
(Flavour note.)
d süß-fruchtig
f douce-fruité
p doce de frutas

5383 **sweet-fruity flavour note**
(Prod.)
(Flavour note, flavour chemicals; elaboration of aromas: organic chemistry.)
d süß-fruchtige Geschmacksnote *f*
f note *f* saveur douce-fruitée
p nota *f* doce de sabor de frutas

5384 **sweetish**
(Prod.)
(Flavour notes.)
d süßlich
f douceâtre; douçâtre
p adocicado

5385 **sweet pepper; bell pepper**
(Agr.)
(Horticulture. "Capsicum" fruit.)
d süßer Paprika *m*
f piment *m* doux
p pimentão *m* doce

5386 **sweet potato**
(Agr.)
(Horticulture. "Ipomoea batatas"; tuberous edible root.)
d Süßkartoffel *f*; Batate *f*

f patate *f*; patate *f* douce
p batata *f* doce

5387 sweets
(Prod.)
(Confectionary; general denomination.)
d Süßigkeiten *fpl*
f sucreries *fpl*; friandises *fpl*
p doces *mpl*

5388 sweet taste
(Prod.)
(Flavour note; e.g. ref. to organoleptic food evaluation.)
d süßer Geschmack *m*
f goût *m* doux; saveur *f* douce
p gosto *m* doce; sabor *m* doce

* **sweet tidbit → 5389**

5389 sweet titbit; sweet tidbit
(Prod.)
(Gastronomy.)
d süßer Leckerbissen *n*
f gourmandise *f*
p iguaria *f* doce

* **sweet whey → 554**

5390 sweet wine
(Prod.)
(Enology; wine type.)
d Süßwein *m*
f vin *m* doux
p vinho *m* doce

5391 swelling
(Prod.)
(Failure in the food preserving and canning process: the tin distends by means of bacteriological action, due to insufficient sterilization.)
d Aufquellung *f*
f bombage *m*
p estufagem *f*

5392 swelling behaviour
(Biochem.)
(Food biochemistry; product characteristic: e.g. ref. to starch.)
d Quellverhalten *m*
f comportement *m* de renflement
p comportamento *m* de inchação; comportamento *m* de inchamento

5393 swelling capacity
(Biochem.)
(Food biochemistry; product characteristic under certain production processes; see modified starch.)
d Quellfähigkeit *f*
f capacité *f* de renflement
p capacidade *f* de inchação; capacidade *f* de inchamento

5394 swelling of gums
(Med.)
(Diseased gums.)
d Zahnfleischschwellung *f*
f enflure *f* des gencives; enflure *f* gingivale
p inchamento *m* das gengivas

5395 swelling pressure
(Prod.)
(Food processing technology; e.g. of powder substances in water.)
d Schwelldruck *m*; Anschwellungsdruck *m*
f pression *f* de gonflement
p pressão *f* de inchação

5396 swelling without gel formation; swelling without gelling
(Prod.)
(Food processing technology.)
d Anschwellen *n* ohne Gelbildung
f gonflement *m* sans formation de gel
p inchação *f* sem formação de gel

* **swelling without gelling → 5396**

5397 swine dysentery
(Med.)
(Veterinary; caused by pathologic intestinal microorganisms, as Treponema and Campylobacter.)
d Schweineruhr *f*
f dysenterie *f* des cochons
p disenteria *f* suína

5398 swine erysipelas
(Med.)
(Veterinary; Bacterium "Erysipelotrix rhusiopathiae".)
d Schweinerotlauf *m*; Schweinerose *f*
f érysipèle *m* dos cochons
p erisipela *f* suína

5399 swine influenza
(Med.)
(Veterinary; virus disease of the hogs.)
d Schweinegrippe *f*
f influenza *f* des porcs
p influenza *f* suína; gripe *f* dos porcos

5400 swine plague
(Med.)
(Veterinary; livestock devastating disease caused by a filterable virus.)
d Schweinepest *f*

f peste *f* porcine
p peste *f* suína

* **Swiss chard → 1029**

5401 **Swiss cheese with holes**
(Prod.)
(Dairy product; hard, mildly flavoured cheese type.)
d Schweizer Käse *m* mit Löchern
f fromage *m* suisse à trous
p queijo *m* suiço com buracos

5402 **symptomatic anthrax**
(Med.)
(Veterinary; caused by "Clostridium chanvoi" affecting the muscles of the hind legs of cattle and horses, causing them to limp; therefore the Brazilian word"manqueira", "mancar" = to limp.)
d symptomatischer Karbunkel *m*
f anthrax *m* symptomatique
p carbúnculo *m* sintomático; manqueira *f*

* **syncline → 5576**

* **syndrome of hyponatraemia → 2818**

* **syndrome of hyponatremia → 2818**

5403 **syneresis**
(Biochem.)
(Nutritional science. Loss of a part of water content in foodstuffs: e.g. cheese production.)
d Synärese *f*
f synérèse *f*
p sinérese *f*

5404 **synergistic effect**
(Biochem.)
(Food biochemistry.)
d synergistischer Effekt *m*; synergistische Auswirkung *f*
f effet *m* synergique
p efeito *m* sinérgico

5405 **synthesis of amino acids**
(Biochem.)
(Nutritional science.)
d Aminosäuresynthese *f*
f synthèse *f* des acides aminés; synthèse *f* d'amino-acides
p síntese *f* dos aminoácidos

5406 **synthesis of fatty acids**
(Biochem.)
(Nutritional science.)
d Fettsäuresynthese *f*
f synthèse *f* des acides gras
p síntese *f* dos ácidos graxos

5407 **synthesis of vitamin E in the plant**
(Med.)
(Veterinary; e.g. in the leaves of alfalfa and lettuce etc.; sources for feed components.)
d Vitamin E-Synthese *f* in der Pflanze
f synthèse *f* de la vitamine E dans la plante
p síntese *f* de vitamina E na planta

5408 **synthetic chemical products**
(Prod.)
(Chemical starting material. Prime material.)
d chemische Syntheseprodukte *npl*
f produits *mpl* chimiques de synthèse
p produtos *mpl* químicos de síntese

5409 **synthetic dyes**
(Prod.)
(Food colorants.)
d synthetische Farbstoffe *mpl*
f colorants *mpl* synthétiques
p corantes *mpl* sintéticos

* **synthetic flavour → 444**

5410 **synthetic molecule**
(Biochem.)
(Food biochemistry; aroma/fragrance research and production.)
d synthetisches Molekül *n*
f molécule *f* de synthèse
p molécula *f* sintética

5411 **synthetic phenolic antioxidant**
(Biochem.)
(Nutritional science; ref. to restructured meat in meat processing.)
d synthetisches phenolisches Antioxidant *n*
f antioxydante *m* phénolique synthétique
p antioxidante *m* fenólico sintético

5412 **synthetic polypeptides**
(Biochem.)
(Food biochemistry: research in nutritional science.)
d künstliche Polypeptide *npl*; synthetische Polypeptide *npl*
f polypeptides *mpl* synthétiques
p polipeptídeos *mpl* sintéticos

5413 **synthetic products; synthetic substances**
(Prod.)
(Organic chemistry. Ref. to the research of synthetic flavour chemicals and flavour notes.)
d Syntheseprodukte *npl*
f produits *mpl* de synthèse; substances *fpl* de synthèse
p produtos *mpl* sintéticos

* **synthetic substances → 5413**

5414 synthetic sweetener
(Prod.)
(Food processing technology; edulcorant, sweetening auxiliary.)
d synthetischer Süßstoff *m*
f édulcorant *m* de synthèse
p adoçante *m* sintético; edulcorante *m* sintético

5415 synthetic tocopherol
(Prod.)
(Vitamin in nutrition. Vit. E. $C_{29}H_{50}O_2$; also obtained from germ oils; used in food as an antioxidant.)
d synthetisches Tocopherol *n*
f tocophérol *m* synthétique
p tocoferol *m* sintético

5416 syrup
(Prod.)
(Food processing technology. Table syrup e.g. to eat on bread. Thick fruit juice from fruit boiling (preservation), drinkable by water addition: "Fruchtsirup" in German.)
d Sirup *m*
f sirop *m*
p xarope *m*

5417 systematic investigation
(Biochem.)
(Biochemical research in nutritional science.)
d systematische Untersuchung *f*
f étude *f* systématique
p estudo *m* sistemático

5418 systematic supplementation
(Biochem.)
(Food biochemistry.)
d systematischer Zuschuss *m*; systematische Ergänzungzufuhr *f*; systematische Supplementierung *f*
f supplémentation *f* systématique
p suplementação *f* sistemática

T

* **table salt → 4803**

5419 table salt substitute; table salt succedaneum
(Prod.)
(Food processing technology: e.g. sodium-free salt types for dietary purposes.)
d Kochsalzersatz *m*
f succédané *m* du sel de cuisine
p sucedâneo *m* do sal de cozinha

* **table salt succedaneum → 5419**

5420 table water
(Prod.)
(Drinking water with carbon dioxide.)
d Selterswasser *n*; Tafelwasser *n*; Sprudel *m*
f eau *f* gazeuse; eau *f* de Seltz
p água *f* mineral com gás

5421 table wine
(Agr.)
(Enology; wine served with dishes.)
d Tafelwein *m*
f vin *m* de table; vin *m* de consommation courante
p vinho *m* de mesa

5422 tachyphagia
(Med.)
(Action of hasty eating, accompanied by insufficient mastication and saliva production for normal digestion.)
d Tachyphagie *f*; hastiges Essen *n*
f tachyphagie *f*; action *f* de manger trop vite
p taquifagia *f*; hábito *m* de comer rápido

5423 tactile stimulation
(Med.)
(Baby nutrition. Stimulation by nursing.)
d Anregung *f* des Tastsinnes
f stimulation *f* tactile
p estimulação *f* tátil

* **taffy → 5510**

5424 tail
(Med.)
(Veterinary anatomy; rear prolongation of animal body.)
d Schwanz *m*
f queue *f*
p cauda *f*

5425 tan bark
(Agr.)
(Agricultural produce, subproduct. Ground oak bark or pine tree (spruce) bark for tanning purposes.)
d Lohe *f*; Gerberlohe *f*
f tan *m*
p matéria *f* curtante

* **tangerine → 3368**

5426 tannic character of the wine
(Agr.)
(Enology; ref. to wine production techniques.)
d Gerbstoffcharakter *m* des Weines
f caractère *m* tannique du vin
p caráter *m* de tanino do vinho

5427 tannic structure of red wine
(Biochem.)
(Enology: vinification of red wines.)
d Gerbstoffstruktur *f* des Rotweines
f structure *f* tannique du vin rouge
p estrutura *f* tanina do vinho tinto

5428 tannin
(Prod.)
(Food processing technology; plant substance of astringent effect: e.g. in tea; soothing effect on the stomach.)
d Gerbstoff *m*
f tanin *m*; tannin *m*
p tanino *m*

5429 tannin contents of the wine
(Agr.)
(Enology; wine characteristic.)
d Gerbstoffgehalt *m* des Weines
f teneur *f* du vin en tanin
p teor *m* de tanino do vinho

5430 tanning
(Agr.)
(Leather treatment.)
d Gerben *n*
f tannage *m*
p curtimento *m*

5431 tanning extract
(Agr.)
(Leather treatment; tanning process.)
d Gerbstoffextrakt *m*
f extrait *m* tannique
p extrato *m* de curtimento

5432 tannin richness
(Biochem.)
(Enology.)
d Gerbstoffreichhaltigkeit *f*

f richesse *f* tannique
p riqueza *f* taninosa; riqueza *f* em taninos

5433 tapioca
(Agr.)
(Horticulture. "Cassava starch"; food ingredient for thickening; extract from the manioc (cassava) root for cooked preparations: tapioca soup. Tapioca from tupi/guarany language.)
d Tapioka *f*
f tapioca *m*
p tapioca *f*

5434 tapioca soup
(Prod.)
(Gastronomy.)
d Tapiokasuppe *f*
f potage *m* au tapioca
p sopa *f* de tapioca

5435 tapping of the wine; drawing of the wine; drawing off of the wine
(Prod.)
(Tapping of wine from a cask.)
d Abzapfen *n* des Weines
f tirage *m* du vin
p tiragem *m* do vinho

5436 tap *v* the wine; draw *v* the wine; draw *v* off the wine
(Prod.)
(To tap the wine from a cask.)
d Wein abzapfen
f tirer le vin
p tirar *m* o vinho

* **tar camphor → 3669**

5437 tarragon
(Prod.)
("Artemisia dracunculus", having aromatic leaves used in salads and other gastronomic preparations, e.g. vinegar aromatizer.)
d Estragon *m*
f estragon *m*
p estragão *m*

5438 tartar; calculus
(Med.)
(Teeth condition.)
d Zahnstein *m*
f tartre *m*
p tártaro *m*

5439 tartaric acid
(Prod.)
($C_4H_6O_6$; used e.g. in the elaboration of baking powder, sherbet powder and soft drinks; prime material.)
d Weinsäure *f*; Weinsteinsäure *f*; Dihydroxybernsteinsäure *f*
f acide *m* tartrique
p ácido *m* tartárico

5440 tartar sauce
(Prod.)
(Gastronomy.)
d Tartarsoße *f*; Tartarsauce *f*
f sauce *f* tartare
p molho *m* tártaro

5441 tartlet
(Prod.)
(Confectionary.)
d Törtchen *n*
f tartelette *f*
p torta *f* pequena

5442 tartrazine
(Prod.)
($C_{16}H_9N_4Na_3O_9S_2$; FD&C yellow no. 5; foodstuff colorant; depending on Government regulations.)
d Tartrazin *n*
f tartrazine *f*
p tartrazina *f*

5443 tarts; layer cakes
(Prod.)
(Confectionary.)
d Torten *fpl*
f tartes *fpl*
p tortas *fpl*

5444 taste
(Prod.)
(Foodstuff composition and aroma/flavour research; flavour-perceiving sense.)
d Geschmack *m*
f saveur *f*; goût *m*
p sabor *m*; gosto *m*

* **taste *v* → 1545**

* **taste improvement → 2859**

* **tasty *adj* → 5295**

5445 tawing mixture
(Agr.)
(Leather treatment; tanning process.)
d Gare *f*
f mélange *m* tannant à l'alun
p mistura *f* à base de alume como aditivo de curtimento

5446 tea
(Agr.)
(Agricultural produce; "Camellia sinensis",

Family "Theaceae"; tea plant.)
d Tee *m*
f thé *m*
p chá *m*

5447 **teal**
(Agr.)
(Livestock. Genus "Anas"; duck.)
d Krickente *f*
f sarcelle *f*
p marreco *m*

5448 **tea of black elder blossoms**
(Prod.)
(Tea of "Sambucus nigra".)
d Tee *m* der Blüten des schwarzen Holunders
f tisane *f* des fleurs de sureau noir
p chá *m* das flores do sabugueiro negro

5449 **teats**
(Med.)
(Veterinary; ref. to dairy cattle anatomy; four projections of the udder for milk passage.)
d Zitzen *fpl*
f tettes *fpl*; trayons *mpl*
p tetas *fpl*

5450 **technique of vinification**
(Prod.)
(Enology: wine production.)
d Technik *f* der Weinbereitung
f technique *f* de vinification
p técnica *f* da vinificação

5451 **technique of wine preservation**
(Agr.)
(Enology: wine production.)
d Technik *f* der Weinkonservierung; Technik *f* der Haltbarmachung des Weines
f technique *f* de conservation du vin
p técnica *f* da conservação do vinho

5452 **temperate climate**
(Agr.)
(Climatology, e.g. for agricultural purposes.)
d gemäßigtes Klima *n*
f climat *m* tempéré
p clima *m* temperado

5453 **temperature control in yeast drying process**
(Prod.)
(Food processing technology. Yeast production plant technology: fluid bed drying process.)
d Temperaturregelung *f* im Hefetrocknungsprozess
f contrôle *m* de la température dans le procédé du séchage de la levure
p controle *m* da temperatura no processo de secagem do fermento; controle *m* de temperatura no processo de secagem de lêvedo

5454 **temporal lobe**
(Med.)
(Anatomy; e.g. brain part related to sensory reception.)
d Schläfenlappen *m* der Großhirnrinde
f lobe *m* temporal
p lobo *m* temporal

5455 **tench**
(Agr.)
("Tinca tinca"; edible fish, similar to carps. In Brazil: genus "Mugi L." of the Atlantic. Portuguese "tenca" is not used in Brazil.)
d Schleie *f*
f tanche *f*
p tainha *f*

5456 **tender** *adj*
(Prod.)
(Gastronomy, ref. to meat quality.)
d zart
f tendre
p macio

5457 **tender foodstuff**
(Prod.)
(Food processing technology; product characteristic.)
d mürbes Nahrungsmittel *n*
f aliment *m* tendre
p produto *m* alimentício tenro; alimento *m* tenro

5458 **tenderloin**
(Prod.)
(Gastronomy; butcher's product.)
d zartes Lendenstück *n*
f filet *m* mignon; pointe *f* du filet
p filé *m* mignon

5459 **tenderness**
(Prod.)
(Food processing technology, meat quality.)
d Zartheit *f*
f tendreté *f*
p maciez *f*

5460 **tendinous** *adj*
(Prod.)
(Food processing technology; meat qualification.)
d sehnig
f tendineux
p nervoso

* **tendril** → **5720**

* **tepid** *adj* → **3294**

* **tepid coffee → 3295**

5461 **termination of biochemical reactions**
(Biochem.)
(Biochemistry in nutritional science.)
d Beendigung *f* biochemischer Reaktionen
f fin *f* des réactions biochimiques
p conclusão *f* das reações bioquímicas

* **ternate leaf → 5565**

5462 **terpenes**
(Prod.)
($(C_5H_8)_n$; hydrocarbons e.g. present in essential oils; prime material in organic synthesis.)
d Terpene *npl*
f terpènes *mpl*
p terpenos *mpl*

5463 **terpenoides**
(Prod.)
(Fragrance prime material: vehicles of specific odoriferous characteristics; they are the main part of essential oils.)
d Terpenoide *npl*
f terpénoïdes *mpl*
p terpenóides *mpl*

5464 **terpineol**
(Prod.)
($C_{10}H_{18}O$; lilac; flavour chemical.)
d Terpineol *n*
f terpinéol *m*
p terpineol *m*; lilacina *f*

5465 **terrace**
(Agr.)
(Soil treatment; ref. to erosion-preventing level constructions on a slope.)
d Terrasse *f*
f terrasse *f*
p terraço *m*

5466 **terrace culture**
(Agr.)
(Soil treatment; ref. to terracing: formation of level areas at different altitudes e.g. for rice culture land: absorption terrace for water holding purposes.)
d Terrassenkultur *f*
f culture *f* en terrasse
p cultura *f* de terraço

5467 **terrace-like rice fields**
(Agr.)
(Soil treatment; soil type for rice culture.)
d terrassenförmige Reisfelder *npl*
f rizières *fpl* en terrasse
p arrozeiras *fpl* de terraço; arrozal *m* de terraço

5468 **tertiary structure of the protein**
(Biochem.)
(Polypeptide chains of amino acids: coiling or pleating of the polypeptides result in secondary structure: the three-dimensional form of these polypeptides are called the tertiary structure.)
d Tertiärstruktur *f* des Proteins
f structure *f* tertiaire de la protéine
p estrutura *f* terciária da proteína

5469 **tetanus**
(Med.)
(Infectious disease caused by "Clostridium tetani" toxin.)
d Tetanus *m*; Wundstarrkrampf *m*
f tétanos *m*
p tétano *m*

5470 **tetany**
(Med.)
(Muscle spasm, due to decreased level of blood calcium.)
d Tetanie *f*
f tétanie *f*
p tetania *f*; espasmofilia *f*

* **tetramethylene → 1481**

5471 **texture**
(Prod.)
(Food processing technology; physical foodstuff quality; its character: e.g. viscosity etc.)
d Textur *f*
f texture *f*
p textura *f*

5472 **textured vegetable protein; texturized vegetable protein; T.V.P.**
(Prod.)
(Food processing technology; protein-rich industrialized products; e.g. meat substitution product; soybean extract.)
d strukturiertes Pflanzeneiweiß *n*; texturiertes Pflanzenprotein *n*
f protéine *f* végétale texturée
p proteína *f* vegetal estruturada; proteína *f* vegetal texturizada

* **texturized vegetable protein → 5472**

5473 **thalamus**
(Med.)
(Anatomy; e.g. brain part related to sensory message reception.)
d Thalamus *m*
f thalamus *m*
p tálamo *m*

5474 **thawing**
(Prod.)
(Food processing technology; frozen food treatment: changing of the deep-freezing temperature to normal temperature.)
d Auftauung *f*; Auftauen *n*
f décongélation *f*
p descongelação *f*; descongelamento *m*

5475 **theobromine**
(Biochem.)
(Nutritional science; $C_7H_8N_4O_2$; caffeine-near plant substance with specific effect on the nervous system; cacao bean alkaloid; purine alkaloid.)
d Theobromin *n*
f théobromine *f*
p teobromina *f*

5476 **theophylline**
(Biochem.)
(Nutritional science; $C_7H_8N_4O_2$; theobromine isomeric; can be found in tea; caffeine-near plant substance with specific effect on the nervous system.)
d Theophyllin *n*
f théophylline *f*
p teofilina *f*

5477 **therapeutical importance of micronutrients**
(Biochem.)
(Nutrition in medicine.)
d therapeutische Wichtigkeit *f* der Mikronährstoffe
f importance *f* thérapeutique des micronutriments
p importância *f* terapêutica dos micronutrientes

5478 **thermal exchange**
(Biochem.)
(Nutritional science, ref. to research and production processes.)
d Wärmeaustausch *m*
f échange *m* thermique
p intercâmbio *m* térmico

* **thermal removal of weeds → 5479**

* **thermal treatment → 2671**

* **thermal treatment in foodstuff processing → 2672**

5479 **thermal weeding; thermal removal of weeds**
(Agr.)
(E.g. with propane gas equipment; in biological agriculture, in certain vegetable cultures.)
d thermische Unkrautvertilgung *f*
f désherbage *m* thermique
p termorremoção *f* de ervas daninhas; remoção *f* de ervas daninhas por meios térmicos

5480 **thermometric titrimetry**
(Prod.)
(Food processing technology: determination method: titration)
d thermometrische Titrimetrie *f*
f titrimétrie *f* thermométrique
p titrimetria *f* termométrica; volumetria *f* termométrica

5481 **thermophagy**
(Med.)
(Habit to swallow very hot food.)
d Thermophagie *f*; heißes Essen *n*
f thermophagie *f*
p termofagia *f*

* **thiamin hydrochloride → 5744**

5482 **thiamin hydrochloride**
(Prod.)
(Vitamin B_1 hydrochloride; $C_{12}H_{17}ClN_4OS.HCl$.)
d Thiaminhydrochlorid *n*
f hydrochlorure *m* de thiamine
p hidrocloreto *m* de tiamina

5483 **thiazole**
(Prod.)
(C_3H_3NS; source of aroma/fragrance prime material.)
d Thiazol *n*
f thiazole *m*
p tiazol *m*

5484 **thickening**
(Prod.)
(Gastronomy; ref. to culinary process of sauce thickening.)
d Abbinden *n*; Abbindung *f*
f liaison *f*
p espessamento *m*

5485 **thickening agent**
(Prod.)
(Food processing technology: auxiliary product.)
d Verdickungsmittel *n*
f agent *m* épaississant
p espessante *m*

* **thin** *v* **→ 1684**

5486 **thin layer chromatography**
(Biochem.)
(Food biochemistry; separation process type for analysis.)

d Dünnschichtchromatographie *f*
f chromatographie *f* en couches minces
p cromatografia *f* de camada fina

* **third fraction of distillation** → 5524

5487 **thistle**
(Agr.)
(Botany; biologic agriculture; "Centaurea melitensis"; weed.)
d Distel *f*
f chardon *m*
p cardo *m*

5488 **thixotropic** *adj*
(Prod.)
(Food processing technology; e.g. characteristic of gels of becoming fluid by shaking: this characteristic is important in some parts of food processing: e.g. cheese elaboration.)
d thixotrop
f thixotrope
p tixotrópico

* **thrash** *v* → **5490**

5489 **threonine**
(Prod.)
($C_4H_9NO_3$. Essential amino acid; ingredient in human and in cow's milk; a nutrient.)
d Threonin *n*
f thréonine *f*
p treonina *f*

5490 **thresh** *v*; **thrash** *v*
(Agr.)
(Agricultural produce treatment: ref. to threshing of grain; separating grain from the husk.)
d dreschen
f battre
p malhar

5491 **thresholds of perception**
(Med.)
(Aroma/flavour perception.)
d Wahrnehmungsschwellen *fpl*
f seuils *mpl* de perception
p limiares *mpl* da percepção

5492 **throat**
(Med.)
(Anatomy.)
d Kehle *f*; Hals *m*; Gurgel *f*; Rachen *m*; Schlund *m*
f gorge *f*; gosier *m*
p garganta *f*; goela *f*

5493 **thrombosis**
(Med.)
(Blood clot (thrombus) formation.)
d Thrombose *f*; Blutpfropfbildung *f*
f thrombose *f*
p trombose *f*

5494 **thyme**
(Agr.)
(Botany. "Thymus vulgaris L."; medicinal herb.)
d Thymian *m*
f thym *m*
p tomilho *m*; timo *m*

5495 **thyroid hormone**
(Med.)
(Essential for development and metabolism; present in human milk; ref. to baby nutrition.)
d Schilddrüsenhormon *n*
f hormone *f* thyroïdienne
p hormônio *m* da tireóide

* **thyroxin** → **5496**

5496 **thyroxine; thyroxin**
(Med.)
($C_{15}H_{11}I_4NO_4$; one of the two thyroid hormones; the other one is triiodothyronine; thyroxin(e) is present in human milk; ref. to baby nutrition.)
d Thyroxin *n*
f thyroxine *f*
p tiroxina *f*

5497 **ticks**
(Med.)
(Veterinary; family "Ixodoidea", order "Acarina"; arachnids, animal parasites.)
d Zecken *fpl*
f tiques *fpl*
p carrapatos *mpl*

5498 **tightness**
(Prod.)
(E.g. of a bottle, cask.)
d Dichte *f*; Dichtigkeit *f*
f étanchéité *f*
p estanquidade *f*; estanqueidade *f*

5499 **tillage; soil cultivation**
(Agr.)
(Soil treatment for agricultural purposes.)
d Bodenbearbeitung *f*; Bodenbewirtschaftung *f*; Bodenbestellung *f*
f culture *f* du sol
p cultivo *m* do solo

5500 **Tilsit; Tilsiter**
(Prod.)
(Tilsit cheese; semisoft, light yellow cheese;

named after the Eastprussian town Tilsit (Sovetsk).)
d Tilsiter *m*; Tilsiter Käse *f*
f tilsitt *m*
p queijo *m* tipo Tilsit

* **Tilsiter → 5500**

* **tincture of bitter wood → 4536**

5501 **tinctures**
(Prod.)
(Aroma/flavour research and production: extraction process: solution of a substance in alcoholic solvent.)
d Tinkturen *fpl*; Auszüge *mpl*
f teintures *fpl*
p tinturas *fpl*

* **tinned food → 890**

* **tinned food production → 891**

* **tinned fruits → 892**

* **tinned meat → 893**

* **tinned milk → 894**

5502 **tissue antioxidant**
(Biochem.)
(Ref. to certain trace elements and vitamins in food biochemistry.)
d Gewebsoxidationsverhinderer *m*
f antioxydant *m* tissulaire
p antioxidante *m* tissular

5503 **tissue construction**
(Med.)
(Anatomy.)
d Gewebeaufbau *m*
f construction *f* tissulaire
p construção *f* dos tecidos

5504 **tissue renewal**
(Med.)
(Anatomy.)
d Gewebserneuerung *f*
f renouvellement *m* tissulaire
p renovação *f* dos tecidos

5505 **titanium dioxide**
(Prod.)
(TiO_2; foodstuff colorant; food surface colouring.)
d Titandioxid *n*
f bioxyde *m* de titane; blanc *m* de titane
p dióxido *m* de titânio

5506 **titrimetry determination method**
(Prod.)
(Food processing technology: determination method: titration)
d Bestimmung *f* durch die Titriermethode
f méthode *f* de dosage par titrimétrie
p método *m* de determinação por titrimetria; método *m* de dosagem por volumetria

5507 **tocopherol concentration in feedstuff ration**
(Biochem.)
(Veterinary; ref. to vitamin E as feedstuff supplement.)
d Tocopherolkonzentration *f* in der Futtermittelration
f concentration *f* de tocophérol dans la ration animale
p concentração *f* de tocoferol na ração animal

5508 **tocopherol extract**
(Prod.)
($C_{29}H_{50}O_2$. Vitamin in nutrition. Vitamin E; antioxidant.)
d Tocopherolextrakt *m*
f extrait *m* de tocophérol
p extrato *m* de tocoferol

5509 **toddy**
(Prod.)
(Beverages; alcoholic hot drink, made of water, rum, sugar and cinnamon.)
d Grog *m*
f grog *m*
p grogue *m*

5510 **toffee; taffy**
(Prod.)
(Confectionary.)
d Karamelbonbon *m*
f bonbon *m* au caramel
p bala *f* de caramelo; bala *f* puxa-puxa

5511 **tofu; bean curd**
(Prod.)
(Food processing technology. Chinese cheese type made from soybean milk.)
d Tofu *m*; Sojabohnenquark *m*
f tofu *m*; pâté *m* de soja
p tofu *m*; queijo *m* de soja

5512 **tolerance limit**
(Med.)
(Excess supply of certain nutrients, mineral salts etc., e.g. in baby nutrition.)
d Toleranzschwelle *f*, Toleranzgrenze *f*
f limite *f* de la tolérance
p limite *m* de tolerância

5513 **tolerated fungicide; permitted fungicide**
(Agr.)
(Biological agriculture.)

d toleriertes Fungizid *n*; zugelassenes Fungizid *n*
f fongicide *m* toléré; fongicide *m* permis
p fungicida *f* tolerada; fungicida *f* permitida

5514 toluene; toluol
(Prod.)
(C_7H_8; synthesis prime material; ref. to aroma/fragrance synthesis.)
d Toluol *n*
f toluène *m*
p tolueno *m*

* **toluol → 5514**

5515 tomato
(Agr.)
(Horticulture. Genus "Lycopersicon", "Lycopersicon esculentum".)
d Tomate *f*
f tomate *f*
p tomate *m*

5516 tomato sauce
(Prod.)
(Gastronomy.)
d Tomatensoße *f*
f sauce *f* tomate
p molho *m* de tomate

5517 tongue
(Med.)
(Anatomy.)
d Zunge *f*
f langue *f*
p língua *f*

5518 tongue root
(Med.)
(Anatomy.)
d Zungenwurzel *f*
f racine *f* de la langue
p raiz *f* da língua

5519 tonic water
(Prod.)
(Carbonated beverage with quinine note.)
d Tonic *n*
f tonic *m*
p água *f* tônica

5520 tonka bean
(Agr.)
(Genus "Dipteryx"; raw material for artificial vanilla aroma.)
d Tonkabohne *f*
f fève *f* de tonka; fève *f* de tonca
p fava-tonca *f*, fava-de-cheiro *f*, fava-da-índia *f*

5521 tooth (*pl* teeth)
(Med.)
(Anatomy.)
d Zahn *m*
f dent *f*
p dente *m*

5522 top fermentation
(Prod.)
(Food processing technology; ref. to beer brewing process and beer characteristic.)
d Obergärung *f*
f fermentation *f* haute
p alta fermentação *f*

5523 top fermenting beer
(Prod.)
(Food processing technology. Beer type; denomination refers to the fermentation process type.)
d obergäriges Bier *n*
f bière *f* de fermentation en surface; bière *f* haute
p cerveja *f* de alta fermentação

5524 topped distillate; overhead distillate; distillation tail; third fraction of distillation
(Prod.)
(Food processing technology; ref. to distillation process: last fraction of distillation, final dropping distillate of components of high boiling point, in the end of the distillation process.)
d Nachlauf *m* der Destillation; Destillationsnachlauf *m*
f queue *f* de distillation; troisième fraction *f* de la distillation
p destilado *m* de cauda

5525 total acidity
(Biochem.)
(Enology. Wine production, wine characteristic.)
d Gesamtsäuregehalt *m*
f acidité *f* totale
p acidez *f* total

5526 total metabolism
(Med.)
(Energy requirement.)
d Gesamtumsatz *m* des Stoffwechsels
f métabolisme *m* total
p metabolismo *m* total

5527 total separation
(Prod.)
(Food processing technology; e.g. of products.)
d vollständige Trennung *f*
f séparation *f* totale
p separação *f* total

5528 **total water hardness**
(Prod.)
(Food processing technology; ref. to the calcium and magnesium ion content of the water.)
d Gesamtwasserhärte *f*
f dureté *f* totale de l'eau
p dureza *f* total da água

* **toxic component → 5529**

5529 **toxic constituent; toxic component**
(Biochem.)
(Food biochemistry.)
d toxischer Bestandteil *m*; giftiger Bestandteil *m*
f constituant *m* toxique
p constituinte *m* tóxico

5530 **toxicity**
(Med.)
(Toxicology dealing with poisons and their effects: alimentary toxins.)
d Toxizität *f*; Giftigkeit *f*
f toxicité *f*
p toxicidade *f*

5531 **toxicity trials**
(Biochem.)
(Food biochemistry.)
d toxikologische Versuche *mpl*
f essais *mpl* de toxicité
p ensaios *mpl* de toxicologia

5532 **toxic metabolite**
(Med.)
(Nutritional science.)
d toxisches Metabolit *n*; giftiges Stoffwechselprodukt *n*
f métabolite *m* toxique
p metabólito *m* tóxico

5533 **toxicological danger**
(Med.)
(Food processing technology.)
d Vergiftungsgefahr *f*
f danger *m* toxicologique
p perigo *m* toxicológico

5534 **toxicological study**
(Med.)
(Food processing technology.)
d toxikologische Untersuchung *f*
f étude *f* toxicologique
p estudo *m* toxicológico

5535 **toxicology**
(Med.)
(Food processing technology: Science dealing with poisons and their effects.)
d Toxikologie *f*
f toxicologie *f*
p toxicologia *f*

5536 **toxigenic** *adj*; **producing toxin** *adj*
(Med.)
(Food processing technology: bacteria, fungi.)
d toxigen; toxogen; Giftstoff erzeugend
f toxigénique
p toxigênico

5537 **toxins**
(Med.)
(Nutritional intolerance; immunity problems.)
d Toxine *npl*; Giftstoffe *mpl*
f toxines *fpl*
p toxinas *fpl*

5538 **trace element-enriched milk**
(Prod.)
(Dairy product; e.g. calcium (Ca) enriched; omega-3 enriched.)
d spurenelementen-angereicherte Milch *f*; mit Spurenelemten angereicherte Milch *f*
f lait *m* enrichi des oligoéléments
p leite *m* enriquecido com microelementos

5539 **trace elements**
(Biochem.)
(Food biochemistry; required for body functioning in very small amounts.)
d Spurenelemente *npl*
f oligo-éléments *mpl*
p microelementos *mpl*

5540 **traces of residual sugar**
(Biochem.)
(Food biochemistry.)
d Spuren *fpl* restlichen Zucker
f traces *fpl* de sucre résiduel
p traços *mpl* de açúcar residual

5541 **trachea**
(Med.)
(Anatomy; the windpipe.)
d Luftröhre *f*
f trachée *f*; trachée-artère *f*
p traquéia *f*; traquéia-artéria *f*

5542 **traditional industrialized milk**
(Med.)
(Baby nutrition; milk types based on human milk.)
d traditionelle industrialisierte Milch *f*
f lait *m* industriel traditionnel
p leite *m* industrializado tradicional

* **tragacanth → 2608**

5543 **transamination**
(Biochem.)
(Oxidation-reduction reaction; ref. e.g. to aroma food biochemistry; aroma synthesis.)

d Transaminierung *f*
f transamination *f*
p transaminação *f*

5544 **transferase**
(Biochem.)
(Nutritional science; transfer promoting enzyme, e.g. ATP-transferase.)
d Transferase-Enzym *n*; Transferase *f*
f transférase *f*
p transferase *f*

5545 **transfer of the odoriferous molecules**
(Biochem.)
(Flavour chemicals, flavour and fragrance biotechnology in food biochemistry.)
d Verlagerung *f* der Riechstoffmoleküle
f transfert *m* des molécules odorantes
p transferência *f* das moléculas odorantes; transferência *f* das moléculas odoríferas

5546 **transformation into wine**
(Prod.)
(Enology: wine production.)
d Transformation *f* in Wein; Umwandlung *f* in Wein
f transformation *f* en vin
p transformação *f* em vinho

5547 **transformation of fluid oils into solid oils**
(Prod.)
(Food processing technology: e.g. margarine production.)
d Umwandlung *f* flüssiger Öle in feste Öle
f transformation *f* des huiles fluides en huiles concrètes
p transformação *f* de óleos líquidos em óleos solidificados

5548 **transformation of lactose into lactic acid**
(Biochem.)
(Nutritional science; dairy products.)
d Umwandlung *f* der Laktose in Milchsäure; Laktoseumwandlung *f* in Milchsäure
f transformation *f* du lactose en acide lactique
p transformação *f* da lactose em ácido láctico

5549 **transformation of sugar in alcohol**
(Biochem.)
(Fermentation process.)
d Verwandlung *f* des Zuckers in Alkohol
f transformation *f* de sucre en alcool
p transformação *f* de açúcar em álcool

5550 **transformation of wheat starch**
(Biochem.)
(Nutritional science; $(C_6H_{10}O_5)_n$; carbohydrate; foodstuff.)
d Verarbeitung *f* von Weizenstärke
f transformation *f* des amidons issus du blé
p transformação *f* do amido de trigo

5551 **transformation process**
(Prod.)
(Food processing technology: Various phases, until obtaining the final product.)
d Verarbeitungsprozess *m*
f processus *m* de transformation
p processo *m* de transformação

5552 **transitory hypogalactia**
(Med.)
(Transitory reduction of milk secretion in breast feeding.)
d vorübergehende Hypogalaktie *f*; transitorische Hypogalaktie *f*
f hypogalactie *f* transitoire
p hipogaláctia *f* transitória

5553 **transmissible disease; communicable disease**
(Med.)
(Veterinary; ref. to diseases which can be transmitted to another person or animal, e.g. from animals to persons and vice versa. E.g. zoonoses: diseases communicable from animals to humans.)
d übertragbare Krankheit *f*; ansteckende Krankheit *f*
f maladie *f* transmissible; maladie *f* contagieuse
p doença *f* transmissível; doença *f* contagiosa

5554 **transport of lipids**
(Med.)
(Nutrition in medicine.)
d Lipidtransport *m*
f transport *m* des lipides
p transporte *m* dos lipídios; transporte *m* dos lípides

5555 **transport of nutrients in the blood**
(Med.)
(Nutrition.)
d Transport *m* der Nährstoffe durch das Blut; Nährstofftransport *m* des Blutes
f transport *m* sanguin des nutriments
p transporte *m* dos nutrientes no sangue

5556 **transport protein**
(Med.)
(Ref. to O_2-transport.)
d Transportprotein *n*
f protéine *f* de transport
p proteína *f* de transporte

5557 **transverse colon**
(Med.)
(Anatomy; part of the large intestine.)
d querliegender Grimmdarm *m*

f côlon *m* transverse
p cólon *m* transverso

* **treacle → 3611**

5558 **treat** *v*; **process** *v*
(Prod.)
(Food processing technology.)
d aufbereiten
f traiter
p tratar; processar

5559 **treated water; processed water**
(Prod.)
(Drinking water (tap water) production.)
d aufbereitetes Wasser *n*
f eau *f* traitée
p água *f* tratada

* **treatment based on nutrition → 3824**

* **treatment by actinism → 65**

5560 **treatment by cooling**
(Biochem.)
(Food biochemistry process.)
d Kältebehandlung *f*
f traitement *m* par le froid
p tratamento *m* pelo frio

5561 **treatment of essential oils; processing of essential oils**
(Prod.)
(Aroma/flavour research and production.)
d Aufbereitung *f* von ätherischen Ölen
f traitement *m* des huiles essentielles
p tratamento *m* de óleos essenciais

5562 **treetop**
(Agr.)
(Botany. The topmost tree part.)
d Baumkrone *f*
f couronne *f* de l'arbre; cime *f* de l'arbre
p copa *f* da árvore

5563 **trichina**
(Med.)
(Veterinary. "Trichinella spiralis", a nematode intestinal worm; parasite in larval form in the muscles of animals and humans, to whom it is transmitted e.g. by pork.)
d Trichine *f*
f trichine *f*
p triquina *f*

5564 **trichloroethylene**
(Prod.)
(C_2HCl_3; trichloroethene; for solvent extraction e.g. in aroma/flavour research and production.)
d Trichloräthylen *n*; Trichlorethylen *n*
f trichloréthylène *m*
p tricoloroetileno *m*

5565 **trifoliate leaf; ternate leaf**
(Agr.)
(Botany. Leaf form.)
d dreiteiliges Blatt *n*
f feuille *f* trifoliée
p folha *f* trifoliada

5566 **triggering of a disease**
(Med.)
(By subnutrition.)
d Auslösung *f* einer Krankheit
f déclenchement *m* d'une maladie
p desencadear uma doença

5567 **triglyceride**
(Biochem.)
(Nutritional science; fats consist of a mixture of triglycerides: compounds of a molecule of glycerine (glycerol $C_3H_8O_3$) with three fatty acid molecules.)
d Triglycerid *n*; Triglyzerid *n*
f triglycéride *m*
p trigliciríideo *m*; triglicídeo *m*

5568 **triglyceride transport in the organism**
(Med.)
(Nutrition in medicine.)
d Triglyceridtransport *m* im Organismus
f transport *m* des triglycérides dans l'organisme
p transporte *m* do trigliciríideo no organismo; transporte *m* do triglicídeo no organismo

5569 **trigonelline**
(Biochem.)
($C_7H_7NO_2$. Coffee treatment, coffee roasting: partial transformation of trigonelline in nicotinic acid (vitamin B group). 4 cups of coffee may correspond to the daily requirement of this vitamin.)
d Trigonellin *n*
f trigonelline *f*
p trigonelina *f*

* **trim** *v* **→ 4484**

* **trimethylene → 1487**

* **trimethylglycocol → 604**

5570 **trimming**
(Agr.)
(Horticulture. Cutting, clipping unfavourable, useless plant parts.)
d Beschneiden *n*; Ausputzen *n*
f taillage *m*
p poda *f*

5571 **tripeptide**
(Biochem.)
(Nutritional science: peptide; e.g. gluthatione ($C_{10}H_{17}N_3O_6S$), to be found in animal and plant cells.)
d Tripeptid *n*
f tripeptide *m*
p tripeptídeo *m*

5572 **triple superphosphate**
(Agr.)
(Soil treatment. Fertilizer type.)
d Triple-Superphosphat *n*
f superphosphate *m* en trois éléments
p superfosfato *m* triplo

5573 **trituration of oily products**
(Prod.)
(Food processing technology.)
d Zerreiben *n* von ölhaltigen Produkten; Zerreiben *n* ölhaltiger Produkte
f trituration *f* des oléagineux
p trituração *f* de produtos oleosos

5574 **trotter; pig's foot**
(Prod.)
(Butchery; meat part.)
d Spitzbein *n*
f pied *m* de porc
p pé *m* de porco

5575 **trough**
(Agr.)
(Livestock nutrition. Agricultural equipment for cattle treatment.)
d Viehtrog *m*
f auge *f*
p cocho *m*

5576 **trough; syncline**
(Agr.)
(Soil formation; a type of depression between hills.)
d Mulde *f*; Synklinale *f*
f cuvette *f*; bassin *m* synclinal
p dobra *f* sinclinal

5577 **trout**
(Agr.)
("Trutta fario L.". Edible fish.)
d Forelle *f*
f truite *f*
p truta *f*

5578 **trout au bleu**
(Prod.)
(Gastronomy.)
d Forelle *f* blau
f truite *f* au bleu
p truta *f* "au bleu"

5579 **trub; break**
(Prod.)
(Food processing technology. Beer brewing.)
d Trub *m*; Kühlgeläger *n*
f moût *m* coagulé et refroidi
p mosto *m* coagulado e resfriado

5580 **truck farming**
(Agr.)
(Horticulture; production of vegetables.)
d Gemüseanbau *m*
f maraîchage *m*; culture *f* des légumes
p horticultura *f*

5581 **truffle**
(Agr.)
(Horticulture. The ascomycetous fungi, genus "Tuber"; and also its edible subterranean fruiting body.)
d Trüffel *f*
f truffe *f*
p trufa *f*

5582 **truffle of chocolate; chocolate truffle**
(Prod.)
(Confectionary; candy.)
d Schokoladentrüffel *f*
f truffes *fpl* au chocolat
p trufa *f* de chocolate

5583 **trunk**
(Agr.)
(Botany. Stem of a tree.)
d Baumstamm *m*
f tronc *m* d'arbre
p tronco *m* da árvore

5584 **trypanosoma**
(Med.)
(Genus "Trypanosoma" parasitic protozoans, transmitted by insect bite; sleeping disease; in Brazil also Chagas disease (by Trypanosoma cruzi), ref. to the Brazilian physician Carlos Chagas.)
d Trypanosoma *n*
f trypanosome *m*
p tripanossomo *m*

5585 **trypsin**
(Med.)
(Parenzyme. Pancreas enzyme; acts in the protein digestion; splitting of proteins and polypeptides.)
d Trypsin *n*
f trypsine *f*
p tripsina *f*

5586 **tryptophan; tryptophane**
(Biochem.)
(Nutritional science: $C_{11}H_{12}O_2N_2$; essential

amino acid; nutrient; pellagra-preventing property; essential amino acid-ingredient in human and in cow's milk.)
d Tryptophan *n*
f tryptophane *m*
p triptofano *m*

5587 **tryptophan deficiency**
(Med.)
(Pellagra risk, as tryptophan can be metabolized to niacin vitamin PP, a pellagra-preventive vitamin.)
d Tryptophanmangel *m*
f carence *f* en tryptophane
p deficiência *f* de triptofânio

* **tryptophane → 5586**

5588 **tryptophan supplementation**
(Med.)
(In nutritional diseases.)
d Tryptophanergänzungszufuhr *f*
f supplémentation *f* en tryptophane
p suplementação *f* de triptofano

5589 **tuber**
(Agr.)
(Botany.)
d Knolle *f*
f tubercule *m*
p tubérculo *m*

5590 **tuberculosis**
(Med.)
(Veterinary; bacteria "Mycobacterium tuberculosis"; treatment of livestock is very expensive and valid only for valuable animals.)
d Tuberkulose *f*
f tuberculose *f*
p tuberculose *f*

5591 **tuberous root**
(Agr.)
(Botany; fleshy storage plant root.)
d Wurzelknolle *f*
f racine *f* tubéreuse; racine *f* tubérisée
p raiz *f* tuberosa

* **tubular pasta products → 3763**

5592 **tuna; tuna fish**
(Agr.)
("Thunnus thunys L."; Fish. The flesh is canned as food.)
d Thunfisch *m*
f thon *m*
p atum *m*

* **tuna fish → 5592**

5593 **turbid** *adj*
(Prod.)
(Food processing technology: ref. to liquids: beer, juices, wine etc.)
d trübe
f trouble
p turvo

5594 **turbidimetry**
(Prod.)
(Food processing technology: Measuring process: beverage production technology, for the determination of the point of turbidity (as to DIN).)
d Trübungsmessung *f*; Turbidimetrie *f*
f turbidimétrie *f*
p turbidimetria *f*

5595 **turbidity; cloudiness; clouding**
(Prod.)
(Food processing technology: ref. to liquids, a beverage: beer, wine, juices.)
d Trübung *f*
f troublement *m*; aspect *m* trouble
p turbidez *f*; turvação *f*

5596 **turbot**
(Agr.)
("Bothus rhombus", "Psetta maxima"; edible fish. Brazil: "Paralichthys brasiliensis (Ranz).)
d Butt *m*; Steinbutt *m*
f turbot *m*; barbue *f*
p rodovalho *m*; catraio *m*

5597 **turkey; gobbler**
(Agr.)
(Poultry farming. "Meleagris gallopavo".)
d Truthahn *m*; Puter *m*
f dindon *m*
p peru *m*

* **turn** *v* **acid → 48**

5598 **turnip**
(Agr.)
(Horticulture. "Brassica napus".)
d weiße Rübe *f*
f navet *m*
p nabo *m* branco

5599 **turpentine oil**
(Prod.)
(Source for pinene which is used as prime material for aroma/fragrance production.)
d Terpentinöl *n*
f essence *f* de térébenthine
p essência *f* de terebintina

* **T.V.P. → 5472**

* **twig → 744**

5600 **twig with panicle**
(Agr.)
(Botany; vine; panicle: compound inflorescence type.)
d Zweig *m* mit Blütenrispe
f tige *f* florale avec panicule
p ramo *m* florífero com panícula

5601 **two-element fertilizer**
(Agr.)
(Soil treatment. Fertilizer type containing two chemical components.)
d Zweinährstoffdünger *m*
f engrais *m* binaire
p adubo *m* binário

5602 **tyndallization**
(Prod.)
(Food processing technology; ref. to fractionated sterilization process.)
d Tyndallisierung *f*, Tyndallisation *f*
f tyndallisation *f*
p tindalização *f*, esterilização *f* conforme Tyndall

* **tyndallometry → 3712**

* **types of bread → 3072**

5603 **typicality of taste; typicalness of taste**
(Prod.)
(Gastronomy; e.g. ref. to wine sorts.)
d Typgerechtheit *f* des Geschmacks
f typicité *f* gustative
p tipicidade *f* gustativa

5604 **typicality of the wine; typicalness of the wine**
(Prod.)
(Enology; e.g. related to the origin of a specific wine.)
d Typgerechtheit *f* des Weines
f typicité *f* du vin
p tipicidade *f* do vinho

* **typicalness of taste → 5603**

* **typicalness of the wine → 5604**

5605 **typical standard formulation**
(Prod.)
(Food processing technology.)
d typische Standardformulation *f*
f formulation *f* type
p formulação *f* padrão

5606 **tyramine**
(Biochem.)
(Nutritional science; $C_8H_{11}NO$; blood pressure increasing substance, occurs e.g. in red wine, cheese etc.)
d Tyramin *n*
f tyramine *f*
p tiramina *f*

5607 **tyrosine**
(Biochem.)
($C_9H_{11}NO_3$; non-essential amino acid; ingredient in human and in cow's milk; precursor of e.g. melanin (dark brown pigment) and epinephrin(e) ($C_9H_{13}NO_3$), a blood pressure raising hormone.)
d Tyrosin *n*
f tyrosine *f*
p tirosina *f*

U

5608 **udder; bag**
(Med.)
(Veterinary; anatomy; esp. of a milk-producing cow; also referring to other milk producing farm animals.)
d Euter *n*
f pis *m*
p úbere *m*

* **U.H.T. process → 5612**

* **U.H.T. sterilized milk → 5613**

* **ulcerative colitis → 5609**

5609 **ulcerous colitis; ulcerative colitis**
(Med.)
(One of the causes is said to be eventually sugar and milk consumption; Colitis ulcerosa.)
d Dickdarmschleimhautentzündung *f* mit Geschwürsbildungen
f colite *f* membraneuse
p colite *f* ulcerosa

5610 **ulcerous gingivitis**
(Med.)
(Inflammation type of the gums.)
d Zahnfleischentzündung *f* mit Geschwürbildung
f gingivite *f* ulcéreuse
p gengivite *f* ulcerosa

5611 **ultrafiltration**
(Prod.)
(Food processing technology.)
d Ultrafiltration *f*
f ultrafiltration *f*
p ultrafiltração *f*

5612 **ultra-high-temperature process; U.H.T. process**
(Prod.)
(Food processing technology of milk; conservation method; milk heat-treatment for some seconds of 130-150° C.)
d Ultrahocherhitzungsverfahren *n*; UHT-Verfahren *n*
f procédé *m* ultra-haute-température; procédé *m* U.H.T.
p processo *m* de tratamemnto a temperaturas ultra-elevadas; processo *m* de tratamento UAT

5613 **ultra-high-temperature sterilized milk; U.H.T. sterilized milk**
(Biochem.)
(Nutritional science: Obtaining a conservation period possibility of 6 months without refrigeration.)
d ultrahocherhitzt-sterilisierte Milch *f*; UHT-Milch *f*
f lait *m* stérilisé ultra-haute-température; lait *m* stérilisé U.H.T
p leite *m* esterilizado à temperatura ultra-elevada; leite *m* esterilizado U.A.T.

5614 **ultraviolet spectrum**
(Biochem.)
(Nutritional science; e.g. ref. to processes of analysis.)
d Ultraviolettspektrum *n*; UV-Spektrum *n*
f spectre *m* ultraviolet; spectre *m* UV
p espectro *m* ultravioleta

5615 **uncooked**
(Prod.)
(Food processing technology.)
d ungekocht
f non-cuit; cru
p não cozido; cru

5616 **uncooked pressed cheese**
(Prod.)
(Dairy plant technology: e.g. Edam-type cheese.)
d ungekochter Presskäse *m*
f fromage *m* à pâte pressée non-cuite
p queijo *m* prensado não cozido

* **uncultivated fruits → 5904**

* **10-undecenoic acid → 5617**

5617 **undecylenic acid; 10-undecenoic acid**
(Prod.)
($C_{11}H_{20}O_2$; prime material in aroma/fragrance production.)
d Undecylensäure *f*; Undecensäure *f*
f acide *m* undécylénique
p ácido *m* undecilênico

* **undercooled → 5341**

* **undercooled foodstuffs → 5342**

5618 **uneven cheese quality**
(Prod.)
(Dairy plant technology: Result of the incontinuous production process)
d ungleichförmige Käsequalität *f*; uneinheitliche Käsequalität *f*

f qualité *f* inégale du fromage; qualité *f* non-homogène du fromage
p qualidade *f* não uniforme do queijo; qualidade *f* não homogênea do queijo

5619 uniform cheese quality
(Prod.)
(Dairy plant technology: Result of the continuous production process.)
d gleichförmige Käsequalität *f*; einheitliche Käsequalität *f*
f qualité *f* uniforme du fromage; qualité *f* homogène du fromage
p qualidade *f* uniforme do queijo; qualidade *f* homogênea do queijo

5620 uniform granules
(Prod.)
(Food processing technology. Physical product presentation form.)
d einheitliches Granulat *n*
f granulé *m* uniforme
p granulado *m* uniforme

5621 unleavened bread
(Prod.)
(Bakery; Jewish Passah-time bread.)
d ungesäuertes Fladenbot *n*; Matze *f*; Matzen *m*
f azyme *m*
p pão *m* ázimo; pão *m* sem fermento

5622 unpeeled
(Agr.)
(Ref. to fruits.)
d ungeschält
f non-épluché
p em casca

5623 unprocessed plant products
(Agr.)
(Biological agriculture.)
d nicht weiterverarbeitete pflanzliche Produkte *npl*
f produits *mpl* végétaux non transformés
p produtos *mpl* vegetais não transformados

5624 unrefined sugar
(Agr.)
(Agricultural produce.)
d Rohzucker *m*; unraffinierter Zucker *m*
f sucre *m* brut; sucre *m* roux
p açúcar *m* não-refinada

* **unsalted butter → 5374**

5625 unsaturated
(Biochem.)
(Nutritional science: organic compound with double or triple bonds between carbon atoms.)
d ungesättigt
f insaturé
p insaturado

5626 unsaturated fatty acid
(Biochem.)
(Nutritional science.)
d ungesättigte Fettsäure *f*
f acide *m* gras insaturé
p ácido *m* graxo insaturado

5627 unsaturated fatty acids in foodstuff
(Med.)
(These acids are sensible to oxygen action, provoking formation of peroxide: phenomenon of rancing; used as food ingredient for high cholesterol and arteriosclerosis prevention in regimens, diets.)
d ungesättigte Fettsäuren *fpl* in den Nahrungsmitteln
f acides *mpl* gras non-saturés dans les aliments; acides *mpl* gras insaturés dans les aliments
p ácidos *mpl* graxos não saturados nos alimentos

5628 unsaturated fatty acid with one double bond
(Biochem.)
(Food biochemistry; oleic acid ($C_{18}H_{34}O_2$).)
d ungesättigte Fettsäure *f* mit einer Doppelbindung
f acide *m* gras non-saturé avec une double liaison; acide *m* gras insaturé avec une double liaison
p ácido *m* graxo insaturado com uma dupla ligação

5629 unsaturated fatty acid with two double bonds
(Biochem.)
(Food biochemistry; linoleic acid ($C_{18}H_{32}O_2$).)
d ungesättigte Fettsäure *f* mit zwei Doppelbindungen
f acide *m* gras non-saturé avec deux doubles liaisons; acide *m* gras insaturé avec deux doubles liaisons
p ácido *m* graxo insaturado com duas duplas ligações

* **unskimmed milk → 5897**

5630 unskimmed powdered milk
(Med.)
(Baby nutrition.)
d Vollmilchpulver *n*
f lait *m* entier en poudre
p leite *m* integral em pó

5631 unstabilized
(Prod.)
(Food processing technology.)
d unstabilisiert; nicht stabilisiert

f non-stabilisé
p não estabilizado

5632 unstabilized form
(Prod.)
(Food processing technology, e.g. product characteristic.)
d unstabilisierte Form *f*
f forme *f* non-stabilisée
p forma *f* não estabilizada

5633 unstable colloidal particle
(Biochem.)
(Food biochemistry: colloidal chemistry.)
d unstabiles Kolloidteilchen *n*; nicht stabiles kolloidales Teilchen *n*
f particule *f* colloïdale instable
p partícula *f* coloidal instável

5634 unsugared unskimmed milk
(Med.)
(Baby nutrition: milk without saccharose addition.)
d ungesüßte Vollmilch *f*
f lait *m* entier non-sucré
p leite *m* integral não açucarado

* **upper jaw → 3416**

* **upper jawbone → 3416**

5635 upper lip
(Med.)
(Anatomy.)
d Oberlippe *f*
f lèvre *f* supérieure
p lábio *m* superior

5636 urea
(Agr.)
(Cattle breeding, nutrition: feed composition: nitrogenous compound (CH_4N_2O), end product of protein break-up, additive in livestock ration.)
d Harnstoff *m*
f urée *f*
p uréia *f*

5637 ureter
(Med.)
(Anatomy; a pair of tubes conduct the urine from the kidney to the bladder.)
d Harnleiter *m*
f uretère *m*
p ureter *f*

5638 urethra
(Med.)
(Anatomy; tube conducting urine from the bladder to the exterior.)
d Harnröhre *f*
f urètre *f*
p uretra *f*

5639 urinary bladder
(Med.)
(Anatomy; urine-storing organ.)
d Harnblase *f*
f vessie *f*
p bexiga *f*

5640 urinary calculus
(Med.)
(Urinary tract calculus; formation, can be inhibited probably by alimentary regimen.)
d Harnstein *m*
f calcul *m* urinaire
p cálculo *m* da bexiga

5641 urine alkalinizing diet
(Med.)
(Alimentary regimen; ovolactovegetable nutrition.)
d Diät *f* der Harnalkalisierung
f diète *f* alcalisante de l'urine
p dieta *f* de alcalinização da urina

5642 useful plant; economic plant
(Agr.)
(Botany; plant type grown for food, feed etc.)
d Nutzpflanze *f*
f plante *f* utile
p planta *f* útil

* **use of canola oil in food → 5643**

* **use of fruit tree culture → 5644**

5643 use of rape oil in food; use of canola oil in food
(Prod.)
(Canola is an improved rape variety, canola oil is an edible vegetable oil.)
d Rapsöleinsatz *m* in Nahrungsmitteln; Gebrauch *m* von Rapsöl in Nahrungsmitteln
f usage *m* alimentaire de l'huile de colza
p uso *m* de óleo de colza em alimentos

5644 utilization of arboriculture; use of fruit tree culture
(Agr.)
(Biological agriculture.)
d Nutzung *f* der Fruchtbaumkultur
f exploitation *f* arboricole; exploitation *f* de l'arboriculture fruitière
p exploração *f* da arboricultura; exploração *f* da cultura de árvores frutíferas

5645 uvula
(Med.)
(Anatomy of the mouth: a soft palate extension; contributes to the closure process of the nasal part of the pharynx during deglutition.)
d Zäpfchen *n*
f luette *f* du palais
p úvula *f* palatina; campainha *f*

V

5646 **vaccination**
(Med.)
(Veterinary; animal sanitation; vaccination e.g. of cattle against brucellosis, foot and mouth disease, paratyphoid, gas gangrene etc.)
d Impfung *f*
f vaccination *f*
p vacinação *f*

5647 **vacuum distillation**
(Prod.)
(Food processing technology. Reduced-pressure distillation process. Prevention from decomposing of the product to be distilled, by using a lower boiling point.)
d Vakuumdestillation *f*
f distillation *f* sous vide
p destilação *f* a vácuo

5648 **vacuum drying**
(Prod.)
(Food processing technology: food conservation process.)
d Vakuumtrocknung *f*
f séchage *m* sous vide
p secagem *f* a vácuo

5649 **valence; valency**
(Biochem.)
(Nutritional science; e.g. the combining power of an atom.)
d Wertigkeit *f*; Valenz *f*
f valence *f*
p valência *f*

* **valency → 5649**

* **valerates → 5651**

5650 **valerian; allheal**
(Agr.)
(Botany; "Valeriana officinalis L."; medicinal plant.)
d Baldrian *m*
f valériane *f*; herbe-à-chats *f*
p valeriana *f*

5651 **valerianates; valerates**
(Prod.)
(Esters of valerianic acid (valeric acid) ($C_5H_{10}O_2$): prime material for thc production of aroma additives.)
d Valerianate *npl*; Valerate *npl*
f valérianates *mpl*
p valerianatos *mpl*; valeratos *mpl*

* **valerianic acid → 5652**

5652 **valeric acid; n-valeric acid; valerianic acid**
(Prod.)
(($C_5H_{10}O_2$); prime material in aroma/fragrance research and production: source in alcoholic beverages, e.g. in whiskey, in dairy products and fruits etc.)
d Valeriansäure; n-Valeriansäure *f*
f acide *m* valérianique; acide *m* n-valérianique
p ácido *m* valérico; ácido *m* n-valérico

* **valeric aldehyde → 171**

5653 **valine**
(Prod.)
($C_5H_{11}NO_2$; essential amino acid-ingredient in human and in cow's milk; nutrient.)
d Valin *n*
f valine *f*
p valina *f*

5654 **valley**
(Agr.)
(Soil; area depression between hills, or drained by waters.)
d Tal *n*
f vallée *f*
p vale *m*

5655 **value attached to food**
(Med.)
(Physiologic and psychologic value interacting with the choice of foodstuffs.)
d Nahrungsmitteln beigelegter Wert *m*
f valeur *f* attachée aux aliments
p valor *m* atribuído ao alimento

* **value of phenolic compounds → 4572**

5656 **vanilla**
(Agr.)
(Botany. Genus "Vanilla"; vanilla bean extract: Flavouring agent.)
d Vanille *f*
f vanille *f*
p baunilha *f*

5657 **vanilla essence**
(Prod.)
(Aroma/flavour prime material.)
d Vanilleessenz *f*
f essence *f* de vanille
p essência *f* de baunilha

5658 **vanilla tincture**
(Prod.)
(Aroma/flavour research and production. "Vanilla planifolia"; extraction process: vanilla is used in confectionary/bakery and beverage flavouring.)
d Vanillentinktur *f*, Auszug *m* der Vanille
f teinture *f* de vanille
p tintura *f* de baunilha

5659 **vanillin**
(Prod.)
($C_8H_8O_3$; natural or synthetically obtained prime material for the elaboration of flavour chemicals.)
d Vanillin *n*
f vanilline *f*
p vanilina *f*

5660 **vanillin sugar**
(Prod.)
(Sugar prepared with vanillin ($C_8H_8O_3$) as aroma additive.)
d Vanillezucker *m*
f sucre *m* vanilliné
p açúcar-baunilha *m*

5661 **vaporization**
(Prod.)
(Food processing technology. Passage of a substance from the liquid to the gaseous aggregate structure by boiling or evaporation; thermal separation process in chemistry.)
d Verdampfung *f*, Verdampfen *n*
f vaporisation *f*
p vaporização *f*

5662 **vaporization velocity**
(Prod.)
(Aroma/flavour research and production: distillation processes.)
d Schnelligkeit *f* der Vaporisierung; Schnelligkeit *f* der Vaporisation
f vitesse *f* de vaporisation
p rapidez *f* da vaporização; velocidade *f* de vaporização

5663 **vapour phase**
(Prod.)
(Aroma/flavour research and production: elaboration processes.)
d Dampfphase *f*
f phase *f* vapeur
p fase *f* de vapor

5664 **vapour pressure**
(Prod.)
(Aroma/fragrance research and production.)
d Dampfdruck *m*
f pression *f* de vapeur
p pressão *f* do vapor

5665 **varied crop rotation**
(Agr.)
(Biological agriculture: planting system for soil preservation.)
d variierte Fruchtfolge *f*, verschiedenartige Fruchtfolge *f*
f assolement *m* varié
p alternação *f* variada de cultura

* **varieties adapted to the climate → 1158**

* **varieties adapted to the soil → 5060**

5666 **varieties of great yield**
(Agr.)
(Agricultural produce characteristic.)
d Abarten *fpl* hohen Ertrages
f variétés *fpl* à haut rendement
p variedades *fpl* de alto rendimento

5667 **variety of strains**
(Biochem.)
(Microbiology: bacteria strains.)
d Verschiedenheit *f* der Stränge
f variété *f* de souches
p variedade *f* de cepas; variedade *f* de raças

5668 **vascular degradation; vascular deterioration**
(Med.)
(Anatomy; pathology.)
d Gefäßverfall *m*
f dégradation *f* vasculaire
p degradação *f* vascular

* **vascular deterioration → 5668**

5669 **veal**
(Prod.)
(Butchery. Calf meat.)
d Kalbfleisch *n*
f viande *f* de veau; veau *m* de boucherie
p vitela *f*, carne *f* de vitela

5670 **veal liver**
(Prod.)
(Gastronomy.)
d Kalbsleber *f*
f foie *f* de veau
p fígado *m* de vitela

5671 **vegetable albumin**
(Prod.)
(Food processing technology; nutrient.)
d pflanzliches Albumin *n*; pflanzliches Eiweiß *n*
f albumine *f* végétale
p albumina *f* vegetal

5672 **vegetable associations**
(Agr.)
(Biological agriculture. Ref. to associated planting of different vegetable types.)
d Zusammenbau *m* von Gemüsesorten
f association *f* végétale
p associação *f* de vegetais

5673 **vegetable concentrate**
(Prod.)
(Food processing technology.)
d Gemüsekonzentrat *n*
f concentré *m* de légumes
p concentrado *m* de legumes

5674 **vegetable farming**
(Agr.)
(Agricultural produce.)
d Feldanbau *m* von Gemüse; Gemüsegroßanbau *m*
f culture *f* maraîchère
p lavoura *f* de legumes e hortaliças

5675 **vegetable fat**
(Prod.)
(Plant fat; prime material.)
d Pflanzenfett *n*; pflanzliches Fett *n*
f graisse *f* végétale
p gordura *f* vegetal

5676 **vegetable garden**
(Agr.)
(Horticulture.)
d Gemüsegarten *m*
f potager *m*; jardin *m* potager
p horta *f*

5677 **vegetable insecticide**
(Agr.)
(Biological agriculture: insecticide made from vegetable extracts, e.g. from legumes.)
d pflanzliches Insektizid *n*; pflanzliches Insektenbekämpfungsmittel *n*
f insecticide *m* végétal
p inseticida *m* vegetal

5678 **vegetable leaves**
(Agr.)
(Horticulture: e.g. salad, cabbage.)
d Blattgemüse *n*
f légumes *mpl* feuilles
p folhas *fpl* de verduras

5679 **vegetable margarine**
(Prod.)
(Food processing technology; vegetable fat/vegetable oil emulsion, with water and skim milk; "vegetable butter".)
d Pflanzenmargarine *f*
f margarine *f* végétale
p margarina *f* vegetal

5680 **vegetable oil**
(Prod.)
(Plant oil; prime material in food processing technology.)
d Pflanzenöl *n*
f huile *f* végétale
p óleo *m* vegetal

5681 **vegetable oil industry**
(Prod.)
(Food processing technology and production: vegetable oil production from fruits and/or seeds.)
d Pflanzenölindustrie *f*
f huilerie *f*; industrie *f* de la fabrication d'huiles végétales
p indústria *f* de óleos vegetais

5682 **vegetable plot**
(Agr.)
(Horticulture; vegetable bed, ref. to truck farming.)
d Gemüsebeet *n*
f planche *f* de légumes
p canteiro *m* de legumes

5683 **vegetable protein**
(Biochem.)
(Food biochemistry.)
d Pflanzenprotein *n*
f protéine *f* végétale
p proteína *f* vegetal

5684 **vegetable soup**
(Prod.)
(Gastronomy; made of vegetable stock as a base.)
d Gemüsesuppe *f*
f bouillon *m* de légumes
p caldo *m* de legumes

5685 **vegetable tanned upper leather**
(Agr.)
(Agricultural industrial product.)
d Fahlleder *n*
f cuir *m* tanné aux extraits tanniques végétaux
p couro *m* curtido com taninos

* **vegetable tissues → 4212**

5686 **vegetal toxin; plant toxin**
(Med.)
(Food processing technology.)
d pflanzliches Toxin *n*; pflanzlicher Giftstoff *m*
f toxine *f* végétale
p toxina *f* vegetal

5687 vegetarian
(Med.)
(Person practicing vegetarianism, i.e. a specific alimentary regimen; preferably raw vegetables and fruit diet, sometimes also incl. dairy products.)
d Vegetarier *m*; Vegetarierin *f*
f végétarien *m*; végétarienne *f*
p vegetariano *m*; vegetariana *f*

5688 vegetarian diet
(Med.)
(Plant/vegetable diet.)
d Vegetarierdiät *f*
f régime *m* végétarien
p regime *m* vegetariano

5689 vegetarianism
(Med.)
(Specific alimentary regimen; preferably raw vegetables and fruit diet, sometimes also incl. dairy products.)
d Vegetarismus *m*
f végétarisme *m*
p vegetarianismo *m*

5690 vegetative branch
(Agr.)
(Horticulture. Branches which do not produce fruits (in Portuguese ramo ladrão = thief branch); they are eliminated by trimming.)
d vegetativer Zweig *m*
f branche *f* végétative
p ramo *m* vegetativo; ramo *m* ladrão

5691 vegetative cycle
(Agr.)
(Botany; plant growth.)
d vegetativer Zyklus *m*
f cycle *m* végétatif
p ciclo *m* vegetativo

5692 vegetative development
(Agr.)
(Botany; plant growth.)
d vegetative Entwicklung *f*
f développement *m* végétatif
p desenvolvimento *m* vegetativo

5693 vegetative phase
(Med.)
(Ref. to the active life stage of parasites, not referring to reproduction.)
d Vegetationsstadium *n*
f phase *f* végétative
p fase *f* vegetativa

5694 vegetative vine cycle
(Agr.)
(Viticulture; wine growing; cultivation of wine grapes.)
d vegetativer Zyklus *m* der Weinrebe
f cycle *m* végétatif de la vigne
p ciclo *m* vegetativo da videira

5695 vein; vena (*pl* venae)
(Med.)
(Anatomy; blood transport vessel towards the heart.)
d Vene *f*
f veine *f*
p veia *f*

* **vein of the leaf → 3719**

5696 velocity of cell multiplication
(Biochem.)
(Nutritional science.)
d Zellvermehrungsgeschwindigkeit *f*
f rapidité *f* de la multiplication cellulaire
p rapidez *f* da multiplicação celular

* **velocity of intestinal passage → 5697**

5697 velocity of intestinal transit; velocity of intestinal passage
(Med.)
(Baby nutrition.)
d Schnelligkeit *f* des Darmdurchganges; Schnelligkeit *f* des Darmdurchlaufes
f rapidité *f* du transit intestinal
p rapidez *f* do trânsito intestinal; rapidez *f* de passagem intestinal

5698 velocity of transfer
(Prod.)
(Flavour molecules: in aroma/flavour research and application in food products.)
d Verlagerungsschnelligkeit *f*
f vitesse *f* de transfert
p velocidade *f* de transferência

* **vena → 5695**

5699 venison
(Agr.)
(Game; animal's edible flesh; flesh of a deer.)
d Wildbret *n*; Wildfleisch *n*
f venaison *f*; chair *f* de grand gibier
p carne *f* de caça; carne *f* de veado; veação *f*

5700 ventilate *v* **the soil**
(Agr.)
(Soil treatment.)
d den Boden ventilieren; den Boden belüften
f aérer le sol
p aerar o solo

5701 verbena tea
(Prod.)
("Verbena officinalis", herb tea.)

d Eisenkrauttee *m*
f tisane *f* de verveine
p chá *m* de verbena

5702 **vermicelli; long cut pasta**
(Prod.)
(Food processing technology; pasta plant product, for spaghetti production; pasta, long, very thin noodle type.)
d Fadennudeln *fpl*; langgeschnittene Teigmasse *f*
f vermicelle *m*; pâtes *fpl* alimentaires du type vermicelles
p aletria *f*; letria *f*; cabelo-de-anjo *m*; pasta *f* cortada ao longo

5703 **vermicelli soup**
(Prod.)
(Gastronomy.)
d Fadennudelnsuppe *f*
f soupe *f* au vermicelle
p sopa *f* de aletria

5704 **vermouth**
(Prod.)
(Beverages; aperitif wine.)
d Wermut *m*
f vermouth *m*; vermout *m*
p vermute *m*

* **vertebral column → 5151**

5705 **vervain**
(Prod.)
(Genus "Verbena", "Verbena officinalis", aromatic herb.)
d Verbene *f*; Eisenkraut *n*
f verveine *f*
p verbena *f*

5706 **vetch**
(Agr.)
(Botany; "Viccia sativa"; forage plant; used also for green manure in biologic agriculture.)
d Wicke *f*; Futterwicke *f*
f vesce *f*; vesce *f* fourragère
p ervilhaca *f*

5707 **veterinary anatomy**
(Med.)
(Veterinary.)
d Tieranatomie *f*; Veterinäranatomie *f*
f anatomie *f* vétérinaire
p anatomia *f* veterinária

5708 **veterinary care**
(Med.)
(Veterinary; ref. to livestock breeding.)
d veterinäre Betreuung *f*; tierärztliche Betreuung *f*
f soin *m* vétérinaire
p acompanhamento *m* veterinário; cuidados *mpl* veterinários

5709 **veterinary sterilization**
(Med.)
(Veterinary science.)
d Veterinärsterilisierung *f*
f stérilisation *f* vétérinaire
p esterilização *f* veterinária

5710 **vibrio**
(Med.)
(Genus "Vibrio bacteria"; ref. to parasitic life.)
d Vibrionen *pl*
f vibrion *m*
p vibrião *m*

* **Vienna cutlet → 5899**

5711 **vigorous stock**
(Agr.)
(Viticulture; ref. to grafting process: the shoot (scion) of the desired variety is grafted into the stock.)
d kräftiger Wildling *m*
f porte-greffe *m* vigoureux
p porta-enxerto *m* vigoroso

5712 **vine**
(Agr.)
(Viticulture. "Vitis vinifera".)
d Weinrebe *f*
f cep *m* de vigne
p videira *f*; parreira *f*; vide *f*; vinha *f*

5713 **vine; climber; creeper**
(Agr.)
(Botany; trailing plant stem which trails e.g. along the ground.)
d Kletterpflanze *f*; Kriechpflanze *f*
f plante *f* grimpante
p planta *f* trepadeira

5714 **vinegar**
(Prod.)
(Food condiment, food preservative; obtained by alcoholic fermentation.)
d Essig *m*
f vinaigre *m*
p vinagre *m*

* **vinegar acid → 25**

5715 **vinegar essence**
(Prod.)
(Food processing technology: synthetic acetic acid diluted with water.)
d Essigessenz *f*

f essence *f* de vinaigre
p essência *f* de vinagre

5716 vine leaf
(Agr.)
(Viticulture. "Vitis vinifera".)
d Weinrebenblatt *n*; Weinblatt *n*; Weinlaub *n*
f feuille *f* de vigne
p folha *f* da parreira; folha *f* da parra

5717 vine protection against the phylloxera
(Agr.)
(Viticulture. Grafting processes, using resistant (American) vine stocks against this type of plant lice pest.)
d Schutz *m* des Rebstocks gegen die Reblaus
f protection *f* de la vigne contre le phylloxéra
p proteção *f* da videira contra a filoxera

5718 viner
(Agr.)
(Threshing machine, in which green peas and beans are separated from the pods and vines, having its best output when pods are of equal size.)
d Erbsendreschmaschine *f*
f batteuse *f* à pois
p debulhadora *f* de ervilhas

5719 vine scion
(Agr.)
(Viticulture; ref. to grafting process: the shoot (scion) of the desired variety is grafted into the stock.)
d Edelreis *n* der Weinrebe
f greffon *m* de vigne; greffe *f* de vigne
p garfo *m* da videira

5720 vine shoot; tendril
(Agr.)
(Viticulture. "Vitis vinifera"; coiling organ of the climbing plant.)
d Weinranke *f*
f sarment *m*; pampre *m*
p ramo *m* de videira; parra *f*; sarmento *m*; pâmpano *m*

5721 vine sort
(Agr.)
(Viticulture; ref. to quality characteristics.)
d Rebsorte *f*
f cépage *m*
p espécie *f* de cepa

5722 vine stem
(Agr.)
(Viticulture; winegrowing.)
d Weinstock *m*; Rebstock *m*
f cep *m*; pied *m* de vigne
p cepa *f*; lenho *m* da videira

5723 vine stock
(Agr.)
(Viticulture; ref. to vine grafting process.)
d Weinrebenwildling *m*
f porte-greffe *m* de vigne
p cepa *f* porta-enxerto; raça *f* porta-enxerto

5724 vineyard
(Agr.)
(Viticulture; ref. to the culture area of grapevines.)
d Weinberg *m*
f vigne *f*; vignoble *m*
p vinha *f*

5725 vineyard of temperate climate
(Agr.)
(Climatology in winegrowing.)
d Weinberge *mpl* gemäßigten Klimas
f vignes *fpl* tempérées; vignobles *mpl* tempérés; vignobles *mpl* de climat tempéré
p vinha *f* de clima temperada

* **viniculture → 5807**

5726 vinification
(Agr.)
(Viticulture.)
d Weinbereitung *f*
f vinification *f*
p vinificação *f*

5727 vinification by direct expression
(Biochem.)
(Enology; technology of wine production.)
d Weinbereitung *f* durch direktes Auspressen
f vinification *f* par pressurage direct
p vinificação *f* sob expressão direta; vinificação *f* sob espremedura direta

5728 vinification of rosé
(Agr.)
(Viticulture; vinification (production) of rosé wine type, a light pink table wine.)
d Roséweinbereitung *f*
f vinification *f* en rosé
p vinificação *f* rosé; vinificação *f* do vinho rosé

5729 vinosity
(Prod.)
(Enology: wine elaboration.)
d Weingehalt *m*
f vinosité *f*
p vinosidade *f*

5730 vintage
(Agr.)
(Viticulture: season's yield of wine.)
d Jahrgang *m*

f année *f*; millésime *m*
p ano *m*

5731 **vintage; yield of grapes of a season; grape harvest**
(Agr.)
(Vintage, vendange and vindima also means grape harvest. In German: Weinernte means harvest, geerntete Weintrauben means yield of grapes.)
d geerntete Weintrauben *fpl*; Weinernte *f*
f vendange *f*; raisin *m* récolté
p vindima *f*; uvas *fpl* vindimadas

5732 **violaxanthin**
(Prod.)
($C_{40}H_{56}O_4$; carotenoid pigment. Foodstuff colorant.)
d Violaxanthin *n*
f violaxanthine *f*
p violaxantina *f*

5733 **violet soil**
(Agr.)
(Soil; ref. to fertile violet Brazilian farm soil, originated by decomposition of effusive basaltic rock.)
d Roterden *fpl*
f terre *f* rouge; terra *f* rossa
p terras *fpl* roxas

5734 **viral mutation**
(Med.)
(Change in the structure of the genetic material of the virus.)
d virale Mutation *f*; Veränderung *f* im Erbgefüge des Virus
f mutation *f* virale
p mutação *f* viral

5735 **viscosity**
(Prod.)
(Food processing technology: flow resistance property of a substance.)
d Viskosität *f*
f viscosité *f*
p viscosidade *f*

5736 **viscosity of the flavour product**
(Prod.)
(Aroma/flavour research and application.)
d Geschmacksstoffviskosität *f*
f viscosité *f* d'arôme
p viscosidade *f* do aroma

5737 **viscous foodstuff**
(Prod.)
(Food processing technology; product characteristic.)
d viskoses Nahrungsmittel *n*
f aliment *m* visqueux
p alimento *m* viscoso; produto *m* alimentício viscoso

5738 **viscous liquid**
(Prod.)
(Food processing technology and flavour research and production.)
d viskose Flüssigkeit *f*
f liquide *m* visqueux
p líquido *m* viscoso

5739 **viscous oil**
(Prod.)
(Food processing technology: product definition.)
d viskoses Öl *n*
f huile *f* visqueuse
p óleo *m* viscoso

5740 **vitamin A acetate in unstabilized form**
(Prod.)
(Vitamins in nutrition.)
d nicht stabilisiertes Vitamin A-Acetat *n*; unstabilisiertes Vitamin A-Acetat *n*
f acétate *m* de vitamine A non stabilisé
p acetato *m* de vitamina A não-estabilizado

5741 **vitamin activity**
(Prod.)
(Vitamins in nutrition: vitamin application.)
d Vitaminaktivität *f*
f activité *f* vitaminique
p atividade *f* vitamínica

5742 **vitamin addition; vitaminization; vitamin reinforcement**
(Prod.)
(Supplementary addition of vitamins to foodstuffs, e.g. vitamin additions to margarines (A, D, E) and dried milks (D); rice (B_1, B_2); fruit juice (C).)
d Vitaminisierung *f*; Vitaminierung *f*; Vitaminzusatz *m*
f vitaminisation *f*; addition *f* des vitamines; renforcement *m* vitaminique
p vitaminização *f*; vitaminação *f*; reforço *m* vitamínico

5743 **vitamin addition to dietary products; vitaminization of dietary products**
(Prod.)
(Vitamins in nutrition: supplementary addition of vitamins to dietary products.)
d Vitaminisierung *f* von Diätprodukten
f vitaminisation *f* des produits diététiques
p vitaminização *f* de produtos dietéticos; vitaminação *f* de produtos dietéticos

5744 **vitamin B_1; thiamin hydrochloride**
(Prod.)
(Vitamins in nutrition. Vitamin B_1, thiamin hydrochloride ($C_{12}H_{17}ClN_4OS.HCl$). Part of the vitamin B complex.)
d Vitamin B_1 *n*; Thiamin *n*
f vitamine B_1 *f*; thiamine *f*
p vitamina B_1 *f*; tiamina *f*

5745 **vitamin B_{12}**
(Prod.)
($C_{63}H_{90}CoN_{14}O_{14}P$; vitamin in nutrition. Cyanocobalamin; dietary supplement.)
d Vitamin B_{12} *n*
f vitamine B_{12} *f*
p vitamina B_{12} *f*

5746 **vitamin B_2; riboflavin**
(Prod.)
($C1_7H_{20}N_4O_6$; lactoflavin. Vitamins in nutrition.)
d Vitamin B_2 *n*; Riboflavin *n*
f vitamine B_2 *f*; riboflavine *f*
p vitamina B_2 *f*; riboflavina *f*

5747 **vitamin B_5; pantothenic acid**
(Prod.)
($C_9H_{17}NO_5$. Vitamins in nutrition. Precursor of coenzyme A. Intervenes in the fatty acid/acetic acid metabolism.)
d Vitamin B_5 *n*; Pantothensäure *f*
f vitamine B_5 *f*; acide *m* pantothénique
p vitamina B_5 *m*; ácido *m* pantotênico

5748 **vitamin B_6; pyridoxine**
(Prod.)
($C_8H_{11}NO_3.HCl$. Vitamin B_6 hydrochloride; pyridoxine hydrochloride. Vitamins in nutrition.)
d Vitamin B_6 *n*; Pyridoxin *n*
f vitamine B_6 *f*; pyridoxine *f*
p vitamina B_6 *f*; piridoxina *f*

5749 **vitamin B_6 in foods**
(Prod.)
(Vitamins in nutrition as supplementary addition.)
d Vitamin B_6 *n* in Nahrungsmitteln
f vitamine B_6 *f* dans les aliments
p vitamina B_6 *f* em alimentos

5750 **vitamin B deficiency**
(Med.)
(See avitaminosis.)
d Vitamin B-Mangelkrankheit *f*; Vitamin B-Hypovitaminose *f*
f maladie *f* de carence en vitamine B; hypovitaminose *f* B
p deficiência *f* de vitamina B; hipovitaminose *f* de vitamina B

5751 **vitamin blend emulsified into the milk**
(Prod.)
(Vitaminization in foodstuff processing.)
d Vitaminmischung *f* in die Milch hineinemulgiert
f mélange *m* des vitamines émulsifié dans le lait
p mistura *f* vitamínica emulsificada dentro do leite

5752 **vitamin blends for further processing**
(Prod.)
(Vitamins in nutrition.)
d Vitaminmischungen *fpl* zur Weiterverarbeitung
f mélanges *mpl* vitaminiques pour transformation
p misturas *fpl* vitamínicas para processamento

5753 **vitamin blends in baby nutrition; vitamin mixtures for baby food**
(Biochem.)
(Vitamin/food biochemistry in nutritional science.)
d Vitaminmischungen *fpl* in der Säuglingsernährung
f mélanges *mpl* de vitamines dans l'alimentation des nourrissons
p misturas *fpl* de vitaminas na alimentação dos récem-nascidos; misturas *fpl* vitamínicas para a alimentação do récem-nascido

5754 **vitamin blends suitable for food-vitaminizing**
(Prod.)
(Vitamins in nutrition: Oily blends in food stuff processing.)
d Vitaminmischungen *fpl* geeignet zur Nahrungsmittelvitaminierung
f mélanges *mpl* vitaminiques conviennent pour l'enrichissement des aliments en vitamines
p misturas *fpl* vitamínicas apropriadas para enriquecimento de produtos alimentícios

5755 **vitamin C; ascorbic acid**
(Prod.)
($C_6H_8O_6$. Vitamins in nutrition; antioxidant, sometimes together with vitamin E.)
d Vitamin C *n*; Ascorbinsäure *f*
f vitamine C *f*; acide *m* ascorbique
p vitamina C *f*; ácido *m* ascórbico

5756 **vitamin contents**
(Prod.)
(Vitamins in nutrition.)
d Vitamingehalt *m*
f teneur *f* en vitamines; teneur *f* vitaminique
p teor *m* de vitaminas; conteúdo *m* em vitaminas

5757 **vitamin contents of the milk**
(Med.)
(Baby nutrition.)

d Vitamingehalt *m* der Milch
f teneur *f* en vitamines du lait
p teor *m* de vitaminas no leite

5758 **vitamin D**
(Prod.)
(Vitamins in nutrition; vitamin D: produced e.g. by UV-irradiation on the skin. Interferes in the calcium exchange between skeleton and blood.)
d Vitamin D *n*
f vitamine D *f*
p vitamina D *f*

5759 **vitamin deficiency disease**
(Med.)
(See avitaminosis.)
d Vitaminmangelkrankheit *f*
f maladie *f* de carence en vitamine; maladie *f* de carence vitaminique
p doença *f* por deficiência vitamínica

5760 **vitamin degradation**
(Biochem.)
(Vitamin/food biochemistry.)
d Vitaminzerfall *m*
f dégradation *f* de vitamines
p degradação *f* de vitaminas

5761 **vitamin D-enriched milk; milk enriched with vitamin D**
(Med.)
(Baby nutrition.)
d Vitamin D-angereicherte Milch *f*; mit Vitamin D angereicherte Milch *f*
f lait *m* enrichi en vitamine D
p leite *m* enriquecido com vitamina D

5762 **vitamin depletion**
(Med.)
(Nutritional diseases; harmful reduction, impoverishment.)
d Vitamindezimierung *f*
f déplétion *f* vitaminique
p depleção *f* vitamínica

5763 **vitamin diluted in oil**
(Prod.)
(Vitamins in nutrition; vitamin presentation form.)
d Vitamin *n* in öliger Verdünnung
f vitamine *f* en dilution huileuse
p vitamine *f* em diluição oleosa

5764 **vitamin E; alpha tocopherol**
(Prod.)
($C_{29}H_{50}O_2$. Vitamins in nutrition; antioxidant, together with vitamin C.)
d Vitamin E *n*; Alpha-Tocopherol *n*
f vitamine E *f*, alpha-tocophérol *m*
p vitamina E *f*, alfa-tocoferol *m*

5765 **vitamin E as quality-enhancing factor**
(Biochem.)
(Food biochemistry, vitamin used in food of animal origin.)
d Vitamin E *n*, als qualitätsfördernder Faktor
f vitamine E *f*, activeur des facteurs qualitatifs
p vitamina E *f*, fator promovedor de qualidade

5766 **vitamin enriched milk**
(Prod.)
(Vitamins in nutrition: vitamin treated dairy products.)
d mit Vitaminen angereicherte Milch *f*
f lait *m* supplémenté en vitamines
p leite *m* enriquecido com vitaminas

5767 **vitamin enrichment; vitamin fortification**
(Prod.)
(Vitamins in nutrition: supplementary addition of vitamins to foodstuffs.)
d Vitaminanreicherung *f*
f enrichissement *m* vitaminique
p enriquecimento *m* com vitaminas

5768 **vitamin enrichment of breakfast cereals**
(Prod.)
(Vitamins in nutrition.)
d Vitaminanreicherung *f* von Frühstückszerealien *fpl*
f enrichissement *m* en vitamines des céréales pour le petit déjeuner
p enriquecimento *m* vitamínico de cereais para o café da manhã

5769 **vitamin enrichment of dietary products**
(Prod.)
(Vitamins in nutrition; e.g. vitamin A.)
d Vitaminanreicherung *f* von Diätprodukten
f enrichissement *m* des produits diététiques
p enriquecimento *m* de produtos para dieta; enriquecimento *m* de produtos dietéticos

5770 **vitamin enrichment of milk**
(Prod.)
(Vitamins in nutrition; e.g. vitamin A.)
d Vitaminanreicherung *f* von Milch
f enrichissement *m* en vitamine du lait
p enriquecimento *m* de leite por vitaminas

5771 **vitamin enrichment of milk powder**
(Prod.)
(Vitamins in nutrition; e.g. vitamin A.)
d Vitaminanreicherung *f* von Milchpulver
f enrichissement *m* en vitamine du lait en poudre
p enriquecimento *m* com vitaminas de leite em pó

5772 **vitamin E provisioning**
(Med.)
(Veterinary: Referring to vitamin supplementation of animal ration.)
d Vitamin-E-Versorgung *f*
f apport *m* en vitamine E
p abastecimento *m* com vitamina E

5773 **vitamin E-rich mixed feed**
(Med.)
(Veterinary: Feed. Vitamin E has an antioxidant effect, stabilization effect on fatty acids in the cellular metabolism and on vitamin A etc.)
d Vitamin E-reiches Mischfutter *n*
f ration *f* équilibrée enrichie à vitamine E
p ração *f* balanceada rica em vitamina E

* **vitamin fortification → 5767**

5774 **vitaminic disequilibrium**
(Med.)
(Nutritional diseases.)
d Missverhältnis *n* an Vitaminen; Unausgeglichenheit *f* an Vitaminen
f déséquilibre *m* en vitamines
p desequilíbrio *m* vitamínico

5775 **vitamin in crystalline form**
(Prod.)
(Vitamins in nutrition: vitamin presentation form.)
d Vitamin *n* in kristalliner Form
f vitamine *f* sous la forme de cristaux
p vitamina *f* sob forma cristalina

5776 **vitamin in fine crystalline form**
(Prod.)
(Vitamins in nutrition: vitamin presentation form.)
d Vitamin *n* in feinkristalliner Form
f vitamine *f* sous forme de cristaux fins
p vitamina *f* sob forma de cristais finos

5777 **vitamin influence in meat quality**
(Med.)
(Veterinary; ref. to feed composition with certain vitamins.)
d Beeinflussung *f* der Fleischqualität durch Vitamine; Einflussnahme *f* der Vitamine auf die Fleischqualität
f influence *f* des vitamines dans la qualité de la viande
p influência *f* das vitaminas na qualidade da carne

5778 **vitamin instability to oxidizing agents**
(Biochem.)
(Food biochemistry; vitamin E.)
d Vitamininstabilität *f* gegenüber oxidierender Substanzen
f instabilité *f* de la vitamine aux oxydants
p instabilidade *f* da vitamina aos oxidantes

* **vitaminization → 5742**

* **vitaminization of dietary products → 5743**

5779 **vitaminization of food; food vitaminization; food vitaminizing**
(Prod.)
(Vitamins in nutrition. Addition of vitamins to foodstuffs during product processing.)
d Vitaminisierung *f* von Nahrungsmitteln; Nahrungsmittelvitaminisierung *f*; Nahrungsmittelvitaminierung *f*
f enrichissement *m* en vitamines de produits alimentaires; enrichissement *m* des aliments en vitamines
p vitaminização *f* de produtos alimentícios; enriquecimento *m* de produtos alimentícios com vitaminas; vitaminização *f* de alimentos

5780 **vitaminized milk**
(Prod.)
(Dairy product; e.g. vitamin D supplementation.)
d vitaminierte Milch *f*; vitaminisierte Milch *f*; vitaminangereicherte Milch *f*
f lait *m* vitaminé; lait *m* vitaminisé
p leite *m* vitaminado; leite *m* vitaminizado

5781 **vitamin K**
(Med.)
(Vit. K_1: phytomenadione: $C_{31}H_{46}O_2$; "Koagulationsvitamin", promotes blood coagulation. Vit.K_3: menadione: $C_{11}H_8O_2$.)
d Vitamin K *n*
f vitamine K *f*
p vitamina K *f*

5782 **vitamin K_3-stability in a mineral premix**
(Med.)
(Veterinary; as various forms of this vitamin show stability problems due to temperature, light, moisture and chemicals, stabilized forms have been developed, e.g. by coating processes.)
d Vitamin K_3-Stabilität *f* in einem Mineral-Prämix
f stabilité *f* de la vitamine K_3 dans d'un prémix minéral
p estabilidade *f* de vitamina K_3 numa pré-mistura mineral

5783 **vitamin levels for immune enhancement**
(Med.)
(Veterinary; ref. to vitamin supplementation of feed for nutritional veterinary treatment; e.g. ref. to vitamin E.)

d Vitaminniveaus *npl* für die Immunitätsanhebung
f niveaux *mpl* vitaminiques pour l'augmentation immunitaire
p níveis *mpl* vitaminicos para o aumento da imunidade

5784 vitamin losses
(Prod.)
(Food processing technology: food preservation process.)
d Vitaminverluste *mpl*
f pertes *fpl* de vitamines
p perdas *fpl* de vitaminas; perdas *fpl* vitamínicas

5785 vitamin losses in foodstuffs
(Biochem.)
(Food biochemistry; food conservation process.)
d Vitaminverluste *mpl* in Nahrungsmitteln
f pertes *fpl* de vitamines dans des produits alimentaires
p perdas *fpl* de vitaminas em produtos alimentícios

5786 vitamin mixture in oily form
(Prod.)
(Vitamins in nutrition.)
d Vitaminmischung *f* in öliger Form
f mélange *m* de vitamines à l'état huileux
p mistura *f* vitamínica em forma oleosa

5787 vitamin mixture in powder form
(Prod.)
(Vitamins in nutrition.)
d Vitaminmischung *f* in Pulverform
f mélange *m* de vitamines sous la forme de poudre
p mistura *f* vitamínica em forma de pó

5788 vitamin mixtures
(Prod.)
(Vitamins in nutrition.)
d Vitaminmischungen *fpl*
f mélanges *mpl* de vitamines
p misturas *fpl* de vitaminas; misturas *fpl* vitamínicas

* **vitamin mixtures for baby food → 5753**

5789 vitamin mixtures for the food industries
(Prod.)
(Vitamins in nutrition. Vitamin presentation form for food stuff processing.)
d Vitaminmischungen *fpl* für die Nahrungsmittelindustrie
f mélanges *mpl* vitaminiques pour l'industrie alimentaire
p misturas *fpl* vitamínicas para a indústria alimentícia

5790 vitamin nutrients
(Biochem.)
(Nutritional science.)
d vitaminreiche Nährstoffe *mpl*
f nutriments *mpl* vitaminiques
p nutrientes *mpl* vitamínicos

5791 vitamin of natural origin
(Agr.)
(Livestock nutrition; feedstuff ration component.)
d Vitamin *n* natürlicher Herkunft
f vitamine *f* d'origine naturelle
p vitamina *f* de origem natural

5792 vitamin plasma concentration
(Med.)
(Veterinary; ref. to vitamin supplementation to feed, vitamin absorption and animal metabolism.)
d Vitaminkonzentration *f* im Plasma
f concentration *f* plasmatique de la vitamine
p concentração *f* plasmática da vitamina

5793 vitamin-poor alimentation
(Biochem.)
(Nutritional science in medicine: incorrect nutritional habits.)
d vitaminarme Ernährung *f*
f alimentation *f* pauvre en vitamines
p alimentação *f* pobre de vitaminas

5794 vitamin processing techniques
(Med.)
(Veterinary purposes: ref. to fodder composition.)
d Vitaminverarbeitungstechnik *f*
f technique *f* de traitement vitaminique
p técnica *f* de processamento de vitaminas

* **vitamin reinforcement → 5742**

5795 vitamin retention
(Biochem.)
(Nutritional science; ref. to oxidation-sensitive active agent retention in products, improving product quality.)
d Vitaminbewahrung *f*
f rétention *f* des vitamines
p retenção *f* das vitaminas

5796 vitamin richness
(Prod.)
(Vitamins in nutrition; ref. to certain vegetables, and fruits.)
d Vitaminreichtum *m*
f richesse *f* vitaminique
p riqueza *f* de vitaminas; riqueza *f* vitamínica

5797 **vitamin safety supplements**
(Agr.)
(Livestock nutrition; feedstuff manipulation; feedstuff composition.)
d Vitaminsicherungszusätze *mpl*
f suppléments *mpl* vitaminiques pour sûreté
p suplementos *mpl* vitamínicos de segurança

5798 **vitamins for food vitaminization**
(Prod.)
(Vitamins in nutrition.)
d Vitamine *npl* für die Nahrungsmittelvitaminisierung
f vitamines *fpl* pour l'enrichissement des produits alimentaires
p vitaminas *fpl* para o enriquecimento de produtos alimentícios

5799 **vitamins for the food industry**
(Prod.)
(Vitamins in nutrition.)
d Vitamine *npl* für die Nahrungsmittelindustrie
f vitamines *fpl* pour l'industrie alimentaire
p vitaminas *fpl* para a indústria alimentícia

5800 **vitamins in animal nutrition**
(Med.)
(Veterinary; ref. to livestock feeding, poultry farming; feed composition.)
d Vitamine *npl* in der Tierernährung
f vitamines *fpl* en nutrition animale
p vitaminas *fpl* na nutrição animal

5801 **vitamins in cellular respiration**
(Med.)
(Vitamin biochemistry in the body; vitamin metabolism.)
d Vitamine *npl* in der Zellatmung
f vitamines *fpl* dans la respiration cellulaire
p vitaminas *fpl* na respiração celular

5802 **vitamins of the A group**
(Prod.)
(Vitamins in nutrition; fat-soluble vitamin.)
d Vitamine *fpl* der A-Gruppe
f vitamines *fpl* du groupe A
p vitaminas *fpl* do grupo A

5803 **vitamins of the B-group**
(Prod.)
(Vitamins in nutrition; water-soluble vitamins.)
d Vitamine *fpl* der B-Gruppe
f vitamines *fpl* du groupe B
p vitaminas *fpl* do grupo B

5804 **vitamin stability in products**
(Biochem.)
(Nutritional science; e.g. ref. to vitamin stability against oxidation processes.)
d Vitaminstabilität *f* in Produkten
f stabilité *f* vitaminique dans les produits
p estabilidade *f* vitamínica nos produtos

* **vitamin stabilization → 5185**

5805 **vitamin transport in the blood plasma**
(Med.)
(Vitamins, proteins, and trace elements carrying blood plasma.)
d Vitamintransport *m* im Blutplasma
f transport *m* plasmatique des vitamines
p transporte *m* plasmático das vitaminas

5806 **vitellus**
(Biochem.)
(Food biochemistry; egg yolk protein.)
d Vitellin *n*; Eidotterprotein *n*
f vitellin *m*
p vitelina *f*

5807 **viticulture; viniculture; winegrowing**
(Agr.)
(Viticulture; ref. to winegrowing; cultivation of wine grapes.)
d Weinbau *m*; Weinanbau *m*
f viticulture *f*; culture *f* de la vigne; activité *f* vinicole
p viticultura *f*; vinicultura *f*; cultura *f* das vinhas

5808 **viticulture production; winegrowing production**
(Agr.)
(Viticulture; ref. to grape harvest (vintage) yield.)
d Weinproduktion *f*; Weinherstellung *f*
f production *f* vinicole
p produção *f* vinícola

5809 **volatile acidity**
(Biochem.)
(Enology. Wine production, wine characteristic: acidity fraction (e.g. acetic acid) which can be eliminated by warming up.)
d flüchtiger Säuregehalt *m*
f acidité *f* volatile
p acidez *f* volátil

5810 **volatile acidity formation by yeast activity**
(Biochem.)
(Fermentation processes in food biochemistry.)
d gärungsbedingte Bildung *f* flüchtigen Säuregehaltes
f formation *f* d'acidité volatile par la levure
p formação *f* de acidez volátil pelo fermento; formação *f* de acidez volátil pelo lêvedo

5811 **volatile constituents of the distillation front**
(Prod.)
(Aroma/flavour research and production, distillation product.)
d flüchtige Bestandteile *fpl* des Destillationsvorlaufes
f constituants *mpl* volatils de tête de la distillation
p componentes *mpl* voláteis de destilado de cabeça

5812 **volatile essence**
(Prod.)
(Aroma/flavour research and production.)
d flüchtige Essenz *f*
f essence *f* volatile
p essência *f* volátil

5813 **volatility of the substance**
(Prod.)
(Aroma/fragrance research and production.)
d Flüchtigkeit *f* der Substanz
f volatilité *f* de la substance
p volatilidade *f* da substância

5814 **volatility point**
(Prod.)
(Aroma/fragrance research and production.)
d Flüchtigkeitsgrad *m*
f point *m* de volatilité
p ponto *m* de volatilidade

W

5815 wafer
(Prod.)
(Confectionary; small waffle type)
d kleine Waffel *f*
f bricelet *m*
p wafer *m* pequeno

5816 waffle
(Prod.)
(Confectionary.)
d Waffel *f*
f gaufre *f*
p wafer *m*

5817 waist
(Med.)
(Anatomy.)
d Taille *f*; Gürtelweite *f*
f taille *f*
p cintura *f*

5818 walls of the arteries
(Med.)
(Anatomy.)
d Artierienwandungen *fpl*
f parois *fpl* artérielles
p paredes *fpl* arteriais

5819 walnut
(Agr.)
(Agricultural produce. Genus "Juglans"; drupe; stone fruit.)
d Walnuss *f*
f noix *f*
p noz *f*

5820 walnut oil
(Prod.)
(Food processing technology: prime material.)
d Walnussöl *n*
f huile *f* de noix
p óleo *m* de nozes

5821 washing; washing out
(Prod.)
(Food processing technology, separation technique.)
d Waschen *n*; Auswaschen *n*
f lavage *m*
p lavagem *f*

* **washing out → 5821**

5822 water/alcohol systems
(Prod.)
(Food processing technology.)
d Wasser/Alkohol-Systeme *mpl*
f systèmes *mpl* eau/alcool
p sistemas *mpl* água/álcool

5823 water analysis
(Prod.)
(Water supply: ref. to water quality control.)
d Wasseranalyse *f*
f analyse *f* d'eau
p análise *f* da água

* **water bath → 1755**

5824 water buffalo; carabao
(Agr.)
(Cattle breeding. "Bubalus bubalis": Asian (Indian) buffalo.)
d Wasserbüffel *m*
f karbau *m*; kérabau *m*
p búfalo *m* (*da Ásia*)

5825 water consumption
(Agr.)
(Biological agriculture.)
d Wasserkonsum *m*; Wasserverbrauch *m*
f consommation *f* d'eau
p consumo *m* de água

5826 water content
(Prod.)
(Food processing technology: e.g. meat quality.)
d Wassergehalt *m*
f teneur *f* en eau
p teor *m* de água

5827 water cycle in nature
(Agr.)
(Botany.)
d Wasserkreislauf *m* in der Natur
f cycle *m* d'eau dans la nature
p ciclo *m* da água na natureza

5828 water-diluted wine
(Prod.)
(Product of a fraudulent wine quality diminution by water adding.)
d "getaufter" Wein *m*; mit Wasser gestreckter Wein *m*
f vin *m* coupé; vin *m* de coupage; vin *m* baptisé
p vinho *m* "batizado"; vinho *m* diluído com água

* **water erosion → 2775**

5829 water for cooking
(Prod.)
(Food processing technology: cooking, boiling

processes.)
d Kochwasser *n*
f eau *f* de cuisson
p água *f* de cozinhar

5830 **water handling**
(Agr.)
(Especially ref. to poultry farming: water makes up to 70% of the fowl body; water loss of 20% results in death; water supply must be clean and abundant.)
d Wasserhandhabung *f*; Wasserbedienung *f*
f manipulation *f* de l'apport d'eau
p manejo *m* da água

5831 **water hardness**
(Prod.)
(Water supply; hardness is caused e.g. by calcium salts; contributes to the calcium supplementation for the human body.)
d Wasserhärte *f*
f dureté *f* de l'eau
p dureza *f* da água

5832 **water-in-oil emulsion; w/o emulsion**
(Prod.)
(Food processing technology; e.g. butter; margarine.)
d Wasser-in-Öl-Emulsion *f*; Wasser/Öl-Emulsion *f*
f émulsion *f* eau/huile; émulsion *f* E/H
p emulsão *f* água/óleo; emulsão *f* água em óleo; emulsão *f* a/o

5833 **watermelon**
(Agr.)
(Horticulture. "Citrullus vulgaris".)
d Wassermelone *f*
f melon *m* d'eau; pastèque *f*
p melancia *m*

5834 **water pollution**
(Prod.)
(Water supply.)
d Wasserverschmutzung *f*; Wasserverseuchung *f*
f pollution *f* des eaux
p poluição *f* da água

5835 **water-retaining soil**
(Agr.)
(Soil; ref. to water retention capacity of the soil after infiltration by rains etc.; this capacity influences the choice of plants for cultivation.)
d wasserhaltender Boden *m*
f sol *m* à retenue d'eau
p solo *m* retentor de água

5836 **water retention in the soil**
(Agr.)
(Soil type, soil characteristics.)
d Wasserzurückhaltung *f* im Boden
f rétention *f* de l'eau dans le sol
p retenção *f* de água no solo

5837 **water softening**
(Prod.)
(Water supply; water quality.)
d Wasserenthärtung *f*
f adoucissement *m* de l'eau; décalcification *f* de l'eau
p descalcificação *f* da água

5838 **water-soluble** *adj*
(Prod.)
(Food processing technology: product characteristic.)
d wasserlöslich
f hydrosoluble
p hidrossolúvel

5839 **water-soluble dyes**
(Prod.)
(Foodstuff colorants.)
d wasserlösliche Farbstoffe *mpl*
f colorants *mpl* hydrosolubles
p corantes *mpl* hidrossolúveis

5840 **water-soluble vitamins**
(Prod.)
(Vitamins in nutrition; e.g. vitamin C and vitamin B group.)
d wasserlösliche Vitamine *npl*
f vitamines *fpl* hydrosolubles
p vitaminas *fpl* hidrossolúveis

5841 **waterspout**
(Agr.)
(Climatology; funnel-like column of rotating wind over a water surface.)
d Trombe *f*; Wasserhose *f*
f trombe *f* d'eau
p tromba-d'água *f*

5842 **water supplies**
(Agr.)
(Water resources; 3/4 of the surface of the earth is occupied by water; the water system, important for the agriculture, is represented by the rivers and its tributaries.)
d Wasserbestände *mpl*
f ressources *fpl* en eau
p recursos *mpl* hídricos

5843 **water vapour**
(Prod.)
(Water supply; water in gaseous state.)
d Wasserdampf *m*
f vapeur *f* d'eau
p vapor *m* de água

5844 water vapour discharge; water vapour release
(Prod.)
(Aroma/flavour research and production, distillation/extraction processes.)
d Wasserdampfabzug *m*
f départ *m* de la vapeur d'eau
p saída *f* de vapor de água; descarga *f* de vapor de água

5845 water vapour microdistillation
(Prod.)
(Aroma/flavour production: ref. to distillation process types.)
d Wasserdampfmikrodestillation *f*
f microdistillation *f* à la vapeur d'eau
p microdestilação *f* sob vapor de água

* **water vapour release → 5844**

5846 wax candle
(Agr.)
(Apiculture: apicultural product.)
d Wachskerze *f*; Bienenwachskerze *f*
f cierge *m*; bougie *f*
p vela *f* de cera de abelha

5847 weak acid
(Biochem.)
(Nutritional science; only partially dissociated in water: e.g. acetic acid ($C_2H_4O_2$).)
d schwache Säure *f*
f acide *m* faible
p ácido *m* fraco

5848 weak biologic activity of the soil
(Agr.)
(Biological agriculture: ref. to earth type, soil treatment.)
d schwache biologische Aktivität *f* des Bodens
f faible activité *f* biologique du sol
p fraca atividade *f* biológica do solo

5849 weakening of the antioxidant defence
(Med.)
(Nutritional disease: could eventually be nutrition-related.)
d Schwächung *m* der antioxidierenden Abwehr
f affaiblissement *m* de la défense antioxydante
p enfraquecimento *m* da defesa antioxidante

5850 weak flavour
(Prod.)
(Aroma/flavour research and application.)
d schwacher Geschmack *m*; mangelnder Geschmack *m*
f flaveur *f* déficiente
p sabor *m* fraco

5851 weakness of nutritional condition
(Med.)
(Nutritional disease; ref. to incorrect nutrition.)
d Ernährungsschwäche *f*
f faiblesse *f* de la condition nutritionnelle
p fraqueza *f* da condição nutricional

5852 weak solubility
(Prod.)
(Aroma/fragrance research and production.)
d schwache Löslichkeit *f*
f solubilité *f* faible
p solubilidade *f* fraca

5853 weak yield; feeble output
(Prod.)
(Aroma/flavour research and production.)
d schwache Ausbeute *f*; geringe Ausgiebigkeit *f*
f rendement *m* faible
p rendimento *m* fraco

5854 weaning
(Agr.)
(Livestock raising; cattle breeding.)
d Entwöhnung *f*
f sevrage *m*
p desmama *f*; desmame *m*

5855 weaning from nursing
(Med.)
(Baby care and nutrition)
d Entwöhnung *f* vom Stillen
f sevrage *m* de l'allaitement maternel
p desmama *f* da amamentação; desmame *m* da amamentação

5856 weaning products
(Prod.)
(Baby nutrition, e.g. fruits, vegetables.)
d Entwöhnungsprodukte *npl*
f produits *mpl* de sevrage
p produtos *mpl* para desmame

5857 weanling pig
(Agr.)
(Livestock; ref. to hog raising; pig raising.)
d entwöhntes Ferkel *n*
f porcelet *m* sevré
p leitão *m* desmamado

5858 weathering
(Agr.)
(Soil. Decomposition of materials on the surface of the earth as a result of the weather.)
d Verwitterung *f*
f effritement *m*
p decomposição *f* pelo clima

5859 **weed control**
(Agr.)
(Biological agriculture. Destruction of weed growth e.g. by tillage.)
d Unkrautbekämpfung *f*
f contrôle *m* des mauvaises herbes
p controle *m* das ervas daninhas

5860 **weeded plant**
(Agr.)
(Biological agriculture; removed plant.)
d gejätete Pflanze *f*
f plante *f* sarclée
p planta *f* mondada; planta sachada

5861 **weeding**
(Agr.)
(Biological agriculture.)
d Jäten *n*
f sarclage *m*
p capinação *f*

5862 **weeding; weed killing**
(Agr.)
(Weed removal, e.g. in biological agriculture.)
d Unkrautvertilgung *f*
f désherbage *m*; enlèvement *m* des mauvaises herbes
p ação *f* herbicida; remoção *f* de ervas daninhas

* **weed killing → 5862**

5863 **weeds**
(Agr.)
(Botany. Undesirable plant.)
d Unkraut *n*
f mauvaise herbe *f*
p erva *f* daninha

5864 **well-balanced nutrition**
(Med.)
(Ref. to dietary problems.)
d ausgeglichene Ernährung *f*
f alimentation *f* équilibrée
p alimentação *f* equilibrada; nutrição *f* equilibrada

5865 **well-balanced ration**
(Agr.)
(Livestock feeding.)
d ausgeglichene Nahrungsration *f*
f ration *f* alimentaire équilibrée
p ração *f* de alimentação equilibrada; ração *f* alimentar equilibrada

5866 **wether**
(Agr.)
(Livestock. Castrated male sheep.)
d Hammel *m*
f mouton *m* mâle
p carneiro *m*

5867 **whale fat**
(Prod.)
(Food processing technology; prime material.)
d Walfischfett *n*
f graisse *f* de baleine
p gordura *f* de baleia

5868 **whalemeat**
(Prod.)
(Order "Cetacea"; food processing technology; edible meat.)
d Walfischfleisch *n*
f viande *f* de baleine
p carne *f* de baleia

5869 **whale oil**
(Prod.)
(Food processing technology; prime material.)
d Walfischöl *n*
f huile *f* de baleine
p óleo *m* de baleia

5870 **wheat**
(Agr.)
(Agricultural produce. Genus "Triticum"; cereal grain.)
d Weizen *m*
f blé *m*; froment *m*
p trigo *m*

5871 **wheat and rye bread**
(Prod.)
(Bakery. Bread type.)
d Roggenmischbrot *n*
f pain *m* de seigle et froment
p pão *m* misto de trigo e centeio

5872 **wheat bran cake**
(Agr.)
(Agricultural produce, subproduct.)
d Weizenkleie *f*
f son *m* de blé; gâteau *m* de son de blé
p farelo *m* de trigo; bolo *m* de farelo de trigo

5873 **wheat bread**
(Prod.)
(Bakery; wheat flour bread.)
d Weizenbrot *n*
f pain *m* de froment
p pão *m* de trigo

5874 **wheat germ**
(Agr.)
(Botany. Genus "Triticum".)
d Weizenkeimling *m*
f germe *m* de blé
p germe *m* de trigo; gérmen *m* de trigo

5875 wheat-germ bread
(Prod.)
(Bakery.)
d Weizenkeimbrot *n*
f pain *m* aux germes de blé
p pão *m* de gérmen de trigo

5876 wheat seed oil
(Prod.)
(Additive.)
d Weizenkeimöl *n*
f huile *f* de germes de blé
p óleo *m* da semente do trigo

5877 wheat sowing
(Agr.)
(Agricultural activity.)
d Weizenaussaat *f*; Aussaat *f* des Weizens *m*
f emblavage *m*
p semeadura *f* do trigo; semeação *f* do trigo

* **whey → 3118**

5878 whey cheese
(Prod.)
(Dairy product. Scandinavian type of cheese.)
d Molkekäse *m*
f fromage *m* de sérum
p queijo *m* de soro

5879 whey separation
(Prod.)
(Dairy product. Yoghurt production.)
d Molkeabsonderung *f*; Molkeabtrennung *f*
f séparation *f* de lactosérum
p separação *f* do soro de leite

5880 whipped cream
(Prod.)
(Dairy product.)
d Schlagsahne *f*; geschlagene Creme *f*
f crème *f* fouettée; chantilly *f*; crème *f* chantilly
p creme *m* chantilly; creme *m* batido

5881 whirlwind
(Agr.)
(Climatology, rotating windstorm.)
d Wirbelwind *m*; Windhose *f*
f tourbillon *m*
p turbilhão *m* de vento

5882 white beeswax
(Agr.)
(Apiculture.)
d gebleichtes Bienenwachs *n*
f cire *f* blanche d'abeille
p cera *f* branca de abelha

5883 white leghorn
(Agr.)
(Poultry farming. Chicken breed of good layers (good egg production).)
d weißes Leghorn *n*
f leghorn *f* blanche
p leghorn *m* da variedade *f* branca

5884 white loaf
(Prod.)
(Bakery: type of very white wheat flour bread.)
d Weißbrot *n*
f pain *m* blanc
p pão *m* branco

5885 white meat
(Prod.)
(Butchery; beef.)
d weißes Fleisch *n*
f viande *f* blanche
p carne *f* branca

5886 white mould spraying
(Prod.)
(Dairy technology of cheese production, occurring in the mould tunnel.)
d Besprühung *f* mit weißem Schimmelpilz
f arrosage *m* à moisissures blanches
p pulverização *f* com bolor branco

* **white of egg → 1865**

5887 white powder
(Prod.)
(Food processing technology; product characteristic.)
d weißes Pulver *n*
f poudre *f* blanche
p pó *m* branco

5888 white radish
(Agr.)
(Horticulture. Family "Cruciferae".)
d Rettich *m*
f radis *m*
p rábano *m*

* **white Rhine wine → 2720**

5889 white rice
(Prod.)
(Food processing technology: Rice type that has undergone pericarp abrasion treatment.)
d gebleichter Reis *m*
f riz *m* blanchi
p arroz *m* branqueado; arroz *m* alvejado

5890 white roll
(Prod.)
(Bakery; bread type.)
d Weizenbrötchen *n*

f petit pain *m* de froment
p pãozinho *m* francês

5891 white vine sort
(Agr.)
(Viticulture; grape selection.)
d weiße Rebsorte *f*
f cépage *m* blanc
p espécie *f* de cepa branca

5892 white wine
(Biochem.)
(Enology.)
d Weißwein *m*
f vin *m* blanc
p vinho *m* branco

5893 white wine vinification
(Agr.)
(Viticulture.)
d Weißweinbereitung *f*
f vinification *f* en blanc
p vinificação *f* de vinhos brancos

5894 whiting
(Agr.)
("Merlangus merlangus"; edible fish of the Northern seas.)
d Merlan *m*; Wittling *m*; Weißling *m*
f merlan *m*
p pescadinha *f*

5895 whole cheese
(Prod.)
(Dairy product; food processing technology.)
d Käselaib *m*; Käserad *n*
f meule *f*; meule *f* de fromage
p peça *f* inteira de queijo

5896 wholemeal bread
(Prod.)
(Bakery.)
d Vollkornbrot *n*
f pain *m* complet
p pão *m* integral

5897 whole milk; unskimmed milk
(Prod.)
(Dairy product; food industrialization.)
d Vollmilch *f*
f lait *m* entier; lait *m* non-écrémé
p leite *m* integral; leite *m* não desnatado

5898 wholesaler
(Prod.)
(Food processing technology and marketing.)
d Großhändler *m*
f grossiste *m*
p atacadista *m*

5899 Wiener schnitzel; Vienna cutlet
(Prod.)
(Gastronomy.)
d Wiener Schnitzel *n*
f escalope *f* à la viennoise
p escalope *m* vienense

5900 wild boar
(Agr.)
("Sus scrofa"; wild hog.)
d Wildschwein *n*; Keiler *m*
f sanglier *m* mâle
p javali *m*; porco-montês *m*

5901 wild caraway
(Agr.)
(Botany. "Carum carvi"; aromatic herb.)
d Feldkümmel *m*
f carvi *m*; cumin *m* des prés
p cominho *m* do campo; cominho *m* silvestre

5902 wild chicory leaf infusion; infusion of the leaves of wild endive
(Prod.)
(Here: tea of "Cichorium intybus".)
d Aufguss *m* der Blätter der Wegwarte; Zichorienblättertee *m*
f tisane *f* des feuilles de chicorée sauvage
p chá *m* das folhas da endívia; infusão *f* das folhas da endívia

5903 wild forest note
(Prod.)
(Taste; aroma research and production.)
d Waldnote *f*
f note *f* sylvestre
p nota *f* silvestre

5904 wild-growing fruits; uncultivated fruits
(Agr.)
(Opposed to fruit culture.)
d wilde Früchte *fpl*; wildwachsende Früchte *fpl*
f fruits *mpl* sauvages
p frutas *fpl* silvestres

5905 wild growing plant
(Agr.)
(Botany. As opposed to cultivated plant.)
d freiwachsende Pflanze *f*
f plante *f* sauvage
p planta *f* silvestre

* **wild-living animal → 2360**

5906 wildsow
(Agr.)
(Wild adult female hog.)
d Bache *f*
f laie *f*
p javalina *f*; gironda *f*

5907 wild vine
(Agr.)
(Viticulture. "Vitis vinifera"; wild vines are resistant against pests, like e.g. "Phylloxera vitifolae". They are used as "stocks" in grafting processes.)
d wilde Weinrebe *f*
f vigne *f* sauvage
p videira *f* selvagem

5908 wilt *v*
(Agr.)
(Botany; plants.)
d welken; verwelken
f se faner; se flétrir
p murchar

* **wind erosion → 1537**

5909 windfall
(Agr.)
(Horticulture: In this specific case: fruits blown down from the tree by the wind.)
d Fallobst *n*
f fruits *mpl* tombés
p frutas *fpl* caídas; frutas *fpl* do chão

5910 wine bouquet when aging
(Biochem.)
(Enology: metaphor ref. to aroma note of the wine during aging process.)
d Alterungsbukett *n* des Weines
f bouquet *m* de vieillissement du vin
p buquê *m* do vinho em fase de envelhecimento

5911 wine cellar
(Agr.)
(Viticulture: Wine storing room; wine stock.)
d Weinkeller *m*
f cellier *m*; cave *f* à vin
p adega *f*

5912 wine clarification
(Biochem.)
(Enology; wine treatment process with addition of additives for sedimentation purposes.)
d Klären *n* des Weines
f collage *m*; clarification *f* du vin
p clarificação *f* do vinho

5913 wine destined for aging
(Biochem.)
(Enology.)
d zur Alterung bestimmter Wein *m*
f vin *m* de garde
p vinho *m* prestes a ser envelhecido; vinho *m* destinado ao envelhecimento

5914 wine fermentation in the vat
(Biochem.)
(Enology.)
d Gärenlassen *n* des Weines im Bottich
f cuvage *m*; cuvaison *f*; fermentation *f* du vin en cuve
p fermentação *f* do vinho na cuba

5915 wine filtration
(Biochem.)
(Enology, wine production and treatment.)
d Weinfiltration *f*; Weinfiltrierung *f*
f filtration *f* des vins
p filtração *f* de vinho

* **wine ground → 2593**

* **winegrowing → 5807**

5916 winegrowing area
(Agr.)
(Viticulture.)
d Weinanbaugebiet *n*
f région *f* vinicole; région *f* viticole
p região *f* vinícola; área *f* vitivinícola

5917 winegrowing countries; wineproducing countries
(Agr.)
(Viticulture: wine production.)
d Weinanbauländer *npl*
f pays *mpl* producteurs de vins
p países *mpl* produtores de vinho

* **winegrowing production → 5808**

5918 wine-like taste
(Prod.)
(Slightly fermented savour; flavour note; e.g. ref. to organoleptic food evaluation.)
d weinartiger Geschmack *m*
f saveur *f* vineuse
p sabor *m* de vinho

5919 wine made from selected grapes
(Biochem.)
(Enology; wine quality.)
d Auslese *f*
f vin *m* de meilleur cru; vin *m* de grand cru
p vinho *m* de colheita selecionada

5920 wine of controlled origin
(Agr.)
(Viticulture. Wine quality classification.)
d Wein *m* kontrollierten Ursprungs
f vin *m* d'origine contrôlée
p vinho *m* de origem controlada; vinho *m* de procedência controlada

5921 wine of maceration process
(Biochem.)
(Enology: technology of wine production; e.g.

ref. to red wine types.)
d Wein *m* des Mazerationsprozesses
f vin *m* du processus de macération
p vinho *m* do processo de maceração

5922 **wine of strong, spicy flavour**
(Biochem.)
(Enology; wine type.)
d kräftiger, würziger Wein *m*
f vin *m* corsé
p vinho *m* forte

* **wineproducing countries → 5917**

* **wine protection against oxidation → 4428**

5923 **wine stability during preservation period**
(Biochem.)
(Enology.)
d Weinstabilität *f* während der Konservierungsdauer
f stabilité *f* du vin au cours de la conservation
p estabilidade *f* do vinho durante a conservação

5924 **wine tasting**
(Agr.)
(Viticulture.)
d Weinprobe *f*
f dégustation *f* de vin
p degustação *f* do vinho

5925 **wine vinegar**
(Prod.)
(Preservation additive; used as a condiment.)
d Weinessig *m*
f vinaigre *m* de vin
p vinagre *m* de vinho

* **winterberry → 537**

5926 **wire trellis**
(Agr.)
(Viticulture: Frame of stretched wires between posts to support vines; the tendrils grow around the wire trellis.)
d Drahtrahmenspaliererziehung *f*
f treillis *m* avec fil de fer
p latada *f*

5927 **wisdom tooth**
(Med.)
(Anatomy.)
d Weisheitszahn *m*
f dent *f* de sagesse
p dente *m* de siso; siso *m*

* **wisent → 664**

5928 **with coffee flavour**
(Prod.)
(Food processing technology: e.g. certain milk products.)
d mit Kaffeegeschmack
f aromatisé au café
p com paladar de café

5929 **withdrawal of nutritional supply**
(Med.)
(Nutritional diseases; ref. to tissue supply, e.g. due to thrombogenic processes which could be caused by incorrect nutrition.)
d Entzug *m* der Nahrungsmittelzufuhr
f privation *f* de l'apport nutritionnel
p privação *f* do aporte nutricional

5930 **within the limits of cold water**
(Prod.)
(Food processing technology.)
d im Kaltwasserbereich
f dans les limites d'eau froide
p dentro dos limites de água fria

5931 **within the limits of hot water**
(Prod.)
(Food processing technology.)
d im Heißwasserbereich
f dans les limites d'eau chaude
p dentro dos limites de água quente

* **w/o emulsion → 5832**

5932 **woody; ligneous** *adj*
(Prod.)
(Food processing technology; product aspect.)
d holzig
f ligneux
p lenhoso

5933 **worker bee**
(Agr.)
(Apiculture.)
d Arbeiterin *f*; Arbeitsbiene *f*
f ouvrière *f*; abeille *f* neutre; abeille *f* femelle travailleuse; butineuse *f*
p abelha *f* operária

5934 **worm**
(Agr.)
(Culture destroying animal, esp. in biological agriculture.)
d Wurm *m*
f ver *m*
p verme *m*

* **wormwood → 437**

5935 **wort**
(Prod.)
(Food processing technology. Beer brewing process.)

d Bierwürze *f*
f moût *m*
p mosto *m*

5936 **wort-boiling**
(Prod.)
(Food processing technology. Beer brewing process.)
d Würzekochen *n*
f cuisson *f* du moût
p fervura *f* do mosto

5937 **wrap** *v*
(Prod.)
(Food processing technology; ref. to food packaging technology.)
d einwickeln; einpacken
f envelopper; emballer; empaqueter
p embrulhar; enrolar

5938 **wrapped in a foil**
(Prod.)
(Food processing technology; ref. to product packaging.)
d in Folie gewickelt
f emballé dans des feuilles; empaqueté dans des feuilles
p embrulhado em folha; enrolado em folha

5939 **wrapping paper**
(Prod.)
(Food processing technology; food packaging.)
d Packpapier *n*
f papier *m* d'emballage
p papel *m* de embrulho

X

* **xanthaemia → 950**

5940 xanthophyll
(Prod.)
($C_{40}H_{56}O_2$; foodstuff colorant (yellow to brown); occurs in nature: vegetable lutein, carotenoid alcohol; E 161.)
d Xanthophyll *n*
f xanthophylle *m*
p xantofila *f*

5941 xerophthalmia
(Med.)
(Conjunctiva dryness, atrophy with opacity of the cornea: Vitamin A deficiency.)
d Xerophthalmie *f*
f xérophtalmie *f*
p xeroftalmia *f*

5942 xerosis
(Med.)
(Conjunctiva dryness: E.g. vitamin A deficiency.)
d Xerose *f*; Augendarre *f*
f xérose *f*
p xerose *f*

5943 xylene; xylol
(Prod.)
(C_8H_{10}; dimethylbenzene; prime material for aroma/fragrance production.)
d Xylol *n*
f xylène *m*
p xileno *m*

5944 xylitol
(Prod.)
($C_5H_{12}O_5$; xylose derivative: sweetening agent: polyalcohol.)
d Xylit *n*
f xylitol *m*
p xilitol *m*

* **xylol → 5943**

Y

5945 **yak**
(Agr.)
("Bos Grunniens" of Central Asia.)
d Jack *m*; Grunzochse *m*
f yack *m*
p jaque *m*; bibovino *m*

5946 **yam**
(Agr.)
(Horticulture. Genus "Dioscorea"; edible starch-containing sweet potato-like root of the tropical plant.)
d Jamswurzel *f*
f igname *f*
p inhame *m*

* **yearling lamb → 3127**

5947 **yeast**
(Biochem.)
(Family "Saccharomycetaceae"; Fermentation-promoting fungus.)
d Hefe *f*
f levure *f*
p fermento *m* cervejeiro

5948 **yeast cake**
(Prod.)
(Food processing technology. Yeast production plant product, obtained by dewatering the yeast cream. The yeast is extruded into small blocks.)
d Hefetablette *f*
f levure *f* en forme de tablette
p lêvedo *m* em tabletes; fermento *m* em tabletes

5949 **yeast cream**
(Prod.)
(Food processing technology. Yeast plant product, obtained in the centrifugal separator.)
d Hefekrem *f/m*
f crème *f* en levure
p creme *m* de fermento; creme *m* de lêvedo

5950 **yeast extract**
(Prod.)
(Food processing technology; yeast plant product.)
d Hefeextrakt *m*
f extrait *m* de levure
p extrato *m* de fermento

5951 **yeast fermentation**
(Biochem.)
(Fermentation. Beer brewery process: Ethanol (alcohol) production process.)
d Hefefermentation *f*; Hefegärung *f*
f fermentation *f* de levure
p fermentação *f* de levedura

5952 **yeast filamentations**
(Biochem.)
(Microbiology.)
d Hefestränge *mpl*
f filamentations *fpl* des levures
p filamentos *mpl* das leveduras

5953 **yeast ground**
(Biochem.)
(Fermentation processes.)
d Hefesatz *m*
f lie *f* de levure
p borra *f* do fermento; borra *f* do lêvedo; lia *f* do fermento; lia *f* do lêvedo

5954 **yeast growth**
(Biochem.)
(Fermentation.)
d Hefewachstum *m*
f croissance *f* levurienne
p crescimento *m* do lêvedo; crescimento *m* da levedura

5955 **yeast inactivation**
(Biochem.)
(Fermentation processes.)
d Hefe-Inaktivierung *f*
f inactivation *f* des levures
p inativação *f* do lêvedo

5956 **yeast in phase of growth**
(Biochem.)
(Fermentation.)
d Hefe *f* in der Wachstumsphase
f levure *f* en phase de croissance
p lêvedo *m* em fase de crescimento; levedura *f* em fase de crescimento

5957 **yeast of vinification**
(Biochem.)
(Enology.)
d Hefe *f* der Weinbereitung
f levure *f* de vinification
p lêvedo *m* de vinificação; levedura *f* de vinificação

5958 **yeast strains used in bakery**
(Biochem.)
(Food biochemistry.)
d in der Bäckerei angewandte Hefestränge *mpl*
f souches *fpl* de levure employées en boulangerie
p cepas *fpl* de lêvedo usadas na panificação

5959 yellow orange lake
(Prod.)
(Foodstuff colorant; E number: E 102.)
d Gelborange-Lack *m*
f laque *m* d'orangé-jaune
p laca *f* amarela-alaranjada

* **yellow plum → 3592**

* **yield of grapes of a season → 5731**

5960 yield per hectare
(Agr.)
(Agricultural produce. Hectare: ha = 10,000 square metres = 2.47 acres, USA.)
d Ausbeute *f* per Hektar
f rendement *m* à l'hectare
p rendimento *m* por hectare

* **yoghourt → 5961**

5961 yoghurt; yoghourt; yogurt
(Prod.)
(Food processing technology; fermented milk product with the action of bacteria cultures: "Lactobacillus bulgaricus" and "Streptococcus thermophilus".)
d Joghurt *m/n*
f yaourt *m*; yogourt *m*
p iogurte *m*

5962 yoghurt enriched with lactobacilli
(Prod.)
(Food processing technology.)
d mit Laktobazillen angereichertes Joghurt *n*
f yaourt *m* enrichi en lactobacilles; yogourt *m* enrichi en lactobacilles
p iogurte *m* enriquecido com lactobacilos

* **yogurt → 5961**

5963 yolk
(Agr.)
(Poultry farming.)
d Eidotter *f*; Eigelb *n*
f jaune *m* d'œuf
p gema *f* do ovo

5964 young bull
(Agr.)
(Livestock raising.)
d Jungstier *m*; Farre *m*; Farren *m*
f jeune taureau *m*
p novilho *m*; bezerro *m*; almalho *m*; vitelo *m*

5965 young cattle
(Agr.)
(Cattle breeding.)
d junges Rindvieh *n*
f jeunes bovins *mpl*
p bovinos *mpl* jovens

* **young chicken → 4492**

5966 young goat; kid
(Agr.)
(Livestock raising. Genus "Capra".)
d Zicklein *n*; Kitzlein *n*; Geißlein *n*
f chevreau *m*
p cabrito *m*; cabrita *f*

5967 young wild boar
(Agr.)
(Livestock. "Sus scrofa"; very young wild hog.)
d Frischling *m*
f marcassin *m*
p filhote *m* de javali

Z

5968 zebu
(Agr.)
(Cattle breeding. "Bos indicus".)
d Zebu *m*; Buckelochse *m*
f zébu *m*
p zebu *m*

5969 zinc
(Med.)
(Baby nutrition: Zn present in human milk: important e.g. for the prevention of enteropathic acrodermatitis.)
d Zink *n*
f zinc *m*
p zinco *m*

5970 zinc deficiency
(Med.)
(Veterinary; mineral (ZN) deficiency, causing e.g. organic troubles: growth delay, infertility of the animals, general dermatitis: scabies.)
d Zinkmangel *m*
f carence *f* en zinc
p deficiência *f* de zinco

* **zucchini → 1383**

* **zygomatic bone → 1034**

Deutsch

Français

Português